Medieval History

Volume I

Readings in
Medieval History

Volume I

edited by
Patrick J. Geary

broadview

Cataloguing In Publication Data

Readings in medieval history

ISBN 0-921149-38-7

1. Middle Ages - History - Sources. I. Geary, Patrick J., 1948-

D113.R42 1989   940.1   C89-093690-0

BROADVIEW PRESS
In Canada: In the United States:
P. O. Box 1243   3576 California Road
Peterborough, Ontario   Orchard Park, NY 14127
Canada, K9J 7H5   USA

Preface

"History is merely the applied utilization of documents." This old dictum of the positivist-historicist tradition, rightly criticized by generations of historians reacting against a mechanical, pseudo-objective approach to history, nevertheless contains a deep and abiding truth. History is after all done with documents — primary sources are at the heart of the historical enterprise. But the dictum should be qualified in two ways. First, we must remember how much this "applied utilization," far from being an objective and naturally imposed process, is rather one of creativity and interpretation. Second, "document" must be understood in a broad sense to denote not just written texts but every echo of the past, written, oral, physical, mental. In this sense every historian must begin with documents, and every student of history must be exposed to these documents in order to understand the creative elaborations that are what historians of every stripe make of them. A healthy introduction to such primary sources is not only vital to the development of historical understanding, but it is also the source of the greatest pleasure to historians, the creative pursuit of meaning in the past, and thus a pleasure which should not be denied students.

It is the modest intention of this volume to place at the disposal of students beginning their exploration of medieval history some of these documents so that they can actually participate in the continuing process of interpretation and debate which is at the heart of the historical enterprise. I hope that these documents will bring them more than merely a deeper knowledge of the received tradition of medieval history. May the recognition of the fragmentary and ambiguous nature of the documentation with which historians have reconstructed the past inspire in students a healthy skepticism toward these syntheses and engender an impatience to acquire the necessary skills to do their own medieval history and to do it better.

Since this volume intends neither to argue for any particular interpretation of medieval history nor to serve as mere illustration of currently fashionable historical theses, four principles have guided the selection of the documents it contains.

First, entire documents or long excerpts have been included whenever possible, since truncated and severely abridged texts do not allow students to understand the form and context of historical sources or to attempt their own analyses of them. The result is a volume containing fewer texts than might be desired, but students and instructors should be able to do more with those that are included. The editor particularly regrets that, with the exception of the Old High German *Song of Hildebrand*, literary texts have been excluded. The reason is that excellent inexpensive translations of the classics of medieval literature are generally available for students and should be included in any history syllabus.

Second, rather than selecting widely different texts to illustrate particular issues, some texts are grouped to form a dossier in which the individual documents relate to each other. This is of course what the practicing historian attempts to compile and examine. These examples, such as the series of documents concerning land holding from Cluny, three contradictory treatises on the eternality of the world, and a group of Florentine catasto filings from the Alberti family, provide students with the opportunity to examine historical questions from a variety of differing documents and perspectives. Likewise, it should be possible for students to make valid connections among documents across units. Thus, for example, the selection from the Theodosian code can be related to texts from the Salic law, Anglo-Saxon law, and twelfth century Italian marriage contracts. Guibert of Nogent's autobiography can be compared with that of the emperor Charles IV and the *Book of Margery Kempe*.

Third, wherever possible the documents presented here have been selected because they have been the object of significant scholarship available in English. Nothing is more frustrating for a student beginning to develop an interest in medieval history than to find that the issues he or she raises in relationship to a particular text have been discussed only in Continental languages. Thus, for example, one reason for the selection of the book of the miracles of St. Foy rather than other hagiographic texts is that it has been the subject of a number of recent studies in English from a variety of perspectives. The example of an inquisitorial dossier comes from Montaillou, brilliantly if controversially studied by Emmanuel Le Roy Ladurie.

Finally, although I have my own prejudices and preferences in terms of how one does history, I have made a sincere effort to provide the raw material for many types of historical investigations. There is no one exercise that can be done with each document, no single way that an instructor can make use of them, nor is there one point of view toward which the selection of documents tacitly points. They can be used equally by the political historian, the cultural historian, the social historian or the historian of mentalities.

Of course, every historical enterprise is limited by the perspective and competence of the investigator, and this volume is no exception. One could easily compile an equally valuable alternative list of readings to this one, and one could validly object to the geographical limitations from which the sources are taken. I have tried to take into account the range of documents my colleagues are currently using by surveying medievalists and by examining syllabi and other source books. I have then selected accurate translations or made new ones. Finally I have included a number of hitherto untranslated texts in order to provide the sorts of documents representative of the types of sources to which medievalists are turning in contemporary research. I sincerely hope that my colleagues will feel free to send me suggestions for additions and deletions so that future editions of the volume may be even more responsive to their needs.

Don LePan, President of Broadview Press, who suggested that a new medieval reader was needed and encouraged me to undertake it, deserves much of the credit for this book. I would like to thank as well Barbara Rosenwein, Susanna Foster Baxandall, George Beech, and Jonathan M. Elukin for their contributions. I owe a lasting debt of gratitude to John William Rooney, Jr., who first introduced me to the joy of reading the sources of medieval history. Wolter Braamhorst and Anne Picard spent many hours assisting me in finding appropriate translations and editions. J. Patout Burns and Richard Kay provided many useful suggestions for revisions.

Patrick J. Geary
Gainesville, April 1989

For my students and especially in memory of

Bridget Bernadette Phillips

1966-1989

whose tragic death cut short a career of great promise.

Contents

Theodosian Code

The Theodosian Code, compiled in 438, was the first official collection of imperial general constitutions. It was ordered by Emperor Theodosius II (401-450) as part of his concern with legal education. It was completed in 438 and adopted in both the eastern and western portions of the empire.

The work is arranged in sixteen books, each composed of a number of titles. In the east it was superceded by the codification of Justinian but continued to be the authoritative collection of Roman law in the barbarian kingdoms of western Europe. As such it had an enormous influence on the formation of western barbarian and medieval law.

The following selection is Book III, which treats contracts, betrothal, marriage, dowries, divorce, and care of minors.

Source: *The Theodosian Code and Novels and the Sirmondian Constitutions*, tr. Clyde Pharr in collaboration with Theresa Sherrer Davidson and Mary Brown Pharr (Princeton: Princeton University Press, 1952).

Title 1: Contracts of Purchase (*De Contrahenda Emptione*)

1.   Emperor Constantine Augustus to Profuturus, Prefect of the Annona.
It is not at all fitting that the good faith of sale and purchase should be broken, when no duress was exerted through fraud. For a contract that has been executed without any flaw must not be disturbed by a litigious controversy because of the sole complaint that the price was too cheap.
Posted on the ides of August in the fifth consulship of Constantine Augustus and the consulship of Licinius Caesar. – August 13, 319.

INTERPRETATION: When a thing has been purchased for a definite price that is agreed upon between the buyer and seller, although it is worth more than it is sold for at the present, this only must be investigated, whether the person who is proved to have purchased it has committed no fraud or violence. If the seller should wish to revoke the sale, by no means shall he be permitted to do so.

2.   The same Augustus to Gregorius.
The purchaser shall assume the tax assessment[1] of property that is purchased, and no person shall be permitted either to buy or sell property without its tax assessment.
1. Moreover, in accordance with this law, there must henceforth be a public or fiscal inspection, so that if any property should be sold without its tax assessment and this fact should be reported by another, the seller, indeed, shall lose the landholding, and the purchaser for his part shall lose the price that he has paid, since the fisc shall vindicate both.
1a. It is also Our pleasure that no person shall engage in the sale of anything whatsoever unless at the time when the contract between the seller and the buyer is formally executed, a certain and true ownership is proved by the neighbors. To such an extent shall the precaution prescribed by this law be observed that even if "benches," or strips of land, as they are commonly called, are sold, the proof of showing ownership shall be fulfilled.
2. Nor shall the formalities between the buyer and the seller be solemnized in hidden corners, but fraudulent sales shall be completely buried and shall perish.
Given on the day before the nones of February at Constantinople in the year of the consulship of Felicianus and Titianus.—February 4, 337.

INTERPRETATION: If any person should purchase a villa, he shall know that he has purchased the obligation of the tribute of the thing itself as well as the right to the landholding, because no person is permitted either to buy or sell a farm without the tribute or

1

fiscal payment. But if any person should dare to sell or presume to purchase anything when the fiscal payment had been concealed, those between whom such a contract has been made by a secret transaction should know that both the purchaser shall lose the price and the seller shall lose the landholding, because it is ordered that the neighbors of the property which is sold must be witnesses and present, to the extent that even in the case of things of slight value, if anything is sold for use, it is Our pleasure that it shall be shown to the neighbors and thus purchased, in order that the property of others may not be sold.

3. Emperor Julian Augustus to Julianus, Count of the Orient.

We order that the constitution of My paternal uncle, Constantine, shall be repealed, in which he commanded that minor women who were united with husbands in marriage should be able to negotiate sales without the interposition of a decree, if their husbands should suppose that they ought to give their consent as well as provide their subscription to the documents. For it is absurd that husbands who are at times needy men should be obligated for their wives, because when the right itself of the sale is not valid, these women are able to recover their own property from those persons who have participated in the illicit contracts. 1. Therefore We revive the old law, that on no account shall any sale whatsoever be valid when it has been contracted by a minor, whether a man or a woman, without the interposition of a decree.

Given on the eighth day before the ides of December at Antioch in the year of the consulship of the Most Noble Mamertinus and Nevitta.–December 6, 362.

INTERPRETATION: It had been ordained by a law of the Emperor Constantine that minor women who had husbands could sell anything from their own resources with the consent of their husbands. But this ordinance is abrogated by the present law, and the following rule must be observed, namely, that if under the compulsion of necessity men or women who are minors should wish to sell anything, whoever should wish to buy it shall be protected by the authorization of the judge or by the consent of the municipal council; for otherwise a sale made by minors will not be valid.

4. Emperors Gratian, Valentinian, and Theodosius Augustusees to Hypatius, Praetorian Prefect.

If a person in his majority and approved as capable of administering his own patrimony should sell a landed estate, even though it is situated at a distance and even though, perchance, in some cases the entire estate has not been sold, he shall not thereafter obtain the right of recovery on the ground that the price was too cheap.

1. He shall not be allowed to contrive delays by means of unfounded objections, namely, that he should allege that the value of the property was unknown to him, since he ought to know the value, that is, the worth and income of his own family property.

Given on the sixth day before the nones of May at Milan in the year of the second consulship of Merobaudes and the consulship of Saturninus.–May 2, 383.

INTERPRETATION: If any person, already of full legal age and able to manage his own household, should sell his villa, house, or anything else at a definite price and if, perchance, later he should wish to claim in opposition that he received a smaller price than the property was worth, because he says, perhaps, that he was ignorant of the value of the land which he sold, since it was located at a distance, the sale cannot be revoked for that reason. For a person of full age could have known what sort of thing he sold or at what price the thing to be sold could be valued.

5. The same Augustuses to Cynegius, Praetorian Prefect.

No Jew whatever shall purchase a Christian slave or contaminate an ex-Christian with Jewish religious rites. But if a public investigation should disclose that this has been done, the slave shall be forcibly taken away, and such masters shall undergo a punishment suitable and appropriate for the crime. It is further added that if there should be found among the Jews any slaves who are either still Christians or ex-Christian Jews, they shall be redeemed from this unworthy servitude by the Christians upon payment of a suitable price.

Received on the tenth day before the kalends of October at Rhegium in the year of the consulship of Richomer and Clearchus.–September 22, 384.

INTERPRETATION: It must be observed above all things else that no Jew shall be permitted to have a Christian slave; indeed, if a Jew should have a Christian slave, he shall under no circumstances dare to presume to transfer him to his own religious faith. If he should do this, he shall know that his slaves will be forcibly taken from him, and he shall undergo a punishment suited to so great a crime. For before this law was issued, it had been decreed that if a Christian slave had been contaminated by Jewish pollution, his master should know that the price which he had paid for the slave would be refunded to him by the Christians in order that the slave might remain in the Christian faith.

6. The same Augustuses to Flavianus, Praetorian Prefect of Illyricum and Italy.

Formerly the right had been granted to near kinsmen and to co-owners to exclude extraneous persons from a purchase,[2] and men could not, in accordance with their own decision, sell any property which they had for sale. But because this appears to be a grave injustice, which is veiled by the empty pretext of honour, that men should be compelled to do anything about their own property against their will, this former law is hereby annulled, and each person shall be able to seek and approve a purchaser according to his own decision.

Given on the sixth day before the kalends of June at Vincentia in the year of the consulship of Titianus and Symmachus.–May 27, 391.

INTERPRETATION: A former ordinance of the law had provided that if one co-owner, because of some necessity, should wish to sell a thing, an extraneous person should not have the opportunity to buy it. But this imperial indulgence is approved as better, namely, that any person shall have the right to use his unconstrained decision concerning his own property. He may pass over his co-owners and near kinsmen and have the unrestricted privilege of selling to whomever he wishes.

7. The same Augustuses to Remigius, Augustal Prefect.

If persons of full legal capacity should once enter into a contract of purchase and sale, it cannot be invalidated on the ground that too small a price has been paid.

Given on the third day before the kalends of April at Constantinople in the year of the fourth consulship of Arcadius Augustus and the third consulship of Honorius Augustus.–March 30, 396.

INTERPRETATION: When an agreement has been made between any two persons concerning the price of anything, although the thing has been bought for a less price than it was worth, the sale shall by no means be revoked.

8. The same Augustuses to Messala, Praetorian Prefect.

(After other matters.) If any persons by flight should desert the compulsory public services, either municipal or provincial, that have been enjoined upon them and should suppose that they may enter into clandestine contracts, they shall understand that these artifices will profit them nothing, and the purchaser shall be fined the price that he has paid. (Etc.)

Given on the twelfth day before the kalends of September in the year of the consulship of the Most Noble Theodorus.–August 21, 399.

INTERPRETATION: If any persons should attempt to escape the compulsory public serv-

ices which are due to the municipal council or their own municipality and should wish
to sell their property secretly, they shall know that what they have done cannot be valid,
and that they themselves will be recalled to the services due. Those persons also who
bought the property shall lose the price.

9.   Emperors Honorius and Theodosius Augustuses to the People.
    We command that the sales, gifts, and compromises which have been extorted
through the exercise of power[3] shall be invalidated.
    *Given on the thirteenth day before the kalends of March at Constantinople in the year of the
tenth consulship of Honorius Augustus and the sixth consulship of Theodosius Augustus.–February 17, 415.*

INTERPRETATION: All men shall know that whatever they have given or sold under the
compulsion of very powerful persons can be recovered.

10. Honorius and Theodosius Augustuses to Palladius, Praetorian Prefect.
    There is said to exist a superfluous belief of some persons that the right to purchase
has been denied to persons placed in administrative offices and in the imperial service,
although a law of the sainted Honorius, issued to Palladius, Praetorian Prefect, and included in the Theodosian corpus, is read as having given this right to such persons.

Title 2: The Annulment of Provisions for Forfeiture (*De Commissoria Rescin-
denda*)

    1. Emperor Constantine Augustus to the People.
    Since among other captious practices, the harshness of the provision for forfeiture
is especially increasing, it is Our pleasure that such provision shall be invalidated and that
hereafter all memory of it shall be abolished. If any person, therefore, is suffering under
such a contract, he shall be relieved by this sanction which cancels all such past and present arguments and prohibits them for the future. For We order that creditors shall surrender the property[4] and recover that which they have given.[5]
    *Given on the day before the kalends of February at Sofia (Serdica) in the year of the seventh
consulship of Constantine Augustus and the consulship of Constantius Caesar.–January 31, 326;
320.*

INTERPRETATION: Those written acknowledgements of debt are called agreements for
forfeiture in which a debtor through necessity promises in a written acknowledgement of
debt to sell to his own creditor a thing which he had pledged for a time to the creditor.
This law cancels any such agreement for forfeiture which has been made and absolutely
prohibits one to be made. Thus if any creditor should appear to have bought property of
his debtor under such a pretext, he shall not delude himself with written documents, but
as soon as the debtor wishes, who sold when oppressed by debt, the creditor shall recover
his money, and the debtor shall receive back his property.

Title 3: Fathers Who Have Sold Their Children (*De Patribus Qui Filios Distrax-
erunt*)

1.   Emperors Valentinian, Theodosius, and Arcadius Augustuses to Tatianus, Praetorian Prefect.
    All those persons whom the piteous fortune of their parents has consigned to slavery
while their parents thereby were seeking sustenance shall be restored to their original
status of free birth. Certainly no person shall demand repayment of the purchase price,
if he has been compensated by the slavery of a freeborn person for a space of time that
is not too short.
    Given on the fifth day before the ides of March at Milan in the year of the consulship of Ta-

tianus and Symmachus.–March 11, 391.

INTERPRETATION: If a father, forced by need, should sell any freeborn child whatsoever, the child cannot remain in perpetual slavery, but if he has made compensation by his slavery, he shall be restored to his freeborn status without even the repayment of the purchase price.

Title 4: Aedilician Actions (*De Aedilicis Actionibus*)

1.   Emperors Valentinian, Theodosius, and Arcadius Augustuses to Nebridius, Prefect of the City.
   Once a contract of good faith has been completed and a slave has been received and the price paid, the right to recover the purchase price shall be granted to the purchaser of the slave only if he can produce the slave who he claims is a fugitive. This rule, indeed, is prescribed by law not only in the case of barbarian slaves, but also in the case of provincial slaves.
   Given on the third day before the kalends of July at Constantinople in the year of the consulship of Emperor Designate Honorious and the Most Noble Evodius.–June 29, 386.

INTERPRETATION: When the price of a slave has been agreed upon between the buyer and seller and a deed of sale has been written, such sale can by no means be revoked, unless by chance the buyer should prove that the slave is a fugitive, and then he shall have permission to recover the price if he should restore the slave to the seller.

Title 5: Betrothal and Antenuptial Gifts (*De Sponsalibus Et Ante Nuptias Donationibus*)

1.   Emperor Constantine Augustus to Rufinus, Praetorian Prefect.
   It was the will of Our father that no act of generosity should be valid unless it was entered in the public records. We decree also that, after the time of promulgation of this law, gifts between betrothed persons, as well as those between all other persons, shall be valid only if they are accompanied by the attestation of the public records.
   Given on the fourth day before the ides of May at Sirmium in the year of the fifth consulship of Constantine Augustus and the consulship of Licinius Caesar.–May 12, 319; 352.

INTERPRETATION: Before the time of the above law, gifts were valid even without the attestation of the public records. But now, after the above law, no nuptial or any other gift of anything whatsoever, between any persons whatsoever, can be valid if it has not been formally registered in the public records.

2.   The same Augustus to Maximus, Prefect of the City.
   Since We are displeased with the opinion of the ancients which decreed that gifts to a betrothed woman were valid even though the marriage did not follow, We order that those negotiations between betrothed persons which are conducted with due legal formality with the intention of making gifts shall be made subject to the following conditions: whether it appears that persons live under paternal power or that they are in any manner legally independent, if, either of their own volition or with the mutual consent of their parents, they should make presents to each other as though with a view to future matrimony, and if indeed the man of his own accord should be unwilling to take the woman as his wife, he shall not recover that which has been given and delivered by him; if any part of the promised gift remains in the possession of the donor, it shall be transferred to the betrothed woman without any evasion. 1. But if the responsibility for failure to contract the marriage is revealed to have been that of the betrothed woman or of the person under whose power she lives, then all gifts shall be returned to the betrothed man or his heirs without any diminution.

5

2. These provisions shall similarly be observed also if a gift has been made to a betrothed man on the part of the woman betrothed to him. There shall be no further inquiry into reasons for failure to contract the marriage. Thus, for example, the morals or the low birth, perhaps, of either party may not be alleged, and no other obstacle may be adduced which anyone might consider unsuitable, since long before the betrothal was contracted, all these things should have been foreseen. Therefore, only the intention shall be investigated, and a change of intention shall suffice for either restitution or recovery of the gifts that have been made, since, after the elimination of all pretexts, it shall be necessary for nothing further to be established, except the evidence as to which party said that the marriage which was to be contracted was not acceptable.

3. Since it is possible that before the marriage is contracted, one of the two may die while his intention to marry is still unchanged, We consider it suitable that when the one to whom a gift has been made completes his days before the marriage, whatever has been given under the title of a betrothal gift or donated in any other way shall be restored to the person who made the gift. Also, if the person who presented a gift should die before the wedding, the gift shall be immediately invalidated and that property which was presented shall be restored to the heirs of the donor without any hindrance.

4. We decree that this benefit shall extend even to the person of the father and mother and of children also, if there were any from a former marriage; if in any manner any of these persons should succeed to the inheritance of the deceased. But if none of these persons should be an heir of the deceased, but some one from the remaining[6] degrees should succeed to the inheritance, the gifts shall become valid even though because of death the marriage was not confirmed, since We believe that suitable provisions should be made only for those persons.[7]

Given on the seventeenth day before the kalends of November: October 16. Posted on the sixth day before the aforesaid kalends at Rome in the year of the fifth consulship of Constantine Augustus and the consulship of Licinius Caesar.–October 27, 319.

INTERPRETATION: Whenever betrothed persons have made a specific agreement concerning their future marriage, and the man, either with the consent of his parents or of his own free will if he is legally independent, has written a deed of gift of his betrothal bounty to his betrothed and has confirmed this deed of gift with all the formality of written documents, provided also that it shall be proved that public records were made in conformity with the law and that formal induction into the land and delivery of movables followed, then if anything should pass into the right and ownership of the betrothed woman by such a formal gift and if later, after the aforesaid formal documents have been executed, the man should voluntarily refuse to accept as his wife the woman whom he betrothed, he shall not demand back anything that has been delivered. If he is proved to have in his possession any of the property thus formally specified and delivered, it shall be transferred without any delay to the ownership of the betrothed woman whom he was unwilling to accept.

It is unnecessary to explain the remainder of the above law because it is annulled by the subsequent laws.

3. The same Augustus to Valerianus, Acting Vicar of the Prefect.

Although in matters of gain it is not customary to assist women who are ignorant of the law, the statutes of former Emperors declare that this rule does not apply as against one who is still under age. 1. Lest, therefore, when marital affection has vanished, some cruel decision should be made, We decree that if property has been given and delivered to a prospective wife who is under age at the time of marriage, this property cannot be recovered on the grounds that the former husband refused to register the gift in the public records.

Given on the fourth day before the kalends of May in the year of the consulship of Gallicanus and Symmachus.–April 28, 330.

INTERPRETATION: Although even in the case of women, who can at times be excused because of their frailty, the law is unwilling to assist them in some cases if they have been negligent, nevertheless, in the above law it was the Emperor's will that especial provision should be made for them, so that if any girl should be united to a husband in her pupillary years and her husband should through negligence fail to register his betrothal bounty in the public records, she shall know that by the benefit of this law, even if public records are lacking, the gift will remain in her ownership with indefeasible title.

4. The same Augustus to Pacatianus, Praetorian Prefect.
If any man should contract for the marriage of a girl to himself and should fail to effect such marriage within two years, and if after this time has elapsed the girl should proceed to marry another, no fraud shall be imputed to her for hastening her marriage and not allowing her marriage vows to be mocked any longer.
Given on the day before the ides of April at Marcianopolis in the year of the consulship of Pacatianus and Hilarianus.–April 12, 332.

5. The same Augustus to Pacatianus, Praetorian Prefect.
The father of a girl or her tutor, curator, or any kinsman, shall not be permitted to give her in marriage to another after having previously betrothed her to a soldier. If the girl should be given in marriage to another within two years, the person guilty of such perfidy shall be exiled by relegation to an island. But if after an interval of two years has elapsed since the marriage was agreed upon, the person who betrothed the girl[8] should marry her to another, it shall be attributed to the fault of the betrothed man[9] rather than to that of the girl, and the person who gave the girl in marriage to another husband after two years shall suffer no injury.
Given on the day before the ides of April at Marcianopolis in the year of the consulship of Pacatianus and Hilarianus.–April 12, 332.

INTERPRETATION: If any person, either a private citizen or a soldier, after his betrothal to a girl, should make a definite agreement concerning the marriage with her father, tutor, curator, or near kinsman, he must effect the marriage within two years after this definite agreement. But if on account of the procrastination or negligence of the betrothed man, a period of two years should elapse and the girl should marry another man, both she herself and the kinsman who delivered her in marriage shall be free from calumny. For the fault is that of the man who, by delaying his own marriage, gave to another man the opportunity to marry the girl. If she should be given in marriage to another man within two years, the rules to be observed will be understood more clearly from the subsequent law.

6. The same Augustus to Tiberianus, Vicar of Spain.
If a man should make gifts to his betrothed when a kiss has been exchanged as a pledge and if it should happen that either the man or the woman should die before the marriage, We order that one half of the things given shall belong to the survivor; the other half shall belong to the heirs of the deceased man or woman, of whatever degree such heirs may be and by whatever right they may succeed to the inheritance, so that it appears that one half the gift shall remain valid and one half shall be annulled. But when no kiss has been exchanged as a pledge, if either of the betrothed persons should die, the whole gift shall be invalidated and shall be restored to the betrothed donor or to his heirs.
1. If a woman should give anything to her betrothed under the title of betrothal gifts, a thing which rarely occurs, and if it happens that either the man or the woman dies before the marriage, whether or not a kiss has been exchanged as a pledge, the whole gift shall be invalidated, and the ownership of the things shall be transferred to the betrothed woman who gave it or to her heirs.

Given on the ides of July at Constantinople: July 15, 335. Received on the fourteenth day be-

fore the kalends of May at Hispalis in the year of the consulship of Nepotianus and Facundus.–
April 18, 336.

INTERPRETATION: If when a betrothal has been solemnized and a kiss has been exchanged as a pledge, the betrothed man should make some gift to the betrothed woman, and if perchance he should die before the marriage, then the girl, in case she survives, shall be able to vindicate one half of the things which had been formally given to her, and the heirs of the deceased shall acquire one half, in whatsoever order, according to the degree of succession, they may come. But if a kiss should not be exchanged as a pledge, and the betrothed man should die, the girl shall not be able to vindicate any of the things given or delivered to her. But if anything should be given by the girl to the betrothed man and she should die, whether or not a kiss has been exchanged as a pledge, the parents or near kinsmen of the girl shall recover all that which the girl gave.

7. [10] ...

...provided that...has been preserved, the gift shall have complete validity, although he did not arrange for the certification of public records in testimony thereof. Certainly, a group of people assembled as witnesses of these vows is sufficiently competent. But in the case of all other gifts, the execution of public records shall be required in accordance with the constitutions of Our sainted father.[11]

Given on the fifth day before the ides of Ju...[12] at Köln in the year of the consulship of Amantius and Albinus.–June 9 (July 11), 345.

8. Emperor Julian Augustus to Hypatius, Vicar of the City of Rome.

Whenever any gifts consisting of landed estates that are subject to either Italian, stipendiary, or tributary rights[13] are given and pledged by a stipulation to a betrothed woman in her minority, with a view to future marriage, such bounty shall be supported by perpetual validity, even though it should appear that the formality of delivery was lacking; provided, however, that even in the case of those gifts which are bestowed upon minors, the execution of public records shall be demanded in all cases.

Given on the ninth day before the kalends of M(arch) at Antioch in the year of the fourth consulship of Julian Augustus and the consulship of Sallustius.–February 21, 363.

9. Emperors Valentinian, Valens, and Gratian Augustuses to Probus, Praetorian Prefect.

Before marriage many things are delivered with all due formality under the title of betrothal gifts, and these gifts must not by any means contribute to loss on the part of the donor. But if the girl should die during the marriage, they shall revert to the advantage of the said donor in disregard, of course, of the old law. Therefore, the claim of the father and other near kinsmen shall be annulled, and such gifts shall be returned without delay to those persons who appear to have presented them before the marriage was contracted.

Given on the third day before the ides of July at Trier in the year of the consulship of Valentinian and Valens Augustuses.–July 13, 368; 367; 373.

10. Emperors Gratian, Valentinian, and Theodosius Augustuses to Eutropius, Praetorian Prefect.

If, after anything has been given as earnest under the title of betrothal gifts, either of the betrothed persons should die, *We order that whatever has been given shall be restored, unless the deceased person had previously given cause for the non-performance of the marriage rites.*

Given on the fifteenth day before the kalends of July at Thessalonica in the year of the fifth consulship of Gratian Augustus and the first consulship of Theodosius Augustus.–June 17, 380.

11. The same Augustuses to Eutropius, Praetorian Prefect.

When betrothal gifts have been made to a girl before her tenth year, We remit the fourfold penalty for the father, mother, tutor, or any person, even though the marriage should not follow; and if the girl should die in the meantime, We order that the betrothal gifts shall be restored to her betrothed. 1. But if the father or any other person who has charge of the girl's affairs should suppose that he should retain the pledges which he has received in the girl's tenth year or later, and before her twelfth year, that is, until the end of her eleventh year, then if, when the time for the marriage arrives, he should be false to his trust, he shall become obligated to the fourfold penalty.

2. But for a widow, since she is not assisted by the privilege of age, there is a different rule, namely, that if she does not effect her marriage, she shall be liable to the fourfold penalty according to the ancient constitution.

3. Moreover, when any person makes an agreement concerning the marriage of a girl after the completion of her twelfth year, if indeed the person making the agreement is the girl's father, he shall obligate himself, but if her mother or a curator or other near kinsman, the girl shall become obligated.

4. But there shall be reserved to the girl against her mother, tutor, curator, or such near kinsman, an unimpaired action, on the basis of what is fair and just with regard to those pledges which she restored from her own resources according to the penalty of the law, provided that she can prove that she had been compelled by the aforesaid persons to consent to receive what was given as earnest.

Given on the fifteenth day before the kalends of July at Thessalonica in the year of the fifth consulship of Gratian Augustus and the first consulship of Theodosius Augustus.–June 17, 380.

11. The same Augustuses to Eutropius, Praetorian Prefect.

When betrothal gifts have been made to a girl before her tenth year, We remit the fourfold penalty for the father, mother, tutor, or any other person, even though the marriage should not follow; and if the girl should die in the meantime, We order that the betrothal gifts shall be restored to her betrothed. 1. But if the father or any other person who has charge of the girl's affairs should suppose that he should retain the pledges which he has received in the girl's tenth year or later, and before her twelfth year, that is, until the end of her eleventh year, then if, when the time for the marriage arrives, he should be false to his trust, he shall be become obligated to the fourfold penalty.

2. But for a widow, since she is not assisted by the privilege of age, there is a different rule, namely, that if she does not effect her marriage, she shall be liable to the fourfold penalty according to the ancient constitution.

3. Moreover, when any person makes an agreement concerning the marriage of a girl after the completion of her twelfth year, if indeed the person making the agreement is the girl's father, he shall obligate himself, but if her mother or a curator or other near kinsman, the girl shall become obligated.

4. But there shall be reserved to the girl against her mother, tutor, curator, or such near kinsman, an unimpaired action, on the basis of what is fair and just with regard to those pledges which she restored from her own resources according to the penalty of the law, provided that she can prove that she had been compelled by the aforesaid persons to consent to receive what was given as earnest.

Given on the fifteenth day before the kalends of July at Thessalonica in the year of the fifth consulship of Gratian Augustus and the first consulship of Theodosius Augustus.–June 17, 380.

INTERPRETATION: If, before a girl has reached her tenth year, her father or mother or, if the father should be lacking, her tutor, curator, or any near kinsman, should make an agreement concerning her marriage and should accept betrothal gifts, and if afterwards he should change his mind and wish to reject the person whom he had formerly accepted, he shall not be condemned to the fourfold penalty, but shall restore only what he had received. Certainly, also if the girl should die, only that shall be returned which had been received. But if, when the girl is in her tenth year and until the completion of her eleventh year, she herself, or her parents, tutors and curators should retain the earnest which had been received, the following rule must be observed, namely, that if the person who made

9

the agreement concerning the marriage of the girl should wish to prove false to the agreement and should reject the man whose betrothal gifts had been received, he shall be liable to the fourfold penalty, without doubt. But if he should return the pledges received before the girl's eleventh year is completed, he shall fear no malicious charges concerning the earnest which had been accepted. On the other hand, if the girl should be a widow, she shall not be able to defend herself on the ground of her age,[11] if she should turn her affections elsewhere and should wish to reject her former betrothed. Then whatever she has accepted under the title of betrothal gifts she shall return fourfold. But if after the girl's twelfth year, her father should wish to do otherwise than he promised concerning her marriage, her father himself shall be held liable to the fourfold penalty. If the father is dead and the mother, tutor, curator or any near kinsman should make a definite agreement concerning the marriage of the girl and the girl should prefer to wed another, she herself out of her own resources shall make reparation to her former betrothed in the amount of four times the value of what she received. This condition, however, shall be observed, that she can bring suit afterwards against the aforesaid persons, if under their compulsion she unwillingly accepted the pledges of the man whom she later refused.

12. Emperors Honorius and Theodosius Augustuses to Marinianus, Praetorian Prefect.
(After other matters.) If a father should enter into a pact concerning the marriage of his daughter and he should not be able to reach the time of the marriage because he perished by human lot, the decision which is proved to have been made by the father shall remain valid and binding between the betrothed, and a compromise shall not be permitted to have any weight if it is proved to have been made by the guardian to whose administration the interests of the minor pertain. 1. For it is thoroughly unjust that the decision of a tutor or curator, who has perhaps been bribed, should be admitted as against the father's wish, since frequently even the determination of a woman herself is found to work against her own interests. (Etc.)
Given on the third day before the nones of November at Ravenna in the year of the thirteenth consulship of Our Lord Honorius Augustus and the tenth consulship of Our Lord Theodosius Augustus.—November 3, 422.

INTERPRETATION: When a definite agreement concerning the marriage of a girl has been made by the decision of her father, if by human lot the father should die before the girl is married, the agreement cannot be changed in any way, and the girl shall not have the liberty to do anything else even if her mother or tutor or curator or near kinsmen should perhaps wish that she accept another rather than the man her father chose. But the promise of her father with reference to the man whom he himself accepted as her betrothed shall remain valid, and in no way shall the girl be permitted in accordance with her own plan to desire anything contrary to the wishes of her father.

13. Emperors Theodosius and Valentinian Augustuses to Hierius, Praetorian Prefect.
(After other matters.) If a deed or gift has been validated before marriage by the formality of registration in the public records, there shall be no inquiry as to whether delivery of the gift either preceded or followed the marriage or was altogether omitted. In the case of a gift which is less than two hundred solidi in its total value, the execution of public records shall not be required. 1. We do not permit these advantages to be denied to a wife or to those persons who succeed to her rights, who may be deceived through the fraud of her husband or the dishonesty of his heirs or through legal technicalities, even though either through ignorance or cunning the deed of gift should make mention of things to be given as dowry, but such gifts shall be extracted from the husband or his heirs and shall be restored. That law also shall remain in force which makes just provision for women of minor age, even when the attestation of the public records has been omitted, if they have been deprived of their father's aid. (Etc.)
Given on the tenth day before the kalends of March at Constantinople in the year of the consulship of Taurus and Felix.—February 21, 428.

INTERPRETATION: If a betrothal gift should be entered in the public records before marriage, it cannot be invalidated even though the thing given is not delivered. But in the case of a gift, the total value of which is found to be less than two hundred solidi, even when a public record of it is lacking, no chicanery can be employed against women under cover of any cunning device or objection, but any writing whatever which indicates the day and the time shall suffice. Therefore, whether a gift is one which is made by entry in the public records without delivery, or whether it is one which is less than two hundred solidi in value, it shall not be invalidated by any arguments resting upon chicanery in any respect, but the things shall be exacted from the husband or his heirs who shall be ordered to restore them to the woman. Nevertheless, the benefit of the law shall remain valid concerning those women who are married during their minority after their father's death, so that a deed of gift of any amount whatever, when made in writing, shall stand with complete validity, even though it has not been registered in the public records.

14. ...

...the betrothed man or the betrothed woman may violate this regulation without any hazard. But the fifteenth constitution of the fifteenth title of the third book of the Theodosian Code confirms the threatened penalty to the extent of double indemnity in cases of agreements for marriage.

Title 6: If the Governor of a Province or Persons Connected with Him Should Give Betrothal Gifts (*Si Provinciae Rector Vel Ad Eum Pertinentes Sponsalia Dederint*)

1. Emperors Gratian, Valentinian, and Theodosius Augustuses to Eutropius, Praetorian Prefect.
(After other matters.) If betrothal gifts should be given by persons who hold positions of public power and honour in the administration of provinces and who, therefore, can intimidate parents, tutors, curators, or the women themselves who are about to contract the marriage, We order that if either the parents or the women themselves should change their minds thereafter, they shall not only be released from the toils of the law and free from the fourfold penalty which it has established, but in addition they shall keep as gain the things given as pledges if they should suppose that they ought not to be returned. 1. So widely do We intend this provision to extend that We decree that it shall apply not only to such administrators, but also to sons, grandsons, near kinsmen, associates and confidential advisers of administrations, provided, however, that the administrators had given them assistance. 2. However, We do not forbid that marriage to be effected thereafter which was obligated by means of an earnest at the time of such administration, on account of those persons about whom We have spoken, if the consent of the betrothed woman should accede thereto.
Given on the fifteenth day before the kalends of July at Thessalonica in the year of the fifth consulship of Our Lord Gratian Augustus and the first consulship of Our Lord Theodosius Augustus.–June 17, 380.

INTERPRETATION: If any judges[15] of provinces or any persons in administrative offices, while holding the aforesaid positions of honour, should have with them their adult sons or near kinsmen or any persons who appear to be associated with them in their administration, if they should use their power to threaten the parents or perchance to intimidate tutors or curators or the girls themselves, if they should give anything in the name of betrothal gifts or as earnest for the purpose of obligating the household of any person, and if the parents or the girls themselves should wish to resist this desire,[16] they shall have the unrestricted right to refuse that which they appear to have thus accepted. They shall know that the fourfold penalty shall not be exacted of them, but also those gifts which it appears that they accepted through terror they shall retain to their own profit, if they so wish, and they cannot be constrained to return them unless perchance they should wish to do so of their own free will. For if, after the end of such administration, the desire of the parents or the girls should remain unchanged with regard to marriage with those persons who had given betrothal gifts, the marriage thus chosen may follow.

Title 7: Marriage (*De Nuptiis*)

1. Emperors Valentinian, Valens and Gratian Augustuses to the Senate.

A widow less than twenty-five years of age, even though she enjoys the freedom derived from emancipation, shall not enter into a subsequent marriage without the consent of her father or in opposition to his will. Therefore, the intermediaries and marriage brokers, the corrupt bearers of secret messages back and forth, shall cease. No person shall purchase a noble marriage,[17] no person shall solicit one; but the kinsmen shall be consulted publicly, and a number of nobles shall be admitted. 1. But if in the choice of a marriage the woman's desire should conflict with the decision of her near kinsmen, it is Our pleasure that, as has been sanctioned in the case of marriages of girls who are pupils, the authority of a judicial trial shall be added to the investigation that must be held, so that if the suitors are equal in birth and character, the person whom the woman herself approves, consulting her own interests, shall be adjudged preferable. 2. But lest perchance even honorable marriages should be impeded by those persons who, as kinsmen in the nearest degree, would be called to the inheritances of such widows, if a suspicion of this kind should arise, it is Our will that the authority and judgment of those persons shall prevail who, even though death should intervene, could not receive the benefit of the inheritance.

Given on the seventeenth day before the kalends of August in the year of the second consulship of Gratian Augustus and the consulship of Probus.–July 16, 371.

INTERPRETATION: If a widow who has not yet arrived at her twenty-fifth year during her father's lifetime should wish to enter into a subsequent marriage, she shall know that, even though she has acquired her freedom by emancipation, her marriage is subject to the control of her father and does not rest upon her own desire, and her consent must conform to the choice of her father and not that of any friends or comrades whatever. But if indeed the father of such a widow is dead, even so she shall not have the right to marry according to her own individual choice, but in the interests of an honorable condition of marriage, the judgment of the near kinsmen must be followed. But if there should be two suitors, the near kinsmen must certainly be consulted, and the judge[18] also must not be ignored, who shall take into consideration the desire of the woman only in the interest of the more honorable man. He shall not give assent to the wishes of those near kinsmen only who labour under the suspicion of desiring the inheritance and who, perhaps, while they delay the wedding, appear to be awaiting the death of the woman with a view to their succession to the inheritance. But if such a condition should arise, the choice of those persons rather must be followed who can acquire nothing from the inheritance of the aforesaid woman.

2. Emperors Valentinian, Theodosius, and Arcadius Augustuses to Cynegius, Praetorian Prefect.

No Jew shall receive a Christian woman in marriage, nor shall a Christian man contract a marriage with a Jewish woman. For if any person should commit an act of this kind, the crime of this misdeed shall be considered as the equivalent of adultery, and freedom to bring accusation shall be granted also to the voices of the public.

Given on the day before the ides of March at Thessalonica in the year of the second consulship of Theodosius Augustus and the consulship of the Most Noble Cynegius.–March 14, 388.

INTERPRETATION: By the severity of this law it is prohibited that a Jew should enjoy marriage with a Christian woman or that a Christian man should receive a Jewish woman as his wife. But if any persons should involve themselves in such a union, contrary to Our prohibition, they shall know that they will be prosecuted and subjected to the same punishment as that which is inflicted upon adulterers, and that the right to bring accusation of this crime and the prosecution of it shall be allowed not only to near kinsmen but also to everyone.

3. Emperors Theodosius and Valentinian Augustuses to Hierius, Praetorian Prefect.
If instruments[19] of prenuptial gifts or dowries should be lacking and if the solemn procession and other wedding ceremonies should be omitted, no person shall suppose that on this account a marriage otherwise legally entered into shall lack validity or that the rights of legitimacy can be taken from children born of such a marriage, when the marriage is contracted of persons of equally honorable status, when it is preceded by no law, and when it is confirmed by the consent of the parties and the reliable testimony of friends.(Etc.)
Given on the tenth day before the kalends of March at Constantinople in the year of the consulship of Felix and Taurus.–February 21, 428.

INTERPRETATION: If any such exigency should arise that a marriage should lack the due formalities, or even that betrothal gifts cannot be made or the bestowal of a dowry executed, yet if the parties should unite in marriage by mutual consent, when they are persons of equal status, a suitable choice and the agreement of the parties shall suffice, provided, however, that the knowledge of friends shall act as surety of the marriage; then if such a situation should occur, the marriage shall be approved as valid and the children as legitimate.

Title 8: Subsequent Marriages (*De Secundis Nuptiis*)

1. Emperors Gratian, Valentinian, and Theodosius Augustuses to Eutropius, Praetorian Prefect.
If any woman who has lost her husband should hasten to marry another man within the period of a year (for We add a small amount of time to be observed after the ten months period, although We consider even that to be very little) she shall be branded with the marks of disgrace and deprived of both the dignity and rights of a person of honorable and noble status. She shall also forfeit all the property which she has obtained from the estate of her former husband, either by the right of betrothal gifts or by the will of her deceased husband. She shall know also that she shall expect no help from Us through either a special grant of imperial favour or an annotation.
Given on the third day before the kalends of June at Constantinople in the year of the consulship of Eucherius and Syagrius.–May 30, 381.

INTERPRETATION: If within a year after the death of her husband a woman should marry another man, she shall know that she will subject herself to infamy and be rendered infamous to such a degree that she shall forfeit any betrothal gifts that she has received by the bounty of her former husband or anything that he has given to her by his testament, and all this property shall go to his children. If there should be no children, the said property shall profit those persons who are akin to the former husband in the nearest degree, and they shall be able to vindicate this property for themselves through the right of inheritance.

2. The same Augustuses to Florus, Praetorian Prefect.
When a woman passes to a subsequent marriage, if she has children born from a prior marriage, anything that she has received from the property of her former husband by right of betrothal gifts, or anything that she has also received upon celebration of the marriage, or anything that she has acquired from the property of her former husband by gifts made in expectation of death or by testament, either by direct right or under the title of a trust or legacy or as a reward through any other form of munificent liberality, all this

13

she shall have the right to transmit undiminished, just as she received it, to the children which she has from her prior marriage, or to any one of these children upon whom the mother believes she ought to bestow the judgment of her liberality in view of the merits of such child, provided that this child should be one of those whom We consider most worthy of such a succession. Such a woman shall not presume or have the power to alienate any part of such property to any extraneous person whatsoever or to successors born from the union of the second marriage. She shall have the right of possession only to the last day of her life, and she shall not be allowed the power of alienation also. For if any of the aforesaid property, through a fraud of evil intent, should be transferred by the mother who possesses it to any other person whatsoever, it must be restored by compensation out of her own resources, whereby the property shall go undiminished and unimpaired to those persons whom We have designated as heirs.

1. We also add to the law the following provision, namely, that if any son from the aforesaid children who are proved to have been born from the former marriage should perhaps die, leaving one or more sisters but no brother, and thus, by benefit of the decree of the Senate, he should appear to provide for the mother a place as heir along with the sisters; or if a daughter should die leaving no brother alive, but only her mother and sisters as survivors and should thus preserve for the mother an opportunity to enter upon the inheritance for a half portion, whatever the mother shall appear to have obtained by the benefit of succession,[20] she shall be granted only the possession thereof to the last day of her life in accordance with her due portion. She shall leave everything to the surviving children who were born of her prior marriage, and she shall not have the power to will such property to any extraneous person or to alienate any of it.

2. But if she should have no children as her successors from the prior marriage, or if such child or children should have died, she shall hold in fully legal ownership all property which she has received in any manner, and she shall have the unlimited power to acquire ownership from these children and to give it by testament to whomever she wishes.

3. It is Our will that husbands also shall be admonished by a similar example of both piety and law. Although We do not constrain them by the bond, so to speak, of a sanction very severely imposed upon them, nevertheless We restrain them by the law of religion, that they may know that which is enjoined upon mothers by the necessity of the law, as here set forth, is more readily expected of them in consideration of justice, in order that, if necessity should so persuade, in the case of men, too, there should not have to be exacted from them by the aid of a sanction that which meanwhile may properly be desired and expected.

Given on the sixteenth day before the kalends of January at Constantinople in the year of the consulship of Antonius and Syagrius.–December 17, 382.

INTERPRETATION: If a woman should lose her husband and afterward should enter into another marriage at the statutory time, that is, when a year has elapsed, and if she should have children by her former husband, she shall preserve for such children all the property which she has received through any betrothal bounty or gift made at the time of the wedding, and she shall know that this property must not be transferred to other or extraneous persons. But whatever the former husband has given to his wife by a testament or trust fund or under the title of legacy or in expectation of death, this property that the wife has received by such a gift, she shall have the unlimited power to bestow, either upon all the children or upon one for the merit of such child's service, if she should so wish; but she shall not be permitted to alienate any of the property of her former husband away from his children. But if she should presume to do this, she must know that compensation must be made out of her own resources.

The Emperor supposed that the following provision especially should be included in this law, namely, that if a woman should proceed to another marriage, and if, of the children which she had born from her prior marriage, a son should die, in case that he leaves surviving a mother and sisters, or at least a sister and does not leave a brother, who would be able to exclude the mother, then by the benefit of the law the mother and the daughters or daughter shall succeed to equal shares. But if a daughter should die and should leave only a mother and sisters, the mother shall acquire half the inheritance of the deceased daughter, and half shall accrue to the sisters, whether there be one or many, under the condition, however, that while the mother lives, she shall possess only in usufruct the half which she has acquired from such inheritance of a son or daughter. After her death she shall leave this property to the remaining children, if any have survived from her former marriage, and she shall not have the liberty to transfer it to other persons either by testament or by gift. But if no children by her former husband should survive, then any property whatever that she has received on this account she shall vindicate for herself as though it were her own property, and she shall lawfully transmit it to whomever she may wish. In this law also it was the Emperor's will that a similar condition should be observed if a father whose wife had died should proceed to a subsequent marriage, so that, if there should be sons or daughters by his former wife, of whom some should die and make a place for the father in the succession to their own portion, after the father's death, this portion which was left to him should accrue to the brothers and sisters who survive from his prior marriage, and it could not pass to other persons through paternal power.

3. Emperors Honorius and Theodosius Augustuses to Johannes, Praetorian Prefect.
   No person shall have any doubt that a woman shall have a usufruct to the last day of her life in the property which she received at the time of her marriage, even though she should perchance proceed to a subsequent marriage after the statutory time has elapsed and even though there should be children of the prior marriage. The ownership of such property shall be preserved for those persons to whom the most sacred imperial laws have reserved the entire right after the death of the woman, which right it is manifestly established is transmitted to the children of the prior marriage.
   Given on the tenth day before the kalends of July at Ravenna in the year of the ninth consulship of Our Lord Honorius Augustus and the fifth consulship of Our Lord Theodosius Augustus.–June 22, 412.

INTERPRETATION: It is very well known that a woman vindicates to her ownership such property as she receives from her husband at the time of her wedding. If her husband should chance to die, leaving children, however, and the woman should lawfully proceed to another marriage after the period of mourning has elapsed, to the last day of her life she shall hold a usufruct of the property thus given to her. But after the death of the woman, all such property shall revert to the children of the former husband, and the mother is not permitted to transfer any of it to the ownership of others while the children are living.

Title 9: If a Woman to Whom Her Husband Left a Usufruct Should Subsequently Marry (*Si Secundo Nupserit Mulier Cui Maritus Usumfructum Reliquerit*)

1. Emperors Arcadius and Honorius Augustuses to Asterius, Count of the Orient.
   By a clear decision We indicate that the regulations which have been established by Our Clemency concerning prenuptial gifts are far different from those which have been established concerning property from a man's own patrimony, the usufruct of which he has left to his wife by his own will. For in the case of such usufruct of a portion of his own property which a man by executing his last will leaves to his wife, it is Our will that the woman shall be threatened with the loss of this usufruct immediately after her subsequent marriage, in accordance with that law which has indubitably been issued concerning this special point. But as to the usufruct of property given before marriage, those rules shall be observed which an earlier, most salutary law has decreed with a full regulation.
   Given on the sixteenth day before the kalends of March at Constantinople in the year of the fourth consulship of Honorius Augustus and the consulship of Eutychianus.–February 14, 398.

INTERPRETATION: With a clear interpretation the Emperor has explained these two legal provisions, namely, that if the husband at his death should leave to his wife, in addition to the betrothal gift, a usufruct on property of his own patrimony, she shall possess that which has been left to her according to his will, on condition that if afterwards the woman should marry another man, she shall immediately restore the usufruct acquired under the will to the children of the man from whom she had obtained the usufruct. But she shall rightfully retain the usufruct of the betrothal gift until her death, just as another law previously indicated. Whence the ownership of this property shall revert after the mother's death to the children of the husband who gave it.

Title 10: If Marriage Should be Petitioned for in Accordance With a Rescript (*Si Nuptiae Ex Rescripto Petantur*)

1. Emperors Honorius and Theodosius Augustuses to Theodorus, Praetorian Prefect.

Some men, in disregard of the provision of the ancient law, suppose that they may request from Us by surreptitious supplication permission for a marriage to which they know they are not entitled, and they pretend that they have the girl's consent. Therefore We prohibit betrothals of such a kind by the ordinance of the present law. 1. If any person, therefore, in violation of this ordinance, should obtain such permission to marry by a surreptitious supplication, he shall not doubt that he will suffer the forfeiture of his goods and the punishment of deportation. He shall also know that he forfeits the right of marriage which he obtained by such a forbidden usurpation; that he cannot have legally born children in this manner; and that he has never obtained an effective permission by the grant of the requested indulgence or the imperial annotation. Excepted herefrom are those persons whom the law of Our father of triumphal memory[21] did not forbid to supplicate, after the pattern of the imperial indulgences, for the marriage of cousins, that is, of persons related in the fourth degree. Those persons also shall be excepted who desire that the solemn engagement of parents as to the marriage of their daughters shall be fulfilled or who request the return of betrothal gifts, that is, of gifts given in the name of earnest, together with the fourfold penalty, under the provisions of the laws. 2. For We forbid that We be requested by supplication to grant permission for a marriage which should properly be impetrated in accordance with the wish of the parents or of the adult girls or the women themselves. But if a marriage is refused which has previously been promised and some lawsuit arises under the provision of these statutes, We do not forbid that We be consulted about the law.

Given on the tenth day before the kalends of February at Ravenna in the year of the eighth consulship of Our Lord Honorius Augustus and the third consulship of Our Lord Theodosius Augustus.–January 23, 409.

INTERPRETATION: Occasionally it happens that some man, forgetful of the severity of the law, dares to employ surreptitious methods in dealing with the imperial majesty, that he seeks for himself permission granted by an imperial order for a marriage which he is not entitled to obtain, and that he lies about the consent of the parents or of the girl; wherefore, the Emperor prohibits such audacity. If any man, therefore, should suppose that he should obtain the right to marry through such surreptitious methods, he shall know that he will be punished by the forfeiture of his property and exile by relegation; that he shall not have the marriage which he sought in such a manner; that the children born of a union contracted through such an arrangement and by such corrupt solicitation shall not be called legitimate, and that not even through a supplication to the Emperor shall he obtain pardon for such presumption. But in the case of persons connected by kinship in the fourth degree who have entered into a presumptuous union, although such a union is infamous, nevertheless, if the parties should supplicate the Emperor, he will grant a pardon. Those persons shall not be prohibited from seeking an ordinance of His Majesty, since they are united in marriage pursuant to an agreement of the parents. But if any man to whom a girl was betrothed while her parents were living is scorned by the girl after the death of her parents, according to the tenor of the law he shall recover fourfold those things which he has given or presented in the name of earnest. But if arrangements have not been previously been made, the Emperor, with all severity, prohibits the request by supplication of permission to marry. But if any man should make a marriage agreement with the parents of a girl or with the girl herself, and one of the contracting parties should wish to abandon the agreement, We do not forbid the person who is scorned to consult Us. (The remainder of this law has already been expounded elsewhere.)

Title 11: If a Person Endowed With Any Administrative Power Should Seek to Marry a Woman Against Her Will (*Si Quacumque Praeditus Potestate Nuptias Petat Invitae*)

1. Emperors Gratian, Valentinian, and Theodosius Augustuses to Neoterius, Praetorian Prefect.

If a person endowed with ordinary authority[22] or with any administrative authority whatever, should use the advantage of his power in connection with contracting a marriage to which the woman herself or her parents are averse, whether the girl is a pupil, a maiden or widow living with her father, a widow of independent status, or in short, a woman of any condition whatever, and if such administrator should be found to show or to have shown his menacing favour toward unwilling persons whose interests are here considered, We decree that he shall be liable to a fine of ten pounds of gold, and We forbid him, when he has retired from his high office, to usurp the high rank thus acquired. If he should refuse to obey the sanction of Our statute with respect to the vindication of the honour which he has wrongfully used, the following penalty is provided, namely, that in every case for a continuous period of two years he shall not be allowed to live in the province in which he committed such usurpation.

1. Because, however, We realize that certain households and certain parents must be further protected against hidden malice, We order that if any parent or any woman whatsoever should be assailed by hidden promises or threats through the judge[23] with regard to that marriage to which the woman has disdained to give her consent, such persons may immediately file an attestation. Whereupon they, together with their household and that of their family, shall cease to belong to his jurisdiction; the defenders of each municipality and the apparitors of the aforesaid judge shall attend to this matter. 2. If such depravity should be that of the judge ordinary, all jurisdiction over the aforesaid household in all matters, civil and criminal, shall belong to the vicar as long as the aforesaid judge ordinary is in authority. However, if the vicar or a person of similar authority should undertake to exercise coercion in contracting such a marriage, the judge ordinary in turn shall become the intercessor. But if the judge and vicar should both be suspected, the protection of such households particularly shall devolve upon the Illustrious prefect as long as the aforesaid judge or vicar is in office.

Given on the fifteenth day before the kalends of July at Thessalonica in the year of the fifth consulship of Gratian Augustus and the first consulship of Theodosius Augustus.–June 17, 380.

INTERPRETATION: If any judge who administers a province, or even if any person to whom is entrusted the administration of municipalities or districts, through his authority should assign to himself for marriage a maiden, against the will of her parents, or even a widow who is either of independent status or a pupil, and if, contrary to the interests of this woman, by means of terror and collusion of any persons whatever, such woman should be assigned against her will to be married to those persons concerning whom the Emperor speaks — if anyone should presume to do this, he shall know that he will be condemned to the payment of ten pounds of gold, stripped of his high rank, and prohibited for a period of two years from entering the province in which he had been judge. But this law provides a special grant of imperial favour, as a protection against such men, to parents and to women themselves when they are of independent status, and to those persons who exercise guardianship over minors, namely, that they shall have the right to file their attestations before other judges or in the nearest municipalities and to be defended by their protection. Thus if there should be another high official in the same province, as, for example, if there should be two judges, one administering private rights and the other imperial rights, and if, in this situation, any person is oppressed by one of these judges, he shall be defended by the protection of the other, or at least he shall have recourse to the magnificent authority,[24] who can bring this information to the ears of the Emperor.

Title 12: Incestuous Marriages (*De Incestis Nuptiis*)

1. Emperors Constantius and Constans Augustuses to the Provincials of Phoenicia.
   If any man should be so abominable as to presume that a daughter of a brother or of a sister should be made his wife, and if he should fly to her embrace, not as her paternal or maternal uncle, he shall be held subject to a sentence of capital punishment.
   Given on the day before the kalends of April at Antioch in the year of the third consulship of consulship of Constantius Augustus and the second consulship of Constans Augustus.–March 31, 342.

INTERPRETATION: If any man should presume to enter into an incestuous union with the daughter of his brother or of his sister, he shall know that he will undergo the peril of capital punishment.

2. Emperors Constantius and Constans Augustuses and Julian Caesar to Volusianus, Praetorian Prefect.
   Although the ancients believed it lawful for a man to marry his brother's wife after the marriage of his brother had been dissolved, and lawful also for a man, after the death or divorce of his wife, to contract a marriage with a sister of the said wife, all men shall abstain from such marriages, and they shall not suppose that legitimate children may be begotten from such a union. For it is established that children so born are spurious.
   Given on the day before the kalends of May at Rome in the year of the consulship of Arbitio and Lollianus.–April 30, 355.

INTERPRETATION: Licence is absolutely denied a man to marry a woman who has been his brother's wife or for the same man to have two sisters to wife, for the children born of such a union are not considered legitimate.

3. Emperors Arcadius and Honorius Augustuses to Eutychianus, Praetorian Prefect.
   The decrees shall remain undisturbed with regard to those persons who have been either absolved or punished in any manner under the law formerly issued. But hereafter, 1. if any person should defile himself by an incestuous marriage with his own first cousin, the daughter of his sister or brother, or finally with any man's wife whose marriage to him has been forbidden and condemned, he shall indeed be exempt from the punishment designated by the law, that is, the punishment of fire and proscription, and he shall have the right to hold his own property as long as he lives. But he shall not be considered as having a wife or as having children born from her. 1. Absolutely nothing shall be given by him during his lifetime or left by him at his death to the aforesaid wife, even through an interposed person. 2. If perchance any dowry has been formally given, specified, or promised, it shall accrue to the resources of Our fisc in accordance with the ancient law. 3. He shall leave nothing by his testament to extraneous persons, but whether he dies testate or intestate, he shall be succeeded, according to the statutes and the law, by those persons, if there be any, who are born of statutory and legal marriage; that is, in the case of descendants, by a son, daughter, grandson, granddaughter, great grandson, great granddaughter; in the case of ascendants, by a father, mother, grandfather, grandmother; in the case of collaterals, by a brother, sister, paternal uncle, or paternal aunt.
   4. Indeed, he shall have the power to make a testament only to the extent that he may

leave what he wishes, subject to the provisions of the law and statutes, to those persons alone whom We order to succeed by the terms of the imperial statute; provided, however, that if any of those persons whom We have mentioned should be proved to have participated in contracting the incestuous marriage and to have entered into the plan, he shall be absolutely barred from the inheritance of the deceased, and into his place shall succeed that person who is found to rank next after him in the order of kinship. 5. Certainly these provisions which We have made concerning men shall be observed also by women who pollute themselves by marriage with the aforesaid persons. 6. But if none of the aforementioned persons should survive, a place shall be open to the fisc.[25] 7. We order to be subject to the restraints and conditions of this law any person who perchance previously, that is, before the promulgation of this law, has been contaminated by the illicit crimes of the aforesaid marriages and has been able in any manner to avoid detection.

Given on the seventh day before the ides of December at Constantinople in the year of the fourth consulship of Arcadius Augustus, and the third consulship of Honorius Augustus.–December 7 (6), 396.[26]

INTERPRETATION: After the provisions of the former law which was issued about such persons, the Emperor commands that the following rules shall be observed, namely, that if any person should unite to himself in a criminal marriage a sister's or a brother's daughter, a cousin of the third degree,[27] or even a cousin of more remote degree, or the wife[28] of his brother, such person shall be exempt from the penalty of the law, that is, severe punishment and proscription, but he shall be subjected to the punishment that he shall be separated from such a union and that if there are any children, they shall not be considered his heirs. But both parties[29] shall be branded with infamy, with the provision that, by special grant of imperial favour, they shall appear only to have possession of their own property; but they shall presume to enter into no contract. They shall be deprived of the right to make gifts and to execute testaments. But such a husband shall bestow nothing upon the woman herself whom he has thus married, and if the husband and wife have exchanged gifts at the time of the marriage, such gifts shall be confiscated to the fisc. Even if they should have children, none of their property shall pass to such children through a supposititious person or any other person or by fictitious gift, but at their death their property shall pass by intestate succession to those lawful heirs who are admitted to the inheritance according to their rank in the line of succession, up to a certain degree of kinship. They are permitted the right to make a testament for the benefit of those persons only for whom they are allowed by law to make testaments, so that from these persons they may designate as heirs those persons whom they choose; provided, however, that if any of these persons are shown to have given their approval to such a union, they shall be excluded from the inheritance, and they shall make place for others who come in the next degree. Indeed, if there should be a lack of such near kinsmen that the law calls to the succession, then the fisc shall take possession of their property.

4.   Emperors Honorius and Theodosius Augustuses to Aurelianus, Praetorian Prefect for the second time.

A man shall be considered as though he had committed incest, if after the death of a former wife he should presume to select her sister for marriage. A woman, also, shall be held to an equal and similar accountability if after the death of her husband she should presume to aspire to a marriage with his own brother. It will undoubtedly follow that the children of such a cohabitation will not be considered legitimate, they shall not be in the power of their father, and they shall not receive the paternal inheritance as family heirs.

Given on the seventeenth day before the kalends of January at Constantinople in the year of the tenth consulship of Our Lord Honorius Augustus and the sixth consulship of Our Lord Theodosius Augustus.–December (May) 16, 415.

INTERPRETATION: If any woman should marry the husband[30] of her sister after the death of the latter, or if any man should be united by a subsequent marriage to his de-

19

ceased wife's sister, such persons shall know that they are infamous as a result of such a union. The children born of this union are excluded from the succession and shall not be reckoned as children.

Title 13: Dowries (*De Dotibus*)

1. Emperors Constantius and Constans Augustuses to Philippus, Praetorian Prefect.
    An action on morals cannot be extended beyond the person accused, and it shall not be granted against an heir nor assigned to an heir.
    Given on the twelfth day before the kalends of October in the year of the consulship of Limenius and Catullinus.–September 20, 349.

INTERPRETATION: If a husband should accuse his wife with respect to her morals, that is, of sorcery, adultery or other similar crimes, and if his wife should then die, her heirs cannot be accused because a crime dies with its author. Also if a husband who has accused his wife should die, the wife cannot be accused by the heir of the husband.

2. Emperor Julian Augustus to Mamertinus, Praetorian Prefect.
    In the restoration of dowries, it is Our pleasure that rights of retention created by law and by pacts shown to be consistent with the law shall also be preserved unbroken and inviolate by the authority of this sanction.
    Given on the fourth day before the kalends of March in the year of the fourth consulship of Julian Augustus and the consulship of Sallustius. —February 26, 363.

INTERPRETATION: This law prescribes that pacts made between a husband and wife, which were made relative to a dowry and which are consistent with the law, shall be valid, just as all other pacts. But since this statute evidently does not set forth the provisions concerning retentions from a dowry, such provisions must be sought in the body of the law, that is, in the Sentences of Paulus under the title, *Dowries*, or at any rate in the *Responses* of Paulus under the title, *A Wife's Property*.

3. Emperors Honorius and Theodosius Augustuses to Marinianus, Praetorian Prefect.
    (After other matters.) If while a marriage subsists it should chance that the husband should be destroyed by the lot of fate, the dowry which is said to have been given or promised out of his wife's property shall revert to the woman, and the heir of the deceased shall not dare to vindicate for himself any of the property which has reverted to the woman as the result of her husband's death.
    1. If perchance, while the marriage subsists, the dowry has been returned to a wife by her husband, a transaction which cannot stand according to the laws, because it is understood to be analogous to a gift,[31] and if the wife should die, the dowry, together with the fruits thereof from the day that the dowry was returned to her, shall be restored to the husband by her heirs; but the ownership of the same cannot be alienated by the husband away from the children born of the aforesaid woman. (Etc.)
    Given on the third day before the nones of November at Ravenna in the year of the thirteenth consulship of Honorius Augustus and the tenth consulship of Theodosius Augustus.–November 3, 422.

INTERPRETATION: If perchance a husband should die and his wife should survive him, the woman shall recover for her own ownership any property which had been given to her husband as a dowry, and the heirs of the deceased husband shall not presume to vindicate it. Indeed, if the husband, while he was living, had perhaps returned that property which he had received from his wife as dowry, since such a return is like a gift, this act shall have no validity. If the woman should die, such property cannot be vindicated by her heirs, but it is ordered that, together with its fruits, it shall be restored to her husband; provided, however, that if there should be children, they shall not vindicate this property

20

for themselves as though a part of their mother's estate during the lifetime of their father, and the father shall have nothing therefrom except the usufruct, nor shall he have the unrestricted right to transfer such property to another person; but after his death all of it shall revert to their common children.

4. Emperors Theodosius and Valentinian Augustuses to Hierius, Praetorian Prefect.
(After other matters.) We decree that any sort of words whatever shall suffice for the exaction of a dowry, if its delivery has once been agreed upon, even though a formal statement or stipulation with reference to the promise of the property of the dowry did not follow.(Etc.)
Given on the tenth day before the kalends of March at Constantinople in the year of the consulship of Felix and Taurus.–February 21, 428.

INTERPRETATION: A dowry, that is, whatever is given by[32] a woman to her husband at the time of marriage, is ordered to be valid with respect to its fulfillment or its exaction, even though a stipulation of the promiser and the legally prescribed words should be lacking.

Title 14: Marriages With Foreigners *(De Nuptiis Gentilium)*

1. Emperors Valentinian and Valens Augustuses to Theodosius, Master of the Horse.
No provincial, of whatever rank or class he may be, shall marry a barbarian wife, nor shall a provincial woman be united with any foreigner. But if there should be any alliances between provincials and foreigners through such marriages and if anything should be disclosed as suspect or criminal among them, it shall be expiated by capital punishment.
Given on the fifth day before the kalends of January in the year of the consulship of Valentinian and Valens Augustuses.–December 28, 373 or 373; May 28, 368.

INTERPRETATION: No Roman shall presume to have a barbarian wife of any nation whatever, nor shall any Roman woman be united in marriage with a barbarian. But if they should do this, they shall know that they are subject to capital punishment.

Title 15: Sureties of Dowries *(De Fidejussoribus Dotium)*

1. Emperors Valentinian, Theodosius, and Arcadius Augustuses to Martinianus, Count of the Orient.
Henceforth We absolve all sponsors or sureties from their promises in guaranteeing any solemn agreement for a dowry.
Given on the third day before the ides of November at Constantinople in the year of the second consulship of Arcadius Augustus, and the consulship of Rufinus.–November 11 (10), 392.

INTERPRETATION: If any person should become surety of a woman for the payment of a dowry, he shall not be held liable for such guaranty.

Title 16: Notices of Divorce *(De Repudiis)*

1. Emperor Constantine Augustus to Ablavius, Praetorian Prefect.
It is Our pleasure that no woman, on account of her own depraved desires, shall be permitted to send a notice of divorce to her husband on trumped up grounds, as, for instance, that he is a drunkard or a gambler or a philanderer, nor indeed shall a husband be permitted to divorce his wife on every sort of pretext. But when a woman sends a notice of divorce, the following criminal charges only shall be investigated, that is, if she should prove that her husband is a homicide, a sorcerer, or a destroyer of tombs, so that the wife may thus earn commendation and at length recover her entire dowry. For if she should send a notice of divorce to her husband on grounds other than these three crimi-

nal charges, she must leave everything, even her last hairpin, in her husband's home, and as punishment for her supreme self confidence, she shall be deported to an island. In the case of a man also, if he should send a notice of divorce, inquiry shall be made as to the following three criminal charges, namely, if he wishes to divorce her as an adultress, a sorceress, or a procuress. For if he should cast off a wife who is innocent of these crimes, he must restore her entire dowry, and he shall not marry another woman. But if he should do this, his former wife shall be given the right to enter and seize his home by force and to transfer to herself to herself the entire dowry of his later wife in recompense for the outrage inflicted upon her.

Given…in the year of the consulship of Bassus and Ablavius. - 331

INTERPRETATION: The right to send a notice of divorce is extended to a wife or husband for certain approved reasons and causes; for they are forbidden to dissolve a marriage for a trivial charge. If perchance a woman should say that her husband is either a drunkard or given to licentiousness, she shall not send him notice of divorce on that account. But if perchance she should prove that he is either a homicide, a sorcerer, or a violator of tombs, the husband who is convicted of these crimes appears to be justly divorced, without any fault of the woman; and she may recover her dowry and depart. If the woman should not be able to prove such crimes, she shall be subjected to the following punishment: namely, that she shall forfeit both the dowry which she had given or which had been given on her behalf and the gift[33] which she received, and she shall also be liable to exile by relegation. But if a man should cast off his wife, he also is not permitted to divorce her for a trivial quarrel, as often happens, unless perhaps he should be able to prove that she is an adultress, a sorceress, or a procuress. But if he cannot prove this, he shall restore her dowry to the woman, and he shall not presume to take another wife. But if perchance he should attempt to do so, the woman who was cast off, though innocent, shall have the right to vindicate for herself her husband's home and all his substance. It is recognized that this is ordained in order that if a woman should be unjustly divorce, she is ordered to acquire the dowry of the second wife also.

2.   Emperors Honorius, Theodosius, and Constantius Augustuses to Palladius, Praetorian Prefect.

If a woman should serve notice of divorce upon her husband and separate from him and if she should prove no grounds for divorce, the gifts shall be annulled which she had received when betrothed. She shall also be deprived of her dowry, and she shall be sentenced to the punishment of deportation. We deny her not only the right to a union with a subsequent husband, but even the right of postliminium. But if a woman who has revolted against her marriage should prove merely flaws of character and ordinary faults, she shall lose her dowry and restore to her husband all gifts, and never at all shall she be associated in marriage with any man. In order that she may not defile her widowhood with wanton debauchery. We grant to the repudiated husband the right to bring an accusation.

1. It remains to say that if a woman who withdraws should prove serious grounds and a conscience involved in great crimes, she shall obtain possession of her dowry and shall also retain the betrothal bounty, and she shall regain the right to marry after a period of five years from the day of the divorce. For then it will appear that she has done this from loathing of her own husband rather than from a desire for another husband.

2(1). Certainly if the husband should be the first to give notice of divorce and if he should charge his wife with a grave crime, he shall prosecute the accused woman in accordance with the law, and when he has obtained his revenge, he shall both get possession of her dowry and recover his bounty to her, and he shall acquire the unrestricted right to marry another woman immediately. 3. If it is a fault of character and not of criminality, the husband shall recover his gifts but relinquish the dowry, and he shall have the right to marry another woman after a period of two years. 4. But if the husband should wish to dissolve the marriage because of a mere disagreement and should charge the repudiated woman with no vices or sins, he shall lose both his gifts and the dowry and be compelled to live in perpetual celibacy; he shall suffer punishment for his insolent divorce in the sadness of solitude; and the woman shall be granted the right to marry after the termination of a year. Moreover, We order to be preserved the guarantees of the ancient law in regard to the retentions of dowries, on account of children.

Given on the sixth day before the ides of March at Ravenna in the year of the consulship of Eustathius and Agricola.–March 10, 421.

INTERPRETATION: If a woman should be the first to serve a notice of divorce upon her husband and should not prove the statutory grounds for divorce, she shall forfeit the betrothal bounty, and she shall not recover that which she gave her husband as dowry. In addition, she shall also be sent into exile by relegation, and she shall not have the right to marry another man. If, however, after divorcing her husband, she should become involved in adultery, her husband shall have the right to prosecute her even after the divorce. But if a woman who has separated from her husband should prove that he is guilty of grave and definite crimes, she shall both recover her dowry and vindicate that which her husband bestowed upon her as a betrothal bounty, and she shall have the unrestricted right of marriage after five years.

Indeed, if the husband should be the first to serve notice of divorce, he shall secure his revenge on grounds approved by law, he shall vindicate his dowry of his repudiated wife, shall recover his betrothal gifts, and shall have the right to marry another woman immediately if he wishes. If indeed there were no definite crimes, but, as often happens, the husband is displeased with the frivolity of his wife's character, he shall recover his gifts and shall restore to her immediately anything which he has received from her, after a period of two years he shall have the right to marry another wife. But if no defect of character should be proved but merely mental discord, the innocent woman who is rejected by her husband shall both vindicate the gifts made to her by the man and shall recover her dowry. But he shall remain alone forever and shall not presume to associate himself in marriage with another woman. The woman, however, is permitted to proceed to another marriage after a year if she should so wish. But for the sake of their common children, if there should be any, the Emperor orders those rules to be observed which have been established in the law concerning retentions according to the number of children, which law Paulus sets forth in his *Book of Responses* under the title *A Wife's Property*.

Title 17: The Creation of Tutors and Curators (*De Tutoribus Et Curatoribus Creandis*)

1. Emperor Constantine Augustus and the Caesar to Bassus, Prefect of the City.

It is Our pleasure that in all litigation, no person who has attained the age of puberty[34] shall have legal capacity unless by the interposition of a decree a curator has been appointed for him, either for the purpose of administering his patrimony or for the purpose of the lawsuit, so that, in accordance with the preceding statutes of Our Providence, when a suit has been legally instituted, the controversy may be tried in the courts and settled.

Given on the fourth day before the ides of October at Aquileia in the year of the fifth consulship of Constantine Augustus and the consulship of Licinius Caesar.–October 12, 319; 318.

INTERPRETATION: If an action is brought as though against a pupil,[35] although he should appear to be an adult,[36] such person cannot take part in the lawsuit unless perchance his age should be confirmed by attestation of the municipal council, or at any rate a curator should be provided who may defend the patrimony or lawsuit of the ward.

2. The same Augustus and Caesar to the People.

A consanguineous paternal uncle shall not refuse the statutory guardianship over a woman.

Given on the day before the kalends of January in the year of the seventh consulship of the Augustus Himself and the consulship of the Caesar.–December 31, 326.

3. Emperors Valentinian, Theodosius, and Arcadius Augustuses to Proculus, Prefect of the City.

The Illustrious prefect of the City, with the assistance of ten men selected from the membership of the Most August Senate, together with the Most Noble praetor who presides over suits involving guardianship, shall provide that suitable persons, of any rank whatever, shall be obligated to act as tutors and curators.

1. Certainly, those who judge this matter shall decide with free judgment and without liability. If one nominee should not be adequate for administering the pupil's property, it shall be proper, according to the ancient law, that several shall be called to this duty and that the person whom the aforesaid group adjudges the most competent for administering the pupil's affairs shall obtain such administration by the decision of the prefect alone.

2. Hence in this manner, those present at the council shall remain free of fear, and from this deliberation of prudent men, legalized protection shall be provided for both young children and adults.

3(1). However, it is evident that We have decreed the preceding regulation concerning those persons for whom there are available neither testamentary nor statutory guardians of a suitable mode of life, age and property. For when, perchance, such men are offered, We rightly prescribe that they can be held obligated if they should acquire no grounds of defense through their privileges. 4(2). Moreover, We decree that all other provisions that have been prescribed by the ancient laws concerning the case of minors shall remain inviolate.

Given on the sixth day before the kalends of January at Milan in the year of the consulship of Timasius and Promotus.–December 27, 389.

INTERPRETATION: As often as the problem arises concerning the guardianship of pupils, the chief decurions of the municipality, along with the judge, must select either a tutor or a curator, according to the age of the minor, so that a person who undertakes a tutelage according to the age of the minor, so that a person who undertakes a tutelage as the result of such a selection can be secure. However, this manner of selection shall be observed in connection with those persons whose appointment has not been directed by testament and who have not been assigned to this office through close kinship. Concerning the other interests of minors, indeed, the Emperor commands that the provisions of former laws shall be observed.

4. The same Augustuses to Tatianus, Praetorian Prefect.

If mothers who have lost their husbands should demand tutelage over their children to administer their affairs, before confirmation of such an office can legally come to them, they shall state in the public records that they will not proceed to another marriage. 1. Certainly, no woman is forced to make such a choice, but she shall comply of her own free will with the conditions which We have prescribed. For if she prefers to choose another marriage, she must not administer the guardianship of her children.

2. In order that such a woman may not easily be taken by storm after she has lawfully undertaken the guardianship, We order that, first of all, the property of any man who eagerly seeks the marriage of a woman who is administering the guardianship shall be obligated and held liable for the accounts of the children, so that nothing may be lost to them through negligence or through fraud. 3. To the aforesaid provisions We add the following: that a woman who has attained her majority shall have the right to petition for a guardianship when a statutory tutor is lacking or when such a person is excused from serving as tutor by reason of his privilege, or when he is excluded as being of the class of suspect, or when he is found to be incapable of managing even his own property because of mental or physical infirmity. 4. But if women should avoid the guardianship and

should prefer marriage, and no statutory tutor can be called to such cases, then only the Illustrious prefect of the City, with the assistance of the praetor who presides over the appointment of tutors or the judges who administer the law in the provinces, shall, after investigation, order guardians of another order to be appointed for minors.

Given on the twelfth day before the kalends of February at Milan in the year of the fourth consulship of Valentinian Augustus and the consulship of Neoterius.–January 21, 390.

INTERPRETATION: If women whose husbands are dead should themselves wish to undertake the guardianship of their children, before they may assume this responsibility, they shall formally declare in the public records that they will not marry. However, this declaration must not be extorted from them, but if they prefer, they shall so state of their own free will. For if they desire to proceed to subsequent marriages, they cannot administer the guardianship of their children. When men request the mothers of young children to marry them, they too shall know that if a woman has begun to administer the tutelage of her children, and later marries, the man whom she takes as her consort in marriage shall know that his property will be obligated, and he himself will be responsible for rendering an account to the minors.

There is the further provision that a woman is forbidden to undertake a guardianship unless she has attained her majority. As to those persons, indeed, who come to a guardianship by statute, if any one of them should appear either to be mistaken as to his resources or to be worthless in character, he cannot be admitted to the guardianship, lest the property of the minors should be lost. But those persons shall undertake the guardianship who are characterized by integrity of mind and who are definitely connected by a near degree of kinship. For if the aforesaid persons should be lacking and the mother should be unwilling to undertake the guardianship, then, as has been previously provided, tutors shall be assigned to minors by the selection of the judges or the provincials.[37]

Title 18: Those Persons Who Shall Petition (*Qui Petant*)

1. Emperors Constantius Augustus and Julian Caesar to Our Very Dear Orfitus, Greetings.

Grandfathers also and grandmothers shall be held obligated to the necessity of requesting the appointment of tutors if both testamentary and statutory guardianship should be lacking for their grandchildren of pupillary age. For if perchance a tutor should not be requested, in accordance with the provisions of the ancient laws, those persons to whom the inheritance could have come shall forfeit the benefit of the succession.

Given on the ides of July in the year of the ninth consulship of Constantius Augustus and the second consulship of Julian Caesar.–July 15, 357.

INTERPRETATION: If there should be no paternal grandfather, the Emperor orders that even the maternal grandfather and the paternal and maternal grandmothers shall be bound by the command of the law to request tutors for young children, provided that testamentary or statutory tutors are proved to be lacking. But if they should scorn to provide tutors for their young grandchildren, the Emperor orders that they shall be subjected to the following penalty, namely, that if perchance the "mournful" inheritance should accrue from the estates of minors for whom they have either not sought or not wished to provide tutors, they shall be considered as extraneous persons.

2.[38] ...

Title 30: The Administration and Liability of Tutors and Curators (*De administratione et periculo tutorum et curatorum*)

1. Emperor Constantine Augustus.
    Minors shall not be prohibited from vindicating for themselves the property of their

tutors or curators, as though it were obligated under title of a pledge, if such tutors or curators should become indebted to them on account of the duties of their administration.

Given on the seventh day before the kalends of April in the year of the consulship of Volusianus and Annianus.–March 26, 314.

INTERPRETATION: If any tutor or curator should be proved to be a debtor to minors through negligence of his administration, he shall know that his own property is so obligated that if he should not render satisfaction, after his account has been deducted,[39] his goods shall be held as a pledge by the minors.

2.   The same Augustus to Maximus, Prefect of the City.

(After other measures.) The guardians of minors shall make good the value of the property lost,[40] if through them the conditions attached to the gifts should be neglected. (Etc.)

Given on the third day before the nones of February at Rome in the year of the consulship of Sabinus and Rufinus Augustus.–(January 30) February 3, 316; 323; 320.

INTERPRETATION: If in the case of gifts which can be made to minors, the formality or condition of a gift should not be fulfilled through the tutor's negligence or collusion, he shall be compelled to pay out of his own property that which the minor has lost.

3.   The same Augustus to the People.

...or curator shall be solicitous to make repeated inspections in order to see that the aforesaid articles are unharmed. As to superfluous animals of minors also, We do not forbid that they be sold.

Given on the ides of March at Sirmium in the year of the seventh consulship of Constantine Augustus and the consulship of Constantius Caesar.–March 15, 326; 329.

4. The same Augustus to all Provincials.

(After other matters.) If guardians of minors, that is, tutors or curators, as co-owners of property that is being sued for in litigation should decline to declare, as the law requires, but contrary to the prohibition, they should name the aforesaid minors, the guardians shall pay to the fisc out of their own resources as much money as is computed to be a third of the estimated value of the property involved in the litigation, since minors, whether pupils or adults, must lose nothing, no matter what the outcome of the suit. However, if the guardians should be paupers, they shall suffer diminution of status and shall cease to be Roman citizens, but in such a way that the rights of the minors themselves shall be preserved unimpaired. (Etc.)

Given on the kalends of August[12] in the year of the consulship of Bassus and Ablavius. –August 1, 331.

5.   The same Augustus to Felix.

Since landholdings held by emphyteutic tenure are being torn from the possessions of minors as a result of default involving forfeiture which occurred through neglect or betrayal by tutors or curators, it is Our pleasure that if during the administration of a tutor or curator, the landed estates of a minor should lose the prerogative of emphyteutic tenure through an offense involving forfeiture, they shall restore to the minor from their own resources, under the threat of a severe sentence, as much as it shall be determined that the property forfeited was worth.

Given on the fourteenth day before the kalends of May at Constantinople in the year of the consulship of Dalmatius and Zenophilus.–April 18, 333.

INTERPRETATION: If perchance it should occur that, subject to any kind of payment whatever, minors should hold by emphyteutic tenure a landed estate, that is, property of the fisc which their parents had obtained the right to hold, and if this estate should be diminished or certainly if it should be taken away from them through the negligence or betrayal of the tutor, whatever may be lost shall be restored by the tutor or curator.

6.   Emperors Arcadius and Honorius Augustuses to Eutychianus, Praetorian Prefect.

The very moment that they are instituted, tutors shall immediately appear before the judges, so that, in the presence of the chief decurions, the defender, and public office staffs,[41] an inventory shall be made with due formality, and all the gold and silver found in the pupil's substance, as well as anything else that does not suffer change with the lapse of time, shall be marked with the seals of the judges, senators and public office staffs, and placed in safest custody by the authorization of a public order. There shall be no expectation of interest, nor shall any change be made in any event whatever, until the ward, having become an adult, attains legal age, when he does not so much begin to have time for lawsuits as to rejoice that he has been restored so soon to his whole patrimony.

1. Since a moderate fortune, too, must be considered, if perchance movables alone, and no immovables, are left to a person as an inheritance, and no income from landed estates can be reckoned upon, out of which the pupil's household or the pupil himself can be supported, either suitable estates shall be purchased with the aforesaid movables, or if perchance, as usually happens, suitable estates cannot be found, in accordance with the general rule of the ancient law, an income shall accrue from interest. Thus in this case also, in which there is no hope for income from landed estates, the needs of the minor shall be provided from the income of his movable property; and in the former case[42] interest shall by no means be sought without the risk of the tutor.

Given on the sixth day before the kalends of March at Constantinople in the year of the fourth consulship of Arcadius Augustus, and the third consulship of Honorius Augustus.–February 25, 396(?).

INTERPRETATION: As soon as any person enters upon a guardianship, he shall immediately summon the chief decurions of the municipality and the defender, together with his office staff, while he takes an inventory and makes a written record of the property of the pupil which he has received. If there should be any money or silver or things which cannot perish with age, he shall deposit them after they have been marked with the seals of the aforesaid officials, and in no event shall such property be diminished. The aforesaid persons shall know that while the pupil is in his minority, this property shall not be entrusted to him for the purpose of lawsuits or for any other reasons, but it shall be preserved in all its entirety until his mature age. In all other matters there shall be profitable diligence. If the resources of a minor are of less value, so that he has no patrimony, and his substance is found to consist of movables only, the tutors shall know that they will be permitted to undertake to sell the movables and to purchase fields, so that they may provide for the minors in this respect. But if there is no substance of such value that a land estate can be purchased with it, the tutors are ordered to use diligence in collecting the money and to acquire profit for the pupil from the earnings of interest or from any other sources. If perchance the substance of the minor should be very small, then the property shall be kept intact, and means of subsistence shall be furnished to the pupil. If this is done, the pupil shall not seek interest from the tutor.

Title 31: Exemption from Tutelage[43] (De excusatione tutelae)

1.   Emperors Arcadius and Honorius Augustuses to Flavianus, Prefect of the City.

(After other matters.) We grant to the shipmasters themselves exemption from tutelage or curatorship to this extent, namely, that they shall be obligated to perform such duties for minors of their own guild only.

Given on the third day before the nones of March at Milan in the year of the consulship of Stilicho and Aurelianus.–March 5, 400.

Title 32: The Landed Estates of Minors Shall Not Be Alienated Without a Decree (*De praendiis minorum sine decreto non alienandis*)

1. Emperor Constantine Augustus to Severus.
    A minor who is less than twenty-five years of age shall be able to vindicate a landed estate or a rustic slave which was alienated without the issuance of a decree, even though he has not applied for restoration to his original condition; provided that if, following upon the publication of this law, so little time before the end of the twenty-fifth year should remain that a lawsuit already begun cannot be terminated within the limits of the aforesaid year, the lawsuit that is begun can be continued. 1. Those persons also whom this same law has found past their twenty-fifth and within their twenty-sixth year shall not delay to commence their petitions, since the time limits for a lawsuit thus begun shall be concluded at the twenty-sixth year.
    2. But if any persons should attempt to sue after this time, they shall be rejected, so that the possessor shall now be certain and secure.[44]
    Given on the fifteenth day before the kalends of January at Sofia (Serdica) in the year of the consulship of Probianus and Julianus.–December 18, 322; 325.

2. Emperors...
    Even if any minor should be found obligated, either in the name of his father or in his own name, on account of urgent fiscal debts only or as a consequence of private contracts, the interposition of a decree shall be granted by the Constantinian Praetor after the reasons have been exactly proved, so that after the reliability of the facts has been revealed, a sale may remain valid.[45] Since these things are so, tutors also who are suspect must be sued in the court of the said praetor; an action also must be granted, provided, of course, that the laws shall be observed and that recourse may be had finally to Your Experience, if, while the trial is being conducted before either of the two praetors, the aid of an appeal should be interposed by one of the parties, so that you as the sublime judge may weigh the merits of the appeal.
    Given ...–December 31, 326(?).

Notes

1   That is, payments of the taxes assessed on the property.
2   Of property held in common.
3   The merciless exploitation of the poor and weak by the rich and powerful was extremely common. It was often forbidden by the Emperors, but the various laws against it were apparently ineffectual.
4   Which they have accepted as a pledge.
5   As a loan.
6   The more remote degrees of kinship than those mentioned above.
7   The ones specified above.
8   To a soldier.
9   The soldier who had thus delayed the marriage of the girl to himself.
10 The first part of the constitution has been lost.
11 Constantine the Great.
12 Since the ms. is defective, the month is uncertain.
13 Estates subject to Italian rights had certain privileges that were not held by stipendiary or tributary estates, since Italian estates were originally those of the Roman conquerors, while stipendiary and tributary estates were originally those of conquered peoples. These distinctions were gradually abolished in the time of the Empire.
14 That is, she may not claim the privileges granted to women who were minors.
15 Governors, the judges ordinary.
16 Of the administrators. Or: if the parents or the girls themselves should wish to oppose their previous agreement.

17 Marriage with a person of noble rank.
18 The governor of the province, the judge ordinary.
19 Documentary evidence, such as deeds of gift and dowry agreements.
20 Benefit of succession; as an heir.
21 Theodosius I. The law is not extant.
22 Administrative authority, as of the governors, the judges ordinary.
23 The governor of the province.
24 The praetorian prefect.
25 That is, the right to receive the inheritance shall be available to the fisc, if the properly qualified heirs are lacking.
26 The date is doubtful, since Caesarius was prefect until July 13, 397, and was succeeded by Eutychianus on September 4, 397.
27 A first cousin.
28 The former wife.
29 Both parties to the union
30 The former husband.
31 Gifts between husbands and wives were forbidden.
32 On behalf of.
33 The betrothal and antenuptial gifts.
34 *puber*, an adult, a male over fourteen or a female over twelve and under twenty-five years of age.
35 Under the age of puberty.
36 Under twenty-five years of age, but over the age of puberty.
37 The municipal councils.
38 A constitution has been lost.
39 An account of his own expenses incurred for the benefit of the minor during the course of his guardianship.
40 To the minors by reason of the negligence of the guardians.
41 The office staffs of the public officials of the district.
42 If suitable estates can be purchased for the minor.
43 The guardianship of minors was a compulsory public service, without remuneration. It could not be evaded except by some legally recognized excuse.
44 In his possession.
45 Minors were not permitted to sell property without a decree which could be granted for various reasons, such as urgent debts.

Martianus Capella

The Marriage of Philology and Mercury

Martianus Capella was a fifth century author from Carthage in North Africa. His The Marriage of Philology and Mercury, composed between 410 and 439, is an encyclopaedia of the seven liberal arts, that is, the trivium: grammar, dialectic and rhetoric, and the quadrivium: geometry, arithmetic, astronomy, and music. The arts are presented in the form of an allegory. Philology ascends to heaven accompanied by her handmaidens, the liberal arts, to marry Mercury, the god of eloquence. Each art is described in turn, thus forming a compendium of information about the liberal arts. The text was the most influential source of information on the seven liberal arts from the ninth through twelfth centuries and was the model for medieval allegories describing heavenly ascents.

The form of the text is a mixture of prose and verse, a popular Classical genre.

Source: *Martianus Capella and the Seven Liberal Arts*, tr. William Harris Stahl and Richard Johnson with E.L. Burge, vol. II *The Marriage of Philology and Mercury* (New York: Columbia University Press, 1977.).

BOOK IV

Dialectic

[327] Into the assembly of the gods came Dialectic, a woman whose weapons are complex and knotty utterances. Without her, nothing follows, and likewise, nothing stands in opposition. She brought with her the elements of speech; and she had ready the school maxim which reminds us that speech consists in words which are ambiguous, and judges nothing as having a standard meaning unless it be combined with other words. Yet, though Aristotle himself pronounce his twice-five categories, and grow pale as he tortures himself in thought; though the sophisms of the Stoics beset and tease the senses, as they wear on their foreheads the horns that they never lost;[1] though Chrysippus[2] heap up and consume his own pile, and Carneades match his mental power through the use of hellebore,[3] no honor so great as this has ever befallen any of these sons of men, nor is it chance that so great an honor has fallen to your lot; it is your right, Dialectic, to speak in the realms of the gods, and to act as teacher in the presence of Jove.

[328] So at the Delian's summons this woman entered, rather pale but very keen-sighted. Her eyes constantly darted about; her intricate coiffure seemed beautifully curled and bound together, and descending by successive stages, it so encompassed the shape of her whole head that you could not have detected anything lacking, nor grasped anything excessive. She was wearing the dress and cloak of Athens, it is true, but what she carried in her hands was unexpected, and had been unknown in all the Greek schools. In her left hand she held a snake twined in immense coils; in her right hand a set of patterns carefully inscribed on wax tablets, which were adorned with the beauty of contrasting color, was held on the inside by a hidden hook; but since her left hand kept the crafty device of the snake hidden under her cloak, her right hand was offered to one and all. Then if anyone took one of those patterns, he was soon caught on the hook and dragged toward the poisonous coils of the hidden snake, which presently emerged and after first biting the man relentlessly with the venomous points of its sharp teeth then gripped him

in its many coils and compelled him to the intended position. If no one wanted to take any of the patterns, Dialectic confronted them with some questions; or secretly stirred the snake to creep up on them until its tight embrace strangled those who were caught and compelled them to accept the will of their interrogator.

[329] Dialectic herself was compact in body, dark in appearance, with thick, bushy hair on her limbs, and she kept saying things that the majority could not understand. For she claimed that the universal affirmative was diametrically opposed to the particular negative, but that it was possible for both of them to be reversed by connecting ambiguous terms to univocal terms;[4] she claimed also that she alone discerned what was true from what was false, as if she spoke with assurance of divine inspiration. [330] She said she had been brought up on an Egyptian crag and then had migrated to Attica to the school of Parmenides, and there, while the slanderous report was spread abroad that she was devoted to deceitful trickery, she had taken to herself the greatness of Socrates and Plato.

[331] This was the woman, well-versed in every deceptive argument and glorying in her many victories, whom the Cyllenian's twofold serpent, rising on its staff, tried to lick at, constantly darting its tongues, while the Tritonian's (Athena's) Gorgon hissed with the joy of recognition. Meanwhile Bromius (Bacchus), the wittiest of the gods, who was completely unacquainted with her, said: "Surely this woman comes from the sands of panting Libya, as her braided hair and her fondness for venom suggest. Otherwise we must believe that she is a Marsian sorceress[5]: she is so well recognized by snakes, and they show their fondness for her in their slimy way. Apart from this, we may deduce from that concealed hook that she is proven a most alluring charlatan, and an inhabitant of the distant parts of Marsia." [332] When he had said this and several of the gods had laughed as much as was seemly, Pallas, rather shocked, restrained them as they were starting to make jokes, reminding them that this was a woman of perfect sobriety, something which had been wholly denied to some of the gods; and even amongst her sisters, who were estimable women, she was the most sharp-witted, and could not be scorned when she uttered her assertions. But Pallas ordered Dialectic to hand over those items which she had brought to illustrate her sharpness and her deadly sure assertions, and told her to put on an appearance suitable for imparting her skill. [333] Grammar was standing close by when the introduction was completed; but she was afraid to accept the coils and gaping mouth of the slippery serpent. Together with the enticing patterns and the rules fitted with the hook, they were entrusted to the great goddess who had tamed the locks of Medusa.[6] Thus Dialectic stood revealed as a genuine Athenian, a daughter of Cecrops, by the beauty of her hair and her especially because she was attended by a crowd in Greek dress, the chosen youth of Greece, who were filled with wonder at the woman's wisdom and intelligence. But, for assessing virtue as well as practicing it, Jupiter considered the levity of the Greeks inferior to the vigour of Romulus (i.e., the Romans), so he ordered her to unfold her field of knowledge in Latin eloquence. [334] Dialectic did not think she could express herself adequately in Latin; but presently her confidence increased, the movements of her eyes were confined to a slight quivering, and formidable as she had been even before she uttered a word, she began to speak as follows:

[335] "Unless amid the glories of the Latin tongue the learning and labour of my beloved and famous Varro had come to my aid, I could have been found to be a Greek by the rest of the Latin speech, or else completely uncultivated or even quite barbarous. Indeed, after the golden flow of Plato and the brilliance of Aristotle it was Marcus Terentius' labors which first enticed me into Latin speech and made it possible for me to express myself throughout the schools of Ausonia. [336] I shall therefore strive to obey my instructions and, without abandoning the Greek order of discussion, I shall not hesitate to express my propositions in the tongue of Laurentum (i.e., Latin.) First, I want you to realize that the toga-clad Romans have not been able to coin a name for me, and that I am called Dialectic just as in Athens; and whatever the other Arts propound is entirely under my authority. [337] Not even Grammar herself, whom you have just heard and approved, nor the lady renowned for the richness of her eloquence,[7] nor the one who draws

various diagrams on the ground with her rod,[8] can unfold her subject without using my reasoning.

[338] Indeed there are six canons on which the other disciplines rely, and they are all under my power and authority. The first concerns terms; the second, complete utterances; the third, propositions; the fourth, syllogisms; the fifth, criticism; that is, of poets and their works; while the sixth concerns the style suitable for orators.

[339] Under the first heading, one inquires what genus is, what is species, difference, accident, property, definition, the whole, the part, the difference between division and partition, and what is meant by equivocal, univocal, and (to coin a word) plurivocal. You should put up with the strangeness of my language, since you have compelled a Greek to treat the subject in Latin.

[340] The first part of my discipline considers the proper senses of words, the transferred senses of words, and the number of ways the sense can be transferred; it considers also substance, quality, quantity, relation, place, time, attitude, state, activity, passivity, opposition, and how many modes of opposition there are.

[341] In the second part, which I have called 'On Complete Utterances,' one investigates what is a noun, a verb, and the result of combining these; which of these is the subject part of a sentence, and which is the predicate part; what is the extent of the subject and of the predicate; how far the noun and the verb are taken; and how far a complete sentence can be a proposition.

[342] Next comes the third part, on propositions. In this one studies, so far as is sufficient for the purpose of today's brief exposition, the differences in propositions as regards quantity, quality; what is the universal, the particular, the indefinite; which are affirmative, which negative; what is their individual force, and how they are related to one another.

[343] Then follows the fourth part, on the syllogism. In this we inquire what is a premise, a conclusion, a syllogism, a related conclusion; a categorical syllogism, a conditional syllogism, and the difference between the two; how many figures of the categorical kind there are and what they are; whether they adhere to a fixed order and, if they do, what is the explanation of that order; how many moods they each have and whether these moods adhere to a fixed order and, if they do, what is the explanation of that order; and, finally, how many fundamental and necessary moods of the conditional syllogism there are; what is the order of those moods, and what is the difference between them. These are the matters which I think are sufficient for our present understanding and exposition.

Therefore, going back to the beginning, in order to survey the whole subject I shall first explain[9] what is meant by *genus*.

[344] *Genus* is the embracing of many forms by means of a single name, as, for example, *animal*; its forms are *man, horse, lion*, and so on. But some forms sometimes fall under genera in such a way that they themselves can comprise a *genus* with other forms subsumed under it. For example, the genus *man*, which has form in relation to *animal*, is a genus to *barbarian* or *Roman*. Genera can extend right down to the point where on dividing it into its forms you reach the individual. For example, suppose you were to divide *men* into *males* and *females*; likewise, *males* into *boys, youths* and *old men*; the likewise, *boys* into *infants* and *those who can speak*. If you wished to divide *boy* into *Ganymede* or some other particular boy, that is not a genus, because you have arrived at the individual. We ought to use the genus which is closest to the matter at hand, so that if we are discussing *man*, we ought to take *animal* as the genus because it is closest to our subject. For if we take as our genus *substance*, that is true in logic but too wide for our needs.

[345] *Forms*, we say, are the same as *species*. *Forms* are those things which being subordinated to a genus retain its definition and name: *man, horse, lion*, since they are forms of *animal*, can each be called an *animal* and a *corporeal living being*; both the name and the definition are recognized as being those of the genus.

[346] *Difference* is a distinction adequate for the matter under discussion. For example, if one is asked what is the difference between a man and a horse, it is enough to say that a man has two legs and a horse four. However, we ought to be aware that, because

there are many differences in individual cases, we are able to distinguish any living thing in different ways, as often as we can discover in it more and more points of difference. For if we want to divide the genus *animal*, we can divide it into *sexes*, since some are masculine, some feminine; we can divide it into *age groups*, since some are infant, some young, some old; we can divide it by *sizes*, since some are small, some large, some of medium size; we can divide it by their various *modes of motion*, since some walk, some crawl, some swim, some fly; or by their different *habitats*, since some live in water, some on land, some in the air, others, it is said, in fire; or by the sound of their *cries*, since some talk, some growl, some bark, some howl. But let us be sure that these individual divisions are complete and that all the members are included within the individual divisions. For male animals can include those recently born, small, walking, terrestrial, two-footed, and speaking. Therefore, of the possible distinctions, you ought to use that which is appropriate to the matter under discussion. For if you are to speak about mankind in a complementary manner, you will have to divide animals into the rational and the brute, so that it may be more readily understood how great a value nature has placed on mankind amongst all the animals— since to men alone she has given the power of reason to come to knowledge of herself.

[347] *Accident* is something found only in a given species but which does not always occur in that species. For example, *rhetoric* occurs only amongst men, but it can fail to occur amongst them, so that although someone may be a man he need not be an orator.

[348] *Property* is what is found only in a given species and always occurs in it, so that it marks off the given thing from the generality of things; for example, *laughter* in man. For no one can laugh unless he is a man, and there is no man who cannot laugh when he wants to, so far as is in his stature. Difference is distinguished from property in this, that difference distinguishes something only by reference to the subject under discussion, whereas property distinguishes it from everything. For when we want to distinguish man from lion by difference, and say that the lion is wild but man is gentle, clearly we make a distinction relevant only to the subject in question. For in saying *The lion is wild, but man is gentle,* we have not distinguished man from other tame animals, nor the lion from other wild animals. But when we call man an animal capable of laughter, we have thereby distinguished him from the generality of all other living beings.

[349] *Definition* is the clear and brief explanation of any involved concept. In definition three things must be avoided: signifying what is false, what is too wide, or what is too narrow. We signify something false as follows: *Man is an immortal, irrational animal.* For although man is an animal, it is false that he is immortal or irrational. We signify too much when we say: *Man is a mortal animal.* For although this is brief, it is too wide, since it is true of all animals. We signify something too narrow when we say: *Man is a grammatical animal.* For although there is no animal except man with a knowledge of grammar, yet not every man has a knowledge of grammar. The full definition is *Man is a rational, mortal animal.* For by adding the word *mortal* we have distinguished him from the gods, and by adding *rational* we have distinguished him from the beasts.

[350] A *whole* is that which sometimes lends its name but never its definition to two or more parts within itself. This is found only in individuals. For example, when we refer to a given man and consider his various limbs as his parts, we understand that the man himself is the whole, since we have decided on a particular man, and that the definition and name of that whole man cannot descend to his parts. For we cannot say that an arm or a head by itself is a man, nor can the separate limbs take the definition that belongs to man himself. Yet we must notice that sometimes it is possible to say *all* instead of *the whole*, but with a difference of meaning. For a whole is recognized in single terms, but *all* is applied to a plurality. For when we say *man*, meaning Cicero, because Cicero is one person the appropriate term is *the whole*; but when we mean 'mankind', because that can include the unskilled and the skilled, men and women, the better term is *all*.

[351] *Parts* are those which are understood to be present in a whole and of which the whole consists.

[352] *Division* ought to be carried to the point at which we reach the individual; this comes when we reduce genera through their differences to cover a smaller number of

items, and then we subordinate species to these in such a way that the separate species themselves can each be genera with other species subordinate to them. For instance, if we want to make a first brief division of *animal*, we can proceed by differences, because some animals walk, some crawl, some swim, and some fly. Again, we can make genera of these divisions, so that we say that walking animals are a genus and we subordinate species to it, because some are human, some beasts. Of these again there can be other species, through which, if need be, it will be possible to reach the individual. This ought not to be done in every statement, but only in minute argument. In a speech we can divide in this way when the obscurity of our subject requires it; if the subject is not obscure, the theory of division should be applied and incorporated but ought not to be very apparent.

[353] In *partition*, specific differences do not often occur, and without them partition can be limitless, if we wish to reach what cannot be further divided. For if we name each particular man as a whole and wish briefly to enumerate his parts, there are no differences of parts available, and we are forced to use the names of the particular parts, so that we say the head, the feet, and the rest. If we want to group these briefly, the fact that there are no specific differences means that we cannot group the particular items; the fact that they are so many means it will be impossible, or else a very long task.

[354] Between *division* and *partition* there is the difference that in division we proceed by species, in partition by parts. Species are what are subordinate to a genus and can retain its definition and name. Parts are those which are included in a whole, and they can never take the definition of the whole but sometimes can take its name. For we can take one and the same thing as both a genus and a whole, but with a certain difference of force. For instance, if we wish to divide *man* into youth, old man, and child, we have a genus and its species; but if we want it to be partitioned into head, feet, and hands, we have a whole and its parts. This is because youth, old man, and child, which as we have said are species, can take the name and definition of man, so that an old man may be called a man and a rational, mortal animal; and so may a child, and also a youth. But the head and the feet, which as we have said are parts, cannot take the definition or name of man, because a head cannot be said to be an animal capable of laughter, nor can the feet or hands.

[355] The *equivocal* occurs when many things have one name, but not the same definition; for instance, *lion*. For *lion* is applied to an actual lion, a picture of a lion, and the zodiac sign Leo, so far as the word goes, but as far as the definition is concerned, the actual lion is defined in one way, the painted lion in another, and the zodiac sign in another again.

[356] The *univocal* occurs when there is one name and one definition for two or more items; as, for instance, *clothing*. For both a cloak and a tunic have the name of clothing and can take its definition. Therefore the univocal is recognized in the genera, which give their name and definition to their subordinate species.

[357] The *plurivocal* occurs when a thing is known by many names; as, for instance, a sword: for *gladius, ensis,* and *mucro* all signify the same thing.

[358] Words are *proper* to things when they are the natural and appropriate terms for them, as *lapis* (stone), *lignum* (wood), and so on.

[359] Words are *transferred* (i.e., are used metaphorically) when they are changed in some way, either from necessity or for imagery: from necessity, as when we say *vites gemmare* (the vines are forming gems; i.e., are budding) or when we say *laetas segetes* (the crops are in good heart; i.e., are abundant). Here, since the proper word is lacking, we have used one transferred from another context: we cannot say that vines do anything except form gems, or that crops are in anything but good heart. But for imagery we say *fluctuare segete* (the crops are rippling); we can say something else—that they are moving—but since that is not decorative, we use a word proper to another subject.

[360] Words have a transferred sense in three ways; through similarity, or contrariety, or difference; through similarity; as are those which are included in the tropes of grammar, like the one I have already mentioned: 'the crops are rippling.' Of this kind also are those which signify the part by the whole or the whole by the part in such a way that there

is some appropriately close relationship between the words. It has been found desirable to include these under the heading of similarity. Words are used through contrariety when they are understood in a sense contrary to what we say, as when we call the Fates the *Parcae* although they are not merciful, or when we use the word *lucus* (grove) although it does not transmit light. Grammarians call this *antiphrasis*. Words are transferred through difference when they are taken from other words without any reason, as if we were to call a man who was neither hard of body nor stupid of mind *lapis* (stone). It is not appropriate to use these words; for it is stupid to bring forward words which either have no meaning or are transferred too far from their proper meaning. It is, however, right to use words that are proper, or similar, or contrary.

[361] Before I speak about substance, there are some things that need to be explained: everything that we say is either a *subject* itself, or *of a subject*, or both *of* and *in a subject*. A *subject* is itself not attributed to anything else in such a way that it is dependent on it for its existence, but other things are attributed to it; as, for instance, *Cicero* (not the name, but what is signified by that name). Something is *of a subject when it is said of the subject itself and gives to it its definition and name; as, for example, man*: for Cicero is a man and is a rational, mortal animal. So both the name and the definition, which is of the subject, have been predicated of the same subject; and thus what is said *of the subject* is found in its genera and species.

[362] Something is *in a subject* when it gives neither its name nor its definition to the subject but is understood to be in the subject itself in such a way that it cannot exist without the subject; as, for instance, *rhetoric*: for a subject cannot take the name and definition of rhetoric. For Cicero is not rhetoric, nor is Cicero the science of speaking well; but rhetoric is understood to be in Cicero, although he himself cannot be called rhetoric. Something is both *of a subject* and *in a subject* when it is of a subject with regard to one thing and in a subject with regard to another; as, for example, *discipline*: for with regard to rhetoric, discipline is of the subject; with regard to Cicero, it is in the subject. A *primary substance*, therefore, is a subject; a *secondary substance* is what is said of a primary substance. For instance, *Cicero* is a primary substance, *man* and *animal* are secondary. Now all the following categories are understood to be in a subject; so let us look at them one by one.

[363] A *quality* is that in accordance with which we say what a thing is like; for instance, *whiteness*. It can be understood that a quality is in a subject; since whiteness necessarily is in something, without which it cannot exist; the thing itself in which the whiteness exists is a subject.

The *relative* is what is so called in relation to something; for instance, *father, brother*. These are undoubtedly in a subject. For necessarily these names relate to something else. There are also some relative terms whose correlates will be evident in the mind.

Place is what we call such expressions as *in Rome*; Rome is a substance, this bears reference to Rome itself. *Time* is, for instance, *yesterday, recently, at evening*. The things by whose movements time is reckoned, are substances; for instance, the sun, by whose course we understand time, and those bodies which give us understanding of interval. *Attitude is, for instance, is-lying, is-sitting. State* is, for instance, *having-shoes-on, having-armour-on*; man is the substance, these bear a reference to him. *Activity* is, for example, cutting, burning. *Passivity* is, for example, *being cut, being burned*.

[364] A *primary substance*, then, is what is not inseparably in a subject and is not predicated of any subject. "Inseparably" has been added to the definition for this reason—that every primary substance, though it may be in some locality, nevertheless can be separated and move from that locality; for example, Cicero is understood to be in the senate house in such a manner that he can go from there to some other place. And a part of a primary substance, though in the whole substance, is not inseparable from it, for our arm can be separated from our body, either in fact or in thought. Rhetoric, on the other hand, is in the mind of Cicero in such a way that, even if by some chance it ceased to be there, we do not understand that it is going somewhere else; for when it has begun to be in Cicero's mind we do not consider it has come from elsewhere.

[365] A *secondary substance* is, as has been said, what is predicated of a primary sub-

35

stance, as *man* is predicated of Cicero, and *animal* is predicated of man and Cicero. Whatever is the genus of a primary substance is understood to be a secondary substance. Therefore it is common to all substances not to be *in* a subject, but primary substance is not *of* a substance either. Substance cannot be extended or reduced; that is, it cannot admit of a more and a less. If no man is more a man than any other man, and no particular man will be more a man tomorrow than he was yesterday, so in different species a horse is not more a horse than a man is a man. But in discussing substances we must be careful to compare within the same class; that is, to compare a primary substance with a primary, a secondary with a secondary. For the primary substance more directly signifies the thing; secondary substance involves the possibility of confusion with these things. When I say *Cicero*, I signify a definite individual; when I say man, it is uncertain what I mean, because we are all subject of this rule. Thus it happens that primary substance is more truly substance than is secondary substance for primary substance is more truly substance than is secondary substance; for primary substance more directly identifies the thing. [366] The concept of more or less a substance cannot apply, therefore, among substances within the same class. Again, substance has no opposite; for there is nothing opposite to man, or horse. If someone says that Clodius was the opposite of Cicero, he means not that the substances were opposed to each other but that the qualities in them were opposites, such as evil opposed to good, vice to virtue, injustice to justice. It is clearly a property of substance that one and the same substance can accept opposite qualities by variation within itself. Thus a stone can be now white, now black, and not cease to be the same stone; and Cicero, at first foolish, later wise, does not cease to be the same Cicero.

[367] A *quality*, as I have said, is that inn accordance ith which we are said to be of a certain kingd. Of qualities, one sort is that in which a certain disposition and habit of mind is understood; as for instance, in all the acquired disciplines —philosophy, grammar, rhetoric, and the rest—which so take root in the mind that it is difficult for them to be lost from it. Amongst this sort, some are perfect, some imperfect; if someone has studied grammar yet often makes mistakes, one cannot refer to the habit (of grammatical knowledge), but only to the disposition. Not every disposition is regarded as a habit, but every habit is regarded as being a disposition. [368] A second sort is what we call the 'affective' qualities, like sweet or bitter, hot or cold; not that the corresponding substances are affected by anything from these qualities, but that they compel our senses to be affected. For heat compels the person who comes in contact with it to be affected, as sweetness compels the person who tastes it. Again, there are the qualities which have been implanted in us by some natural affection, in accordance with which each of us is said to be pale or ruddy, without any sudden cause making us pale or ruddy. These are more rightly called *affections* than qualities, if we are not said to be of a certain kind because of them. For it does not follow that he who grows pale is a pale person, that he who loves is a lover, that he who drinks is a drunkard. The former instances are affections; the latter, qualities.

[369] There is a third kind of qualities which are understood not from what actually exists in an individual case ut from what can exist; for instance, we say that wood is breakable, not because it is already broken, but because it can be broken. Again, we speak of a body as *athletic* in two senses; both as one that has been athletically trained and as one so formed by nature that it is well-suited to athletics even though it has not in fact been athletically trained. The former kind of body is rightly called athlete from its athletic skill, because the skill is ingrained in it; but there does not exist any name for the quality itself from which the abjective has been derived and named to apply to a body which is able to be athletically trained but is not so yet. Therefore we must recognize that some substances are said to be what they are from qualities for which there are no names. For though we speak of good as derived from goodness, we do not speak of best as derived from 'bestness.' In the same way athletic, which we understand from the fact that a body can acquire athletic skill, does not have a definite name for the quality from which it is seen to be so called, yet we agree that it is so called from a quality. [370] The fourth kind of quality covers those according to which we understand the shapes and configurations

of things, such as *square, round, beautiful, ugly*, and the like. Quality accepts the idea of a more and a less, but not in every instance. For nothing square is more square than any other square thing; but something can be said to be more white than another white thing. And it is a question often discussed, whether one person may be said to be more just than another. But there appear to be many who have given careful thought to the question and say that the qualities themselves cannot accept the idea of a more and a less, but only the items named after them. For instance, justice is in itself one single perfect concept, so that we cannot say *This man is more just than that*. Similarly, we cannot say *This is more health than that*, but we can say *This man is more healthy than that*. So it happens that a substance does not accept the idea of a more and a less, but qualities can accept it through substances. Again, quality can have a contrary, but not in every case; for although infirmity is the contrary of health, there is no contrary for square or round. It must be noted that when anything is contrary to a quality it must itself be a quality; for instance, sweetness is a quality; therefore bitterness is a quality; and so on.

[371] *Quantity* is of two kinds, discrete or continuous; discrete, as of number or speech; continuous, as of a line or time. There is another division of quantity, whereby one form of it has its parts in a certain position while the other does not. For a line is understood by the position of its parts, since one can say which part of it is where, and it is seen to have a left and a right. But number or speech or time have none of these, although they can have order so that there is in them something that is first and second and last and midmost, but nothing which is understood as being in any *place*.

[372] Quantity has no contrary whatever. For what can be contrary to a two-foot length or a three-foot length? If anyone were to say that *greater* and *smaller*, which seem to be words of quantity, are contraries, he should realize that it is not quantity which is indicated. If he says that something is greater, it seems to be contrary to that which is less. But if I ask: 'Greater than what?' and he replies: 'Than three feet long,' it is clear that there is no contrary. For things which are said to be greater or less are clearly said to be so in a relative sense. For whatever is greater when compared to a less is less when compared to a greater. If therefore greater and less are contraries, we are compelled to admit to an absurdity, that one and the same thing can be contrary to itself, if one thing compared to different quantities can be at the same time both greater and less. [373] Quantity does not accept the idea of greater and less; for five is not more five than two is two, and two are not more two than any other two, and they will not be any more two tomorrow than they are today. It is a distinguishing characteristic of quantity that according to it we speak of equal and unequal, just as it is a characteristic of quantity that according to it we speak of equal and unequal, just as it is a characteristic of quality that according to it we speak of similar and dissimilar, although with different things it is possible to abuse and misapply either term.

[374] *Relation* is the term used when the thing we are discussing is *of* some other thing, or can be referred *to* some other thing in some way; as, for instance, *son* cannot be understood without *father* and *mother*, *slave* without *master*, and vice versa. [375] There are three kinds of relation: either *of* something, as in the case of *son*; or *to* something, as in the case of *neighbor*; or *in comparison with* something, as in the case of *double*, since it is double in comparison with something *single*. All relatives have correlatives; just as a son is the son of the father, so is a father the father of some son. In correlation some correlatives use the same grammatical cases as their relatives, some use different cases. For what I have said of a son, we can also say of a slave, since a slave is the slave of a master and a master is the master of a slave. These correlate in such a way that they retain the same grammatical cases in the reverse relationship. Similarly what is double is double with respect to something single, and the single is single with respect to something double; the greater is greater than the smaller, and the smaller is smaller than the greater. It is therefore obvious that those instances keep the same cases when the relationships are reversed. But, although knowledge is a relative (for knowledge is of some knowable thing), in the reverse relationship it changes its case. For because we say: *Knowledge is knowledge of some knowable thing* we cannot therefore say: *The knowable thing is knowable of knowledge*.

Similarly, perception is perception of something perceptible, whereas the perceptible is perceptible by perception. These instances, therefore, when they reverse their relationships, do not like the previous instances retain the same cases, but change their cases. [376] Some things are coextensive in time with their correlates, and begin and cease to exist at the same time as they. For instance, there cannot be a slave until there is a master, and when there ceases to be a master there ceases to be a slave; and the master, when he has no slave, cannot be termed a master. But the knowable thing is prior in nature to the knowledge of it; for if you remove knowable things there will be no knowledge; if, however, you remove the knowledge of it the knowable thing can still exist, although there is no one who knows it. [377] Relatives can have contraries, but not in every case. For knowledge is the contrary of ignorance, friendship of enmity, but there is no contrary to the double or the greater or the smaller. Anyone who thinks that those are contraries is compelled to admit that one and the same thing at one and the same time can be contrary to itself, for the greater is greater when compared to a smaller, and the same thing can be smaller when compared at the same time to a greater, which is quite impossible for contraries. For a man cannot be both a fool and a wise man at the same time, nor both white and black at the same time. Since we have shown that this can happen in the case of the greater and smaller, we must admit that greater and smaller are not contraries; similarly, double cannot be the contrary of single, since the same thing which is double can be single in relation to something else. Therefore not all relatives can be contraries. Similarly, some can accept the idea of more and less, but some cannot. For this man can be more a friend than that, but this double item cannot be more double than that; for if it is double it is implicit that if it were in any way more or less it would not be double.

[378] It is argued whether any substance can be spoken of relatively. There is no question about a primary substance; for Cicero cannot be said to be *of* anything, nor can he be so called *in relation to* anything. Similarly, someone's horse—say Rhoebus—is not of anything for the sole reason that he is Rhoebus, but it is because he is a beast of burden that he is someone else's beast of burden. Therefore a primary substance cannot be said to be relative; nor can any part of it, since without doubt that too is itself a primary substance. For in the same way as Cicero is a primary substance, so his hand. ...cannot be so termed relatively. For the terms do not reciprocate when they are interchanged; for instance, we can say *The hand is the hand of Cicero*, not *Cicero is the Cicero of the hand*. Nor is the hand itself a hand for the reason that it is Cicero's, but it is called a hand because it has such and such characteristics. Therefore, as we said, neither a primary substance nor its parts can be so called in relation to something else. Therefore the question arises, What of the parts of secondary substance? There is no question about a substance itself, for a man is not a man *of* anyone. But a hand in its general character as a hand is the hand of some man, and (so that the relationship can be reversed) it is the hand of a handed person. We can reverse the relationship in this way because something handed is handed with a hand. Similarly, a hoof is not a hoof of a primary substance but the hoof of something hoofed, because something hoofed is hoofed with a hoof, so that it can accept the reciprocating of relationships which I have said is proper to relatives. If, therefore, that definition of the relative stands—that the relative is that which can be said to be of something else—we can scarcely refrain from allowing that the parts of secondary substance are relative. But if the definition is changed, so that relatives are those things which are referred to something else when we except the fact that the items considered are already *in* the something else, then no substance comes under this definition. For instance, consider servitude; when we except the fact that it is in the slave himself—that is, in some man—it is still related to a master. But a wing is the wing of something winged in such a way that if we except the fact that it is in something winged we cannot relate it to anything. [379] We must bear in mind not to be ashamed to coin new words where necessary to express correlations. For if correlation is not possible, we are not expressing a relative. For instance, when I say *wing*, wanting to show it as a relative, I should not be ashamed of saying something is *winged* to express the correlation; for *winged* is familiar enough not to offend our ears. If I am speaking of the foot, I should not be ashamed to form, by a similar derivation, a word

suitable for expressing the correlation.

Again, we should be aware that a man who does not know what some relative refers to cannot know whether the alleged relation can apply. For example, when you say, *This is double*, you know the single of it; that is, in comparison with what it is double—or if you do not know that, then you cannot know at all whether it is double.

[380] *Activity* and *passivity* can have contraries; for instance, 'to heat, to chill'; 'to be heated, to be chilled.' They also have more and less, as 'to burn more and less'; 'to be burned more and less.'

[381] The terms for *attitude* are all derivative; for example, 'to sit' from *sitting*, 'to stand' from *standing*. Although sometimes there are no words from which the names of postures may be derived, yet the corresponding notion exists in thought.

[382] Of the three categories that remain, the examples I have given above are sufficient. For we indicated *when* by, for example, *yesterday, tomorrow*; *where* by, for example, *in Rome, in Athens*; and *state* by *shod, armed*. Which of these will accept the idea of more or less is easily seen when an instance occurs in everyday speech.

[383] Those are the ten categories from which every individual thing we utter must come. For whatever we say which has some meaning but yet cannot be understood as true or false is within these ten categories, except only those words which are, in a sense, the joints of speech. For there are many words listed by the grammarians amongst the parts of speech which have no meaning at all by themselves, or else make no complete sense, but only become meaningful when they are joined to other words; such as conjunctions, prepositions, and such similar items as the grammarians lay down.

[384] It remains for me to speak about opposites. *Opposites* are what are seen to confront each other, as it were, face to face, for instance, contraries. Not all opposites are contraries, but all contraries are opposites. Opposites are opposed either as relatives, as large is opposed to small, or half to double; or as contraries, as foolishness is opposed to wisdom; or as possession to privation, as sight to sightlessness; or as affirmation to negation, as *Cicero discusses* to *Cicero does not discuss*. These forms of opposites differ greatly among themselves. A *relative* is opposed to another in such a way that it either is *of* that to which it is opposed or else it is related to it in some way. Thus half is opposed to double, and the half is the half of the double. It is therefore opposed to it in such a way that it is *of* an opposite. And small is opposite to large (so as to be its contrary) in such a way that the small item is small in relation to the large to which it is opposed. [385] *Contraries*, on the other hand, are opposites, but not in a way that makes them *of* their opposites or so that they are in any way related to their opposites; foolishness is opposed to wisdom without being the foolishness *of* wisdom or *in relation to* it. However, we should realize that some contraries have something intermediate between them, while others do not. Those contraries which are such that either one or the other *must* necessarily occur in a thing in which they *can* occur, have no intermediate; for instance, health and sickness. These two contraries are present by nature in the bodies of animals, and either one or the other must necessarily be present, as I have said. So where health is not present in the body of the animal there must be sickness, and where there is not sickness there must be health. But white and black, although contraries and naturally found in bodies, may nevertheless have an intermediate, once it is not necessary for a body to be either white or black; it can lack whiteness without having blackness, and vice versa. Therefore some intermediate color can be found, like yellow or green. [386] *Possession* and *privation* are opposed to each other in such a way that, in instances where they can occur, one or the other of them must necessarily be present from the moment when nature allows it. For instance, we call 'toothed' that which has teeth, but we do not call 'toothless' that which does not have teeth, but only that which can have them in nature, and that from the time when nature allows it to have them. For we do not properly call a stone 'toothless,' since it never has teeth; nor an infant—although it can at some stage have teeth, nature does not permit it to have them at that time. This third kind of opposites differs from the first, the relatives, because sight is opposed to blindness in such a way that sight is not *of* blindness and is not referred to it in any way. It differs from the second kind, the contraries, between which

there is something intermediate, because sight and blindness are understood with respect to eyes, so that either the one or the other of them must be present in them. They differ, then, from the contraries which have intermediates in that it is not necessary for one of the contraries which have an intermediate to be present in any substance, but it is necessary for one of these. But they differ from those contraries where there is nothing intermediate because one or the other of them must always be present in any substance in which they are naturally possible, like health or sickness in the body of an animal. One or the other of these is always present in the body of an animal. But these opposites can sometimes be present in a thing where they are naturally possible, and at another time they can both be absent. For instance, an infant for whom it is not yet time to have teeth is not said to be either toothed or toothless; and the eyes of some animal, before the time comes for them to have sight, are not said to be either sighted or blind, and at that time there is no intermediate condition either. (Therefore there are two kinds of contraries which have nothing intermediate between them: those of which either one or the other is present in any item in which it is possible for them to be present, and which allow nothing intermediate; as, for instance, health and sickness; and those which, when they are so lacking, have no mean in their place; for instance, sight and blindness, or possession and privation.) [387] The fourth kind of opposites is affirmation and denial, such as *Cicero is discussing, Cicero is not discussing.* These differ from the former kinds because the members of those pairs are used as single terms but in this fourth kind the terms are used in combination. They differ from relatives in that relatives are used relative to something, but these are not so used; for *discussing* is not relative to *not discussing.* They differ from contraries in that if contraries are used in combination, they are true or false for as long as that in which they can be present exists; but when it has ceased to exist, they are neither true nor false. For instance, of the statements *He is a fool* and *He is a wise man* one is true as long as the 'he' is alive; when the 'he' has ceased to exist, both are false, since he who does not exist cannot be either a fool or a wise man. On the other hand, the statements *Cicero is discussing* and *Cicero is not discussing* are opposites of such a kind that as long as Cicero lives one of them is necessarily the case, and when he is dead the statement that he is discussing is false, but the statement that he is not discussing is true. Thus these opposites are distinguished from privation and possession; for he who does not exist is neither blind nor sighted. Do not be concerned because we seem to have touched on the subject of propositions, which is a subject for later consideration; I have done so because it was appropriate to this discussion of opposites.

[388] A *noun* is that which signifies a certain thing and which can be inflected in cases; a verb is that which signifies something and can be inflected in tenses; for instance, *Cicero* is a noun, *discusses* is a verb. Nouns or verbs in separation from each other can signify something, but cannot be said to be true or false. However, when used in combination they can be either affirmed or denied. For instance, just as we can say *Cicero discusses*, we can also say *Cicero does not discuss.* (What must be present are the nominative case of the noun and the third person of the verb). The first person signifies something which can already be affirmed or denied and applies only to a man. In this person the noun is understood even if it is not expressed; for instance, *disputo* (I discuss) is complete, even if *ego* (I) is not expressed. The second person, too, is itself already subject to truth or falsity, and it also applies to a human being. We cannot correctly say *You discuss* to something which can neither hear nor understand what is said; when this is said without a noun expressed, again a noun is understood. We can, however, use the first and second persons in a different way, figuratively, to introduce as speaking one who cannot speak, or to address speech to one who can neither hear or understand. [389] The third person, however, is used not only with a human being as subject but for other subjects also; and the subject is not understood as soon as the verb is used, unless we happen to be speaking about a god and saying something that could only be used of a god; when, for example, we say *It is raining*, that can be true or false even when we do not add a name, since it is known who is sending rain. But when we say *disputat* (...is discussing), although this signifies something, it cannot be said to be true or false, unless a noun is added. And al-

we say *It is raining*, that can be true or false even when we do not add a name, since it is known who is sending rain. But when we say *disputat* (…is discussing), although this signifies something, it cannot be said to be true or false, unless a noun is added. And although *He is discussing* can be understood only of a man, it can be said of more than one man, and therefore it is necessary to add a noun as subject. And when we say *resistit* (…resists), this is the third person of the verb and requires as a subject a name, not necessarily of a man but of anything which is capable of resisting. So the first and second persons can be understood only of a human being as subject, and when used alone can be said to be either true or false, since with them the nouns are understood; but the third person cannot always stand alone, nor is it understood only of a human being. But the union of the third person of the verb and the nominative case of a noun [390] in such a way that it must be either true or false or doubtful is called a *proposition*. For we all judge *Man is an animal* to be true; and *Every animal is a man*, we all judge to be false. *He is discussing* is doubtful; although 'he' must either be discussing or not discussing, the assertion is doubtful to us. We understand that one or the other is necessarily true, but we do not know which one is true. When we use those verbs which are called impersonal, the sentence is not completed by the use of a nominative case; it accepts other cases, as when we say *disputatur* (it is being discussed) the sentence is complete when one adds an ablative such as *a Cicerone* (by Cicero). When we say *paenitet* (it grieves) the sentence is complete if one adds the accusative *Ciceronem* (Cicero). There are many such; [391] but the fact remains that personal verbs do not make up a complete sentence unless the third person of the verb occurs with the nominative case. There are also sentences which consist indeed of a noun and a verb but cannot be affirmed or denied. Some have chosen to call these not *propositions* but *complete utterances*; an example is the imperative mood. When we say *Run!* the sentence is already complete; for what you say can not only be understood but even acted upon. It cannot, however, be denied, for it is no denial to say *Don't run!* This is not in opposition to the utterance *Run!* so that the question can arise which is true and which false. The question certainly arises in affirmation and denial. For instance, in *He runs* and *He does not run* there is the question whether he runs. But *Run!* and *Don't run!* do not give rise to the question whether he runs. There cannot be understood here any question whether he ought to run. That arises from affirmation and denial: for example, *He should run, he should not run*. The same applies to expressions of wishing. For although the sentence is complete when we say *Would that I were writing!* no question can arise here of whether or not writing is being done. [392] There are many such sentences; these will suffice for illustration. The combination of a complete noun and a complete verb necessarily makes a sentence, but does not necessarily make a proposition, if there is nothing that can be affirmed or denied. *Every man is an animal* is, therefore, a complete proposition. Although nature demands that the noun should be uttered first and then the verb, as above, it does not cease to be a true proposition even if you say *An animal is every man*.[10]

[393] If anything is added to the sentence, one must consider carefully to which part it is added. For there are two parts of a proposition; one, which is the province of the noun, is called the *subject*; the other, which is the province of the verb, is called the *predicate* (*pars declarativa*). For what it is we are talking about is 'laid down' as subject; and what can be understood about it is 'declared' or predicated of it. So when we say *Cicero is discussing*, if we add to this sentence *in the Tusculan Disputations*, these words are added to the predicate of the sentence; if we add *the Roman*, these words are added to the subject; if we add *wisely and fully*, it is to the predicate; again, if we say *with Cato*, it is added to the predicate. So whatever is added in the nominative case is added to the subject; whatever is added to the predicate is added in various cases and ways. For no other cases can be added, with the exception of the nominative.

[394] It is noted that it is possible for a verb to be in the subject, and a noun in the predicate, but the verb then is in the subject in such a way that some pronoun is associated with it in place of a noun. And a noun is in the predicate in association with some verb through which it fulfills the function of a verb. Suppose, for example, we say *qui disputat Cicero est* ([He] who discusses is Cicero), then *qui disputat* ([He] who discusses) is sub-

nevertheless cannot form a complete sentence on their own; and if they do form one, how there are sentences which, though complete, are not subject to truth or falsity; and how we arrive at what is not merely a complete sentence but is also of necessity true or false. And this is the *proposition*.

[396] Now follows the third part, in which I must discuss propositions themselves; we achieved an understanding of what they are in the preceding section. Propositions differ from one another in two ways, in *quantity* and in *quality*. The distinction of quantity is that some are *universal*, some *particular*, some *indefinite*. An instance of the universal is *Every man is an animal*; of the particular, *Some man is walking*; of the indefinite, *(A) man is walking*.[11] What we call an indefinite assertion we perforce take as particular, and not perforce as general and universal. Since the safe interpretation is the one to be counted by preference, an indefinite proposition is taken as a particular. There will be then a twofold distinction of quantity; namely, that between universal and particular propositions; and likewise a twofold distinction of quality, that between *affirmative* and *negative* propositions. An example of the affirmative is *Every pleasure is good*; and of the negative, *All pleasure is not good*.

[397] The converse of a universal affirmative proposition does not necessarily follow. For it is not the case that if every man is an animal, every animal is a man. The converse of a universal negative proposition does, however, necessarily follow. For if no pleasure is a good thing, no good thing is a pleasure; and if no dumb animal is a man, then no man is a dumb animal. A particular affirmative proposition, however, is necessarily convertible. For if some man is an animal, then some animal is a man. The particular negative, on the other hand, is not necessarily convertible. For it is not the case that if some animal is not rational then some rational being is not an animal. Therefore the universal affirmative and the particular negative are not necessarily reversible. But the universal negative and the particular affirmative propositions are necessarily convertible, in such a way, however, that when the conversion is made, the negation remains in the predicate. At any rate, the conversion is to be made in such a way that the former predicate term becomes the subject term. Therefore, when I say *Every pleasure is not good*, *Every pleasure* is the subject, but the negative remains with the predicate. If I wanted to express it as *No pleasure is good*, it should be converted as *No good thing is a pleasure*.

[398) But because of the two kinds of propositions which, as I have said, are not necessarily convertible, we ought to look at all the attributions made in propositions which enable them to be propounded correctly or incorrectly, in order to be able to indicate what is true or false. These five attributes have already been set out above genus, difference, accident, definition, and property. Definition and property make those propositions convertible; the other three do not do so in any way. For just as every man is a rational mortal animal, so every rational mortal animal is a man; and just as every man is capable of laughter, so every being that is capable of laughter is a man. Again, in the particular negative proposition we must see what negative attribute is a property. For just as it is a property of man to be capable of laughter, so it is a property of beings other than man not to be able to laugh. Therefore if we propound the particular negative proposition *Something capable of laughter is not other than man*, it is without doubt convertible as *Something other than man is not capable of laughter*. Similarly, *Something inanimate, irrational, and immortal is not a man;* and *Some man is not inanimate, irrational, and immortal*.

[399] Again, there are other forms of conversion which make the same terms of propositions indefinite while the sign of negation moves from its place. Indefinite terms are formed in this way: *man, nonman; animal, nonanimal*. It is indefinite, then, because you say only that this is not something and do not say what it is. Therefore, when I say *Every man is an animal*, if I want to convert that correctly, I add signs of negation so that the terms become indefinite. For if it is true that every man is an animal, it is also true that every nonanimal is nonman. Cicero used this conversion in his *Rhetoric*: *Then if the issue itself or any part of it is in rebuttal of an accusation, anything that is not in rebuttal of the accusation is not the issue nor part of the issue.*

[400] Likewise the particular negative proposition can be converted in this way. For

42

if some animal is not a man, then some nonman is an animal. In this conversion we should note that in the place where there is no negative when we express the proposition directly a negative occurs when we convert. The two forms of proposition which did not necessarily take the first kind can take this kind of conversion; only the universal negative does not take the other kind. So for the sake of exposition let us call the former kind *primary conversion*; the latter, *secondary*.

The mutual relations of these propositions will be shown more clearly in the following way.

[401] With four lines let us draw a square figure. In the first corner of the upper line let us write *universal affirmative*, and in the other corner of the same line let us write *universal negative*. Below that, in the first corner of the lower line let us write *particular affirmative*, and in the remaining corner *particular negative*. Then let us draw diagonal lines from the universal affirmative to the particular negative and from the universal negative to the particular affirmative. The two upper propositions cannot both be asserted but can both be denied at the same time, [402] for *Every pleasure is good* and *No pleasure is good* cannot both be true at the same time. But it is possible for it not to be the case that every

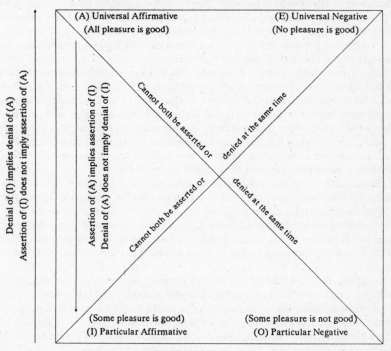

Cannot both be asserted but can both be denied at the same time

Can both be asserted but can both be denied at the same time

pleasure is good, and at the same time for it not to be the case that no pleasure is good. The two lower propositions can both be asserted but cannot both be denied at the same time, but we can at the same time assert both *Some pleasure is good* and *Some pleasure is not good*. Those propositions joined by the diagonals cannot both be asserted or denied at the same time. For if *Every pleasure is good* is true, *Some pleasure is not good* is false. Again, if *Every pleasure is good* is false, *Some pleasure is not good* is true. This also happens if you mention the particular proposition first in each case.

Again, if *No pleasure is good* is true, *Some pleasure is good* is false; and if *No pleasure is good* is false, then *Some pleasure is good* is true. [403] Again, the assertion of a universal affirmative proposition necessarily implies the assertion of the corresponding particular;

but its denial does not necessarily imply the denial of the corresponding particular. For if *All pleasure is good* is true, *Some pleasure is good* is necessarily true. But if we deny the first proposition and say it is not the case that all pleasure is good, it can still be true that some pleasure is good. Again, the assertion of a particular affirmative proposition does not necessarily imply the assertion of the corresponding universal, but its denial necessarily implies the denial of the universal. For if *Some pleasure is good* is true it does not follow that all pleasure is good, but if some pleasure is not good, then *Every pleasure is good* is false. You can observe this in the two remaining instances.

[404] When we have propounded a complete sentence with the purpose of deducing something from it, after it has been granted it is termed a *premise*. Another sentence should be joined to this sentence in a particular way, and of course this needs to be granted for the sake of what we want to infer; and when it has been granted, it is called a premise.

[405] From two premises rightly connected there results a *conclusion*. This conclusion cannot be called a premise, because you do not expect your opponent to concede it to you; rather, it follows despite his efforts, provided it has been inferred by keeping the rules. To make this clear by an example, let us suppose that the question is whether pleasure is advantageous. If we begin by asserting *Every pleasure is good*, we have a complete sentence; if our opponent grants this, it becomes a premise. When this has been conceded, the further sentence must be joined to it, *Everything good is advantageous*. If that also is granted, it becomes a premise; from these two premises there follows, despite our opponent, the conclusion: *Therefore all pleasure is advantageous*.

[406] The whole which consists of two premises and a conclusion is termed by us *ratiocinatio* and by the Greeks *syllogismos*. A syllogism, then, is the necessary progression from two or more conceded positions to one not conceded. There can therefore be more than two premises but there cannot be fewer. For it is a complete syllogism if we wish to reach what we desire to show (that pleasure is advantageous) by means of even three premises, as in *Every pleasure is in accordance with nature; everything in accordance with nature is good; every good is advantageous; therefore every pleasure is advantageous*. From this it is clear that even more premises may be added if appropriate.

[407] Sometimes we reach a conclusion by inferring not what follows directly from the premises but what necessarily follows from what we ought to infer; for example, *Every virtue is good; everything good is advantageous; therefore every virtue is free from harm*. The proper inference would be *therefore all virtue is advantageous*; but from that it necessarily follows that it is free from harm, because what is advantageous is never harmful. This is called by the Greeks symperasma and by us it can be called *confinis conclusio* (related conclusion).

The syllogism, then, whether it has its own proper conclusion or a related conclusion, is divided into two kinds: the categorical and the conditional syllogism.

[408] A *categorical syllogism* is one in which the premises are connected in such a way that they are completed by something else added from outside, as in the example given above: *Every pleasure is good; everything good is advantageous*. We see here that not all that was in the first premise has been mentioned (in the second), but from the first premise one part, the predicate, has been taken and has become the subject in the second proposition. To form a complete sentence the second proposition has taken something from outside; namely, *is advantageous*. The conclusion is formed from the term which is added and the term which is not repeated; *therefore every pleasure is advantageous*.

This kind of syllogism has three figures. The first is the one in which the predicate of the leading premise becomes the subject of the subsequent premise, or the subject of the leading premise becomes the predicate of the subsequent one. The predicate of the leading premise becomes the subject of the subsequent one, for instance, in the example given above. The subject of the leading premise becomes the predicate of the subsequent one if you should wish to convert in the following way: *Everything good is advantageous; every pleasure is good; therefore every pleasure is advantageous*.

The second figure is that in which the predicate of the leading premise is also the predicate of the subsequent premise, as in *Every virtue is good; no pleasure is good; therefore no pleasure is a virtue.*

The third figure is that in which the subject of the first premise is also the subject of the subsequent one, as in *Some good is a pleasure; every good is advantageous; therefore something advantageous is a pleasure.*

[409] In the first figure a conclusion can be universal or particular, affirmative or negative; in the second figure no conclusion can be reached except negatively; in the third figure only a particular conclusion can be reached. There is, therefore, a point in keeping this order. For that figure is deservedly called first in which every kind of conclusion can be reached; and that is rightly called second in which a universal conclusion can be reached, albeit negatively; and that is rightly called third, being lesser in range, in which only a particular conclusion can be reached.

[410] I must now discuss how many moods each of these figures can have; these are restricted to a definite number and one should not lightly grant that any conclusion has been reached except in one of these moods. The first figure can have nine moods; the second, four; the third, six.

[411] In the first figure the *first mood* is that in which a universal affirmative is concluded directly from two universal affirmatives; for example, *Everything just is honorable; everything honorable is good; therefore everything just is good.* If you make the inference conversely *therefore everything good is just,* it does not follow; but one can make the particular inference *therefore something good is just,* and that forms the *fifth mood.* The *second mood* is that in which a universal negative is concluded directly from a universal affirmative and a universal negative; for example, *Everything just is honorable; nothing honorable is base; therefore nothing just is base.* If you convert *therefore nothing base is just,* it forms the *sixth mood.* We have said above that a universal negative can be converted. The *third mood* is that in which a particular affirmative is concluded directly from a particular affirmative and a universal affirmative; for instance, *Something just is honorable; everything honorable is advantageous; therefore something just is advantageous.* But if you convert you form the *seventh mood, therefore something advantageous is just,* since it has been said above that the particular affirmative can be converted. The *fourth mood is that in which a particular negative is concluded directly from a particular affirmative and a universal negative; for example, Something just is honorable; nothing honorable is base; therefore something just is not base.* It cannot be converted, for we have said above that the particular negative cannot be converted. The *eighth mood* is that in which a particular negative is concluded conversely from a universal negative and a universal affirmative; for instance, *Nothing base is honorable; everything honorable is just; therefore something just is not base.* The *ninth mood* is that in which a particular negative is concluded conversely from a universal negative and a particular affirmative; for instance, *Nothing base is honorable; something honorable is just; therefore something just is not base.*

[412] Of the second figure the *first mood* is that in which a universal negative is concluded directly from a universal affirmative and a universal negative; *for example, Everything just is honorable; nothing base is honorable; therefore nothing just is base.* If you employ conversion here, the result is not another mood, since the conclusion is formed from the subjects of the two premises. The *second mood* is that in which a universal negative is concluded directly from a universal negative and a universal affirmative; for example, *Nothing base is honorable; everything just is honorable; therefore nothing base is just.* The *third mood* is that in which a particular negative is concluded directly from a particular affirmative and a universal negative; for example, *Something just is honorable; nothing base is honorable; therefore something just is not base.* The *fourth mood* is that in which a particular negative is concluded directly from a particular negative and a universal affirmative; *for example, Something just is not base; everything evil is base; therefore something just is not evil.*

[413] In the third figure the *first mood* is that in which a particular affirmative is concluded directly from two universal affirmatives; for example, Everything just is honorable; everything just is good; therefore something honorable is good. The *second mood* is that in which a particular affirmative is concluded directly from a particular affirmative and a universal affirmative; for example, *Something just is honorable; everything just is good;*

therefore something honorable is good. The *third mood* is that in which a particular affirmative is concluded directly from a universal affirmative and a particular affirmative; for example, *Everything honorable is just; something honorable is good; therefore something just is good.* The *fourth mood* is that in which a particular negative is concluded directly from a universal affirmative and a universal negative; for example, Everything just is honorable; nothing just is evil; therefore something honorable is not evil. The *fifth mood* is that in which a particular negative is concluded directly from a particular affirmative and a universal negative; for example, Something just is honorable; nothing just is evil; therefore something honorable is not evil. The *sixth mood* is that in which a particular negative is concluded directly from a universal affirmative and a particular negative; *for example, Everything just is honorable; something just is not evil; therefore something honorable is not evil.* So all the moods keep to a fixed order, and the reason for the order is as has been shown in the figures themselves.

[414] A *conditional syllogism* is one in which the initial premise contains both a full statement of the evidential proposition and a full statement of the demonstrandum, in such a way that when the evidential proposition has been taken as an additional premise the demonstrandum can be inferred with certainty. For instance, let us suppose the demonstrandum to be whether rhetoric is advantageous. As we wish to show that it is advantageous, let us form an evidential proposition from its definition, "the science of speaking well." From this evidential proposition and the earlier demonstrandum a conditional syllogism is formed of which the first premise is *If rhetoric is the science of speaking well, it is advantageous*; as second premise we take the evidential proposition. *But rhetoric is the art of speaking well.* Whoever grants the truth of these two must grant, even against his will, that rhetoric is advantageous, which was in doubt before the first and second premises were granted. No term occurs in the second premise from outside the first, for that is a characteristic of the categorical syllogism. This is called by dialecticians the *first mode, from antecedents*, for the reason that the evidential proposition forms the second premise just as it occurs in the first, with the difference only that it occurs conditionally in the first and categorically in the second.

[415] The *second mode*, which is called *from consequents*, is one in which the evidential proposition follows the demonstrandum and not the other way round, for instance; *If rhetoric is not advantageous, it is not the science of speaking well.* The negation of the evidential proposition is taken as the additional premise, thus: *But rhetoric is the science of speaking well; therefore it is advantageous.*

[416] The *third mode* is called *from incompatibles*. In this mode it is shown that it is not possible at the same time for one thing to be so and another not to be. When one of these two is asserted as an additional premise the other will necessarily be rejected, so that when the affirmative one is asserted the negative one is rejected. For example, *It is not the case both that rhetoric is the science of speaking well and that it is not advantageous; but in fact it is the science of speaking well; therefore it is advantageous.* Here the conclusion that it is advantageous is established by rejecting the negative disjunct in the first premise. These three modes can all be formed from one evidential proposition or the demonstrandum, provided that the conditional form is preserved. When you say *If rhetoric is the science of speaking well, it is advantageous*, this can also be expressed as *Rhetoric is advantageous if it is the science of speaking well.* The same can be tried with the other two modes.

[417] The *fourth mode* is formed by disjunction in such a way that when the truth of one disjunct is granted, the other is necessarily denied; for example, *Either he is healthy or he is sick; but he is healthy; therefore he is sick.*

[418] The *fifth mode* is also formed by disjunction in such a way that when one disjunct is denied the other is necessarily the case. For example, *Either he is healthy or he is sick; but it is not the case that he is healthy; therefore he is sick.*

[419] There are two further modes which can be formed through the evidential proposition used in the fourth and fifth, though not by disjunction but *by negation*. There is then a *sixth mode*, in which it is shown that two things cannot both be the case at the same time. The second premise is formed by the assertion of one, and the conclusion by

the negation of the other; for example, *It is not the case both that he is healthy and that he is sick; but he is healthy; therefore he is not sick.* The *seventh mode* has the same initial premise as the sixth, but the same second premise and conclusion as the fifth. [420] To enable the matter to be more easily understood, some formulas follow below, in such a way that their logical force may be appreciated through the facts themselves, not through the stated examples. This is the formula for the first mode. *If the first, then the second; but the first; therefore the second.* For the second mode: *If not the first, then not the second; but the second; therefore the first.* For the third mode: Not both the first and not the second; but the first; therefore the second. For the fourth mode: *Either the first or the second; but the first; therefore not the second.* For the fifth mode: *Either the first or the second; but not the first; therefore the second.* For the sixth mode: *Not both the first and the second; but the first; therefore not the second.* For the seventh mode: *Not both the first and not the second; but not the first; therefore the second.*

[421] We must recognize that from one evidential proposition three of the above modes can be formed, and from a different one the other four. The reason for this order is so that the first mode may be the one called *from antecedents*, because what is antecedent comes first; and the one called *from consequents* is second, on the same principle, so that by its name it seems to show that it ought to follow the first in order. There remains the third one using the same evidential proposition, that *from incompatibles*; for we cannot leap across to *disjunction*, since it cannot be formed from the same evidential proposition. This will therefore be the fourth mode, but, as it were, the first of those using another evidential proposition and in that class the one which asserts its second premise affirmatively ought to come first; for affirmation is prior to negation. The fifth mode ought to be through disjunction also, but after the fourth because in the fourth the second premise is formed by affirmation, in the fifth by negation. This may be understood also in the two remaining modes.

[422] Syllogisms are combined in many ways, so that in one process of reasoning you may recognize the forms of both the categorical and conditional syllogisms. For example, if the question is whether dialectic itself is advantageous, the argument should be set out: *If it is advantageous to discuss well, the science of discussing well is advantageous; but to discuss well is advantageous; therefore dialectic is advantageous.* However, we must observe in the categorical syllogism what the second premise takes over from the first; for it is clear that it takes something from outside. But as I said, in what the second premise takes over from the first, we must note whether it takes it over correctly, in accordance with the patterns properly kept and remembered. For it happens that what was observed in the first premise to belong to the predicate, in the second premise clearly belongs to the subject; and again, if you form the second premise in a different way, the same phrase will belong to the predicate. For example, it is known that in the first figure the second premise is the same as the subject of the second, or else that the subject of the first is the predicate of the second; but in the second figure the predicates of the first premise and of the second are the same. So that if you were to advance an argument like this—*Every art is to be practiced by frequent exercise; but speech is the exercise of rhetoric; therefore rhetoric is to be practiced by frequent speech*—then in the first premise *exercise* was seen to belong to the predicate, and in the second premise again it belongs to the predicate. Then how has the form been preserved? Surely, because something has been left in the predicate of the second, from which a conclusion could be formed; and that is, *is to be practiced.* For if I wished to form the second premise thus—*Rhetoric is an art*—the whole would be kept to form the conclusion: *Therefore rhetoric is to be practiced by frequent exercise.* From this it is clear that there are many common elements which can be joined to either the subject or the predicate, according to the style of the second premise."

[423] While Dialectic was holding forth in this way and getting on to matters as complicated as they are obscure, Maia's son (Mercury) grew impatient and nodded to Pallas, who cut in:

"Madam, you speak with great skill; but now stop your exposition before you get entangled in the complexities of your subject, and its knotty problems exhaust the goodwill of Hymen. You have said in summary all that is fitting from that which learned discussion who cut in:

"Madam, you speak with great skill; but now stop your exposition before you get entangled in the complexities of your subject, and its knotty problems exhaust the goodwill of Hymen. You have said in summary all that is fitting from that which learned discussion has contributed for the development of the subject in a large volume. A modest spring from deep learning is sufficient; it brings to light things hidden from sight, and avoids tedious discussion, without passing over anything and leaving it unrecognized. The matters that remain[12] are founded on great deceit, and false deception encompasses those who are caught by them, while you prepare sophisms fraught with guile, or seductively make sport with trickeries from which one cannot get free. And when you gradually build up a sorites, or fashion errors which truth condemns, then your sin, your wicked deed, resounds in the ears of the Thunderer, since the lofty denizens of heaven hate everything false in a woman of shame. If you ponder it, what is more cruel than making sport of people? You have had your say, and you will surely become a more disreputable and itinerant charlatan if you go on to build up your snares. Away then with shifty profundity, and leave what time remains to your sisters."

[424]When Dialectic heard this she hesitated a little, but in obedience to the orders of the goddess she replied:

"I must respect your word, and in obedience to commands that I must honor I shall refrain and shall not say what I had commenced. But one indulgence should have been allowed me, that as a matter of honor I should have been permitted to refute the story which Bromius invented; he would then know that we daughters of Cecrops (i.e., the women of Athens) know very well how to feel insulted; he would be able to see that I am more viperish than he had thought; his 'clumsy Marsian' would indeed become a magician; and he would not catch *me* asleep or drunk and babbling commonplaces when Jupiter's stars are rising. But I must wait upon you alone, lady; I shall be quiet."

With these words she fell silent, as if restrained, and many of the gods who had at first laughed at her trembled before her.

Notes

1   This refers to the sophism: "What you have not lost, you have; you have not lost horns from your head; therefore you have horns on your head."

2   A celebrated stoic philosopher of the third century B.C., author of numerous logical works, including a book on the sorites—"the heap." See Diogenes Laertius 7. 192. Cf. Persius 6. 80.

3   Carneades, a skeptic philosopher of the second century B.C., is said to have used hellebore, a purgative drug, to make his mind keener and more subtle before disputing with Chrysippus (a chronological impossibility). See Valerius Maximus 8. 7. 5.

4   This sentence remains opaque. If *vertier* (here translated as "reversed") means "converted" rather than "overthrown," the first part taken alone is nonsense, since it is precisely these two kinds of propositions which cannot be converted *simpliciter*. In this case, the second part ("connecting ambiguous terms to univocal terms") may refer to some fallacious way of effecting the conversions. If *vertier* means "overthrown," there may be a reference to the "fallacy of four terms," where an ambiguous middle term is used in different senses in the premises of a syllogism. It is hard not to suspect the text.

5   The Marsi, an Italian tribe, had a reputation for sorcery, poisoning, and snake-charming. The reputation may originate in their claim to be descended from Circe.

6   Arhena bore the representation of Medusa's head on her shield to commemorate her slaying of the Gorgon or her part in helping Perseus to do so.

7   Rhetoric.

8   Geometry.

9   Sections 344-54 correspond in subject matter to Porphyry's *Introduction* (3d cent. A.D.) to Aristotle's *Categories* and deal with what came to be called the *quinque voces* (the five terms, or predicables). This became the standard order of expression among the medieval logicians.

10   This curious utterance should be understood as having "every man" as the subject. Despite Martianus' claim of what order is "natural," the inverted sentence is far more natural in Latin

necessarily conversely.

12 Martianus' failure to include a discussion of fallacies is strange in the work of one supposedly teaching the science of disputation. Athena apparently does not recognize the value of being able to detect fallacious reasoning, whether in an opponent or oneself.

Augustine of Hippo

City of God and *On Christian Doctrine*

Augustine of Hippo (354-430) had the most profound influence in medieval culture of any ancient writer. Two of his most influential works were his treatise On Christian Doctrine *and his great* City of God.

In the first, finished in 426, Augustine outlined what became the universal means of interpreting Sacred Scripture and other texts through the twelfth century. The particular passages below discuss his fundamental distinction between use and enjoyment of creation, and his theory of signs.

Augustine wrote The City of God *over a long period, completing it only in 426. The work began as a defense against the charge that Christianity had led to the misfortunes of the Roman Empire culminating in the sacking of Rome by the Visigoths in 410. It became a broad-ranging meditation on the nature of good and evil, human society and government and formed the foundation of all medieval political theory.*

Source: Marcus Dods (tr.), *A Select Library of the Nicene and Post-Nicene Fathers of the Christian Church*, vol. II (Buffalo: the Christian Literature Co., 1987);

On Christian Doctrine

Preface: Showing that to teach rules for the interpretation of scripture is not a superfluous task.

1.   There are certain rules for the interpretation of Scripture which I think might with great advantage be taught to earnest students of the word, that they might profit not only from reading the works of others who have laid open the secrets of sacred writings, but also from themselves opening such secrets to others. These rules I propose to teach to those who are able and willing to learn, if God our Lord do not withhold from me, while I write, the thoughts He is wont to vouchsafe to me in my meditations on this subject. But before I enter upon this undertaking, I think it well to meet the objections of those who are likely to take exception to the work, or who would do so, did I not conciliate them beforehand. And if, after all, men should still be found to make objections, yet at least they will not prevail with others over whom they might have influence, did they not find them forearmed against their assaults), to turn them back from a useful study to the dull sloth of ignorance.

2.   There are some, then, likely to object to this work of mine, because they have failed to understand the rules here laid down. Others, again, will think that I have spent my labour to no purpose, because, though they understand the rules, yet in their attempts to apply them and to interpret Scripture by them, they have failed to clear up the point they wish cleared up; and these, because they have received no assistance from this work themselves, they will give it as their opinion that it can be of no use to anybody. There is a third class of objectors who either really do understand Scripture well, or think they do, and who, because they know (or imagine) that they have attained a certain power of interpreting the sacred books without reading any directions of the kind that I propose to lay down here, will cry out that such rules are not necessary for any one, but that everything rightly done towards clearing up the obscurities of Scripture could be better done by the unas-

sisted grace of God.

3.   To reply briefly to all these: To those who do not understand what is here set down, my answer is, that I am not to be blamed for their want of understanding. It is just as if they were anxious to see the new or the old moon, or some very obscure star, and I should point it out with my finger; if they had not sight enough to see even my finger, they would surely have no right to fly into a passion with me on that account. As for those who, even though they know and understand my directions, fail to penetrate the meaning of obscure passages in Scripture, they may stand for those who, in the case I have imagined, are just able to see my finger, but cannot see the stars at which it is pointed. And so both these classes had better give up blaming me, and pray instead that God would grant them the sight of their eyes. For though I can move my finger to point out an object, it is out of my power to open men's eyes that they may see either the fact that I am pointing, or the object at which I point.

4.   But now as to those who talk vauntingly of Divine Grace, and boast that they understand and can explain Scripture without the aid of such directions as those I now propose to lay down, and who think, therefore, that what I have undertaken to write is entirely superfluous. I would such persons could calm themselves so far as to remember that, however justly they may rejoice in God's great gift, yet it was from human teachers that they themselves learned to read. Now, they would hardly think it right that they should be held in contempt by the Egyptian monk Antony, a just and holy man, who, not being able to read himself, is said to have committed the Scriptures to memory through hearing them read by others, and by dint of wise meditations to have arrived at a thorough understanding of them; or by that barbarian slave Christianus, of whom I have lately heard from very respectable and trustworthy witnesses, who, without any teaching from man, attained a full knowledge of the art of reading simply through prayer that it might be revealed to him; after three days' supplication obtaining his request that he might read through a book presented to him on the spot by the astonished bystanders.

5.   But if any one thinks that these stories are false, I do not strongly insist on them. For, as I am dealing with Christians who profess to understand the Scriptures without any directions from man (and if the fact be so, they boast of a real advantage, and one of no ordinary kind), they must surely grant that every one of us learnt his own language by hearing it constantly from childhood, and that any other language we have learnt,—Greek, or Hebrew, or any of the rest,—we have learnt either in the same way, by hearing it spoken, or from a human teacher. Now, then, suppose we advise all our brethren not to teach their children any of these things, because on the outpouring of the Holy Spirit the apostles immediately began to speak the language of every race; and warn every one who has not had a like experience that he need not consider himself a Christian, or may at least doubt whether he has yet received the Holy Spirit? No, no; rather let us put away false pride and learn whatever can be learnt from man; and let him who teaches another communicate what he has himself received without arrogance and without jealousy. And do not let us tempt Him in whom we have believed, lest, being ensnared by such wiles of the enemy and by our own perversity, we may even refuse to go to the churches to hear the gospel itself, or to read a book, or to listen to another reading or preaching, in the hope that we shall be carried up to the third heaven, "whether in the body or out of the body," as the apostle says, and there hear unspeakable words, such as it is not lawful for man to utter, or see the Lord Jesus Christ and hear the gospel from his own lips rather than from those of men.

6.   Let us beware of such dangerous temptations of pride, and let us rather consider the facts that the Apostle Paul himself, although stricken down and admonished by the voice of God from heaven, yet was sent to a man to receive the sacraments and be admitted into the Church; and that Cornelius the centurion, although an angel announced to him that

his prayers were heard and his alms had in remembrance, yet was handed over to Peter for instruction, and not only received the sacraments from the apostle's hands, but was also instructed by him as to the proper objects of faith, hope, and love. And without doubt it was *possible* to have done everything through the instrumentality of angels, but the condition of our race would have been more degraded if God had not chosen to make use of men as the ministers of His word to their fellow-men. For how could that be true which is written, "The temple of God is holy, which temple ye are," if God gave forth no oracles from His human temple, but communicated everything that He wished to be taught to men by voices from heaven, or through the ministration of angels? Moreover, love itself, which binds men together in the bond of unity, would have no means of pouring soul into soul, and, as it were, mingling them one with another, if men never learnt anything from their fellow-men.

7.   And we know that the eunuch who was reading Isaiah the prophet, and did not understand what he read, was not sent by the apostle to an angel, nor was it an angel who explained to him what he did not understand, nor was he inwardly illuminated by the grace of God without the interposition of man; on the contrary, at the suggestion of God, Philip, who *did* understand the prophet, came to him, and sat with him, and in human words, and with a human tongue, opened to him the Scriptures. Did not God talk with Moses, and yet he, with great wisdom and entire absence of jealous pride, accepted the plan of his father-in-law, a man of an alien race, for ruling and administering the affairs of the great nation entrusted to him? For Moses knew that a wise plan, in whatever mind it might originate, was to be ascribed not to the man who devised it, but to Him who is the Truth, the unchangeable God.

8.   In the last place, every one who boasts that he, through divine illumination, understands the obscurities of Scripture, though not instructed in any rules of interpretation, at the same time believes, and rightly believes, that this power is not his own, in the sense of originating with himself, but is the gift of God. For so he seeks God's glory, not his own. But reading and understanding, as he does, without the aid of any human interpreter, why does he himself undertake to interpret for others? Why does he not rather send them direct to God, that they too may learn by the inward teaching of the Spirit without the help of man? The truth is, he fears to incur the reproach: "Thou wicked and slothful servant, thou oughtest to have put my money to the exchangers." Seeing, then, that these men teach others, either through speech or writing, what they understand, surely they cannot blame me if I likewise teach not only what they understand, but also the rules of interpretation they follow. For no one ought to consider anything as his own, except perhaps what is false. All truth is of Him who says, "I am the truth." For what have we that we did not receive? and if we have received it, why do we glory, as if we had not received it?

9.   He who reads to an audience pronounces aloud the words he sees before him: he who teaches reading, does it that others may be able to read for themselves. Each, however, communicates to others what he has learnt himself. Just so, the man who explains to an audience the passages of Scripture he understands is like one who reads aloud the words before him. On the other hand, the man who lays down rules for interpretation is like one who teaches reading, that is, shows others how to read for themselves. So that, just as he who knows how to read is not dependent on some one else, when he finds a book, to tell him what is written in it, so the man who is in possession of the rules which I here attempt to lay down, if he meet with an obscure passage in the books which he reads, will not need an interpreter to lay open the secret to him, but, holding fast by certain rules, and following up certain indications, will arrive at the hidden sense without any error, or at least without falling into any gross absurdity. And so although it will sufficiently appear in the course of the work itself that no one can justly object to this undertaking of mine, which has no other object than to be of service, yet as it seemed convenient to reply at the outset

to any who might make preliminary objections, such is the start I have thought good to make on the road I am about to traverse in this book.

BOOK I. Containing a general view of the subjects treated in Holy Scripture.

Chapter 1. — The interpretation of Scripture depends on the discovery and enunciation of the meaning, and is to be undertaken in dependence on God's aid.

1.   There are two things on which all interpretation of Scripture depends: the mode of ascertaining the proper meaning, and the mode of making known the meaning when it is ascertained. We shall treat first of the mode of ascertaining, next of the mode of making known, the meaning;—a great and arduous undertaking, and one that, if difficult to carry out, it is, I fear, presumptuous to enter upon. And presumptuous it would undoubtedly be, if I were counting on my own strength; but since my hope of accomplishing the work rests on Him who has already supplied me with many thoughts on this subject, I do not fear but that He will go on to supply what is yet wanting when once I have begun to use what He has already given. For a possession which is not diminished by being shared with others, if it is possessed and not shared, is not yet possessed as it ought to be possessed. The Lord saith, "Whosoever hath, to him shall be given," He will give, then, to those who have; that is to say, if they use freely and cheerfully what they have received, He will add to and perfect His gifts. The loaves in the miracle were only five and seven in number before the disciples began to divide them among the hungry people. But when once they began to distribute them, though the wants of so many thousands were satisfied, they filled baskets with the fragments that were left. Now, just as that bread increased in the very act of breaking it, so those thoughts which the Lord has already vouchsafed to me with a view to undertaking this work will, as soon as I begin to impart them to others, be multiplied by His grace, so that, in this very work of distribution in which I have engaged, so far from incurring loss and poverty, I shall be made to rejoice in a marvellous increase of wealth.

Chapter 2. — What a thing is, and what a sign.

2.   All instruction is either about things or about signs; but things are learnt by means of signs. I now use the word "thing" in a strict sense, to signify that which is never employed as a sign of anything else: for example, wood, stone, cattle, and other things of that kind. Not, however, the wood which we read Moses cast into the bitter waters to make them sweet, nor the stone which Jacob used as a pillow, nor the ram which Abraham offered up instead of his son; for these, though they are things, are also signs of other things. They are signs of another kind, those which are never employed except as signs: for example, words. No one uses words except as signs of something else; and hence may be understood what I call signs: these things, to wit, which are used to indicate something else. Accordingly, every sign is also a thing; for what is not a thing is nothing at all. Every thing, however, is not also a sign. And so, in regard to this distinction between things and signs, I shall, when I speak of things, speak in such a way that even if some of them may be used as signs also, that will not interfere with the division of the subject according to which I am to discuss things first and signs afterwards. But we must carefully remember that what we have now to consider about things is what they are in themselves, not what other things they are signs of.

Chapter 3 — Some things are for use, some for enjoyment.

3.   There are some things, then, which are to be enjoyed, others which are to be used, others still which enjoy and use. Those things which are objects of enjoyment make us

happy. Those things which are objects of use assist, and (so to speak) support us in our efforts after happiness, so that we can attain the things that make us happy and rest in them. We ourselves, again, who enjoy and use these things, being placed among both kinds of objects, if we set ourselves to enjoy those which we ought to use, are hindered in our course, and sometimes even led away from it; so that, getting entangled in the love of lower gratifications, we lag behind in, or even altogether turn back from, the pursuit of the real and proper objects of enjoyment.

Chapter 4. — Difference of use and enjoyment.

4.   For to enjoy a thing is to rest with satisfaction in it for its own sake. To use, on the other hand, is to employ whatever means are at one's disposal to obtain what one desires, if it is a proper object of desire; for an unlawful use ought rather to be called an abuse. Suppose, then, we were wanderers in a strange country, and could not live happily away from our fatherland, and that we felt wretched in our wandering, and wishing to put an end to our misery, determined to return home. We find, however, that we must make use of some mode of conveyance, either by land or water, in order to reach that fatherland where our enjoyment is to commence. But the beauty of the country through which we pass, and the very pleasure of the motion, charm our hearts, and turning these things which we ought to use into objects of enjoyment, we become unwilling to hasten the end of our journey; and becoming engrossed in a factitious delight, our thoughts are diverted from that home whose delights would make us truly happy. Such is a picture of our condition in this life of mortality. We have wandered far from God; and if we wish to return to our Father's home, this world must be used, not enjoyed, that so the invisible things of God may be clearly seen, being understood by the things that are made,—that is, that by means of what is material and temporary we may lay hold upon that which is spiritual and eternal.

BOOK II.

Chapter 1. — Signs, their nature and variety.

1.   As when I was writing about things, I introduced the subject with a warning against attending to anything but what they are in themselves, even though they are signs of something else, so now, when I come in its turn to discuss the subject of signs, I lay down this direction, not to attend to what they are in themselves, but to the fact that they are signs, that is, to what they signify. For a sign is a thing which, over and above the impression it makes on the senses, causes something else to come into the mind as a consequence of itself: as when we see a footprint, we conclude that an animal whose footprint this is has passed by; and when we see smoke, we know that there is fire beneath; and when we hear the voice of a living man, we think of the feeling in his mind; and when the trumpet sounds, soldiers know that they are to advance or retreat, or do whatever else the state of battle requires.

2.   Now some signs are natural, others conventional. Natural signs are those which, apart from any intention or desire of using them as signs, do yet lead to the knowledge of something else, as, for example, smoke when it indicates fire. For it is not from any intention of making it a sign that it is so, but through attention to experience we come to know that fire is beneath, even when nothing but smoke can be seen. And the footprint of an animal passing by belongs to this class of signs. And the countenance of an angry or sorrowful man indicates the feeling in his mind, independently of his will: and in the same way every other emotion of the mind is betrayed by the tell-tale countenance, even though we do nothing with the intention of making it known. This class of signs, however, it is no part of my design to discuss at present. But as it comes under this division of the subject, I could not altogether pass it over. It will be enough to have noticed it thus far.

Chapter 2. — Of the kind of signs we are now concerned with.

3. Conventional signs, on the other hand, are those which living beings mutually exchange for the purpose of showing, as well as they can, the feelings of their minds, or their perceptions, or their thoughts. Nor is there any reason for giving a sign except the desire of drawing forth and conveying into another's mind what the giver of the sign has in his own mind. We wish, then, to consider and discuss this class of signs so far as men are concerned with it, because even the signs which have been given us of God, and which are contained in the Holy Scriptures, were made known to us through men—those, namely, who wrote the Scriptures. The beasts, too, have certain signs among themselves by which they make known the desires in their mind. For when the poultry-cock has discovered food, he signals with his voice for the hen to run to him, and the dove by cooing calls his mate, or is called by her in turn; and many signs of the same kind are matters of common observation. Now whether these signs, like the expression or the cry of a man in grief, follow the movement of the mind instinctively and apart from any purpose, or whether they are really used with the purpose of signification, is another question, and does not pertain to the matter in hand. And this part of the subject I exclude from the scope of this work as not necessary to my present object.

Chapter 3. — Among signs, words hold the chief place.

4. Of the signs, then, by which men communicate their thoughts to one another, some relate to the sense of sight, some to that of hearing, a very few to the other senses. For, when we nod, we give no sign except to the eyes of the man to whom we wish by this sign to impart our desire. And some convey a great deal by the motion of the hands: and actors by movements of all their limbs give certain signs to the initiated, and, so to speak, address their conversation to the eyes: and the military standards and flags convey through the eyes the will of the commanders. And all these signs are as it were a kind of visible words. The signs that address themselves to the ear are, as I have said, more numerous, and for the most part consist of words. For though the bugle and the flute and the lyre frequently give not only a sweet but a significant sound, yet all these signs are very few in number compared with words. For among men words have obtained far and away the chief place as a means of indicating the thoughts of the mind. Our Lord, it is true, gave a sign through the odour of the ointment which was poured out upon his feet; and in the sacrament of His body and blood He signified His will through the sense of taste; and when by touching the hem of His garment the woman was made whole, the act was not wanting in significance. But the countless multitude of the signs through which men express their thoughts consist of words. For I have been able to put into words all those signs, the various classes of which I have briefly touched upon, but I could by no effort express words in terms of those signs...

Chapter 17.—Origin of the legend of the nine Muses.

27. For we must not listen to the falsities of heathen superstition, which represent the nine muses as daughters of Jupiter and Mercury. Varro refutes these, and I doubt whether any one can be found among them more curious or more learned in such matters. He says that a certain state (I don't recollect the name) ordered from each of three artists a set of statues of the Muses, to be placed as an offering in the temple of Apollo, intending that whichever of the artists produced the most beautiful statues, they should select and purchase from him. It so happened that these artists executed their works with equal beauty, that all nine pleased the state, and that all were bought to be dedicated in the temple of Apollo; and he says that afterwards Hesiod the poet gave names to them all. It was not Jupiter, therefore, that begat the nine Muses, but three artists created three each. And the state had originally given the order for three, not because it had seen them in visions, nor because they had presented themselves in that number to the eyes of any

of the citizens, but because it was obvious to remark that all sound, which is the material of song, is by nature of three kinds. For it is either produced by the voice, as in the case of those who sing with the mouth without an instrument; or by blowing, as in the case of trumpets and flutes; or by striking, as in the case of harps and drums, and all other instruments that give their sound when struck.

Chapter 18 — No help is to be despised, even though it come from a profane source.

28. But whether the fact is as Varro has related, or is not so, still we ought not to give up music because of the superstition of the heathen, if we can derive anything from it that is not of use for the understanding of Holy Scripture; nor does it follow that we must busy ourselves with their theatrical trumpery because we enter upon an investigation about harps and other instruments, that may help us to lay hold upon spiritual things. For we ought not to refuse to learn letters because they say that Mercury discovered them; nor because they have dedicated temples to Justice and Virtue, and prefer to worship in the form of stones things that ought to have their place in the heart, ought we on that account to forsake justice and virtue. Nay, but let every good and true Christian understand that wherever truth may be found, it belongs to his Master; and while he recognizes and acknowledges the truth, even in their religious literature, let him reject the figments of superstition, and let him grieve over and avoid men who, "when they knew God, glorified him not as God, neither were thankful; but became vain in their imaginations, and their foolish heart was darkened. Professing themselves to be wise, they became fools, and changed the glory of the uncorruptible God into an image made like to corruptible man, and to birds, and four-footed beasts, and creeping things."

Chapter 19 — Two kinds of heathen knowledge.

29. But to explain more fully this whole topic (for it is one that cannot be omitted), there are two kinds of knowledge which are in vogue among the heathen. One is the knowledge of things instituted by men, the other of things which they have noted, either as transacted in the past or as instituted by God. The former kind, that which deals with human institutions, is partly superstitious, partly not.

Chapter 20 — The superstitious nature of human institutions.

30. All the arrangements made by men for the making and worshipping of idols are superstitious, pertaining as they do either to the worship of what is created or of some part of it as God, or to consultations and arrangements about signs and leagues with devils, such, for example, as are employed in the magical arts, and which the poets are accustomed not so much to teach as to celebrate. And to this class belong, but with a bolder reach of deception, the books of the haruspices and augurs. In this class we must place also all amulets and cures which the medical art condemns, whether these consist in incantations, or in marks which they call *characters*, or in hanging or tying on or even dancing in a fashion certain articles, not with reference to the condition of the body, but to certain signs hidden or manifest; and these remedies they call by the less offensive name of *physica*, so as to appear not to be engaged in superstitious observances, but to be taking advantage of the forces of nature. Examples of these are the ear-rings on the top of each ear, or the rings of ostrich bone on the fingers, or telling you when you hiccup to hold your left thumb in your right hand.

31. To these we may add thousands of the most frivolous practices, that are to be observed if any part of the body should jump, or if, when friends are walking arm-in-arm, a stone, or a dog, or a boy, should come between them. And the kicking of a stone, as if it were a divider of friends, does less harm than to cuff an innocent boy if he happens to

run between men who are walking side by side. But it is delightful that the boys are sometimes avenged by the dogs; for frequently men are so superstitious as to venture upon striking a dog who has run between them,—not with impunity however, for instead of a superstitious remedy, the dog sometimes makes his assailant run in hot haste for a real surgeon. To this class, too, belong the following rules: To tread upon the threshold when you go back to bed if any one should sneeze when you are putting on your slippers; to return home if you stumble when going to a place; when your clothes are eaten by mice, or to be more frightened at the prospect of coming misfortune than grieved by your present loss. Whence that witty saying of Cato, who, when consulted by a man who told him that mice had eaten his boots, replied, "That is not strange, but it would have been very strange indeed if the boots had eaten the mice."

Chapter 21 — Superstition of astrologers.

32. Nor can we exclude from this kind of superstition those who were called *genethliaci*, on account of their attention to birthdays, but are now commonly called *mathematici*. For these, too, although they may seek with pains for the true position of the stars at the time of our birth, and may sometimes even find it out, yet in so far as they attempt thence to predict our actions, grievously err, and sell inexperienced men into a miserable bondage. For when any freeman goes to an astrologer of this kind, he gives money that he may come away the slave either of Mars or of Venus, or rather, perhaps, of all the stars to which those who first fell into this error, and handed it on to posterity, have given the names either of beasts, or of men with a view to confer honor on those men. And this is not to be wondered at, when we consider that even in times more recent and nearer our own, the Romans made an attempt to dedicate the star which we call Lucifer to the name and honor of Caesar. And this would, perhaps, have been done, and the name handed down to distant ages, only that his ancestress Venus had given her name to this star before him, and could not by any law transfer to her heirs what she had never possessed, nor sought to possess, in life. For where a place was vacant, or not held in honor of any of the dead of former times, the usual proceeding in such cases was carried out. For example, we have changed the names of the months Quintilis and Sextilis to July and August, naming them in honor of the men Julius Cæsar and Augustus Cæsar; and from this instance any one who cares can easily see that the stars spoken of above formerly wandered in the heavens without the names they now bear. But as the men were dead whose memory people were either compelled by royal power or impelled by human folly to honor, they seemed to think that in putting their names upon the stars they were raising the dead men themselves to heaven. But whatever they may be called by men, still there are stars which God has made and set in order after His own pleasure, and they have a fixed movement, by which the seasons are distinguished and varied. And when any one is born, it is easy to observe the point at which this movement has arrived, by use of the rules discovered and laid down by those who are rebuked by Holy Writ in these terms: "For if they were able to know so much that they could weigh the world, how did they not more easily find out the Lord thereof?"

Chapter 22. — The folly of observing the stars in order to predict the events of a life.

33. But to desire to predict the characters, the acts, and the face of those who are born from such an observation, is a great delusion and great madness. And among those at least who have any sort of acquaintance with matters of this kind (which, indeed, are only fit to be unlearnt again), this superstition is refuted beyond the reach of doubt. For the observation is of the position of the stars, which they call constellations, at the time when the person was born about whom these wretched men are consulted by their still more wretched dupes. Now it may happen that, in the case of twins, one follows the other out of the womb so closely that there is no interval of time between them that can be appre-

hended and marked in the position of the constellations. Whence it necessarily follows that twins are in many cases born under the same stars, while they do not meet with equal fortune either in what they do or what they suffer, but often meet with fates so different that one of them has a most fortunate life, the other a most unfortunate. As, for example, we are told that Esau and Jacob were born twins, and in such close succession, that Jacob, who was born last, was found to have laid hold with his hand upon the heel of his brother, who preceded him. Now, assuredly, the day and the hour of the birth of these two could not be marked in any way that would not give both the same constellation. But what a difference there was between the characters, the actions, the labors, and the fortunes of these two, the Scriptures bear witness, which are now so widely spread as to be in the mouth of all nations.

34. Nor is it to the point to say that the very smallest and briefest moment that separates the birth of twins, produces great effects in nature, and in the extremely rapid motion of the heavenly bodies. For, although I may grant that it does produce the greatest effects, yet the astrologer cannot discover this in the constellations, and it is by looking into these that he professes to read the fates. If, then, he does not discover the difference when he examines the constellations, which must, of course, be the same whether he is consulted about Jacob or his brother, what does it profit him that there is a difference in the heavens, which he rashly and carelessly brings into disrepute, when there is no difference in his chart, which he looks into anxiously but in vain? And so these notions also, which have their origin in certain signs of things being arbitrarily fixed upon by the presumption of men, are to be referred to the same class as if they were leagues and covenants with devils.

Chapter 23. — Why we repudiate arts of divination.

35. For in this way it comes to pass that men who lust after evil things are, by a secret judgment of God, delivered over to be mocked and deceived, as the just reward of their evil desires. For they are deluded and imposed on by the false angels, to whom the lowest part of the world has been put in subjection by the law of God's providence, and in accordance with His most admirable arrangement of things. And the result of these delusions and deceptions is, that through these superstitions and baneful modes of divination, many things in the past and future are made known, and turn out just as they are foretold; and in the case of those who practice superstitious observances, many things turn out agreeably to their observances, and ensnared by these successes, they become more eagerly inquisitive, and involve themselves further and further in a labyrinth of most pernicious error. And to our advantage, the Word of God is not silent about this species of fornication of the soul; and it does not warn the soul against following such practices on the ground that those who profess them speak lies, but it says, "Even if what they tell you should come to pass, hearken not unto them." For though the ghost of the dead Samuel foretold the truth to King Saul, that does not make such sacrilegious observances as those by which his ghost was brought up the less detestable; and though the ventriloquist woman in the Acts of the Apostles bore true testimony to the apostles of the Lord, the Apostle Paul did not spare the evil spirit on that account, but rebuked and cast it out, and so made the woman clean.

36. All arts of this sort, therefore, are either nullities, or are part of a guilty superstition, springing out of a baleful fellowship between men and devils, and are to be utterly repudiated and avoided by the Christian as the covenants of a false and treacherous friendship. "Not as if the idol were anything," says the apostle; "but because the things which they sacrifice they sacrifice to devils and not to God; and I would not that ye should have fellowship with devils." Now, what the apostle has said about idols and the sacrifices offered in their honor, that we ought to feel in regard to all fancied signs which lead either to the worship of idols, or to worshipping creation or its parts instead of God, or which

are connected with attention to medicinal charms and other observances; for these are not appointed by God as the public means of promoting love towards God and our neighbor, but they waste the hearts of wretched men in private and selfish striving after temporal things. Accordingly, in regard to all these branches of knowledge, we must fear and shun the Devil their prince, strive only to shut and bar the door against our return. As, then, from the stars which God created and ordained, men have drawn lying omens of their own fancy, so also from things that are born, or in any other way come into existence under the government of God's providence, if there chance only to be something unusual in the occurrence,—as when a mule brings forth young, or an object is struck by lightning,—men have frequently drawn omens by conjectures of their own, and have committed them to writing, as if they had drawn them by rule.

Chapter 24. — The intercourse and agreement with demons which superstitious observances maintain.

37. And all these omens are of force just so far as has been arranged with the devils by that previous understanding in the mind which is, as it were, the common language, but they are all full of hurtful curiosity, torturing anxiety, and deadly slavery. For it was not because they had meaning that they were attended to, but it was by attending to and marking them that they came to have meaning. And so they are made different for different people, according to their several notions and prejudices. For those spirits which are bent upon deceiving, take care to provide for each person the same sort of omens as they see his own conjectures and preconceptions have already been entangled in. For, to take an illustration, the same figure of the letter X, which is made in the shape of a cross, means one thing among the Greeks and another among the Latins, not by nature, but by agreement and pre-arrangement as to its signification; and so, any one who knows both languages uses this letter in a different sense when writing to a Greek from that in which he uses it when writing to a Latin. And the same sound, *beta*, which is the name of a letter among the Greeks, is the name of a vegetable among the Latins; and when I say, *lege*, these two syllables mean one thing to a Greek and another to a Latin. Now, just as all these signs affect the mind according to the arrangements of the community in which each man lives, and affect different men's minds differently, because these arrangements are different; and as, further, men did not agree upon them as signs because they were already significant, but on the contrary they are now significant because they have agreed upon them; in the same way also, those signs by which the ruinous intercourse with devils is maintained have meaning just in proportion to each man's observations. And this appears quite plainly in the rites of the augurs; for they, both before they observe the omens and after they have completed their observations, take pains not to see the flight or hear the cry of the birds, because these signs are of no significance apart from the previous arrangement in the mind of the observer.

Chapter 25.—In human institutions which are not superstitious, there are some things superfluous and some convenient and necessary.

38. But when all these have been cut away and rooted out of the mind of the Christian, we must then look at human institutions which are not superstitious, that is, such as are not set up in association with devils, but by men in association with one another. For all arrangements that are in force among men, because they have agreed among themselves that they should be in force, are human institutions; and of these, some are matters of superfluity and luxury, some of convenience and necessity. For if those signs which the actors make in dancing were of force by nature, and not by the arrangement and agreement of men, the public crier would not in former times have announced to the people of Carthage, while the pantomime was dancing, what it meant to express,—a thing still remembered by many old men from whom we have frequently heard it. And we may well believe this, because even now, if any one who is unaccustomed to such follies goes into

the theatre, unless some one tells him what these movements mean, he will give his whole attention to them in vain. Yet all men aim at a certain degree of likeness in their choice of signs, that the signs may as far as possible be like the things they signify. But because one thing may resemble another in many ways, such signs are not always of the same significance among men, except when they have mutually agreed upon them.

39. But in regard to pictures and statues, and other works of this kind, which are intended as representations of things, nobody makes a mistake, especially if they are executed by skilled artists, but every one, as soon as he sees the likenesses, recognizes the things they are likenesses of. And this whole class are to be reckoned among the superfluous devices of men, unless when it is a matter of importance to inquire in regard to any of them, for what reason, where, when, and by whose authority it was made. Finally, the thousands of fables and fictions, in whose lies men take delight, are human devices, and nothing is to be considered more peculiarly man's own and derived from himself than anything that is false and lying. Among the convenient and necessary arrangements of men with men are to be reckoned whatever differences they choose to make in bodily dress and ornament for the purpose of distinguishing sex or rank; and the countless varieties of signs without which human intercourse either could not be carried on at all, or would be carried on at great inconvenience; and the arrangements as to weights and measures, and the stamping and weighing of coins, which are peculiar to each state and people, and other things of the same kind. Now these, if they were not devices of men, would not be different in different nations, and could not be changed among particular nations at the discretion of their respective sovereigns.

40. This whole class of human arrangements, which are of convenience for the necessary intercourse of life, the Christian is not by any means to neglect, but on the contrary should pay a sufficient degree of attention to them, and keep them in memory.

Chapter 26.—What human contrivances we are to adopt, and what we are to avoid.

For certain institutions of men are in a sort of way representations and likenesses of natural objects. And of these, such as have relation to fellowship with devils must, as has been said, be utterly rejected and held in detestation; those, on the other hand, which relate to the mutual intercourse of men, are, so far as they are not matters of luxury and superfluity, to be adopted, especially the forms of letters which are necessary for reading, and the various languages as far as is required—a matter I have spoken of above. To this class also belong shorthand characters, those who are acquainted with which are called shorthand writers. All these are useful, and there is nothing unlawful in learning them, nor do they involve us in superstition, or enervate us by luxury, if they only occupy our minds so far as not to stand in the way of more important objects to which they ought to be subservient.

Chapter 27. — Some departments of knowledge, not of mere human invention, aid us in interpreting scripture.

41. But, coming to the next point, we are not to reckon among human institutions those things which men have handed down to us, not as arrangements of their own, but as the result of investigation into the occurrences of the past, and into the arrangements of God's providence. And of course, some pertain to the bodily senses, some to the intellect. Those which are reached by the bodily senses we either believe on testimony, or perceive when they are pointed out to us, or infer from experience.

Chapter 28. — To what extent history is an aid.

42. Anything, then, that we learn from history about the chronology of past times assists us very much in understanding the Scriptures, even if it be learnt without the pale of the Church as a matter of childish instruction. For we frequently seek information about a variety of matters by use of the Olympiads, and the names of the consuls; and ignorance of the consulship in which our Lord was born, and that in which He suffered, has led some into the error of supposing that He was forty-six years of age when He suffered, that being the number of years He was told by the Jews the temple (which He took as a symbol of His body) was in building. Now we know on the authority of the evangelist that He was baptized; but the number of years He lived afterwards, although by putting His actions together we can make it out, yet that no shadow of doubt might arise from another source, can be ascertained more clearly and more certainly from a comparison of profane history with the gospel. It will still be evident, however, that it was not without a purpose it was said that the temple was forty and six years in building; so that, as this cannot be referred to our Lord's age, it may be referred to the more secret formation of the body which, for our sakes, the only-begotten Son of God, by whom all things were made, condescended to put on.

43. As to the utility of history, moreover, passing over the Greeks, what a great question our own Ambrose has set at rest! For, when the readers and admirers of Plato dared calumniously to assert that our Lord Jesus Christ learnt all those sayings of His, which they are compelled to admire and praise, from the books of Plato—because (they urged) it cannot be denied that Plato lived long before the coming of our Lord!—did not the illustrious bishop, when by his investigations into profane history he had discovered that Plato was through Jeremiah's means initiated into our literature, so as to be able to teach and write those views of his which are so justly praised? For not even Pythagoras himself, from whose successors these men assert Plato learnt theology, lived at a date prior to the books of that Hebrew race, among whom the worship of one God sprang up, and of whom as concerning the flesh our Lord came. And thus, when we reflect upon the dates, it becomes much more probable that those philosophers learnt whatever they said that was good and true from our literature, than that the Lord Jesus Christ learnt from the writings of Plato,—a thing which it is the height of folly to believe.

44. And even when in the course of an historical narrative former institutions of men are described, the history itself is not to be reckoned among human institutions; because things that are past and gone and cannot be undone are to be reckoned as belonging to the course of time, of which God is the author and governor. For it is one thing to tell what has been done, another to show what ought to be done. History narrates what has been done, faithfully and with advantage; but the books of the haruspices, and all writings of the same kind, aim at teaching what ought to be done or observed, using the boldness of an adviser, not the fidelity of a narrator.

Chapter 29. — To what extent natural science is an exegetical aid.

45. There is also a species of narrative resembling description, in which not a past but an existing state of things is made known to those who are ignorant of it. To this species belongs all that has been written about the situation of places, and the nature of animals, trees, herbs, stones, and other bodies. And of this species I have treated above, and have shown that this kind of knowledge is serviceable in solving the difficulties of Scripture, not that these objects are to be used conformably to certain signs as nostrums or the instruments of superstition; for that kind of knowledge I have already set aside as distinct from the lawful and free kind now spoken of. For it is one thing to say: If you bruise down this herb and drink it, it will remove the pain from your stomach; and another to say: If you hang this herb round your neck, it will remove the pain from your stomach. In the for-

mer case the wholesome mixture is approved of, in the latter the superstitious charm is condemned; although indeed, where incantations and invocations and marks are not used, it is frequently doubtful whether the thing that is tied or fixed in any way to the body to cure it, acts by a natural virtue, in which case it may be freely used; or acts by a sort of charm, in which case it becomes the Christian to avoid it the more carefully, the more efficacious it may seem to be. But when the reason why a thing is of virtue does not appear, the intention with which it is used is of great importance, at least in healing or in tempering bodies, whether in medicine or in agriculture.

46. The knowledge of the stars, again, is not a matter of narration, but of description. Very few of these, however, are mentioned in Scripture. And as the course of the moon, which is regularly employed in reference to celebrating the anniversary of our Lord's passion, is known to most people; so the rising and setting and other movements of the rest of the heavenly bodies are thoroughly known to very few. And this knowledge, although in itself it involves no superstition, renders very little, indeed almost no assistance, in the interpretation of Holy Scripture, and by engaging the attention unprofitably is a hindrance rather; and as it is closely related to the very pernicious error of the diviners of the fates, it is more convenient and becoming to neglect it. It involves, moreover, in addition to a description of the present state of things, something like a narrative of the past also; because one may go back from the present position and motion of the stars, and trace by rule their past movements. It involves also regular anticipations of the future, not in the way of forebodings and omens, but by way of sure calculation; not with the design of drawing any information from them as to our own acts and fates, in the absurd fashion of the *genethliaci*, but only as to the motions of the heavenly bodies themselves. For, as the man who computes the moon's age can tell, when he has found out her age to-day, what her age was any number of years ago, or what will be her age any number of years hence, in just the same way men who are skilled in such computations are accustomed to answer like questions about every one of the heavenly bodies. And I have stated what my views are about all this knowledge, so far as regards its utility.

Chapter 30. — What the mechanical arts contribute to exegetics.

47. Further, as to the remaining arts, whether those by which something is made which, when the effort of the workman is over, remains as a result of his work, as, for example, a house, a bench, a dish, and other things of that kind; or those which, so to speak, assist God in His operations, as medicine, and agriculture, and navigation; or those whose sole result is an action, as dancing, and racing, and wrestling;—in all these arts experience teaches us to infer the future from the past. For no man who is skilled in any of these arts moves his limbs in any operation without connecting the memory of the past with the expectation of the future. Now of these arts a very superficial and cursory knowledge is to be acquired, not with a view to practicing them (unless some duty compel us, a matter on which I do not touch at present), but with a view to forming a judgment about them, that we may not be wholly ignorant of what Scripture means to convey when it employs figures of speech derived from these arts.

Chapter 31. — Use of dialectics. Of fallacies.

48. There remain those branches of knowledge which pertain not to the bodily senses, but to the intellect, among which the science of reasoning and that of number are the chief. The science of reasoning is of very great service in searching into and unravelling all sorts of questions that come up in Scripture, only in the use of it we must guard against the love of wrangling, and the childish vanity of entrapping an adversary. For there are many of what are called *sophisms*, inferences in reasoning that are false, and yet so close an imitation of the true, as to deceive not only dull people, but clever men too, when they are not on their guard. For example, one man lays before another with whom he is talk-

ing, the proposition, "What I am, you are not." The other assents, for the proposition is in part true, the one man being cunning and the other simple. Then the first speaker adds: "I am a man;" and when the other has given his assent to this also, the first draws his conclusion: "Then you are not a man." Now of this sort of ensnaring arguments, Scripture, as I judge, expresses detestation in that place where it is said, "There is one that showeth wisdom in words, and is hated;" although indeed, a style of speech which is not intended to entrap, but only aims at verbal ornamentation more than is consistent with seriousness of purpose, is also called sophistical.

49. There are also valid processes of reasoning which lead to false conclusions, by following out to its logical consequences the error of the man with whom one is arguing; and these conclusions are sometimes drawn by a good and learned man, with the object of making the person from whose error these consequences result, feel ashamed of them, and of thus leading him to give up his error, when he finds that if he wishes to retain his old opinion, he must of necessity also hold other opinions which he condemns. For example, the apostle did not draw true conclusions when he said, "Then is Christ not risen," and again, "Then is our preaching vain, and your faith is also vain;" and further on drew other inferences which are all utterly false; for Christ has risen, the preaching of those who declared this fact was not in vain, nor was their faith in vain who had believed it. But all these false inferences followed legitimately from the opinion of those who said that there is no resurrection of the dead. These inferences, then, being repudiated as false, it follows that since they would be true if the dead rise not, there will be a resurrection of the dead. As, then, valid conclusions may be drawn not only from true but from false propositions, the laws of valid reasoning may easily be learnt in the schools, outside the pale of the Church. But the truth of propositions must be inquired into in the sacred books of the Church.

Chapter 32. — Valid logical sequence is not devised but only observed by man.

50. And yet the validity of logical sequences is not a thing devised by men, but is observed and noted by them that they may be able to learn and teach it; for it exists eternally in the reason of things, and has its origin with God. For as the man who narrates the order of events does not himself create that order; and as he who describes the situations of places, or the natures of animals, or roots, or minerals, does not describe arrangements of man; and as he who points out the stars and their movements does not point out anything that he himself or any other man has ordained;—in the same way, he who says, "When the consequent is false, the antecedent must also be false," says what is most true; but he does not himself make it so, he only points out that it is so. And it is upon this rule that the reasoning I have quoted from the Apostle Paul proceeds. For the antecedent is, "There is no resurrection of the dead,"—the position taken up by those whose error the apostle wished to overthrow. Next, from this antecedent, the assertion, viz., that there is no resurrection of the dead, the necessary consequence is, "Then Christ is not risen." But this consequence is false, for Christ has risen; therefore the antecedent is also false. But the antecedent is, that there is no resurrection of the dead. Now all this is briefly expressed thus: If there is no resurrection of the dead, then is Christ not risen; but Christ is risen, therefore there is a resurrection of the dead. This rule, then, that when the consequent is removed, the antecedent must also be removed, is not made by man, but only pointed out by him. And this rule has reference to the validity of the reasoning, not to the truth of the statements.

Chapter 33. — False inferences may be drawn from valid reasonings, and vice

versa.

51. In this passage, however, where the argument is about the resurrection, both the law of the inference is valid, and the conclusion arrived at is true. But in the case of false conclusions, too, there is a validity of inference in some such way as the following. Let us suppose some man to have admitted: If a snail is an animal, it has a voice. This being admitted, then, when it has been proved that the snail has no voice, it follows (since when the consequent is proved false, the antecedent is also false) that the snail is not an animal. Now this conclusion is false, but it is a true and valid inference from the false admission. Thus, the truth of a statement stands on its own merits; the validity of an inference depends on the statement or the admission of the man with whom one is arguing. And thus, as I said above, a false inference may be drawn by a valid process of reasoning, in order that he whose error we wish to correct may be sorry that he has admitted the antecedent, when he sees that its logical consequences are utterly untenable. And hence it is easy to understand that as the inferences may be unsound where the opinions are false, so the inferences may be unsound where the opinions are true. For example, suppose that a man propounds the statement, "If this man is just, he is good," and we admit its truth. Then he adds, "But he is not just;" and when we admit this too, he draws the conclusion, "Therefore he is not good." Now although every one of these statements may be true, still the principle of the inference is unsound. For it is not true that, as when the consequent is proved false the antecedent is also false, so when the antecedent is proved false the consequent is false. For the statement is true, "If he is an orator, he is a man." But if we add, "He is not an orator," the consequence does not follow, "He is not a man."

Chapter 34. — It is one thing to know the laws of inference, another to know the truth of opinions.

52. Therefore it is one thing to know the laws of inference, and another to know the truth of opinions. In the former case we learn what is consequent, what is inconsequent, and what is incompatible. An example of a consequent is, "If he is an orator, he is a man;" of an inconsequent, "If he is a man, he is an orator;" of an incompatible, "If he is a man, he is a quadruped." In these instances we judge of the connection. In regard to the truth of opinions, however, we must consider propositions as they stand by themselves, and not in their connection with one another; but when propositions that we are sure about are joined by a valid inference to propositions that are true and certain, they themselves, too, necessarily become certain. Now some, when they have ascertained the validity of the inference, plume themselves as if this involved also the truth of the propositions. Many, again, who hold the true opinions have an unfounded contempt for themselves, because they are ignorant of the laws of inference; whereas the man who knows that there is a resurrection of the dead is assuredly better than the man who only knows that it follows that if there is no resurrection of the dead, then is Christ not risen.

Chapter 35. — The science of definition is not false, though it may be applied to falsities.

53. Again, the science of definition, of division, and of partition, although it is frequently applied to falsities, is not itself false, nor framed by man's device, but is evolved from the reason of things. For although poets have applied it to their fictions, and false philosophers, or even heretics—that is, false Christians—to their erroneous doctrines, that is no reason why it should be false, for example, that neither in definition, nor in division, nor in partition, is anything to be included that does not pertain to the matter in hand, nor anything to be omitted that does. This is true, even though the things to be defined or divided are not true. For even falsehood itself is defined when we say that falsehood is the declaration of a state of things which is not as we declare it to be; and this definition is true, although falsehood itself cannot be true. We can also divide it, saying that

64

there are two kinds of falsehood, one in regard to things that cannot be true at all, the other in regard to things that are not, though it is possible that they might be, true. For example, the man who says that seven and three are eleven, says what cannot be true under any circumstances; but he who says that it rained on the kalends of January, although perhaps the fact is not so, says what possibly might have been. The definition and division, therefore, of what is false may be perfectly true, although what is false cannot, of course, itself be true.

Chapter 36. — The rules of eloquence are true, though sometimes used to persuade men of what is false.

54. There are also certain rules for a more copious kind of argument, which is called eloquence, and these rules are not the less true that they can be used for persuading men of what is false; but as they can be used to enforce the truth as well, it is not the faculty itself that is to be blamed, but the perversity of those who put it to a bad use. Nor is it owing to an arrangement among men that the expression of affection conciliates the hearer, or that a narrative, when it is short and clear, is effective, and that variety arrests men's attention without wearying them. And it is the same with other directions of the same kind, which, whether the cause in which they are used be true or false, are themselves true just in so far as they are effective in producing knowledge or belief, or in moving men's minds to desire and aversion. And men rather found out that these things are so, than arranged that they should be so.

Chapter 37. — Use of rhetoric and dialectic.

55. This art, however, when it is learnt, is not to be used so much for ascertaining the meaning as for setting forth the meaning when it is ascertained. But the art previously spoken of, which deals with inferences, and definitions, and divisions, is of the greatest assistance in the discovery of the meaning, provided only that men do not fall into the error of supposing that when they have learnt these things they have learnt the true secret of a happy life. Still, it sometimes happens that men find less difficulty in attaining the object for the sake of which these sciences are learnt, than in going through the very intricate and thorny discipline of such rules. It is just as if a man wishing to give rules for walking should warn you not to lift the hinder foot before you set down the front one, and then should describe minutely the way you ought to move the hinges of the joints and knees. For what he says is true, and one cannot walk in any other way; but men find it easier to walk by executing these movements than to attend to them while they are going through them, or to understand when they are told about them. Those, on the other hand, who cannot walk, care still less about such directions, as they cannot prove them by making trial of them. And in the same way a clever man often sees that an inference is unsound more quickly than he apprehends the rules for it. A dull man, on the other hand, does not see the unsoundness, but much less does he grasp the rules. And in regard to all these laws, we derive more pleasure from them as exhibitions of truth, than assistance in arguing or forming opinions, except perhaps that they put the intellect in better training. We must take care, however, that they do not at the same time make it more inclined to mischief or vanity,—that is to say, that they do not give those who have learnt them an inclination to lead people astray by plausible speech and catching questions, or make them think that they have attained some great thing that gives them an advantage over the good and innocent.

Chapter 38. — The science of numbers not created, but only discovered, by man.

56. Coming now to the science of number, it is clear to the dullest apprehension that this was not created by man, but was discovered by investigation. For, though Virgil could at

his own pleasure make the first syllable of *Italia* long, while the ancients pronounced it short, it is not in any man's power to determine at his pleasure that three times three are not nine, or not not make a square, or are not the triple of three, nor one and a half times the number six, or that it is not true that they are not the double of any number because odd numbers have no half. Whether, then, numbers are considered in themselves, or as applied to the laws of figures, or of sounds, or of other motions, they have fixed laws which were not made by man, but which the acuteness of ingenious men brought to light.

57. The man, however, who puts so high a value on these things as to be inclined to boast himself one of the learned, and who does not rather inquire after the source from which those things which he perceives to be true derive their truth, and from which those others which he perceives to be unchangeable also derive their truth and unchangeableness, and who, mounting up from bodily appearances to the mind of man, and finding that it too is changeable (for it is sometimes instructed, at other times uninstructed), although it holds a middle place between the unchangeable truth above it and the changeable things beneath it, does not strive to make all things redound to the praise and love of the one God from whom he knows that all things have their being;—the man, I say, who acts in this way may seem to be learned, but wise he cannot in any sense be deemed.

Chapter 39. — To which of the above-mentioned studies attention should be given, and in what spirit.

58. Accordingly, I think that it is well to warn serious and able young men, who fear God and are seeking for happiness of life, not to venture heedlessly upon the pursuit of the branches of learning that are in vogue beyond the pale of the Church of Christ, as if these could secure for them the happiness they seek; but soberly and carefully to discriminate among them. And if they find any of those which have been instituted by men varying by reason of the varying pleasure of their founders, and unknown by reason of erroneous conjectures, especially if they involve entering into fellowship with devils by means of leagues and covenants about signs, let these be utterly rejected and held in detestation. Let the young men also withdraw their attention from such institutions of men as are unnecessary and luxurious. But for the sake of the necessities of this life we must not neglect the arrangements of men that enable us to carry on intercourse with those around us. I think, however, there is nothing useful in the other branches of learning that are found among the heathen, except information about objects, either past or present, that relate to the bodily senses, in which are included also the experiments and conclusions of the useful mechanical arts, except also the sciences of reasoning and of number. And in regard to all these we must hold by the maxim, "Not too much of anything;" especially in the case of those which, pertaining as they do to the senses, are subject to the relations of space and time.

59. What, then, some men have done in regard to all words and names found in Scripture, in the Hebrew, and Syriac, and Egyptian, and other tongues, taking up and interpreting separately such as were left in Scripture without interpretation; and what Eusebius has done in regard to the history of the past with a view to the questions arising in Scripture that require a knowledge of history for their solution;—what, I say, these men have done in regard to matters of this kind, making it unnecessary for the Christian to spend his strength on many subjects for the sake of a few items of knowledge, the same, I think, might be done in regard to other matters, if any competent man were willing in a spirit of benevolence to undertake the labour for the advantage of his brethren. In this way he might arrange in their several classes, and give an account of the unknown places, and animals, and plants, and trees, and stones, and metals, and other species of things that are mentioned in Scripture, taking up these only, and committing his account to writing. This might also be done in relation to numbers, so that the theory of those numbers, and those only, which are mentioned in Holy Scripture, might be explained and written

down. And it may happen that some or all of these things have been done already (as I have found that many things I had no notion of have been worked out and committed to writing by good and learned Christians), but are either lost amid the crowds of the careless, or are kept out of sight by the envious. And I am not sure whether the same thing can be done in regard to the theory of reasoning; but it seems to me it cannot, because this runs like a system of nerves through the whole structure of Scripture, and on that account is of more service to the reader in disentangling and explaining ambiguous passages, of which I shall speak hereafter, than in ascertaining the meaning of unknown signs, the topic I am now discussing.

Chapter 40. — Whatever has been rightly said by the heathen, we must appropriate to our use.

60. Moreover, if those who are called philosophers, and especially the Platonists, have said aught that is true and in harmony with our faith, we are not only not to shrink from it, but to claim it for our own use from those who have unlawful possession of it. For, as the Egyptians had not only the idols and heavy burdens which the people of Israel hated and fled from, but also the vessels and ornaments of gold and silver, which the same people when going out of Egypt appropriated to themselves, designing them for a better use, not doing this on their own authority, but by the command of God, the Egyptians themselves, in their ignorance, providing them with things which they themselves were not making a good use of; in the same way all branches of heathen learning have not only false and superstitious fancies and heavy burdens of unnecessary toil, which every one of us, when going out under the leadership of Christ from the fellowship of the heathen, ought to abhor and avoid; but they contain also liberal instruction which is better adapted to the use of the truth, and some most excellent precepts of morality; and some truths in regard even to the worship of the One God are found among them. Now these are, so to speak, their gold and silver, which they did not create themselves, but dug out of the mines of God's providence which are everywhere scattered abroad, and are perversely and unlawfully prostituting to the worship of devils. These, therefore, the Christian, when he separates himself in spirit from the miserable fellowship of these men, ought to take away from them, and to devote to their proper use in preaching the gospel. Their garments, also,—that is, human institutions such as are adapted to that intercourse with men which is indispensable in this life,—we must take and turn to a Christian use.

61. And what else have many good and faithful men among our brethren done? Do we not see with what a quantity of gold and silver and garments Cyprian, that most persuasive teacher and most blessed martyr, was loaded when he came out of Egypt? How much Lactantius brought with him? And Victorinus, and Optatus, and Hilary, not to speak of living men! How much Greeks out of number have borrowed! And prior to all these, that most faithful servant of God, Moses, had done the same thing; for of him it is written that he was learned in all the wisdom of the Egyptians. And to none of all these would heathen superstition (especially in those times when, kicking against the yoke of Christ, it was persecuting the Christians) have ever furnished branches of knowledge it held useful, if it had suspected they were about to turn them to the use of worshipping the One God, and thereby overturning the vain worship of idols. But they gave their gold and their silver and their garments to the people of God as they were going out of Egypt, not knowing how the things they gave would be turned to the service of Christ. For what was done at the time of the exodus was no doubt a type prefiguring what happens now. And this I say without prejudice to any other interpretation that may be as good, or better.

Chapter 41. — What kind of spirit is required for the study of Holy Scripture.

62. But when the student of the Holy Scriptures, prepared in the way I have indicated, shall enter upon his investigations, let him constantly meditate upon that saying of the

apostle's, "Knowledge puffeth up, but charity edifieth." For so he will feel that, whatever may be the riches he brings with him out of Egypt, yet unless he has kept the passover, he cannot be safe. Now Christ is our passover sacrificed for us, and there is nothing the sacrifice of Christ more clearly teaches us than the call which He himself addresses to those whom He sees toiling in Egypt under Pharoah: "Come unto me, all ye that labour and are heavy laden, and I will give you rest. Take my yoke upon you, and learn of me; for I am meek and lowly in heart; and ye shall find rest unto your souls. For my yoke is easy, and my burden is light." To whom is it light but to the meek and lowly in heart, whom knowledge doth not puff up, but charity edifieth? Let them remember, then, that those who celebrated the passover at that time in type and shadow, when they were ordered to mark their door-posts with the blood of the lamb, used hyssop to mark them with. Now this is a meek and lowly herb, and yet nothing is stronger and more penetrating than its roots; that being rooted and grounded in love, we may be able to comprehend with all saints what is the breadth, and length, and depth, and height,—that is, to comprehend the cross of our Lord, the breadth of which is indicated by the transverse wood on which the hands are stretched, its length by the part from the ground up to the cross-bar on which the whole body from the head downwards is fixed, its height by the part which is hidden, being fixed in the earth. And by this sign of the cross all Christian action is symbolized, viz., to do good works in Christ, to cling with constancy to Him, to hope for heaven, and not to desecrate the sacraments. And purified by this Christian action, we shall be able to know even "the love of Christ which passeth knowledge," who is equal to the Father, by whom all things, were made, "that we may be filled with all the fullness of God." There is besides in hyssop a purgative virtue, that the breast may not be swollen with that knowledge which puffeth up, nor boast vainly of the riches brought out from Egypt. "Purge me with hyssop," the psalmist says, "and I shall be clean; wash me, and I shall be whiter than snow. Make me to hear joy and gladness." Then he immediately adds, to show that it is purifying from pride that is indicated by hyssop, "that the bones which Thou hast broken may rejoice."

Chapter 42. — Sacred Scripture compared with profane authors.

63. But just as poor as the store of gold and silver and garments which the people of Israel brought with them out of Egypt was in comparison with the riches which they afterwards attained at Jerusalem, and which reached their height in the reign of King Solomon, so poor is all the useful knowledge which is gathered from the books of the heathen when compared with the knowledge of Holy Scripture. For whatever man may have learnt from other sources, if it is hurtful, it is there condemned; if it is useful, it is therein contained. And while every man may find there all that he has learnt of useful elsewhere, he will find there in much greater abundance things that are to be found nowhere else, but can be learnt in the wonderful sublimity and wonderful simplicity of the Scriptures.

When, then, the reader is possessed of the instruction here pointed out, so that unknown signs have ceased to be a hindrance to him; when he is meek and lowly of heart, subject to the easy yoke of Christ, and loaded with His light burden, rooted and grounded and built up in faith, so that knowledge cannot puff him up, let him then approach the consideration and discussion of ambiguous signs in Scripture. And about these I shall now, in a third book, endeavor to say what the Lord shall be pleased to vouchsafe.

The City of God

Book I.

Preface, explaining his design in undertaking this work.

The glorious city of God is my theme in this work, which you, my dearest son Marcellinus,[1] suggested, and which is due to you by my promise. I have undertaken its defence against those who prefer their own gods to the Founder of this city,—a city surpassingly glorious, whether we view it as it still lives by faith in this fleeting course of time, and sojourns as a stranger in the midst of the ungodly, or as it shall dwell in the fixed stability of its eternal seat, which it now with patience waits for, expecting until "righteousness shall return unto judgment," and it obtain, by virtue of its excellence, final victory and perfect peace. A great work this, and an arduous; but God is my helper. For I am aware what ability is requisite to persuade the proud how great is the virtue of humility, which raises us, not by a quite human arrogance, but by a divine grace, above all earthly dignities that totter on this shifting scene. For the King and Founder of this city of which we speak, has in Scripture uttered to His people a dictum of the divine law in these words: "God resisteth the proud, but giveth grace unto the humble." But this, which is God's prerogative, the inflated ambition of a proud spirit also affects, and dearly loves that this be numbered among its attributes, to

"Show pity to the humbled soul,
    And crush the sons of pride."

And therefore, as the plan of this work we have undertaken requires, and as occasion offers, we must speak also of this earthly city, which, though it be mistress of the nations, is itself ruled by its lust of rule.

Chapter 1. — Of the adversaries of the name of Christ, whom the barbarians for Christ's sake spared when they stormed the city.

For to this earthly city belong the enemies against whom I have to defend the city of God. Many of them, indeed, being reclaimed from their ungodly error, have become sufficiently creditable citizens of this city; but many are so inflamed with hatred against it, and are so ungrateful to its Redeemer for His signal benefits, as to forget that they would now be unable to utter a single word to its prejudice, had they not found in its sacred places, as they fled from the enemy's steel, that life in which they now boast themselves.[2] Are not those very Romans, who were spared by the barbarians through their respect for Christ, become enemies to the name of Christ? The reliquaries of the martyrs and the churches of the apostles bear witness to this; for in the sack of the city they were open sanctuary for all who fled to them, whether Christian or Pagan. To their very threshold the blood-thirsty enemy raged; there his murderous fury owned a limit. Thither did such of the enemy as had any pity convey those to whom they had given quarter, lest any less mercifully disposed might fall upon them. And, indeed, when even those murderers who everywhere else showed themselves pitiless came to those spots where that was forbidden which the license of war permitted in every other place, their furious rage for slaughter was bridled, and their eagerness to take prisoners was quenched. Thus escaped multitudes who now reproach the Christian religion, and impute to Christ the ills that have befallen their city; but the preservation of their own life—a boon which they owe to the respect entertained for Christ by the barbarians—they attribute not to our Christ, but to their own good luck. They ought rather, had they any right perceptions, to attribute the severities and hardships inflicted by their enemies, to that divine providence which is wont to reform the depraved manners of men by chastisement, and which exercises with similar afflictions the righteous and praiseworthy,—either translating them, when they have passed through the trial, to a better world, or detaining them still on earth for ulterior purposes. And they ought to attribute it to the spirit of these Christian times, that, contrary to the custom of war, these bloodthirsty barbarians spared them, and spared them for Christ's sake, whether this mercy was actually shown in promiscuous places, or in those places specially dedicated to Christ's name, and of which the very largest were selected as sanctuaries, that full scope might thus be given to the expansive compassion which desired that a large multitude might find shelter there. Therefore ought they to give God thanks, and with sincere confession flee for refuge to His name, that so they may escape the punishment of eternal fire—they who with lying lips took upon them this name, that they might escape the punishment of present destruction. For of those whom you see insolently and shamelessly insulting the servants of Christ, there are numbers who would not have escaped that destruction and slaughter had they not pretended that they themselves were Christ's servants. Yet now, in ungrateful pride and most impious madness, and at the risk of being punished in everlasting darkness, they perversely oppose that name under which they fraudulently protected themselves for the sake of enjoying the fruits of this brief life....

Chapter 8. — Of the advantages and disadvantages which often indiscriminately accrue to good and wicked men.

Will some one say, Why, then, was this divine compassion extended even to the ungodly and ungrateful? Why, but because it was the mercy of Him who daily "maketh His sun to rise on the evil and on the good, and sendeth rain on the just and on the unjust." For though some of these men, taking thought of this, repent of their wickedness and reform, some, as the apostle says, "despising the riches of His goodness and long-suffering, after their hardness and impenitent heart, treasure up unto themselves wrath against the day of wrath and revelation of the righteous judgment of God, who will render to every man according to his deeds:" nevertheless does the patience of God still invite the wicked to repentance, even as the scourge of God educates the good to patience. And so, too, does the mercy of God embrace the good that it may cherish them, as the severity of God arrests the wicked to punish them. To the divine providence it has seemed good to prepare in the world to come for the righteous good things, which the unrighteous shall not enjoy; and for the wicked evil things, by which the good shall not be tormented. But as for the good things of this life, and its ills, God has willed that these should be common to both; that we might not too eagerly covet the things which wicked men are seen equally to enjoy, nor shrink with an unseemly fear from the ills which even good men must suffer.

There is, too, a very great difference in the purpose served both by those events which we call adverse and those called prosperous. For the good man is neither uplifted with the good things of time, nor broken by its ills; but the wicked man, because he is corrupted by this world's happiness, feels himself punished by its unhappiness. Yet often, even in the present distribution of temporal things, does God plainly evince His own interference. For if every sin were now visited with manifest punishment, nothing would seem to be reserved for the final judgment; on the other hand, if no sin received now a plainly divine punishment, it would be concluded that there is no divine providence at all. And so of the good things of this life: if God did not by a very visible liberality confer these on some of those persons who ask for them, we should say that these good things were not at His disposal; and if He gave them to all who sought them, we should suppose that such were the only rewards of His service; and such a service would make us not godly, but greedy rather, and covetous. Wherefore, though good and bad men suffer alike, we must not suppose that there is no difference between the men themselves, because there is no difference in what they both suffer. For even in the likeness of the sufferings, there remains an unlikeness in the sufferers; and though exposed to the same anguish, virtue and vice are not the same thing. For as the same fire causes gold to glow brightly, and chaff to smoke; and under the same flail the straw is beaten small, while the grain is cleansed; and as the lees are not mixed with the oil, though squeezed out of the vat by the same pressure, so the same violence of affliction proves, purges, clarifies the good, but damns, ruins, exterminates the wicked. And thus it is that in the same affliction the wicked detest God and blaspheme, while the good pray and praise. So material a difference does it make, not what ills are suffered, but what kind of man suffers them. For, stirred up with the same movement, mud exhales a horrible stench, and ointment emits a fragrant odour.

Chapter 9. — Of the reasons for administering correction to bad and good together.

What, then, have the Christians suffered in that calamitous period, which would not profit every one who duly and faithfully considered the following circumstances? First of all, they must humbly consider those very sins which have provoked God to fill the world with such terrible disasters; for although they be far from the excesses of wicked, immoral, and ungodly men, yet they do not judge themselves so clean removed from all faults as to be too good to suffer for these even temporal ills. For every man, however laudably he lives, yet yields in some points to the lust of the flesh. Though he do not fall into gross enormity of wickedness, and abandoned viciousness, and abominable profanity, yet he slips into some sins, either rarely or so much the more frequently as the sins seem of less account. But not to mention this, where can we readily find a man who holds in fit and just estimation those persons on account of whose revolting pride, luxury, and avarice, and cursed iniquities and impiety, God now smites the earth as His predictions threatened? Where is the man who lives with them in the style in which it becomes us to live with them? For often we wickedly blind ourselves to the occasions of teaching and admonishing them, sometimes even of reprimanding and chiding them, either because we shrink from the labour or are ashamed to offend them, or because we fear to lose good friendships, lest this should stand in the way of our advancement, or injure us in some worldly matter, which either our covetous disposition desires to obtain, or our weakness shrinks from losing. So that, although the conduct of wicked men is distasteful to the good, and therefore they do not fall with them into that damnation which in the next life awaits such persons, yet, because they spare their damnable sins through fear, therefore, even though their own sins be slight and venial, they are justly scourged with the wicked in this world, though in eternity they quite escape punishment. Justly, when God afflicts them in common with the wicked, do they find this life bitter, through love of whose sweetness they declined to be bitter to these sinners.

If anyone forbears to reprove and find fault with those who are doing wrong, because he seeks a more seasonable opportunity, or because he fears they may be made worse by his rebuke, or that other weak persons may be disheartened from endeavoring to lead a good and pious life, and may be driven from the faith; this man's omission seems to be occasioned not by covetousness, but by a charitable consideration. But what is blameworthy is, that they who themselves revolt from the conduct of the wicked, and live in quite another fashion, yet spare those faults in other men which they ought to reprehend and wean them from; and spare them because they fear to give offence, lest they should injure their interests in those things which good men may innocently and legitimately use,— though they use them more greedily than becomes persons who are strangers in this world, and profess the hope of a heavenly country. For not only the weaker brethren who enjoy married life, and have children (or desire to have them), and own houses and establishments, whom the apostle addresses in the churches, warning and instructing them how they should live, both the wives with their husbands, and the husbands with their wives, the children with their parents, and parents with their children, and servants with their masters, and masters with their servants,—not only do these weaker brethren gladly obtain and grudgingly lose many earthly and temporal things on account of which they dare not offend men whose polluted and wicked life greatly displeases them; but those also who live at a higher level, who are not entangled in the meshes of married life, but use meager food and raiment, do not often take thought of their own safety and good name, and abstain from finding fault with the wicked, because they fear their wiles and violence. And although they do not fear them to such an extent as to be drawn to the commission of like iniquities, nay, not by any threats or violence soever; yet those very deeds which they refuse to share in the commission of, they often decline to find fault with, when possibly they might by finding fault prevent their commission. They abstain from interference, because they fear that, if it fail of good effect, their own safety or reputation may be damaged or destroyed; not because they see that their preservation and good name are needful, that they may be able to influence those who need their instruction, but rather because they weakly relish the flattery and respect of men, and fear the judgments of the people, and the pain or death of the body; that is to say, their non-intervention is the result of selfishness, and not of love.

Accordingly this seems to me to be one principal reason why the good are chastised along with the wicked, when God is pleased to visit with temporal punishments the profligate manners of a community. They are punished together, not because they have spent an equally corrupt life, but because the good as well as the wicked, though not equally with them, love this present life; while they ought to hold it cheap, that the wicked, being admonished and reformed by their example, might lay hold of life eternal. And if they will not be the companions of the good in seeking life everlasting, they should be loved as enemies, and be dealt with patiently. For so long as they live, it remains uncertain whether they may not come to a better mind. These selfish persons have more cause to fear than those to whom it was said through the prophet, "He is taken away in his iniquity, but his blood I will require at the watchman's hand." For watchmen or overseers of the people are appointed in churches, that they may unsparingly rebuke sin. Nor is that man guiltless of the sin we speak of, who, though he be not a watchman, yet sees in the conduct of those with whom the relationships of this life bring him into contact, many things that should be blamed, and yet overlooks them, fearing to give offence, and lose such worldly blessings as may legitimately be desired, but which he too eagerly grasps. Then, lastly, there is another reason why the good are afflicted with temporal calamities—the reason which Job's case exemplifies: that the human spirit may be proved, and that it may be manifested with what fortitude of pious trust, and with how unmercenary a love, it cleaves to God....

(Book XIX)

Chapter 4. — What the Christians believe regarding the supreme good and evil, in opposition to the philosophers, who have maintained that the supreme good is in themselves.

If, then, we be asked what the city of God has to say upon these points, and, in the first place, what its opinion regarding the supreme good and evil is, it will reply that life eternal is the supreme good, death eternal the supreme evil, and that to obtain the one and to escape the other we must live rightly. And thus it is written, "The just lives by faith," for we do not as yet see our good, and must therefore live by faith; neither have we in ourselves power to live rightly, but can do so only if He who has given us faith to believe in His help do help us when we believe and pray. As for those who have supposed that the sovereign good and evil are to be found in this life, and have placed it either in the soul or the body, or, to speak more explicitly, either in pleasure or in virtue, or in both; in repose or in virtue, or in both; in pleasure and repose, or in virtue, or in all combined; in the primary objects of nature, or in virtue, or in both,—all these have, with a marvelous shallowness, sought to find their blessedness in this life and in themselves. Contempt has been poured upon such ideas by the Truth, saying by the prophet, "The Lord knoweth the thoughts of men" (or, as the Apostle Paul cites the passage, "The Lord knoweth the thoughts of the *wise*") "that they are vain."

For what flood of eloquence can suffice to detail the miseries of this life? Cicero, in the *Consolation* on the death of his daughter, has spent all his ability in lamentation; but how inadequate was even his ability here? For when, where, how, in this life can these primary objects of nature be possessed so that they may not be assailed by unforeseen accidents? Is the body of the wise man exempt from any pain which may dispel pleasure, from any disquietude which may banish repose? The amputation or decay of the members of the body puts an end to its integrity, deformity blights its beauty, weakness its health, lassitude its vigour, sleepiness or sluggishness its activity,—and which of these is it that may not assail the flesh of the wise man? Comely and fitting attitudes and movements of the body are numbered among the prime natural blessings; but what if some sickness makes the members tremble? what if a man suffers from curvature of the spine to such an extent that his hands reach the ground, and he goes upon all-fours like a quadruped? Does not this destroy all beauty and grace in the body, whether at rest or in motion? What shall I say of the fundamental blessings of the soul, sense and intellect, of which the one is given for the perception, and the other for the comprehension of truth? But what kind of sense is it that remains when a man becomes deaf and blind? where are reason and intellect when disease makes a man delirious? We can scarcely, or not at all, refrain from tears, when we think of or see the actions and words of such frantic persons, and consider how different from and even opposed to their own sober judgment and ordinary conduct their present demeanor is. And what shall I say of those who suffer from demoniacal possession? Where is their own intelligence hidden and buried while the malignant spirit is using their body and soul according to his own will? And who is quite sure that no such thing can happen to the wise man in this life? Then, as to the perception of truth, what can we hope for even in this way while in the body, as we read in the true book of Wisdom, "The corruptible body weigheth down the soul, and the earthly tabernacle presseth down the mind that museth upon many things?" And eagerness, or desire of action, if this is the right meaning to put on the Greek ὁρμή, is also reckoned among the primary advantages of nature; and yet is it not this which produces those pitiable movements of the insane, and those actions which we shudder to see, when sense is deceived and reason deranged?

In fine, virtue itself, which is not among the primary objects of nature, but succeeds to them as the result of learning, though it holds the highest place among human good things, what is its occupation save to wage perpetual war with vices,—not those that are outside of us, but within; not other men's, but our own,—a war which is waged especially by that virtue which the Greeks call σωφροσύνη, and we temperance, and which bridles carnal lusts, and prevents them from winning the consent of the spirit to wicked deeds? For we must not fancy that there is no vice in us, when, as the apostle says, "The flesh lusteth against the spirit;" for to this vice there is a contrary virtue, when, as the same writer says, "The spirit lusteth against the flesh." "For those two," he says, "are contrary one to the other, so that you cannot do the things which you would." But what is it we wish to do when we seek to attain the supreme good, unless that the flesh should cease to lust against the spirit, and that there be no vice in us against which the spirit may lust? And as we cannot attain to this in the present life, however ardently we desire it, let us by God's help accomplish at least this, to preserve the soul from succumbing and yielding to the flesh that lusts against it, and to refuse our consent to the perpetration of sin. Far be it from us, then, to fancy that while we are still engaged in this intestine war, we have already found the happiness which we seek to reach by victory. And who is there so wise that he has no conflict at all to maintain against his vices?

What shall I say of that virtue which is called prudence? Is not all its vigilance spent in the discernment of good from evil things, so that no mistake may be admitted about what we should desire and what avoid? And thus it is itself a proof that we are in the midst of evils, or that evils are in us; for it teaches us that it is an evil to consent to sin, and a good to refuse this consent. And yet this evil, to which prudence teaches and temperance enables us not to consent, is removed from this life neither by prudence nor by temperance. And justice, whose office it is to render to every man his due, whereby there is in man himself a certain just order of nature, so that the soul is subjected to God, and the flesh to the soul, and consequently both soul and flesh to God,—does not this virtue demonstrate that it is as yet rather laboring towards its end than resting in its finished work? For the soul is so much the less subjected to God as it is less occupied with the thought of God; and the flesh is so much the less subjected to the spirit as it lusts more vehemently against the spirit. So long, therefore, as we are beset by this weakness, this plague, this disease, how shall we dare to say that we are safe? and if not safe, then how can we be already enjoying our final beatitude? Then that virtue which goes by the name of fortitude is the plainest proof of the ills of life, for it is these ills which it is compelled to bear patiently. And this holds good, no matter though the ripest wisdom co-exists with it. And I am at a loss to understand how the Stoic philosophers can presume to say that these are no ills, though at the same time they allow the wise man to commit suicide and pass out of this life if they become so grievous that he cannot or ought not to endure them. But such is the stupid pride of these men who fancy that the supreme good can be found in this life, and that they can become happy by their own resources, that their wise man, or at least the man whom they fancifully depict as such, is always happy, even though he become blind, deaf, dumb, mutilated, racked with pains, or suffer any conceivable calamity such as may compel him to make away with himself; and they are not ashamed to call the life that is beset with these evils happy. O happy life, which seeks the aid of death to end it? If it is happy, let the wise man remain in it; but if these ills drive him out of it, in what sense is it happy? Or how can they say that these are not evils which conquer the virtue of fortitude, and force it not only to yield, but so to rave that it in one breath calls life happy and recommends it to be given up? For who is so blind as not to see that if it were happy it would not be fled from? And if they say we should flee from it on account of the infirmities that beset it, why then do they not lower their pride and acknowledge that it is miserable? Was it, I would ask, fortitude or weakness which prompted Cato to kill himself? for he would not have done so had he not been too weak to endure Cæsar's victory. Where, then, is his fortitude? It has yielded, it has succumbed, it has been so thoroughly overcome as to abandon, forsake, flee this happy life. Or was it no longer happy? Then it was miserable. How, then, were these not evils which made life miserable, and a thing to be escaped from?

And therefore, those who admit that these are evils, as the Peripatetics do, and the Old Academy, the sect which Varro advocates, express a more intelligible doctrine; but theirs also is a surprising mistake, for they contend that this is a happy life which is beset by these evils, even though they be so great that he who endures them should commit suicide to escape them. "Pains and anguish of body," says Varro, "are evils, and so much the worse in proportion to their severity; and to escape them you must quit this life." What life, I pray? This life, he says, which is oppressed by such evils. Then it is happy in the midst of these very evils on account of which you say we must quit it? Or do you call it happy because you are at liberty to escape these evils by death? What, then, if by some secret judgment of God you were held fast and not permitted to die, nor suffered to live without these evils? In that case, at least, you would say that such a life was miserable. It is soon relinquished, no doubt, but this does not make it not miserable; for were it eternal, you yourself would pronounce it miserable. Its brevity, therefore, does not clear it of misery; neither ought it to be called happiness because it is a brief misery. Certainly there is a mighty force in these evils which compel a man—according to them, even a wise man—to cease to be a man that he may escape them, though they say, and say truly, that it is as it were the first and strongest demand of nature that a man cherish himself, and naturally therefore avoid death, and should so stand his own friend as to wish and vehemently aim at continuing to exist as a living creature, and subsisting in this union of soul and body. There is a mighty force in these evils to overcome this natural instinct by which death is by every means and with all a man's efforts avoided, and to overcome it is desired, sought after, and if it cannot in any other way be obtained, is inflicted by the man on himself. There is a mighty force in these evils which make fortitude a homicide,—if, indeed, that is to be called fortitude which is so thoroughly overcome by these evils, that it not only cannot preserve by patience the man whom it undertook to govern and defend, but is it-self obliged to kill him. The wise man, I admit, ought to bear death with patience, but when it is inflicted by another. If, then, as these men maintain, he is obliged to inflict it on himself, certainly it must be owned that the ills which compel him to this are not only evils, but intolerable evils. The life, then, which is either subject to accidents, or envi-roned with evils so considerable and grievous, could never have been called happy, if the men who give it this name had condescended to yield to the truth, and to be conquered by valid arguments, when they inquired after the happy life, as they yield to unhappiness, and are overcome by overwhelming evils, when they put themselves to death, and if they had not fancied that the supreme good was to be found in this mortal life; for the very vir-tues of this life, which are certainly the best and most useful possessions, are all the more telling proofs of its miseries in proportion as they are helpful against the violence of its dangers, toils, and woes. For if these are true virtues,—and such cannot exist save in those who have true piety,—they do not profess to be able to deliver the men who possess them from all miseries; for true virtues tell no such lies, but they profess that by the hope of the future world this life, which is miserably involved in the many and great evils of this world, is happy as it is also safe. For if not yet safe, how could it be happy? And therefore the Apostle Paul, speaking not of men without prudence, temperance, fortitude, and justice, but of those whose lives were regulated by true piety, and whose virtues were therefore true, says, "For we are saved by hope: now hope which is not seen is not hope; for what a man seeth, why doth he yet hope for? But if we hope for that we see not, then do we with patience wait for it." As, therefore, we are saved, so we are made happy by hope. And as we do not as yet possess a present, but look for a future salvation, so is it with our happi-ness, and this "with patience;" for we are encompassed with evils, which we ought pa-tiently to endure, until we come to the ineffable enjoyment of unmixed good; for there shall be no longer anything to endure. Salvation, such as it shall be in the world to come, shall itself be our final happiness. And this happiness these philosophers refuse to be-lieve in, because they do not see it, and attempt to fabricate for themselves a happiness in this life, based upon a virtue which is as deceitful as it is proud.

Chapter 5. — Of the social life, which, though most desirable, is frequently disturbed by many distresses.

We give a much more unlimited approval to their idea that the life of the wise man must be social. For how could the city of God (concerning which we are already writing no less than the nineteenth book of this work) either take a beginning or be developed, or attain its proper destiny, if the life of the saints were not a social life? But who can enu-merate all the great grievances with which human society abounds in the misery of this mortal state? Who can weigh them? Hear how one of their comic writers makes one of his characters express the common feelings of all men in this matter: "I am married; this is one misery. Children are born to me; they are additional cares." What shall I say of the miseries of love which Terence also recounts—slights, suspicions, quarrels, war to-day, peace to-morrow?" Is not human life full of such things? Do they not often occur even in honorable friendships? On all hands we experience these slights, suspicions, quarrels, war, all of which are undoubted evils; while, on the other hand, peace is a doubtful good, because we do not know the heart of our friend, and though we did know it to-day, we should be as ignorant of what it might be to-morrow. Who ought to be, or who are more friendly than those who live in the same family? And yet who can rely even upon this friendship, seeing that secret treachery has often broken it up, and produced enmity as bitter as the amity was sweet, or seemed sweet by the most perfect dissimulation? It is on this account that the words of Cicero so move the heart of every one, and provoke a sigh: "There are no snares more dangerous than those which lurk under the guise of duty or the name of the relationship. For the man who is your declared foe you can easily baffle by precaution; but this hidden, intestine, and domestic danger not merely exists, but over-whelms you before you can foresee and examine it." It is also to this that allusion is made by the divine saying, "A man's foes are those of his own household,"—words which one cannot hear without pain; for though a man have sufficient fortitude to endure it with equanimity, and sufficient sagacity to baffle the malice of a pretended friend, yet if he himself is a good man, he cannot but be greatly pained at the discovery of the perfidy of wicked men whether they have always been wicked and merely feigned goodness, or have fallen from a better to a malicious disposition. If, then, home, the natural refuge from the ills of life, is itself not safe, what shall we say of the city, which, as it is larger, is so much the more filled with lawsuits civil and criminal, and is never free from the fear, if sometimes from the actual outbreak, of disturbing and bloody insurrections and civil wars?...

Chapter 9. — Of the friendship of the holy angels, which men cannot be sure of in this life, owing to the deceit of the demons who hold in bondage the worshippers of a plurality of gods.

The philosophers who wished us to have the gods for our friends rank the friendship of the holy angels in the fourth circle of society, advancing now from the three circles of society on earth to the universe, and embracing heaven itself. And in this friendship we have indeed no fear that the angels will grieve us by their death or deterioration. But as we cannot mingle with them as familiarly as with men (which itself is one of the grievances of this life), and as Satan, as we read, sometimes transforms himself into an angel of light, to tempt those whom it is necessary to discipline, or just to deceive, there is great need of God's mercy to preserve us from making friends of demons in disguise, while we fancy we have good angels for our friends; for the astuteness and deceitfulness of these wicked spirits is equalled by their hurtfulness. And is this not a great misery of human life, that we are involved in such ignorance as, but for God's mercy, makes us a prey to these demons? And it is very certain that the philosophers of the godless city, who have maintained that the gods were their friends, had fallen a prey to the malignant demons who rule that city, and whose eternal punishment is to be shared by it. For the nature of these beings is sufficiently evinced by the sacred or rather sacrilegious observances which form their worship, and by the filthy games in which their crimes are celebrated, and which they themselves originated and exacted from their worshippers as a fit propitiation.

Chapter 10. — The reward prepared for the Saints after they have departed the trial of this life.

But not even the saints and faithful worshippers of the one true and most high God are safe from the manifold temptations and deceits of the demons. For in this abode of weakness, and in these wicked days, this state of anxiety has also its use, stimulating us to seek with keener longing for that security where peace is complete and unassailable. There we shall enjoy the gifts of nature, that is to say, all that God the Creator of all natures has bestowed upon ours,—gifts not only good, but eternal,—not only of the spirit, healed now by wisdom, but also of the body renewed by the resurrection. There the virtues shall no longer be struggling against any vice or evil, but shall enjoy the reward of victory, the eternal peace which no adversary shall disturb. This is the final blessedness, this the ultimate consummation, the unending end. Here, indeed, we are said to be blessed when we have such peace as can be enjoyed in a good life; but such blessedness is mere misery compared to that final felicity. When we mortals possess such peace as this mortal life can afford, virtue, if we are living rightly, makes a right use of the advantages of this peaceful condition; and when we have it not, virtue makes a good use even of the evils a man suffers. But this is true virtue, when it refers all the advantages it makes a good use of, and all that it does in making good use of good and evil things, and itself also, to that end in which we shall enjoy the best and greatest peace possible.

Chapter 11. — Of the happiness of the eternal peace, which constitutes the

end or true perfection of the Saints.

And thus we may say of peace, as we have said of eternal life, that it is the end of our good; and the rather because the Psalmist says of the city of God, the subject of this laborious work, "Praise the Lord, O Jerusalem; praise thy God, O Zion: for He hath strengthened the bars of thy gates; He hath blessed thy children within thee; who hath made thy borders peace." For when the bars of her gates shall be strengthened, none shall go in or come out from her; consequently we ought to understand the peace of her borders as that final peace we are wishing to declare. For even the mystical name of the city itself, that is, *Jerusalem*, means, as I have already said, "Vision of Peace." But as the word peace is employed in connection with things in this world in which certainly life eternal has no place, we have preferred to call the end or supreme good of this city life eternal rather than peace. Of this end the apostle says, "But now, being freed from sin, and become servants to God, ye have your fruit unto holiness, and the end life eternal." But, on the other hand, as those who are not familiar with Scripture may suppose that the life of the wicked is eternal life, either because of the endless punishment of the wicked, which forms a part of our faith, and which seems impossible unless the wicked live for ever, it may therefore be advisable, in order that every one may readily understand what we mean, to say that the end or supreme good of this city is either peace in eternal life, or eternal life in peace. For peace is a good so great, that even in this earthly and mortal life there is no word we hear with such pleasure, nothing we desire with such zest, or find to be more thoroughly gratifying. So that if we dwell for a little longer on this subject, we shall not, in my opinion, be wearisome to our readers, who will attend both for the sake of understanding what is the end of this city of which we speak, and for the sake of the sweetness of peace which is dear to us all....

Chapter 21. — Whether there ever was a Roman Republic answering to the definitions of Scipio in Cicero's dialogue.

This, then, is the place where I should fulfill the promise gave in the second book of this work, and explain, as briefly and clearly as possible, that if we are to accept the definitions laid down by Scipio in Cicero's *De Republica*, there never was a Roman republic; for he briefly defines a republic as the weal of the people. And if this definition be true, there never was a Roman republic, for the people's weal was never attained among the Romans. For the people, according to his definition, is an assemblage associated by a common acknowledgement of right and by a community of interests. And what he means by a common acknowledgement of right he explains at large, showing that a republic cannot be administered without justice. Where, therefore, there is no true justice, there can be no right. For that which is done right is justly done, and what is unjustly done cannot be done by right. For the unjust inventions of men are neither to be considered nor spoken of as rights; for even they themselves say that right is that which flows from the fountain of justice, and deny the definition which is commonly given by those who misconceive the matter, that right is that which is useful to the stronger party. Thus, where there is not true justice there can be no assemblage of men associated by a common acknowledgment of right, and therefore there can be no people, as defined by Scipio or Cicero; and if no people, then no weal of the people, but only of some promiscuous multitude unworthy of the name of people. Consequently, if the republic is the weal of the people, and there is no people if it be not associated by a common acknowledgement of right, and if there is no right where there is no justice, then most certainly it follows that there is no republic where there is no justice. Further, justice is that virtue which gives every one his due. Where, then, is the justice of man, when he deserts the true God and yields himself to impure demons? Is this to give every one his due? Or is he who keeps back a piece of ground from the purchaser, and gives it to a man who has no right to it, unjust, while he who keeps back himself from the God who made him, and serves wicked spirits, is just?

This same book, *De Republica*, advocates the cause of justice against injustice with great force and keenness. The pleading for injustice against justice was first heard, and it was asserted that without injustice a republic could neither increase nor even subsist, for it was laid down as an absolutely unassailable position that it is unjust for some men to rule and some to serve; and yet the imperial city to which the republic belongs cannot rule her provinces without having recourse to this injustice. It was replied in behalf of justice, that this ruling of the provinces is just, because servitude may be advantageous to the provincials, and is so when rightly administered,—that is to say, when lawless men are prevented from doing harm. And further, as they became worse and worse so long as they were free, they will improve by subjection. To confirm this reasoning, there is added an eminent example drawn from nature: for "why," it is asked, "does God rule man, the soul the body, the reason the passions and other vicious parts of the soul?" This example leaves no doubt that, to some, servitude is useful; and, indeed, to serve God is useful to all. And it is when the soul serves God that it exercises a right control over the body; and in the soul itself the reason must be subject to God if it is to govern as it ought the passions and other vices. Hence, when a man does not serve God, what justice can we ascribe to him, since in this case his soul cannot exercise a just control over the body, nor his reason over his vices? And if there is no justice in such an individual, certainly there can be none in a community composed of such persons. Here, therefore, there is not that common acknowledgement of right which makes an assemblage of men a people whose affairs we call a republic. And why need I speak of the advantageousness, the common participation in which, according to the definition, makes a people? For although, if you choose to regard the matter attentively, you will see that there is nothing advantageous to those who live godlessly, as every one lives who does not serve God but demons, whose wickedness you may measure by their desire to receive the worship of men though they are most impure spirits, yet what I have said of the common acknowledgement of right is enough to demonstrate that, according to the above definition, there can be no people, and therefore no republic, where there is no justice. For if they assert that in their republic the Romans did not serve unclean spirits, but good and holy gods, must we therefore again reply to this evasion, though already we have said enough, and more than enough, to expose it? He must be an uncommonly stupid, or a shamelessly contentious person, who has read through the foregoing books to this point, and can yet question whether the Romans served wicked and impure demons. But, not to speak of their character, it is written in the law of the true God, "He that sacrificeth unto any god save unto the Lord only, he shall be utterly destroyed." He, therefore, who uttered so menacing a commandment decreed that no worship should be given either to good or bad gods....

Chapter 24. — The definition which must be given of a people and a republic, in order to vindicate the assumption of these titles by the Romans and by other kingdoms.

But if we discard this definition of a people, and, assuming another, say that a people is an assemblage of reasonable beings bound together by a common agreement as to the objects of their love, then, in order to discover the character of any people, we have only to observe what they love. Yet whatever it loves, if only it is an assemblage of reasonable beings and not of beasts, and is bound together by an agreement as to the objects of love, it is reasonably called a people; and it will be a superior people in proportion as it is bound together by lower. According to this definition of ours, the Roman people is a people, and its weal is without doubt a commonwealth or republic. But what its tastes were in its early and subsequent days, and how it declined into sanguinary seditions and then to social and civil wars, and so burst asunder or rotted off the bond of concord in which the health of a people consists, history shows, and in the preceding books I have related at large. And yet I would not on this account say either that it was not a people, or that its administration was not a republic, so long as there remains an assemblage of reasonable beings bound together by a common agreement as to the objects of love. But what

I say of this people and of this republic I must be understood to think and say of the Athenians or any Greek state, of the Egyptians, of the early Assyrian Babylon, and of every other nation, great or small, which had a public government. For, in general, the city of the ungodly, which did not obey the command of God that it should offer no sacrifice save to Him alone, and which, therefore, could not give to the soul its proper command over the body, nor to the reason its just authority over the vices, is void of true justice.

Chapter 25. — That where there is no true religion there are no true virtues.

For though the soul may seem to rule the body admirably, and the reason the vices, if the soul and reason do not themselves obey God, as God has commanded them to serve Him, they have no proper authority over the body and the vices. For what kind of mistress of the body and the vices can that mind be which is ignorant of the true God, and which, instead of being subject to His authority, is prostituted to the corrupting influences of the most vicious demons? It is for this reason that the virtues which it seems to itself to possess, and by which it restrains the body and the vices that it may obtain and keep what it may obtain and keep what it desires, are rather vices than virtues so long as there is no reference to God in the matter. For although some suppose that virtues which have a reference only to themselves, and are desired only on their own account, are yet true and genuine virtues, the fact is that even then they are inflated with pride, and therefore to be reckoned vices rather than virtues. For as that which gives life to the flesh is not derived from the flesh, but is above it, so that which gives blessed life to man is not derived from man, but is something above him; and what I say of man is true of every celestial power and virtue whatsoever.

Chapter 26. — Of the peace which is enjoyed by the people that are alienated from God, and the use made of it by the people of God in the time of its pilgrimage.

Wherefore, as the life of the flesh is the soul, so the blessed life of man is God, of whom the sacred writings of the Hebrews say, "Blessed is the people whose God is the Lord." Miserable, therefore, is the people which is alienated from God. Yet even this people has a peace of its own which is not to be lightly esteemed, though, indeed, it shall not in the end enjoy it, because it makes no good use of it before the end. But it is our interest that it enjoy this peace meanwhile in this life; for as long as the two cities are commingled, we also enjoy the peace of Babylon. For from Babylon the people of God is so freed that it meanwhile sojourns in its company. And therefore the apostle also admonished the Church to pray for kings and those in authority, assigning as the reason, "that we may live a quiet and tranquil life in all godliness and love." And the prophet Jeremiah, when predicting the captivity that was to befall the ancient people of God, and giving them the divine command to go obediently to Babylonia, and thus serve their God, counselled them also to pray for Babylonia, saying, "In the peace thereof shall ye have peace,"—the temporal peace which the good and the wicked together enjoy.

Chapter 27. — That the peace of those who serve God cannot in this mortal life be apprehended in its perfection.

But the peace which is peculiar to ourselves we enjoy now with God by faith, and shall hereafter enjoy eternally with Him by sight. But the peace which we enjoy in this life, whether common to all or peculiar to ourselves, is rather the solace of our misery than the positive enjoyment of felicity. Our very righteousness, too, though true in so far as it has respect to the true good, is yet in this life of such a kind that it consists rather in the remission of sins than in the perfecting of virtues. Witness the prayer of the whole city of God in its pilgrim state, for it cries to God by the mouth of all its members, "Forgive us our debts as we forgive our debtors." And this prayer is efficacious not for those whose faith is "without works and dead," but for those whose faith "worketh by love." For as reason, though subjected to God, is yet "pressed down by the corruptible body," so long as it is in this mortal condition, it has not perfect authority over vice, and therefore this prayer is needed by the righteous. For though it exercises authority, the vices do not submit without a struggle. For however well one maintains the conflict, and however thoroughly he has subdued these enemies, there steals in some evil thing, which, if it do not find ready expression in act, slips out by the lips, or insinuates itself into the thought; and therefore his peace is not full so long as he is at war with his vices. For it is a doubtful conflict he wages with those that resist, and his victory over those that are defeated is not secure, but full of anxiety and effort. Amidst these temptations, therefore, of all which it has been summarily said in the divine oracles, "Is not human life upon earth a temptation?" who but a proud man can presume that he so lives that he has no need to say to God, "Forgive us our debts?" And such a man is not great, but swollen and puffed up with vanity, and is justly resisted by Him who abundantly gives grace to the humble." In this, then, consists the righteousness of a man, that he submit himself to God, his body to his soul, and his vices, even when they rebel, to his reason, which either defeats or at least resists them; and also that he beg from God grace to do his duty, and the pardon of his sins, and that he render to God thanks for all the blessings he receives. But, in that final peace to which all our righteousness has reference, and for the sake of which it is maintained, as our nature shall enjoy a sound immortality and incorruption, and shall have no more vices, and as we shall experience no resistance either from ourselves or from others, it will not be necessary that reason should rule vices which no longer exist, but God shall rule the man, and the soul shall rule the body, with a sweetness and facility suitable to the felicity of a life which is done with bondage. And this condition shall there be eternal, and we shall be assured of its eternity; and thus the peace of this blessedness and the blessedness of this peace shall be the supreme good.

Chapter 28. — The end of the wicked.

But, on the other hand, they who do not belong to this city of God shall inherit eternal misery, which is also called the second death, because the soul shall then be separated from God its life, and therefore cannot be said to live, and the body shall be subjected to eternal pains. And consequently this second death shall be the more severe, because no death shall terminate it. But war being contrary to peace, as misery to happiness, and life to death, it is not without reason asked what kind of war can be found in the end of the wicked answering to the peace which is declared to be the end of the righteous? The person who puts this question has only to observe what it is in war that is hurtful and destructive, and he shall see that it is nothing else than the mutual opposition and conflict of things. And can he conceive a more grievous and bitter war than that in which the will is so opposed to passion, and passion to the will, that their hostility can never be terminated by the victory of either, and in which the violence of pain so conflicts with the nature of the body, that neither yields to the other? For in this life, when this conflict has arisen, either pain conquers and death expels the feeling of it, or nature conquers and health expels the pain. But in the world to come the pain continues that it may torment, and the nature endures that it may be sensible of it; and neither ceases to exist, lest punishment also should cease. Now, as it is through the last judgment that men pass to these ends, the good to the supreme good, the evil to the supreme evil, I will treat of this judgment in the following book.

Notes

1 Marcellinus was a friend of Augustine, and urged him to write this work. He was commissioned by the Emperor Honorius to convene a conference of Catholic and schismatic Donatist bishops in the summer of 411, and conceded the victory to the Catholics; but on account of his rigour in executing the laws against the Donatists, he fell a victim to their revenge, and was

honored by a place among the martyrs.

2   Augustine refers to the sacking of the city of Rome by the West-Gothic King Alaric, 410. He was the most humane of the barbaric invaders and conquerors of Rome, and had embraced Arian Christianity (probably from the teaching of Ulphilas, the Arian bishop and translator of the Bible). He spared the Catholic Christians.

St. Perpetua

The Passion of Saints Perpetua and Felicity

Vibia Perpetua, a member of a high ranking Roman family, was arrested under a decree of Septimus Severus in 202. She was executed in the arena in Carthage on 7 March, 203. Her Passion is one of the earliest historical accounts by a Christian woman. Most of the text was written by Perpetua herself while in prison. The introductory and concluding materials were added by contemporaries.

Source: W.H. Shewring, tr. *The Passion of Perpetua and Felicity* (London: 1931).

1.   If ancient examples of faith kept, both testifying the grace of God and working the edification of man, have to this end been set in writing, that by their reading as though by the again showing of the deeds God may be glorified and man strengthened; why should not new witnesses also be so set forth which likewise serve either end? Yea, for these things also shall at some time be ancient and necessary to our sons, though in their own present time (through some reverence of antiquity presumed) they are made of but slight account. But let those take heed who judge the one power of the Holy Spirit according to the succession of times; whereas those things which are later ought for their very lateness to be thought the more eminent, according to the abundance of grace appointed for the last periods of time. For *In the last days*, saith the Lord, *I will pour My Spirit upon all flesh, and their sons and daughters shall prophesy; and upon My servants and upon My hand-maids I will pour forth of My Spirit; and the young men shall see visions, and the old men shall dream dreams.* We also therefore, by whom both the prophecies and the new visions promised are received and honored, and by whom those other wonders of the Holy Spirit are assigned unto the service of the Church, to which also was sent the same Spirit administering all gifts among all men, *according as the Lord hath distributed unto each*—do of necessity both write them and by reading celebrate them to the glory of God; that no weakness or failing of faith may presume that among those of old time only was the grace of divinity present, whether in martyrs or in revelations vouchsafed; since God ever works that which He has promised, for a witness to them that believe not and a benefit to them that believe. Wherefore we too, brethren and dear sons, *declare to you* likewise *that which we have heard and handled*; that both ye who were present may call to mind the glory of the Lord, and ye who now know by hearing may have communion with those holy martyrs, and through them with the Lord Jesus Christ, to Whom is glory and honor for ever and ever. Amen.

2.   There were apprehended the young catechumens, Revocatus and Felicity his fellow-servant, Saturninus and Secundulus. With them also was Vibia Perpetua, nobly born, reared in a liberal manner, wedded honorably; having a father and mother and two brothers, one of them a catechumen likewise, and a son, a child at the breast; and she herself was about twenty-two years of age. What follows here shall she tell herself; the whole order of her martyrdom as she left it written with her own hand and in her own words.

3.   When, saith she, we were yet with our sureties and my father was fain to vex me with his words and continually strove to hurt my faith because of his love: Father, said I, seest thou (for example's sake) this vessel lying, a pitcher or whatsoever it may be?[1] And he

said, I see it. And I said to him, Can it be called by any other name than that which it is? And he answered, No. So can I call myself nought other than that which I am, a Christian. Then my father moved with this word came upon me to tear out my eyes; but he vexed me only, and he departed vanquished, he and the arguments of the devil. Then because I was without my father for a few days I gave thanks unto the Lord; and I was comforted because of his absence. In this same space of a few days we were baptised, and the Spirit declared to me, I must pray for nothing else after that water save only endurance of the flesh. A few days after we were taken into prison, and I was much afraid because I had never known such darkness. O bitter day! There was a great heat because of the press, there was cruel handling of the soldiers. Lastly I was tormented there by care for the child. Then Tertius and Pomponius, the blessed deacons who ministered to us, obtained with money that for a few hours we should be taken forth to a better part of the prison and be refreshed. Then all of them going out from the dungeon took their pleasure; I suckled my child that was now faint with hunger. And being careful for him, I spoke to my mother and strengthened my brother and commended my son unto them. I pined because I saw they pined for my sake. Such cares I suffered for many days; and I obtained that the child should abide with me in prison; and straightway I became well, and was lightened of my labour and care for the child; and suddenly the prison was made a palace for me, so that I would sooner be there than anywhere else.

4. Then said my brother to me: Lady my sister, thou art now in high honor, even such that thou mightest ask for a vision; and it should be shown thee whether this be a passion or else a deliverance. And I, as knowing that I conversed with the Lord, for Whose sake I had suffered such things, did promise him, nothing doubting; and I said: To-morrow I will tell thee. And I asked, and this was shown me.

I beheld a ladder of bronze, marvellously great, reaching up to heaven; and it was narrow, so that not more than one might go up at one time. And in the sides of the ladder were planted all manner of things of iron. There were swords there, spears, hooks, and knives; so that if any that went up took not good heed or looked not upward, he would be torn and his flesh cling to the iron. And there was right at the ladder's foot a serpent lying, marvellously great, which lay in wait for those that would go up, and frightened them that they might not go up. Now Saturus went up first (who afterwards had of his own free will given up himself for our sakes, because it was he who had edified us; and when we were taken he had not been there). And he came to the ladder's head; and he turned and said: Perpetua, I await thee; but see that serpent bite thee not. And I said: it shall not hurt me, in the name of Jesus Christ. And from beneath the ladder, as though it feared me, it softly put forth its head; and as though I trod on the first step I trod on its head. And I went up, and I saw a very great space of garden, and in the midst a man sitting, white-headed, in shepherd's clothing, tall, milking his sheep; and standing around in white were many thousands. And he raised his head and beheld me and said to me: Welcome, child. And he cried to me, and from the curd he had from the milk he gave me as it were a morsel; and I took it with joined hands and ate it up; and all that stood around said, Amen. And at the sound of that word I awoke, yet eating I know not what of sweet.

And forthwith I told my brother, and we knew it should be a passion; and we began to have no hope any longer in this world.

5. A few days after, the report went abroad that we were to be tried. Also my father returned from the city spent with weariness; and he came up to me to cast down my faith, saying: Have pity, daughter, on my grey hairs; have pity on thy father, if I am worthy to be called father by thee; if with these hands I have brought thee unto this flower of youth— and I have preferred thee before all thy brothers; give me not over to the reproach of men. Look upon thy brothers; look upon thy mother and mother's sister; look upon thy son, who will not endure to live after thee. Forbear thy resolution; destroy us not all together; for none of us will speak openly against men again if thou sufferest aught. This he said fatherwise in his love, kissing my hands and grovelling at my feet; and with tears

he named me, not daughter, but lady. And I was grieved for my father's case because he would not rejoice at my passion out of all my kin; and I comforted him, saying: That shall be done at this tribunal, whatsoever God shall please; for know that we are not stablished in our own power, but in God's. And he went from me very sorrowful.

DUT HE DID NOT BEG HER MERCILESSLY

6.   Another day as we were at meat we were suddenly snatched away to be tried; and we came to the forum. Therewith a report spread abroad through the parts near to the forum, and a very great multitude gathered together. We went up to the tribunal. The others being asked, confessed. So they came to me. And my father appeared there also, with my son, and would draw me from the step, saying: Sacrifice; have mercy on the child. And Hilarian the procurator—he that after the death of Minucius Timinian the proconsul had received in his room the right and power of the sword—Spare, said he, thy father's grey hairs; spare the infancy of the boy. Make sacrifice for the Emperors' prosperity. And I answered: I am a Christian. And when my father stood by me yet to cast down my faith, he was bidden by Hilarian to be cast down and was smitten with a rod. And I sorrowed for my father's harm as though I had been smitten myself; so sorrowed I for his unhappy old age. Then Hilarian passed sentence upon us all and condemned us to the beasts; and cheerfully we went down to the dungeon. Then because my child had been wont to take suck of me and to abide with me in the prison, straightway I sent Pomponius the deacon to my father, asking for the child. But my father would not give him. And as God willed, neither is he fain to be suckled any more, nor did I take fever; that I might not be tormented by care for the child and by the pain of my breasts.

7.   A few days after, while we were all praying, suddenly in the midst of the prayer I uttered a word and named Dinocrates; and I was amazed because he had never come into my mind save then; and I sorrowed, remembering his fate. And straightway I knew that I was worthy, and that I ought to ask for him. And I began to pray for him long, and to groan unto the Lord. Forthwith the same night, this was shown me.
   I beheld Dinocrates coming forth from a dark place, where were many others also; being both hot and thirsty, his raiment foul, his color pale; and the wound on his face which he had when he died. This Dinocrates had been my brother in the flesh, seven years old, who being diseased with ulcers of the face had come to a horrible death, so that his death was abominated of all men. For him therefore I had made my prayer; and between him and me was a great gulf, so that either might not go to the other. There was moreover, in the same place where Dinocrates was, a font full of water, having its edge higher than was the boy's stature; and Dinocrates stretched up as though to drink. I was sorry that the font had water in it, and yet for the height of the edge he might not drink.
   And I awoke, and I knew that my brother was in travail. Yet I was confident I should ease his travail; and I prayed for him every day till we passed over into the camp prison. (For it was in the camp games that we were to fight; and the time was the feast of Geta Cæsar.) And I made supplication for him day and night with groans and tears, that he might be given me.

8.   On the day when we abode in the stocks, this was shown me.
   I saw that place which I had before seen, and Dinocrates clean of body, finely clothed, in comfort; and the font I had seen before, the edge of it being drawn to the boy's navel; and he drew water thence which flowed without ceasing. And on the edge was a golden cup full of water; and Dinocrates came up and began to drink therefrom; which cup failed not. And being satisfied he departed away from the water and began to play as children will, joyfully.
   And I awoke. Then I understood that he was translated from his pains.

9.   Then a few days after, Pudens the adjutant, in whose charge the prison was, who also began to magnify us because he understood that there was much grace in us, let in many to us that both we and they in turn might be comforted. Now when the day of the games

drew near, there came in my father to me, spent with weariness, and began to pluck out his beard and throw it on the ground and to fall on his face cursing his years and saying such words as might move all creation. I was grieved for his unhappy old age. *She mentions only his old age that she is sorry for.*

10. The day before we fought, I saw in a vision that Pomponius the deacon had come hither to the door of the prison, and knocked hard upon it. And I went out to him and opened to him; he was clothed in a white robe ungirdled, having shoes curiously wrought. And he said to me: Perpetua, we await thee; come. And he took my hand, and we began to go through rugged and winding places. At last with much breathing hard we came to the amphitheatre, and he led me into the midst of the arena. And he said to me: Be not afraid; I am here with thee and labour together with thee. And he went away. And I saw much people watching closely. And because I knew that I was condemned to the beasts I marvelled that beasts were not sent out against me. And there came out against me a certain ill-favored Egyptian with his helpers, to fight with me. Also there came to me comely young men, my helpers and aiders. And I was stripped, and I became a man. And my helpers began to rub me with oil as their custom is for a contest; and over against me I saw that Egyptian wallowing in the dust. And there came forth a man of very great stature, so that he overpassed the very top of the amphitheatre, wearing a robe ungirdled, and beneath it between the two stripes over the breast a robe of purple[2]; having also shoes curiously wrought in gold and silver; bearing a rod like a master of gladiators, and a green branch whereon were golden apples. And he besought silence and said: The Egyptian, if he shall conquer this woman, shall slay her with the sword; and if she shall conquer him, she shall receive this branch. And he went away. And we came nigh to each other, and began to buffet one another. He was fain to trip up my feet, but I with my heels smote upon his face. And I rose up into the air and began so to smite him as though I trod not the earth. But when I saw that there was yet delay, I joined my hands, setting finger against finger of them. And I caught his head, and he fell upon his face; and I trod upon his head. And the people began to shout, and my helpers began to sing. And I went up to the master of gladiators and received the branch. And he kissed me and said to me: Daughter, peace be with thee. And I began to go with glory to the gate called the Gate of Life.

And I awoke; and I understood that I should fight, not with beasts but against the devil; but I knew that mine was the victory.

Thus far I have written this, till the day before the games; but the deed of the games themselves let him write who will.

11. And blessed Saturus too delivered this vision which he himself wrote down.

We had suffered, saith he, and we passed out of the flesh, and we began to be carried towards the east by four angels whose hand touched us not. And we went not as though turned upwards upon our backs, but as though we went up an easy hill. And passing over the world's edge we saw a very great light; and I said to Perpetua (for she was at my side): This is which the Lord promised us; we have received His promise. And while we were being carried by these same four angels, a great space opened before us, as it had been a pleasure garden, having rose-trees and all kinds of flowers. The height of the trees was after the manner of the cypress, and their leaves sang without ceasing. And there in the garden were four other angels, more glorious than the rest; who when they saw us gave us honor and said to the other angels: Lo, here are they, here are they: and marvelled. And the four angels who bore us set us down trembling; and we passed on foot by a broad way over a plain. There we found Jocundus and Saturninus and Artaxius who in the same persecution had been burned alive; and Quintus, a martyr also, who in prison had departed this life; and we asked of them where were the rest. The other angels said to us: Come first, go in, and salute the Lord.

12. And we came near to a place, of which place the walls were such, they seemed built of light; and before the door of that place stood four angels who clothed us when we went in with white raiment. And we went in, and we heard as it were one voice crying *Sanctus,*

Sanctus, Sanctus without any end. And we saw sitting in that same place as it were a man, white-headed, having hair like snow; youthful of countenance; whose feet we saw not. And on his right hand and on his left, four elders; and behind them stood many other elders. And we went in with wonder and stood before the throne; and the four angels raised us up; and we kissed him, and with his hand he passed over our faces. And the other elders said to us: Stand ye. And we stood, and gave the kiss of peace. And the elders said to us: Go ye and play. And I said to Perpetua: Thou hast that which thou desirest. And she said to me: Yea, God be thanked; so that I that was glad in the flesh am now more glad.

13. And we went out, and we saw before the doors, on the right Optatus the bishop, and on the left Aspasius the priest and teacher, being apart and sorrowful. And they cast themselves at our feet and said: Make peace between us, because ye went forth and left us thus. And we said to them: Art not thou our Father, and thou our priest, that ye should throw yourselves at our feet? And we were moved, and embraced them. And Perpetua began to talk with them in Greek; and we set them apart in the pleasure garden beneath a rose tree. And while we yet spoke with them, the angels said to them: Let these go and be refreshed; and whatsoever dissensions ye have between you, put them away from you each for each. And they made them to be confounded. And they said to Optatus: Correct thy people; for they come to thee as those that return from the games and wrangle concerning the parties there. And it seemed to us as though they would shut the gates. And we began to know many brothers there, martyrs also. And we were all sustained there with a savour inexpressible which satisfied us. Then in joy I awoke.

14. These were the glorious visions of those martyrs themselves, the most blessed Saturus and Perpetua, which they themselves wrote down. But Secundulus by an earlier end God called from this world while he was yet in prison; not without grace, that he should escape the beasts. Yet if not his soul, his flesh at least knew the sword.[3]

15. As for Felicity, she too received this grace of the Lord. For because she was now gone eight months (being indeed with child when she was taken) she was very sorrowful as the day of the games drew near, fearing lest for this cause she should be kept back (for it is not lawful for women that are with child to be brought forth for torment) and lest she should shed her holy and innocent blood after the rest, among strangers and malefactors. Also her fellow martyrs were much afflicted lest they should leave behind them so good a friend and as it were their fellow-traveller on the road of the same hope. Wherefore with joint and united groaning they poured out their prayer to the Lord, three days before the games. Incontinently after their prayer her pains came upon her. And when by reason of the natural difficulty of the eighth month she was oppressed with her travail and made complaint, there said to her one of the servants of the keepers of the door: Thou that thus makest complaint now, what wilt thou do when thou art thrown to the beasts, which thou didst contemn when thou wouldst not sacrifice? And she answered, I myself now suffer that which I suffer, but there another shall be in me who shall suffer for me, because I am to suffer for him. So she was delivered of a daughter, whom a sister reared up to be her own daughter.

16. Since therefore the Holy Spirit has suffered, and suffering has willed, that the order of the games also should be written; though we are unworthy to finish the recounting of so great glory, yet we accomplish the will of the most holy Perpetua, nay rather her sacred trust, adding one testimony more of her own steadfastness and height of spirit. When they were being more cruelly handled by the tribune because through advice of certain most despicable men he feared lest by magic charms they might be withdrawn secretly from the prisonhouse, Perpetua answered him to his face: Why dost thou not suffer us to take some comfort, seeing we are victims most noble, namely Cæsar's, and on his feast day we are to fight? Or is it not thy glory that we should be taken out thither fatter of flesh? The tribune trembled and blushed, and gave order that they should be more gently han-

dled, granting that her brothers and the rest should come in and rest with them. Also the adjutant of the prison now believed.

17. Likewise on the day before the games, when at the last feast which they call Free[4] they made (as far as they might) not a Free Feast but a Love Feast, with like hardihood they cast these words at the people; threatening the judgment of the Lord, witnessing to the felicity of their passion, setting at nought the curiosity of those that ran together. And Saturus said: Is not to-morrow sufficient for you? Why do ye favorably behold that which ye hate? Ye are friends to-day, foes to-morrow. Yet mark our faces diligently, that ye may know us again on that day. So they began all to go away thence astonished; of whom many believed.

18. Now dawned the day of their victory, and they went forth from the prison into the amphitheatre as it were into heaven, cheerful and bright of countenance; if they trembled at all, it was for joy, not for fear. Perpetua followed behind, glorious of presence, as a true spouse of Christ and darling of God; at whose piercing look all cast down their eyes. Felicity likewise, rejoicing that she had borne a child in safety, that she might fight with the beasts, came now from blood to blood, from the midwife to the gladiator, to wash after her travail in a second baptism. And when they had been brought to the gate and were being compelled to put on, the men the dress of the priests of Saturn, the women the dress of the priestesses of Ceres, the noble Perpetua remained of like firmness to the end, and would not. For she said: For this cause came we willingly unto this, that our liberty might not be obscured. For this cause have we devoted our lives, that we might do no such thing as this; this we agreed with you. Injustice acknowledged justice; the tribune suffered that they should be brought forth as they were, without more ado. Perpetua began to sing, as already treading on the Egyptian's head. Revocatus and Saturninus and Saturus threatened the people as they gazed. Then when they came into Hilarian's sight, they began to say to Hilarian, stretching forth their hands and nodding their heads: Thou judgest us, said they, and God thee. At this the people being enraged besought that they should be vexed with scourges before the line of gladiators (those namely who fought with beasts). Then truly they gave thanks because they had received somewhat of the sufferings of the Lord.

19. But He Who had said *Ask, and ye shall receive* gave to them asking that end which each had desired. For whenever they spoke together of their desire in their martyrdom, Saturninus for his part would declare that he wished to be thrown to every kind of beast, that so indeed he might wear the more glorious crown. At the beginning of the spectacle therefore himself with Revocatus first had ado with a leopard and was afterwards torn by a bear on a raised bridge. Now Saturus detested nothing more than a bear, but was confident already he should die by one bite of a leopard. Therefore when he was being given to a boar, the gladiator instead who had bound him to the boar was torn asunder by the same beast and died after the days of the games; nor was Saturus more than dragged. Moreover when he had been tied on the bridge to be assaulted by a bear, the bear would not come forth from his den. So Saturus was called back unharmed a second time.

20. But for the women the devil had made ready a most savage cow, prepared for this purpose against all custom; for even in this beast he would mock their sex. They were stripped therefore and made to put on nets; and so they were brought forth. The people shuddered, seeing one a tender girl, the other her breasts yet dropping from her late childbearing. So they were called back and clothed in loose robes. Perpetua was first thrown, and fell upon her loins. And when she had sat upright, her robe being rent at the side, she drew it over to cover her thigh, mindful rather of modesty than of pain. Next, looking for a pin, she likewise pinned up her dishevelled hair; for it was not meet that a martyr should suffer with hair dishevelled, lest she should seem to grieve in her glory. So she stood up; and when she saw Felicity smitten down, she went up and gave her her hand

and raised her up. And both of them stood up together and (the hardness of the people being now subdued) were called back to the Gate of Life. There Perpetua being received by one named Rusticus, then a catechumen, who stood close at her side, and as now awakening from sleep (so much was she in the Spirit and in ecstasy) began first to look about her; and then (which amazed all there), When, forsooth, quoth she, are we to be thrown to the cow? And when she heard that this had been done already, she would not believe till she perceived some marks of mauling on her body and on her dress. Thereupon she called her brother to her, and that catechumen, and spoke to them, saying: Stand fast in the faith, and love ye all one another; and be not offended because of our passion.

21. Saturus also at another gate exhorted Pudens the soldier, saying: So then indeed, as I trusted and foretold, I have felt no assault of beasts until now. And now believe with all thy heart. Behold, I go out thither and shall perish by one bite of the leopard. And forthwith at the end of the spectacle, the leopard being released, with one bite of his he was covered with so much blood that the people (in witness to his second baptism) cried out to him returning: Well washed, well washed. Truly it was well with him who had washed in this wise. Then said he to Pudens the soldier: Farewell; remember the faith and me; and let not these things trouble thee, but strengthen thee. And therewith he took from Pudens' finger a little ring, and dipping it in his wound gave it back again for an heirloom, leaving him a pledge and memorial of his blood. Then as the breath left him he was cast down with the rest in the accustomed place for his throat to be cut. And when the people besought that they should be brought forward, that when the sword pierced through their bodies their eyes might be joined thereto as witnesses to the slaughter, they rose of themselves and moved whither the people willed them, first kissing one another, that they might accomplish their martyrdom with the rites of peace. The rest not moving and in silence received the sword; Saturus much earlier gave up the ghost; for he had gone up earlier also, and now he waited for Perpetua likewise. But Perpetua, that she might have some taste of pain, was pierced between the bones and shrieked out; and when the swordsman's hand wandered still (for he was a novice), herself set it upon her own neck. Perchance so great a woman could not else have been slain (being feared of the unclean spirit) had she not herself so willed it.

O most valiant and blessed martyrs! O truly called and elected unto the glory of Our Lord Jesus Christ! Which glory he that magnifies, honors and adores, ought to read these witnesses likewise, as being no less than the old, unto the Church's edification; that these new wonders also may testify that one and the same Holy Spirit works ever until now, and with Him God the Father Almighty, and His Son Jesus Christ Our Lord, to Whom is glory and power unending for ever and ever. Amen.

Notes

1 In the symbolism of early Christian art such a vessel was used to signify a Christian's good works, or sometimes the Christian himself as the "vessel of Christ." S. Perpetua may have had this in mind.

2 The interpretation of this difficult passage is probably this: The man wears a white *tunica*, purple-edged and open in front (somewhat like a white cope with purple orphreys); beneath it is a purple undergarment, visible between the purple bands of the *tunica*.

3 The narrator's words are not clear, but seem to mean that Secundulus was beheaded in prison.

4 At which ancient, as modern, custom allowed the condemned choice of food and drink. The martyrs used the occasion for the celebration of the *Agape*.

Tacitus

Germania

In 98 the Roman historian Cornelius Tacitus (ca. 56 -ca. 120) wrote a brief description of the Germanic peoples living beyond the Rhine. His account is based on the writings of previous geographers and historians, especially, Pliny the Elder's lost German Wars *as well as on interviews with people who had first-hand experience with the Germanic peoples. Although largely accurate in its details, the treatise organizes and filters Tacitus' data through the classical ethnological categories. Its purpose was less to inform Romans about the Germans than to criticize Roman customs and morals by contrasting them with those of the barbarians.*

Source: Tacitus. Dialogus, Agricola, Germania, (London: Heineman, 1914) Germania translated by Maurice Hutton, revised by D. LePan, 1989.

1   Undivided Germany is separated from the Gauls, Rhaetians, and Pannonians by the rivers Rhine and Danube: from the Sarmatians and Dacians by mutual fear or mountains: the rest of it is surrounded by the ocean, which enfolds wide peninsulas and islands of vast expanse, some of whose people and kings have but recently become known to us: war has lifted the curtain.

The Rhine, rising from the inaccessible and precipitous crest of the Rhaetian Alps, after turning west for a reach of some length is lost in the North Sea. The Danube pours from the sloping and not very lofty ridge of Mount Abnoba, and visits several peoples on its course, until at length it emerges by six of its channels into the Pontic Sea: the seventh mouth is swallowed in marshes.

2   As for the Germans themselves, I should suppose them to be native to the area and only very slightly blended with new arrivals from other races or regions; for in ancient times people who sought to migrate reached their destination by sea and not by land; while, in the second place, the great ocean on the further side of Germany—at the opposite end of the world, so to speak, from us—is rarely visited by ships from our world. Besides, even apart from the perils of an awful and unknown sea, who would have left Asia or Africa or Italy to look for Germany? With its wild scenery and harsh climate it is pleasant neither to live in nor look upon unless it be one's home.

Their ancient hymns—the only record of history which they possess—celebrate a god Tuisto, a scion of the soil, and his son Mannus as the founders of their race. To Mannus they ascribe three sons, from whose names the tribes of the seashore came to be known as Ingaevones, the central tribes as Herminones, and the rest as Istaevones. Some authorities, using the license which pertains to antiquity, claim more sons for the god and a larger number of race names: Marsi, Gambrivii, Suebi, Vandilii. These are, they say, real and ancient names, while the name of "Germany" is new. The first tribes in fact to cross the Rhine and expel the Gauls, though now called Tungri, were then styled Germans: so little by little the name—a tribal, not a national, name—prevailed, until the whole people were called by the artificial name of "Germans," first only by the victorious tribe in order to intimidate the Gauls, but afterwards among themselves also.

3   The authorities also record how Hercules appeared among the Germans, and on the

eve of battle the natives chant "Hercules, the first of brave men." They use as well another chant—"barritus" is the name they use for it—to inspire courage; and they forecast the results of the coming battle from the sound of the cry. Intimidation or timidity depends on the concert of the warriors; the chant seems to them to mean not so much unison of voices as union of hearts; the object they specially seek is a certain volume of hoarseness, a crashing roar, their shields being brought up to their lips, that the voice may swell to a fuller and deeper note by means of the echo.

To return. Ulysses also—in the opinion of some authorities—was carried during his long and legendary wanderings into this ocean, and reached the lands of Germany. Asciburgium, which stands on the banks of the Rhine and has inhabitants today, was founded, they say, and named by him; further, they say that an altar dedicated by Ulysses, who added to his own inscription that of his father Laertes, was once found at the same place, and that certain monuments and barrows, marked with Greek letters, are still extant on the borderland between Germany and Rhaetia. I have no intention of furnishing evidence to establish or refute these assertions: every one according to his temperament may minimize or magnify their credibility.

4   Personally, I agree with those who hold that in the peoples of Germany there has been given to the world a nation untainted by inter-marriage with other peoples, a peculiar people and pure, like no one but themselves; whence it comes that their physique, in spite of their vast numbers, is identical: fierce blue eyes, red hair, tall frames. They are powerful too, but only spasmodically; they have no fondness for feats of endurance or for hard work. Nor are they well able to bear thirst and heat; to cold and hunger, thanks to the climate and the soil, they are accustomed.

5   There are some varieties in the appearance of the country, but in general it is a land of bristling forests and unhealthy marshes; the rainfall is heavier on the side of Gaul; the winds are higher on the side of Noricum and Pannonia.

It is fertile in cereals, but unkind to fruit-bearing trees; it is rich in flocks and herds, but for the most part they are undersized. Even the cattle lack natural beauty and majestic brows. The pride of the people is rather in the number of their beasts, which constitute the only form of wealth they value.

The gods have denied them gold and silver, whether in mercy or in wrath I find it hard to say. Not that I would assert that Germany has no veins bearing gold or silver, for who has explored there? At any rate, they are not affected, like their neighbours, by the use and possession of such things. One may see among them silver vases, given as gifts to their commanders and chieftains, but treated as of no more value than earthenware. Although the border tribes for purposes of trade treat gold and silver as precious metals, and recognise and collect certain coins of our money, the tribes of the interior practise barter in the simpler and older fashion. The coinage which appeals to them is the old and long-familiar: the denarii with milled edges, showing the two-horsed chariot. They prefer silver to gold: not that they have any feeling in the matter, but because a number of silver pieces is easier to use for people whose purchases consist of cheap objects of general utility.

6   Even iron is not plentiful among them, as may be gathered from the style of their weapons. Few have swords or the longer kind of lance: they carry short spears, in their language *"frameae,"* with a narrow and small iron head, so sharp and so handy in use that they fight with the same weapon, as circumstances demand, both at close quarters and at a distance. The mounted man is content with a shield and *framea*: the infantry launch showers of spears as well, each man a volley, and are able to hurl these great distances, for they wear no outer clothing, or at most a light cloak.

Their garb is for the most part quite plain; only shields are decorated, each a few colours. Few have breast–plates: scarcely one or two at most have metal or hide helmets. The horses are conspicuous for neither beauty nor speed; but then neither are they trained like our horses to run in shifting circles: the Germans ride them forwards only or to the right, with but one turn from the straight, dressing the line so closely as they wheel that no one is left behind. In general there is more strength in their infantry, and accordingly cavalry and infantry fight in one body; the swift-footed infantryman, whom they pick out of the whole body of warriors and place in front of the line, are well-adapted to cavalry battles. The number of these men is fixed—one hundred from each canton, and among themselves "the Hundred" is the precise name they use. What was once a number only has become a title and a distinction. The battle-line itself is arranged in wedges. To retire, provided you press on again, they treat as a question of tactics, not of cowardice; they carry off their dead and wounded even in drawn battles. To have abandoned one's shield is the height of disgrace. The man so dishonoured cannot be present at religious rites, nor attend a council; many survivors of war have ended their infamy with a noose.

7   They choose their kings on the grounds of birth, their generals on the basis of courage. The authority of their kings is not unlimited or arbitrary; their generals control them by example rather than command, the troops admiring their energy and the conspicuous place they take in front of the line. But anything beyond this—capital punishment, imprisonment, even a blow—is permitted only to the priests, and then not as a penalty or under the general's orders, but in obedience to the god whom they believe accompanies them on campaign. Certain totems, in fact, and emblems are fetched from groves and carried into battle. The strongest incentive to courage lies in this, that neither chance nor casual grouping makes the squadron or the wedge, but family and kinship. Close at hand, too, are their dearest, so that they hear the wailing voices of women and cries of children. Here are the witnesses who are in each man's eyes most precious; here the praise he covets most. The warriors take their wounds to mother and wife, who do not shrink from counting the hurts and demanding a sight of them: they give to the combatants food and encouragement.

8   Tradition relates that some battles that seemed lost have been restored by the women, by their incessant prayers and by the baring of their breasts; for so it is brought home to the men that slavery, which they dread much more keenly on their women's account, is close at hand. It follows that the loyalty of those tribes is more effectively guaranteed if you hold, among other hostages, girls of noble birth.

Further, they conceive that in women is a certain uncanny and prophetic sense: they neither scorn to consult them nor slight their answers. In the reign of Vespasian of happy memory we saw Velaeda treated as a deity by many during a long period; but in ancient times they also reverenced Albruna and many other women—in no spirit of flattery, nor for the manufacture of goddesses.

9   Of the gods they most worship Mercury, to whom on certain days they count even the sacrifice of human life lawful. Hercules and Mars they appease with such animal life as is permissible. A section of the Suebi sacrifices also to Isis: the cause and origin of this foreign worship I have not succeeded in discovering, except that the emblem itself, which takes the shape of a Liburnian galley, shows that the ritual is imported.

Apart from this they deem it incompatible with the majesty of the heavenly host to confine the gods within walls, or to mould them into any likeness of the human face. They consecrate groves and coppices, and they give divine names to that mysterious presence which is visible only to the eyes of faith.

10   To divination and casting lots they pay as much attention as any one. The method of drawing lots is uniform. A bough is cut from a nut–bearing tree and divided into slips. These are distinguished by certain runes and spread casually and at random over white cloth. Afterwards, should the inquiry be official the priest of the state, if private the father of the family in person, after prayers to the gods and with eyes turned to heaven takes up one slip at a time till he has done this on three separate occasions. After taking the

three he interprets them according to the runes which have already been stamped on them. If the massage is a prohibition, no inquiry on the same matter is made during the same day; if the message gives permission, further confirmation is required by means of divination. Among the Germans divination by consultation of the cries and flight of birds is well known. Another form of divination peculiar to them is to seek the omens and warnings furnished by horses.

In the same groves and coppices are fed certain white horses, never soiled by mortal use. These are yoked to a sacred chariot and accompanied by the priest and king, or other chief of the state, who then observe their neighing and snorting. On no other form of divination is more reliance placed, not merely by the people but also by their leaders. The priests they regard as the servants of the gods, but the horses are their confidants.

They have another method of taking divinations, by means of which they probe the issue of serious wars. A member of the tribe at war with them is somehow or other captured and pitted against a selected champion of their own countrymen, each in his tribal armour. The victory of one or the other is taken as a presage.

11 On small matters the chiefs consult, on larger questions the community; but with this limitation: even when the decision rests with the people, the matter is considered first by the chiefs. They meet, unless there is some unforeseen and sudden emergency, on days set apart—when the moon is either new or full. They regard these times as the most auspicious for the transaction of business. They count not days as we do, but by nights and their decisions and proclamations are subject to this principle; the night, that is, seems to take precedence over the day.

It is a foible of their freedom that they do not meet at once and when commanded, but waste two or three days by dilatoriness in assembling. When they are finally ready to begin, they take their seats carrying arms. Silence is called for by the priests, who then have the power to force obedience. Then a king or a chief is listened to, in order of age, birth, glory in war, or eloquence. Such figures command attention through the prestige which belongs to their counsel rather than any prescriptive right to command. If the advice tendered is displeasing, the people reject it with groans; if it pleases them, they clash their spears. The most complimentary expression of assent is this martial approbation.

12 At this assembly it is also permissible to lay accusations and to bring capital charges. The nature of the death penalty differs according to the offence: traitors and deserters are hung from trees; cowards, poor fighters and notorious evil-livers are plunged in the mud of marshes with a hurdle on their heads. These differences of punishment follow the principle that crime should be blazoned abroad by its retribution, but shameful actions hidden. Lighter offences have also a measured punishment. Those convicted are fined a certain number of horses or cattle. Part of the fine goes to the king or the state; part is paid to the person who has brought the charge or to his relatives. At the same gatherings are selected chiefs, who administer law through the cantons and villages: each of them has one hundred assessors from the people to act as his responsible advisors.

13 They do no business, public or private, without arms in their hands; yet the custom is that no one takes arms until the state has endorsed this competence. Then in the assembly itself one of the chiefs or his father or his relatives equip the young man with shield and spear. This corresponds with them to the toga, and is youth's first public distinction; before that he was merely a member of the household, now he becomes a member of the state. Conspicuously high birth, or great services on the part of their ancestors may win the chieftain's approval even for the very young men. They mingle with the others, men of maturer strength and tested by long years and have no shame to be seen among the chief's retinue. In the retinue itself degrees are observed at the chief's discretion; there is great rivalry among the retainers to decide who shall have the first place with chief, and among the chieftains as to who shall have the largest and most enthusiastic retinue. It is considered desirable to be surrounded always with a large band of chosen youths—glory

in peace, in war protection. Nor is this only so with a chief's own people; with neighbouring states also it means name and fame for a man that his retinue be conspicuous for number and character. Such men are in demand for embassies, and are honoured with gifts; often, by the mere terror of their name, they are able to break the back of opposition in war.

14 When the battlefield is reached it is a reproach for a chief to be surpassed in prowess and a reproach for his retinue not to equal the prowess of its chief. Much worse, though, is to have left the field and survived one's chief; this means lifelong infamy and shame. To protect and defend the chief and to devote one's own feats to his glorification is the gist of their allegiance. The chief fights for victory, but the retainers for the chief.

Should it happen that the community where they are born has been drugged with long years of peace and quiet, many of the high-born youth voluntarily seek those tribes which are at the time engaged in some war; for rest is unwelcome to the race, and they distinguish themselves more readily in the midst of uncertainties: besides, you cannot keep up a great retinue except by war and violence. It is the generous chief that the warriors expect to give them a particular war-horse or murderous and masterful spear. Banquetings and a certain rude but lavish outfit take the place of salary. The material for this generosity comes through war and foray. You will not so readily persuade a German to plough the land and wait for the year's returns as to challenge the enemy and earn wounds. Besides, it seems limp and slack to get with the sweating of your brow what you can gain with the shedding of your blood.

15 When they are not warring, they spend much time hunting, but more in idleness—creatures who eat and sleep, the best and bravest warriors doing nothing, having handed over the charge of their home, hearth and estate to the women and the old men and the weakest members of the family. For themselves they vegetate by that curious incongruity of temperament which makes of the same men such lovers of slumber and such haters of quiet.

It is the custom in their states for each man to bestow upon the chief unasked some portion of his cattle or crops. It is accepted as a compliment, but also serves the chief's needs. The chiefs appreciate still more the gifts of neighboring tribes, which are sent not merely by individuals but by the community—selected horses, heavy armour, bosses and bracelets; by this time we have taught them to accept money also.

16 It is well known that none of the German tribes live in cities, that individually they do not permit houses to touch each other. They live separated and scattered, according as spring-water, meadow, or grove appeals to each man. They lay out their villages not, after our fashion, with buildings contiguous and connected; everyone keeps a clear space round his house, whether it be a precaution against the chances of fire or just ignorance of building. They have not even learned to use quarry-stone or tiles: the timber they use for all purposes is unshaped, and stops short of all ornament or attraction. Certain buildings are smeared with a stucco bright and glittering enough to be a substitute for paint and frescoes. They are in the habit also of opening pits in the earth and piling dung in quantities on the roof, as a refuge from the winter or a root-house, because such places lessen the harshness of frost. If an enemy comes, he lays waste the open, but the hidden and buried houses are either missed outright or escape detection just because they require a search.

17 For clothing all wear a cloak, fastened with a clasp, or, in its absence a thorn. They spend whole days on the hearth round the fire with no other covering. The richest men are distinguished by the wearing of underclothes—not loose, like those of Parthians and Sarmatians, but drawn tight, throwing each limb into relief.

They wear also the skins of wild beasts: the tribes adjoining the river-bank in casual fashion, the inland tribes with more attention, since they cannot depend on traders for clothing. The beasts for this purpose are selected, and the hides so taken are chequered with the pied skins of the creatures native to the outer ocean and its unknown waters.

The women have the same dress as the men, except that very often long linen garments, striped with purple, are in use for the women. The upper part of this costume does not widen into sleeves; their arms and shoulders are therefore bare, as is the adjoining portion of the breast.

18 None the less the marriage tie with them is strict; you will find nothing in their character to praise more highly. They are almost the only barbarians who are content with a wife apiece. The very few exceptions have nothing to do with passion, but consist of those with whom polygamous marriage is eagerly sought for the sake of their high birth.

As for the dowry, it is not the wife who brings it to the husband, but the husband to the wife. The parents and relations are present to approve these gifts—gifts not devised for ministering to females fads, nor for the adornment of the person of the bride, but oxen, a horse and bridle, a shield and spear or sword. It is to share these things that the wife is taken by the husband, and she in turn brings some piece of armour to her husband. Here is the gist of the bond between them, here in their eyes its mysterious sacrament, the divinity which hedges it. Thus the wife may not imagine herself released from the practice of heroism, released from the chances of war; she is warned by the very rites with which her marriage begins that she comes to share with her husband hard work and peril. Her fate will be the same as his in peace and in panic, her risks the same. This is the moral of the yoked oxen, of the bridled horse, of the exchange of arms; so she must live and so she must die. The things she takes she is to hand over inviolate to her children, fit to be taken by her daughters–in–law and passed on again to her grandchildren.

19 So their life is one of fenced-in chastity. There is no arena with its seductions, no dinner-tables with their provocations to corrupt them. Of the exchange of secret letters men and women alike are innocent. Adultery is very rare among these people. Punishment is prompt and is the husband's prerogative: the wife's hair is close-cropped, she is stripped of her clothes, her husband drives her from his house in the presence of his relatives and pursues her with blows through the length of the village. For lost chastity there is no pardon; neither beauty nor youth nor wealth will find the sinner a husband. No one laughs at vice there; no one calls seduction the spirit of the age. Better still are those tribes where only maids marry and where a woman makes an end, once and for all, with the hopes and vows of a wife. So they take one husband only, just as one body and one life, in order that there may be second thoughts, no belated fancies, and in order that their excessive desire may be not for the man, but for marriage. To limit the number of their children or to put to death any of the later children is considered abominable. Good habits have more force with them than good laws elsewhere.

20 The children in every house, grow up amid nakedness and squalour into that girth of limb and frame which is to our people a marvel. Its own mother suckles each at her breast; children are not passed on to nursemaids and wet–nurses.

Nor can master be recognised from servant by having been spoiled in his upbringing. Master and servant live in the company of the same cattle and on the same mud floor till years separate the free–born and character claims her own.

The virginity of young men is long preserved, and their powers are therefore inexhaustible. Nor for the girls is there any hot–house forcing; they pass their youth in the same way as the boys. Their stature is as tall; when they reach the same strength they are mated, and the children reproduce the vigour of the parents. Sisters' children mean as much to their uncle as to their father: some tribes regard this blood-tie as even closer and more sacred than that between son and father, and in taking hostages make it the basis of their demand, as though they thus secure loyalty more surely and have a wider hold on the family.

However, so far as succession is concerned, each man's children are his heirs, and there is no will. If there are no children, the nearest degrees of relationship for the holding of property are brothers, paternal uncles, and maternal uncles. The more relations a man has and the larger the number of his connections by marriage, the more influence has he in his age; it does not pay to have no ties.

21   It is incumbent to take up the feuds of one's father or kinsman no less than his friendships. But such feuds do not continue unappeasable; even homicide may be atoned for by a fixed number of cattle and sheep. The whole family thereby receives satisfaction to the public advantage, for feuds are more dangerous among a free people.

No race indulges more lavishly in hospitality and entertainment. To close the door against any human being is a crime. Everyone according to his means welcomes guests generously. Should there not be enough, he who is your host goes with you next door, without an invitation, but it makes no difference; you are received with the same courtesy. Stranger or acquaintance no one distinguishes them where the right of hospitality is concerned. It is customary to speed the parting guest with anything he fancies. There is the same readiness in turn to ask of him: gifts are the Germans delight, but they neither count upon what they have given, nor are bound by what they have received.

22   On waking from sleep, which they generally prolong in the day, they wash, usually in warm water, since winter bulks so large in their lives. After washing they take a meal, seated apart, each at his own table. Then, arms in hand, they proceed to business, or, just as often, to revelry. To drink heavily day and night is a reproach to no man. Brawls are frequent, as you would expect among heavy drinkers: these seldom terminate with abuse, more often in wounds and bloodshed. Nevertheless the mutual reconciliation of enemies, the forming of family alliances, the appointment of chiefs, the question even of war or peace, are usually debated at these banquets; as though at no other time were the mind more open to obvious, or better warmed to larger, thoughts. The people are without craft or cunning, and expose in the freedom of revelry the heart's secrets; so every mind is bared to nakedness. On the next day the matter is handled afresh. So the principle of each debating season is justified: deliberation comes when people are incapable of pretence, but decision when they are secure from illusion.

23   For drink they use a liquid distilled from barley or wheat, after fermentation has given it a certain resemblance to wine. The tribes nearest the river also buy wine. Their diet is simple: wild fruit, fresh venison, curdled milk. They banish hunger without sauce or ceremony, but there is not the same temperance in facing thirst: if you humour their drunkenness by supplying as much as they crave, they will be vanquished through their vices as easily as on the battlefield.

24   Their shows are all of one kind, and the same whatever the gathering may be: naked youths, for whom this a form of professional acting, jump and bound between swords and upturned spears. Practice has made them dexterous and graceful. Yet they do not perform for hire or gain: however daring be the sport, the spectator's pleasure is the only price they ask.

Gambling, one may be surprised to find, they practise in all seriousness in their sober hours, with such recklessness in winning or losing that, when all else has failed, they stake personal liberty on the last and final throw.

The loser faces voluntary slavery; though he may be the younger and the stronger man, he will still allow himself to be bound and sold. Such is the Germans' persistence in wrong-doing, or their good faith, as they themselves style it. Slaves so acquired they trade, in order to deliver themselves, as well as the slave from the humiliation involved in such victory.

25   Their other slaves are not organised in our fashion: that is, by a division of the services of life among them. Each of them remains master of his own house and home: the

master requires from the slave as serf a certain quantity of grain or cattle or clothing. The slave so far is subservient; but the other services of the household are discharged by the master's wife and children. To beat a slave or coerce him with hard labor and imprisonment is rare. If slaves are killed, it is not usually to preserve strict discipline, but in a fit of fury like an enemy, except that there is no penalty to be paid.

Freedmen are not much above slaves. Rarely are they of any weight in the household, never in politics, except in those states which have kings. Then they climb above the freeborn and above the nobles; in other states the disabilities of the freedman are the evidence of freedom.

26 To charge interest, let alone interest at high rates, is unknown and the principal or avoiding usury is accordingly better observed than if there had been actual prohibition.

Land is taken up by a village as a whole, in quantity according to the number of cultivators. They then distribute it among themselves on the basis of rank, such distribution being made easy by the amount of land available. They change the arable land yearly, and there is still land to spare, for they do not strain the fertility and resources of the soil by tasking them, through the planting of vineyards, the setting apart of water–meadows, or the irrigation of vegetable gardens. Grain is the only harvest required of the land. Accordingly the year itself is not divided into as many parts as with us: winter, spring, summer have a meaning and a name; the gifts of autumn and its name are alike unknown.

27 In burial there is no ostentation. The only ceremony is to burn the bodies of their notables with special kinds of wood. They build a pyre, but do not load it with palls or spices. The man's armour and some of his horse also is added to the fire. The tomb is a mound of turf: the difficult and tedious tribute of a monument they reject as too heavy on the dead. Weeping and wailing they put away quickly; sorrow and sadness linger. Lamentation becomes women: men must restrain their emotion.

So much in general we have ascertained concerning the origin of the undivided Germans and their customs. I shall now set forth the habits and customs of the several nations, and the extent to which they differ from each other; and explain what tribes have migrated from Germany to the Gallic provinces.

28 That the fortunes of Gaul were once higher than those of Germany is recorded on the supreme authority of Julius of happy memory. Therefore it is easy to believe that the Gauls at one time crossed over into Germany; small chance there was of the river preventing each tribe, as it became powerful, from seizing new land, which had not yet been divided into powerful kingdoms. Accordingly the country between the Hercynian forest and the rivers Rhine and Moenus was occupied by the Helvetii, and the country beyond the Boii, both Gallic races. The name Boihaemum still testifies to the old traditions of the place, though here has been a change of occupants.

Whether, however, the Aravisci migrated into Pannonia from the Osi, or the Osi into Germany from the Aravisci, must remain uncertain, since their speech, habits, and type of character are still the same. Originally, in fact, there was the same misery and the same freedom on either bank of the river, the same advantages and the same drawbacks.

The Treveri and Nervi conversely go out of their way in their ambition to claim a German origin, as though this illustrious ancestry delivers them from any affinity with the indolent Gaul.

On the river bank itself are planted certain peoples who are unquestionably German: Vangiones, Triboci, Nemetes. Not even the Ubii, though they have earned the right to be a Roman colony and prefer to be called "Agrippinenses" after the name of their founder, blush to own their German origin. They originally came from beyond the river. After they had given proof of their loyalty, they were placed in charge of the bank itself, in order to block the way to others, not in order to be under supervision.

Of all these races the most manly are the Batavi, who occupy only a short stretch of the river bank, but with it the island in the stream. They were once a tribe of the Chatti, and on account of a rising at home they crossed the river onto lands which later became part of the Roman Empire. Their distinction persists and the emblem of their ancient alliance with us; they are not insulted, that is, by the exaction of tribute, and there is no tax-farmer to oppress them. Immune from burdens and contributions, and set apart for fighting purposes only, they are reserved for war to be, as it were, our arms and weapons. Equally loyal are the tribe of the Mattiaci; for the greatness of the Roman nation has projected the awe felt for our Empire beyond the Rhine, and beyond the long-established frontier. So by site and territory they belong to their own bank, but by sentiment and thought they act with us, and are similar in all respects to the Batavi, except that hitherto both the soil and the climate of their land make them more lively.

I should not count among the people of Germany, though they have established themselves beyond the Rhine and Danube, the tribes who cultivate "the tithe-lands." All the wastrels of Gaul, plucking courage from misery, took possession of that disputed land. Later, since the frontier line has been drawn and the garrisons pushed forward, these lands have been counted as an outlying corner of the Empire and a part of the Roman province.

30 Beyond these people are the Chatti. The front of their settlements begins with the Hercynian forest. The land is not so low and marshy as the other states of the level German plain; yet even where the hills cover a considerable territory they gradually fade away, and so the Hercynian forest, after escorting its Chatti to the full length of their settlement, drops them in the plain. This tribe has hardier bodies than the others, close-knit limbs, a forbidding expression, and more strength of the intellect. There is much method in what they do, for Germans at least, and much shrewdness. They elect magistrates and listen to the man elected; know their place in the ranks and recognise opportunities; reserve their attack; have a time for everything; entrench at night; distrust luck, but rely on courage; and—the rarest thing of all, and usually attained only through Roman discipline—depend on the initiative of the general rather than on that of the soldier. Their whole strength lies in their infantry, whom they load with iron tools and baggage, in addition to their arms. Other Germans may be seen going to battle, but the Chatti go to war. Forays and casual fighting are rare with them. The latter method no doubt is part of the strength of cavalry—to win suddenly, that is, and as suddenly to retire. For the speed of cavalry is near allied to panic, but the deliberate action of infantry is more likely to be resolute.

31 One ceremony that is practised by other German peoples only occasionally, depending on preference, has with the Chatti become a convention: to let the hair and beard grow when a youth has attained manhood, and to remove this manly facial garb only after an enemy has been slain. Standing above the bloody spoil, they dismantle their faces again, and advertise that then and not before have they paid the price of their birthpangs, and are worthy of their kin and country. Cowards and weaklings remain unkempt. The bravest also wear a ring of iron—the badge of shame on other occasions among this people—as a symbolic band from which each man frees himself by the slaughter of an enemy. This symbolism is very popular, and men already growing grey still wear this uniform for the pointing finger of friend and foe. Every battle begins with these men: the front rank is made up of them and is a curious sight. But, even in peace they do not allow a tamer life to enervate them. None of them has a house or land or any business. Wherever they go they are entertained; they waste the possessions of others and are indifferent to their own, until age and loss of blood make them unequal to such demanding heroism.

32 Next to the Chatti come the Usipi and Tencteri, on the Rhine banks where the river has ceased to shift its bed and has become fit to serve as a boundary. The Tencteri, in addition to the general reputation as the race as warriors, excel in the accomplishments of trained horsemen. Even the fame of the Chattan infantry is not greater than that of their cavalry. Their ancestors established the precedent, and succeeding generations vie with

them. Horsemanship is the diversion of children, the centre of competition for youth, and the abiding interest of age. Horses descend with servants, house, and regular inheritance. The heir to the horse, however, is not as in other things the eldest son but the confident soldier and the better man.

33 Next to the Tencteri one originally came across the Bructeri. The Chamavi and Angrivarii are said to have trekked there recently, after the Bructeri had been expelled or cut to pieces by the joint action of neighboring peoples. Whether this was from disgust at their arrogance or from the attractions of plunder, or because Heaven leans to the side of Rome cannot be said. But Heaven did not grudge us a dramatic battle; over sixty thousand men fell, not before the arms and spears of Rome, but—what was even a greater triumph for us—merely to delight our eyes. Long may such behaviour last, I pray, and persist among the German nations—if they feel no love for us, at least may they feel hatred for each other. Now that the destinies of the Empire have passed their zenith, Fortune can guarantee us nothing better than discord among our foes.

34 The Angrivarii and Chamavi are surrounded to the south by the Dulgubnii and the Chasuarii and other tribes not so well known to history. To the north follow the Frisii: they are called the Greater or Lesser Frisii according to the measure of their strength. These two tribes border the Rhine down to the ocean, and also fringe the great lakes which the fleets of Rome navigate. In that quarter we have even reached the ocean itself, and beyond our range are rumoured to stand the pillars of Hercules. Did Hercules really visit those shores, or is it only that we have agreed to credit all marvels everywhere to him. Nor did Drusus Germanicus lack audacity as an explorer but Ocean vetoed inquiry into either itself or Hercules. Soon the attempt was abandoned, and it came to be judged more reverent to believe in the works of deities than to comprehend them.

35 Thus far we have been enquiring into Western Germany. At this point the country falls away with a great bend towards the north. First in this area come the Chauci. Though they start next to the Frisii and occupy part of the seaboard, they also border on all of the tribes just mentioned, and finally edge away south as far as the Chatti. This vast block of territory is not merely held by the Chauci but filled by them. They are the noblest of the German tribes, and prefer to protect their vast domain by justice alone. They are neither grasping nor lawless; in peaceful seclusion they provoke no wars and despatch no raiders on marauding forays. The special proof of their great strength is, indeed, just this, that they do not depend for their superior position on injustice. Yet they are ready with arms, and, if circumstances should require, with armies, men and horse in abundance. So, even though they keep the peace, their reputation does not suffer.

36 Bordering the Chauci and the Chatti are the Cherusci. For long years they have been unassailed and have encouraged an abnormal and languid peacefulness. It has been a pleasant rather than a sound policy. With lawlessness and strength on either side of you, you will find no true peace; where might is right, self-control and righteousness are titles reserved for the stronger. Accordingly, the Cherusci, who were once styled just and generous, are now described as indolent and shortsighted, while the good luck of the victorious Chatti has been credited to them as wisdom. The fall of the Cherusci dragged down the Fosi also, a neighboring tribe. They share the adversity of the Cherusci on even terms, though they have only been dependents in their prosperity.

37 This same "sleeve" or peninsula of Germany is the home of the Cimbri, who dwell nearest the ocean. They are a small state to–day, but rich in memories. Broad traces of their ancient fame are still extant—a spacious camp on each bank (of the Rhine), by the circuit of which you can even to–day measure the size and skill of the nation and get some sense of that mighty trek.

Our city was in its six hundred and fortieth year when the Cimbrian armies were first heard of, in the consulship of Caecilius Metellus and Papirius Carbo. If we count from that date to the second consulship of the Emperor Trajan, the total amounts to about two hundred and ten years. For that length of time the conquest of Germany has been in process. Between the beginning and end of that long period there have been many mutual losses. Neither Samnite nor Carthaginian, neither Spain nor Gaul, nor even the Parthians have taught us more lessons. The German fighting for liberty has been a keener enemy than the absolutism of Arsaces. What has the East to taunt us with, apart from the overthrow of Crasus—the East which itself fell at the feet of a Ventidius and lost Pacorus?

But the Germans routed or captured Carbo and Cassius and Aurelius Scaurus and Servilius Caepio and Gnaeus Mallius, and rested five consular armies in one campaign from the people of Rome, and even from a Caesar rested Varus and three legions with him. Nor was it without paying the price that Marius smote them in Italy, and Julius of happy memory in Gaul, and Drusus, Nero, and Germanicus in their own homes. Soon after that the great tragedy threatened by Gaius Caesar turned into a farce. Then came peace until, on the opportunity offered by our own dissensions and by civil war, the Germans carried the legions' winter quarters by storm and even aspired to the Gallic provinces. Finally they were repulsed, and they have in recent years gratified us with more triumphs than victories.

38   Now I must speak of the Suebi, who do not comprise only one tribe, as with the Chatti and the Tencteri. Rather they occupy the greater part of Germany, and are still distinguished by special national names, though styled in general Suebi. One mark of the race is to comb the hair back over the side of the face and tie it low in a knot behind. This distinguishes the Suebi from other Germans, and the free–born of the Suebi from the slave. In other tribes, whether from some relationship to the Suebi or, as often happens, from imitation, the same thing may be found, but it is rare and confined to the period of youth. Among the Suebi, even till the hair is grey they twist the rough locks backward, and often knot them on the very crown. The chieftains wear theirs somewhat more ornamentally, and are to this extent interested in appearances, but innocently so. It is not for making love or being made love to, but rather that men who are to face battle are—in the eyes of their foes—more terrifying with these adornments heightening their stature.

39   The Semnones are described as the most ancient and best–born tribe of the Suebi; this is confirmed by religious rite. At fixed seasons all the tribes of the same blood gather with their delegations at a certain forest that is hallowed by visions beheld by their ancestors and by the awe of the ages. After publicly offering up a human life, they celebrate the grim "initiation" of their barbarous worship. There is a further tribute which they pay to the grove; no one enters it until he has been bound with a chain. He puts off his freedom, and advertises in his person the might of the deity. If he chances to fall, he must not be lifted up or rise—he must writhe along the ground until he is out again. The whole superstition comes to this, that it was here where the race arose, here where dwells the god who is lord of all things; everything else is subject to him. The prosperity of the Semnones enforces the idea; they occupy one hundred cantons, and their magnitude leads them to consider themselves the head of the Suebi.

40   The Langobardi, conversely, are distinguished by lack of number. Set in the midst of numberless and powerful tribes, they find safety not in submissiveness, but in peril and pitched battle. Then come the Reudigni and the Aviones, and the Anglii and the Varini, the Eudoses and Suardones and Nuithones. These tribes are protected by forests and rivers. There is nothing noteworthy about them individually, except that they worship in common Nerthus, or Mother Earth, and conceive her as intervening in human affairs, and riding in procession through the cities of men. In an island of the ocean is a holy grove, and in it a consecrated chariot, covered with robes. A single priest is permitted to touch it; he interprets the presence of the goddess in her shrine, and follows with deep

reverence as she rides away, drawn by cows. Then come days of rejoicing, and all places keep holiday, as many as she thinks worthy to receive and entertain her. They make no war, take no arms. Every weapon is put away; peace and quiet rules until the same priest returns the goddess to her temple, when she has had her fill of the society of mortals. After this the chariot and the robes, and, if you are willing to credit it, the deity in person, are washed in a sequestered lake. Slaves perform this duty and are then straightaway swallowed by the same lake. Hence a mysterious terror and ignorance full of piety as to what it may be which men only behold to die.

41   These sections on the Suebi extend into the more secluded parts of Germany. Nearer to us—to follow the course of the Danube, as before I followed the Rhine—comes the state of the Hermunduri. They are loyal to Rome, and with them alone among Germans business is transacted not on the river bank, but far within the frontier in the most thriving colony of the province of Rhaetia. They cross the river everywhere without supervision, and while we let other peoples see only our fortified camps, to them we have thrown open our houses and homes because they do not covet them. Among the Hermunduri rises the River Albis—a river once famous, now a name only.

42   Next to the Hermunduri are the Naristi and then the Marcomani and the Quadi. The fame and strength of the Marcomani are outstanding; their very home was won by their bravery, through the expulsion in ancient times of the Boii. Nor are the Naristi and Quadi inferior to them. These tribes are, so to speak, the brow of Germany, so far as Germany is wreathed by the Danube. The Marcomani and the Quadi retained kings of their own race down to our time—the noble houses of Maroboduus and Tudrus. Now they submit to foreign kings also, but the force and power of their kings rest on the influence of Rome. Occasionally they are assisted by our armed intervention: more often by subsidies, out of which they get as much help.

43   Behind them are the Marsigni, Cotini, Osi, and Buri, enclosing the Marcomani and Quadi from the rear. Among these the Marsigni and Buri in language and culture recall the Suebi. As for the Cotini and Osi, the Gallic tongue of the first and the Pannonian of the second prove not to be Germans; so does their submission to tribute. This tribute is imposed upon them as foreigners in part by the Sarmatae, in part by the Quadi. The Cotini, to their shame, even have iron–mines to work. All these peoples have little level land, but occupy the summits and ridges of mountains. In fact, a continuous range parts and cuts Suebia in two.

Beyond the range are many races. The most widely diffused name is that of the Lugii, which extends over several states. It will be sufficient to have named the strongest: Harii, Helvecones, Manimi, Elisii, Nahanarvali. Among the Nahanarvali one is shown a grove, the seat of a prehistoric ritual. A priest presides in female dress; but according to the Roman interpretation the gods recorded in this fashion are Castor and Pollux. That at least is the spirit of the godhead here recognised, whose name is the Alci. No images are in use; there is no sign of foreign superstition. Nevertheless they worship these deities as brothers and as youths.

But to return. The Harii, apart from the strength in which they surpass the peoples just enumerated, are fierce in nature, and augment this natural ferocity by the help of art and season. They blacken their shields and dye their bodies; they choose pitchy nights for their battles; by sheer panic and darkness they strike terror like an army of ghosts. No enemy can face this novel and, as it were, phantasmagorial vision. In every battle, after all, the eye is conquered first.

Beyond the Lugii is the monarchy of the Gotones. The hand upon the reins closes somewhat tighter here than among the other tribes of Germans, but not so tight yet as to destroy freedom. Then immediately following them and on the ocean are the Rugii and the Lemovii. The distinguishing features of all these tribes are round shields, short swords, and a submissive bearing before their kings.

44　Beyond these tribes the states of the Suiones, on the ocean, possess not merely arms and mens but powerful fleets. The style of their ships differs in this respect: there is a prow at each end, with a beak ready to be driven forwards. They neither work a ship with sails, nor add oars in banks to the side; the gearing of the oars is detached as on certain rivers, and reversible as occasion demands for movement in either direction.

Among these peoples respect is paid to wealth, and one man is accordingly supreme, with no restrictions and with an unchallenged right to obedience. Nor is there any general carrying of arms here, as among the other Germans. Rather they are locked up in charge of a custodian, who is a slave. The ocean forbids sudden inroads from enemies; and, besides, bands of armed men, with nothing to do, easily become riotous: it is not in the king's interest to put a noble or a freeman or even a freedman in charge of the arms.

45　Beyond the Suiones is another sea, sluggish and almost motionless, with which the earth is girdled and bounded. Evidence for this is furnished by the brilliance of the last rays of the sun, which remain so bright from his setting to his rising again as to dim the stars. Faith adds further that the sound of the sun's emergence is audible and the forms of his horses visible, with the spikes of his crown.

So far (and here rumour speaks the truth), and so far only, does Nature reach.

We must now turn to the right-hand shore of the Suebic Sea. Here it washes the tribes of the Aestii; there customs and dress are Suebic, but their language is nearer British.

They worship the mother of the gods. As an emblem of that superstition they wear the figures of wild boars; this boar takes the place of arms or of any other protection, and guarantees to the votary of the goddess a mind at rest even in the midst of foes. They use swords rarely, clubs frequently. Grain and other products of the earth they cultivate with a patience out of keeping with the lethargy customary to Germans. They ransack the sea also, and are the only people who gather in the shallows and on the shore itself amber, which they call in their tongue "glaesum."

Nor have they, being barbarians, inquired or learned what substance or process produces it. It lay there long among the rest of the flotsam and jetsam of the sea, until Roman luxury gave it a name. To the natives it is useless. It is gathered crude and is forwarded to Rome unshaped; the barbarians are astonished to be paid for it. Yet you may infer that it is the gum of trees; certain creeping and even winged creatures are continually found embedded in it. They have been entangled in its liquid form, and, as the material hardens, are imprisoned. I should suppose therefore that just as in the secluded places in the East, where frankincense and balsam are exuded, so in the islands and lands of the West there are groves and glades more than ordinarily luxuriant. These are tapped and liquified by the rays of the sun as it approached, and ooze into the nearest sea, whence by the force of tempests they are stranded on the shores opposite. If you try the qualities of amber by setting fire to it, it kindles like a torch, feeds an oily and odorous flame, and soon dissolves into something like pitch and resin.

Adjacent to the Suiones come the tribes of the Sitones, resembling them in all other respects, and differing only in this, that among them the woman rules. To this extent they have fallen lower not merely than freeman but even than slaves.

46　Here Suebia ends. As for the tribes of the Peucini, Venedi, and Fenni, I am in doubt whether to count them as Germans or Sarmatians. Though the Peucini, whom some men call Bastarnae, in language, culture, fixity of habitation, and house-building, conduct themselves as Germans, all are dirty and lethargic. The faces of the chiefs, too, owing to intermarriage, wear to some extent the degraded aspect of Sarmatians while the Venedi have contracted many Sarmatian habits; they are caterans, infesting all the hills and forests which lie between the Peucini and the Fenni.

And yet these peoples are preferably entered as Germans, since they have fixed abodes, and carry shields, and delight to use their feet and to run fast, all of which are traits opposite to those of the Sarmatians, who live in wagons and on horseback.

The Fenni live in astonishing barbarism and disgusting misery: no arms, no horses, no fixed homes; herbs for their food, skins for their clothing, earth for their bed. Arrows are all their wealth and for want of iron they tip them with bone. This same hunting is the support of the women as well as of the men, for they accompany the men freely and claim a share of the spoil. Nor have their infants any shelter against wild beasts and rain, except the covering afforded by a few intertwined branches. To these the hunters return: these are the refuse of age; and yet the people think it happier so than to groan over field labour, be encumbered with house–service, and be for ever exchanging their own and their neighbours' goods with alternate hopes and fears. Unconcerned towards men, unconcerned towards Heaven, they have achieved a consummation very difficult: they have nothing even to ask for.

Beyond this all else that is reported is legendary: that the Hellusii and Oxiones have human faces and features, the limbs and bodies of beasts. It has not been so ascertained, and I shall leave it an open question.

Jordanes

History of the Goths

Jordanes was a sixth century Goth or Alan who had been bishop of Kronton and who spent part of his later life in Constantinople. His History of the Goths *is largely a summary of Cassidorus' now lost work of the same name. It combines genuine Gothic oral traditions into the traditional framework of classical ethnography to present the Goths within the broader perspective of Roman and Christian history.*

Source: Charles C. Mierow, tr. *The Gothic History of Jordanes* (Princeton: 1915).

The United Goths

IV Now from this island of Scandza, as from a hive of races of a womb of nations, the Goths are said to have come forth long ago under their king, Berig by name. As soon as they disembarked from their ships and set foot on the land, they straightway gave their name to the place. And even to-day it is said to be called Gothiscandza. Soon they moved from here to the abodes of the Ulmerugi, who then dwelt on the shores of Ocean, where they pitched camp, joined battle with them and drove them from their homes. Then they subdued their neighbours, the Vandals, and thus added to their victories. But when the number of the people increased greatly and Filimer, son of Gadaric, reigned as king— about the fifth since Berig—he decided that the army of the Goths with their families should move from that region. In search of suitable homes and pleasant places they came to the land of Scythia, called *Oium* in that tongue. Here they were delighted with the great richness of the country, and it is said that when half the army had been brought over, the bridge whereby they had crossed the river fell in utter ruin, nor could anyone thereafter pass to or fro. For the place is said to be surrounded by quaking bogs and an encircling abyss, so that by this double obstacle nature has made it inaccessible. And even to-day one may hear in that neighborhood the lowing of cattle and may find traces of men, if we are to believe the stories of travellers, although we must grant that they hear these things from afar.

This part of the Goths, which is said to have crossed the river and entered with Filimer into the country of Oium, came into possession of the desired land, and there they soon came upon the race of the Spali, joined battle with them and won the victory. Thence the victors hastened to the farthest part of Scythia, which is near the sea of Pontus; for so the story is generally told in their early songs, in almost historic fashion. Ablabius also, a famous chronicler of the Gothic race, confirms this in his most trustworthy account. Some of the ancient writers also agree with the tale. Among these we may mention Josephus, a most reliable relator of annals, who everywhere follows the truth and unravels from the beginning the origin of things;—but why he has omitted the beginnings of the race of the Goths, of which I have spoken, I do not know. He barely mentions Magog of that stock, and says they were Scythians by race and were called so by name.

Before we enter on our history, we must describe the boundaries of this land, as it lies.

V Now Scythia borders on the land of Germany as far as the source of the river Ister and the expanse of the Morsian Swamp. It reaches even to the rivers Tyra, Danaster and Vagosola, and the great Danaper, extending to the Taurus range—not the mountains in

Asia but our own, that is, the Scythian Taurus—all the way to Lake Maeotis. Beyond Lake Maeotis it spreads on the other side of the straits of Bosphorus to the Caucasus Mountains and the river Araxes. Then it bends back to the left behind the Caspian Sea, which comes from the northeastern ocean in the most distant parts of Asia, and so is formed like a mushroom, at first narrow and then broad and round in shape. It extends as far as the Huns, Albani and Seres. This land, I say—namely, Scythia, stretching far and spreading wide—has on the east the Seres, a race that dwelt at the very beginning of their history on the shore of the Caspian Sea. On the west are the Germans and the river Vistula; on the arctic side, namely the north, it is surrounded by Ocean; on the south by Persis, Albania, Hiberia, Pontus and the farthest channel of the Ister, which is called the Danube all the way from the mouth to the source. But in that region where Scythia touches the Pontic coast it is dotted with towns of no mean fame:—Borysthenis, Olbia, Callipolis, Cherson, Theodosia, Careon, Myrmicion and Trapezus. These towns the wild Scythian tribes allowed the Greeks to build to afford them the means of trade. In the midst of Scythia is the place that separates Asia and Europe, I mean the Rhipaeian mountains, from which the mighty Tanais flows. This river enters Maeotis, a marsh having circuit of one hundred and four miles and never subsiding to a depth of less than eight cubits.

In the land of Scythia to the westward dwells, first of all, the race of the Gepidae, surrounded by great and famous rivers. For the Tisia flows through it on the north and northwest, and on the southwest is the great Danube. On the east it is cut by the Flutausis, a swiftly eddying stream that sweeps whirling into the Ister's waters. Within these rivers lies Dacia, encircled by the lofty Alps as by a crown. Near their left ridge, which inclines toward the north, and beginning at the source of the Vistula, the populous race of the Venethi dwell, occupying a great expanse of land. Though their names are now dispersed amid various clans and places, yet they are chiefly called Sclaveni and Antes. The abode of the Sclaveni extends from the city of Noviodunum and the lake called Mursianus to the Danaster, and northward as far as the Vistula. They have swamps and forests for their cities. The Antes, who are the bravest of these peoples dwelling in the curve of the sea of Pontus, spread from the Danaster to the Danaper, rivers that are many days' journey apart. But on the shore of Ocean, where the floods of the river Vistula empty from three mouths, the Vidivarii dwell, a people gathered out of various tribes. Beyond them the Aesti, a subject race, likewise hold the shore of Ocean. To the south dwell the Acatziri, a very brave tribe ignorant of agriculture, who subsist on their flocks and by hunting. Farther away and above the Sea of Pontus are the abodes of the Bulgares, well known from the disasters our neglect has brought upon us. From this region the Huns, like a fruitful root of bravest races, sprouted into two hordes of people. Some of these are called Altziagiri, others Sabiri; and they have different dwelling places. The Altziagiri are near Cherson, where the avaricious traders bring in the goods of Asia. In summer they range the plains, their broad domains, wherever the pasturage for their cattle invites them, and betake themselves in winter beyond the sea of Pontus. Now the Hunuguri are known to us from the fact that they trade in marten skins. But they have been cowed by their bolder neighbors.

We read that in their first abode the Goths dwelt in the land of Scythia near Lake Maeotis; in their second in Moesia, Thrace and Dacia, and in their third they dwelt again in Scythia, above the sea of Pontus. Nor do we find anywhere in their written records legends which tell of their subjection to slavery in Britain or in some other island, or of their redemption by a certain man at the cost of a single horse. Of course if anyone in our city says that the Goths had an origin different from that I have related, let him object. For myself, I prefer to believe what I have read, rather than put trust in old wives' tales.

To return, then, to my subject. The aforesaid race of which I speak is known to have had Filimer as king while they remained in their first home in Scythia near Maeotis. In their second home, that is, in the countries of Dacia, Thrace and Moesia, Zalmoxes reigned, whom many annals mention as a man of remarkable learning in philosophy. Yet even before this they had a learned man Zeuta, and after him Dicineus; and the third was Zalmoxes of whom I have made mention above. Nor did they lack teachers of wisdom.

Wherefore the Goths have ever been wiser than other barbarians and were nearly like the Greeks, as Dio relates, who wrote their history and annals with a Greek pen. He says that those of noble birth among them, from whom their kings and priests were appointed, were called first Tarabostesei and then Pilleati. Moreover so highly were the Getae praised that Mars, whom the fables of poets call the god of war, was reputed to have been born among them. Hence Vergil says:

"Father Gradivus rules the Getic fields."

Now Mars has always been worshipped by the Goths with cruel rites, and captives were slain as his victims. They thought that he who is lord of war ought to be appeased by the shedding of human blood. To him they devoted the first share of the spoil, and in his honor arms stripped from the foe were suspended from trees. And they had more than all other races a deep spirit of religion, since the worship of this god seemed to be really bestowed upon their ancestor.

In their third dwelling place, which was above the Sea of Pontus, they had now become more civilized and, as I have said before, were more learned. Then the people were divided under ruling families. The Visigoths served the family of the Balthi and the Ostrogoths served the renowned Amali. They were the first race of men to string the bow with cords, as Lucan, who is more of a historian than a poet, affirms:

"They string Armenian bows with Getic cords."

In earliest times they sang of the deeds of their ancestors in strains of song accompanied by the cithara; chanting of Eterpamara, Hanala, Fritigern, Vidigoia and others whose fame among them is great; such heroes as admiring antiquity scarce proclaims its own to be. Then, as the story goes, Vesosis waged a war disastrous to himself against the Scythians, whom ancient tradition asserts to have been the husbands of the Amazons. Concerning these female warriors Orosius speaks in convincing language. Thus we can clearly prove that Vesosis then fought with the Goths, since we know surely that he waged war with the husbands of the Amazons. They dwelt at that time along a bend of Lake Maeotis, from the river Borysthenes, which the natives call the Danaper, to the stream of the Tanais. By the Tanais I mean the river which flows down from the Rhipaeian mountains and rushes with so swift a current that when the neighboring streams or Lake Maeotis and the Bosphorus are frozen fast, it is the only river that is kept warm by the rugged mountains and is never solidified by the Scythian cold. It is also famous as the boundary of Asia and Europe. For the other Tanais is the one which rises in the mountains of the Chrinni and flows into the Caspian Sea. The Danaper begins in a great marsh and issues from it as from its mother. It is sweet and fit to drink as far as half-way down its course. It also produces fish of a fine flavour and without bones, having only cartilage as the frame-work of their bodies. But as it approaches the Pontus it receives a little stream called Exampaeus, so very bitter that although the river is navigable for the length of a forty days' voyage, it is so altered by the water of this scanty stream as to become tainted and unlike itself, and flows thus tainted into the sea between the Greek towns of Callipidae and Hypanis. At its mouth there is an island named Achilles. Between these two rivers is a vast land filled with forests and treacherous swamps.

VI This was the region where the Goths dwelt when Vesosis, king of the Egyptians, made war upon them. Their king at that time was Tanausis. In a battle at the river Phasis (whence come the birds called pheasants, which are found in abundance at the banquets of the great all over the world) Tanausis, king of the Goths, met Vesosis, king of the Egyptians, and there inflicted a severe defeat upon him, pursuing him even to Egypt. Had he not been restrained by the waters of the impassable Nile and the fortifications which Vesosis had long ago ordered to be made against the raids of the Ethiopians, he would have slain him in his own land. But finding he had no power to injure him there, he returned and conquered almost all Asia and made it subject and tributary to Sornus, king of the Medes, who was then his dear friend. At that time some of his victorious army, seeing that the subdued provinces were rich and fruitful, deserted their companies and of their own accord remained in various parts of Asia. From their name or race Pompeius

Trogus says the stock of the Parthians had its origin. Hence even to-day in the Scythian tongue they are called Parthi, that is, Deserters. And in consequence of their descent they are archers—almost alone among the nations of Asia—and are very valiant warriors. Now in regard to the name, though I have said they were called Parthi because they were deserters, some have traced the derivation of the word otherwise, saying that they were called Parthi because they fled from their kinsmen. Now when this Tanausis, king of the Goths, was dead, his people worshipped him as one of their gods.

VII After his death, while the army under his successors was engaged in an expedition in other parts, a neighboring tribe attempted to carry off women of the Goths as booty. But they made a brave resistace, as they had been taught to do by their husbands, and routed in disgrace the enemy who had come upon them. When they had won this victory, they were inspired with greater daring. Mutually encouraging each other, they took up arms and chose two of the bolder, Lampeto and Marpesia, to act as their leaders. While they were in command, they cast lots both for the defense of their own country and the devastation of other lands. So Lampeto remained to guard their native land and Marpesia took a company of women and led this novel army into Asia. After conquering various tribes in war and making others their allies by treaties, she came to the Caucasus. There she remained for some time and gave the place the name Rock of Marpesia, of which also Vergil makes mention:
"Like to hard flint or the Marpesian Cliff."
It was here Alexander the Great afterwards built gates and named them the Caspian Gates, which now the tribe of the Lazi guard as a Roman outpost. Here, then, the Amazons remained for some time and were much strengthened. Then they departed and crossed the river Halys, which flows near the city of Gangra, and with equal success subdued Armenia, Syria, Cilicia, Galatia, Pisidia and all the places of Asia. Then they turned to Ionia and Aeolia, and made provinces of them after their surrender. Here they ruled for some time and even founded cities and camps bearing their name. At Ephesus also they built a very costly and beautiful temple for Diana, because of her delight in archery and the chase—arts to which they were themselves devoted. Then these Scythian-born women, who had by such a chance gained control over the kingdoms of Asia, held them for almost a hundred years, and at last came back to their own kinsfolk in the Marpesian rocks I have mentioned above, namely in the Caucasus mountains....

VIII Fearing their race would fail, they sought marriage with neighboring tribes. They appointed a day for meeting once in every year, so that when they should return to the same place on that day in the following year each mother might give over to the father whatever male child she had borne, but should herself keep and train for warfare whatever children of the female sex were born. Or else, as some maintain, they exposed the males, destroying the life of the ill-fated child with a hate like that of a stepmother. Among them childbearing was detested, though everywhere else it is desired. The terror of their cruelty was increased by common rumour; for what hope, pray, would there be for a captive, when it was considered wrong to spare even a son? Hercules, they say fought against them and overcame Menalippe, yet more by guile than by valour. Theseus, moreover, took Hippolyte captive, and of her he begat Hippolytus. And in later times the Amazons had a queen named Penthesilea, famed in the tales of the Trojan war. These women are said to have kept their power even to the time of Alexander the Great.

IX But say not "Why does a story which deals with the men of the Goths have so much to say of their women?" Hear, then, the tale of the famous and glorious valour of the men. Now Dio, the historian and diligent investigator of ancient times, who gave to his work the title "Getica" (and the Getae we have proved in a previous passage to be Goths, on the testimony of Orosius Paulus)—this Dio, I say, makes mention of a later king of theirs named Telefus. Let no one say that this name is quite foreign to the Gothic tongue, and let no one who is ignorant cavil at the fact that the tribes of men make use of many names, even as the Romans borrow from the Macedonians, the Greeks from the Romans, the Sarmatians from the Germans, and the Goths frequently from the Huns. This Telefus, then, a son of Hercules by Auge, and the husband of a sister of Priam, was of towering stature and terrible strength. He matched his father's valour by virtues of his own and also recalled the traits of Hercules by his likeness in appearance. Our ancestors called his kingdom Moesia. This province has on the east the mouths of the Danube, on the south Macedonia, on the west Histria and on the north the Danube. Now this king we have mentioned carried on wars with the Greeks, and in their course he slew in battle Thesander, the leader of Greece. But while he was making a hostile attack upon Ajax and was pursuing Ulysses, his horse became entangled in some vines and fell. He himself was thrown and wounded in the thigh by a javelin of Achilles, so that for a long time he could not be healed. Yet, despite his wound, he drove the Greeks from his land. Now when Telefus died, his son Eurypylus succeeded to the throne, being a son of the sister of Priam, king of the Phrygians. For love of Cassandra he sought to take part in the Trojan war, that he might come to the help of her parents and his own father-in-law; but soon after his arrival he was killed....

XI Then when Buruista was king of the Goths, Dicineus came to Gothia at the time when Sulla ruled the Romans. Buruista received Dicineus and gave him almost royal power. It was by his advice that the Goths ravaged the lands of the Germans, which the Franks now possess. Then came Caesar, the first of all the Romans to assume imperial power and to subdue almost the whole world, who conquered all kingdoms and even seized islands lying beyond our world, reposing in the bosom of Ocean. He made tributary to the Romans those that knew not the Roman name even by hearsay, and yet was unable to prevail against the Goths, despite his frequent attempts. Soon Gaius Tiberius reigned as third emperor of the Romans, and yet the Goths continued in their kingdom unharmed. Their safety, their advantage, their one hope lay in this, that whatever their counsellor Dicineus advised should by all means be done; and they judged it expedient that they should labour for its accomplishment. And when he saw that their minds were obedient to him in all things and that they had natural ability, he taught them almost the whole of philosophy, for he was a skilled master of this subject. Thus by teaching them ethics he restrained their barbarous customs; by imparting a knowledge of physics he made them live naturally under laws of their own, which they possess in written form to this day and call *belagines*. He taught them logic and made them skilled in reasoning beyond all other races; he showed them practical knowledge and so persuaded them to abound in good works. By demonstrating theoretical knowledge he urged them to contemplate the courses of the twelve signs and the planets passing through them, and the whole of astronomy. He told them how the disc of the moon gains increase or suffers loss, and showed them how much the fiery globe of the sun exceeds in size our earthly planet. He explained the names of the three hundred and forty-six stars and told through what signs in the arching vault of the heavens they glide swiftly from their rising to their setting. Think, I pray you, what pleasure it was for these brave men, when for a little space they had leisure from warfare, to be instructed in the teachings of philosophy! You might have seen one scanning the position of the heavens and another investigating the nature of plants and bushes. Here stood one who studied the waxing and waning of the moon, while still another regarded the labors of the sun and observed how these bodies which were hastening to go toward the east are whirled around and borne back to the west by the rotation of the heavens. When they had learned the reason, they were at rest. These and various other matters Dicineus taught the Goths in his wisdom and gained marvellous repute among them, so that he ruled not only the common men but their kings. He chose from among them those that were at that time of noblest birth and superior wisdom and taught them theology, bidding them worship certain divinities and holy places. He gave the name of Pilleati to the priests he ordained, I suppose because they offered sacrifice having their heads covered with tiaras, which we otherwise call *pillei*. But he bade them call the rest of their race Capillati. This name the Goths accepted and prized highly, and they retain it to this day in their songs.

After the death of Dicineus, they held Comosicus in almost equal honor, because he was not inferior in knowledge. By reason of his wisdom he was accounted their priest and king, and he judged the people with the greatest uprightness.

XII When he too had departed from human affairs, Coryllus ascended the throne as king of the Goths and for forty years ruled his people in Dacia. I mean ancient Dacia, which the race of the Gepidae now possesses. This country lies across the Danube within sight of Moesia, and is surrounded by a crown of mountains. It has only two ways of access, one by way of Boutae and the other by Tapae. This Gothia, which our ancestors called Dacia and now, as I have said, is called Gepidia, was then bounded on the east by the Roxolani, on the west by the Iazygres, on the north by the Sarmatians and Basternae and on the south by the river Danube. The Iazyges are separated from the Roxolani by the Aluta river only.

And since mention has been made of the Danube, I think it not out of place to make brief notice of so excellent a stream. Rising in the fields of the Alamanni, it receives sixty streams which flow into it here and there in the twelve hundred miles from its source to its mouths in the Pontus, resembling a spine interwoven with ribs like a basket. It is indeed a most vast river. In the language of the Bessi it is called the Hister, and it has profound waters in its channel to a depth of quite two hundred feet. This stream surpasses in size all other rivers, except the Nile. Let this much suffice for the Danube. But let us now with the Lord's help return to the subject from which we have digressed.

XIII Now after a long time, in the reign of the Emperor Domitian, the Goths, through fear of his avarice, broke the truce they had long observed under other emperors. They laid waste the bank of the Danube, so long held by the Roman Empire, and slew the soldiers and their generals. Oppius Sabinus was then governor of that province, after Agrippa, while Dorpaneus held command over the Goths. Thereupon the Goths made war and conquered the Romans, cut off the head of Oppius Sabinus and invaded and boldly plundered many castles and cities belonging to the Emperor. In this plight of his countrymen Domitian hastened with all his might to Illyricum, bringing with him the troops of almost the entire empire. He sent Fuscus before him as his general with picked soldiers. Then joining boats together like a bridge, he made his soldiers cross the river Danube above the army of Dorpaneus. But the Goths were on the alert. They took up arms and presently overwhelmed the Romans in the first encounter. They slew Fuscus, the commander, and plundered the soldiers' camp of its treasure. And because of the great victory they had won in this region, they thereafter called their leaders, by whose good fortune they seemed to have conquered, not mere men, but demigods, that is *Ansis*. Their genealogy I shall run through briefly, telling the lineage of each and the beginning and the end of this line. And do thou, O reader, hear me without repining; for I speak truly.

XIV Now the first of these heroes, as they themselves relate in their legends, was Gapt, who begat Hulmul. And Hulmul begat Augis; and Augis begat him who was called Amal, from whom the name of Amali comes. This Amal begat Hisarnis. Hisarnis moreover begat Ostrogotha, and Ostrogotha begat Hunuil, and Hunuil likewise begat Athal. Athal begat Achiulf and Oduulf. Now Achiulf begat Ansila and Ediulf, Vultuulf and Hermanaric. And Vultuulf begat Valaravans and Valaravans begat Vandalarius; Vandalarius begat Thiudimer and Valamir and Vidimer; and Thiudimer begat Theodoric. Theodoric begat Amalasuentha; Amalasuentha bore Athalatic and Mathesuentha to her husband Eutharic, whose race was thus joined to hers in kinship. For the aforesaid Hermanaric, the son of Achiulf, begat Hunimund, and Hunimund begat Thorismud. Now Thorismud begat Beremud, Beremud begat Veteric, and Veteric likewise begat Eutharic, who married Amalasuentha and begat Athalaric and Mathesuentha. Athalaric died in the years of his childhood, and Mathesuentha married Vitiges, to whom she bore no child. Both of them were taken together by Belisarius to Constantinople. When Vitiges passed from human affairs, Germanus the patrician, a nephew of the Emperor Justinian, took Mathesuentha in marriage and made her a Patrician Ordinary. And of her he begat a son, also called Germanus. But upon the death of Germanus, she determined to remain a widow. Now how and in what wise the kingdom of the Amali was overthrown we shall keep to tell in its proper place, if the Lord help us....

... ...

XVII From this city [Marcianople], as we were saying, the Getae returned after a long siege to their own land, enriched by the ransom they had received. Now the race of the Gepidae was moved with envy when they saw them laden with booty and so suddenly victorious everywhere, and made war on their kinsmen. Should you ask how the Getae and Gepidae are kinsmen, I can tell you in a few words. You surely remember that in the beginning I said the Goths went forth from the bosom of the island of Scandza with Berig, their king, sailing in only three ships toward the hither shore of Ocean, namely to Gothiscandza. One of these three ships proved to be slower than the others, as is usually the case, and thus is said to have given the tribe their name, for in their language *gepanta* means slow. Hence it came to pass that gradually and by corruption the name Gepidae was coined for them by way of reproach. For undoubtedly they too trace their origin from the stock of the Goths, but because, as I have said, *gepanta* means something slow and stolid, the word Gepidae arose as a gratuitous name of reproach. I do not believe this is very far wrong, for they are slow of thought and too sluggish for quick movement of their bodies.

These Gepidae were then smitten by envy while they dwelt in the province of Spesis on an island surrounded by the shallow waters of the Vistula. This island they called, in the speech of their fathers, Gepedoios; but it is now inhabited by the race of the Vividarii, since the Gepidae themselves have moved to better lands. The Vividarii are gathered from various races into this one asylum, if I may call it so, and thus they form a nation. So then, as we were saying, Fastida, king of the Gepidae, stirred up his quiet people to enlarge their boundaries by war. He overwhelmed the Burgundians, almost annihilating them, and conquered a number of other races also. He unjustly provoked the Goths, being the first to break the bonds of kinship by unseemly strife. He was greatly puffed up with vain glory, but in seeking to acquire new lands for his growing nation, he only reduced the numbers of his own countrymen. For he sent ambassadors to Ostrogotha, to whose rule Ostrogoths and Visigoths alike, that is, the two peoples of the same tribe, were still subject. Complaining that he was hemmed in by rugged mountains and dense forests, he demanded one of two things, that Ostrogotha should either prepare for war or give up part of his lands to them. Then Ostrogotha, king of the Goths, who was a man of firm mind, answered the ambassadors that he did indeed dread such a war and that it would be a grievous and infamous thing to join battle with their kin—but he would not give up his lands. And why say more? The Gepidae hastened to take arms and Ostrogotha likewise moved his forces against them, lest he should seem a coward. They met at the town of Galtis, near which the river Auha flows, and there both sides fought with great valour; indeed the similarity of their arms and of their manner of fighting turned them against their own men. But the better cause and their natural alertness aided the Goths. Finally night put an end to the battle as a part of the Gepidae were giving way. Then Fastida, king of the Gepidae, left the field of slaughter and hastened to his own land, as much humiliated with shame and disgrace as formerly he had been elated with pride. The Goths returned victorious, content with the retreat of the Gepidae, and dwelt in peace and happiness in their own land as long as Ostrogotha was their leader.

XVIII After his death, Cniva divided the army into two parts and sent some to waste Moesia, knowing that it was undefended through the neglect of the emperors. He himself with seventy thousand men hastened to Euscia, that is, Novae. When driven from this place by the general Gallus, he approached Nicopolis, a very famous town situated near the Iatrus river. This city Trajan built when he conquered the Sarmatians and named it the City of Victory. When the Emperor Decius drew near, Cniva at last withdrew to the regions of Haemus, which were not far distant. Thence he hastened to Philippopolis, with his forces in good array. When the Emperor Decius learned of his departure, he was eager to bring relief to his own city and, crossing Mount Haemus, came to Beroa. While he was resting his horses and his weary army in that place, all at once Cniva and his Goths fell upon him like a thunderbolt. He cut the Roman army to pieces and drove the Emperor, with a few who had succeeded in escaping, across the Alps again to Euscia in Moesia, where Gallus was then stationed with a large force of soldiers as guardian of the frontier. Collecting an army from this region as well as from Oescus, he prepared for the conflict of the coming war. But Cniva took Philippopolis after a long siege and then, laden with spoil, allied himself to Priscus, the commander in the city, to fight against Decius. In the battle that followed they quickly pierced the son of Decius with an arrow and cruelly slew him. His father saw it, and although he is said to have exclaimed, to cheer the hearts of his soldiers: "Let no one mourn; the death of one soldier is not a great loss to the republic," he was yet unable to endure it, because of his love for his son. So he rode against the foe, demanding either death or vengeance, and when he came back to Abrittus, a city of Moesia, he was himself cut off by the Goths and slain, thus making an end of his dominion and of his life. This place is to-day called the Altar of Decius, because he there offered strange sacrifices to idols before the battle.

XIX Then upon the death of Decius, Gallus and Volusianus succeeded to the Roman Empire. At this time a destructive plague, almost like death itself, such as we suffered nine years ago, blighted the face of the whole earth and especially devastated Alexandria and all the land of Egypt. The historian Dionysius gives a mournful account of it and Cyprian, our own bishop and venerable martyr in Christ, also describes it in his own book entitled "On Mortality." At this time the Goths frequently ravaged Moesia, through the neglect of the Emperors. When a certain Aemilianus saw that they were free to do this, and that they could not be dislodged by anyone without great cost to the republic, he thought that he too might be able to achieve fame and fortune. So he seized the rule in Moesia and, taking all the soldiers he could gather, began to plunder cities and people. In the next few months, while an armed host was being gathered against him, he wrought no small harm to the state. Yet he died almost at the beginning of his evil attempt, thus losing at once his life and the power he coveted. Now though Gallus and Volusianus, the Emperors we have mentioned, departed this life after remaining in power for barely two years, yet during this space of two years which they spent on earth they reigned amid universal peace and favour. Only one thing was laid to their charge, namely the great plague. But this was an accusation made by ignorant slanderers, whose custom it is to wound the lives of others with their malicious bite. Soon after they came to power they made a treaty with the race of the Goths. When both rulers were dead, it was no long time before Gallienus usurped the throne.

XX While he was given over to luxurious living of every sort, Respa, Veduc and Thuruar, leaders of the Goths, took ship and sailed across the strait of the Hellespont to Asia. There they laid waste many populous cities and set fire to the renowned temple of Diana at Ephesus, which, as we have said before, the Amazons built. Being driven from the neighborhood of Bithynia, they destroyed Chalcedon, which Cornelius Avitus afterwards restored to some extent. Yet even to-day, though it is happily situated near the royal city, it still shows some traces of its ruin as a witness to posterity. After their success, the Goths recrossed the strait of the Hellespont, laden with booty and spoil, and returned along the same route by which they had entered Asia, sacking Troy and Ilium on the way. These cities, which had scarce recovered a little from the famous war with Agamemnon, were thus destroyed anew by the hostile sword. After the Goths had thus devastated Asia, Thrace next felt their ferocity. For they went thither and presently attacked Anchiali, a city at the foot of Haemus and not far from the sea. Sardanapalus, king of the Parthians, had built this city long ago between an inlet of the sea and the base of Haemus. There they are said to have stayed for many days, enjoying the baths of the hot springs which are situated about twelve miles from the city of Anchiali. There they gush from the depths of their fiery source, and among the innumerable hot springs of the world they are particularly famous and efficacious to heal the sick.

XXI After these events, the Goths had already returned home when they were summoned at the request of the Emperor Maximian to aid the Romans against the Parthians. They fought for him faithfully, serving as auxiliaries. But after Caesar Maximian by their aid had routed Narseus, king of the Persians, the grandson of Sapor the Great, taking as spoil all his possessions, together with his wives and his sons, and when Diocletian had conquered Achilles in Alexandria and Maximianus Herculius had broken the Quinquegentiani in Africa, thus winning peace for the empire, they began rather to neglect the Goths.

Now it had been a hard matter for the Roman army to fight against any nations whatsoever without them. This is evident from the way in which the Goths were so frequently called upon. Thus they were summoned by Constantine to bear arms against his kinsman Licinius. Later, when he was vanquished and shut up in Thessalonica and deprived of his power, they slew him with the sword of Constantine the victor. In like manner it was the aid of the Goths that enabled him to build the famous city that is named after him, the rival of Rome, inasmuch as they entered into a truce with the Emperor and furnished him forty thousand men to aid him against various peoples. This body of men, namely, the Allies, and the service they rendered in war are still spoken of in the land to this day. Now at that time they prospered under the rule of their kings Ariaric and Aoric. Upon their death Geberich appeared as successor to the throne, a man renowned for his valour and noble birth.

XXII For he was the son of Hilderith, who was the son of Ovida, who was the son of Nidada; and by his illustrious deeds he equalled the glory of his race. Soon he sought to enlarge his country's narrow bounds at the expense of the race of the Vandals and Visimar, their king. This Visimar was of the stock of the Asdingi, which is eminent among them and indicates a most warlike descent, as Dexippus the historian relates. He states furthermore that by reason of the great extent of their country they could scarcely come from Ocean to our frontier in a year's time. At that time they dwelt in the land where the Gepidae now live, near the rivers Marisia, Miliare, Gilpil and the Grisia, which exceeds in size all previously mentioned. They then had on the east the Goths, on the west the Marcomanni, on the north the Hermunduli and on the south the Hister, which is also called the Danube. At the time when the Vandals were dwelling in this region, was begun against them by Geberich, king of the Goths, on the shore of the river Marisia which I have mentioned. Here the battle raged for a little while on equal terms. But soon Visimar himself, the king of the Vandals, was overthrown, together with the greater part of his people. When Geberich, the famous leader of the Goths, had conquered and spoiled the Vandals, he returned to his own place whence he had come. Then the remnant of the Vandals who had escaped, collecting a band of their unwarlike folk, left their ill-fated country and asked Emperor Constantine for Pannonia. Here they made their home for about sixty years and obeyed the commands of the emperors like subjects. A long time afterward they were summoned thence by Stilicho, Master of the Soldiery, Ex-Consul and Patrician, and took possession of Gaul. Here they plundered their neighbors and had no settled place of abode.

XXIII Soon Geberich, king of the Goths, departed from human affairs and Hermanaric, noblest of the Amali, succeeded to the throne. He subdued many warlike peoples of the north and made them obey his laws, and some of our ancestors have justly compared him to Alexander the Great. Among the tribes he conquered were the Golthescytha, Thiudos, Inaunxis, Vasinabroncae, Merens, Mordens. Imniscaris, Rogas, Tadzans, Athaul,

Navego, Bubegenae and Coldae. But though famous for his conquest of so many races, he gave himself no rest until he had slain some in battle and then reduced to his sway the remainder of the tribe of the Heruli, whose chief was Alaric. Now the aforesaid race, as the historian Ablabius tells us, dwelt near Lake Maeotis in swampy places which the Greeks call *hele*; hence they were named Heluri. They were a people swift of foot, and on that account were the more swollen with pride, for there was at that time no race that did not choose from them its light-armed troops for battle. But though their quickness often saved them from others who made war upon them, yet they were overthrown by the slowness and steadiness of the Goths; and the lot of fortune brought it to pass that they, as well as the other tribes, had to serve Hermanaric, king of the Getae. After the slaughter of the Heruli, Hermanaric also took arms against the Venethi. This people, though despised in war, was strong in numbers and tried to resist him. But a multitude of cowards is of no avail, particularly when God permits an armed multitude to attack them. These people, as we started to say at the beginning of our account or catalogue of nations, though offshoots from one stock, have now three names, that is, Venethi, Antes and Sclaveni. Though they now rage in war far and wide, in consequence of our neglect, yet at that time they were all obedient to Hermanaric's commands. This ruler also subdued by his wisdom and might the race of the Aesti, who dwell on the farthest shore of the German Ocean, and ruled all the nations of Scythia and Germany by his own prowess alone.

XXIV But after a short space of time, as Orosius relates, the race of the Huns, fiercer than ferocity itself, flamed forth against the Goths. We learn from old traditions that their origin was as follows: Filimer, king of the Goths, son of Gadaric the Great, who was the fifth in succession to hold the rule of the Getae after their departure from the island of Scandza—and who, as we have said, entered the land of Scythia with his tribe—found among his people certain witches, whom he called in his native tongue *Haliurunnae*. Suspecting these women, he expelled them from the midst of his race and compelled them to wander in solitary exile afar from his army. There the unclean spirits, who beheld them as they wandered through the wilderness, bestowed their embraces upon them and begat this savage race, which dwelt at first in the swamps, a stunted, foul and puny tribe, scarcely human and having no language save one which bore but slight resemblance to human speech. Such was the descent of the Huns who came to the country of the Goths.

This cruel tribe, as Priscus the historian relates, settled on the farther bank of the Maeotic swamp. They were fond of hunting and had no skill in any other art. After they had grown to a nation, they disturbed the peace of neighboring races by theft and rapine. At one time, while hunters of their tribe were as usual seeking for game on the farthest edge of Maeotis, they saw a doe unexpectedly appear to their sight and enter the swamp, acting as guide of the way; now advancing and again standing still. The hunters followed and crossed on foot the Maeotic swamp, which they had supposed was impassable as the sea. Presently the unknown land of Scythia disclosed itself and the doe disappeared. Now in my opinion the evil spirits, from whom the Huns are descended, did this from envy of the Scythians. And the Huns, who had been wholly ignorant that there was another world beyond Maeotis, were now filled with admiration for the Scythian land. As they were quick of mind, they believed that this path, utterly unknown to any age of the past, had been divinely revealed to them. They returned to their tribe, told them what had happened, praised Scythia and persuaded the people to hasten thither along the way they had found by the guidance of the doe. As many as they captured, when they thus entered Scythia for the first time, they sacrificed to Victory. The remainder they conquered and made subject to themselves. Like a whirlwind of nations they swept across the great swamp and at once fell upon the Alpidzuri, Alcildzuri, Itimari, Tuncarsi and Boisci, who bordered on that part of Scythia. The Alani also, who were their equals in battle, but unlike them in civilization, manners and appearance, they exhausted by their incessant attacks and subdued. For by the terror of their features they inspired great fear in those whom perhaps they did not really surpass in war. They made their foes flee in horror because their swarthy aspect was fearful, and they had, if I may call it so, a sort of shapeless lump, not a head, with pin-holes rather than eyes. Their hardihood is evident in their wild appearance, and they are beings who are cruel to their children on the very day they are born. For they cut the cheeks of the males with a sword, so that before they receive the nourishment of milk they must learn to endure wounds. Hence they grow old beardless and their young men are without comeliness, because a face furrowed by the sword spoils by its scars the natural beauty of a beard. They are short in stature, quick in bodily movement, alert horsemen, broad shouldered, ready in the use of bow and arrow, and have firm-set necks which are ever erect in pride. Though they live in the form of men, they have the cruelty of wild beasts.

When the Getae beheld this active race that had invaded many nations, they took fright and consulted with their king how they might escape from such a foe. Now although Hermanaric, king of the Goths, was the conqueror of many tribes, as we have said above, yet while he was deliberating on this invasion of the Huns, the treacherous tribe of the Rosomoni, who at that time were among those who owed him their homage, took this chance to catch him unawares. For when the king had given orders that a certain woman of the tribe I have mentioned, Sunilda by name, should be bound to wild horses and torn apart by driving them at full speed in opposite directions (for he was roused to fury by her husband's treachery to him), her brothers Sarus and Ammius came to avenge their sister's death and plunged a sword into Hermanaric's side. Enfeebled by this blow, he dragged out a miserable existence in bodily weakness. Balamber, king of the Huns, took advantage of his ill health to move an army into the country of the Ostrogoths, from whom the Visigoths had already separated because of some dispute. Meanwhile Hermanaric, who was unable to endure either the pain of his wound or the inroads of the Huns, died full of days at the great age of one hundred and ten years. The fact of his death enabled the Huns to prevail over those Goths who, as we have said, dwelt in the east and were called Ostrogoths.

The Divided Goths: Visigoths

XXV The Visigoths, who were their other allies and inhabitants of the western country, were terrified as their kinsmen had been, and knew not how to plan for their safety against the race of the Huns. After long deliberation by common consent they finally sent ambassadors into Romania to the Emperor Valens, brother of Valentinian, the elder Emperor, to say that if he would give them part of Thrace or Moesia to keep, they would submit themselves to his laws and commands. That he might have greater confidence in them, they promised to become Christians, if he would give them teachers who spoke their language. When Valens learned this, he gladly and promptly granted what he had himself intended to ask. He received the Getae into the region of Moesia and placed them there as a wall of defense for his kingdom against other tribes. And since at that time the Emperor Valens, who was infected with the Arian perfidy, had closed all the churches of our party, he sent as preachers to them those who favored his sect. They came and straightway filled a rude and ignorant people with the poison of their heresy. Thus the Emperor Valens made the Visigoths Arians rather than Christians. Moreover, from the love they bore them, they preached the gospel both to the Ostrogoths and to their kinsmen the Gepidae, teaching them to reverence the heresy, and they invited all people of their speech everywhere to attach themselves to this sect. They themselves, as we have said, crossed the Danube and settled Dacia Ripensis, Moesia and Thrace by permission of the Emperor.

XXVI Soon famine and want came upon them, as often happens with a people not yet well settled in a country. Their princes and the leaders who ruled them in place of kings, that is Fritigern, Alatheus and Safrac, began to lament the plight of their army and begged Lupicinus and Maximus, the Roman commanders, to open a market. But to what will not the "cursed lust for gold" compel men to assent? The generals, swayed by avarice, sold them at a high price not only the flesh of sheep and oxen, but even the carcasses of dogs and unclean animals, so that a slave would be bartered for a loaf of bread or ten pounds of meat. When their goods and chattels failed, the greedy trader demanded their sons in return for the necessities of life. And the parents consented even to this, in order to provide for the safety of their children, arguing that it was better to lose liberty than life; and indeed it is better that one be sold, if he will be mercifully fed, than that he should be kept free only to die.

Now it came to pass in that troublous time that Lupicinus, the Roman general, invited Fritigern, a chieftain of the Goths, to a feast and, as the event revealed, devised a plot against him. But Fritigern, thinking no evil, came to the feast with a few followers. While he was dining in the praetorium he heard the dying cries of his ill-fated men, for, by order of the general, his soldiers were slaying his companions who were shut up in another part of the house. The loud cries of the dying fell upon ears already suspicious, and Fritigern at once perceived the treacherous trick. He drew his sword and with great courage dashed quickly from the banqueting-hall, rescued his men from their threatening doom and incited them to slay the Romans. Thus these valiant men gained the chance they had longed for—to be free to die in battle rather than to perish of hunger—and immediately took arms to kill the generals Lupicinus and Maximus. Thus that day put an end to the famine of the Goths and the safety of the Romans, for the Goths no longer as strangers and pilgrims, but as citizens and lords, began to rule the inhabitants and to hold in their own right all the northern country as far as the Danube.

When the Emperor Valens heard of this at Antioch, he made ready an army at once and set out for the country of Thrace. Here a grievous battle took place and the Goths prevailed. The Emperor himself was wounded and fled to a farm near Hadrianople. The Goths, not knowing that an emperor lay hidden in so poor a hut, set fire to it (as is customary in dealing with a cruel foe), and thus he was cremated in royal splendour. Plainly it was a direct judgment of God that he should be burned with fire by the very men whom he had perfidiously led astray when they sought the true faith, turning them aside from the flame of love into the fire of hell. From this time the Visigoths, in consequence of their glorious victory, possessed Thrace and Dacia Ripensis as if it were their native land.

XXVII Now in the place of Valens, his uncle, the Emperor Gratian established Theodosius the Spaniard in the Eastern Empire. Military discipline was soon restored to a high level, and the Goths, perceiving that the cowardice and sloth of former princes had ended, became afraid. For the Emperor was famed alike for his acuteness and discretion. By stern commands and by generosity and kindness he encouraged a demoralized army to deeds of daring. But when the soldiers, who had obtained a better leader by the change, gained new confidence, they sought to attack the Goths and drive them from the borders of Thrace. But as Emperor Theodosius fell so sick at this time that his life was almost despaired of, the Goths were again inspired with courage. Dividing the Gothic army, Fritigern set out to plunder Thessaly, Epirus and Achaia, while Alatheus and Safrac with the rest of the troops made for Pannonia. Now the Emperor Gratian had at this time retreated from Rome to Gaul because of the invasions of the Vandals. When he learned that the Goths were acting with greater boldness because Theodosius was in despair of his life, he quickly gathered an army and came against them. Yet he put no trust in arms, but sought to conquer them by kindness and gifts. So he entered on a truce with them and made peace, giving them provisions.

XXVIII When the Emperor Theodosius afterwards recovered and learned that the Emperor Gratian had made a compact between the Goths and the Romans, as he had himself desired, he was very well pleased and gave his assent. He gave gifts to King Athanaric, who had succeeded Fritigern, made an alliance with him and in the most gracious manner invited him to visit him in Constantinople. Athanaric very gladly consented and as he entered the royal city exclaimed in wonder, "Lo, now I see what I have often heard of with unbelieving ears," meaning the great and famous city. Turning his eyes hither and thither, he marvelled as he beheld the situation of the city, the coming and going of the ships, the splendid walls, and the people of divers nations gathered like a flood of waters streaming from different regions into one basin. So too, when he saw the army in array, he said, "Truly the Emperor is a god on earth, and whoso raises a hand against him is guilty of his own blood." In the midst of his admiration and the enjoyment of even greater honors at the hand of the Emperor, he departed this life after the space of a few months. The Emperor had such affection for him that he honored Athanaric even more when he was dead than during his lifetime, for he not only gave him a worthy burial, but himself walked before the bier at the funeral. Now when Athanaric was dead, his whole army continued in the service of the Emperor Theodosius and submitted to the Roman rule, forming as it were one body with the imperial soldiery. The former service of the Allies under the Emperor Constantine was now renewed and they were again called Allies. And since the Emperor knew that they were faithful to him and his friends, he took from their number more than twenty thousand warriors to serve against the tyrant Eugenius who had slain Gratian and seized Gaul. After winning the victory over this usurper, he wreaked his vengeance upon him.

XXIX But after Theodosius, the lover of peace and of the Gothic race, had passed from human cares, his sons began to ruin both empires by their luxurious living and to deprive their Allies, that is to say the Goths, of the customary gifts. The contempt of the Goths for the Romans soon increased, and for fear their valour would be destroyed by long peace, they appointed Alaric king over them. He was of famous stock, and his nobility was second only to that of the Amali, for he came from the family of the Balthi, who because of their daring valour had long ago received among their race the name *Baltha*, that is, The Bold. Now when this Alaric was made king, he took counsel with his men and persuaded them to seek a kingdom by their own exertions rather than serve others in idleness. In the consulship of Stilicho and Aurelian he raised an army and entered Italy, which seemed to be bare of defenders, and came through Pannonia and Sirmium along the right side. Without meeting any resistance, he reached the bridge of the river Candidianus at the third milestone from the royal city of Ravenna.

This city lies amid the streams of the Po between swamps and the sea, and is accessible only on one side. Its ancient inhabitants, as our ancestors relate, were called *αἰνεροὶ*, that is "Laudable." Situated in a corner of the Roman Empire above the Ionian Sea, it is hemmed in like an island by a flood of rushing waters. On the east it has no sea, and one who sails straight to it from the region of Corcyra and those parts of Hellas sweeps with his oars along the right hand coast, first touching Epirus, then Dalmatia, Liburnia and Histria and at last the Venetian Isles. But on the west it has swamps through which a sort of door has been left by a very narrow entrance. To the north is an arm of the Po, called the Fossa Asconis. On the south likewise is the Po itself, which they call the King of the rivers of Italy; and it has also the name Eridanus. This river was turned aside by the Emperor Augustus into a very broad canal which flows through the midst of the city with a seventh part of its stream, affording a pleasant harbor at its mouth. Men believed in ancient times, as Dio relates, that it would hold a fleet of two hundred and fifty vessels in its safe anchorage. Fabius says that this, which was once a harbor, now displays itself like a spacious garden full of trees; but from them hang not sails but apples. The city boasts of three names and is happily placed in its threefold location. I mean to say the first is called Ravenna and the most distant part Classis; while midway between the city and the sea is Caesarea, full of luxury. The sand of the beach is fine and suited for riding.

XXX But as I was saying, when the army of the Visigoths had come into the neighborhood of the city, they sent an embassy to the Emperor Honorius, who dwelt within. They said that if he would permit the Goths to settle peaceably in Italy, they would so live with the Roman people that men might believe them both to be of one race; but if not, whoever prevailed in war should drive out the other, and the victor should henceforth rule unmolested. But the Emperor Honorius feared to make either promise. So he took counsel with his senate and considered how he might drive them from the Italian borders. He finally decided that Alaric and his race, if they were able to do so, should be allowed to seize for their own home the provinces farthest away, namely Gaul and Spain. For at this time he had almost lost them, and moreover they had been devastated by the invasion of Gaiseric, king of the Vandals. The grant was confirmed by an imperial rescript, and the Goths, consenting to the arrangement, set out for the country given them.

When they had gone away without doing any harm in Italy, Stilicho, the Patrician and father-in-law of the Emperor Honorius—for the Emperor had married both his daughters, Maria and Thermantia, in succession, but God called both from this world in their virgin purity—this Stilicho, I say, treacherously hurried to Pollentia, a city in the Cottian Alps. There he fell upon the unsuspecting Goths in battle, to the ruin of all Italy and his own disgrace. When the Goths suddenly beheld him, at first they were terrified. Soon regaining their courage and arousing each other by brave shouting, as is their custom, they turned to flight the entire army of Stilicho and almost exterminated it. Then forsaking the journey they had undertaken, the Goths with hearts full of rage returned again to Liguria whence they had set out. When they had plundered and spoiled it, they also laid waste Aemilia, and then hastened toward the city of Rome along the Flaminian Way, which runs between Picenum and Tuscia, taking as booty whatever they found on either hand. When they finally entered Rome, by Alaric's express command they merely sacked it and did not set the city on fire, as wild peoples usually do, nor did they permit serious damage to be done to the holy places. Thence they departed to bring like ruin upon Campania and Lucania, and then came to Bruttii. Here they remained a long time and planned to go to Sicily and thence to the countries of Africa.

Now the land of the Bruttii is at the extreme southern bound of Italy, and a corner of it marks the beginning of the Apennine mountains. It stretches out like a tongue into the Adriatic Sea and separates it from the Tyrrhenian waters. It chanced to receive its name in ancient times from a Queen Bruttia. To this place came Alaric, king of the Visigoths, with the wealth of all Italy which he had taken as spoil, and from there, as we have said, he intended to cross over by way of Sicily to the quiet land of Africa. But since man is not free to do anything he wishes without the will of God, that dread strait sunk several of his ships and threw all into confusion. Alaric was cast down by his reverse and, while deliberating what he should do, was suddenly overtaken by an untimely death and departed from human cares. His people mourned for him with the utmost affection. Then turning from its course the river Busentus near the city of Consentia—for this stream flows with its wholesome waters from the foot of a mountain near that city—they led a band of captives into the midst of its bed to dig out a place for his grave. In the depths of the pit they buried Alaric, together with many treasures, and then turned the waters back into their channel. And that none might ever know the place, they put to death all the diggers. They bestowed the kingdom of the Visigoths on Athavulf his kinsman, a man of imposing beauty and great spirit; for though not tall of stature, he was distinguished for beauty of face and form.

XXXI When Athavulf became king, he returned again to Rome, and whatever had escaped the first sack his Goths stripped bare like locusts, not merely despoiling Italy of its private wealth, but even of its public resources. The Emperor Honorius was powerless to resist even when his sister Placidia, the daughter of the Emperor Theodosius by his second wife, was led away captive from the city. But Athavulf was attracted to her nobility, beauty and chaste purity, and so he took her to wife in lawful marriage at Forum Julii, a city of Aemilia. When the barbarians learned of this alliance, they were the more effectually terrified, since the Empire and the Goths now seemed to be made one. Then Athavulf set out for Gaul, leaving Honorius Augustus stripped of his wealth, to be sure, yet pleased at heart because he was now a sort of kinsman of his. Upon his arrival the neighboring tribes who had long made cruel raids into Gaul—Franks and Burgundians alike—were terrified and began to keep within their own borders. Now the Vandals and the Alani, as we have said before, had been dwelling in both Pannonias by permission of the

Roman Emperors. Yet fearing they would not be safe even here if the Goths should return, they crossed over into Gaul. But no long time after they had taken possession of Gaul they fled thence and shut themselves up in Spain, for they still remembered from the tales of their forefathers what ruin Geberich, king of the Goths, had long ago brought on their race, and how by his valour he had driven them from their native land. And thus it happened that Gaul lay open to Athavulf when he came. Now when the Goth had established his kingdom in Gaul, he began to grieve for the plight of the Spaniards and planned to save them from the attacks of the Vandals. So Athavulf left with a few faithful men at Barcelona his treasures and those who were unfit for war, and entered the interior of Spain. Here he fought frequently with the Vandals and, in the third year after he had subdued Gaul and Spain, fell pierced through the groin by the sword of Euervulf, a man whose short stature he had been wont to mock. After his death Segeric was appointed king, but he too was slain by the treachery of his own men and lost both his kingdom and his life even more quickly than Athavulf.

XXXII Then Valia, the fourth from Alaric, was made king, and he was an exceeding stern and prudent man. The Emperor Honorius sent an army against him under Constantius, who was famed for his achievements in war and distinguished in many battles, for he feared that Valia would break the treaty long ago made with Athavulf and that, after driving out the neighboring tribes, he would again plot evil against the Empire. Moreover Honorius was eager to free his sister Placidia from the disgrace of servitude, and made an agreement with Constantius that if by peace or war or any means soever he could bring her back to the kingdom, he should have her in marriage. Pleased with this promise, Constantius set out for Spain with an armed force and in almost royal splendor. Valia, king of the Goths, met him at a pass in the Pyrenees with as great a force. Hereupon embassies were sent by both sides and it was decided to make peace on the following terms, namely that Valia should give up Placidia, the Emperor's sister, and should not refuse to aid the Roman Empire when occasion demanded.

Now at that time a certain Constantine usurped imperial power in Gaul and appointed as Caesar his son Constans, who was formerly a monk. But when he had held for a short time the Empire he had seized, he was himself slain at Arelate and his son at Vienne. Jovinus and Sebastian succeeded them with equal presumption and thought they might seize the imperial power; but they perished by a like fate.

Now in the twelfth year of Valia's reign the Huns were driven out of Pannonia by the Romans and Goths, almost fifty years after they had taken possession of it. Then Valia found that the Vandals had come forth with bold audacity from the interior of Galicia, whither Athavulf had long ago driven them, and were devastating and plundering everywhere in his own territories, namely in the land of Spain. So he made no delay but moved his army against them at once, at about the time when Hierius and Ardabures had become consuls.

XXXIII But Gaiseric, king of the Vandals, had already been invited into Africa by Boniface, who had fallen into a dispute with the Emperor Valentinian and was able to obtain revenge only by injuring the Empire. So he invited them urgently and brought them across the narrow strait known as the Strait of Gades, scarcely seven miles wide, which divides Africa from Spain and unites the mouth of the Tyrrhenian Sea with the waters of Ocean. Gaiseric, still famous in the City for the disaster of the Romans, was a man of moderate height and lame in consequence of a fall from his horse. He was a man of deep thought and few words, holding luxury in disdain, furious in his anger, greedy for gain, shrewd in winning over the barbarians and skilled in sowing the seeds of dissension to arouse enmity. Such was he who, as we have said, came at the solicitous invitation of Boniface to the country of Africa. There he reigned for a long time, receiving authority, as they say, from God Himself. Before his death he summoned the band of his sons and ordained that there should be no strife among them because of desire for the kingdom, but that each should reign in his own rank and order as he survived the others; that is, the next younger should succeed his elder brother, and he in turn should be followed by his junior. By giving heed to this command they ruled their kingdom in happiness for the space of many years and were not disgraced by civil war, as is usual among other nations; one after another receiving the kingdom and ruling the people in peace.

Now this is their order of succession: first, Gaeseric who was the father and lord, next Huneric, the third Gunthamund, the fourth Thrasamund, and the fifth Ilderich. He was driven from his throne and slain by Gelimer, who destroyed his race by disregarding his ancestor's advice and setting up a tyranny. But what he had done did not remain unpunished, for soon the vengeance of the Emperor Justinian was manifested against him. With his whole family and that wealth over which he gloated like a robber, he was taken to Constantinople by that most renowned warrior Belisarius, Master of the Soldiery of the East, Ex-Consul Ordinary and Patrician. Here he afforded a great spectacle to the people in the Circus. His repentance, when he cast himself down from his royal state, came too late. He died as a mere subject and in retirement, though he had formerly been unwilling to private life. Thus after a century Africa, which in the division of the earth's surface is regarded as the third part of the world, was delivered from the yoke of the Vandals and brought back to the liberty of the Roman Empire. The country which the hand of the heathen had long ago cut off from the body of the Roman Empire, by reason of the cowardice of emperors and the treachery of generals, was now restored by a wise prince and a faithful leader and to-day is happily flourishing. And though, even after this, it had to deplore the misery of civil war and the treachery of the Moors, yet the triumph of the Emperor Justinian, vouchsafed him by God, brought to a peaceful conclusion what he had begun. But why need we speak of what the subject does not require? Let us return to our theme.

Now Valia, king of the Goths, and his army fought so fiercely against the Vandals that he would have pursued them even into Africa, had not such a misfortune recalled him as befell Alaric when he was setting out for Africa. So when he had won great fame in Spain, he returned after a bloodless victory to Tolosa, turning over to the Roman Empire, as he had promised, a number of provinces which he had rid of his foes. A long time after this he was seized with sickness and departed this life. Just at that time Beremud, the son of Thorismud, whom we have mentioned above in the genealogy of the family of the Amali, departed with his son Veteric from the Ostrogoths, who still submitted to the oppression of the Huns in the land of Scythia, and came to the kingdom of the Visigoths. Well aware of his valour and noble birth, he believed that the kingdom would be more readily bestowed upon him by his kinsmen, inasmuch as he was known to be the heir of many kings. And who would hesitate to choose one of the Amali, if there were an empty throne? But he was not himself eager to make known who he was, and so upon the death of Valia the Visigoths made Theodorid his successor. Beremud came to him and, with the strength of mind for which he was noted, concealed his noble birth by prudent silence, for he knew that those of royal lineage are always distrusted by kings. So he suffered himself to remain unknown, that he might not bring the established order into confusion. King Theodorid received him and his son with special honor and made him partner in his counsels and a companion at his board; not for his noble birth, which he knew not, but for his brave spirit and strong mind, which Beremud could not conceal.

XXXIV And what more? Valia (to repeat what we have said) had but little success against the Gauls, but when he died the more fortunate and prosperous Theodorid succeeded to the throne. He was a man of the greatest moderation and notable for vigor of mind and body. In the consulship of Theodosius and Festus the Romans broke the truce and took up arms against him in Gaul, with the Huns as their auxiliaries. For a band of the Gallic Allies, led by Count Gaina, had aroused the Romans by throwing Constantinople into a panic. Now at that time the Patrician Aëtius was in command of the army. He was of the bravest Moesian stock, the son of Gaudentius and born in the city of Durostorum. He was a man fitted to endure the toils of war, born expressly to serve the Roman state; and by inflicting crushing defeats he had compelled the proud Suavi and barbarous

Franks to submit to Roman sway. So then, with the Huns as allies under their leader Litorius, the Roman army moved in array against the Goths. When the battle lines of both sides had been standing for a long time opposite each other, both being brave and neither side the weaker, they struck a truce and returned to their ancient alliance. And after the treaty had been confirmed by both and an honest peace was established, they both withdrew.

During this peace Attila was lord over all the Huns and almost the sole earthly ruler of all the tribes of Scythia; a man marvellous for his glorious fame among all nations. The historian Priscus, who was sent to him on an embassy by the younger Theodosius, says this among other things: "Crossing mighty rivers—namely, the Tisia and Tibisia and Dricca—we came to the place where long ago Vidigoia, bravest of the Goths, perished by the guile of the Sarmatians. At no great distance from that place we arrived at the village where King Attila was dwelling, a village, I say, like a great city, in which we found wooden walls made of smooth-shining boards, whose joints so counterfeited solidity that the union of the boards could scarcely be distinguished by close scrutiny. There you might see dining halls of large extent and porticoes planned with great beauty, while the courtyard was bounded by so vast a circuit that its very size showed it was the royal palace." This was the abode of Attila, the king of all the barbarian world; and he preferred this as a dwelling to the cities he captured.

XXXV Now this Attila was the son of Mundiuch, and his brothers were Octar and Ruas who are said to have ruled before Attila, though not over quite so many tribes as he. After their death he succeeded to the throne of the Huns, together with his brother Bleda. In order that he might first be equal to the expedition he was preparing, he sought to increase his strength by murder. Thus he proceeded from the destruction of his own kindred to the menace of all others. But though he increased his power by this shameful means, yet by the balance of justice he received the hideous consequences of his own cruelty. Now when his brother Bleda, who ruled over a great part of the Huns, had been slain by his treachery, Attila united all the people under his own rule....

XXXVI Now when Gaiseric, king of the Vandals, whom we mentioned shortly before, learned that his mind was bent on the devastation of the world, he incited Attila by many gifts to make war on the Visigoths, for he was afraid that Theodorid, king of the Visigoths, would avenge the injury done to his daughter. She had been joined in wedlock with Huneric, the son of Gaiseric, and at first was happy in this union. But afterwards he was cruel even to his own children, and because of the mere suspicion that she was attempting to poison him, he cut off her nose and mutilated her ears. He sent her back to her father in Gaul thus despoiled of her natural charms. So the wretched girl presented a pitiable aspect ever after, and the cruelty which would stir even strangers still more surely incited her father to vengeance. Attila, therefore, in his efforts to bring about the wars long ago instigated by the bribe of Gaiseric, sent ambassadors into Italy to the Emperor Valentinian to sow strife between the Goths and the Romans, thinking to shatter by civil discord those whom he could not crush in battle. He declared that he was in no way violating his friendly relations with the Empire, but that he had a quarrel with Theodorid, king of the Visigoths. As he wished to be kindly received, he filled the rest of the letter with the usual flattering salutations, striving to win credence for his falsehood. In like manner he despatched a message to Theodorid, king of the Visigoths, urging him to break his alliance with the Romans and reminding him of the battles to which they had recently provoked him. Beneath his great ferocity he was a subtle man, and fought with craft before he made war.

Then the Emperor Valentinian sent an embassy to the Visigoths and their king Theodorid, with this message: "Bravest of nations, it is the part of prudence for us to unite against the lord of the earth who wishes to enslave the whole world; who requires no just cause for battle, but supposes whatever he does is right. He measures his ambition by his might. License satisfies his pride. Despising law and right, he shows himself an enemy to

Nature herself. And thus he, who clearly is the common foe of each, deserves the hatred of all. Pray remember—what you surely cannot forget—that the Huns do not overthrow nations by means of war, where there is an equal chance, but assail them by treachery, which is a greater cause for anxiety. To say nothing about ourselves, can you suffer such insolence to go unpunished? Since you are mighty in arms, give heed to your own danger and join hands with us in common. Bear aid also to the Empire, of which you hold a part. If you would learn how such an alliance should be sought and welcomed by us, look into the plans of the foe."

By these and like arguments the ambassadors of Valentinian prevailed upon King Theodorid. He answered them, saying: "Romans, you have attained your desire; you have made Attila our foe also. We will pursue him wherever he summons us, and though he is puffed up by his victories over divers races, yet the Goths know how to fight this haughty foe. I call no war dangerous save one whose cause is weak; for he fears no ill on whom Majesty has smiled." The nobles shouted assent to the reply and the multitude gladly followed. All were fierce for battle and longed to meet the Huns, their foe. And so a countless host was led forth by Theodorid, king of the Visigoths, who sent home four of his sons, namely Friderich and Eurich, Retemer and Himnerith, taking with him only the two elder sons, Thorismud and Theodorid, as partners of his toil. O brave array, sure defense and sweet comradeship, having the aid of those who delight to share in the same dangers!

On the side of the Romans stood the Patrician Aëtius, on whom at that time the whole Empire of the West depended; a man of such wisdom that he had assembled warriors from everywhere to meet them on equal terms. Now these were his auxiliaries: Franks, Sarmatians, Armoricians, Liticians, Burgundians, Saxons, Riparians, Olibriones (once Roman soldiers and now the flower of the allied forces), and some other Celtic or German tribes. And so they met in the Catalaunian Plains, which are also called Mauriacian, extending in length one hundred *leuva*, as the Gauls express it, and seventy in width. Now a Gallic *leuva* measures a distance of fifteen hundred paces. That portion of the earth accordingly became the threshing-floor of countless races. The two hosts bravely joined battle. Nothing was done under cover, but they contended in open fight. What just cause can be found for the encounter of so many nations, or what hatred inspired them all to take arms against each other? It is proof that the human race lives for its kings, for it is at the mad impulse of one mind a slaughter of nations takes place, and at the whim of a haughty ruler that which nature has taken ages to produce perishes in a moment.

XXXVII But before we set forth the order of the battle itself, it seems needful to relate what had already happened in the course of the campaign, for it was not only a famous struggle but one that was complicated and confused. Well then, Sangiban, king of the Alani, smitten with fear of what might come to pass, had promised to surrender to Attila, and to give into his keeping Aureliani, a city of Gaul wherein he dwelt. When Theodorid and Aëtius learned of this, they cast up great earthworks around that city before Attila's arrival and kept watch over the suspected Sangiban, placing him with his tribe in the midst of their auxiliaries. Then Attila, king of the Huns, was taken aback by this event and lost confidence in his own troops, so that he feared to begin the conflict. While he was meditating on flight—a greater calamity than death itself—he decided to inquire into the future through soothsayers. So, as was their custom, they examined the entrails of cattle and certain streaks in bones that had been scraped, and foretold disaster to the Huns. Yet as a slight consolation they prophesied that the chief commander of the foe they were to meet should fall and mar by his death the rest of the victory and the triumph. Now Attila deemed the death of Aëtius a thing to be desired even at the cost of his own life, for Aëtius stood in the way of his plans. So although he was disturbed by this prophecy, yet inasmuch as he was a man who sought counsel of omens in all warfare, he began the battle with anxious heart at about the ninth hour of the day, in order that the impending darkness might come to his aid if the outcome should be disastrous.

XXXVIII The armies met, as we have said, in the Catalaunian Plains. The battle field was a plain rising by a sharp slope to a ridge, which both armies sought to gain; for advantage of position is a great help. The Huns with their forces seized the right side, the Romans, the Visigoths and their allies the left, and then began a struggle for the yet untaken crest. Now Theodorid with the Visigoths held the right wing and Aëtius with the Romans the left. They placed in the centre Sangiban (who, as said before, was in command of the Alani), thus contriving with military caution to surround by a host of faithful troops the man in whose loyalty they had little confidence. For one who has difficulties placed in the way of his flight readily submits to the necessity of fighting. On the other side, however, the battle line of the Huns was arranged so that Attila and his bravest followers were stationed in the centre. In arranging them thus the king had chiefly his own safety in view, since by his position in the very midst of his race he would be kept out of the way of threatening danger. The innumerable peoples of the divers tribes, which he had subjected to his sway, formed the wings. Amid them was conspicuous the army of the Ostrogoths under the leadership of the brothers Valamir, Thiudimer and Vidimer, nobler even than the king they served, for the might of the family of the Amali rendered them glorious. The renowned king of the Gepidae, Ardaric, was there also with a countless host, and because of his great loyalty to Attila, he shared his plans. For Attila, comparing them in his wisdom, prized him and Valamir, king of the Ostrogoths, above all the other chieftains. Valamir was a good keeper of secrets, bland of speech and skilled in wiles, and Ardaric, as we have said, was famed for his loyalty and wisdom. Attila might well feel sure that they would fight against the Visigoths, their kinsmen. Now the rest of the crowd of kings (if we may call them so) and the leaders of various nations hung upon Attila's nod like slaves, and when he gave a sign even by a glance, without a murmur each stood forth in fear and trembling, or at all events did as he was bid. Attila alone was king of all kings over all and concerned for all.

So then the struggle began for the advantage of position we have mentioned. Attila sent his men to take the summit of the mountain, but was outstripped by Thorismud and Aëtius, who in their effort to gain the top of the hill reached higher ground and through this advantage of position easily routed the Huns as they came up.

XXXIX Now when Attila saw his army was thrown into confusion by this event, he thought it best to encourage them by an extemporaneous address on this wise: "Here you stand, after conquering mighty nations and subduing the world. I therefore think it foolish for me to goad you with words, as though you were men who had not been proved in action. Let a new leader or an untried army resort to that. It is not right for me to say anything common, nor ought you to listen. For what is war but your usual custom? Or what is sweeter for a brave man than to seek revenge with his own hand? It is a right of nature to glut the soul with vengeance. Let us then attack the foe eagerly; for they are ever the bolder who make the attack. Despise this union of discordant races! To defend oneself by alliance is proof of cowardice. See, even before our attack they are smitten with terror. They seek the heights, they seize the hills and, repenting too late, clamour for protection against battle in the open fields. You know how slight a matter the Roman attack is. While they are still gathering in order and forming in one line with locked shields, they are checked, I will not say by the first wound, but even by the dust of battle. Then on to the fray with stout hearts, as is your wont. Despise their battle line. Attack the Alani, smite the Visigoths! Seek swift victory in that spot where the battle rages. For when the sinews are cut the limbs soon relax, nor can a body stand when you have taken away the bones. Let your courage rise and your own fury burst forth! Now show your cunning, Huns, now your deeds of arms! Let the wounded exact in return the death of his foe; let the unwounded revel in the slaughter of the enemy. No spear shall harm those who are sure to live; and those who are sure to die Fate overtakes even in peace. And finally, why should Fortune have made the Huns victorious over so many nations, unless it were to prepare them for the joy of this conflict. Who was it revealed to our sires the path through the Maeotian swamp, for so many ages a closed secret? Who, moreover, made armed men yield to you, when you were as yet unarmed? Even a mass of federated nations could not endure the sight of the Huns. I am not deceived in the issue; here is the field so many victories have promised us. I shall hurl the first spear at the foe. If any can stand at rest while Attila fights, he is a dead man." Inflamed by these words, they all dashed into battle.

XL And although the situation was itself fearful, yet the presence of their king dispelled anxiety and hesitation. Hand to hand they clashed in battle, and the fight grew fierce, confused, monstrous, unrelenting—a fight whose like no ancient time has ever recorded. There such deeds were done that a brave man who missed this marvellous spectacle could not hope to see anything so wonderful all his life long. For, if we may believe our elders, a brook flowing between low banks through the plain was greatly increased by blood from the wounds of the slain. It was not flooded by showers, as brooks usually rise, but was swollen by a strange stream and turned into a torrent by the increase of blood. Those whose wounds drove them to slake their parching thirst drank water mingled with gore. In their wretched plight they were forced to drink what they thought was the blood they had poured from their own wounds.

Here King Theodorid, while riding by to encourage his army, was thrown from his horse and trampled under foot by his own men, thus ending his days at a ripe old age. But others say he was slain by the spear of Andag of the host of the Ostrogoths, who were then under the sway of Attila. This was what the soothsayers had told to Attila in prophecy, though he understood it of Aëtius. Then the Visigoths, separating from the Alani, fell upon the horde of the Huns and nearly slew Attila. But he prudently took flight and straightway shut himself and his companions within the barriers of the camp, which he had fortified with wagons. A frail defense indeed; yet there they sought refuge for their lives, whom but a little while before no walls of earth could withstand. But Thorismud, the son of King Theodorid, who with Aëtius had seized the hill and repulsed the enemy from the higher ground, came unwittingly to the wagons of the enemy at night, thinking he had reached his own lines. As he was fighting bravely, someone wounded him in the head and dragged him from his horse. Then he was rescued by the watchful care of his followers and withdrew from the fierce conflict. Aëtius also became separated from his men in the confusion of night and wandered about in the midst of the enemy. Fearing disaster had happened, he went about in search of the Goths. At last he reached the camp of his allies and passed the remainder of the night in the protection of their shields.

At dawn on the following day, when the Romans saw the fields were piled high with bodies and that the Huns did not venture forth, they thought the victory was theirs, but knew that Attila would not flee from the battle unless overwhelmed by a great disaster. Yet he did nothing cowardly, like one that is overcome, but with clash of arms sounded the trumpets and threatened an attack. He was like a lion pierced by hunting spears, who paces to and fro before the mouth of his den and dares not spring, but ceases not to terrify the neighborhood by his roaring. Even so this warlike king at bay terrified his conquerors. Therefore the Goths and Romans assembled and considered what to do with the vanquished Attila. They determined to wear him out by a siege, because he had no supply of provisions and was hindered from approaching by a shower of arrows from the bowmen placed within the confines of the Roman camp. But it was said that the king remained supremely brave even in this extremity and had heaped up a funeral pyre of horse saddles, so that if the enemy should attack him, he was determined to cast himself into the flames, that none might have the joy of wounding him and that the lord of so many races might not fall into the hands of his foes.

XLI Now during these delays in the siege, the Visigoths sought their king and the king's sons their father, wondering at his absence when success had been attained. When, after a long search, they found him where the dead lay thickest, as happens with brave men, they honored him with songs and bore him away in the sight of the enemy. You might have seen bands of Goths shouting with dissonant cries and paying honor to the dead while the battle still raged. Tears were shed, but such as they were accustomed to devote to brave men. It was death indeed, but the Huns are witness that it was a glorious one. It was a death whereby one might well suppose the pride of the enemy would be lowered, when they beheld the body of so great a king borne forth with fitting honors. And so the Goths, still continuing the rites due to Theodorid, bore forth the royal majesty with sounding arms, and valiant Thorismud, as befitted a son, honored the glorious spirit of his dear father by following his remains.

When this was done, Thorismud was eager to take vengeance for his father's death on the remaining Huns, being moved to this both by the pain of bereavement and the impulse of that valour for which he was noted. Yet he consulted with the Patrician Aëtius (for he was an older man and of more mature wisdom) with regard to what he ought to do next. But Aëtius feared that if the Huns were totally destroyed by the Goths, the Roman Empire would be overwhelmed, and urgently advised him to return to his own dominions to take up the rule which his father had left. Otherwise his brothers might seize their father's possessions and obtain the power over the Visigoths. In this case Thorismud would have to fight fiercely and, what is worse, disastrously with his own countrymen. Thorismud accepted the advice without perceiving its double meaning, but followed it with an eye toward his own advantage. So he left the Huns and returned to Gaul. Thus while human frailty rushes into suspicion, it often loses an opportunity of doing great things.

In this most famous war of the bravest tribes, one hundred and sixty-five thousand are said to have been slain on both sides, leaving out of account fifteen thousand of the Gepidae and Franks, who met each other the night before the general engagement and fell by wounds mutually received, the Franks fighting for the Romans and the Gepidae for the Huns.

Now when Attila learned of the retreat of the Goths, he thought it a ruse of the enemy—for so men are wont to believe when the unexpected happens—and remained for some time in his camp. But when a long silence followed the absence of the foe, the spirit of the mighty king was aroused to the thought of victory and the anticipation of pleasure, and his mind turned to the old oracles of his destiny.

Thorismud, however, after the death of his father on the Catalaunian Plains where he had fought, advanced in royal state and entered Tolosa. Here although the throng of his brothers and brave companions were still rejoicing over the victory he yet began to rule so mildly that no one strove with him for the succession to the kingdom.

XLII But Attila took occasion from the withdrawal of the Visigoths, observing what he had often desired—that his enemies were divided. At length feeling secure, he moved forward his array to attack the Romans. As his first move he besieged the city of Aquileia, the metropolis of Venetia, which is situated on a point or tongue of land by the Adriatic Sea. On the eastern side its walls are washed by the river Natissa, flowing from Mount Piccis. The siege was long and fierce, but of no avail, since the bravest soldiers of the Romans withstood him from within. At last his army was discontented and eager to withdraw. Attila chanced to be walking around the walls, considering whether to break camp or delay longer, and noticed that the white birds, namely, the storks, who build their nests in the gables of houses, were bearing their young from the city and, contrary to their custom, were carrying them out into the country. Being a shrewd observer of events, he understood this and said to his soldiers: "You see the birds foresee the future. They are leaving the city sure to perish and are forsaking strongholds doomed to fall by reason of imminent peril. Do not think this a meaningless or uncertain sign; fear, arising from the things they foresee, has changed their custom." Why say more? He inflamed the hearts of his soldiers to attack Aquileia again. Constructing battering rams and bringing to bear all manner of engines of war, they quickly forced their way into the city, laid it waste, divided the spoil and so cruelly devastated it as scarcely to leave a trace to be seen. Then growing bolder and still thirsting for Roman blood, the Huns raged madly through the remaining cities of the Veneti. They also laid waste Mediolanum, the metropolis of Liguria, once an imperial city, and gave over Ticinum to a like fate. Then they destroyed the neighboring country in their frenzy and demolished almost the whole of Italy.

Attila's mind had been bent on going back to Rome. But his followers, as the historian Priscus relates, took him away, not out of regard for the city to which they were hostile, but because they remembered the case of Alaric, the former king of the Visigoths. They distrusted the good fortune of their own king, inasmuch as Alaric did not live long after the sack of Rome, but straightway departed this life. Therefore while Attila's spirit was wavering in doubt between going and not going, and he still lingered to ponder the matter, an embassy came to him from Rome to seek peace. Pope Leo himself came to meet him in the Ambuleian district of the Veneti at the well-travelled ford of the river Mincius. Then Attila quickly put aside his usual fury, turned back on the way he had advanced from beyond the Danube and departed with the promise of peace. But above all he declared and avowed with threats that he would bring worse things upon Italy, unless they sent him Honoria, the sister of the Emperor Valentinian and daughter of Augusta Placidia, with her due share of the royal wealth. For it was said that Honoria, although bound to chastity for the honor of the imperial court and kept in constraint by command of her brother, had secretly despatched a eunuch to summon Attila that she might have his protection against her brother's power; a shameful thing, indeed, to get license for her passion at the cost of the public weal.

XLIII So Attila returned to his own country, seeming to regret the peace and to be vexed at the cessation of war. For he sent ambassadors to Marcian, Emperor of the East, threatening to devastate the provinces, because that which had been promised him by Theodosius, a former emperor, was in no wise performed, and saying that he would show himself more cruel to his foes than ever. But as he was shrewd and crafty, he threatened in one direction and moved his army in another; for in the midst of these preparations he turned his face towards the Visigoths who had yet to feel his vengeance. But here he had not the same success as against the Romans. Hastening back by a different way than before, he decided to reduce to his sway that part of the Alani which was settled across the river Loire, in order that by attacking them, and thus changing the aspect of the war, he might become a more terrible menace to the Visigoths. Accordingly he started from the provinces of Dacia and Pannonia, where the Huns were then dwelling with various subject peoples, and moved his array against the Alani. But Thorismud, king of the Visigoths, with like quickness of thought perceived Attila's trick. By forced marches he came to the Alani before him, and was well prepared to check the advance of Attila when he came after him. They joined battle in almost the same way as before at the Catalaunian Plains, and Thorismud dashed his hopes of victory, for he routed him and drove him from the land without a triumph, compelling him to flee to his own country. Thus while Attila, the famous leader and lord of many victories, sought to blot out the fame of his destroyer and in this way to annul what he had suffered at the hands of the Visigoths, he met a second defeat and retreated ingloriously. Now after the bands of the Huns had been repulsed by the Alani, without any hurt to his own men, Thorismud departed for Tolosa. There he established a settled peace for his people and in the third year of his reign he fell sick. While letting blood from a vein, he was betrayed to his death by Ascalc, a client, who told his foes that his weapons were out of reach. Yet grasping a foot-stool in the one hand he had free, he became the avenger of his own blood by slaying several of those that were lying in wait for him.

XLIV After his death, his brother Theodorid succeeded to the kingdom of the Visigoths and soon found that Riciarius his kinsman, the king of the Suavi, was hostile to him. For Riciarius, presuming on his relationship to Theodorid, believed that he might seize almost the whole of Spain, thinking the disturbed beginning of Theodorid's reign made the time opportune for this trick. The Suavi formerly occupied as their country Galicia and Lusitania, which extend on the right side of Spain along the shore of Ocean. To the east is Austrogonia, to the west, on a promontory, is the sacred Monument of the Roman general Scipio, to the north Ocean, and to the south Lusitania and the Tagus river, which mingles golden grains in its sands and thus carries wealth in its worthless mud. So then Riciarius, king of the Suavi, set forth and strove to seize the whole of Spain. Theodorid, his kinsman, a man of moderation, sent ambassadors to him and told him quietly that he must not only withdraw from the territories that were not his own, but furthermore that he should not presume to make such an attempt, as he was becoming hated for his ambition. But with arrogant spirit he replied: "If you murmur here and find fault with my coming, I shall come to Tolosa where you dwell. Resist me there, if you can." When he heard this, Theodorid was angry and, making a compact with all the other tribes, moved his array against the Suavi. He had as his close allies Gundiuch and Hilperic, kings of the Burgundians. They came to battle near the river Ulbius, which flows between Asturica and Hiberia, and in the engagement Theodorid with the Visigoths, who fought for the right, came off victorious, overthrowing the entire tribe of the Suavi and almost exterminating them. Their king Riciarius fled from the dread foe and embarked upon a ship. But he was beaten back by another foe, the adverse wind of the Tyrrhenian Sea, and so fell into the hands of the Visigoths. Thus though he changed from sea to land, the wretched man did not avert his death.

When Theodorid had become the victor, he spared the conquered and did not suffer the rage of conflict to continue, but placed over the Suavi whom he had conquered one of his own retainers, named Agrivulf. But Agrivulf soon treacherously changed his mind, through the persuasion of the Suavi, and failed to fulfil his duty. For he was quite puffed up with tyrannical pride, believing he had obtained the province as a reward for the valour by which he and his lord had recently subjugated it. Now he was a man born of the stock of the Varni, far below the nobility of Gothic blood, and so was neither zealous for liberty nor faithful toward his patron. As soon as Theodorid heard of this, he despatched a force to cast him out from the kingdom he had usurped. They came quickly and conquered him in the first battle, inflicting a punishment befitting his deeds. For he was captured, taken from his friends and beheaded. Thus at last he was made aware of the wrath of the master he thought might be despised because he was kind. Now when the Suavi beheld the death of their leader, they sent priests of their country to Theodorid as suppliants. He received them with the reverence due their office and not only granted the Suavi exemption from punishment, but was moved by compassion and allowed them to choose a ruler of their own race for themselves. The Suavi did so, taking Rimismund as their prince. When this was done and peace was everywhere assured, Theodorid died in the thirteenth year of his reign.

XLV His brother Eurich succeeded him with such eager haste that he fell under dark suspicion. Now while these and various other matters were happening among the people of the Visigoths, the Emperor Valentinian was slain by the treachery of Maximus, and Maximus himself, like a tyrant, usurped the rule. Gaiseric, king of the Vandals, heard of this and came from Africa to Italy with ships of war, entered Rome and laid it waste. Maximus fled and was slain by a certain Ursus, a Roman soldier. After him Majorian undertook the government of the Western Empire at the bidding of Marcian, Emperor of the East. But he too ruled but a short time. For when he had moved his forces against the Alani who were harassing Gaul, he was killed at Dertona near the river named Ira. Severus succeeded him and died at Rome in the third year of his reign. When the Emperor Leo, who had succeeded Marcian in the Eastern Empire, learned of this, he chose as emperor his Patrician Anthemius and sent him to Rome. Upon his arrival he sent against the Alani his son-in-law Ricimer, who was an excellent man and almost the only one in Italy at that time fit to command the army. In the very first engagement he conquered and destroyed the host of the Alani, together with their king, Beorg.

Now Eurich, king of the Visigoths, perceived the frequent change of Roman Emperors and strove to hold Gaul by his own right. The Emperor Anthemius heard of it and asked the Brittones for aid. Their King Riotimus came with twelve thousand men into the state of the Bituriges by the way of Ocean, and was received as he disembarked from his ships. Eurich, king of the Visigoths, came against them with an innumerable army, and after a long fight he routed Riotimus, king of the Brittones, before the Romans could join him. So when he had lost a great part of his army, he fled with all the men he could gather together, and came to the Burgundians, a neighboring tribe then allied to the Romans. But Eurich, king of the Visigoths, seized the Gallic city of Arverna; for the Emperor Anthemius was now dead. Engaged in fierce war with his son-in-law Ricimer, he had worn out Rome and was himself finally slain by his son-in-law and yielded the rule to Olybrius.

At that time Aspar, first of the Patricians and a famous man of the Gothic race was wounded by the swords of the eunuchs in his palace at Constantinople and died. With him were slain his sons Ardabures and Patriciolus, the one long a Patrician, and the other styled a Caesar and son-in-law of the Emperor Leo. Now Olybrius died barely eight months after he had entered upon his reign, and Glycerius was made Caesar at Ravenna, rather by usurpation than by election. Hardly had a year been ended when Nepos, the son of the sister of Marcellinus, once a Patrician, deposed him from his office and ordained him bishop at the Port of Rome.

When Eurich, as we have already said, beheld these great and various changes, he seized the city of Arverna, where the Roman general Ecdicius was at that time in command. He was a senator of most renowned family and the son of Avitus, a recent emperor who had usurped the reign for a few days—for Avitus held the rule for a few days before Olybrius, and then withdrew of his own accord to Placentia, where he was ordained bishop. His son Ecdicius strove for a long time with the Visigoths, but had not the power to prevail. So he left the country and (what was more important) the city of Arverna to the enemy and betook himself to safer regions. When the Emperor Nepos heard of this, he ordered Ecdicius to leave Gaul and come to him, appointing Orestes in his stead as Master of the Soldiery. This Orestes thereupon received the army, set out from Rome against the enemy and came to Ravenna. Here he tarried while he made his son Romulus Augustulus emperor. When Nepos learned of this, he fled to Dalmatia and died there, deprived of his throne, in the very place where Glycerius, who was formerly emperor, held at that time the bishopric of Salona.

XLVI Now when Augustulus had been appointed Emperor by his father Orestes in Ravenna, it was not long before Odoacer, king of the Torcilingi, invaded Italy, as leader of the Sciri, the Heruli and allies of various races. He put Orestes to death, drove his son Augustulus from the throne and condemned him to the punishment of exile in the Castle of Lucullus in Campania. Thus the Western Empire of the Roman race, which Octavianus Augustus, the first of the Augusti, began to govern in the seven hundred and ninth year from the founding of the city, perished with this Augustulus in the five hundred and twenty-second year from the beginning of the rule of his predecessors and those before them, and from this time onward kings of the Goths held Rome and Italy. Meanwhile Odoacer, king of nations, subdued all Italy and then at the very outset of his reign slew Count Bracila at Ravenna that he might inspire a fear of himself among the Romans. He strengthened his kingdom and held it for almost thirteen years, even until the appearance of Theodoric, of whom we shall speak hereafter.

XLVII But first let us return to that order from which we have digressed and tell how Eurich, king of the Visigoths, beheld the tottering of the Roman Empire and reduced Arelate and Massilia to his own sway. Gaiseric, king of the Vandals, enticed him by gifts to do these things, to the end that he himself might forestall the plots which Leo and Zeno had contrived against him. Therefore he stirred the Ostrogoths to lay waste the Eastern Empire and the Visigoths the Western, so that while his foes were battling in both empires, he might himself reign peacefully in Africa. Eurich perceived this with gladness and, as he already held all of Spain and Gaul by his own right, proceeded to subdue the Burgundians also. In the nineteenth year of his reign he was deprived of his life at Arelate, where he then dwelt. He was succeeded by his own son Alaric, the ninth in succession from the famous Alaric the Great to receive the kingdom of the Visigoths. For even as it happened to the line of the Augusti, as we have stated above, so too it appears in the line of the Alarici, that kingdoms often come to an end in kings who bear the same name as those at the beginning. Meanwhile let us leave this subject, and weave together the whole story of the origin of the Goths, as we promised.

The Divided Goths: Ostrogoths

XLVIII Since I have followed the stories of my ancestors and retold to the best of my ability the tale of the period when both tribes, Ostrogoths and Visigoths, were united, and then clearly treated of the Visigoths apart from the Ostrogoths. It appears that at the death of their king, Hermanaric, they were made a separate people by the departure of the Visigoths, and remained in their country subject to the sway of the Huns; yet Vinitharius of the Amali retained the insignia of his rule. He rivalled the valour of his grandfather Vultuulf, although he had not the good fortune of Hermanaric. But disliking to remain under the rule of the Huns, he withdrew a little from them and strove to show his courage by moving his forces against the country of the Antes. When he attacked them, he was beaten in the first encounter. Thereafter he did valiantly and, as a terrible example, crucified their king, named Boz, together with his sons and seventy nobles, and left their bodies hanging there to double the fear of those who had surrendered. When he had ruled with such license for barely a year, Balamber, king of the Huns, would no longer endure it, but sent for Gesimund, son of Hunimund the Great. Now Gesimund, together with a great part of the Goths, remained under the rule of the Huns, being mindful of his oath of fidelity. Balamber renewed his alliance with him and led his army up against Vinitharius. After a long contest, Vinitharius prevailed in the first and in the second conflict, nor can any say how great slaughter he made of the army of the Huns. But in the third battle, when they met each other unexpectedly at the river named Erac, Balamber shot an arrow and wounded Vinitharius in the head, so that he died. Then Balamber took to himself in marriage Vadamerca, the grand-daughter of Vinitharius, and finally ruled all the people of the Goths as his peaceful subjects, but in such a way that one ruler of their own number always held the power over the Gothic race, though subject to the Huns.

And later, after the death of Vinitharius, Hunimund ruled them, the son of Hermanaric, a mighty king of yore; a man fierce in war and of famous personal beauty, who afterwards fought successfully against the race of the Suavi. And when he died, his son Thorismud succeeded him, in the very bloom of youth. In the second year of his rule he moved an army against the Gepidae and won a great victory over them, but is said to have been killed by falling from his horse. When he was dead, the Ostrogoths mourned for him so deeply that for forty years no other king succeeded in his place, and during all this time they had ever on their lips the tale of his memory. Now as time went on, Valamir grew to man's estate. He was the son of Thorismud's cousin Vandalarius. For his son Beremud, as we have said before, at last grew to despise the race of the Ostrogoths because of the overlordship of the Huns, and so had followed the tribe of the Visigoths to the western country, and it was from him Veteric was descended. Veteric also had a son Eutharic, who married Amalasuentha, the daughter of Theodoric, thus uniting again the stock of the Amali which had divided long ago. Eutharic begat Athalaric and Mathesuentha. But since Athalaric died in the years of his boyhood, Mathesuentha was taken to Constantinople by her second husband, namely Germanus, a nephew of the Emperor Justinian, and bore a posthumous son, whom she named Germanus.

But that the order we have taken for our history may run its due course, we must return to the stock of Vandalarius, which put forth three branches. This Vandalarius, the great grand-nephew of Hermanaric and cousin of the aforesaid Thorismud, vaunted himself among the race of the Amali because he had begotten three sons, Valamir, Thiudimer and Vidimer. Of these Valamir ascended the throne after his parents, though the Huns as yet held the power over the Goths in general as among other nations. It was pleasant to behold the concord of these three brothers; for the admirable Thiudimer served as a soldier for the empire of his brother Valamir, and Valamir bade honors be given him, while Vidimer was eager to serve them both. Thus regarding one another with common affection, not one was wholly deprived of the kingdom which two of them held in mutual peace. Yet, as has often been said, they ruled in such a way that they respected the dominion of Attila, king of the Huns. Indeed they could not have refused to fight against their kinsmen the Visigoths, and they must even have committed parricide at their lord's command. There was no way whereby any Scythian tribe could have been wrested from the power of the Huns, save by the death of Attila—an event the Romans and all other nations desired. Now his death was as base as his life was marvellous....

We shall not omit to say a few words about the many ways in which his shade was honored by his race. His body was placed in the midst of a plain and lay in state in a silken tent as a sight for men's admiration. The best horsemen of the entire tribe of the Huns rode around in circles, after the manner of circus games, in the place to which he had been brought and told of his deeds in a funeral dirge in the following manner: "The chief of the Huns, King Attila, born of his sire Mundiuch, lord of bravest tribes, sole possessor of the Scythian and German realms—powers unknown before—captured cities and terrified both empires of the Roman world and, appeased by their prayers, took annual tribute to save the rest from plunder. And when he had accomplished all this by the favour of fortune, he fell not by wound of the foe, nor by treachery of friends, but in the midst of his nation at peace, happy in his joy and without sense of pain. Who can rate this as death, when none believes it calls for vengeance?" When they had mourned him with such lamentations, a *strava*, as they call it, was celebrated over his tomb with great revelling. They gave way in turn to the extremes of feeling and displayed funereal grief alternating with joy. Then in the secrecy of night they buried his body in the earth. They bound his coffins, the first with gold, the second with silver and the third with the strength of iron, showing by such means that these three things suited the mightiest of kings; iron because he subdued the nations, gold and silver because he received the honors of both empires. They also added the arms of foemen won in the fight, trappings of rare worth, sparkling with various gems, and ornaments of all sorts whereby princely state is maintained. And that so great riches might be kept from human curiosity, they slew those appointed to the work—a dreadful pay for their labour; and thus sudden death was the lot of those who buried him as well as of him who was buried.

L ...When Ardaric, king of the Gepidae, learned this, he became enraged because so many nations were being treated like slaves of the basest condition, and was the first to rise against the sons of Attila. Good fortune attended him, and he effaced the disgrace of servitude that rested upon him. For by his revolt he freed not only his own tribe, but all the others who were equally oppressed; since all readily strive for that which is sought for the general advantage. They took up arms against the destruction that menaced all and joined battle with the Huns in Pannonia, near a river called Nedao. There an encounter took place between the various nations Attila had held under his sway. Kingdoms with their peoples were divided, and out of one body were made many members not responding to a single impulse. Being deprived of their head, they madly strove against each other. They never found their equals ranged against them without harming each other by wounds mutually given. And so the bravest nations tore themselves to pieces. For then, I think, must have occurred a most remarkable spectacle, where one might see the Goths fighting with pikes, the Gepidae raging with the sword, the Rugi breaking off the spears in their own wounds, the Suavi fighting on foot, the Huns with bows, the Alani drawing up a battle-line of heavy-armed and the Heruli of light-armed warriors.

Finally, after many bitter conflicts, victory fell unexpectedly to the Gepidae. For the sword and conspiracy of Ardaric destroyed almost thirty thousand men, Huns as well as those of the other nations who brought them aid. In this battle fell Ellac, the elder son of Attila, whom his father is said to have loved so much more than all the rest that he preferred him to any child or even to all the children in his kingdom. But fortune was not in accord with his father's wish. For after slaying many of the foe, it appears that he met his death so bravely that if his father had lived, he would have rejoiced at his glorious end. When Ellac was slain, his remaining brothers were put to flight near the shore of the Sea of Pontus, where we have said the Goths first settled. Thus did the Huns give way, a race to which men thought the whole world must yield. So baneful a thing is division, that they who used to inspire terror when their strength was united, were overthrown separately. The cause of Ardaric, king of the Gepidae, was fortunate for the various nations who were unwillingly subject to the rule of the Huns, for it raised their long downcast spirits to the glad hope of freedom. Many sent ambassadors to the Roman territory, where they were most graciously received by Marcian, who was then emperor, and took the abodes allotted them to dwell in. But the Gepidae by their own might won for themselves the territory of the Huns and ruled as victors over the extent of Dacia, demanding of the Roman Empire nothing more than peace and an annual gift as a pledge of their friendly alliance. This the Emperor freely granted at the time, and to this day that race receives its customary gifts from the Roman Emperor.

Now when the Goths saw the Gepidae defending for themselves the territory of the Huns, and the people of the Huns dwelling again in their ancient abodes, they preferred to ask for lands from the Roman Empire, rather than invade the lands of others with danger to themselves. So they received Pannonia, which stretches in a long plain, being bounded on the east by Upper Moesia, on the south by Dalmatia, on the west by Noricum and on the north by the Danube. This land is adorned with many cities, the first of which is Sirmium and the last Vindobona. But the Sauromatae, whom we call Sarmatians, and the Cemandri and certain of the Huns dwelt in Castra Martis, a city given them in the region of Illyricum. Of this race was Blivila, Duke of Pentapolis, and his brother Froila and also Bessa, a Patrician in our time. The Sciri, moreover, and the Sadagarii and certain of the Alani with their leader, Candac by name, received Scythia Minor and Lower Moesia. Paria, the father of my father Alanoviiamuth (that is to say, my grandfather), was secretary to this Candac as long as he lived. To his sister's son Gunthigis, also called Baza, the Master of the Soldiery, who was descended from the stock of the Amali, I also, Jordanes, although an unlearned man before my conversion, was secretary. The Rugi, however, and some other races asked that they might inhabit Bizye and Arcadiopolis. Hernac, the younger son of Attila, with his followers, chose a home in the most distant part of Lesser Scythia. Emnetzur and Ultzindur, kinsmen of his, won Oescus and Utus and Almus in Dacia on the banks of the Danube, and many of the Huns, then swarming everywhere, betook themselves into Romania, and from them the Sacromontisi and the Fossatisii of this day are said to be descended.

LI There were other Goths also, called the Lesser, a great people whose priest and primate was Vulfila, who is said to have taught them to write. And to-day they are in Moesia, inhabiting the Nicopolitan region as far as the base of Mount Haemus. They are a numerous people, but poor and unwarlike, rich in nothing save flocks of various kinds and pasture-lands for cattle and forests for wood. Their country is not fruitful in wheat and other sorts of grain. Some of them do not know that vineyards exist elsewhere, and they buy their wine from neighboring countries. But most of them drink milk.

LII Let us now return to the tribe with which we started, namely the Ostrogoths, who were dwelling in Pannonia under their king Valamir and his brothers Thiudimer and Vidimer. Although their territories were separate, yet their plans were one. For Valamir dwelt between the rivers Scarniunga and Aqua Nigra, Thiudimer near Lake Pelso and Vidimer between them both. Now it happened that the sons of Attila, regarding the Goths as deserters from their rule, came against them as though they were seeking fugitive slaves, and attacked Valamir alone, when his brothers knew nothing of it. He sustained their attack, though he had but few supporters, and after harassing them a long time, so utterly overwhelmed them that scarcely any portion of the enemy remained. The remnant turned in flight and sought the parts of Scythia which border on the stream of the river Danaper, which the Huns call in their own tongue the Var. Thereupon he sent a messenger of good tidings to his brother Thiudimer, and on the very day the messenger arrived he found even greater joy in the house of Thiudimer. For on that day his son Theodoric was born, of a concubine Erelieva indeed, and yet a child of good hope.

Now after no great time King Valamir and his brothers Thiudimer and Vidimer sent an embassy to the Emperor Marcian, because the usual gifts which they received like a New Year's present from the Emperor, to preserve the compact of peace, were slow in arriving. And they found that Theodoric, son of Triarius, a man of Gothic blood also, but born of another stock, not of the Amali, was in great favour, together with his followers. He was allied in friendship with the Romans and obtained an annual bounty, while they themselves were merely held in disdain. Thereat they were aroused to frenzy and took up arms. They roved through almost the whole of Illyricum and laid it waste in their search for spoil. Then the Emperor quickly changed his mind and returned to his former state of friendship. He sent an embassy to give them the past gifts, as well as those now due, and furthermore promised to give these gifts in future without any dispute. From the Goths the Romans received as a hostage of peace Theodoric, the young child of Thiudimer, whom we have mentioned above. He had now attained the age of seven years and was entering upon his eighth. While his father hesitated about giving him up, his uncle Valamir besought him to do it, hoping that peace between the Romans and the Goths might thus be assured. Therefore Theodoric was given as a hostage by the Goths and brought to the city of Constantinople to the Emperor Leo and, being a goodly child, deservedly gained the imperial favour.

LIII Now after firm peace was established between Goths and Romans, the Goths found that the possessions they had received from the Emperor were not sufficient for them. Furthermore, they were eager to display their wonted valour, and so began to plunder the neighboring races around them, first attacking the Sadagis who held the interior of Pannonia. When Dintzic, king of the Huns, a son of Attila, learned this, he gathered to him the few who still seemed to have remained under his sway, namely, the Ultzinzures, the Angisciri, the Bittugures and the Bardores. Coming to Bassiana, a city of Pannonia, he beleaguered it and began to plunder its territory. Then the Goths at once abandoned the expedition they had planned against the Sadagis, turned upon the Huns and drove them so ingloriously from their own land that those who remained have been in dread of the arms of the Goths from that time even down to the present day.

When the tribe of the Huns was at last subdued by the Goths, Hunimund, chief of the Suavi, who was crossing over to plunder Dalmatia, carried off some cattle of the Goths which were straying over the plains; for Dalmatia was near Suavia and not far distant from the territory of Pannonia, especially that part where the Goths were then staying. So then, as Hunimund was returning with the Suavi to his own country, after he had devastated Dalmatia, Thiudimer the brother of Valamir, king of the Goths, kept watch on their line of march. Not that he grieved so much over the loss of his cattle, but he feared that if the Suavi obtained this plunder with impunity, they would proceed to greater license. So in the dead of night, while they were asleep, he made an unexpected attack on them, near Lake Pelso. Here he so completely crushed them that he took captive and sent into slavery under the Goths even Hunimund, their king, and all of his army who had escaped the sword. Yet as he was a great lover of mercy, he granted pardon after taking vengeance and became reconciled to the Suavi. He adopted as his son the same man whom he had taken captive, and sent him back with his followers into Suavia. But Hunimund was unmindful of his adopted father's kindness. After some time he brought forth a plot he had contrived and aroused the tribe of the Sciri, who then dwelt above the Danube and abode peaceably with the Goths. So the Sciri broke off their alliance with them, took up arms, joined themselves to Hunimund and went out to attack the race of the Goths. Thus war came upon the Goths who were expecting no evil, because they relied upon both of their neighbors as friends. Constrained by necessity they took up arms and avenged themselves and their injuries by recourse to battle. In this battle, as King Valamir rode on his horse before the line to encourage his men, the horse was wounded and fell, overthrowing its rider. Valamir was quickly pierced by his enemies' spears and slain. Thereupon the Goths proceeded to exact vengeance for the death of their king, as well as for the injury done them by the rebels. They fought in such wise that there remained of all the race of the Sciri only a few who bore the name, and they with disgrace. Thus were all destroyed.

LIV The kings [of the Suavi], Hunimund and Alaric, fearing the destruction that had come upon the Sciri, next made war upon the Goths, relying upon the aid of the Sarmatians, who had come to them as auxiliaries with their kings Beuca and Babai. They summoned the last remnants of the Sciri, with Edica and Hunuulf, their chieftains, thinking they would fight the more desperately to avenge themselves. They had on their side the Gepidae also, as well as no small reinforcements from the race of the Rugi and from others gathered here and there. Thus they brought together a great host at the river Bolia in Pannonia and encamped there. Now when Valamir was dead, the Goths fled to Thiudimer, his brother. Although he had long ruled along with his brothers, yet he took the insignia of increased authority and summoned his younger brother Vidimer and shared with him the cares of war, resorting to arms under compulsion. A battle was fought and the party of the Goths was found to be so much the stronger that the plain was drenched in the blood of their fallen foes and looked like a crimson sea. Weapons and corpses, piled up like hills, covered the plain for more than ten miles. When the Goths saw this, they rejoiced with joy unspeakable, because by this great slaughter of their foes they had avenged the blood of Valamir their king and the injury done themselves. But those of the innumerable and motley throng of the foe who were unable to escape, though they got away, nevertheless came to their own land with difficulty and without glory.

LV After a certain time, when the wintry cold was at hand, the river Danube was frozen over as usual. For a river like this freezes so hard that it will support like a solid rock an army of foot-soldiers and wagons and sledges and whatsoever vehicles there may be—nor is there need of skiffs and boats. So when Thiudimer, king of the Goths, saw that it was frozen, he led his army across the Danube and appeared unexpectedly to the Suavi from the rear. Now this country of the Suavi has on the east the Baiovari, on the west the Franks, on the south the Burgundians and on the north the Thuringians. With the Suavi there were present the Alamanni, then their confederates, who also ruled the Alpine heights, whence several streams flow into the Danube, pouring in with a great rushing sound. Into a place thus fortified King Thiudimer led his army in the winter-time and conquered, plundered and almost subdued the race of the Suavi as well as the Alamanni, who were mutually banded together. Thence he returned as victor to his own home in Pannonia and joyfully received his own son Theodoric, once given as hostage to Constantinople and now sent back by the Emperor Leo with great gifts. Now Theodoric had reached man's estate, for he was eighteen years of age and his boyhood was ended. So he summoned certain of his father's adherents and took to himself from the people his friends and retainers—almost six thousand men. With these he crossed the Danube, without his father's knowledge, and marched against Babai, king of the Sarmatians, who had just won a victory over Camundus, a general of the Romans, and was ruling with insolent pride. Theodoric came upon him and slew him, and taking as booty his slaves and treasure, returned victorious to his father. Next he invaded the city of Singidunum, which the Sarmatians themselves had seized, and did not return to the Romans, but reduced it to his own sway.

LVI Then as the spoil taken from one and another of the neighboring tribes diminished, the Goths began to lack food and clothing, and peace became distasteful to men for whom war had long furnished the necessaries of life. So all the Goths approached their king Thiudimer and, with great outcry, begged him to lead forth his army in whatsoever direction he might wish. He summoned his brother and, after casting lots, bade him go into the country of Italy, where at this time Glycerius ruled as emperor, saying that he himself as the mightier would go to the east against a mightier empire. And so it happened. Thereupon Vidimer entered the land of Italy, but soon paid the last debt of fate and departed from earthly affairs, leaving his son and namesake Vidimer to succeed him. The Emperor Glycerius bestowed gifts upon Vidimer and persuaded him to go from Italy to Gaul, which was then harassed on all sides by various races, saying that their own kinsmen, the Visigoths, there ruled a neighboring kingdom. And what more? Vidimer accepted the gifts and, obeying the command of the Emperor Glycerius, pressed on to Gaul. Joining with his kinsmen the Visigoths, they again formed one body, as they had been long ago. Thus they held Gaul and Spain by their own right and so defended them that no other race won the mastery there.

But Thiudimer, the elder brother, crossed the river Savus with his men, threatening the Sarmatians and their soldiers with war if any should resist him. From fear of this they kept quiet; moreover they were powerless in the face of so great a host. Thiudimer, seeing prosperity everywhere awaiting him, invaded Naissus, the first city of Illyricum. He was joined by his son Theodoric and the Counts Astat and Invilia, and sent them to Ulpiana by way of Castrum Herculis. Upon their arrival the town surrendered, as did Stobi later; and several places of Illyricum, inaccessible to them at first, were thus made easy of approach. For they first plundered and then ruled by right of war Heraclea and Larissa, cities of Thessaly. But Thiudimer the king, perceiving his own good fortune and that of his son, was not content with this alone, but set forth from the city of Naissus, leaving only a few men behind as a guard. He himself advanced to Thessalonica, where Hilarianus the Patrician, appointed by the Emperor, was stationed with his army. When Hilarianus beheld Thessalonica surrounded by an entrenchment and saw that he could not resist attack, he sent an embassy to Thiudimer the king and by the offer of gifts turned him aside from destroying the city. Then the Roman general entered upon a truce with the Goths and of his own accord handed over to them those places they inhabited, namely Cyrrhus, Pella, Europus, Methone, Pydna, Beroea, and another which is called Dium. So the Goths and their king laid aside their arms, consented to peace and became quiet. Soon after these events, King Thiudimer was seized with a mortal illness in the city of Cyrrhus. He called the Goths to himself, appointed Theodoric his son as heir of the kingdom and presently departed this life.

LVII When the Emperor Zeno heard that Theodoric had been appointed king over his own people, he received the news with pleasure and invited him to come and visit him in the city, sending an escort of honor. Receiving Theodoric with all due respect, he placed him among the princes of his palace. After some time Zeno increased his dignity by adopting him as his son-in-arms and gave him a triumph in the city at his expense. Theodoric was made Consul Ordinary also, which is well known to be the supreme good and highest honor in the world. Nor was this all, for Zeno set up before the royal palace an equestrian statue to the glory of this great man.

Now while Theodoric was in alliance by treaty with the Empire of Zeno and was himself enjoying every comfort in the city, he heard that his tribe, dwelling as we have said in Illyricum, was not altogether satisfied or content. So he chose rather to seek a living by his own exertions, after the manner customary to his race, rather than to enjoy the advantages of the Roman Empire in luxurious ease while his tribe lived apart. After pondering these matters, he said to the Emperor: "Though I lack nothing in serving your Empire, yet if Your Piety deem it worthy, be pleased to hear the desire of my heart." And when as usual he had been granted permission to speak freely, he said: "The western country, long ago governed by the rule of your ancestors and predecessors, and that city which was the head and mistress of the world—wherefore is it now shaken by the tyranny of the Torcilingi and the Rugi? Send me there with my race. Thus if you but say the word, you may be freed from the burden of expense here, and, if by the Lord's help I shall conquer, the fame of Your Piety shall be glorious there. For it is better that I, your servant and your son, should rule that kingdom, receiving it as a gift from you if I conquer, than that one whom you do not recognize should oppress your Senate with his tyrannical yoke and a part of the republic with slavery. For if I prevail, I shall retain it as your grant and gift; if I am conquered, Your Piety will lose nothing—nay, as I have said, it will save the expense I now entail." Although the Emperor was grieved that he should go, yet when he heard this he granted what Theodoric asked, for he was unwilling to cause him sorrow. He sent him forth enriched by great gifts and commended to his charge the Senate and the Roman People.

Therefore Theodoric departed from the royal city and returned to his own people. In company with the whole tribe of the Goths, who gave him their unanimous consent, he set out for Hesperia. He went in straight march through Sirmium to the places bordering on Pannonia and, advancing into the territory of Venetia as far as the bridge of the Sontius, encamped there. When he had halted there for some time to rest the bodies of his men and pack-animals, Odoacer sent an armed force against him, which he met on the plains of Verona and destroyed with great slaughter. Then he broke camp and advanced through Italy with greater boldness. Crossing the river Po, he pitched camp near the royal city of Ravenna, about the third milestone from the city in the place called Pineta. When Odoacer saw this, he fortified himself within the city. He frequently harassed the army of the Goths at night, sallying forth stealthily with his men, and this not once or twice, but often; and thus he struggled for almost three whole years. But he labored in vain, for all Italy at last called Theodoric its lord and the Empire obeyed his nod. But Odoacer, with his few adherents and the Romans who were present, suffered daily from war and famine in Ravenna. Since he accomplished nothing, he sent an embassy and begged for mercy. Theodoric first granted it and afterwards deprived him of his life.

It was in the third year after his entrance into Italy, as we have said, that Theodoric, by advice of the Emperor Zeno, laid aside the garb of a private citizen and the dress of his race and assumed a costume with a royal mantle, as he had now become the ruler over both the Goths and Romans. He sent an embassy to Lodoin, king of the Franks, and asked for his daughter Audefleda in marriage. Lodoin freely and gladly gave her, and also his sons Celdebert and Heldebert and Thiudebert, believing that by this alliance a league would be formed and that they would be associated with the race of the Goths. But that union was of no avail for peace and harmony, for they fought fiercely with each other again and again for the lands of the Goths; but never did the Goths yield to the Franks while Theodoric lived.

LVIII Now before he had a child from Audefleda, Theodoric had children of a concubine, daughters begotten in Moesia, one named Thiudigoto and another Ostrogotho. Soon after he came to Italy, he gave them in marriage to neighboring kings, one to Alaric, king of the Visigoths, and the other to Sigsimund, king of the Burgundians. Now Alaric begat Amalaric. While his grandfather Theodoric cared for and protected him—for he had lost both parents in the years of childhood—he found that Eutharic, the son of Veteric, grandchild of Beremud and of Thorismud, and a descendant of the race of the Amali, was living in Spain, a young man strong in wisdom and valour and health of body. Theodoric sent for him and gave him his daughter Amalasuentha in marriage. And that he might extend his family as much as possible, he sent his sister Amalafrida (the mother of Theodahad, who was afterwards king) to Africa as wife of Thrasamund, king of the Vandals, and her daughter Amalaberga, who was his own niece, he united with Herminefred, king of the Thuringians.

Now he sent his Count Pitza, chosen from among the chief men of his kingdom, to hold the city of Sirmium. He got possession of it by driving out its king Thrasaric, son of Thraustila, and keeping his mother captive. Thence he came with two thousand infantry and five hundred horsemen to aid Mundo against Sabinian, Master of the Soldiery of Illyricum, who at that time had made ready to fight with Mundo near the city named Margoplanum, which lies between the Danube and Margus rivers, and destroyed the Army of Illyricum. For this Mundo, who traced his descent from the Attilani of old, had fled from the tribe of the Gepidae and was roaming around beyond the Danube in waste places where no man tilled the soil. He had gathered around him many outlaws and ruffians and robbers from all sides and had seized a tower called Herta, situated on the bank of the Danube. There he plundered his neighbors in wild license and made himself king over his vagabonds. Now Pitza came upon him when he was nearly reduced to desperation and was already thinking of surrender. So he rescued him from the hands of the Sabinian and made him a grateful subject of his king Theodoric.

Theodoric won an equally great victory over the Franks through his Count Ibba in Gaul, when more than thirty thousand Franks were slain in battle. Moreover, after the death of his son-in-law Alaric, Theodoric appointed Thiudis, his armour-bearer, guardian of his grandson Amalaric in Spain. But Amalaric was ensnared by the plots of the Franks in early youth and lost at once his kingdom and his life. Then his guardian Thiusis, advancing from the same kingdom, assailed the Franks and delivered the Spaniards from their disgraceful treachery. So long as he lived he kept the Visigoths united. After him Thiudigisclus obtained the kingdom and, ruling but a short time, met his death at the hands of his own followers. He was succeeded by Agil, who holds the kingdom to the present day. Athanagild has rebelled against him and is even now provoking the might of the Roman Empire. So Liberius the Patrician is on the way with an army to oppose him. Now there was not a tribe in the west that did not serve Theodoric while he lived, either in friendship or by conquest.

LIX When he had reached old age and knew that he should soon depart this life, he called together the Gothic counts and chieftains of his race and appointed Athalaric as king. He was a boy scarce ten years old, the son of his daughter Amalasuentha, and he had lost his father Eutharic. As though uttering his last will and testament, Theodoric adjured and commanded them to honor their king, to love the Senate and Roman People and to make sure of the peace and good will of the Emperor of the East, as next after God.

They kept this command fully so long as Athalaric their king and his mother lived, and ruled in peace for almost eight years. But as the Franks put no confidence in the rule of a child and furthermore held him in contempt, and were also plotting war, he gave back to them those parts of Gaul which his father and grandfather had seized. He possessed all the rest in peace and quiet. Therefore when Athalaric was approaching the age of manhood, he entrusted to the Emperor of the East both his own youth and his mother's widowhood. But in a short time the ill-fated boy was carried off by an untimely death and departed from earthly affairs. His mother feared she might be despised by the Goths on account of the weakness of her sex. So after much thought she decided, for the sake of relationship, to summon her cousin Theodahad from Tuscany, where he led a retired life at home, and thus she established him on the throne. But he was unmindful of their kinship and, after a little time, had her taken from the palace at Ravenna to an island of the Bulsinian lake where he kept her in exile. After spending a very few days there in sorrow, she was strangled in the bath by his hirelings.

LX When Justinian, the Emperor of the East, heard this, he was aroused as if he had suffered personal injury in the death of his wards. Now at that time he had won a triumph over the Vandals in Africa, through his most faithful Patrician Belisarius. Without delay he sent his army under this leader against the Goths at the very time when his arms were yet dripping with the blood of the Vandals. This sagacious general believed he could not overcome the Gothic nation, unless he should first seize Sicily, their nursing-mother. Accordingly he did so. As soon as he entered Trinacria, the Goths, who were besieging the town of Syracuse, found that they were not succeeding and surrendered of their own accord to Belisarius, with their leader Sinderith. When the Roman general reached Sicily, Theodahad sought out Evermud, his son-in-law, and sent him with an army to guard the strait which lies between Campania and Sicily and sweeps from a bend of the Tyrrhenian Sea into the vast tide of the Adriatic. When Evermud arrived, he pitched his camp by the town of Rhegium. He soon saw that his side was the weaker. Coming over with a few close and faithful followers to the side of the victor and willingly casting himself at the feet of Belisarius, he decided to serve the rulers of the Roman Empire. When the army of the

Goths perceived this, they distrusted Theodahad and clamored for his expulsion from the kingdom and for the appointment as king of their leader Vitiges, who had been his armour bearer. This was done; and presently Vitiges was raised to the office of king on the Barbarian Plains. He entered Rome and sent on to Ravenna the men most faithful to him to demand the death of Theodahad. They came and executed his command. After King Theodahad was slain, a messenger came from the king—for he was already king in the Barbarian Plains—to proclaim Vitiges to the people.

Meanwhile the Roman army crossed the strait and marched toward Campania. They took Naples and pressed on to Rome. Now a few days before they arrived, King Vitiges had set forth from Rome, arrived at Ravenna and married Mathesuentha, the daughter of Amalasunetha and grand-daughter of Theodoric, the former king. While he was celebrating his new marriage and holding court at Ravenna, the imperial army advanced from Rome and attacked the strongholds in both parts of Tuscany. When Vitiges learned of this through messengers, he sent a force under Hunila, a leader of the Goths, to Perusia - which was beleaguered by them. While they were endeavoring by a long siege to dislodge Count Magnus, who was holding the place with a small force, the Roman army came upon them, and they themselves were driven away and utterly exterminated. When Vitiges heard the news, he raged like a lion and assembled all the host of the Goths. He advanced from Ravenna and harassed the walls of Rome with a long siege. But after fourteen months his courage was broken and he raised the siege of the city of Rome and prepared to overwhelm Ariminum. Here he was baffled in like manner and put to flight; and so he retreated to Ravenna. When besieged there, he quickly and willingly surrendered himself to the victorious side, together with his wife Mathesuentha and the royal treasure.

And thus a famous kingdom and most valiant race, which had long held sway, was at last overcome in almost its two thousand and thirtieth year by that conqueror of many nations, the Emperor Justinian, through his most faithful consul Belisarius. He gave Vitiges the title of Patrician and took him to Constantinople, where he dwelt for more than two years, bound by ties of affection to the Emperor, and then departed this life. But his consort Mathesuentha was bestowed by the Emperor upon the Patrician Germanus, his nephew. And of them was born a son (also called Germanus) after the death of his father Germanus. This union of the race of the Anicii with the stock of the Amali gives hopeful promise, under the Lord's favour, to both peoples.

Conclusion

And now we have recited the origin of the Goths, the noble line of the Amali and the deeds of brave men. This glorious race yielded to a more glorious prince and surrendered to a more valiant leader, whose fame shall be silenced by no ages or cycles of years; for the victorious and triumphant Emperor Justinian and his consul Belisarius shall be named and known as Vandalicus, Africanus and Geticus.

Thou who readest this, know that I have followed the writings of my ancestors, and have culled a few flowers from their broad meadows to weave a chaplet for him who cares to know these things. Let no one believe that to the advantage of the race of which I have spoken—though indeed I trace my own descent from it—I have added aught besides what I have read or learned by inquiry. Even thus I have not included all that is written or told about them, nor spoken so much to their praise as to the glory of him who conquered them.

Hildebrandlied

The fragmentary Song of Hildebrand and Hadubrand, *the oldest extant Continental Germanic heroic poem, was copied into a manuscript in the monastery of Fulda around 800. The current scholarly opinion is that the poem was composed in the eighth century in Lombardy, drawing on a much older Gothic tradition of the fifth and sixth centuries concerning the family of the Brandings, Heribrand, Hildebrand, and Hadubrand. Versions of the legend spread throughout the Germanic and Celtic worlds from Germany to Scandinavia to Ireland. The poem presents the complex world of Late Antiquity from the perspective of the Barbarians as well as the tragic conflict between honor and kindred. We know from other, later allusions to the legend that Hildebrand is victorious and kills his son.*

Source: Sigfried Gutenbrunner,trans. *Von Hildrebrand und Hadubrand: Lied–Sage–Mythos* (Heidelberg: 1976).

The Song of Hildebrand and Hadubrand

That I heard it said...
that two warriors encountered each other
Hildebrand and Hadubrand, between their two armies.
Son and father looked to their armour,
They prepared their battle-dress, their swords the heroes belted fast
Over their ring-armour, and then they rode to the battle.
Hildebrand spoke, (Heribrand's son); he was the older man,
Experienced in the world. He began to ask
With few words, who his father was
From among the heroes of the people...
..."or of what ancestry are you?
Name but one, the others I will know,
Youth, in the kingdoms all the kindreds are known to me."
Hadubrand spoke, Hildebrand's son:
"Long ago our people told me,
The elders and sages who had lived long,
That my father was called Hildebrand, I am called Hadubrand.
Long ago he went east, fled the anger of Otaker,
With Dietrich [Theoderic] and his many swordsmen.
He established misery in the land
The woman in the home, the small child,
He robbed of their inheritance, and then rode east.
Therefore my father was and remained for Dietrich
Indispensable, he was such a reliable man.
He was a great enemy of Odoaker
But he was the best of the swords with Dietrich;
He was always at the head of the army; swordplay was always
dear to him.
He was known to many brave men.
I do not imagine that he still wanders the earth."
Hildebrand spoke, Heribrand's son:

"The Father of All above in heaven knows
That never before have you exchanged speech with so close a kinsman."
Then he took from his arm a twisted ring,
Made from Emperor's gold, as the king had given it to him,
The lord of the Hunns: "This I give to you as a gift!"
Hadubrand spoke, Hildebrand's son:
"With the spear should one receive gifts,
Point against point.
You old Hun, outrageous trickster,
You entice me with your words, you want to cast me down with the spear,
You have become so old that you intend only treachery.
This men have told me who have traveled to the sea
And westward over the earth-encircling sea: War took him away,
Hildebrand is dead, Heribrand's son."
Hildebrand spoke, Heribrand's son:
"In truth I hear it and see it in your war-gear,
That you have at home a lord so good
That under this prince you would never be exiled."...
"Now sorrow, ruling god, the destiny of woe fulfills itself!
I have traveled through sixty summers and winters,
Always I was counted among the most forward
But before none of the cities did I come to die;
Now my child must kill me with the sword,
Must lay me low with the death-ax, or else I must become his killer!
Now you lightly wish, if you have the power,
To win the armour of so old a hero,
To capture the spoils if you have the right to them!"
He would be the most repulsive of all the East people (said Hildebrand)
Who would refuse you battle, now he gladly desires
Hand to hand battle with you! May the encounter decide
Which of us must today loose his armour
Or possess both coats of mail.
Then first they sprang at each other with spears
In hard attacks; the shields protect them.
Then they rush together to bitter swordplay,
The bright shields strike sorrowfully
Until the linden wood became light to them
Ground away by the weapons...

The Tomb of Childeric, Father of Clovis

In 1653 the tomb of the Frankish chieftain Childeric (died 481 or 482) was discovered at Tournai, Belgium. Most of the extremely precious objects from the tomb were stolen and destroyed in the nineteenth century. However, descriptions and sketches of them, as well as objects recently discovered in the area surrounding the tomb, have made it possible to reconstruct the poly-ethnic and poly-cultural world of such Germanic chieftains.

These objects include a lance and an ax typical of northern Gaul and particularly of "Frankish" warriors. Childeric's cruciform broach or fibula is of Roman origin and similar pieces have been found in Hungary and Czechoslovakia. His signet ring with its inscription "Childirici regis" is also typically Roman, although the inscription is not. Another fibula found recently near the tomb appears to be Anglo Saxon. Childeric's long sword and shorter sword with a single blade resemble others found in Pannonia and the cloisonné enamels of bees and other zoomorphic style indicate a strong oriental influence although they were probably produced in northern Gaul. Finally, the form of burial itself, although difficult to interpret, apparently was a tumulus or mound in which the chieftain and at least one horse were buried while a herd of at least thirty horses were killed and buried around his tomb. Such a burial is much more typical of Alans and Sarmats from Iran than of western Germanic peoples.

Source: Patrick Périn and Laure-Charlotte Feffer, *Les Francs* vol. I *À la conquête de la Gaule* (Paris: 1987), 119-133. Translation: Joelle Favreau.

Childeric's tomb was discovered on May 27, 1653 at 3 p.m. by a deaf-mute mason, Adrien Quinquin, during the Saint-Brice hospice reconstructions in Tournai. At 2.50 m deep, Quinquin brought to light the remnants of a leather bag full of gold coins, then a gold bracelet, fragments of iron and, most importantly, a large quantity of jewellery cloisonné with garnet. Among these objects was a gold signet ring with the inscription CHIL-DERICI REGIS. In fact it was the tomb of the Childeric, Clovis' father.

Exceptional in its value, the funeral artifacts found in Childeric's tomb are also remarkable for their precise dating. It was in 481 or 482 that Clovis succeeded his father. The date of his father's death is corroborated by the signet ring. Indeed, this date constitutes an exact terminus ante quem for the dating of the objects gathered in Tournai in 1653, corroborated by the period of issue of the most recent coins found in the royal grave (bearing the effigy of the Emperor Zeno).

Dated to the third quarter of the fifth century, these funeral artifacts still raise two problems: first, the identification of some of their components because of the almost total ignorance of their original sites in the tomb; second, the appreciation of the circumstances that led to the accumulation of all these objects, modest or precious.

While it is possible to allocate precisely the cloisonné ornaments which belonged to the long sword and to the scramasax and to attribute to the royal costume some accessories (belt and shoe buckles, cruciform buckle, purse clasp) and jewels (bracelets, signet ring, ring), archeologists still remain divided as to the identification of other objects, considered by some as clothing accessories and by others as ornaments for the harness of the royal horse. It is the same for the possibility of an adjacent woman's burial place, granted to Basine (second skullcap, sphere of rock crystal characteristic of a woman's costume). The apparent presence of the tomb of a horse (whose head was found) also divides the archeologists: was the entire horse buried, or the head only, or merely the harness? The three possibilities are all plausible, taking into account other similar discoveries.

As controversial is the question of influences reflected by the components of Childeric's funeral artifacts. In a schematic manner, one can try to isolate several lines of influence. The spear and the axe, classic during that era in northern Gaul, must be attributed to the "Frankish" warlike style. The gold cruciform buckle of Roman origin (similar to those found in the tombs of Barbarian princes of Apahida, in Hungary, and of Blucina, in Czechoslovakia), as well as the signet ring (also present in Apahida), illustrate in an eloquent way that the "Roman" style was adopted by Barbarian princes in contact with the Empire. Childeric's tomb also reveals the style then common to the Germans as a whole and even to other Barbarians such as the Alani-Sarmatians (Iranians): the actual funeral pomp (possibly completed by the presence of an adjacent tomb for a horse, with the collective sacrifice of a herd of domestic horses); the presence on the right wrist of a permanently fixed solid gold bracelet which, as in the Apahida, Blucina and Pouan (Aube) tombs, showed the princely status of these wealthy warriors.

Of other influences, perhaps the most spectacular can be termed "Danubian". Parallels between the tombs of Tournai and Pouan and those of wealthy warriors from the oriental Germanic world, (more precisely of the Danubian regions such as the Gepide burial places of Apahida and the Lombard or Skire tombs of Blucina), were identified long ago. In all these cases the tomb has held a long sword and a straight sword with a narrow blade and only one cutting edge; clothing accessories such as massive belt buckles equipped with tongues with large shields; and the ornaments of cloisonné jewellery. These parallels suggest that Childeric's tomb must be directly related to the Germanic tombs which were part of the contemporary Germanic culture that survived the fall of the Hunnic Empire in 455. The parallels should not be assumed to result from Attila and the Huns' raid in Gaul in 451. Indeed, at the end of the fourth century and during the first half of the fifth century, some rare discoveries in occidental Europe (men's tombs at Wolfsheim, Altussheim and Mundolsheim, in the Middle Rhine or vicinity; Béja in Portugal; women's tombs of Hochfelden in Alsace and of Airan in Calvados) testify that there were already contacts with the Danubian regions. These contacts were broadened during the second half of the fifth century and facilitated the adoption and imitation by the occidental Barbarian courts of some styles popular in the oriental Germanic world.

While the cloisonné objects of Childeric's tomb, and in particular the sword and scramasax sword, testify to the remarkable work of several workshops or of several goldsmiths, it does not seem possible today to try to separate those that could have been imported from the Danubian regions or fabricated at the Frankish court by goldsmiths who were native to these regions from those which were produced by local craftsmen imitating the oriental productions. The most plausible hypothesis, supported by the presence of decorated designs which were totally foreign to the oriental world, is that all of Childeric's funeral artifacts were made in northern Gaul by goldsmiths who were either of oriental origin or were working largely according to the traditions of oriental goldsmiths (among which some probably were not "Barbarians", but, for example, Greeks).

Recent excavations in Tournai around the Saint-Brice church have shed some new light on the archeological environment of Childeric's tomb. For example, until 1983 it was thought that this royal burial, established on the site of an old Roman necropolis of the first and second centuries, was isolated. While the recent research had not been able to date this graveyard to the late Empire, it nonetheless has revealed the presence of a series of Merovingian burial places dating from the second half of the fifth century to the seventh century. However, it has not been possible to determine whether the oldest ones among them were prior or contemporary to Childeric's tomb. Therefore it is now established that the royal grave was part of an original core of a Merovingian necropolis and may have marked its beginning.

Several Merovingian burial places have been found to contain rich funeral artifacts: proof that Tournai remained an important town at the beginning of the Early Middle-Ages, even though it was no longer a Merovingian capital. Also significant has been the discovery of three collective burial places of horses, each containing a dozen animals, most of them stallions. These burial places, which lacked artifacts, have been dated to the second half of the fifth century or to the beginning of the sixth century (C14 dating, between 430 and 560 and more probably 440 and 540). Taking into consideration that their location was around 20 m from Childeric's tomb, it is likely that they bear some direct relation to the royal burial. Thus a new detail may be added to our picture of the funeral splendour of Clovis' father: the collective sacrifice of a whole herd of domestic horses. There are no precise parallels for this exceptional ritual in the occidental Germanic world; indeed, in Westphalia as well as in Thuringia, such burials only involved two or three horses.

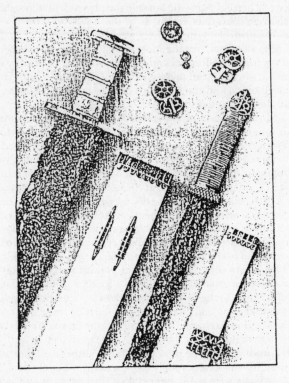

"Treasure of Pouan". The sword and the scramasax.

Childeric's tomb. Zoomorphic purse claps.

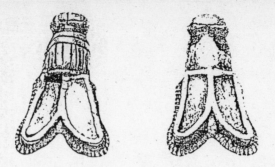

Two gold bees cloisonné with garnet from the "Childeric's treasure".

The signet ring of Childeric I.

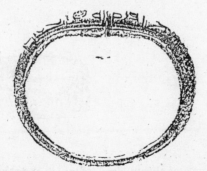

Gilded silver bracelet with zoomorphic ends.

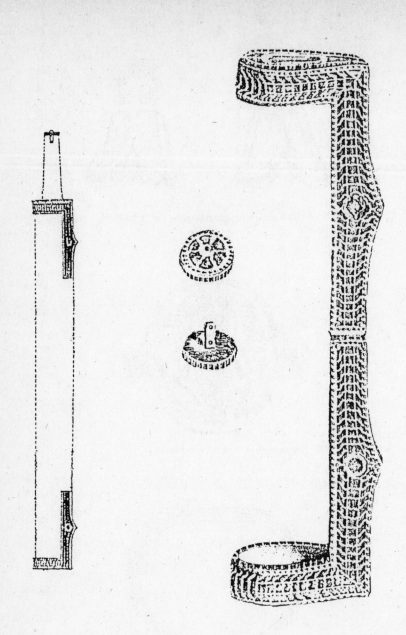

Reconstruction of the scramasax sheath. Knob of button and scramasax appliqués of cloisonné goldsmith work. Childeric's tomb.

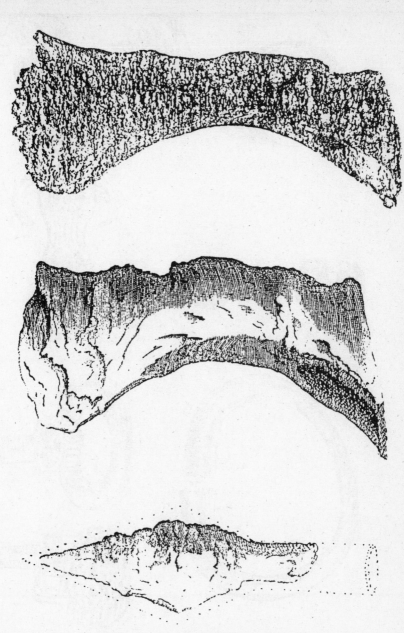

Childeric's tomb. Frankish battle-axe. Spear.

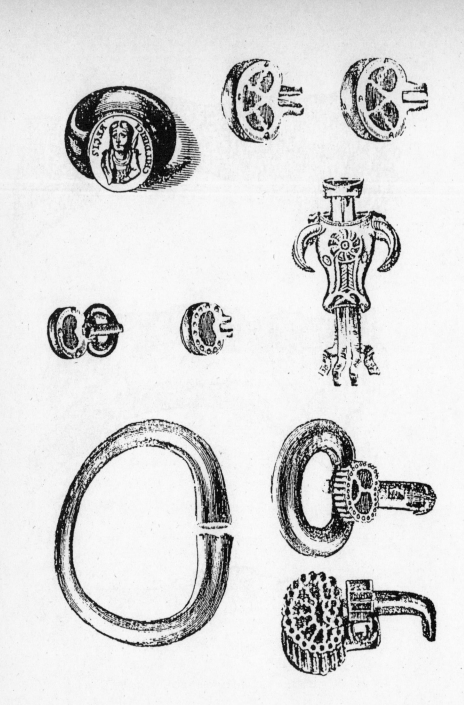

Childeric's tomb. Signet ring and gold bracelet. Belt and shoe buckles and appliqués.

Collective tomb of horses near Childeric's tomb

Reconstruction of the sheath
of the sword.

Hilt and mouth of the sheath of Childeric's sword.

145

Anglo-saxon type buckle with zoomorphic and anthropomorphic design, sixth century.

Salic Law

The first codification of Salic law took place under king Clovis (481-511). The laws were drawn up with the assistance of Gallo-Romans trained in Roman legal tradition. However they also contain much that may date from Salic traditions as early as the fourth century.

Source: E. F. Henderson, *Select Historical Documents of the Middle Ages* (London: George Bell, 1892) p.176-189. (Gengler, "Germanische Rechtsdenkmaeler," p. 267.)

Title I. Concerning Summonses.

1.   If any one be summoned before the "Thing" by the king's law, and do not come, he shall be sentenced to 600 denars, which make 15 shillings (solidi).

2.   But he who summons another, and does not come himself, shall, if a lawful impediment have not delayed him, be sentenced to 15 shillings, to be paid to him whom he summoned.

3.   And he who summons another shall walk with witnesses to the home of that man, and, if he be not at home, shall bid the wife or any one of the family to make known to him that he has been summoned to court.

4.   But if he be occupied in the king's service he can not summon him.

5.   But if he shall be inside the hundred seeing about his own affairs, he can summon him in the manner explained above.

Title II. Concerning Thefts of Pigs, etc.

1.   If any one steal a sucking pig, and it be proved against him, he shall be sentenced to 120 denars, which make three shillings.

2.   If any one steal a pig that can live without its mother, and it be proved on him, he shall be sentenced to 40 denars—that is, 1 shilling.

3.   If any one steal 25 sheep where there were no more in that flock, and it be proved on him, he shall be sentenced to 2500 denars—that is, 62 shillings.

Title III. Concerning Thefts of Cattle.

4.   If any one steal that bull which rules the herd and never has been yoked, he shall be sentenced to 1800 denars, which make 45 shillings.

5.   But if that bull is used for the cows of three villages in common, he who stole him shall be sentenced to three times 45 shillings.

6.   If any one steal a bull belonging to the king he shall be sentenced to 3600 denars, which make 90 shillings.

Title IV. Concerning Damage done among Crops or in any Enclosure.

1. If any one finds cattle or a horse, or flocks of any kind in his crops, he shall not at all mutilate them.

2. If he do this and confess it, he shall restore the worth of the animal in place of it, and shall himself keep the mutilated one.

3. But if he have not confessed it, and it have been proved on him, he shall be sentenced, besides the value of the animal and the fines for delay, to 600 denars, which make 15 shillings.

Title XI. Concerning Thefts or Housebreakings of Freemen.

1. If any freeman steal, outside of the house, something worth 2 denars, he shall be sentenced to 600 denars, which make 15 shillings.

2. But if he steal, outside of the house, something worth 40 denars, and it be proved on him, he shall be sentenced, besides the amount and the fines for delay, to 1400 denars, which make 35 shillings.

3. If a freeman break into a house and steal something worth 2 denars, and it be proved on him, he shall be sentenced to 15 shillings.

4. But if he shall have stolen something worth more than 5 denars, and it have been proved on him, he shall be sentenced, besides the worth of the object and the fines for delay, to 1400 denars, which make 35 shillings.

5. But if he have broken, or tampered with, the lock, and thus have entered the house and stolen anything from it, he shall be sentenced, besides the worth of the object and the fines for delay, to 1800 denars, which make 45 shillings.

6. And if he have taken nothing, or have escaped by flight, he shall, for the housebreaking alone, be sentenced to 1200 denars, which makes 30 shillings.

Title XII. Concerning Thefts or Housebreakings on the Part of Slaves.

1. If a slave steal, outside of the house, something worth two denars, he shall, besides paying the worth of the object and the fines for delay, be stretched out and receive 120 blows.

2. But if he steal something worth 40 denars, he shall either be castrated or pay 6 shillings. But the lord of the slave who committed the theft shall restore to the plaintiff the worth of the object and the fines for delay.

Title XIII. Concerning Rape committed by Freemen.

1. If three men carry off a free born girl, they shall be compelled to pay 30 shillings.

2. If there are more than three, each one shall pay 8 shillings.

3. Those who shall have been present with boats shall be sentenced to three shillings.

4. But those who commit rape shall be compelled to pay 2500 denars, which make 63 shillings.

5. But if they have carried off that girl from behind lock and key, or from the spinning room, they shall be sentenced to the above price and penalty.

6. But if the girl who is carried off be under the king's protection, then the "frith" (peace-money) shall be 2500 denars, which make 63 shillings.

7. But if a bondsman of the king, or a leet, should carry off a free woman, he shall be sentenced to death.

8. But if a free woman have followed a slave of her own will, she shall lose her freedom.

9. If a freeborn man shall have taken an alien bondswoman, he shall suffer similarly.

10. If any body take an alien spouse and join her to himself in matrimony, he shall be sentenced to 2500 denars, which make 63 shillings.

Title XIV. Concerning Assault and Robbery.

1. If any one have assaulted and plundered a free man, and it be proved on him, he shall be sentenced to 2500 denars, which make 63 shillings.

2. If a Roman have plundered a Salian Frank, the above law shall be observed.

3. But if a Frank have plundered a Roman, he shall be sentenced to 35 shillings.

4. If any man should wish to migrate, and has permission from the king, and shall have shown this in the public "Thing:" whoever, contrary to the decree of the king, shall presume to oppose him, shall be sentenced to 8000 denars, which make 200 shillings.

Title XV. Concerning Arson.

1. If any one shall set fire to a house in which men were sleeping, as many freemen as were in it can make complaint before the "Thing;" and if any one shall have been burned in it, the incendiary shall be sentenced to 2500 denars, which make 63 shillings.

Title XVII. Concerning Wounds.

1. If any one have wished to kill another person, and the blow have missed, he on whom it was proved shall be sentenced to 2500 denars, which make 63 denars.

2. If any person have wished to strike another with a poisoned arrow, and the arrow have glanced aside, and it shall be proved on him; he shall be sentenced to 2500 denars, which make 63 shillings.

3. If any person strike another on the head so that the brain appears, and the three bones which lie above the brain shall project, he shall be sentenced to 1200 denars, which make 30 shillings.

4. But if it shall have been between the ribs or in the stomach, so that the wound appears and reaches to the entrails, he shall be sentenced to 1200 denars—which make 30 shillings—besides five shillings for the physician's pay.

5. If any one shall have struck a man so that blood falls to the floor, and it be proved on him, he shall be sentenced to 600 denars, which make 15 shillings.

6.   But if a freeman strike a freeman with his fist so that blood does not flow, he shall be sentenced for each blow—up to 3 blows—to 120 denars, which make 3 shillings.

Title XVIII. Concerning him who, before the King, accuses an innocent Man.

If any one, before the king, accuse an innocent man who is absent, he shall be sentenced to 2500 denars, which make 63 shillings.

Title XIX. Concerning Magicians.

1.   If any one have given herbs to another so that he die, he shall be sentenced to 200 shillings (or shall surely be given over to fire).

2.   If any person have bewitched another, and he who was thus treated shall escape, the author of the crime, who is proved to have committed it, shall be sentenced to 2500 denars, which make 63 shillings.

Title XXIV. Concerning the Killing of little children and women.

1.   If any one have slain a boy under 10 years—up to the end of the tenth—and it shall have been proved on him, he shall be sentenced to 24000 denars, which make 600 shillings.

3.   If any one have hit a free woman who is pregnant, and she dies, he shall be sentenced to 28000 denars, which make 700 shillings.

6.   If any one have killed a free woman after she has begun bearing children, he shall be sentenced to 24000 denars, which make 600 shillings.

7.   After she can have no more children, he who kills her shall be sentenced to 8000 denars, which make 200 shillings.

Title XXX. Concerning Insults.

3.   If any one, man or woman, shall have called a woman harlot, and shall not have been able to prove it, he shall be sentenced to 1800 denars, which make 45 shillings.

4.   If any person shall have called another "fox," he shall be sentenced to 3 shillings.

5.   If any man shall have called another "hare," he shall be sentenced to 3 shillings.

6.   If any man shall have brought it up against another that he have thrown away his shield, and shall not have been able to prove it, he shall be sentenced to 120 denars, which make 3 shillings.

7.   If any man shall have called another "spy" or "perjurer," and shall not have been able to prove it, he shall be sentenced to 600 denars, which make 15 shillings.

Title XXXIII. Concerning the Theft of hunting animals.

2.   If any one have stolen a tame marked stag (-hound?), trained to hunting, and it shall have been proved through witnesses that his master had him for hunting, or had killed him with two or three beasts, he shall be sentenced to 1800 denars, which make 45 shillings.

Title XXXIV. Concerning the Stealing of Fences.

1.   If any man shall have cut 3 staves by which a fence is bound or held together, or have stolen or cut the heads of 3 stakes, he shall be sentenced to 600 denars, which make 15 shillings.

2.   If any one shall have drawn a harrow through another's harvest after it has sprouted, or shall have gone through it with a wagon where there was no road, he shall be sentenced to 120 denars. which make 3 shillings.

3.   If any one shall have gone, where there is no way or path, through another's harvest which has already become thick, he shall be sentenced to 600 denars, which make 15 shillings.

Title XLI. Concerning the Murder of Free Men.

1.   If any one shall have killed a free Frank, or a barbarian living under the Salic law, and it have been proved on him, he shall be sentenced to 8000 denars.

2.   But if he shall have thrown him into a well or into the water, or shall have covered him with branches or anything else, to conceal him, he shall be sentenced to 24000 denars, which make 600 shillings.

3.   But if any one has slain a man who is in the service of the king, he shall be sentenced to 24000 denars, which make 600 shillings.

4.   But if he have put him in the water or a well, and covered him with anything to conceal him, he shall be sentenced to 72000 denars, which make 1800 shillings.

5.   If any one have slain a Roman who eats in the king's palace, and it have been proved on him, he shall be sentenced to 12000 denars, which make 300 shillings.

6.   But if the Roman shall not have been a landed proprietor and table companion of the king, he who killed him shall be sentenced to 4000 denars, which make 100 shillings.

7.   But if he shall have killed a Roman who was obliged to pay tribute, he shall be sentenced to 63 shillings.

9.   If any one have thrown a free man into a well, and he have escaped alive, he (the criminal) shall be sentenced to 4000 denars, which make 100 shillings.

Title XLV. Concerning Migrators.

1.   If any one wish to migrate to another village and if one or more who live in that village do not wish to receive him,—if there be only one who objects, he shall not have leave to move there.

2.   But if he shall have presumed to settle in that village in spite of his rejection by one or two men, then some one shall give him warning. And if he be unwilling to go away, he who gives him warning shall give him warning, with witnesses, as follows: I warn thee that thou may'st remain here this next night as the Salic law demands, and I warn thee that within 10 nights thou shalt go forth from this village. After another 10 nights he shall again come to him and warn him again within 10 nights to go away. If he still refuse to go, again 10 nights shall be added to the command, that the number of 30 nights may be full. If he will not go away even then, then he shall summon him to the "Thing," and pre-

sent his witnesses as to the separate commands to leave. If he who has been warned will not then move away, and no valid reason detains him, and all the above warnings which we have mentioned have been given according to law: then he who gave him warning shall take the matter into his own hands and request the "comes" to go to that place and expel him. And because he would not listen to the law, that man shall relinquish all that he has earned there, and, besides, shall be sentenced to 1200 denars, which make 30 shillings.

3. But if anyone have moved there, and within 12 months no one have given him warning, he shall remain as secure as the other neighbours.

Title XLVI. Concerning Transfers of Property.

1. The observance shall be that the Thunginus or Centenarius shall call together a "Thing," and shall have his shield in the "Thing," and shall demand three men as witnesses for each of the three transactions. He (the owner of the land to be transferred) shall seek a man who has no connection with himself, and shall throw a stalk into his lap. And to him into whose lap he has thrown the stalk he shall tell, concerning his property, how much of it—or whether the whole or a half—he wishes to give. He in whose lap he threw the stalk shall remain in his (the owner's) house, and shall collect three or more guests, and shall have the property—as much as is given him—in his power. And, afterwards, he to whom that property is entrusted shall discuss all these things with the witnesses collected afterwards, either before the king or in the regular "Thing," he shall give the property up to him for whom it was intended. He shall take the stalk in the "Thing," and, before 12 months are over, shall throw it into the lap of him whom the owner has named heir; and he shall restore not more nor less, but exactly as much as was entrusted to him.

2. And if any one shall wish to say anything against this, three sworn witnesses shall say that they were in the "Thing" which the "Thunginus" or "Centenarius" called together, and that they saw that man who wished to give his property throw a stalk into the lap of him whom he had selected. They shall name by name him who threw his property into the lap of the other, and, likewise, shall name him whom he named his heir. And three other sworn witnesses shall say that he in whose lap the stalk was thrown had remained in the house of him who gave his property, and had there collected three or more guests, and that they had eaten porridge at table, and that he had collected those who were bearing witness, and that those guests had thanked him for their entertainment. All this those other sworn witnesses shall say, and that he who received that property in his lap in the "Thing" held before the king, or in the regular public "Thing," did publicly, before the people, either in the presence of king or in public "Thing"—namely on the Mallberg, before the "Thunginus"—throw the stalk into the lap of him whom the owner had named as heir. And thus 9 witnesses shall confirm all this.

Title L. Concerning Promises to Pay.

1. If any freeman or leet have made to another a promise to pay, then he to whom the promise was made shall, within 40 days or within such term as was agreed when he made the promise, go to the house of that man with witnesses, or with appraisers. And if he (the debtor) be unwilling to make the promised payment, he shall be sentenced to 15 shillings above the debt which he had promised.

2. If he then be unwilling to pay, he (the creditor) shall summon him before the "Thing" and thus accuse him: "I ask thee, 'Thunginus,' to bann my opponent who made me a promise to pay and owes me a debt." And he shall state how much he owes and promised to pay. Then the "Thunginus" shall say: "I bann thy opponent to what the Salic law decrees." Then he to whom the promise was made shall warn him (the debtor) to make no

payment or pledge of payment to any body else until he have fulfilled his promise to him (the creditor). And straightway on that same day, before the sun sets, he shall go to the house of that man with witnesses, and shall ask if he will pay that debt. If he will not, he (the creditor) shall wait until after sunset; then, if he shall have waited until after sunset, 120 denars, which make 3 shillings shall be added on to the debt. And this shall be done up to 3 times in 3 weeks. And if at the third time he will not pay all this, it (the sum) shall increase to 360 denars, or 9 shillings: so, namely, that, after each admonition or waiting until after sunset, 3 shillings shall be added to the debt.

3. If any one be unwilling to fulfil his promise in the regular assembly,—then he to whom the promise was made shall go to the count of that place, in whose district he lives, and shall take the stalk and shall say: oh count, that man made me a promise to pay, and I have lawfully summoned him before the court according to the Salic law on this matter; I pledge thee myself and my fortune that thou may'st safely seize his property. And he shall state the case to him, and shall tell how much he (the debtor) had agreed to pay. Then the count shall collect 7 suitable bailiffs, and shall go with them to the house of him who made the promise and shall say: thou who art here present pay voluntarily to that man what thou didst promise, and choose any two of these bailiffs who shall appraise that from which thou shalt pay; and make good what thou dost owe, according to a just appraisal. But if he will not hear, or be absent, then the bailiffs shall take from his property the value of the debt which he owes. And, according to the law, the accuser shall take two thirds of that which the debtor owes, and the count shall collect for himself the other third as peace money; unless the peace money shall have been paid to him before in this same matter.

4. If the count have been appealed to, and no sufficient reason, and no duty of the king, have detained him—and if he have put off going, and have sent no substitute to demand law and justice: he shall answer for it with his life, or shall redeem himself with his "wergeld."

Title LIV. Concerning the Slaying of a Count.

1. If any one slay a count, he shall be sentenced to 24000 denars, which make 600 shillings.

Title LV. Concerning the Plundering of Corpses.

2. If any one shall have dug up and plundered a corpse already buried, and it shall have been proved on him, he shall be outlawed until the day when he comes to an agreement with the relatives of the dead man, and they ask for him that he be allowed to come among men. And whoever, before he come to an arrangement with the relative, shall give him bread or shelter—even if they are his relations or his own wife—shall be sentenced to 600 denars which make 15 shillings.

3. But he who is proved to have committed the crime shall be sentenced to 8000 denars, which make 200 shillings.

Title LVI. Concerning him who shall have scorned to come to Court.

1. If any man shall have scorned to come to court, and shall have put off fulfilling the injunction of the bailiffs, and shall have not been willing to consent to undergo the fine, or the kettle ordeal, or anything prescribed by law: then he (the plaintiff) shall summon him to the presence of the king. And there shall be 12 witnesses who—3 at a time being sworn—shall testify that they were present when the bailiff enjoined him (the accused) either to go to the kettle ordeal, or to agree concerning the fine; and that he had scorned

the injunction. Then 3 others shall swear that they were there on the day when the bailiffs enjoined that he should free himself by the kettle ordeal or by composition; and that 40 days after that, in the "mallberg," he (the accuser) had again waited until after sunset, and that he (the accused) would not obey the law. Then he (the accuser) shall summon him before the king for a fortnight thence; and three witnesses shall swear that they were there when he summoned him and when he waited for sunset. If he does not then come, those 9, being sworn, shall give testimony as we have above explained. On that day likewise, if he do not come, he (the accuser) shall let the sun go down on him, and shall have 3 witnesses who shall be there when he waits till sunset. But if the accuser shall have fulfilled all this, and the accused shall not have been willing to come to any court, then the king, before whom he has been summoned, shall withdraw his protection from him. Then he shall be guilty, and all his goods shall belong to the fisc, or to him to whom the fisc may wish to give them. And whoever shall have fed or housed him—even if it were his own wife—shall be sentenced to 600 denars, which make 15 shillings; until he (the debtor) shall have made good all that has been laid to his charge.

Title LVII. Concerning the "Chrenecruda."

1. If any one have killed a man, and, having given up all his property, has not enough to comply with the full terms of the law, he shall present 12 sworn witnesses to the effect that, neither above the earth nor under it, has he any more property than he has already given. And he shall afterwards go into his house, and shall collect in his hand dust from the four corners of it, and shall afterwards stand upon the threshold, looking inwards into the house. And then, with his left hand, he shall throw over his shoulder some of that dust on the nearest relative that he has. But if his father and (his father's) brothers have already paid, he shall then throw that dust on their (the brothers') children—that is, over three (relatives) who are nearest on the father's and three on the mother's side. And after that, in his shirt, without girdle and without shoes, a staff in his hand, he shall spring over the hedge. And then those three shall pay half of what is lacking of the compounding money or the legal fine; that is, those others who are descended in the paternal line shall do this.

2. But if there be one of those relatives who has not enough to pay his whole indebtedness, he, the poorer one, shall in turn throw the "chrenecruda" on him of them who has the most, so that he shall pay the whole fine.

3. But if he also have not enough to pay the whole, then he who has charge of the murderer shall bring him before the "Thing," and afterwards to 4 Things, in order that they (his friends) may take him under their protection. And if no one have taken him under his protection. And if no one have taken him under his protection—that is, so as to redeem him for what he can not pay—then he shall have to atone with his life.

Title LIX. Concerning private Property.

1. If any man die and leave no sons, if the father and mother survive, they shall inherit.

2. If the father and mother do not survive, and he leave brothers or sisters, they shall inherit.

3. But if there are none, the sisters of the father shall inherit.

4. But if there are no sisters of the father, the sisters of the mother shall claim that inheritance.

5. If there are none of these, the nearest relatives on the father's side shall succeed to that inheritance.

6. But of Salic land no portion of the inheritance shall come to a woman; but the whole inheritance of the land shall come to the male sex.

Title LXII. Concerning Wergeld.

1. If any one's father have been killed, the sons shall have half the compounding money (wergeld); and the other half the nearest relatives, as well on the mother's as on the father's side, shall divide among themselves.

2. But if there are no relatives, paternal or maternal, that portion shall go to the fisc.

Bishops Remigius of Reims and Avitus of Vienne

Letters to Clovis

The following two letters are the only contemporary records directly addressed to Clovis. Remigius of Reims (ca. 437-533) wrote Clovis shortly after he succeeded his father in 481/82 and well before his victory over Syagrius at Soissons in 486 or his conversion. The letter of Avitus was written after Clovis' conversion to Orthodox Christianity. From the letter it is unclear whether Clovis was converted from paganism, as Gregory of Tours asserts, or from Arianism.

Translation: J.N. Hillgarth, *Christianity and Paganism, 350-750* (Philadelphia: University of Pennsylvania Press, 1986).

Bishop Remigius of Reims to Clovis (*c.*481).

To the celebrated and rightly magnificent Lord, King Clovis, Bishop Remigius.

A strong report has come to us that you have taken over the administration of the Second Belgic Province. There is nothing new in that you now begin to be what your parents always were. First of all, you should act so that God's Judgment may not abandon you and that your merits should maintain you at the height where you have arrived by your humility. For, as the proverb says, man's acts are judged. You ought to associate with yourself counselors who are able to do honor to your reputation. Your deeds should be chaste and honest. You should defer to your bishops and always have recourse to their advice. If you are on good terms with them your province will be better able to stand firm. Encourage your people, relieve the afflicted, protect widows, nourish orphans, so shine forth that all may love and fear you. May justice proceed from your mouth. Ask nothing of the poor or of strangers, do not allow yourself to receive gifts from them. Let your tribunal be open to all men, so that no man may leave it with the sorrow [of not having been heard]. You possess the riches your father left you. Use them to ransom captives and free them from servitude. If someone is admitted to your presence let him not feel he is a stranger. Amuse yourself with young men, deliberate with the old. If you wish to reign, show yourself worthy to do so.

Bishop Avitus to King Clovis.

The followers of [Arian] error have in vain, by a cloud of contradictory and untrue opinions, sought to conceal from your extreme subtlety the glory of the Christian name. While we committed these questions to eternity and trusted that the truth of each man's belief would appear at the Future Judgment, the ray of truth has shone forth even among present shadows. Divine Providence has found the arbiter of our age. Your choice is a general sentence. Your Faith is our victory. Many others, in this matter, when their bishops or friends exhort them to adhere to the True Faith, are accustomed to oppose the traditions of their race and respect for their ancestral cult; thus they culpably prefer a false shame to their salvation. While they observe a futile reverence for their parents [by continuing to share their] unbelief, they confess that they do not know what they should choose to do. After this marvelous deed guilty shame can no longer shelter behind this excuse. Of all your ancient genealogy you have chosen to keep only your own nobility, and you have willed that your race should derive from you all the glories which adorn high birth. Your ancestors have prepared a great destiny for you; you willed to prepare better things [for those who will follow you]. You follow your ancestors in reigning in this world; you have opened the way to your descendants to a heavenly reign. Let Greece indeed rejoice it has elected an emperor who shares our Faith; it is no longer alone in deserving such a favour. Your sphere also burns with its own brilliance, and, in the person of a king, the light of a rising sun shines over the Western lands. It is right that this light began at the Nativity of Our Redeemer, so that the waters of rebirth have brought you forth to salvation the very day that the world received the birth of its Redemption, the Lord of Heaven. The day celebrated as the Lord's Nativity is also yours, in which you have consecrated your soul to God, your life to your contemporaries, your glory to posterity.

What should be said of the glorious solemnity of your regeneration? If I could not assist in person among the ministers [of the rite] I shared in its joy. Thanks to God, our land took part in the thanksgiving, for, before your Baptism, a messenger of Your Most Subtle Humility informed us that you were a "competens" [that is, to be baptized within forty days]. Therefore the sacred night [of Christmas] found us sure of what you would do. We saw (with the eyes of the spirit) that great sight, when a crowd of bishops around you, in the ardour of their holy ministry, poured over your royal limbs the waters of life; when that head feared by the peoples bowed down before the servants of God; when your royal locks, hidden under a helmet, were steeped in holy oil; when your breast, relieved of its cuirass, shone with the same whiteness as your baptismal robes. Do not doubt, most flourishing of kings, that this soft clothing will give more force to your arms: whatever Fortune has given up to now, this Sanctity will bestow.

I would wish to add some exhortations to your praises if anything escaped either your knowledge or your attention. Should we preach the Faith to the convert who perceived it without a preacher; or humility, which you have long shown toward us [bishops], although you only owe it to us now, after your profession of Faith; or mercy, attested, in tears and joy to God and men, by a people once captive, now freed by you? One wish remains for me to express. Since God, thanks to you, will make of your people His own possession, offer a part of the treasure of Faith which fills your heart to the peoples living beyond you, who, still living in natural ignorance, have not been corrupted by the seeds of perverse doctrines [that is, Arianism]. Do not fear to send them envoys and to plead with them the cause of God, who has done so much for your cause. So that the other pagan peoples, at first being subject to your empire for the sake of religion, while they still seem to have another ruler, may be distinguished rather by their race than by their prince. [End of letter missing.]

Gregory of Tours

History of the Franks

Gregory of Tours (ca. 540-594) was a member of an illustrious Gallo-Roman family that had dominated the episcopal see of Tours for centuries. His History of the Franks *is the most important source for early Frankish history. Gregory was primarily concerned in his history with Orthodox Christianity, with his community of Tours, and with his Gallo-Roman aristocratic colleagues. He worked closely with the Frankish kings, whom he saw as instruments of divine providence. These concerns are evident in the following passages. The first is his account of Clovis. Written almost a century after the events it describes, it is largely unreliable for a detailed account of Clovis but essential for understanding the meaning of Clovis to later Frankish history. The other selections show Gregory's activities as peacemaker in Tours and his involvement with his contemporary kings of the Franks.*

Source: Lewis Thorpe, tr. *Gregory of Tours, The History of the Franks* (Harmondsworth: Penguin Books, 1974).

Excerpts from Book II

12. Childeric, King of the Franks, whose private life was one long debauch, began to seduce the daughters of his subjects. They were so incensed about this that they forced him to give up his throne. He discovered that they intended to assassinate him and he fled to Thuringia. He left behind a close friend of his who was able to soothe the minds of his angry subjects with his honeyed words. Childeric entrusted to him a token which should indicate when he might return to his homeland. They broke a gold coin into two equal halves. Childeric took one half with him and the friend kept the other half. 'When I send my half to you,' said his friend, 'and the two halves placed together make a complete coin, you will know that you may return home safe and sound.' Childeric then set out for Thuringia and took refuge with King Bisinus and his wife Basina. As soon as Childeric had gone, the Franks unanimously chose as their king that same Aegidius who, as I have already said, had been sent out of Rome as commander of the armies. When Aegidius had reigned over the Franks for eight years, Childeric's faithful friend succeeded in pacifying them secretly and he sent messengers to the exile with the half of the broken coin which he had in his possession. By this token Childeric knew for sure that the Franks wanted him back, indeed that they were clamoring for him to return, and he left Thuringia and was restored to his throne. Now that Bisinus and Childeric were both kings, Queen Basina, about whom I have told you, deserted her husband and joined Childeric. He questioned her closely as to why she had come from far away to be with him, and she is said to have answered: 'I know that you are a strong man and I recognize ability when I see it. I have therefore come to live with you. You can be sure that if I knew anyone else, even far across the sea, who was more capable than you, I should have sought him out and gone to live with him instead.' This pleased Childeric very much and he married her. She became pregnant and bore a son whom she named Clovis. He was a great man and became a famous soldier.

13. After the death of Saint Arthemius, Venerandus, a man of senatorial rank, was con-

secrated as Bishop of Clermont-Ferrand. Paulinus gives us information as to what sort of man this Bishop was:

> Today when you see Bishops as worthy of the Lord as Emperius of Toulouse, Simplicius of Vienne, Armandus of Bordeaux, Diogenianus of Albi, Venerandus of Clermont, Alithius of Cahors and now Pegasus of Périgueux, you will see that we have excellent guardians of all our faith and religion, however great may be the evils of our age.

Venerandus is said to have died on Christmas Eve. The next morning the Christmas procession was also his funeral cortège. After his death the most shameful argument arose among the local inhabitants concerning the election of a bishop to replace him. Different factions were formed some of which wanted this man and others that, and there was great dissension among the people. One Sunday when the electing bishops were sitting in conclave, a woman wearing a veil over her head to mark the fact that she was a true servant of God came boldly in and said: 'Listen to me, priests of the Lord! You must realize that it is true that not one of those whom they have put forward for the bishopric finds favour in the sight of God. This very day the Lord in person will choose Himself a bishop. Do not inflame the people or allow any more argument among them, but be patient for a little while, for the Lord will now send to us the man who is to rule over our church.' As they sat wondering at her words, there came in a man called Rusticus, who was himself a priest of the diocese of this city of Clermont-Ferrand. He was the very man who had been pointed out to the woman in a vision. As soon as she set eyes on him she cried: 'That is the man whom the Lord elects! That is the man whom He has chosen to be your bishop! That is the man whom you must consecrate!' As she spoke the entire population forgot all its previous disagreement and shouted that this was the correct and proper choice. To the great joy of the populace Rusticus was set on the episcopal throne and inducted as Bishop. He was the seventh to be made Bishop in Clermont-Ferrand.

14. In the city of Tours Bishop Eustochius died in the seventeenth year of his episcopate. Perpetuus was consecrated in his place, being the fifth bishop after Saint Martin. When Perpetuus saw how frequently miracles were being performed at Saint Martin's tomb and when he observed how small was the chapel erected over the Saint's body, he decided that it was unworthy of these wonders. He had the chapel removed and he built in its place the great church which is still there some five hundred and fifty yards outside the city. It is one hundred and sixty feet long by sixty feet broad; and its height up to the beginning of the vaulting is forty-five feet. It has thirty-two windows in the sanctuary and twenty in the nave, with forty-one columns. In the whole building there are fifty-two windows, one hundred and twenty columns and eight doorways, three in the sanctuary and five in the nave. The great festival of the church has a threefold significance: it marks the dedication of the building, the translation of the Saint's body and his ordination as a bishop. You should observe this feast-day on 4 July; and you should remember that Saint Martin died on 11 November. If you celebrate this faithfully you will gain the protection of the saintly Bishop in this world and the next. The vault of the tiny chapel which stood there before was most elegantly designed, and so Bishop Perpetuus thought it wrong to destroy it. He built another church in honor of the blessed Apostles Peter and Paul, and he fitted this vault over it. He built many other churches which still stand firm today in the name of Christ.

15. At this time the church of the blessed martyr Symphorian of Autun was built by the priest Eufronius, and later on Eufronius was elected as Bishop of that city. It was he who, in great devotion, sent the marble lid which covers the tomb of Saint Martin.

16. After the death of Bishop Rusticus, Saint Namatius became the eighth Bishop of Clermont-Ferrand. It was he who built by his effort the church which still stands and

which is considered to be the oldest within the city walls. It is one hundred and fifty feet long, sixty feet wide inside the nave and fifty feet high as far as the vaulting. It has a rounded apse at the end, and two wings of elegant design on either side. The whole building is constructed in the shape of a cross. It has forty-two windows, seventy columns and eight doorways. In it one is conscious of the fear of God and of a great brightness, and those at prayer are often aware of a most sweet and aromatic odour which is being wafted towards them. Round the sanctuary it has walls which are decorated with mosaic work made of many varieties of marble. When the building had been finished for a dozen years, the saintly Bishop sent priests to Bologna, the city in Italy, to procure for him the relics of Saint Agricola and Saint Vitalis, who, as I have shown, were assuredly crucified in the name of Christ our Lord.

17. The wife of Namatius built the church of Saint Stephen in the suburb outside the walls of Clermont-Ferrand. She wanted it to be decorated with colored frescoes. She used to hold in her lap a book from which she would read stories of events which happened long ago, and tell the workmen what she wanted painted on the walls. One day as she was sitting in the church and reading these stories, there came a poor man to pray. He saw her in her black dress, a woman already far advanced in age. He thought that she was one of the needy, so he produced a piece of bread, put it in her lap and went on his way. She did not scorn the gift of this poor man, who had not understood who she was. She took it, and thanked him, and put it on one side. She ate it instead of her other food and each day she received a blessing from it until it was all eaten up.

18. Childeric fought a battle at Orleans. Odovacar with his Saxons penetrated as far as Angers. A great pestilence caused the death of many people. Aegidius died and left a son called Syagrius. After the death of Aegidius, Odovacar took hostages from Angers and other places. The Bretons were expelled from Bourges by the Goths and many were killed at Bourg-de-Déois. Count Paul, who had Roman and Frankish troops under his command, attacked the Goths and seized booty from them. Odovacar reached Angers, but King Childeric arrived there on the following day: Count Paul was killed and Childeric occupied the city. On that day the church-house was burnt down in a great fire.

19. While these things were happening a great war was waged between the Saxons and the Romans. The Saxons fled and many of their men were cut down by the Romans who pursued them. Their islands[1] were captured and laid waste by the Franks, and many people were killed. In the ninth month of that year there was an earthquake. Odovacar made a treaty with Childeric and together they subdued the Alamanni, who had invaded a part of Italy.

20. During the fourteenth year of his reign, Euric, King of the Goths, put Duke Victorius in charge of the seven cities. Victorius went straight to Clermont-Ferrand and made certain additions to the city. The underground chapels which he constructed are still there today. It was he who had erected in the church of Saint Julian the columns which are still part of the building. He also built the church of Saint Lawrence and the church of Saint Germanus in Saint-Germain-Lanbron. Victorius was nine years in Clermont. He spread a number of scandalous rumors about the Senator Eucherius. Eucherius was thrown into prison. In the middle of the night Victorius had him brought out, he was attached to an old wall and then Victorius had the wall knocked down on top of him. Victorius was far too much given to irregular affairs with women. He was afraid of being assassinated by the men of Clermont and he fled to Rome. There he began to live the same loose life and he was stoned to death. Euric reigned for another four years after the death of Victorius. He died in the twenty-seventh year of his reign. There again occurred a big earthquake.

21. When Bishop Namatius died in Clermont-Ferrand, Eparchius succeeded him. He was a most saintly and devout man. At that time the church had very little property inside

the city walls. The Bishop had his lodging in what is now called the sacristy. He was in the habit of getting up in the middle of the night to give thanks to God before the high altar in his cathedral. One night it happened that as he went into the church he found it full of devils and Satan himself sitting on his own episcopal throne made up to look like a painted woman. 'You hideous prostitute,' said the Bishop, 'is it not enough that you infect other places with every imaginable sort of foulness, without your defiling the throne consecrated to the Lord by sitting your revolting body down on it? Leave the house of God this instant and stop polluting it with your presence!' 'Since you give me the title of prostitute,' said Satan, 'I will see that you yourself are constantly harassed with sexual desire.' As he said this he disappeared into thin air. It is true that the Bishop was tempted by lusts of the flesh, but he was protected by the sign of the Cross and the Devil was unable to harm him.

According to all accounts it was Eparchius who built the monastery on top of Mont Chantoin, where the oratory now is, and there he would go into retreat during the holy days of Lent. On the day of the Lord's Supper he would process down to his cathedral, escorted by his clergy and the townsfolk, and accompanied by a great singing of psalms.

When Eparchius died he was succeeded by Sidonius Apollinaris, one-time Prefect of the City, a man of most noble birth as honors are counted in this world, and one of the leading Senators of Gaul, so noble indeed that he married the daughter of the Emperor Avitus. In his time, while Victorius, about whom I have already told you, was still in Clermont, there lived in the monastery of Saint-Cyr in the same city an abbot called Abraham, who, thanks to his predecessor and namesake, was greatly distinguished by his faith and good works, as I have told you in my other book where his life is recorded.

22. The saintly Sidonius was so eloquent that he would often speak extempore in public without hesitating in the slightest and express whatever he had to say with the greatest clarity. One day it happened that he went to the monastery church of which I have told you, for he had been invited there for a festival. Some malicious person removed the book with which it was his habit to conduct the church service. Sidonius was so well versed in the ritual that he took them through the whole service of the festival without pausing for a moment. This was a source of wonder to everyone present and they had the impression that it must be an angel speaking rather than a man. I have described this in more detail in the preface of the book which I wrote about the Masses composed by Sidonius. He was a very saintly man and, as I have said, a member of one of the foremost senatorial families. Without saying anything to his wife he would remove silver vessels from his home and give them away to the poor. When she found out what he had done, she used to grumble at him; then he would buy the silver vessels back from the poor folk and bring them home again.

23. At the time when Sidonius was living a saintly life here on earth and was completely devoted to the service of the Lord, two priests rebelled against him. They removed from him all control over the property of his church, reduced him to a very straitened way of life and submitted him to every kind of contumely. God in His clemency did not permit this insult to go long unpunished. One of these two insidious men, who was unworthy to be called by the name of priest, had threatened the night before to drag Sidonius out of his own church. When he got up the next morning on hearing the bell which called to matins, this man was full of spite against the holy man of God, and was busy turning over in his mind how he could best carry out a plan which he had formed the previous evening. He went off to the lavatory and while he was occupied in emptying his bowels he lost his soul instead. A boy was waiting outside with a candle, expecting his master to emerge at any moment. Day dawned. His accomplice, the other priest, sent someone to see what had happened. 'Come quickly,' said the messenger, 'don't hang about in there any longer, we must do together what we planned yesterday.' The dead man gave no answer. The boy lifted up the curtain of the lavatory and found his master dead on the seat. From this we may deduce that this man was guilty of a crime no less serious than that of Arius, who in

the same way emptied out his entrails through his back passage in the lavatory. This, too, smacks of heresy, that one of God's bishops should not be obeyed in his own church, the man to whom had been entrusted the task of feeding God's flock, and that someone else to whom nothing at all had been entrusted, either by God or by man, should have dared to usurp his authority.

After that the saintly Bishop, to whom, mark you, there still remained one of his two enemies, was restored to his authority. Some time later Sidonius fell ill with a very high temperature. He ordered his attendants to carry him into the church. He was borne inside and a great crowd of men and women, and of little children, too, gathered round him, weeping and saying: 'Good shepherd, why are you deserting us? To whom will you abandon us, your orphan children? If you die, what sort of life can we expect? Will there be anyone left to season our lives with the salt of wisdom and to inspire in us the fear of the Lord's name with the same insight which you have shown?' The citizens of Clermont wept as they said these things and others like them. Finally Bishop Sidonius answered them, for the Holy Spirit moved him to do so. 'Do not be afraid, my people,' said he. 'My brother Aprunculus is still alive and he will be your Bishop.' Those who were present did not understand him, and they thought that he was wandering in his mind.

After the death of Sidonius, the evil priest, the second of the two, the one who was still alive, blinded with greed, immediately laid hands on the property of the church, as if he were already bishop. 'God has at last taken notice of me,' said he, 'for He knows that I am more just than Sidonius and He has granted me this power.' He rode proudly through the whole city. On the Sunday following the death of the holy Bishop, this priest prepared a feast in the church-house and ordered all the townspeople to be invited. He showed no respect for the senior among them, but took his place at the table first. The cup-bearer passed him a goblet of wine and said: 'My lord, I have just seen a vision and this I will describe to you, if you permit. I saw it this very Sunday evening. I perceived a great hall, and in this hall there was placed a throne, and on this throne there sat a man, a sort of judge who seemed to have authority over everyone else present. A great throng of priests in white garments stood round him, and there were immense crowds of people of all sorts, so many that I could not count them. While I watched, and trembled as I watched, I saw the blessed Sidonius standing far off as if on a dais, and he was rebuking that dear friend of yours, the priest who died some years ago. The priest was worsted in this argument, and the King had him shut up in the deepest and smallest dungeon. When he had been put away, Sidonius turned on you, saying that you had been implicated in the crime for which the other had just been condemned. Then the judge began to make urgent inquiries to find someone whom he could send to you. I hid myself in the crowd and stood well back, holding my own counsel, for fear that I myself should be sent, for after all I know you very well. While I stood silent and lost in thought everyone else disappeared and I was left all alone in this public place. The judge called me forward and I went up to him. At the sight of him in all his dignity and splendour I lost control of myself and began to sway on my feet from sheer panic. "Do not be afraid, my boy," said he. "Go and tell that priest: 'Be present to answer the charge, for Sidonius has stipulated that you be summoned.'" You must go quickly, for the King commanded me to say what I have said, and he made this dire threat to me: "If you do not speak you will die a frightful death." As his servant said this the priest fell down dead on the spot and the goblet slid out of his hand. He was picked up dead from the couch on which he was reclining, and they buried him and so despatched him to join his accomplice in hell. The Lord passed this earthly judgement on those two unruly priests: one suffered the fate of Arius, and the other was dashed headlong from the very summit of his pride, like Simon Magus at the behest of the holy Apostle. No one can doubt that these two who plotted together against their holy Bishop now have their place side by side in nethermost hell.

Meanwhile rumors of the approach of the Franks were being repeated on all sides in these regions and everyone looked forward with great excitement to the moment when they would take over the government. Saint Aprunculus, the Bishop of the city of Langres, had fallen into ill-favour with the Burgundes. The hatred which they bore him became daily more bitter and an order went out that he should be executed in secret. This came to his ears and one night he was lowered down from the walls of Dijon. He escaped to Clermont-Ferrand and in accordance with the word of God, placed in the mouth of Sidonius, he became the eleventh bishop of that city.

24. In the days of Bishop Sidonius there was a great famine in Burgundy. The inhabitants were widely scattered over the countryside and there was nobody to distribute food to the poor. Then Ecdicius, one of the Senators and a close relative of Sidonius, with the help of God found a wonderful solution. He sent his servants and horses and carts through the neighboring cities and brought in those who were suffering from starvation. They went out and collected all the poor and needy they could find and brought them in to where Ecdicius lived. Throughout the long period of famine he provided them with food and so saved them from dying of hunger. There were, so they say, more than four thousand of them, both men and women. When the time of plenty returned, he arranged transport home again for them and took each man and woman back to where he or she lived. After they had gone a voice was heard from Heaven, saying to him: 'Ecdicius, Ecdicius, because you have done this thing you and your descendants will never lack food; for you have obeyed my word and by feeding the poor you have stayed my hunger, too.' Many witnesses have reported how swift this Ecdicius was to take action. There is a story that he once repelled a strong force of Goths with only ten men to help him. Saint Patiens, Bishop of Lyons, is said to have succored his people in just the same way during the famine. There is still in existence a letter written by Saint Sidonius in which he praises Patiens very highly for this.

25. At the same time Euric, King of the Goths, crossed the Spanish frontier and began a terrible persecution of the Christians in Gaul. Without ado he cut off the heads of all who would not subscribe to his heretical opinions, he imprisoned the priests, and the bishops he either drove into exile or had executed. He ordered the doorways of the churches to be blocked with briers so that the very difficulty of finding one's way in might encourage men to forget their Christian faith. It was mainly the district between the River Garonne and the Pyrenees and the towns of the two Aquitaines which suffered from this violent attack.[2] We still possess a letter by the noble Sidonius written to Bishop Basilus about this, in which he gives full details. Soon afterwards the persecutor died, struck down by the vengeance of God.

26. Not long afterwards Saint Perpetuus, Bishop of the city of Tours, reached the end of his life, having been bishop for thirty years. Volusianus, a man of senatorial rank, was appointed in his place. He was regarded with suspicion by the Goths. In the seventh year of his episcopate he was dragged off as a captive to Spain and there he soon died. Verus succeeded him and was ordained as the seventh Bishop after Saint Martin.

27. The next thing which happened was that Childeric died. His son Clovis replaced him on the throne. In the fifth year of his reign, Syagrius, the King of the Romans and the son of Aegidius, was living in the city of Soissons, where Aegidius himself used to have his residence. Clovis marched against him with his blood-relation Ragnachar, who also had high authority, and challenged him to come out to fight. Syagrius did not hesitate to so do, for he was not afraid of Clovis. They fought each other and the army of Syagrius was annihilated. He fled and made his way as quickly as he could to King Alaric II in Toulouse. Clovis summoned Alaric to surrender the fugitive, informing him that he would attack him in his turn for having given Syagrius refuge. Alaric was afraid to incur the wrath of the Franks for the sake of Syagrius and handed him over bound to the envoys, for the Goths are a timorous race. When Clovis had Syagrius in his power he ordered him to be imprisoned. As soon as he had seized the kingdom of Syagrius he had him killed in secret....Clovis waged many wars and won many victories. In the tenth year of his reign he invaded the Thuringians and subjected them to his rule.

28. The King of the Burgundes was called Gundioc; he was of the family of that King Athanaric who persecuted the Christians and about whom I have told you. He had four sons: Gundobad, Godigisel, Chilperic and Gundomar. Gundobad killed his brother Chilperic and drowned Chilperic's wife after tying a stone round her neck. He drove Chilperic's two daughters into exile: the elder, whose name was Chroma, became a religious, and the younger was called Clotild. Clovis often sent envoys to Burgundy and they saw the girl Clotild. They observed that she was an elegant young woman and clever for her years, and they discovered that she was of the blood royal. They reported all this to Clovis and he immediately sent more messengers to Gundobad to ask for her hand in marriage. Gundobad was afraid to refuse and he handed Clotild over to them. They took her back with them, and presented her to their King. Clovis already had a son called Theuderic by one of his mistresses, but he was delighted when he saw Clotild and made her his wife.

29. The first child which Clotild bore for Clovis was a son. She wanted to have her baby baptized, and she kept on urging her husband to agree to this. 'The gods whom you worship are no good,' she would say. 'They haven't even been able to help themselves, let alone others. They are carved out of stone or wood or some old piece of metal. The very names which you have given them were the names of men, not of gods. Take your Saturn, for example, who ran away from his own son to avoid being exiled from his kingdom, or so they say; and Jupiter, that obscene perpetrator of all sorts of mucky deeds, who couldn't keep his hands off other men, who had his fun with all his female relatives and couldn't even refrain from intercourse with his own sister,

'...Jovisque
Et soror et coniunx,'

to quote her own words. What have Mars and Mercury ever done for anyone? They may have been endowed with magic arts, but they were certainly not worthy of being called divine. You ought instead to worship Him who created at a word and out of nothing heaven, and earth, the sea and all that therein is, who made the sun to shine, who lit the sky with stars, who peopled the water with fish, the earth with beasts, the sky with flying creatures, at whose nod the fields became fair with fruits, the trees with apples, the vines with grapes, by whose hand the race of man was made, by whose gift all creation is constrained to serve in deference and devotion the man He made.' However often the Queen said this, the King came no nearer to belief. 'All these things have been created and produced at the command of *our* gods,' he would answer. 'It is obvious that *your* God can do nothing, and there is no proof that he is a God at all.'

The Queen, who was true to her faith, brought her son to be baptized. She ordered the church to be decorated with hangings and curtains, in the hope that the King, who remained stubborn in the face of argument, might be brought to the faith by ceremony. The child was baptized; he was given the name Ingomer; but no sooner had he received baptism than he died in his white robes. Clovis was extremely angry. He began immediately to reproach his Queen. 'If he had been dedicated in the name of my gods,' he said, 'he would have lived without question; but now that he has been baptized in the name of your God he has not been able to live a single day!' 'I give thanks to Almighty God,' replied Clotild, 'the Creator of all things, who has not found me completely unworthy, for he Has deigned to welcome into His kingdom a child conceived in my womb. I am not at all cast down in my mind because of what has happened, for I know that my child, who was called away from this world in his white baptismal robes, will be nurtured in the sight of God.'

Some time later Clotild bore a second son. He was baptized Chlodomer. He began to ail and Clovis said: 'What else do you expect? It will happen to him as it happened to his brother: no sooner is he baptized in the name of your Christ than he will die!' Clotild prayed to the Lord and at His command the baby recovered.

30. Queen Clotild continued to pray that her husband might recognize the true God and

give up his idol-worship. Nothing could persuade him to accept Christianity. Finally war broke out against the Alamanni and in this conflict he was forced by necessity to accept what he had refused of his own free will. It so turned out that when the two armies met on the battlefield there was a great slaughter and the troops of Clovis were rapidly being annihilated. He raised his eyes to heaven when he saw this, felt compunction in his heart and was moved to tears. 'Jesus Christ,' he said, 'you who Clotild maintains to be the Son of the living God, you who deign to give help to those in travail and victory to those who trust in you, in faith I beg the glory of your help. If you will give me victory over my enemies, and if I may have evidence of that miraculous power which the people dedicated to your name say that they have experienced, then I will believe in you and I will be baptized in your name. I have called upon my own gods, but, as I see only too clearly, they have no intention of helping me. I therefore cannot believe that they possess any power, for they do not come to the assistance of those who trust them. I now call upon you. I want to believe in you, but I must first be saved from my enemies.' Even as he said this the Alamanni turned their backs and began to run away. As soon as they saw that their King was killed, they submitted to Clovis. 'We beg you,' they said, 'to put an end to this slaughter. We are prepared to obey you.' Clovis stopped the war. He made a speech in which he called for peace. Then he went home. He told the Queen how he had won a victory by calling on the name of Christ. This happened in the fifteenth year of his reign.

31. The Queen then ordered Saint Remigius, Bishop of the town of Rheims, to be summoned in secret. She begged him to impart the word of salvation to the King. The Bishop asked Clovis to meet him in private and began to urge him to believe in the true God, Maker of heaven and earth, and to forsake his idols, which were powerless to help him or anyone else. The King replied: 'I have listened to you willingly, holy father. There remains one obstacle. The people under my command will not agree to forsake their gods. I will go and put to them what you have just said to me.' He arranged a meeting with his people, but God in his power had preceded him, and before he could say a word all those present shouted in unison: 'We will give up worshipping our mortal gods, pious King, and we are prepared to follow the immortal God about whom Remigius preaches.' This news was reported to the Bishop. He was greatly pleased and he ordered the baptismal pool to be made ready. The public squares were draped with colored cloths, the churches were adorned with white hangings, the baptistry was prepared, sticks of incense gave off clouds of perfume, sweet-smelling candles gleamed bright and the holy place of baptism was filled with divine fragrance. God filled the hearts of all present with such grace that they imagined themselves to have been transported to some perfumed paradise. King Clovis asked that he might be baptized first by the Bishop. Like some new Constantine he stepped forward to the baptismal pool, ready to wash away the sores of his old leprosy and to be cleansed in flowing water from the sordid stains which he had borne so long. As he advanced for his baptism, the holy man of God addressed him in these pregnant words: 'Bow your head in meekness, Sicamber.[3] Worship what you have burnt, burn what you have been wont to worship.'

Saint Remigius was a bishop of immense learning and a great scholar more than anything else, but he was also famous for his holiness and he was the equal of Saint Silvester for the miracles which he performed. We still have an account of his life, which tells how he raised a man from the dead. King Clovis confessed his belief in God Almighty, three in one. He was baptized in the name of the Father, the Son and the Holy Ghost, and marked in holy chrism with the sign of the Cross of Christ. More than three thousand of his army were baptized at the same time. His sister Albofled was baptized, but she soon after died and was gathered to the Lord. The King grieved over her death, but Saint Remigius sent him a consoling letter which began with these words:

I am greatly distressed and I share your grief at the loss of your sister of pious memory. We can take consolation in this, that she has met her death in such a way that we can look up to her instead of mourning for her.

Another sister of Clovis, called Lanthechild, was converted at the same time. She had accepted the Arian heresy, but she confessed the triune majesty of the Father, the Son and the Holy Ghost, and received the holy chrism.

32. At this time the two brothers Gundobad and Godigisel ruled over the territory round the Rhône and the Saône and the province of Marseilles. Like their subjects they belonged to the Arian sect. They were enemies, and when Godigisel heard of the victories won by King Clovis he sent envoys to him in secret. 'If you help me to attack my brother,' he said, I will pay you any annual tribute which you may care to exact.' Clovis gladly accepted the offer and in his turn promised to help Godigisel wherever occasion should arise. They chose a suitable moment and Clovis marched his army against Gundobad. As soon as he heard of this, Gundobad, who knew nothing of his brother's treachery, sent a message to Godigisel. 'Come to my assistance,' he said, 'for the Franks are marching against us and are invading our territory which they plan to capture. Let us make a common front against this people which hates us, for if we are not united we shall suffer the same fate which others have met before us.' Godigisel answered: 'I am coming with my army and I will support you.' The three kings each put his army in the field, Clovis marching against Gundobad and Godigisel. They arrived with all their military equipment at a fortified place called Dijon. When battle was joined on the River Ouche Godigisel went over to Clovis and their united forces crushed the army of Gundobad. Gundobad turned his back and fled when he saw the treachery of his brother, about whom he had no suspicion. He made his way along the banks of the Rhône and took refuge in the city of Avignon. As for Godigisel, once the victory was won, he promised to hand over part of his kingdom to Clovis and then went home in peace and entered Vienne in triumph, as if he were still master of his own territory. Clovis called up more troops and set out in pursuit of Gundobad, planning to extract him from Avignon and kill him. When Gundobad learned this he was panic-stricken, for he was afraid of being killed at any moment. He had with him a man of some distinction called Aridius. Aridius was astute and full of energy. Gundobad summoned this man to him and said: 'I am surrounded by pitfalls and what to do I cannot tell. These barbarians have launched this attack against me. If they kill us two they will ravage the whole neighborhood.' 'You must do all you can to propitiate this savage creature,' answered Aridius, 'or else you are done for. If you agree, I will run away from you and pretend to go over to his side. When I have joined him I will see to it that no harm is done to you or to this region. If you will only carry out my plan in all its details, the Lord God in his compassion will assure you a happy outcome.' 'I will do whatever you say,' replied Gundobad. Having received his answer, Aridius bade him good-bye and left him. He made his way to Clovis. 'I am your humble slave, most pious King,' said he. 'I have deserted the wretched Gundobad and come to join your forces. If you are prepared to accept me kindly, then you and your descendants will find in me a faithful and trustworthy retainer.' Clovis accepted this offer without hesitating for a moment and kept Aridius by his side. He was a wonderful raconteur, full of good advice, sound in judgement and apparently trustworthy. Clovis remained encamped with his entire army round the city walls. 'If you who are a king with absolute power would deign to accept a little advice from me who am no one,' said Aridius to him, 'this is the loyal proposition which I should like to put to you. What I am going to say will be to your advantage and at the same time to the advantage of the cities through which you propose to pass. What is the point of keeping all these troops under arms when your enemy is safe in a stronghold which is too well fortified for you to capture? You are destroying the fields, spoiling the meadows, cutting up the vineyards, ruining the olive-groves and ravaging the whole countryside, which is a very fruitful one. In doing this you are causing no harm whatsoever to Gundobad. Why don't you send an ultimatum to him to say that he must pay whatever annual tribute you care to exact? In that way the region will be saved and he will have to submit to you and pay tribute to you for ever. If he doesn't accept this, you can do whatever you wish.' Clovis accepted the advice of Aridius and sent his army home. Then he dispatched envoys to Gundobad and ordered him to pay yearly tribute. Gundo-

bad paid up for the year in question and promised that he would do the same from then onwards.

33. Later on Gundobad recovered his strength and scorned to pay King Clovis the tribute which he had been promised. He marched his army against his brother Godigisel and besieged him inside his city of Vienne. Once provisions began to run short among the common people, Godigisel was afraid that the lack of food might extend to him also, and he ordered them to be driven out of the town. This was done, but along with them was expelled the engineer who was in charge of the aqueduct. He was very indignant at having been ejected with the others. He went in a rage to Gundobad and revealed to him how he might break into the city and take vengeance on his brother. With this engineer to show them the way, Gundobad's army was led along the aqueduct. At their head marched a number of sappers with iron crowbars. There was a water-gate blocked by a great stone. Under the direction of the engineer they heaved this stone on one side with their crowbars, made their way into the city and attacked from the rear the defenders, who were still busy shooting their arrows from the wall. A trumpet-call was sounded from the centre of the city, the besiegers attacked the gateways, burst them open and rushed in. The townsfolk were caught between two fires and cut to pieces by two forces. Godigisel took refuge in one of the heretic churches, but he was killed there and his Arian bishop with him. The Franks who had been with Godigisel banded together in one of the towers. Gundobad gave orders that none of them should be maltreated. When he had disarmed them he sent them in exile to King Alaric in Toulouse. All the Gallo-Roman senators and the Burgundes who had sided with Godigisel were killed out of hand. This whole region, which is now called Burgundy, Gundobad took under his own rule. He instituted milder laws among the Burgundes, to stop them treating the Romans unjustly.

34. Gundobad came to realize that the religious tenets of the heretics were of no avail. He accepted that Christ, the Son of God, and the Holy Ghost are equal with the Father, and he asked the saintly Bishop of Vienne to arrange for him to be anointed with the chrism in secret. 'If you really believe what the Lord has Himself taught us,' said the Bishop, 'then you should carry it out. Christ said: "Whosoever therefore shall confess me before men, him I will confess also before my Father which is in heaven. But whosoever shall deny me before men, him will I also deny before my Father which is in heaven." In the same way He gave advice to the holy and blessed Apostles, whom He loved so much, saying: "But beware of men: for they will deliver you up to the councils, and they will scourge you in their synagogues; and ye shall be brought before governors and kings for my sake, for a testimony against them and the Gentiles." You are a king and you need not fear to be taken in charge by anyone: yet you are afraid of your subjects and you do not dare to confess in public your belief in the Creator of all things. Stop being so foolish and confess in front of them all what you say you believe in your heart. The blessed Apostle said: "For with the heart man believeth unto righteousness; and with the mouth confession is made unto salvation." Similarly the prophet said: "I will give thee thanks in the great congregation: I will praise thee among much people." And again: "I will praise thee, O Lord, among the people: I will sing unto thee among the nations." You are afraid of your people. Do you not realize that it is better that the people should accept your belief, rather than that you, a king, should pander to their every whim? You are the leader of your people; your people is not there to lord it over you. When you go to war, you yourself march at the head of the squadrons of your army and they follow where you lead. It is therefore preferable that they should learn the truth under your direction, rather than that at your death they should continue in their errors. For "God is not mocked," nor can He love the man who for an earthly kingdom refuses to confess Him before all the world.' Gundobad was worsted in this argument, but to his life's end he persisted in his obstinacy, refusing to confess in public that the three persons of the Trinity are equal.

    At this time Saint Avitus was at the height of his eloquence. Certain heresies began to be current in the town of Constantinople, first that of Eutyches and then that of Sabellius, who maintained that our Lord Jesus Christ had nothing about Him which was divine. At the request of King Gundobad Avitus wrote polemics against these heresies. We still possess these admirable letters, which at once denounced the heresy and supported the Church of God. He wrote a book of *Homilies*, six books in verse on the creation of the world and other cognate subjects, and nine books of *Letters*, among which are included the ones already mentioned. In the homily which he composed on the Rogations he says that these ceremonies, which we celebrate before the triumph of our Lord's Ascension, were instituted by Mamertus, Bishop of that same town of Vienne of which Avitus held the episcopate when he was writing, at a time when the townsfolk were terrified by a series of portents. Vienne was shaken by frequent earthquakes, and savage packs of wolves and stags came in through the gates and ranged through the entire city, fearing nothing and nobody, or so he writes. These portents continued throughout the whole year. As the season of the feast of Easter approached, the common people in their devotion expected God's compassion on them, hoping that this day of great solemnity might see an end of their terror. However, on the very vigil of the holy night, when the rite of Mass was being celebrated, the King's palace inside the city walls was set ablaze by fire sent by God. The congregation was panic-stricken. They rushed out of the church, for they thought that the whole town would be destroyed by this fire, or else that the earth would open and swallow it up. The holy Bishop was prostrate before the altar, imploring God's mercy with tears and lamentations. What more should I say? The prayers of this famous Bishop rose to heaven above and, so to speak, his floods of tears put out the fire in the palace. While this was going on, the feast of the Ascension of our Lord was coming nearer, as I have told you. Mamertus told the people to fast, he instituted a special form of prayer, a religious service and a grant of alms to the poor in thanksgiving. All the horrors came to an end. The story of what had happened spread through all the provinces and led all the bishops to copy what this particular prelate had done in faith. Down to our own times these rites are celebrated with a contrite spirit and a grateful heart in all our churches to the glory of God.

35. When Alaric II, the King of the Goths, observed that King Clovis was beating one race of people after another, he sent envoys to him. 'If you agree,' said he, 'it seems to me that it would be a good thing, my dear brother, if, with God's approval, we two were to meet.' Clovis did agree. He travelled to meet Alaric and the two of them came together near the village of Amboise, on an island in the Loire, in territory belonging to Tours. They conferred with each other, sat side by side at the meal table, swore eternal friendship and went home again in peace. At that time a great many people in Gaul were very keen on having the Franks as their rulers.

36. It was as a direct result of this that Quintianus, the Bishop of Rodez, fell into disfavour and was driven out of his city. The townsfolk started saying to him: 'If you had your way, the Franks would take over our territory.' Not long after this an open quarrel started between him and his flock. The Goths who were resident in Rodez suspected him, and the Rhuténois themselves went so far as to accuse him of wishing to accept the rule of the Franks. They plotted together and planned to assassinate him. When Quintianus came to hear of this, he fled one night and left the city with the more trustworthy among his attendants. He reached Clermont-Ferrand and there he was kindly received by Saint Eufrasius, who had succeeded to Aprunculus, himself a native of Dijon. Eufrasius gave him accommodation, with fields around and vineyards, for, as he said: "The resources of this diocese are sufficient to support us both: that charity which the blessed Apostle preached must continue between God's ministers.' The Bishop of Lyons also made over to Quintianus certain church property which he administered in Clermont. Other details concerning Saint Quintianus, the wrongs which were done to him and the miracles which the Lord deigned to perform through his agency, are described in my *Vitae Patruum*, in the chapter devoted to him.

37. 'I find it hard to go on seeing these Arians occupy a part of Gaul,' said Clovis to his ministers. 'With God's help let us invade them. When we have beaten them, we will take over their territory.' They all agreed to this proposal. An army was assembled and Clovis marched on Poitiers. Some of his troops passed through land belonging to Tours. In respect for Saint Martin Clovis ordered that they should requisition nothing in this neighborhood except fodder and water. One of the soldiers found some hay belonging to a poor man. 'The King commanded that nothing should be requisitioned except fodder, didn't he?' said this man. 'Well, this is fodder. We shan't be disobeying his orders if we take it.' He laid hands on the poor man and took his hay by main force. This was reported to Clovis. He drew his sword and killed the soldier on the spot. 'It is no good expecting to win this fight if we offend Saint Martin,' said he. This was enough to ensure that the army took nothing else from this region. The King sent messengers to the church of Saint Martin. 'Off with you,' he said, 'and see if you can bring me some good tidings from God's house.' He loaded them with gifts which they were to offer to the church. 'Lord God,' said he, 'if You are on my side and if You have decreed that this people of unbelievers, who have always been hostile to You, are to be delivered into my hands, deign to show me a propitious sign as these men enter Saint Martin's church, so that I may know that You will support your servant Clovis.' The messengers set out on their journey and came to Tours as Clovis had commanded. As they entered the church, it happened that the precentor was just beginning to intone this antiphon: 'For thou hast girded me with strength unto the battle: thou hast subdued under me those that rose up against me. Thou hast also given me the necks of mine enemies: that I might destroy them that hate me.' When the messengers heard this psalm, they gave thanks to God. They made their vows to the Saint and went happily back to report to the King. When Clovis reached the Vienne with his army, he was at a loss to know where to cross, for the river was swollen with heavy rains. That night he prayed that God might deign to indicate a ford by which he might make the crossing. As day dawned an enormous doe entered the water, as if to lead them at God's command. The soldiers knew that where the doe had crossed they could follow. The King marched towards Poitiers, and while he and his army were encamped there a pillar of fire rose from the church of Saint Hilary. It seemed to move towards Clovis as a sign that with the support of the blessed Saint he might the more easily overcome the heretic host, against which Hilary himself had so often done battle for the faith. Clovis forbade his troops to take any booty as they marched in, or to rob any man of his possessions.

At that time on the outskirts of Poitiers there dwelt a saintly Abbot called Maxentius, who lived as a God-fearing recluse in his monastery. There is no point in my giving the name of the monastery, as it is now called the Cell of Saint Maxentius. When the monks saw a squadron of troops coming nearer and nearer to their monastery they begged their Abbot to come out of his cell to give his blessing to the soldiers. He was a long time coming, and they were so frightened that they burst the door open and pushed him out of his cell. He showed no fear. He walked towards the troops, as if to ask them not to molest him. One of the soldiers drew his sword to strike Maxentius over the head. His arm went stiff on a level with the Saint's feet and asked his forgiveness. When his companions saw what had happened, they rushed back to the army in great consternation, for they were afraid that they might all pay for it with their lives. The blessed Saint rubbed the man's arm with holy oil, made the sign of the Cross over him, and he immediately recovered. As a result of what Maxentius had done the monastery remained unharmed. He performed many other miracles, as the diligent reader will discover if he peruses the Abbot's *Vita*. This happened in the fifteenth year of the reign of Clovis.

Meanwhile King Clovis met Alaric II, King of the Goths, on the battlefield of Vouillé, near the tenth milestone outside Poitiers. Some of the soldiers engaged hurled their javelins from a distance, others fought hand to hand. The Goths fled, as they were prone to do, and Clovis was the victor, for God was on his side. As one of his allies he had the son of Sigibert the Lame,[4] called Chloderic. Sigibert had been lame since he was wounded in the knee when fighting against the Alamanni at the fortress of Zülpich. Clovis killed Alaric, but, as the Goths fled, two of them suddenly rushed up in the scrum, one on this

169

side and one on that, and struck at the Frankish King with their spears. It was his leather corselet which saved him and the sheer speed of his horse, but he was very near to death. A large force of Auvergnats took part in the battle, for they had come under the command of Apollinaris; their leaders, who were of senatorial rank, were killed. Amalaric, the son of Alaric, escaped from the conflict and fled to Spain, where he later ruled his father's kingdom wisely. Clovis sent his own son Theuderic through Albi and the town of Rodez to Clermont-Ferrand. As he moved forward Theuderic subjected to his father's rule all the towns which lay between the two frontiers of the Goths and the Burgundes. Alaric II had reigned for twelve years. Clovis wintered in the town of Bordeaux. He removed all Alaric's treasure from Toulouse and went to Angoulême. There the Lord showed him such favour that the city walls collapsed of their own weight as he looked at them. Clovis drove the Goths out of Angoulême and took command of the city. With his victory consolidated he then returned to Tours. There he gave many gifts to the church of Saint Martin.

38. Letters reached Clovis from the Emperor Anastasius to confer the consulate on him. In Saint Martin's church he stood clad in a purple tunic and the military mantle, and he crowned himself with a diadem. He then rode out on his horse and with his own hand showered gold and silver coins among the people present all the way from the doorway of Saint Martin's church to Tours cathedral. From that day on he was called Consul or Augustus. He left Tours and travelled to Paris, where he established the seat of his government. Theuderic came to join him in Paris.

39. When Eustochius, Bishop of Tours, died, Licinius was ordained Bishop in his place. He was the eighth after Saint Martin. The war which I have just described was waged during the episcopate of Licinius, and it was in his time that King Clovis came to Tours. Licinius is said to have been in the East and to have visited the holy places. They even say that he went to Jerusalem and saw on a number of occasions the site of our Lord's Passion and Resurrection, about which we read in the Gospels.

40. While Clovis was resident in Paris he sent secretly to the son of Sigibert, saying: 'Your father is old and he is lame in one leg. If he were to die, his kingdom would come to you of right, and my alliance would come with it.' Chloderic was led astray by his lust for power and began to plot his father's death. One day Sigibert went out of the city of Cologne and crossed the Rhine, for he wanted to walk in the forest of Buchau. At midday he took a siesta in his tent, and his son set assassins on him and had him murdered, so that he might gain possession of his kingdom. By the judgement of God Chloderic fell into the pit which he had dug for his own father. He sent messengers to King Clovis to announce his father's death. 'My father is dead,' said he, 'and I have taken over his kingdom and his treasure. Send me your envoys and I will gladly hand over to you anything which you may care to select from this treasure.' 'I thank you for your goodwill,' answered Clovis. 'I ask you to show all your treasure to my messengers, but you may keep it.' The envoys came and Chloderic showed his father's treasure to them. They inspected everything. 'It was in this coffer that my father used to keep all his gold coins,' said Chloderic. 'Plunge your hand right to the bottom,' they answered, 'to see how much is there.' As he leant forward to do this, one of the Franks raised his hand and split Chloderic's skull with his double-headed axe. This unworthy son thus shared the fate of his father. When Clovis heard that both Sigibert and his son were dead, he came to Cologne himself and ordered the inhabitants to assemble. 'While I was out sailing on the River Scheldt,' said he, 'Chloderic, the son of your King, my brother, was busy plotting against his father and putting it out that I wanted him killed. As Sigibert fled through the forest of Buchau, Chloderic set assassins on him and had him murdered. While Chloderic was showing his father's treasure, he in his turn was killed by somebody or other. I take no responsibility for what has happened. It is not for me to shed the blood of one of my fellow kings, for that is a crime; but since things have turned out in this way, I will give you my advice and you must make of it what

you will. It is that you should turn to me and put yourself under my protection.' When they heard what he had to say, they clashed their shields and shouted their approval. Then they raised Clovis up on a shield and made him their ruler. In this way he took over both the kingship and the treasure of Sigibert and submitted Sigibert's people to his own rule. Day in day out God submitted the enemies of Clovis to his dominion and increased his power, for he walked before Him with an upright heart and did what was pleasing in His sight.

41. Clovis next marched against Chararic.[5] When Clovis was fighting against Syagrius, this Chararic, who had been summoned to his aid, remained neutral, giving help to neither side and awaiting the issue of the conflict, so that he might offer the hand of friendship to whichever leader was victorious. This was the reason why Clovis now attacked him in his wrath. He hemmed Chararic in by some stratagem and made him prisoner. Chararic and his son were both bound and then Clovis had their hair cut short. He ordered Chararic to be ordained as a priest and he made his son a deacon. Chararic objected to this humiliation and burst into tears. His son is said to have exclaimed: 'These leaves have been cut from wood which is still green and not lacking in sap. They will soon grow again and be larger than ever; and may the man who has done this deed perish equally quickly.' The statement came to the ears of Clovis. As they were threatening to let their hair grow again and then to kill him, he had their heads cut off. When they were dead he took possession of their kingdom, their treasure and their people.

42. There lived in Cambrai at this time a king called Ragnachar who was so sunk in debauchery that he could not even keep his hands off the women of his own family. He had an adviser named Farro who was given to the same filthy habits. It was said of Farro that when food, or a present, or indeed any gift was brought to the King, Ragnachar would say that it was good enough for him and his dear Farro. This situation roused their Frankish subjects to the utmost fury. Clovis gave a bribe, of golden arm-bands and sword-belts to the *leudes*[6] of Ragnachar, to encourage them to call him in against their King. These ornaments looked like gold, but they were really of bronze very cleverly gilded. Clovis marched his army against Ragnachar. Ragnachar sent spies to discover the strength of the invaders. When the spies returned, he asked them just how strong the enemy was. 'Strong enough for you and your dear Farro,' they replied. Clovis arrived in person and drew up his line of battle. Ragnachar witnessed the defeat of his army and prepared to slip away in flight. He was arrested by his own troops and with his arms tied behind his back he was brought before Clovis. His brother Ricchar was dragged in with him. 'Why have you disgraced our Frankish people by allowing yourself to be bound?' asked Clovis. 'It would have been better for you had you died in battle.' He raised his axe and split Ragnachar's skull. Then he turned to Ricchar and said: 'If you had stood by your brother, he would not have been bound in this way.' He killed Ricchar with a second blow of his axe. When these two were dead, those who had betrayed them discovered that the gold which they had received from Clovis was counterfeit. When they complained to Clovis, he is said to have answered: 'This is the sort of gold which a man can expect when he deliberately lures his lord to death.' He added that they were lucky to have escaped with their lives, instead of paying for the betrayal of their rulers by being tortured to death. When they heard this, they chose to beg forgiveness, saying that it was enough for them if they were allowed to live. The two Kings of whom I have told you, Ragnachar and Ricchar, were relatives of Clovis. At his command their brother Rignomer was also put to death in Le Mans. As soon as all three were slain, Clovis took over their kingdom and their treasure. In the same way he encompassed the death of many other kings and blood-relations of his whom he suspected of conspiring against his kingdom. By doing this he spread his dominion over the whole of Gaul. One day when he had called a general assembly of his subjects, he is said to have made the following remark about the relatives whom he had destroyed: 'How sad a thing it is that I live among strangers like some solitary pilgrim, and that I have none of my own relations left to help me when disaster threatens!' He said this

not because he grieved for their deaths, but because in his cunning way he hoped to find some relative still in the land of the living whom he could kill.

43. At long last Clovis died in Paris. He was buried in the Church of the Holy Apostles, which he and his Queen Clotild had built. He expired five years after the battle of Vouillé. He had reigned for thirty years and he was forty-five years old. From the passing of Saint Martin until the death of King Clovis, which happened in the eleventh year of the episcopate of Licinius, Bishop of Tours, there are counted one hundred and twelve years. After the death of her husband Queen Clotild came to live in Tours. She served as a religious in the church of Saint Martin. She lived all the rest of her days in this place, apart from an occasional visit to Paris. She was remarkable for her great modesty and her loving kindness.

Excerpts from Book IX

19. The civil discord between the townsfolk of Tours, which I described above as having spent its force, broke out once more with renewed fury. After having murdered Chramnesind's relatives, Sichar formed a great friendship with him, and they became so devoted to each other that they often had meals together and even slept in the same bed. One day as twilight was falling Chramnesind ordered his supper to be prepared and then invited Sichar round to eat with him. He came, and they both sat down to table. Sichar drank far more wine than he could carry and began to boast at Chramnesind's expense. He is reported to have said: 'Dear brother, you ought to be grateful to me for having killed off your relations. There is plenty of gold and silver in your house now that I have recompensed you for what I did to them. If it weren't for the fact that the fine which I've paid has restored your finances, you would still today be poor and destitute.' When he heard Sichar's remarks, Chramnesind was sick at heart. 'If I don't avenge my relatives,' he said to himself, 'they will say that I am as weak as a woman, for I no longer have the right to be called a man!' Thereupon he blew the lights out and hacked Sichar's skull in two. Sichar uttered a low moan as life left his body, then he fell dead to the floor. The servants who had come with him lost no time in making off. Chramnesind stripped Sichar's corpse of its clothes and hung it from a post in his garden-fence. He then climbed on a horse and went off to find the King. He entered a church and threw himself at Childebert's feet. 'Mighty King!' he said, 'I come to plead for my life. I have killed the man who in secret destroyed my relations and then stole all their possessions.' He explained what had happened, point by point. Queen Brunhild took it very ill that Sichar, who was under her protection, should have been killed in this way, and she began to rage at Chramnesind. When he saw that she was against him, he fled to the village of Bouges in the Bourges area, where his people came from, this being under the jurisdiction of King Guntram. Tranquilla, Sichar's wife, abandoned her children and her husband's property in Tours and Poitiers, and went off to join her own relations in the village of Pont-sur-Seine. There she married again.

Sichar was only about twenty when he died. He was a loose-living young man, drunken and murderous, causing trouble to all sorts of people when he was in liquor. Chramnesind went to the King a second time. The judgement was that he must prove that he had taken life in order to avenge an affront, and this he did. In view of the fact that she had taken Sichar under her protection, Queen Brunhild ordered Chramnesind's property to be sequestered. Eventually his goods were handed back by Flavinius, one of the Queen's retainers. Chramnesind rushed off to Count Aginus and obtained a letter of restitution from him. It was to Flavinius that the Queen had made over his possessions.

20. In the thirteenth year of Childebert's reign, just as I had hurried off to Metz to meet the King, I received a command to go to King Guntram on an embassy. I found him in the town of Chalon-sur-Saône. 'Noble King,' said I, 'your illustrious nephew Childebert

172

sends to you his sincerest greetings. He thanks you warmly for your loving kindness and the constant encouragement which you give him to do that which is pleasing in God's sight, which is acceptable to you and in the best interests of his own people. He promises to carry out everything that was agreed between you, and he pledges himself not to contravene any article of the treaty he signed by you both.' 'As far as I am concerned,' replied the King, 'I have little reason to feel grateful to Childebert. Why, he has already broken the promises which he made to me! He has not made over to me my part of the town of Senlis. He has not returned to me those men who, for my own well-being, I wished to summon back from his kingdom, seeing that they were hostile to my interests. How then can you stand there and say that this precious nephew of mine is determined in no way to contravene any article of the treaty signed by us both?'

To this I made the following reply: 'Childebert has no intention of contravening any of the provisions. On the contrary, he really is determined to see that they are all carried out. As for the one to which you refer, if you wish to proceed to a partition of Senlis, it can be made immediately and you can take over your third of the town without delay. As far as the men to whom you have referred are concerned, give me their names in writing and you will see that all the promises made in the treaty will be honored.'

When I had finished my speech, the King ordered the treaty to be read aloud once more in the hearing of all who were present.

Text of the Treaty. When, in the name of Christ, the most noble Lords King Guntram and King Childebert, and the most renowned Lady Queen Brunhild, met at Andelot to reaffirm their friendship and, after full debate, to put to an end any circumstance whatsoever which might prove to be a cause of dispute between them, it was settled, approved and mutually agreed, by the grace of God, and with the approval of their bishops and their military leaders that, for as long as Almighty God should preserve them in their lives here below, they should maintain good faith one with another, in pure loving kindness and singleness of heart.

§. Insofar as King Guntram, according to the terms of the alliance into which he had entered with King Sigibert of blessed memory, has claimed as his own the entire domain which King Sigibert had inherited from the lands owned by Charibert, and in so far as King Childebert has wished to recover from all this that portion which his own father had possessed, it is agreed between them and after full debate decided that the third part of the city of Paris, with its territory and its inhabitants, which came to King Sigibert by signed treaty from the lands ruled over by Charibert, together with the castles of Châteaudun and Vendôme, and all that the aforesaid King possessed with right of free passage in the region of Etampes and Chartres, with the lands concerned and the people who lived there, shall remain in perpetuity under the jurisdiction and dominion of King Guntram, this in addition to what he, Guntram, had already inherited from the lands ruled over by Charibert during the lifetime of King Sigibert.

§. It is further agreed that from this day forward King Childebert shall hold under his dominion the city of Meaux, two thirds of Senlis, and the cities of Tours, Poitiers, Avranches, Aire, Couserans, Labourd and Albi, with their territories.

§. The following condition shall be observed, that whichever of the aforesaid Kings may by God's decree survive the other, given that other has passed away from the light of this world without male issue, shall inherit the kingdom of that other, in its entirety and in perpetuity, and, by God's grace, hand it down to his own descendants.

§. It is further most specifically agreed, and it shall be observed come what may, that whatsoever King Guntram has donated to his daughter Clotild, or may, by God's grace, in the future donate, in property of all kinds, in men, cities, lands or revenues, shall remain in her power and under her control. It is agreed that if she shall decide of her own free will to dispose of any part of the lands or revenues or monies, or to donate them to any person, by God's grace they shall not be taken from him at any time or by any other person. Moreover, she herself shall, under the protection and guardianship of King Childebert, hold secure, in all honor and dignity, everything of which she shall stand possessed at the death of her father.

§. In addition to this and under the same terms, King Guntram promises that if, in the light of human frailty, it should come to pass, and may God in His compassion not permit this, for Guntram himself would certainly not wish to live to see the day, that King Childebert should pass away from the light of this world leaving Guntram still alive, he, Guntram, will take under his own guardianship and protection, with all loving-kindness, her Majesty the Queen Brunhild, mother of King Childebert, Brunhild's daughter Chlodosind, the sister of King Childebert, as long as she remain in the land of the Franks, and Childebert's Queen, Faileuba, as if she were his own dear sister, and her daughters, too; and he will ensure that they may hold in all security and peace, and in all honor and dignity, such men and such goods, such cities, lands, revenues, rights of all sorts and wealth of all kinds, as at this present time they are seen to hold, or as, in the future, with Christ to guide them, they are able lawfully to acquire. If of their own free will they wish to dispose of or to grant to any person any part of their lands, revenues or monies, this shall be secured in safe possession in perpetuity, and their wish shall not be annulled at any time by any other person.

§. As to the cities of Bordeaux, Limoges, Cahors, Lescar and Cieutat, which, as is unquestioned, Galswinth, sister of the Lady Brunhild, acquired as dowry, or as *morgengabe*, that is as a morning-gift, on her first coming to the land of the Franks, and which the Lady Brunhild is recognized to have inherited, by the decree of King Guntram and with the agreement of the Franks, during the lifetime of Chilperic and King Sigibert, it is agreed that the Lady Brunhild shall forthwith receive into her possession the city of Cahors, with its lands and all its inhabitants, but that King Guntram shall hold the other cities named above as long as he lives, on this condition, that after his death they shall pass, God willing, in all security, into the possession of the Lady Brunhild, it being understood that, as long as King Guntram lives, they shall not under any pretext or at any time be claimed by the Lady Brunhild, or by her son King Childebert, or by his sons.

§. It is further agreed that King Childebert shall hold in its entirety the town of Senlis, but that, by the transfer to his lands of that third part of Ressons which is in King Childebert's possession, compensation shall be given to King Guntram for that third part of Senlis which is rightly claimed by him.

§. It is furthermore agreed that in accordance with the treaty made between King Guntram and King Sigibert of blessed memory, those *leudes* who, on the death of King Lothar, first took oaths of loyalty to King Guntram, but who can be shown since then to have transferred their allegiance elsewhere, shall be brought back from the places in which they are known to have taken up residence. In the same way those *leudes* who, after the death of King Lothar, are known first to have taken oaths of loyalty to King Sigibert, and then to have transferred their allegiance elsewhere, shall be brought back.

§. Furthermore, whatsoever the afore-mentioned Kings have conferred upon the churches or upon their own faithful subjects, or may in future, by God's grace, and in lawful fashion, wish to confer upon them, shall be held by them in all security.

§. Whatsoever any faithful subject, in either of the two kingdoms, may justly and legally hold in his possession, shall in no way be open to question, for he shall be permitted to retain the things which are his. If, during interregna, anything is taken away from anyone through no fault of his own, an inquiry shall be held and restoration shall be made. Whatsoever, through the munificence of earlier kings, down to the death of King Lothar of blessed memory, any man has possessed, let him continue to possess it in security. Whatsoever has been taken away from our faithful subjects since then must be restored immediately.

§. Insofar as one single unequivocal treaty has now been accepted in God's name by the aforesaid Kings, it is agreed that, in both kingdoms and for the faithful subjects of both kingdoms, the right of free passage shall at no time be refused to any person who may wish to travel on public affairs or on private business. It is furthermore agreed that neither King shall invite the *leudes* of the other King to join him, and that, if they should come, he shall not receive them. If, as the result of some misdemeanour, the *leudes* of one King seek refuge in the territory of the other King, they shall be handed back and punished in accordance with their crime.

§. It is further resolved to add to the treaty that, if at any time, on any pretext, any one of the parties concerned should fail to observe its provisions, he must forfeit all benefits conferred in the present or promised for the future, to the advantage of him who shall have carried out all the provisions in full detail, this latter then being absolved in all respects from being bound by his oath.

§. Now that agreement has been come to on all these points, the parties concerned swear in the name of God Almighty, and by the inseparable Trinity, by all things divine and by the awful Day of Judgement, that they will observe, in full detail, without fraud or treachery or wish to deceive, each and every provision as it is written above.

§. This treaty was made on 28 November, in the twenty-sixth year of the reign of King Guntram and in the twelfth year of the reign of King Childebert.

When this treaty had been read aloud, the King said: 'May I be struck by the judgement of God, if I break any of the provisions contained in that!' Then he turned to Felix, who had come with me. 'Tell me, Felix,' he said, 'is it really true that you have established friendly relations between my sister Brunhild and that enemy of God and man, Fredegund?' Felix said that it was not. I spoke up and said: 'The King need not question the fact that the "friendly relations" which have bound them together for so many years are still being fostered by them both. That is to say, you may be quite sure that the hatred which they have borne each other for many a long year, far from withering away, is still as strong as ever. Noble King, it is a great pity that you cannot bring yourself to be less kindly disposed towards Queen Fredegund. We have so often remarked that you receive her envoys with more consideration than you give to ours.' 'You may be quite sure in your turn, Bishop,' answered King Guntram, 'that I receive Fredegund's envoys in this way simply in order to maintain friendly relations with my nephew Childebert. I can hardly be offering ties of genuine friendship to a woman who on more than one occasion has sent her men to murder me!'

As soon as the King stopped speaking, Felix said: 'I believe that it has come to your august ears that Recared has sent envoys to your nephew to ask for the hand in marriage of Chlodosind, your own niece and your brother's daughter. Childebert has, however, refused to give any promise without your express approval.' 'It cannot be a good thing,' answered the King, 'that my niece should set out for a land in which her sister met her end. I cannot accept it as right that my niece Ingund's death should go unavenged.' 'They are very keen to prove themselves guiltless of this,' said Felix, 'either by swearing oaths, or by any other means which you may propose. Only give your consent that Chlodosind may be betrothed to Recared as he asks!' 'If my nephew carries out all that has been written into the treaty, and that with his full approval,' answered Guntram, 'I, for my part, will agree to what he wishes in this other matter.' We promised that Childebert would fulfil all the conditions.

'Childebert further asks of you, in your loyalty to your own kith and kin,' went on Felix, 'that you send him help against the Longobards, so that he may drive them out of Italy and win back the territory which his father claimed during his lifetime. Then, with your assistance, the rest of Italy can be restored to Imperial rule.' 'I will never send my troops to Italy,' answered the King, 'for in doing so I should encompass their certain death. A terrible epidemic is raging in that country at this moment.'

'You have put the request to your nephew,' said I in my turn, 'that all the bishops of his realm should meet together, since there are so many other matters which need to be settled. Your nephew has always been of the opinion, and in this he follows the canonical use, that each metropolitan should hold a meeting of the bishops of his own province, and then anything which is wrong in his own diocese can be put right as they may decide. What reason can there be for calling such a huge council together in one place? No threat is being made to the doctrine of the Church. No new heresy is being spawned. What need can there be for so many bishops to meet together in a single council?' 'There are many matters which need to be settled,' answered Guntram. 'Many evil deeds are being committed, there is a decline in personal morality, for instance, and there are many other things which we need to discuss together. Above all, and more important than all the rest, for the issue concerns God Himself, you need to discover how Bishop Praetextatus came to be struck down in his own cathedral. Then there should be an inquiry into the case of those who are accused of the crime of *luxuria*. If they are proved guilty, they should be punished as their fellow-bishops decide, but if they are found to be innocent, the injustice of the accusation should be made public.' He then ordered the council to be deferred until the first day of June.

As soon as our interview was over, we processed to the cathedral. It was the feast-day of our Lord's Resurrection. When Mass was over, Guntram asked us to eat with him. The abundance of dishes on the table was only rivalled by the full contentment which we felt in our hearts. The King talked of God, of building new churches, of succoring the poor. From time to time he laughed out loud, as he coined some witty phrase, thereby ensuring that we shared his happiness. Among the other things which he said, he kept returning to this: 'If only my nephew keeps his promises! All that I have is his! If he takes offence because I grant an audience to my nephew Lothar's envoys, am I such a fool that I cannot mediate between them and so stop their quarrel from spreading? I am quite sure that it is better to end that quarrel, instead of letting it drag on. If I do recognize Lothar as my nephew, I will give him two or three cities in some part or other of my dominions, so that he may not feel that he is disinherited from my kingdom. Childebert has no reason to take offence if I make these gifts to Lothar.' He also said a number of things. He was extremely friendly towards us and loaded us with gifts. He then bade us farewell, exhorting us always to give Childebert such counsel as would make his life easier.

21. As I have often told you, King Guntram was well known for his charity and much given to vigils and fasting.

At this time it was reported that Marseilles was suffering from a severe epidemic of swelling in the groin and that this disease had quickly spread to Saint Symphorien-d'Ozon, a village near Lyons. Like some good bishop providing the remedies by which the wounds of a common sinner might be healed, King Guntram ordered the entire people to assemble in church and Rogations to be celebrated there with great devotion. He then commanded that they should eat and drink nothing else but barley bread and pure water, and that all should be regular in keeping the vigils. His orders were obeyed. For three days his own alms were greater than usual, and he seemed so anxious about all his people that he might well have been taken for one of our Lord's bishops, rather than for a king. He put his hope in the compassion of our Lord, directing all his prayers towards Him, for through His agency he believed with perfect faith that his wishes would be realized.

The faithful had a story which they used to tell about Guntram. There was a woman whose son was seriously ill of a quartan ague. As the boy lay tossing on his bed, his mother pushed her way through the vast crowds and came up behind the King. Without his noticing she cut a few threads from his cloak. She steeped these threads in water and then gave the infusion to her son to drink. The fever left him immediately and he became well again. I accept this as true, for I have often heard men possessed of a devil call upon Guntram's name when the evil spirit was in them, and through his miraculous powers confess their crimes.

22. As I have just said, the city of Marseilles was suffering from a most serious epidemic. I want to tell you exactly how this came about. At the time Bishop Theodore had gone to see King Childebert, for he had some complaint or other to make against the patrician Nicetius. The King paid little attention to what Theodore had to say, so the Bishop prepared to return home. In the meantime a ship from Spain put into port with the usual kind of cargo, unfortunately also bringing with it the source of this infection. Quite a few of the townsfolk purchased objects from the cargo and in less than no time a house in which eight people lived was left completely deserted, all the inhabitants having caught the disease. The infection did not spread through the residential quarter immediately. Some time passed and then, like a cornfield set alight, the entire town was suddenly ablaze with the pestilence. For all that Bishop Theodore came back and took up residence in Saint Victor's Church,[7] together with the seven poor folk who remained at his side. There he stayed throughout the whole of the catastrophe which assailed his city, giving up all his time to prayers and vigils, and imploring God in his mercy to put an end to the slaughter and to allow the people some peace and quiet. At the end of two months the plague burned itself out. The population returned to Marseilles, thinking themselves safe. Then the disease started again and all who had come back died. On several occasions later on Marseilles suffered from an epidemic of this sort.

23. Ageric, Bishop of Verdun, fell seriously ill. Day after day he tortured himself with the thought that it was his fault that Guntram Boso had been killed, in that he had stood surety for him. The fact that Berthefried had been slain in the oratory of his church-house was another cause of chagrin to him. Then there was this last straw, that he faced the daily reminder of having Guntram's sons living with him. 'It is my fault that you are left orphans,' he kept saying to them. As I have told you, these things weighed heavily upon him. He suffered from black depression, virtually giving up eating, and so died and was buried. Abbot Buccovald put in for the bishopric, but he had no success. By royal decree the Referendary Charimer was appointed, this also being the wish of the people. Abbot Buccovald was passed over, but they used to say that he was a proud man, hence his nickname, Buccus Validus.

Licerius, Bishop of Arles, died. With the backing of Bishop Syagrius, Virgil, Abbot of Autun, replaced him in his cathedral....

30. At the request of Bishop Maroveus King Childebert sent tax inspectors to Poitiers: Florentianus, Mayor of the Queen's Household, and Romulf, Count of his own Palace. Their orders were to prepare new tax-lists and to instruct the people to pay the taxes which had been levied from them in the time of Childebert's father. Many of those who were on the lists had died, and, as a result, widows, orphans and infirm folk had to meet a heavy assessment. The inspectors looked into each case in turn: they granted relief to the poor and infirm, and assessed for taxation all who were justly liable.

After this they came to Tours. When they announced that they were about to tax the townsfolk, and that they had in their possession tax-lists showing how the people had been assessed in the time of earlier kings, I gave them this answer: 'It is undeniable that

177

the town of Tours was assessed in the days of King Lothar. The books were taken off to be submitted to the King. Lothar had them thrown into the fire, for he was greatly over-awed by our Bishop, Saint Martin. When Lothar died, my people swore an oath of loyalty to King Charibert, and he swore in his turn that he would not make any new laws or customs, but would secure to them the conditions under which they had lived in his father's reign. He promised that he would not inflict upon them any new tax-laws which would be to their disadvantage. Gaiso, who was Count at that time, took the tax-lists, which, as I have said, had been drawn up by earlier tax inspectors, and began to exact payment. He was opposed by Bishop Eufronius, but he went off to the King with the money which he had collected illegally and showed to him the tax-lists in which the assessment was set down. King Charibert sighed, for he feared the miraculous power of Saint Martin, and he threw the lists into the fire. The money which had been collected he sent back to Saint Martin's church, swearing that no public taxation should ever again be forced upon the people of Tours. King Sigibert held this city after Charibert's death, but he did not burden it with taxation. In the same way Childebert has made no demands in the fourteen years during which he has reigned since his father's death. The city has not had to face any tax-assessment at all. It lies in your power to decide whether or not tax should be collected; but beware of the harm which you will do if you act contrary to the King's sworn agreement.' When I had finished speaking, they made the following reply: 'You see that we hold in our hands the book which lists the tax-assessment for your people.' 'That book was not issued by the King's treasury,' I answered. 'For all these long years it has been in abeyance. I would not be at all surprised if it had been kept carefully in someone's house out of hatred for these townsfolk of mine. God will surely punish the individuals who have produced it after such a long passage of time, just to despoil my citizens.' That very day the son of Audinus, the man who had produced the inventory, caught a fever. He died three days later. We then sent representatives to the King, to ask that he send instructions and make clear just what his orders were. An official letter came back almost immediately, confirming the immunity from taxation of the people of Tours, out of respect for Saint Martin. As soon as they had read it, the men who had been sent on the mission returned home.

Notes

1   These were islands in the River Loire between Saumur and Angers which had been occupied by piratical bands of Saxons.

2   The district between the Garonne and the Pyrenees, then known as Novempopulana, is now Gascony. The 'two Aquitaines', Aquitania Prima and Aquitania Secunda, are the district between the River Garonne and the River Loire.

3   The Merovingians claimed to be descended from the Sicambri.

4   Sigibert the Lame, King of the Ripuarian Franks.

5   Chararic, King of the Salian Franks.

6   The *leudes*, ep. MG *Leute*, were the nobles who had sworn a special oath of loyalty to the king and from whom his personal bodyguard was formed.

7   Saint Victor, a Christian soldier in the Roman army, was martyred in A.D. 303.

Saint Benedict

Rule for Monasteries

Benedict of Nursia (ca. 480-547) began his religious life as a hermit near Subiaco. He went on to found twelve monasteries, the most important being Monte Cassino. His Rule, largely derived from an earlier anonymous Rule of the Master, first became widely known in the middle of the seventh century. By the ninth century it had become the dominant monastic rule in the West, a position that it holds to today.

Source: Leonard J. Doyle, *St. Benedict's Rule for Monasteries* (Collegeville: 1948).

PROLOGUE

Jan. 1—May 2—Sept. 1

Listen, my son, to your master's precepts, and incline the ear of your heart. Receive willingly and carry out effectively your loving father's advice, that by the labour of obedience you may return to Him from whom you had departed by the sloth of disobedience.

To you, therefore, my words are now addressed, whoever you may be, who are renouncing your own will to do battle under the Lord Christ, the true King, and are taking up the strong, bright weapons of obedience.

And first of all, whatever good work you begin to do, beg of Him with most earnest prayer to perfect it, that He who has now deigned to count us among His sons may not at any time be grieved by our evil deeds. For we must always so serve Him with the good things he has given us, that He will never as an angry Father disinherit His children, nor ever as a dread Lord, provoked by our evil actions, deliver us to everlasting punishment as wicked servants who would not follow Him to glory.

Jan. 2—May 3—Sept. 2

Let us arise, then, at last, for the Scripture stirs us up, saying, "Now is the hour for us to rise from sleep." Let us open our eyes to the deifying light, let us hear with attentive ears the warning which the divine voice cries daily to us, "Today if you hear His voice, harden not your hearts." And again, "He who has ears to hear, let him hear what the Spirit says to the churches." And what does He say? "Come, My children, listen to Me; I will teach you the fear of the Lord. Run while you have the light of life, lest the darkness of death overtake you."

Jan. 3—May 4—Sept. 3

And the Lord, seeking His laborer in the multitude to whom He thus cries out, says again, "Who is the man who will have life, and desires to see good days?" And if, hearing Him, you answer, "I am he," God says to you, "If you will have true and everlasting life, keep your tongue from evil and your lips that they speak no guile. Turn away from evil and do good; seek after peace and pursue it. And when you have done these things, My eyes shall be upon you and My ears open to your prayers; and before you call upon Me, I will say to you, 'Behold, here I am.'"

What can be sweeter to us, dear brethren, than this voice of the Lord inviting us? Behold, in His loving kindness the Lord shows us the way of life.

Having our loins girded, therefore, with faith and the performance of good works, let us walk in His paths by the guidance of the Gospel, that we may deserve to see Him who has called us to His kingdom.

For if we wish to dwell in the tent of that kingdom, we must run to it by good deeds or we shall never reach it.

But let us ask the Lord, with the Prophet, "Lord, who shall dwell in Your tent, or who shall rest upon Your holy mountain?"

After this question, brethren, let us listen to the Lord as He answers and shows us the way to that tent, saying, "He who walks without stain and practices justice; he who speaks truth from his heart; he who has not used his tongue for deceit; he who has done no evil to his neighbor; he who has given no place to slander against his neighbor."

It is he who, under any temptation from the malicious devil, has brought him to naught by casting him and his temptation from the sight of his heart; and who has laid hold of his thoughts while they were still young and dashed them against Christ.

It is they who, fearing the Lord, do not pride themselves on their good observance; but, convinced that the good which is in them cannot come from themselves and must be from the Lord, glorify the Lord's work in them, using the words of the Prophet, "Not to us, O Lord, not to us, but to Your name give the glory." Thus also the Apostle Paul attributed nothing of the success of his preaching to himself, but said, "By the grace of God I am what I am." And again he says, "He who glories, let him glory in the Lord."

Hence the Lord says in the Gospel, "Whoever listens to these words of Mine and acts upon them, I will liken him to a wise man who built his house on rock. The floods came, the winds blew and beat against that house, and it did not fall, because it was founded on rock."

Having given us these assurances, the Lord is waiting every day for us to respond by our deeds to His holy admonitions. And the days of this life are lengthened and a truce granted us for this very reason, that we may amend our evil ways. As the Apostle says, "Do you not know that God's patience is inviting you to repent?" For the merciful Lord tells us, "I desire not the death of the sinner, but that he should be converted and live."

So, brethren, we have asked the Lord who is to dwell in His tent, and we have heard His commands to anyone who would dwell there; it remains for us to fulfil those duties.

Therefore we must prepare our hearts and our bodies to do battle under the holy obedience of His commands; and let us ask God that He be pleased to give us the help of His grace for anything which our nature finds hardly possible. And if we want to escape the pains of hell and attain life everlasting, then, while there is still time, while we are still in the body and are able to fulfil all these things by the light of this life, we must hasten to do now what will profit us for eternity.

And so we are going to establish a school for the service of the Lord. In founding it we hope to introduce nothing harsh or burdensome. But if a certain strictness results from the dictates of equity for the amendment of vices or the preservation of charity, do not be at once dismayed and fly from the way of salvation, whose entrance cannot but be narrow. For as we advance in the religious life and in faith, our hearts expand and we run the way of God's commandments and with unspeakable sweetness of love. Thus, never departing from His school, but persevering in the monastery according to His teaching until death, we may by patience share in the sufferings of Christ and deserve to have a share also in His kingdom.

CHAPTER 1 — On the Kinds of Monks

Jan. 8—May 9—Sept. 8

It is well known that there are four kinds of monks. The first kind are the Cenobites: those who live in monasteries and serve under a rule and an Abbot.

The second kind are the Anchorites or Hermits: those who, no longer in the first fervour of their reformation, but after long probation in a monastery, having learned by the help of many brethren how to fight against the devil, go out well armed from the ranks of the community to the solitary combat of the desert. They are able now, with no help save from God, to fight single-handed against the vices of the flesh and their own evil thoughts.

The third kind of monks, a detestable kind, are the Sarabaites. These, not having been tested, as gold in the furnace, by any rule or by the lessons of experience, are as soft as lead. In their works they still keep faith with the world, so that their tonsure marks them as liars before God. They live in twos or threes, or even singly, without a shepherd, in their own sheepfolds and not in the Lord's. Their law is the desire for self-gratification: whatever enters their mind or appeals to them, that they call holy; what they dislike, they regard as unlawful.

The fourth kind of monks are those called Gyrovagues. These spend their whole lives tramping from province to province, staying as guests in different monasteries for three or four days at a time. Always on the move, with no stability, they indulge their own wills and succumb to the allurements of gluttony, and are in every way worse than the Sarabaites. Of the miserable conduct of such men it is better to be silent than to speak.

Passing these over, therefore, let us proceed, with God's help, to lay down a rule for the strongest kind of monks, the Cenobites.

CHAPTER 2 — What Kind of Man the Abbot Ought to Be

Jan. 9—May 10—Sept. 9

An Abbot who is worthy to be over a monastery should always remember what he is called, and live up to the name of Superior. For he is believed to hold the place of Christ in the monastery, being called by a name of His, which is taken from the words of the Apostle: "You have received a Spirit of adoption as sons, by virtue of which we cry, 'Abba—Father!'"

Therefore the Abbot ought not to teach or ordain or command anything which is against the Lord's precepts; on the contrary, his commands and his teaching should be a leaven of divine justice kneaded into the minds of his disciples.

Jan. 10—May 11—Sept. 10

Let the Abbot always bear in mind that at the dread Judgment of God there will be an examination of these two matters: his teaching and the obedience of his disciples. And let the Abbot be sure that any lack of profit the master of the house may find in the sheep will be laid to the blame of the shepherd. On the other hand, if the shepherd has bestowed all his pastoral diligence on a restless, unruly flock and tried every remedy for their unhealthy behaviour, then he will be acquitted at the Lord's Judgment and may say to the Lord with the Prophet: "I have not concealed Your justice within my heart; Your truth and Your salvation I have declared. But they have despised and rejected me." And then finally let death itself, irresistible, punish those disobedient sheep under his charge.

Jan. 11—May 12—Sept. 11

Therefore, when anyone receives the name of Abbot, he ought to govern his disciples with a twofold teaching. That is to say, he should show them all that is good and holy by his deeds even more than by his words, expounding the Lord's commandments in words to the intelligent among his disciples, but demonstrating the divine precepts by his actions for those of harder hearts and ruder minds. And whatever he has taught his disciples to be contrary to God's law, let him indicate by his example that it is not to be done, lest, while preaching to others, he himself be found reprobate, and lest God one day say to him in his sin, "Why do you declare My statutes and profess My covenant with your lips, whereas you hate discipline and have cast My words behind you?" And again, "You were looking at the speck in your brother's eye, and did not see the beam in your own."

Jan. 12—May 13—Sept. 12

Let him make no distinction of persons in the monastery. Let him not love one more than another, unless it be one whom he finds better in good works or in obedience. Let him not advance one of noble birth ahead of one who was formerly a slave, unless there be some other reasonable ground for it. But if the Abbot for just reason think fit to do so, let him advance one of any rank whatever. Otherwise let them keep their due places; because, whether slaves or freemen, we are all one in Christ and bear an equal burden of service in the army of the same Lord. For with God there is no respect of persons. Only for one reason are we preferred in His sight: if we be found better than others in good works and humility. Therefore let the Abbot show equal love to all and impose the same discipline on all according to their deserts.

Jan. 13—May 14—Sept. 13

In his teaching the Abbot should always follow the Apostle's formula: "Reprove, entreat, rebuke"; threatening at one time and coaxing at another as the occasion may require, showing now the stern countenance of a master, now the loving affection of a father. That is to say, it is the undisciplined and restless whom he must reprove rather sharply; it is the obedient, meek and patient whom he must entreat to advance in virtue; while as for the negligent and disdainful, these we charge him to rebuke and correct.

And let him not shut his eyes to the faults of offenders; but, since he has the authority, let him cut out those faults by the roots as soon as they begin to appear, remembering the fate of Heli, the priest of Silo. The well-disposed and those of good understanding let him correct with verbal admonition the first and second time. But bold, hard, proud and disobedient characters he should curb at the very beginning of their ill-doing by stripes and other bodily punishments, knowing that it is written, "The fool is not corrected with words," and again, "Beat your son with the rod and you will deliver his soul from death."

Jan. 14—May 15—Sept. 14

The Abbot should always remember what he is and what he is called, and should know that to whom more is committed, from him more is required. Let him understand also what a difficult and arduous task he has undertaken: ruling souls and adapting himself to a variety of characters. One he must coax, another scold, another persuade, according to each one's character and understanding. Thus he must adjust and adapt himself to all in such a way that he may not only suffer no loss in the flock committed to his care, but may even rejoice in the increase of a good flock.

Jan. 15—May 16—Sept. 15

Above all let him not neglect or undervalue the welfare of the souls committed to him, in a greater concern for fleeting, earthly, perishable things; but let him always bear in mind that he has undertaken the government of souls and that he will have to give an account of them.

And if he be tempted to allege a lack of earthly means, let him remember what is written: "First seek the kingdom of God and His justice, and all these things shall be given you besides." And again: "Nothing is wanting to those who fear Him."

Let him know, then, that he who has undertaken the government of souls must prepare himself to render an account of them. Whatever number of brethren he knows he has under his care, he may be sure beyond doubt on Judgment Day he will have to give the Lord an account of all these souls, as well as of his own soul.

Thus the constant apprehension about his coming examination as shepherd concerning the sheep entrusted to him, and his anxiety over the account that must be given for others, make him careful of his own record. And while by his admonitions he is helping others to amend, he himself is cleansed of his faults.

CHAPTER 3 — On Calling the Brethren for Counsel

Jan. 16—May 17—Sept. 16
Whenever any important business has to be done in the monastery, let the Abbot call together the whole community and state the matter to be acted upon. Then, having heard the brethren's advice, let him turn the matter over in his own mind and do what he shall judge to be most expedient. The reason we have said that all should be called for counsel is that the Lord often reveals to the younger what is best.

Let the brethren give their advice with all the deference required by humility, and not presume stubbornly to defend their opinions; but let the decision rather depend on the Abbot's judgment, and all submit to whatever he shall decide for their welfare.

However, just as it is proper for the disciples to obey their master, so also it is his function to dispose all things with prudence and justice.

Jan. 17—May 18—Sept. 17
In all things, therefore, let us all follow the Rule as guide, and let no one be so rash as to deviate from it. Let no one in the monastery follow his own heart's fancy; and let no one presume to contend with his Abbot in an insolent way or even outside of the monastery. But if anyone should presume to do so, let him undergo the discipline of the Rule. At the same time, the Abbot himself should do all things in the fear of God and in observance of the Rule, knowing that beyond a doubt he will have to render an account of all his decisions to God, the most just Judge.

But if the business to be done in the interests of the monastery be of lesser importance, let him take counsel with the seniors only. It is written, "Do everything with counsel, and you will not repent when you have done it."

CHAPTER 4 — What Are the Instruments of Good Works

Jan. 18—May 19—Sept. 18
1. In the first place, to love the Lord God with the whole heart, the whole soul, the whole strength.
2. Then, one's neighbor as oneself.
3. Then not to murder.
4. Not to commit adultery.
5. Not to steal.
6. Not to covet.
7. Not to bear false witness.
8. To respect all men.
9. And not to do to another what one would not have done to oneself.
10. To deny oneself in order to follow Christ.
11. To chastise the body.
12. Not to become attached to pleasures.
13. To love fasting.
14. To relieve the poor.
15. To clothe the naked.
16. To visit the sick.
17. To bury the dead.
18. To help in trouble.
19. To console the sorrowing.
20. To become a stranger to the world's ways.
21. To prefer nothing to the love of Christ.

Jan. 19—May 20—Sept. 19

22. Not to give way to anger.
23. Not to nurse a grudge.
24. Not to entertain deceit in one's heart.
25. Not to give a false peace.
26. Not to forsake charity.
27. Not to swear, for fear of perjuring oneself.
28. To utter truth from heart and mouth.
29. Not to return evil for evil.
30. To do no wrong to anyone, and to bear patiently wrongs done to oneself.
31. To love one's enemies.
32. Not to curse them who curse us, but rather to bless them.
33. To bear persecution for justice' sake.
34. Not to be proud.
35. Not addicted to wine.
36. Not a great eater.
37. Not drowsy.
38. Not lazy.
39. Not a grumbler.
40. Not a detractor.
41. To put one's hope in God.
42. To attribute to God, and not to self, whatever good one sees in oneself.
43. But to recognize always that the evil is one's own doing, and to impute it to oneself.

Jan. 20—May 21—Sept. 20

44. To fear the Day of Judgment.
45. To be in dread of hell.
46. To desire eternal life with all the passion of the spirit.
47. To keep death daily before one's eyes.
48. To keep constant guard over the actions of one's life.
49. To know for certain that God sees one everywhere.
50. When evil thoughts come into one's heart, to dash them against Christ immediately.
51. And to manifest them to one's spiritual father.
52. To guard one's tongue against evil and depraved speech.
53. Not to love much talking.
54. Not to speak useless words or words that move to laughter.
55. Not to love much or boisterous laughter.
56. To listen willingly to holy reading.
57. To devote oneself frequently to prayer.
58. Daily in one's prayers, with tears and sighs, to confess one's past sins to God, and to amend them for the future.
59. Not to fulfil the desires of the flesh; to hate one's own will.
60. To obey in all things the commands of the Abbot, even though he himself (which God forbid) should act otherwise, mindful of the Lord's precept, "Do what they say, but not what they do."
61. Not to wish to be called holy before one is holy; but first to be holy, that one may be truly so called.

Jan. 21—May 22—Sept. 21

62. To fulfil God's commandments daily in one's deeds.
63. To love chastity.
64. To hate no one.
65. Not to be jealous, not to harbour envy.

184

66. Not to love contention.
67. To beware of haughtiness.
68. And to respect the seniors.
69. To love the juniors.
70. To pray for one's enemies in the love of Christ.
71. To make peace with one's adversary before the sun sets.
72. And never to despair of God's mercy.

These, then, are the tools of the spiritual craft. If we employ them unceasingly day and night, and return them on the Day of Judgment, our compensation from the Lord will be that wage He has promised: "Eye has not seen, nor ear heard, what God has prepared for those who love Him."

Now the workshop in which we shall diligently execute all these tasks is the enclosure of the monastery and stability in the community.

CHAPTER 5 — On Obedience

Jan. 22—May 23—Sept. 22

The first degree of humility is obedience without delay. This is the virtue of those who hold nothing dearer to them than Christ; who, because of the holy service they have professed, and the fear of hell, and the glory of life everlasting, as soon as anything has been ordered by the Superior, receive it as a divine command and cannot suffer any delay in executing it. Of these the Lord says, "As soon as he heard, he obeyed Me." And again to teachers He says, "He who hears you, hears Me."

Such as these, therefore, immediately leaving their own affairs and forsaking their own will, dropping the work they were engaged in and leaving it unfinished, with the ready step of obedience follow up with their deeds the voice of him who commands. And so as it were at the same moment the master's command is given and the disciple's work is completed, the two things being speedily accomplished together in the swiftness of the fear of God by those who are moved with the desire of attaining life everlasting. That desire is their motive for choosing the narrow way, of which the Lord says, "Narrow is the way that leads to life," so that, not living according to their own choice nor obeying their own desires and pleasures but walking by another's judgment and command, they dwell in monasteries and desire to have an Abbot over them. Assuredly such as these are living up to that maxim of the Lord in which he says, "I have come not to do My own will, but the will of Him who sent Me."

Jan. 23—May 24—Sept. 23

But this very obedience will be acceptable to God and pleasing to men only if what is commanded is done without hesitation, delay, lukewarmness, grumbling, or objection. For the obedience given to Superiors is given to God, since He Himself has said, "He who hears you, hears Me." And the disciples should offer their obedience with a good will, for "God loves a cheerful giver." For if the disciple obeys with an ill will and murmurs, not necessarily with his lips but in his heart, then even though he fulfil the command yet his work will not be acceptable to God, who sees that his heart is murmuring. And, far from gaining a reward for such work as this, he will incur the punishment due to murmurers, unless he amend and make satisfaction.

CHAPTER 6 — On the Spirit of Silence

Jan. 24—May 25—Sept. 24

Let us do what the Prophet says: "I said, 'I will guard my ways, that I may not sin with my tongue. I have set a guard to my mouth.' I was mute and was humbled, and kept silence even from good things." Here the Prophet shows that if the spirit of silence ought to lead us at times to refrain even from good speech, so much the more ought the punishment for sin make us avoid evil words.

Therefore, since the spirit of silence is so important, permission to speak should rarely be granted even to perfect disciples, even though it be for good, holy, edifying conversation; for it is written, "In much speaking you will not escape sin," and in another place, "Death and life are in the power of the tongue."

For speaking and teaching belong to the master; the disciple's part is to be silent and to listen. And for that reason if anything has to be asked of the Superior, it should be asked with all the humility and submission inspired by reverence.

But as for coarse jests and idle words or words that move to laughter, these we condemn everywhere with a perpetual ban, and for such conversation we do not permit a disciple to open his mouth.

CHAPTER 7 – On Humility

Jan. 25—May 26—Sept. 25
Holy Scripture, brethren, cries out to us, saying, "Everyone who exalts himself shall be humbled, and he who humbles himself shall be exalted." In saying this it shows us that all exaltation is a kind of pride, against which the Prophet proves himself to be on guard when he says, "Lord, my heart is not exalted, nor are mine eyes lifted up; neither have I walked in great matters, nor in wonders above me." But how has he acted? "Rather have I been of humble mind than exalting myself; as a weaned child on its mother's breast, so You solace my soul."

Hence, brethren, if we wish to reach the very highest point of humility and to arrive speedily at that heavenly exaltation to which ascent is made through the humility of this present life, we must by our ascending actions erect the ladder Jacob saw in his dream, on which Angels appeared to him descending and ascending. By that descent and ascent we must surely understand nothing else than this, that we descend by self-exaltation and ascend by humility. And the ladder thus set up is our life in the world, which the Lord raises up to heaven if our heart is humbled. For we call our body and soul the sides of the ladder, and into these sides our divine vocation has inserted the different steps of humility and discipline we must climb.

Jan. 26—May 27—Sept. 26
The first degree of humility, then, is that a person keep the fear of God before his eyes and beware of ever forgetting it. Let him be ever mindful of all that God has commanded; let his thoughts constantly recur to the hell-fire which will burn for their sins those who despise God, and to the life everlasting which is prepared for those who fear Him. Let him keep himself at every moment from sins and vices, whether of the mind, the tongue, the hands, the feet, or the self-will, and check also the desires of the flesh.

Jan. 27—May 28—Sept. 27
Let a man consider that God is always looking at him from heaven, that his actions are everywhere visible to the divine eyes and are constantly being reported to God by the Angels. This is what the Prophet shows us when he represents God as ever present within our thoughts, in the words "Searcher of minds and hearts is God" and again in the words "The Lord knows the thoughts of men." Again he says, "You have read my thoughts from afar" and "The thoughts of men will confess to You."

In order that he may be careful about his wrongful thoughts, therefore, let the faithful brother say constantly in his heart, "Then shall I be spotless before Him if I have kept myself from my iniquity."

Jan. 28—May 29—Sept. 28
As for self-will, we are forbidden to do our own will by the Scripture, which says to us, "Turn away from your own will," and likewise by the prayer in which we ask God that His will be done in us. And rightly we are taught not to do our own will when we take heed to the warning of Scripture: "There are ways which to men may seem right, but the ends

of them plunge into the depths of hell"; and also when we tremble at what is said of the careless: "They are corrupt and have become abominable in their wills."

And as for the desires of the flesh, let us believe with the Prophet that God is ever present to us, when he says to the Lord, "Every desire of mine is before You."

Jan. 29—May 30—Sept. 29

We must be on our guard, therefore, against evil desires, for death lies close by the gate of pleasure. Hence the Scripture gives this command: "Go not after your concupiescences."

So therefore, since the eyes of the Lord observe the good and the evil and the Lord is always looking down from heaven on the children of men "to see if there be anyone who understands and seeks God," and since our deeds daily, day and night, reported to the Lord by the Angels assigned to us, we must constantly beware, brethren, as the Prophet says in the Psalm, lest at any time God see us falling into evil ways and becoming unprofitable; and lest, having spared us for the present because in His kindness He awaits our reformation, He say to us in the future, "These things you did, and I held My peace."

Jan. 30—May 31—Sept. 30

The second degree of humility is that a person love not his own will nor take pleasure in satisfying his desires, but model his actions on the saying of the Lord, "I have come not to do My own will, but the will of Him who sent Me." It is written also, "Self-will has its punishment, but constraint wins a crown."

Jan. 31—June 1—Oct. 1

The third degree of humility is that a person for love of God submit himself to his Superior in all obedience, imitating the Lord, of whom the Apostle says, "He became obedient even unto death."

Feb. 1—June 2—Oct. 2

The fourth degree of humility is that he hold fast to patience with a silent mind when in this obedience he meets with difficulties and contradictions and even any kind of injustice, enduring all without growing weary or running away. For the Scripture says, "He who perseveres to the end, he it is who shall be saved"; and again, "Let your heart take courage, and wait for the Lord!"

And to show how those who are faithful ought to endure all things, however contrary, for the Lord, the Scripture says in the person of the suffering, "For Your sake we are put to death all the day long; we are considered as sheep marked for slaughter." Then, secure in their hope of a divine recompense, they go on with joy to declare, "But in all these trials we conquer, through Him who has granted us His love." Again, in another place the Scripture says, "You have tested us, O God; You have tried us as silver is tried, by fire; You have brought us into a snare; You have laid afflictions on our back." And to show that we ought to be under a Superior, it goes on to say, "You have set men over our heads."

Moreover, by their patience those faithful ones fulfil the Lord's command in adversities and injuries: when struck on one cheek, they offer the other; when deprived of their tunic, they surrender also their cloak; when forced to go a mile, they go two; with the Apostle Paul they bear with the false brethren and bless those who curse them.

Feb. 2—June 3—Oct. 3

The fifth degree of humility is that he hide from his Abbot none of the evil thoughts that enter his heart or the sins committed in secret, but that he humbly confess them. The Scripture urges us to this when it says, "Reveal your way to the Lord and hope in Him," and again, "Confess to the Lord, for He is good, for His mercy endures forever." And the Prophet likewise says, "My offense I have made known to You, and my iniquities I have not covered up. I said: 'I will declare against myself my iniquities to the Lord;' and 'You forgave the wickedness of my heart.'"

Feb. 3—June 4—Oct. 4

The sixth degree of humility is that a monk be content with the poorest and worst of everything, and that in every occupation assigned him he consider himself a bad and worthless workman, saying with the Prophet, "I am brought to nothing and I am without understanding; I have become as a beast of burden before You, and I am always with You."

Feb. 4—June 5—Oct. 5

The seventh degree of humility is that he consider himself lower and of less account than anyone else, and this not only in verbal protestation but also with the most heartfelt inner conviction, humbling himself and saying with the Prophet, "But I am a worm and no man, the scorn of men and the outcast of the people. After being exalted, I have been humbled and covered with confusion." And again, "It is good for me that You have humbled me, that I may learn Your commandments."

Feb. 5—June 6—Oct. 6

The eighth degree of humility is that a monk do nothing except what is commended by the common Rule of the monastery and the example of the elders.

Feb. 6—June 7—Oct. 7

The ninth degree of humility is that a monk restrain his tongue and keep silence, not speaking until he is questioned. For the Scripture shows that "in much speaking there is no escape from sin" and that "the talkative man is not stable on the earth."

Feb. 7—June 8—Oct. 8

The tenth degree of humility is that he be not ready and quick to laugh, for it is written, "The fool lifts up his voice in laughter."

Feb. 8—June 9—Oct. 9

The eleventh degree of humility is that when a monk speaks he do so gently and without laughter, humbly and seriously, in few and sensible words, and that he be not noisy in his speech. It is written, "A wise man is known by the fewness of his words."

Feb. 9—June 10—Oct. 10

The twelfth degree of humility is that a monk not only have humility in his heart but also by his very appearance make it always manifest to those who see him. That is to say that whether he is at the Work of God, in the oratory, in the monastery, in the garden, on the road, in the fields or anywhere else, and whether sitting, walking or standing, he should always have his head bowed and his eyes towards the ground. Feeling the guilt of his sins at every moment, he should consider himself already present at the dread Judgment and constantly say in his heart what the publican in the Gospel said with his eyes fixed on the earth: "Lord, I am a sinner and not worthy to lift up my eyes to heaven"; and again with the Prophet: "I am bowed down and humbled everywhere."

Having climbed all these steps of humility, therefore, the monk will presently come to that perfect love of God, which casts out fear. And all those precepts which formerly he had not observed without fear, he will now begin to keep by reason of that love, without any effort, as though naturally and by habit. No longer will his motive be the fear of hell, but rather the love of Christ, good habit and delight in the virtues which the Lord will deign to show forth by the Holy Spirit in His servant now cleansed from vice and sin.

CHAPTER 8 — On the Divine Office During the Night

Feb. 10—June 11—Oct. 11

In winter time, that is, from the Calends of November until Easter, the brethren shall rise at what is calculated to be the eighth hour of the night, so that they may sleep somewhat longer than half the night and rise with their rest completed. And the time that remains after the Night Office should be spent in study by those brethren who need a better knowledge of the Psalter or the lessons.

From Easter to the aforesaid Calends of November, the hour of rising should be so arranged that the Morning Office, which is to be said at daybreak, will follow the Night Office after a very short interval, during which the brethren may go out for the necessities of nature.

CHAPTER 9 — How Many Psalms Are to Be Said at the Night Office

Feb. 11—June 12—Oct. 12

In winter time as defined above, there is first this verse to be said three times: "O Lord, open my lips, and my mouth shall declare Your praise." To it is added Psalm 3 and the "Glory be to the Father," and after that Psalm 94 to be chanted with an antiphon or even chanted simply. Let the Ambrosian hymn follow next, and then six Psalms with antiphons. When these are finished and the verse said, let the Abbot give a blessing; then, all being seated on the benches, let three lessons be read from the book on the lectern by the brethren in their turns, and after each lesson let a responsory be chanted. Two of the responsories are to be said without a "Glory be to the Father"; but after the third lesson let the chanter say the "Glory to the Father," and as soon as he begins it let all rise from their seats out of honor and reverence to the Holy Trinity.

The books to be read at the Night Office shall be those of divine authorship, of both the Old and New Testament, and also the explanations of them which have been made by well known and orthodox Catholic Fathers.

After these three lessons with their responsories let the remaining six Psalms follow, to be chanted with "Alleluia." After these shall follow the lesson from the Apostle, to be recited by heart, the verse and the petition of the litany, that is "Lord have mercy on us." And so let the Night Office come to an end.

CHAPTER 10 — How the Night Office Is to Be Said in Summer Time

Feb. 12—June 13—Oct. 13

From Easter until the Calends of November let the same number of Psalms be kept as prescribed above; but no lessons are to be read from the book, on account of the shortness of the nights. Instead of those three lessons let one lesson from the Old Testament be said by heart and followed by a short responsory. But all the rest should be done as has been said, that is to say that never fewer than twelve Psalms should be said at the Night Office, not counting Psalm 3 and Psalm 94.

CHAPTER 11 — How the Night Office Is to Be Said on Sundays

Feb. 13—June 14—Oct. 14

On Sunday the hour of rising for the Night Office should be earlier. In that Office let the measure already prescribed be kept, namely the singing of six Psalms and a verse. Then let all be seated on the benches in their proper order while the lessons and their responsories are read from the book, as we said above. These shall be four in number, with the chanter saying the "Glory be to the Father" in the fourth responsory only, and all rising reverently as soon as he begins it.

After these lessons let six more Psalms with antiphons follow in order, as before, and a verse; and then let four more lessons be read with their responsories in the same way as the former.

After these let there be three canticles from the book of the Prophets, as the Abbot shall appoint, and let these canticles be chanted with "Alleluia." Then when the verse has been said and the Abbot has given the blessing, let four more lessons be read, from the New Testament, in the manner prescribed above.

After the fourth responsory let the Abbot begin the hymn "We praise You, O God."

When this is finished the Abbot shall read the lesson from the book of the Gospels, while all stand in reverence and awe. At the end let all answer "Amen," and let the Abbot proceed at once to the hymn "To You be praise." After the blessing has been given, let them begin the Morning Office.

This order for the Night Office on Sunday shall be observed the year around, both summer and winter; unless it should happen (which God forbid) that the brethren be late in rising, in which case the lessons or the responsories will have to be shortened somewhat. Let every precaution be taken, however, against such an occurrence; but if it does happen, then the one through whose neglect it has come about should make due satisfaction to God in the oratory.

CHAPTER 12 — How the Morning Office Is to Be Said

Feb. 14—June 15—Oct. 15

The Morning Office on Sunday shall begin with Psalm 66 recited straight through without an antiphon. After that let Psalm 50 be said with "Alleluia," then Psalms 117 and 62, the Canticle of Blessing and the Psalms of praise; then a lesson from the Apocalypse to be recited by heart, the responsory, the Ambrosian hymn, the verse, the canticle from the Gospel book, the litany and so the end.

CHAPTER 13 — How the Morning Office Is to be Said on Weekdays

Feb. 15—June 16—Oct. 16

On weekdays the Morning Office shall be celebrated as follows. Let Psalm 66 be said without an antiphon and somewhat slowly, as on Sunday, in order that all may be in time for Psalm 50, which is to be said with an antiphon. After that let two other Psalms be said according to custom, namely: on Monday Psalms 5 and 35, on Tuesday Psalms 42 and 56, on Wednesday Psalms 63 and 64, on Thursday Psalms 87 and 89, on Friday Psalms 75 and 91, and on Saturday Psalm 142 and the canticle from Deuteronomy, which is to be divided into two sections each terminated by a "Glory to the Father." But on the other days let there be a canticle from the Prophets, each on its own day as chanted by the Roman Church. Next follow the Psalms of praise, then a lesson of the Apostle to be recited from memory, the responsory, the Ambrosian hymn, the verse, the canticle from the Gospel book, the litany, and so the end.

Feb. 16—June 17—Oct. 17

The Morning and Evening Offices should never be allowed to pass without the Superior saying the Lord's Prayer in its place at the end so that all may hear it, on account of the thorns of scandal which are apt to spring up. Thus those who hear it, being warned by the covenant which they make in that prayer when they say, "Forgive us as we forgive," may cleanse themselves of faults against that covenant.

But at the other Offices let the last part only of that prayer be said aloud, so that all may answer, "But deliver us from evil."

CHAPTER 14 — How the Night Office Is to Be Said on the Feasts of the Saints

Feb. 17—June 18—Oct. 18

On the feasts of Saints and on all festivals let the Office be performed as we have prescribed for Sundays, except that the Psalms, the antiphons and the lessons belonging to that particular day are to be said. Their number, however, shall remain as we have specified above.

CHAPTER 15 — At What Times "Alleluia" Is to Be Said

Feb. 18—June 19—Oct. 19

From holy Easter until Pentecost without interruption let "Alleluia" be said both in the Psalms and in the responsories. From Pentecost to the beginning of Lent let it be said every night with the last six Psalms of the Night Office only. On every Sunday, however, outside of Lent, the canticles, the Morning Office, Prime, Terce, Sext and None shall be said with "Alleluia," but Vespers with antiphons.

The responsories are never to be said with "Alleluia" except from Easter to Pentecost.

CHAPTER 16 — How the Work of God Is to Be Performed During the Day

Feb. 19—June 20—Oct. 20

"Seven times in the day," says the Prophet, "I have rendered praise to You." Now that sacred number of seven will be fulfilled by us if we perform the Offices of our service at the time of the Morning Office, of Prime, of Terce, of Sext, of None, of Vespers and of Compline, since it was of these day Hours that he said, "Seven times in the day I have rendered praise to You." For as to the Night Office the same Prophet says, "In the middle of the night I arose to glorify You."

Let us therefore bring our tribute of praise to our Creator "for the judgments of His justice" at these times: the Morning Office, Prime, Terce, Sext, None, Vespers, and Compline; and in the night let us arise to glorify Him.

CHAPTER 17 — How Many Psalms Are to Be Said at These Hours

Feb. 20—June 21—Oct. 21

We have already arranged the order of the psalmody for the Night and Morning Offices; let us now provide for the remaining Hours. At Prime let three Psalms be said, separately and not under one "Glory to the Father." The hymn of that Hour is to follow the verse "Incline unto my aid, O God," before the Psalms begin. Upon completion of the three Psalms let one lesson be recited, then a verse, the "Lord, have mercy on us" and the concluding prayers.

The Offices of Terce, Sext and None are to be celebrated in the same order, that is: "Incline unto my aid, O God," the hymn proper to each Hour, three Psalms, lesson and verse, "Lord, have mercy on us" and concluding prayers.

If the community is a large one, let the Psalms be sung with antiphons; but if small, let them be sung straight through.

Let the Psalms of the Vesper Office be limited to four, with antiphons. After these Psalms the lesson is to be recited, then the responsory, the Ambrosian hymn, the verse, the canticle from the Gospel book, the litany, the Lord's Prayer and the concluding prayers.

Let Compline be limited to the saying of three Psalms, which are to be said straight through without antiphon, and after them the hymn of that Hour, one lesson, a verse, the "Lord, have mercy on us," the blessing and the concluding prayers.

CHAPTER 18 — In What Order the Psalms Are to Be Said

Feb. 21—June 22—Oct. 22

Let this verse be said: "Incline unto my aid, O God: O Lord, make haste to help me," and the "Glory be to the Father"; then the hymn proper to each Hour.

Then at Prime on Sunday four sections of Psalm 118 are to be said; and at each of the remaining Hours, that is Terce, Sext and None, three sections of the same Psalm 118.

At Prime on Monday let three Psalms be said, namely Psalms 1, 2 and 6. And so each day at Prime until Sunday let three Psalms be said in numerical order, to Psalm 19, but with Psalms 9 and 17 each divided into two parts. Thus it comes about that the Night Office on Sunday always begins with Psalm 20.

Feb. 22—June 23—Oct. 23
At Terce, Sext and None on Monday let the nine remaining sections of Psalm 118 be said, three at each of these Hours.

Psalm 118 having been completed, therefore, on two days, Sunday and Monday, let the nine Psalms from Psalm 119 to Psalm 127 be said at Terce, Sext and None, three at each Hour, beginning with Tuesday. And let these same Psalms be repeated every day until Sunday at the same Hours, while the arrangement of hymns, lessons and verse is kept the same on all days; and thus Prime on Sunday will always begin with Psalm 118.

Feb. 23—June 24—Oct. 24
Vespers are to be sung with four Psalms every day. These shall begin with Psalm 109 and go on to Psalm 147, omitting those which are set apart for other Hours; that is to say that with the exception of Psalms 117 to 127 and Psalms 133 and 142, all the rest of these are to be said at Vespers. And since there are three Psalms too few, let the longer ones of the above number be divided, namely Psalms 138, 143 and 144. But let Psalm 116 because of its brevity be joined to Psalm 115.

The order of the Vesper Psalms being thus settled, let the rest of the Hour—lesson, responsory, hymn, verse and canticle—be carried out as we prescribed above.

At Compline the same Psalms are to be repeated every day, namely Psalms 4, 90 and 133.

(Feb. 24 in leap year; otherwise added to the preceding)—June 25—Oct. 25
The order of psalmody for the day Hours being thus arranged, let all the remaining Psalms be equally distributed among the seven Night Offices by dividing the longer Psalms among them and assigning twelve Psalms to each night.

We strongly recommend, however, that if this distribution of the Psalms is displeasing to anyone, he should arrange them otherwise, in whatever way he considers better, but taking care that the Psalter with its full number of 150 Psalms be chanted every week and begun again every Sunday at the Night Office. For those monks show themselves too lazy in the service to which they are vowed, who chant less than the Psalter with the customary canticles in the course of a week, whereas we read that our holy Fathers strenuously fulfilled that task in a single day. May we, lukewarm that we are, perform it at least in a whole week!

CHAPTER 19 — On the Manner of Saying the Divine Office

Feb. 24 (25)—June 26—Oct. 26
We believe that the divine presence is everywhere and that "the eyes of the Lord are looking on the good and the evil in every place." But we should believe this especially without any doubt when we are assisting at the Work of God. To that end let us be mindful always of the Prophet's words, "Serve the Lord in fear" and again "Sing praises wisely" and "In the sight of the Angels I will sing praise to You." Let us therefore consider how we ought to conduct ourselves in the sight of the Godhead and of His Angels, and let us take part in the psalmody in such a way that our mind may be in harmony with our voice.

CHAPTER 20 — On Reverence in Prayer

Feb. 25 (26)—June 27—Oct. 27
When we wish to suggest our wants to men of high station, we do not presume to do so except with humility and reverence. How much the more, then, are complete humility and pure devotion necessary in supplication of the Lord who is God of the universe! And let us be assured that it is not in saying a great deal that we shall be heard, but in purity of heart and in tears of compunction. Our prayer, therefore, ought to be short and pure, unless it happens to be prolonged by an inspiration of divine grace. In community, how-

ever, let prayer be very short, and when the Superior gives the signal let all rise together.

CHAPTER 21 — On the Deans of the Monastery

Feb. 26 (27)–June 28–Oct. 28
If the community is a large one, let there be chosen out of it brethren of good repute and holy life, and let them be appointed deans. These shall take charge of their deaneries in all things, observing the commandments of God and the instructions of their Abbot.

Let men of such character be chosen deans that the Abbot may with confidence share his burdens among them. Let them be chosen not by rank but according to their worthiness of life and the wisdom of their doctrine.

If any of these deans should become inflated with pride and found deserving of censure, let him be corrected once, and again, and a third time. If he will not amend, then let him be despised and another put in his place who is worthy of it.

And we order the same to be done in the case of the Prior.

CHAPTER 22 — How the Monks Are to Sleep

Feb. 27 (28)–June 29–Oct. 29
Let each one sleep in a separate bed. Let them receive bedding suitable to their manner of life, according to the Abbot's directions. If possible let all sleep in one place; but if the number does not allow this, let them take their rest by tens and twenties with the seniors who have charge of them.

A candle shall be kept burning in the room until morning.

Let the monks sleep clothed and girded with belts and cords—but not with their knives at their sides, lest they cut themselves in their sleep—and thus be always ready to rise without delay when the signal is given and hasten to be before one another at the Work of God, yet with all gravity and decorum.

The younger brethren shall not have beds next to one another, but among those of the older ones.

When they rise for the Work of God let them gently encourage one another, that the drowsy may have no excuse.

CHAPTER 23 — On Excommunication for Faults

Feb. 28 (29)–June 30–Oct. 30
If a brother is found to be obstinate, or disobedient, or proud, or murmuring, or habitually transgressing the Holy Rule in any point and contemptuous of the orders of his seniors, the latter shall admonish him secretly a first and a second time, as Our Lord commands. If he fails to amend, let him be given a public rebuke in front of the whole community. But if even then he does not reform, let him be placed under excommunication, provided that he understands the seriousness of that penalty; if he is perverse, however, let him undergo corporal punishment.

CHAPTER 24 — What the Measure of Excommunication Should Be

Mar. 1–July 1–Oct. 31
The measure of excommunication or of chastisement should correspond to the degree of fault, which degree is estimated by the Abbot's judgment.

If a brother is found guilty of lighter faults, let him be excluded from the common table. Now the program for one deprived of the fellowship of the table shall be as follows: In the oratory he shall intone neither Psalm nor antiphon nor shall he recite a lesson until he has made satisfaction; in the refectory he shall take his food alone after the community meal, so that if the brethren eat at the sixth hour, for instance, that brother shall eat at the ninth, while if they eat at the ninth hour he shall eat at the evening, until by a suitable satisfaction he obtains pardon.

CHAPTER 25 — On Weightier Faults

Mar. 2—July 2—Nov. 1

Let the brother who is guilty of a weightier fault be excluded both from the table and from the oratory. Let none of the brethren join him either for company or for conversation. Let him be alone at the work assigned him, abiding in penitential sorrow and pondering that terrible sentence of the Apostle where he says that a man of that kind is handed over for the destruction of the flesh, that the spirit may be saved in the day of the Lord. Let him take his meals alone in the measure and at the hour which the Abbot shall consider suitable for him. He shall not be blessed by those who pass by, nor shall the food that is given him be blessed.

CHAPTER 26 — On Those Who Without an Order Associate With the Excommunicated

Mar. 3—July 3—Nov. 2

If any brother presumes without an order from the Abbot to associate in any way with an excommunicated brother, or to speak with him, or to send him a message, let him incur a similar punishment of excommunication.

CHAPTER 27 — How Solicitous the Abbot Should Be for the Excommunicated

Mar. 4—July 4—Nov. 3

Let the Abbot be most solicitous in his concern for delinquent brethren, for "it is not the healthy but the sick who need a physician." And therefore he ought to use every means that a wise physician would use. Let him send "senpectae," that is, brethren of mature years and wisdom, who may as it were secretly console the wavering brother and induce him to make humble satisfaction; comforting him that he may not "be overwhelmed by excessive grief," but that, as the Apostle says, charity may be strengthened in him. And let everyone pray for him.

For the Abbot must have the utmost solicitude and exercise all prudence and diligence lest he lose any of the sheep entrusted to him. Let him know that what he has undertaken is the care of weak souls and not a tyranny over strong ones; and let him fear the Prophet's warning through which God says, "What you saw to be fat you took to yourselves, and what was feeble you cast away." Let him rather imitate the loving example of the Good Shepherd who left the ninety-nine sheep in the mountains and went to look for the one sheep that had gone astray, on whose weakness He had such compassion that He deigned to place it on His own sacred shoulders and thus carry it back to the flock.

CHAPTER 28 — On Those Who Will Not Amend After Repeated Corrections

Mar. 5—July 5—Nov. 4

If a brother who has been frequently corrected for some fault, and even excommunicated, does not amend, let a harsher correction be applied, that is, let the punishment of the rod be administered to him.

But if he still does not reform or perhaps (which God forbid) even rises up in pride and wants to defend his conduct, then let the Abbot do what a wise physician would do. Having used applications, the ointments of exhortation, the medicines of the Holy Scriptures, finally the cautery of excommunication and of the strokes of the rod, if he sees that his efforts are of no avail, let him apply a still greater remedy, his own prayers and those of his own brethren, that the Lord, who can do all things, may restore health to the sick brother.

But if he is not healed even in this way, then let the Abbot use the knife of amputation, according to the Apostle's words, "Expel the evil one from your midst," and again, "If the faithless one departs, let him depart," lest one diseased sheep contaminate the whole flock.

CHAPTER 29 — Whether Brethren Who Leave the Monastery Should Be Received Again

Mar. 6—July 6—Nov. 5

If a brother who through his own fault leaves the monastery should wish to return, let him first promise full reparation for his having gone away; and then let him be received in the lowest place, as a test of his humility. And if he should leave again, let him be taken back again, and so a third time; but he should understand that after this all way of return is denied him.

CHAPTER 30 — How Boys Are to Be Corrected

Mar. 7—July 7—Nov. 6

Every age and degree of understanding should have its proper measure of discipline. With regard to boys and adolescents, therefore, or those who cannot understand the seriousness of the penalty of excommunication, whenever such as these are delinquent let them be subjected to terms by harsh beatings, that they may be cured.

CHAPTER 31 — What Kind of Man the Cellarer of the Monastery Should Be

Mar. 8—July 8—Nov. 7

As cellarer of the monastery let there be chosen from the community one who is wise, of mature character, sober, not a great eater, not haughty, not excitable, not offensive, not slow, not wasteful, but a God-fearing man who may be like a father to the whole community.

Let him have charge of everything. He shall do nothing without the Abbot's orders, but keep to his instructions. Let him not vex the brethren. If any brother happens to make some unreasonable demand of him, instead of vexing the brother with a contemptuous refusal he should humbly give the reason for denying the improper request.

Let him keep guard over his own soul, mindful always of the Apostle's saying that "he who has ministered well acquires for himself a good standing."

Let him take the greatest care of the sick, of children, of guests and of the poor, knowing without doubt that he will have to render an account for all these on the Day of Judgment.

Let him regard all the utensils of the monastery and its whole property as if they were the sacred vessels of the altar. Let him not think that he may neglect anything. He should be neither a miser nor a prodigal and squanderer of the monastery's substance, but should do all things with a measure and in accordance with the Abbot's instructions.

Mar. 9—July 9—Nov. 8

Above all things let him have humility; and if he has nothing else to give let him give a good word in answer, for it is written: "A good word is above the best gift."

Let him have under his care all that the Abbot has assigned to him, but not presume to deal with what he has forbidden him.

Let him give the brethren their appointed allowance of food without any arrogance or delay, that they may not be scandalized, mindful of the Word of God as to what he deserves "who shall scandalize one of the little ones."

If the community is a large one, let helpers be given him, that by their assistance he may fulfil with a quiet mind the office committed to him. The proper times should be observed in giving the things that have to be given and asking for the things that have to be asked for, that no one may be troubled or vexed in the house of God.

CHAPTER 32 — On the Tools and Property of the Monastery

Mar. 10—July 10—Nov. 9
For the care of the monastery's property in tools, clothing and other articles let the Abbot appoint brethren on whose manner of life and character he can rely; and let him, as he shall judge to be expedient, consign the various articles to them, to be looked after and to be collected again. The Abbot shall keep a list of these articles, so that as the brethren succeed one another in their assignments he may know what he gives and what he receives back.

If anyone treats the monastery's property in a slovenly or careless way, let him be corrected. If he fails to amend, let him undergo the discipline of the Rule.

CHAPTER 33 — Whether Monks Ought to Have Anything of Their Own

Mar. 11—July 11—Nov. 10
This vice especially is to be cut out of the monastery by the roots. Let no one presume to give or receive anything without the Abbot's leave, or to have anything as his own—anything whatever, whether book or tablets or pen or whatever it may be—since they are not permitted to have even their bodies or wills at their own disposal; but for all their necessities let them look to the Father of the monastery. And let it be unlawful to have anything which the Abbot has not given or allowed. Let all things be common to all, as it is written, and let no one say or assume that anything is his own. But if anyone is caught indulging in this most wicked vice, let him be admonished once and a second time. If he fails to amend, let him undergo punishment.

CHAPTER 34 — Whether All Should Receive in Equal Measure What Is Necessary

Mar. 12—July 12—Nov. 11
Let us follow the Scripture, "Distribution was made to each according as anyone had need." By this we do not mean that there should be respecting of persons (which God forbid), but consideration for infirmities. He who needs less should thank God and not be discontented; but he who needs more should be humbled by the thought of his infirmity rather than feeling important on account of the kindness shown him. Thus all the members will be at peace.

Above all, let not the evil of murmuring appear for any reason whatsoever in the least word or sign. If anyone is caught at it, let him be placed under very severe discipline.

CHAPTER 35 — On the Weekly Servers in the Kitchen

Mar. 13—July 13—Nov. 12
Let the brethren serve one another, and let no one be excused from the kitchen service except by reason of sickness or occupation in some important work. For this service brings increase of reward and of charity. But let helpers be provided for the weak ones, that they may not be distressed by this work; and indeed let everyone have help, as required by the size of the community or the circumstances of the locality. If the community is a large one, the cellarer shall be excused from the kitchen service; and so also those whose occupations are of greater utility, as we said above. Let the rest serve one another in charity.

The one who is ending his week of service shall do the cleaning on Saturday. He shall wash the towels with which the brethren wipe their hands and feet; and this server who is ending his week, aided by the one who is about to begin, shall wash the feet of all the brethren. He shall return the utensils of his office to the cellarer clean and in good condition, and the cellarer in turn shall consign them to the incoming server, in order that he may know what he gives out and what he receives back.

Mar. 14—July 14—Nov. 13

An hour before the meal let the weekly servers each receive a drink and some bread, over and above the appointed allowance, in order that at the meal time they may serve their brethren without murmuring and without excessive fatigue. On solemn days, however, let them wait until after Mass.

Immediately after the Morning Office on Sunday, the incoming and outgoing servers shall prostrate themselves before all the brethren in the oratory and ask their prayers. Let the server who is ending his week say this verse: "Blessed are You, O Lord God, who have helped me and consoled me." When this has been said three times and the outgoing server has received his blessing, then let the incoming server follow and say, "Incline unto my aid, O God; O Lord, make haste to help me." Let this also be repeated three times by all, and having received his blessing let him enter his service.

CHAPTER 36 — On the Sick Brethren

Mar. 15—July 15—Nov. 14

Before all things and above all things, care must be taken of the sick, so that they will be served as if they were Christ in person; for He Himself said, "I was sick, and you visited Me," and, "What you did for one of these least ones, you did for Me." But let the sick on their part consider that they are being served for the honor of God, and let them not annoy their brethren who are serving them by their unnecessary demands. Yet they should be patiently borne with, because from such as these is gained a more abundant reward. Therefore the Abbot shall take the greatest care that they suffer no neglect.

For these sick brethren let there be assigned a special room and an attendant who is God-fearing, diligent and solicitous. Let the use of baths be afforded the sick as often as may be expedient; but to the healthy, and especially to the young, let them be granted more rarely. Moreover, let the use of meat be granted to the sick who are very weak, for the restoration of their strength; but when they are convalescent, let all abstain from meat as usual.

The Abbot shall take the greatest care that the sick be not neglected by the cellarers or the attendants; for he also is responsible for what is done wrongly by his disciples.

CHAPTER 37 — On Old Men and Children

Mar. 16—July 16—Nov. 15

Although human nature itself is drawn to special kindness towards these times of life, that is towards old men and children, still the authority of the Rule should also provide for them. Let their weakness be always taken into account, and let them by no means be held to the rigour of the Rule with regard to food. On the contrary, let a kind consideration be shown to them, and let them eat before the regular hours.

CHAPTER 38 — On the Weekly Reader

Mar. 17—July 17—Nov. 16

The meals of the brethren should not be without reading. Nor should the reader be anyone who happens to take up the book; but there should be a reader for the whole week, entering that office on Sunday. Let this incoming reader, after Mass and Communion, ask all to pray for him that God may keep him from the spirit of pride. And let him intone the following verse, which shall be said three times by all in the oratory: "O Lord, open my lips, and my mouth shall declare thy praise." Then, having received a blessing, let him enter on the reading.

And let absolute silence be kept at table, so that no whispering may be heard nor any voice except the reader's. As to the things they need while they eat and drink, let the brethren pass them to one another so that no one need ask for anything. If anything is needed, however, let it be asked for by means of some audible sign rather than by speech. Nor shall anyone at table presume to ask questions about the reading or anything else, lest that give occasion for talking; except that the Superior may perhaps wish to say something briefly for the purpose of edification.

The brother who is reader for the week shall take a little refreshment before he begins to read, on account of the Holy Communion and lest perhaps the fast be hard for him to bear. He shall take his meal afterwards with the kitchen and table servers of the week.

The brethren are not to read or chant in order, but only those who edify their hearers.

CHAPTER 39 — On the Measure of Food

Mar. 18—July 18—Nov. 17

We think it sufficient for the daily dinner, whether at the sixth or the ninth hour, that every table have two cooked dishes, on account of individual infirmities, so that he who for some reason cannot eat of the one may make his meal of the other. Therefore let two cooked dishes suffice for all the brethren; and if any fruit or fresh vegetables are available, let a third dish be added.

Let a good pound weight of bread suffice for the day, whether there by only one meal or both dinner and supper. If they are to have supper, the cellarer shall reserve a third of that pound, to be given them at supper.

But if it happens that the work was heavier, it shall lie within the Abbot's discretion and power, should it be expedient, to add something to the fare. Above all things, however, over-indulgence must be avoided and a monk must never be overtaken by indigestion; for there is nothing so opposed to the Christian character as over-indulgence, according to Our Lord's words, "See to it that your hearts be not burdened with over-indulgence."

Young boys shall not receive the same amount of food as their elders, but less; and frugality shall be observed in all circumstances.

Except the sick who are very weak, let all abstain entirely from eating the flesh of four-footed animals.

CHAPTER 40 — On the Measure of Drink

Mar. 19—July 19—Nov. 18

"Everyone has his own gift from God, one in this way and another in that." It is therefore with some misgiving that we regulate the measure of other men's sustenance. Nevertheless, keeping in view the needs of weaker brethren, we believe that a hemina of wine a day is sufficient for each. But those to whom God gives the strength to abstain should know that they will receive a special reward.

If the circumstances of the place, or the work, or the heat of summer require a greater measure, the Superior shall use his judgment in the matter, taking care always that there be no occasion for surfeit or drunkenness. We read, it is true, that wine is by no means a drink for monks; but since the monks of our day cannot be persuaded of this, let us at least agree to drink sparingly and not to satiety, because "wine makes even the wise fall away."

But where the circumstances of the place are such that not even the measure prescribed above can be supplied, but much less or none at all, let those who live there bless God and not murmur. Above all things do we give this admonition, that they abstain from murmuring.

CHAPTER 41 — At What Hours the Meals Should Be Taken

Mar. 20—July 20—Nov. 19

From holy Easter until Pentecost let the brethren take dinner at the sixth hour and supper in the evening.

From Pentecost throughout the summer, unless the monks have work in the fields or the excessive heat of summer oppresses them, let them fast on Wednesdays and Fridays until the ninth hour; on the other days let them dine at the sixth hour. This dinner at the sixth hour shall be the daily schedule if they have work in the fields or the heat of summer is extreme; the Abbot's foresight shall decide on this. Thus it is said that he should adapt and arrange everything in such a way that souls may be saved and that the brethren may do their work without just cause for murmuring.

From the Ides of September until the beginning of Lent let them always take their dinner at the ninth hour.

In Lent let them dine in the evening. But this evening hour shall be so determined that they will not need the light of a lamp while eating, but everything will be accomplished while it is still daylight. Indeed at all seasons let the hour, whether for supper or for dinner, be so arranged that everything will be done by daylight.

CHAPTER 42 — That No One Speak After Compline

Mar. 21—July 21—Nov. 20

Monks ought to be zealous for silence at all times, but especially during the hours of the night. For every season, therefore, whether there be fasting or two meals, let the program be as follows:

If it be a season when there are two meals, then as soon as they have risen from supper they shall all sit together, and one of them shall read the Conferences or the Lives of the Fathers or something else that may edify the hearers; not the Heptateuch or the Book of Kings, however, because it will not be expedient for weak minds to hear those parts of Scripture at that hour; but they shall be read at other times.

If it be a day of fast, then having allowed a short interval after Vespers they shall proceed at once to the reading of the Conferences, as prescribed above; four or five pages being read, or as much as time permits, so that during the delay provided by this reading all may come together, including those who may have been occupied in some work assigned them.

When all, therefore, are gathered together, let them say Compline; and when they come out from Compline, no one shall be allowed to say anything from that time on. And if anyone should be found evading this rule of silence, let him undergo severe punishment. An exception shall be made if the need of speaking to guests should arise or if the Abbot should give someone an order. But even this should be done with the utmost gravity and the most becoming restraint.

CHAPTER 43 — On Those Who Come Late to the Work of God or to Table

Mar. 22—July 22—Nov. 21

At the hour for the Divine Office, as soon as the signal is heard, let them abandon whatever they have in hand and hasten with the greatest speed, yet with seriousness, so that there is no excuse for levity. Let nothing, therefore, be put before the Work of God.

If at the Night Office anyone arrives after the "Glory be to the Father" of Psalm 94— which Psalm for this reason we wish to be said very slowly and protractedly—let him not stand in his usual place in the choir; but let him stand last of all, or in a place set aside by the Abbot for such negligent ones in order that they may be seen by him and by all. He shall remain there until the Work of God has been completed, and then do penance by a public satisfaction. The reason why we have judged it fitting for them to stand in the last place or in a place apart is that, being seen by all, they may amend for very shame. For if they remain outside of the oratory, there will perhaps be someone who will go back to bed and sleep or at least seat himself outside and indulge in idle talk, and thus an occasion will be provided for the evil one. But let them go inside, that they may not lose the whole Office, and may amend for the future.

At the day Hours anyone who does not arrive at the Work of God until after the verse and the "Glory be to the Father" of the first Psalm following it shall stand in the last place, according to our ruling above. Nor shall he presume to join the choir in their chanting until he has made satisfaction, unless the Abbot should pardon him and give him permission; but even then the offender must make satisfaction for his fault.

Mar. 23—July 23—Nov. 22

Anyone who does not come to table before the verse, so that all together may say the verse and the oration and all sit down to table at the same time—anyone who through his own carelessness or bad habit does not come on time shall be corrected for this up to the second time. If then he does not amend, he shall not be allowed to share in the common table, but shall be separated from the company of all and made to eat alone, and his portion of wine shall be taken away from him, until he has made satisfaction and has amended. And let him suffer a like penalty who is not present at the verse said after the meal.

And let no one presume to take any food or drink before or after the appointed time. But if anyone is offered something by the Superior and refuses to take it, then when the time comes that he desires what he formerly refused or something else, let him receive nothing whatever until he has made proper satisfaction.

CHAPTER 44 — How the Excommunicated Are to Make Satisfaction

Mar. 24—July 24—Nov. 23

One who for serious faults is excommunicated from oratory and table shall make satisfaction as follows. At the hour when the celebration of the Work of God is concluded in the oratory, let him lie prostrate before the door of the oratory, saying nothing, but only lying prone with his face to the ground at the feet of all as they come out of the oratory. And let him continue to do this until the Abbot judges that satisfaction has been made. Then, when he has come at the Abbot's bidding, let him cast himself first at the Abbot's feet and then at the feet of all, that they may pray for him.

And next, if the Abbot so orders, let him be received into the choir, to the place which the Abbot appoints, but with the provision that he shall not presume to intone Psalm or lesson or anything else in the oratory without a further order from the Abbot. Moreover, at every Hour, when the Work of God is ended, let him cast himself on the ground in the place where he stands. And let him continue to satisfy in this way until the Abbot again orders him finally to cease from this satisfaction.

But those who for slight faults are excommunicated only from table shall make satisfaction in the oratory, and continue in it till an order from the Abbot, until he blesses them and says, "It is enough."

CHAPTER 45 — On Those Who Make Mistakes in the Oratory

Mar. 25—July 25—Nov. 24

When anyone has made a mistake while reciting a Psalm, a responsory, an antiphon or a lesson, if he does not humble himself there before all by making a satisfaction, let him undergo a greater punishment because he would not correct by humility what he did wrong through carelessness.

But boys for such faults shall be whipped.

CHAPTER 46 — On Those Who Fail in Any Other Matters

Mar. 26—July 26—Nov. 25

When anyone is engaged in any sort of work, whether in the kitchen, in the cellar, in a shop, in the bakery, in the garden, while working at some craft, or in any other place, and he commits some fault, or breaks something, or loses something, or transgresses in any other way whatsoever, if he does not come immediately before the Abbot and the community of his own accord to make satisfaction and confess his fault, then when it becomes known through another, let him be subjected to a more severe correction.

But if the sin-sickness of the soul is a hidden one, let him reveal it only to the Abbot or to a spiritual father, who knows how to cure his own and others' wounds without exposing them and making them public.

CHAPTER 47 — On Giving the Signal for the Time of the Work of God

Mar. 27—July 27—Nov. 26

The indicating of the hour of the Work of God by day and by night shall devolve upon the Abbot, either to give the signal himself or to assign this duty to such a careful brother that everything will take place at the proper hours.

Let the Psalms and the antiphons be intoned by those who are appointed for it, in their order after the Abbot. And no one shall presume to sing or read unless he can fulfil that office in such a way as to edify the hearers. Let this function be performed with humility, gravity and reverence, and by him whom the Abbot has appointed.

CHAPTER 48 — On the Daily Manual Labour

Mar. 28—July 28—Nov. 27

Idleness is the enemy of the soul. Therefore the brethren should be occupied at certain times in manual labour, and again at fixed hours in sacred reading. To that end we think that the times for each may be prescribed as follows.

From Easter until the Calends of October, when they come out from Prime in the morning let them labour at whatever is necessary until about the fourth hour, and from the fourth hour until about the sixth let them apply themselves to reading. After the sixth hour, having left the table, let them rest on their beds in perfect silence; or if anyone may perhaps want to read, let him read to himself in such a way as not to disturb anyone else. Let None be said rather early, at the middle of the eighth hour, and let them again do what work has to be done until Vespers.

And if the circumstances of the place or their poverty should require that they themselves do the work of gathering the harvest, let them not be discontented; for then are they truly monks when they live by the labour of their hands, as did our Fathers and the Apostles. Let all things be done with moderation, however, for the sake of the faint-hearted.

Mar. 29—July 29—Nov. 28

From the Calends of October until the beginning of Lent, let them apply themselves to reading up to the end of the second hour. At the second hour let Terce be said, and then let all labour at the work assigned them until None. At the first signal for the Hour of None let everyone break off from his work, and hold himself ready for the sounding of the second signal. After the meal let them apply themselves to their reading or to the Psalms.

On the days of Lent, from morning until the end of the third hour let them apply themselves to their reading, and from then until the end of the tenth hour let them do the work assigned them. And in these days of Lent they shall each receive a book from the library, which they shall read straight through from the beginning. These books are to be given out at the beginning of Lent.

But certainly one or two of the seniors should be deputed to go about the monastery at the hours when the brethren are occupied in reading and see that there be no lazy brother who spends his time in idleness or gossip and does not apply himself to the reading, so that he is not only unprofitable to himself but also distracts others. If such a one be found (which God forbid), let him be corrected once and a second time; if he does not amend, let him undergo the punishment of the Rule in such a way that the rest may take warning.

Moreover, one brother shall not associate with another at unseasonable hours.

Mar. 30—July 30—Nov. 29

On Sundays, let all occupy themselves in reading, except those who have been appointed to various duties. But if anyone should be so negligent and shiftless that he will not or cannot study or read, let him be given some work to do so that he will not be idle.

Weak or sickly brethren should be assigned a task or craft of such a nature as to keep them from idleness and at the same time not to overburden them or drive them away with excessive toil. Their weakness must be taken into consideration by the Abbot.

CHAPTER 49 — On the Observance of Lent

Mar. 31—July 31—Nov. 30

Although the life of a monk ought to have about it at all times the character of a Lenten observance, yet since few have the virtue for that, we therefore urge that during the actual days of Lent the brethren keep their lives most pure and at the same time wash away during these holy days all the negligences of other times. And this will be worthily done if we restrain ourselves from all vices and give ourselves up to prayer with tears, to reading, to compunction of heart and to abstinence.

During these days, therefore, let us increase somewhat the usual burden of our service, as by private prayers and by abstinence in food and drink. Thus everyone of his own will may offer God "with joy of the Holy Spirit" something above the measure required of him. From his body, that is, he may withhold some food, drink, sleep, talking and jesting; and with the joy of spiritual desire he may look forward to holy Easter.

Let each one, however, suggest to his Abbot what it is that he wants to offer, and let it be done with his blessing and approval. For anything done without the permission of the spiritual father will be imputed to presumption and vainglory and will merit no reward. Therefore let everything be done with the Abbot's approval.

CHAPTER 50 — On Brethren Who Are Working Far From the Oratory or Are on a Journey

Apr. 1—Aug. 1—Dec. 1

Those brethren who are working at a great distance and cannot get to the oratory at the proper time—the Abbot judging that such is the case—shall perform the Work of God in the place where they are working, bending their knees in reverence before God.

Likewise those who have been sent on a journey shall not let the appointed Hours pass by, but shall say the Office by themselves as well as they can, and not neglect to render the task of their service.

CHAPTER 51 — On Brethren Who Go Not Very Far Away

Apr. 2—Aug. 2—Dec. 2

A brother who is sent out on some business and is expected to return to the monastery that same day shall not presume to eat while he is out, even if he is urgently requested to do so by any person whomsoever, unless he has permission from his Abbot. And if he acts otherwise, let him be excommunicated.

CHAPTER 52 — On the Oratory of the Monastery

Apr. 3—Aug. 3—Dec. 3

Let the oratory be what it is called, a place of prayer; and let nothing else be done there or kept there. When the Work of God is ended, let all go out in perfect silence, and let reverence for God be observed, so that any brother who may wish to pray privately will not be hindered by another's misconduct. And at other times also, if anyone should want to pray by himself, let him go in simply and pray, not in a loud voice but with tears and fervour of heart. He who does not say his prayers in this way, therefore, shall not be permitted to remain in the oratory when the Work of God is ended, lest another be hindered, as we have said.

CHAPTER 53 — On the Reception of Guests

Apr. 4—Aug. 4—Dec. 4

Let all guests who arrive be received like Christ, for He is going to say, "I came as a guest, and you received Me." And to all let due honor be shown, especially to the domestics of the faith and to pilgrims.

As soon as a guest is announced, therefore, let the Superior or the brethren meet him with all charitable service. And first of all let them pray together, and then exchange the kiss of peace. For the kiss of peace should not be offered until after the prayers have been said, on account of the devil's deceptions.

In the salutation of all guests, whether arriving or departing, let all humility be shown. Let the head be bowed or the whole body prostrated on the ground in adoration of Christ, who indeed is received in their persons.

After the guests have been received and taken to prayer, let the Superior or someone appointed by him sit with them. Let the divine law be read before the guest for his edification, and then let all kindness be shown him. The Superior shall break his fast for the sake of a guest, unless it happens to be a principal fast day which may not be violated. The brethren, however, shall observe the customary fasts. Let the Abbot give the guests water for their hands; and let both Abbot and community wash the feet of all guests. After the washing of the feet let them say this verse: "We have received Your mercy, O God, in the midst of Your temple."

In the reception of the poor and of pilgrims the greatest care and solicitude should be shown, because it is especially in them that Christ is received; for as far as the rich are concerned, the very fear which they inspire wins respect for them.

Apr. 5—Aug. 5—Dec. 5

Let there be a separate kitchen for the Abbot and guests, that the brethren may not be disturbed when guests, who are never lacking in a monastery, arrive at irregular hours. Let two brethren capable of filling the office well be appointed for a year to have charge of this kitchen. Let them be given such help as they need, that they may serve without murmuring. And on the other hand, when they have less to occupy them, let them go out to whatever work is assigned them.

And not only in their case but in all the offices of the monastery let this arrangement be observed, that when help is needed it be supplied, and again when the workers are unoccupied they do whatever they are bidden.

The guest house also shall be assigned to a brother whose soul is possessed by the fear of God. Let there be a sufficient number of beds made up in it; and let the house of God be managed by prudent men and in a prudent manner.

On no account shall anyone who is not so ordered associate or converse with guests. But if he should meet them or see them, let him greet them humbly, as we have said, ask their blessing and pass on, saying that he is not allowed to converse with a guest.

CHAPTER 54 — Whether a Monk Should Receive Letters or Anything Else

Apr. 6—Aug. 6—Dec. 6

On no account shall a monk be allowed to receive letters, tokens or any little gift whatsoever from his parents or anyone else, or from his brethren, or to give the same, without the Abbot's permission. But if anything is sent him even by his parents, let him not presume to take it before it has been shown to the Abbot. And it shall be in the Abbot's power to decide to whom it shall be given, if he allows it to be received; and the brother to whom it was sent should not be grieved, lest occasion be given to the devil.

Should anyone presume to act otherwise, let him undergo the discipline of the Rule.

CHAPTER 55 — On the Clothes and Shoes of the Brethren

Apr. 7—Aug. 7—Dec. 7

Let clothing be given to the brethren according to the nature of the place in which they dwell and its climate; for in cold regions more will be needed, and in warm regions less. This is to be taken into consideration, therefore, by the Abbot.

We believe, however, that in ordinary places the following dress is sufficient for each monk: a tunic, a cowl (thick and woolly for winter, thin or worn for summer), a scapular for work, stockings and shoes to cover the feet.

The monks should not complain about the color or the coarseness of any of these things, but be content with what can be found in the district where they live and can be purchased cheaply.

The Abbot shall see to the size of the garments, that they be not too short for those who wear them, but of the proper fit.

Let those who receive new clothes always give back the old ones at once, to be put away in the wardrobe for the poor. For it is sufficient if a monk has two tunics and two cowls, to allow for night wear and for the washing of these garments; more than that is superfluity and should be taken away. Let them return their stockings also and anything else that is old when they receive new ones.

Those who are sent on a journey shall receive drawers from the wardrobe, which they shall wash and restore on their return. And let their cowls and tunics be somewhat better than what they usually wear. These they shall receive from the wardrobe when they set out on a journey, and restore when they return.

Apr. 8—Aug. 8—Dec. 8

For bedding let this suffice: a mattress, a blanket, a coverlet and a pillow.

The beds, moreover, are to be examined frequently by the Abbot, to see if any private property be found in them. If anyone should be found to have something that he did not receive from the Abbot, let him undergo the most severe discipline.

And in order that this vice of private ownership may be cut out by the roots, the Abbot should provide all the necessary articles: cowl, tunic, stockings, shoes, girdle, knife, pen, needle, handkerchief, tablets; that all pretext of need may be taken away. Yet the Abbot should always keep in mind the sentence from the Acts of the Apostles that "distribution was made to each according as anyone had need." In this manner, therefore, let the Abbot consider the weaknesses of the needy and not the ill-will of the envious. But in all his decisions let him think about the retribution of God.

CHAPTER 56 — On the Abbot's Table

Apr. 9—Aug. 9—Dec. 9

Let the Abbot's table always be with the guests and the pilgrims. But when there are no guests, let it be in his power to invite whom he will of the brethren. Yet one or two seniors must always be left with the brethren for the sake of discipline.

CHAPTER 57 — On the Craftsmen of the Monastery

Apr. 10—Aug. 10—Dec. 10

If there are craftsmen in the monastery, let them practice their crafts with all humility, provided the Abbot has given permission. But if any one of them becomes conceited over his skill in his craft, because he seems to be conferring a benefit on the monastery, let him be taken from his craft and no longer exercise it unless, after he has humbled himself, the Abbot again gives him permission.

If any of the work of the craftsmen is to be sold, let those through whose hands the transactions pass see to it that they do not presume to practice any fraud. Let them always remember Ananias and Saphira, lest perhaps the death which these incurred in the body, they themselves and any others who would deal dishonestly with the monastery's property should suffer in the soul. And in the prices let not the sin of avarice creep in, but let the goods always be sold a little cheaper than they can be sold by people in the world, "that in all things God may be glorified."

CHAPTER 58 — On the Manner of Receiving Brethren

Apr. 11—Aug. 11—Dec. 11

When anyone is newly come for the reformation of his life, let him not be granted an easy entrance; but, as the Apostle says, "Test the spirits to see whether they are from God." If the newcomer, therefore, perseveres in his knocking, and if it is seen after four or five days that he bears patiently the harsh treatment offered him and the difficulty of admission, and that he persists in his petition, then let entrance be granted him, and let him stay in the guest house for a few days.

After that let him live in the novitiate, where the novices study, eat and sleep. A senior shall be assigned to them who is skilled in winning souls, to watch over them with the utmost care. Let him examine whether the novice is truly seeking God, and whether he is zealous for the Work of God, for obedience and for humiliations. Let the novice be told all the hard and rugged ways by which the journey to God is made.

If he promises stability and perseverance, then at the end of two months let this Rule be read through to him, and let him be addressed thus: "Here is the law under which you wish to fight. If you can observe it, enter; if you cannot, you are free to depart." If he still stands firm, let him be taken to the above-mentioned novitiate and again tested in all patience. And after the lapse of six months let the Rule be read to him, that he may know on what he is entering. And if he still remains firm, after four months let the same Rule be read to him again.

Then, having deliberated with himself, if he promises to keep it in its entirety and to observe everything that is commanded him, let him be received into the community. But let him understand that, according to the law of the Rule, from that day forward he may not leave the monastery nor withdraw his neck from under the yoke of the Rule which he was free to refuse or to accept during that prolonged deliberation.

Apr. 12—Aug. 12—Dec. 12

He who is to be received shall make a promise before all in the oratory of his stability and of the reformation of his life and of obedience. This promise he shall make before God and His Saints, so that if he should ever act otherwise, he may know that he will be condemned by Him whom he mocks. Of this promise of his let him draw up a petition in the name of the Saints whose relics are there and of the Abbot who is present. Let him write this petition with his own hand; or if he is illiterate, let another write it at his request, and let the novice put his mark to it. Then let him place it with his own hand upon the altar; and when he has placed it there, let the novice at once intone this verse: "Receive me, O Lord, according to Your word, and I shall live: and let me not be confounded in my hope." Let the whole community answer this verse three times and add the "Glory be to the Father." Then let the novice brother prostrate himself at each one's feet, that they may pray for him. And from that day forward let him be counted as one of the community.

If he has any property, let him either give it beforehand to the poor or by solemn donation bestow it on the monastery, reserving nothing at all for himself, as indeed he knows that from that day forward he will no longer have power even over his own body. At once, therefore, in the oratory, let him be divested of his own clothes which he is wearing and dressed in the clothes of the monastery. But let the clothes of which he was divested be put aside in the wardrobe and kept there. Then if he should ever listen to the persuasions of the devil and decide to leave the monastery (which God forbid), he may be divested of the monastic clothes and cast out. His petition, however, which the Abbot has taken from the altar, shall not be returned to him, but shall be kept in the monastery.

CHAPTER 59 — On the Sons of Nobles and of the Poor Who Are Offered

Apr. 13—Aug. 13—Dec. 13

If anyone of the nobility offers his son to God in the monastery and the boy is very young, let his parents draw up the petition which we mentioned above; and at the oblation let them wrap the petition and the boy's hand in the altar cloth and so offer him.

As regards their property, they shall promise in the same petition under oath that they will never of themselves, or through an intermediary, or in any way whatever, give him anything or provide him with the opportunity of owning anything. Or else, if they are unwilling to do this, and if they want to offer something as an alms to the monastery for their advantage, let them make a donation of the property they wish to give to the monastery, reserving the income to themselves if they wish. And in this way let everything be barred, so that the boy may have no expectations whereby (which God forbid) he might be deceived and ruined, as we have learned by experience.

Let those who are less well-to-do make a similar offering. But those who have nothing at all shall simply draw up the petition and offer their son before witnesses at the oblation.

CHAPTER 60 — On Priests Who May Wish to Live in the Monastery

Apr. 14—Aug. 14—Dec. 14

If anyone of the priestly order should ask to be received into the monastery, permission shall not be granted him too readily. But if he is quite persistent in his request, let him know that he will have to observe the whole discipline of the Rule and that nothing will be relaxed in his favour, that it may be as it is written: "Friend, for what have you come?"

It shall be granted him, however, to stand next after the Abbot and to give blessings and celebrate Mass, but only by order of the Abbot. Without such order let him not presume to do anything, knowing that he is subject to the discipline of the Rule; but rather let him give an example of humility to all.

If there happens to be question of an appointment or of some business in the monastery, let him expect the rank due him according to the date of his entrance into the monastery, and not the place granted him out of reverence for the priesthood.

If any clerics, moved by the same desire, should wish to join the monastery, let them be placed in a middle rank. But they too are to be admitted only if they promise observance of the Rule and their own stability.

CHAPTER 61 — How Pilgrim Monks Are to be Received

Apr. 15—Aug. 15—Dec. 15

If a pilgrim monk coming from a distant region wants to live as a guest of the monastery, let him be received for as long a time as he desires, provided he is content with the customs of the place as he finds them and does not disturb the monastery by superfluous demands, but is simply content with what he finds. If, however, he censures or points out anything reasonably and with the humility of charity, let the Abbot consider prudently whether perhaps it was for that very purpose that the Lord sent him.

If afterwards he should want to bind himself to stability, his wish should not be denied him, especially since there has been opportunity during his stay as a guest to discover his character.

But if as a guest he was found exacting or prone to vice, not only should he be denied membership in the community, but he should even be politely requested to leave, lest others be corrupted by his evil life.

If, however, he has not proved to be the kind who deserves to be put out, he should not only on his own application be received as a member of the community, but he should even be persuaded to stay, that the others may be instructed by his example, and because in every place it is the same Lord who is served, the same King for whom the battle is fought.

Moreover, if the Abbot perceives that he is a worthy man, he may put him in a somewhat higher rank. And not only with regard to a monk but also with regard to those in priestly or clerical orders previously mentioned, the Abbot may establish them in a higher rank than would be theirs by date of entrance if he perceives that their life is deserving.

Let the Abbot take care, however, never to receive a monk from another known monastery as a member of his community without the consent of his Abbot or a letter of recommendation; for it is written, "Do not to another what you would not want done to yourself."

CHAPTER 62 — On the Priests of the Monastery

If an Abbot desire to have a priest or a deacon ordained for his monastery, let him choose one of his monks who is worthy to exercise the priestly office.

But let the one who is ordained beware of self-exaltation or pride; and let him not presume to do anything except what is commanded him by the Abbot, knowing that he is so much the more subject to the discipline of the Rule. Nor should he by reason of his priesthood forget the obedience and the discipline required by the Rule, but make ever more and more progress towards God.

Let him always keep the place which he received on entering the monastery, except in his duties at the altar or in case the choice of the community and the will of the Abbot should promote him for the worthiness of his life. Yet he must understand that he is to observe the rules laid down by deans and Priors.

Should he presume to act otherwise, let him be judged not as a priest but as a rebel. And if he does not reform after repeated admonitions, let even the Bishop be brought in as a witness. If then he still fails to amend, and his offenses are notorious, let him be put out of the monastery, but only if his contumacy is such that he refuses to submit or to obey the Rule.

CHAPTER 63 — On the Order of the Community

Let all keep their places in the monastery established by the time of their entrance, the merit of their lives and the decision of the Abbot. Yet the Abbot must not disturb the flock committed to him, nor by an arbitrary use of his power ordain anything unjustly; but let him always think of the account he will have to render to God for all his decisions and his deeds.

Therefore in that order which he has established or which they already had, let the brethren approach to receive the kiss of peace and Communion, intone the Psalms and stand in choir. And in no place whatever should age decide the order or be prejudicial to it; for Samuel and Daniel as mere boys judged priests.

Except for those already mentioned, therefore, whom the Abbot has promoted by a special decision or demoted for definite reasons, all the rest shall take their order according to the time of their entrance. Thus, for example, he who came to the monastery at the second hour of the day, whatever be his age or his dignity, must know that he is junior to one who came at the first hour of the day. Boys, however, are to be kept under discipline in all matters and by everyone.

Apr. 19—Aug. 19—Dec. 19

The juniors, therefore, should honor their seniors, and the seniors love their juniors.

In the very manner of address, let no one call another by the mere name; but let the seniors call their juniors Brothers, and the juniors call their seniors Fathers, by which is conveyed the reverence due to a father. But the Abbot, since he is believed to represent Christ, shall be called Lord and Abbot, not for any pretensions of his own but out of honor and love for Christ. Let the Abbot himself reflect on this, and show himself worthy of such an honor.

And wherever the brethren meet one another the junior shall ask the senior for his blessing. When a senior passes by, a junior shall rise and give him a place to sit, nor shall the junior presume to sit with him unless his senior bid him, that it may be as was written, "In honor anticipating one another."

Boys, both small and adolescent, shall keep strictly to their rank in oratory and at table. But outside of that, wherever they may be, let them be under supervision and discipline, until they come to the age of discretion.

CHAPTER 64 — On Constituting an Abbot

Apr. 20—Aug. 20—Dec. 20

In the constituting of an Abbot let this plan always be followed, that the office be conferred on the one who is chosen either by the whole community unanimously in the fear of God or else by a part of the community, however small, if its counsel is more wholesome.

Merit of life and wisdom of doctrine should determine the choice of the one to be constituted, even if he be the last in the order of the community.

But if (which God forbid) the whole community should agree to choose a person who will acquiesce in their vices, and if those vices somehow become known to the Bishop to whose diocese the place belongs, or to the Abbots or the faithful of the vicinity, let them prevent the success of this conspiracy of the wicked, and set a worthy steward over the house of God. They may be sure that they will receive a good reward for this action if they do it with a pure intention and out of zeal for God; as, on the contrary, they will sin if they fail to do it.

Apr. 21—Aug. 21—Dec. 21

Once he has been constituted, let the Abbot always bear in mind what a burden he has undertaken and to whom he will have to give an account of his stewardship, and let him know that his duty is rather to profit his brethren than to preside over them. He must therefore be learned in the divine law, that he may have a treasure of knowledge from which to bring forth new things and old. He must be chaste, sober and merciful. Let him exalt mercy above judgment, that he himself may obtain mercy. He should hate vices; he should love the brethren.

In administering correction he should act prudently and not go to excess, lest in seeking too eagerly to scrape off the rust he break the vessel. Let him keep his own frailty ever before his eyes and remember that the bruised reed must not be broken. By this we do not mean that he should allow vices to grow; on the contrary, as we have already said, he should eradicate them prudently and with charity, in the way which may seem best in each case. Let him study rather to be loved than to be feared.

Let him not be excitable and worried, nor exacting and headstrong, nor jealous and over-suspicious; for then he is never at rest.

In his commands let him be prudent and considerate; and whether the work which he enjoins concerns God or the world, let him be discreet and moderate, bearing in mind the discretion of holy Jacob, who said, "If I cause my flocks to be overdriven, they will all die in one day." Taking this, then, and other examples of discretion, the mother of virtues, let him so temper all things that the strong may have something to strive after, and the weak may not fall back in dismay.

And especially let him keep this Rule in all its details, so that after a good ministry he may hear from the Lord what the good servant heard who gave his fellow-servants wheat in due season: "Indeed, I tell you, he will set him over all his goods."

CHAPTER 65 — On the Prior of the Monastery

Apr. 22—Aug. 22—Dec. 22

It happens all too often that the constituting of a Prior gives rise to grave scandals in monasteries. For there are some who become inflated with the evil spirit of pride and consider themselves second Abbots. By usurping power they foster scandals and cause dissensions in the community. Especially does this happen in those places where the Prior is constituted by the same Bishop or the same Abbots who constitute the Abbot himself. What an absurd procedure this is can easily be seen; for it gives the Prior an occasion for becoming proud from the very time of his constitution, by putting the thought into his mind that he is freed from the authority of his Abbot: "For," he will say to himself, "you were constituted by the same persons who constituted the Abbot." From this source are stirred up envy, quarrels, detraction, rivalry, dissensions and disorders. For while the Abbot and the Prior are at variance, their souls cannot but be endangered by this dissension; and those who are under them, currying favour with one side or the other, go to ruin. The guilt for this dangerous state of affairs rests on the heads of those whose action brought about such disorder.

Apr. 23—Aug. 23—Dec. 23

To us, therefore, it seems expedient for the preservation of peace and charity that the Abbot have in his hands the full administration of his monastery. And if possible let all the affairs of the monastery, as we have already arranged, be administered by deans according to the Abbot's directions. Thus, with the duties being shared by several, no one person will become proud.

But if the circumstances of the place require it, or if the community asks for it with reason and with humility, and the Abbot judges it to be expedient, let the Abbot himself constitute as his Prior whomsoever he shall choose with the counsel of God-fearing brethren.

That Prior, however, shall perform respectfully the duties enjoined on him by his Abbot and do nothing against the Abbot's will or direction; for the more he is raised above the rest, the more carefully should he observe the precepts of the Rule.

If it should be found that the Prior has serious faults, or that he is deceived by his exaltation and yields to pride, or if he should be proved to be a despiser of the Holy Rule, let him be admonished verbally up to four times. If he fails to amend, let the correction of regular discipline be applied to him. But if even then he does not reform, let him be deposed from the office of Prior and another be appointed in his place who is worthy of it. And if afterwards he is not quiet and obedient in the community, let him even be expelled from the monastery. But the Abbot, for his part, should bear in mind that he will have to render an account to God for all his judgments, lest the flame of envy or jealousy be kindled in his soul.

CHAPTER 66 — On the Porters of the Monastery

Apr. 24—Aug. 24—Dec. 24

At the gate of the monastery let there be placed a wise old man, who knows how to receive and to give a message, and whose maturity will prevent him from straying about. This porter should have a room near the gate, so that those who come may always find someone at hand to attend to their business. And as soon as anyone knocks or a poor man hails him, let him answer "Thanks be to God" or "A blessing!" Then let him attend to them promptly, with all the meekness inspired by the fear of God and with the warmth of charity.

Should the porter need help, let him have one of the younger brethren.

If it can be done, the monastery should be so established that all the necessary things, such as water, mill, garden and various workshops, may be within the enclosure, so that there is no necessity for the monks to go about outside of it, since that is not at all profitable for their souls.

We desire that this Rule be read often in the community, so that none of the brethren may excuse himself on the ground of ignorance.

CHAPTER 67 — On Brethren Who Are Sent on a Journey

Apr. 25—Aug. 25—Dec. 25

Let the brethren who are sent on a journey commend themselves to the prayers of all the brethren and of the Abbot; and always at the last prayer of the Work of God let a commemoration be made of all absent brethren.

When brethren return from a journey, at the end of each canonical Hour of the Work of God on the day they return, let them lie prostrate on the floor of the oratory and beg the prayers of all on account of any faults that may have surprised them on the road, through the seeing or hearing of something evil, or through idle talk. And let no one presume to tell another whatever he may have seen or heard outside of the monastery, because this causes very great harm. But if anyone presumes to do so, let him undergo the punishment of the Rule. And let him be punished likewise who would presume to leave the enclosure of the monastery and go anywhere or do anything, however small, without an order from the Abbot.

CHAPTER 68 — If a Brother Is Commanded to Do Impossible Things

Apr. 26—Aug. 26—Dec. 26

If it happens that difficult or impossible tasks are laid on a brother, let him nevertheless receive the order of the one in authority with all meekness and obedience. But if he sees that the weight of the burden altogether exceeds the limit of his strength, let him submit the reasons for his inability to the one who is over him and in a quiet way and at an opportune time, without pride, resistance, or contradiction. And if after these representations the Superior still persists in his decision and command, let the subject know that this is for his good, and let him obey out of love, trusting in the help of God.

CHAPTER 69 — That the Monks Presume Not to Defend One Another

Apr. 27—Aug. 27—Dec. 27

Care must be taken that no monk presume on any ground to defend another monk in the monastery, or as it were to take him under his protection, even though they be united by some tie of blood-relationship. Let not the monks dare to do this in any way whatsoever, because it may give rise to most serious scandals. But if anyone breaks this rule, let him be severely punished.

CHAPTER 70 — That No One Venture to Punish at Random

Apr. 28—Aug. 28—Dec. 28

Every occasion of presumption shall be avoided in the monastery, and we decree that no one be allowed to excommunicate or to strike any of his brethren unless the Abbot has given him the authority. Those who offend in this matter shall be rebuked in the presence of all, that the rest may have fear.

But boys up to 15 years of age shall be carefully controlled and watched by all, yet this too with all moderation and discretion. Anyone, therefore, who presumes without the Abbot's instructions to punish those above that age or who loses his temper with the boys, shall undergo the discipline of the Rule; for it is written, "Do not to another what you would not want done to yourself."

CHAPTER 71 — That the Brethren Be Obedient to One Another

Apr. 29—Aug. 29—Dec. 29

Not only is the boon of obedience to be shown by all to the Abbot, but the brethren are also to obey one another, knowing that by this road of obedience they are going to God. Giving priority, therefore, to the commands of the Abbot and of the Superiors appointed by him (to which we allow no private orders to be preferred), for the rest let all the juniors obey their seniors with all charity and solicitude. But if anyone is found contentious, let him be corrected.

And if any brother, for however small a cause, is corrected in any way by the Abbot or by any of his Superiors, or if he faintly perceives that the mind of any Superior is angered or moved against him, however little, let him at once, without delay, prostrate himself on the ground at his feet and lie there making satisfaction until that emotion is quieted with a blessing. But if anyone should disdain to do this, let him undergo corporal punishment or, if he is stubborn, let him be expelled from the monastery.

CHAPTER 72 — On the Good Zeal Which Monks Ought to Have

Apr. 30—Aug. 30—Dec. 30

Just as there is an evil zeal of bitterness which separates from God and leads to hell, so there is a good zeal which separates from vices and leads to God and to life everlasting. This zeal, therefore, the monks should practice with the most fervent love. Thus they should anticipate one another in honor; most patiently endure one another's infirmities, whether of body or of character; vie in paying obedience one to another—no one following what he considers useful for himself, but rather what benefits another—; tender the charity of brotherhood chastely; fear God in love; love their Abbot with a sincere and humble charity; prefer nothing whatever to Christ. And may He bring us all together to life everlasting!

CHAPTER 73 — On the Fact That the Full Observance of Justice Is Not Established in This Rule

May 1—Aug. 31—Dec. 31

Now we have written this Rule in order that by its observance in monasteries we may show that we have attained some degree of virtue and the rudiments of the religious life.

But for him who would hasten to the perfection of that life there are the teachings of the holy Fathers, the observance of which leads a man to the height of perfection. For what page or what utterance of the divinely inspired books of the Old and New Testaments is not a most unerring role for human life? Or what book of the holy Catholic Fathers does not loudly proclaim how we may come by a straight course to our Creator? Then the Conferences and the Institutes and the Lives of the Fathers, as also the Rule of our holy Father Basil—what else are they but tools of virtue for right-living and obedient monks? But for us who are lazy and ill-living and negligent they are a source of shame and confusion.

Whoever you are, therefore, who are hastening to the heavenly homeland, fulfil with the help of Christ this minimum Rule which we have written for beginners; and then at length under God's protection you will attain to the loftier heights of doctrine and virtue which we have mentioned above.

Gregory the Great

Dialogues

The book of Dialogues *traditionally attributed to Pope Gregory the Great (589-604) spread the fame of Benedict across Europe and was one of the most important hagiographical texts of the Middle Ages. The second book, A Life of Benedict of Nursia, became a model for lives of monastic saints.*

Source: Saint Gregory the Great Dialogues tr. Odo John Zimmerman, O.S.B. The Fathers of the Church (New York: 1959).

Book II

Life and Miracles of St. Benedict Founder and Abbot of the Monastery Which Is Known as the Citadel of Campania.

There was a man of saintly life; blessed Benedict was his name, and he was blessed also with God's grace. Even in boyhood he showed mature understanding, for he kept his heart detached from every pleasure with a strength of character far beyond his years. While still living in the world, free to enjoy its earthly advantages, he saw how barren it was with its attractions and turned from it without regret.

He was born in the district of Norcia[1] of distinguished parents, who sent him back to Rome for a liberal education. But when he saw many of his fellow students falling headlong into vice, he stepped back from the threshold of the world in which he had just set foot. For he was afraid that if he acquired any of its learning, he, too, would later plunge, body and soul, into the dread abyss. In his desire to please God alone, he turned his back on further studies, gave up home and inheritance and resolved to embrace the religious life. He took this step, well aware of his ignorance, yet wise, uneducated though he was.

I was unable to learn about all his miraculous deeds. But the few that I am going to relate I know from the lips of four of his own disciples: Constantine, the holy man who succeeded him as abbot; Valentinian, for many years superior of the monastery at the Lateran; Simplicius, Benedict's second successor; and Honoratus, who is still abbot of the monastery where the man of God first lived.

(1) When Benedict abandoned his studies to go into solitude, he was accompanied only by his nurse, who loved him dearly. As they were passing through Affile, a number of devout men invited them to stay there and provided them with lodging near the Church of St. Peter. One day, after asking her neighbors to lend her a tray for cleaning wheat, the nurse happened to leave it on the edge of the table and when she came back found it had slipped off and broken in two. The poor woman burst into tears; she had only borrowed this tray and now it was ruined. Benedict, who had always been a devout and thoughtful boy, felt sorry for his nurse when he saw her weeping. Quietly picking up both the pieces, he knelt down by himself and prayed earnestly to God, even to the point of tears. No sooner had he finished his prayer than he noticed that the two pieces were

213

joined together again, without even a mark to show where the tray had been broken. Hurrying back at once, he cheerfully reassured his nurse and handed her the tray in perfect condition.

News of the miracle spread to all the country around Affile and stirred up so much admiration among the people that they hung the tray at the entrance to their church. Ever since then it has been a reminder to all of the great holiness Benedict had acquired at the very outset of his monastic life. The tray remained there many years for everyone to see, and it is still hanging over the doorway of the church in these days of Lombard rule.[2] Benedict, however, preferred to suffer ill-treatment from the world rather than enjoy its praises. He wanted to spend himself laboring for God, not to be honored by the applause of men. So he stole away secretly from his nurse and fled to a lonely wilderness about thirty-five miles from Rome called Subiaco. A stream of cold, clear water running through the region broadens out at this point to form a lake, then flows off and continues on its course.[3] On his way there Benedict met a monk named Romanus, who asked him where he was going. After discovering the young man's purpose, Romanus kept it secret and even helped him carry it out by clothing him with the monastic habit and supplying his needs as well as he could.

At Subiaco, Benedict made his home in a narrow cave and for three years remained concealed there, unknown to anyone except the monk Romanus, who lived in a monastery close by under the rule of Abbot Deodatus. With fatherly concern this monk regularly set aside as much bread as he could from his own portion; then from time to time, unnoticed by his abbot, he left the monastery long enough to take the bread to Benedict. There was no path leading from the monastery down to his cave because of a cliff that rose directly over it. To reach him Romanus had to tie the bread to the end of a long rope and lower it over the cliff. A little bell attached to the rope let Benedict know when the bread was there, and he would come out to get it. The ancient Enemy of mankind grew envious of the kindness shown by the older monk in supplying Benedict with food, and one day, as the bread was being lowered, he threw a stone at the bell and broke it. In spite of this, Romanus kept on with his faithful service.

At length the time came when almighty God wished to grant him rest from his toil and reveal Benedict's virtuous life to others. Like a shining lamp his example was to be set on a lampstand to give light to everyone in God's house. The Lord therefore appeared in a vision to a priest some distance away, who had just prepared his Easter dinner. 'How can you prepare these delicacies for yourself,' He asked, 'while my servant is out there in the wilds suffering from hunger?'

Rising at once, the priest wrapped up the food and set out to find the man of God that very day. He searched for him along the rough mountainsides, in the valleys, and through the caverns, until he found him hidden in the cave. They said a prayer of thanksgiving together and then sat down to talk about the spiritual life. After a while the priest suggested that they take their meal. 'Today is the great feast of Easter,' he added.

'It must be a great feast to have brought me this kind visit,' the man of God replied, not realizing after his long separation from men that it was Easter Sunday.

'Today is really Easter,' the priest insisted, 'the feast of our Lord's Resurrection. On such a solemn occasion you should not be fasting. Besides, I was sent here by almighty God so that both of us could share in His gifts.'

After that they said grace and began their meal. When it was over they conversed some more and then the priest went back to his church.

At about the same time some shepherds also discovered Benedict's hiding place. When they first looked through the thickets and caught sight of him clothed in rough skins, they mistook him for some wild animal. Soon, however, they recognized in him a servant of God, and many of them gave up their sinful ways for a life of holiness. As a result, his name became known to all the people in that locality and great numbers visited his cave, supplying him with the food he needed and receiving from his lips in return spiritual food for their souls.

(2) One day, while the saint was alone, the Tempter came in the form of a little black-

bird, which began to flutter in front of his face. It kept so close that he could easily have caught it in his hand. Instead, he made the sign of the cross and the bird flew away. The moment it left, he was seized with an unusually violent temptation. The evil spirit recalled to his mind a woman he had once seen, and before he realized it his emotions were carrying him away. Almost overcome in the struggle, he was on the point of abandoning the lonely wilderness, when suddenly with the help of God's grace he came to himself.

He then noticed a thick patch of nettles and briers next to him. Throwing his garment aside he flung himself into the sharp thorns and stinging nettles. There he rolled and tossed until his whole body was in pain and covered with blood. Yet, once he had conquered pleasure through suffering, his torn and bleeding skin served to drain the poison of temptation from his body. Before long, the pain that was burning his whole body had put out the fires of evil in his heart. It was by exchanging these two fires that he gained the victory over sin. So complete was his triumph that from then on, as he later told his disciples, he never experienced another temptation of this kind.

Soon after, many forsook the world to place themselves under his guidance, for now that he was free from these temptations he was ready to instruct others in the practice of virtue. That is why Moses commanded the Levites to begin their service when they were twenty-five years old or more and to become guardians of the sacred vessels only at the age of fifty.

Peter: The meaning of the passage you quote is becoming a little clearer to me now. Still, I wish you would explain it more fully.

Gregory: It is a well-known fact, Peter, that temptations of the flesh are violent during youth, whereas after the age of fifty concupiscence dies down. Now, the sacred vessels are the souls of the faithful. God's chosen servants must therefore obey and serve and tire themselves out with strenuous work as long as they are still subject to temptations. Only when full maturity has left them undisturbed by evil thoughts are they put in charge of the sacred vessels, for then they become teachers of souls.

Peter: I like the way you interpreted that passage. Now that you have explained what it means, I hope you will continue with your account of the holy man's life.

Gregory: (3) With the passing of this temptation, Benedict's soul, like a field cleared of briers, soon yielded a rich harvest of virtues. As word spread of his saintly life, the renown of his name increased. One day the entire community from a nearby monastery[4] came to see him. Their abbot had recently died, and they wanted the man of God to be their new superior. For some time he tried to discourage them by refusing their request, warning them that his way of life would never harmonize with theirs. But they kept insisting, until in the end he gave his consent.

At the monastery he watched carefully over the religious spirit of the monks and would not tolerate any of their previous disobedience. No one was allowed to turn from the straight path of monastic discipline either to the right or to the left. Their waywardness, however, clashed with the standards he upheld, and in their resentment they started to reproach themselves for choosing him as abbot. It only made them the more sullen to find him curbing every fault and every evil habit. They could not see why they should have to force their settled minds into new ways of thinking.

At length, proving once again that the very life of the just is a burden to the wicked, they tried to find a means of doing away with him and decided to poison his wine. A glass pitcher containing this poisoned drink was presented to the man of God during his meal for the customary blessing. As he made the sign of the cross over it with his hand, the pitcher was shattered, even though it was well beyond his reach at the time. It broke at his blessing as if he had struck it with stone.

Then he realized it had contained a deadly drink which could not bear the sign of life. Still calm and undisturbed, he rose at once and, after gathering the community together, addressed them. 'May almighty God have mercy on you,' he said. 'Why did you conspire to do this? Did I not tell you at the outset that my way of life would never harmonize with yours? Go and find yourselves an abbot to your liking. It is impossible for me to stay here any longer.' Then he went back to the wilderness he loved, to live alone with himself in the presence of his heavenly Father.

Peter: I am not quite sure I understand what you mean by saying 'to live with himself.'

Gregory: These monks had an outlook on religious life entirely unlike his own and were all conspiring against him. Now, if he had tried to force them to remain under his rule, he might have forfeited his own fervour and peace of soul and even turned his eyes from the light of contemplation. Their persistent daily faults would have left him almost too weary to look to his own needs, and he would perhaps have forsaken himself without finding them. For, whenever anxieties carry us out of ourselves unduly, we are no longer with ourselves even though we still remain what we are. We are too distracted with other matters to give any attention whatever to ourselves.

Surely we cannot describe as 'with himself' the young man who traveled to a distant country where he wasted his inheritance and then, after hiring himself out to one of its citizens to feed swine, had to watch them eat their fill of pods while he went hungry. Do we not read in Scripture that, as he was considering all he had lost, 'he came to himself and said, "how many hired servants there are in my father's house that have more bread than they can eat"? If he was already 'with himself,' how could he have come 'to himself'?

Blessed Benedict, on the contrary, can be said to have lived 'with himself' because at all times he kept such close watch over his life and actions. By searching continually into his own soul he always beheld himself in the presence of his Creator. And this kept his mind from straying off to the world outside.

Peter: But what of Peter the Apostle when he was led out of prison by an angel? According to the Scriptures, he, too, 'came to himself.' 'Now I can tell for certain, he said, that the Lord has sent his angel, to deliver me out of Herod's hands, and from all that the people of the Jews hoped to see.'

Gregory: There are two ways in which we can be carried out of ourselves, Peter. Either we fall below ourselves through sins of thought or we are lifted above ourselves by the grace of contemplation. The young man who fed the swine sank below himself as a result of his shiftless ways and his unclean life. The Apostle Peter was also out of himself when the angel set him free and raised him to a state of ecstasy, but he was above himself. In coming to themselves again, the former had to break with his sinful past before he could find his true and better self, whereas the latter merely returned from the heights of contemplation to his ordinary state of mind.

Now, the saintly Benedict really lived 'with himself' out in that lonely wilderness by always keeping his thoughts recollected. Yet he must have left his own self far below each time he was drawn heavenward in fervent contemplation.

Peter: I am very grateful to you for that explanation. Do you think it was right, though, for him to forsake this community, once he had taken it under his care?

Gregory: In my opinion, Peter, a superior ought to bear patiently with a community of evil men as long as it has some devout members who can benefit from his presence. When none of the members is devout enough to give any promise of good results, his efforts to help such a community will prove to be a serious mistake, especially if there are opportunities nearby to work more fruitfully for God. Was there anyone the holy man could have hoped to protect by staying where he was, after he saw that they were all united against him?

In this matter we cannot afford to overlook the attitude of the saints. When they find their work producing no results in one place, they move on to another where it can do some good. This explains the action of the blessed Apostle Paul. In order to escape from Damascus, where he was being persecuted, he secured a basket and a rope and had himself secretly lowered over the wall. Yet this outstanding preacher of the Gospel longed to depart and be with Christ, since for him life meant Christ, and death was a prize to be won. Besides being eager for the trials of persecution himself, he even inspired others to endure them. Can we say that Paul feared death, when he expressly declared that he longed to die for the love of Christ? Surely not. But, when he saw how little he was accomplishing at Damascus in spite of all his toil, he saved himself for more fruitful labors elsewhere. God's fearless warrior refused to be held back inside the walls and sought the open field of battle.

Peter: I am sure your conclusion is correct, after the simple proof you gave and that striking example from sacred Scripture. Would you be good enough to return now to the story of this great abbot's life?

Gregory: As Benedict's influence spread over the surrounding countryside because of his signs and wonders, a great number of men gathered round him to devote themselves to God's service. Christ blessed his work and before long he had established twelve monasteries there, with an abbot and twelve monks in each of them. There were a few monks whom he kept with him, since he felt that they still needed his personal guidance.

It was about this time that pious noblemen from Rome first came to visit the saint and left their sons with him to be schooled in the service of God. Thus, Euthicius brought his son Maurus; and Senator Tertullus, Placid—both very promising boys. Maurus, in fact, who was a little older, had already acquired solid virtue and was soon very helpful to his saintly master. But Placid was still only a child.

(4) In one of the monasteries Benedict had founded in that locality, there was a monk who would never remain with the rest of the community for silent prayer. Instead, he left the chapel as soon as they knelt down to pray, and passed the time aimlessly at whatever happened to interest him. His abbot corrected him repeatedly and at length sent him to the man of God. This time the monk received a stern rebuke for his folly and after his return took the correction to heart for a day or two, only to fall back the third day into his old habit of wandering off during the time of prayer. On learning of this from the abbot, the man of God sent word that he was coming over himself to see that the monk mended his ways.

Upon his arrival at the monastery, Benedict joined the community in the chapel at the regular hour. After they had finished chanting the psalms and had begun their silent prayer, he noticed that the restless monk was drawn outside by a little black boy who was pulling at the edge of his habit.

'Do you see who is leading that monk out of the chapel?' he whispered to Abbot Pompeianus and Maurus.

'No,' they replied.

'Let us pray, then,' he said, 'that you may see what is happening to him.'

They prayed for two days, and after that Maurus also saw what was taking place, but Abbot Pompeianus still could not. The next day, when prayers were over, Benedict found the offender loitering outside and struck him with his staff for being so obstinate of heart. From then on the monk remained quietly at prayer like the rest, without being bothered again by the tempter. It was as if that ancient Enemy had been struck by the blow himself and was afraid to domineer over the monk's thoughts any longer.

(5)Three of the monasteries the saint had built close by stood on the bare rocky heights. It was a real hardship for these monks always to go down to the lake to get water for their daily needs. Besides, the slope was steep and they found the descent very dangerous. The members of the three communities therefore came in a body to see the servant of God. After explaining how difficult it was for them to climb down the

217

mountainside every day for their water supply, they assured him that the only solution was to have the monasteries moved somewhere else.

Benedict answered them with fatherly words of encouragement and sent them back. That same night, in company with the little boy Placid, he climbed to the rocky heights and prayed there for a long time. On finishing his prayer, he placed three stones together to indicate the spot where he had knelt and then went back to his monastery, unnoticed by anyone.

The following day, when the monks came again with their request, he told them to go to the summit of the mountain. 'You will find three stones there,' he said, 'one on top of the other. If you dig down a little, you will see that almighty God has the power to bring forth water even from that rocky summit and in His goodness relieve you of the hardship of such a long climb.'

Going back to the place he had described, they noticed that the surface was already moist. As soon as they had dug the ground away, water filled the hollow and welled up in such abundance that today a full stream is still flowing from the top of the mountain into the ravine below.

(6) At another time a simple, sincere Goth came to Subiaco to become a monk, and blessed Benedict was very happy to admit him. One day he had him take a brush hook and clear away the briers from a place at the edge of the lake where a garden was to be planted. While the Goth was hard at work cutting down the thick brush, the iron blade slipped off the handle and flew into a very deep part of the lake, where there was no hope of recovering it.

At this the poor man ran trembling to Maurus and, after describing the accident, told him how sorry he was for his carelessness. Maurus in turn informed the servant of God, who on hearing what had happened went down to the lake, took the handle from the Goth and thrust it in the water. Immediately the iron blade rose from the bottom of the lake and slipped back onto the handle. Then he handed the tool back to the Goth and told him, 'Continue with your work now. There is no need to be upset.'

(7) Once while blessed Benedict was in his room, one of his monks, the boy Placid, went down to the lake to draw water. In letting the bucket fill too rapidly, he lost his balance and was pulled into the lake, where the current quickly seized him and carried him about a stone's throw from the shore. Though inside the monastery at the time, the man of God was instantly aware of what had happened and called out to Maurus: 'Hurry, Brother Maurus! The boy who just went down for water has fallen into the lake, and the current is carrying him away.'

What followed was remarkable indeed, and unheard of since the time of Peter the Apostle! Maurus asked for the blessing and on receiving it hurried out to fulfill his abbot's command. He kept on running even over the water till he reached the place where Placid was drifting along helplessly. Pulling him up by the hair, Maurus rushed back to shore, still under the impression that he was on dry land. It was only when he set foot on the ground that he came to himself and looking back realized that he had been running on the surface of the water. Overcome with fear and amazement at a deed he would never have thought possible, he returned to his abbot and told him what had taken place.

The holy man would not take any personal credit for the deed, but attributed it to the obedience of his disciple. Maurus, on the contrary, claimed that it was due entirely to his abbot's command. He could not have been responsible for the miracle himself, he said, since he had not even known he was performing it. While they were carrying on this friendly contest of humility, the question was settled by the boy who had been rescued. 'When I was being drawn out of the water,' he told them, 'I saw the abbot's cloak over my head; he is the one I thought was bringing me to shore.'

Peter: What marvelous deeds these are! They are sure to prove inspiring to all who hear of them. Indeed, the more you tell me about this great man, the more eager I am to keep on listening.

Gregory: (8) By this time the people of that whole region for miles around had grown fervent in their love for Christ, and many of them had forsaken the world in order to bring their hearts under the light yoke of the Saviour. Now, in a neighboring church there was a priest named Florentius, the grandfather of our subdeacon Florentius. Urged on by the bitter Enemy of mankind, this priest set out to undermine the saint's work. And envious as the wicked always are of the holiness in others which they are not striving to acquire themselves, he denounced Benedict's way of life and kept everyone he could from visiting him.

The progress of the saint's work, however, could not be stopped. His reputation for holiness kept on growing, and with it the number of vocations to a more perfect state of life. This infuriated Florentius all the more. He still longed to enjoy the praise the saint was receiving, yet he was unwilling to lead a praiseworthy life himself. At length, his soul became so blind with jealousy that he decided to poison a loaf of bread and send it to the servant of God as though it was a sign of Christian fellowship.

Though aware at once of the deadly poison it contained, Benedict thanked him for the gift.

At mealtime a raven used to come out of the nearby woods to receive food from the saint's hands. On this occasion he set the poisoned loaf in front of it and said, 'In the name of our Lord Jesus Christ, take this bread and carry it to a place where no one will be able to find it.' The raven started to caw and circled round the loaf of bread with open beak and flapping wings as if to indicate that it was willing to obey, but found it impossible to do so. Several times the saint repeated the command. 'Take the bread,' he said, 'and do not be afraid! Take it away from here and leave it where no one will find it.' After hesitating a long while, the raven finally took the loaf in its beak and flew away. About three hours later, when it had disposed of the bread, it returned and received its usual meal from the hands of the man of God.

The saintly abbot now realized how deep the resentment of his enemy was, and he felt grieved not so much for his own sake as for the priest's. But Florentius, after his failure to do away with the master, determined instead to destroy the souls of the disciples and for this purpose sent seven depraved women into the garden of Benedict's monastery. There they joined hands and danced together for some time within sight of his followers, in an attempt to lead them into sin.

When the saint noticed this from his window, he began to fear that some of his younger monks might go astray. Convinced that the priest's hatred for him was the real cause of this attack, he let envy have its way, and, taking only a few monks with him, set out to find a new home. Before he left, he reorganized all the monasteries he had founded, appointing priors to assist in governing them, and adding some new members to the communities

Hardly had the man of God made his humble escape from all this bitterness when almighty God struck the priest down with terrible vengeance. As he was standing on the balcony of his house congratulating himself on Benedict's departure, the structure suddenly collapsed, crushing him to death, though the rest of the building remained undamaged. This accident occurred before the saint was even ten miles away. His disciple Maurus immediately decided to send a messenger with the news and ask him to return, now that the priest who had caused him so much trouble was dead. Benedict was overcome with sorrow and regret on hearing this, for not only had his enemy been killed, but one of his own disciples had rejoiced over his death. And for showing pleasure in such a message he gave Maurus a penance to perform.

Peter: This whole account is really amazing. The water streaming from the rock reminds me of Moses, and the iron blade that rose from the bottom of the lake, of Eliseus. The walking on the water recalls St. Peter, the obedience of the raven, Elias, and the grief at the death of an enemy, David. This man must have been filled with the spirit of all the just.

Gregory: Actually, Peter, blessed Benedict possessed the Spirit of only one Person, the Saviour who fills the hearts of all the faithful by granting them the fruits of His Redemption. For St. John says of Him, 'There is one who enlightens every soul born into the world; he was the true light.' And again, 'we have all received something out of his abundance.' Holy men never were able to hand on to others the miraculous powers which they received from God. Our Saviour was the only one to give His followers the power to work signs and wonders, just as He alone could assure His enemies that He would give them the sign of the prophet Jonas. Seeing this sign fulfilled in His death, the proud looked on with scorn. The humble, who saw its complete fulfillment in His rising from the dead, turned to Him with reverence and love. In this mystery, then, the proud beheld Him dying in disgrace, whereas the humble witnessed His triumph over death.

Peter: Now that you have finished explaining this, please tell me where the holy man settled after his departure. Do you know whether he performed any more miracles?

Gregory: Although he moved to a different place, Peter, his enemy remained the same. In fact, the assaults he had to endure after this were all the more violent, because the very Master of evil was fighting against him in open battle.

The fortified town of Cassino lies at the foot of a towering mountain that shelters it within its slope and stretches upward over a distance of nearly three miles.[5] On its summit stood a very old temple, in which the ignorant country people still worshipped Apollo as their pagan ancestors had done, and went on offering superstitious and idolatrous sacrifices in groves dedicated to various demons.

When the man of God arrived at this spot, he destroyed the idol, overturned the altar and cut down the trees in the sacred groves.[6] Then he turned the temple of Apollo into a chapel dedicated to St. Martin,[7] and where Apollo's altar had stood, he built a chapel in honor of St. John the Baptist. Gradually, the people of the countryside were won over to the true faith by his zealous preaching.

Such losses the ancient Enemy could not bear in silence. This time he did not appear to the saint in a dream or under a disguise, but met him face to face and objected fiercely to the outrages he had to endure. His shouts were so loud that the brethren heard him, too, although they were unable to see him. According to the saint's own description, the Devil had an appearance utterly revolting to human eyes. He was enveloped in fire and, when he raged against the man of God, flames darted from his eyes and mouth. Everyone could hear what he was saying. First he called Benedict by name. Then, finding that the saint would not answer, he broke out in abusive language. 'Benedict, Benedict, blessed Benedict!' he would begin, and then add, 'You cursed Benedict! Cursed, not blessed! What do you want with me? Why are you tormenting me like this?'

From now on, Peter, as you can well imagine, the Devil fought against the man of God with renewed violence. But, contrary to his plans, all these attacks only supplied the saint with further opportunities for victory.

(9) One day while the monks were constructing a section of the abbey, they noticed a rock lying close at hand and decided to use it in the building. When two or three did not succeed in lifting it, others joined in to help. Yet it remained fixed in its place as though it was rooted to the ground. Then they were sure that the Devil himself was sitting on this stone and preventing them from moving it in spite of all their efforts.

Faced with this difficulty, they asked Abbot Benedict to come and use his prayers to drive away the Devil who was holding down the rock. The saint began to pray as soon as he got there, and after he had finished and made the sign of the cross, the monks picked up the rock with such care that it seemed to have lost all its previous weight.

(10) The abbot then directed them to spade up the earth where the stone had been. When they had dug a little way into the ground they came upon a bronze idol, which they threw into the kitchen for the time being. Suddenly the kitchen appeared to be on fire and everyone felt that the entire building was going up in flames. The noise and commo-

tion they made in their attempt to put out the blaze by pouring on buckets of water brought Benedict to the scene. Unable to see the fire which appeared so real to his monks, he quietly bowed his head in prayer and soon had opened their eyes to the foolish mistake they were making. Now, instead of the flames the evil spirit had devised, they once more saw the kitchen standing intact.

(11) On another occasion they were working on one of the walls that had to be built a little higher. The man of God was in his room at the time, praying, when the Devil appeared to him and remarked sarcastically that he was on his way to visit the brethren at their work. Benedict quickly sent them word to be on their guard against the evil spirit who would soon be with them. Just as they received his warning, the Devil overturned the wall, crushing under its ruins the body of a very young monk who was the son of a tax collector.

Unconcerned about the damaged wall in their grief and dismay over the loss of their brother, the monks hurried to Abbot Benedict to let him know of the dreadful accident. He told them to bring the mangled body to his room. It had to be carried in on a blanket, for the wall had not only broken the boy's arms and legs but had crushed all the bones in his body. The saint had the remains placed on the reed matting where he used to pray and after that told them all to leave. Then he closed the door and knelt down to offer his most earnest prayers to God. That very hour, to the astonishment of all, he sent the boy back to his work as sound and healthy as he had been before. Thus, in spite of the Devil's attempt to mock the man of God by causing this tragic death, the young monk was able to rejoin his brethren and help them finish the wall.

Meanwhile, Benedict began to manifest the spirit of prophecy by foretelling future events and by describing to those who were with him what they had done in his absence.

(12) It was a custom of the house, strictly observed as a matter of regular discipline, that monks away on business did not take food or drink outside the monastery. One day, a few of them went out on assignment which kept them occupied till rather late. They stopped for a meal at the house of a devout woman they knew in the neighborhood. On their return, when they presented themselves to the abbot for the usual blessing, he asked them where they had taken their meal.

'Nowhere,' they answered.

'Why are you lying to me?' he said. 'Did you not enter the house of this particular woman and eat these various foods and have so many cups to drink?'

On hearing him mention the woman's hospitality and exactly what she had given them to eat and drink, they clearly recalled the wrong they had done, fell trembling at his feet, and confessed their guilt. The man of God did not hesitate to pardon them, confident that they would do no further wrong in his absence, since they now realized he was always present with them in spirit.

(13) The monk Valentinian, mentioned earlier in our narrative, had a brother who was a very devout layman. Every year he visited the abbey in order to get Benedict's blessing and see his brother. On the way he always used to fast. Now, one time as he was making this journey he was joined by another traveler who had brought some food along.

'Come,' said the stranger after some time had passed, 'let us have something to eat before we become too fatigued.'

'I am sorry,' the devout layman replied. 'I always fast on my way to visit Abbot Benedict.'

After that the traveler was quiet for a while. But when they had walked along some distance together, he repeated his suggestion. Still mindful of his good resolve, Valentinian's brother again refused. His companion did not insist and once more agreed to accompany him a little further without eating.

Then, after they had covered a great distance together and were very tired from the long hours of walking, they came upon a meadow and a spring. The whole setting seemed ideal for a much needed rest. 'Look,' said the stranger, 'water and a meadow! What a delightful spot for us to have some refreshments! A little rest will give us strength to finish our journey without any discomfort.'

It was such an attractive sight and this third invitation sounded so appealing that the devout layman was completely won over and stopped there to eat with his companion. Toward evening he arrived at the monastery and was presented to the abbot. As soon as he asked for the blessing, however, the holy man reproved him for his conduct on the journey. 'How is it,' he said, 'that the evil spirit who spoke with you in the person of your traveling companion could not persuade you to do his will the first and second time he tried, but succeeded on his third attempt?' At this Valentinian's brother fell at Benedict's feet and admitted the weakness of his will. The thought that even from such a distance the saint had witnessed the wrong he had done filled him with shame and remorse.

Peter: This proves that the servant of God possessed the spirit of Eliseus. He, too, was present with one of his followers who was far away.

Gregory: If you will listen a little longer, Peter, I have an incident to tell you that is even more astonishing. (14) Once while the Goths were still in power, Totila their king happened to be marching in the direction of Benedict's monastery.[8] When still some distance away, he halted with his troops and sent a messenger ahead to announce his coming, for he had heard that the man of God possessed the gift of prophecy. As soon as he received word that he would be welcomed, the crafty king decided to put the saint's prophetic powers to a test. He had Riggo, his sword-bearer, fitted out with royal robes and riding boots and directed him to go in this disguise to the man of God. Vul, Ruderic and Blidin, three men from his own bodyguard, were to march at his side as if he really were king of the Goths. To supplement these marks of kingship, Totila also provided him with a sword-bearer and other attendants.

As Riggo entered the monastery grounds in his kingly robes and with all his attendants, Benedict caught sight of him and as soon as the company came within hearing called out from where he sat, 'Son, lay aside the robes you are wearing,' he said. 'Lay them aside. They do not belong to you.' Aghast at seeing what a great man he had tried to mock, Riggo sank to the ground, and with him all the members of his company. Even after they had risen to their feet they did not dare approach the saint, but hurried back in alarm to tell their king how quickly they had been detected.

(15) King Totila then went to the monastery in person. The moment he noticed the man of God sitting at a distance, he was afraid to come any closer and fell down prostrate where he was. Two or three times Benedict asked him to rise. When Totila still hesitated to do so in his presence, the servant of Christ walked over to him and with his own hands helped him from the ground. Then he rebuked the king for his crimes and briefly foretold everything that was going to happen to him. 'You are the cause of many evils,' he said. 'You have caused many in the past. Put an end now to your wickedness. You will enter Rome and cross the sea. You will have nine more years to rule, and in the tenth year you will die.'

Terrified at these words, the king asked for a blessing and went away. From that time on he was less cruel. Not long after, he went to Rome and then crossed over to Sicily. In the tenth year of his reign he lost his kingdom and his life as almighty God had decreed.

There is also a story about the bishop of Canosa,[9] who made regular visits to the abbey and stood high in Benedict's esteem because of his saintly life. Once while they were discussing Totila's invasion and the downfall of Rome, the bishop said, 'The city will be destroyed by this king and left without a single inhabitant.'

'No,' Benedict assured him, 'Rome will not be destroyed by the barbarians. It will be shaken by tempests and lightnings, hurricanes and earthquakes, until finally it lies buried in its own ruins.'

The meaning of this prophecy is perfectly clear to us now. We have watched the walls of Rome crumble and have seen its homes in ruins, its churches destroyed by violent storms, and its dilapidated buildings surrounded by their own debris.

Benedict's disciple Honoratus, who told me about the prophecy, admits he did not hear it personally, but he assures me that some of his brethren gave him this account of it.

(16) At about the same time there was a cleric from the church at Aquino[10] who was being tormented by an evil spirit. Constantius, his saintly bishop, had already sent him to the shrines of various martyrs in the hope that he would be cured. But the holy martyrs did not grant him this favour, preferring instead to reveal the wonderful gifts of the servant of God.

As soon as the cleric was brought to him, Benedict drove out the evil spirit with fervent prayers to Christ. Before sending him back to Aquino, however, he told him to abstain from meat thereafter and never to advance to sacred orders.[11] 'If you ignore this warning,' he added, 'and present yourself for ordination, you will find yourself once more in the power of Satan.'

The cleric left completely cured, and as long as his previous torments were still fresh in his mind he did exactly as the man of God had ordered. Then with the passing of years, all his seniors in the clerical state died, and he had to watch newly ordained young men moving ahead of him in rank. Finally, he pretended to have forgotten about the saint's warning and, disregarding it, presented himself for ordination. Instantly he was seized by the Devil and tormented mercilessly until he died.

Peter: The servant of God must even have been aware of the hidden designs of Providence, to have realized that this cleric had been handed over to Satan to keep him from aspiring to holy orders.

Gregory: Is there any reason why a person who has observed the commandments of God should not also know God's secret designs? 'The man who unites himself to the Lord becomes one spirit with him,' we read in sacred Scripture.

Peter: If everyone who unites himself to the Lord becomes one spirit with him, what does the renowned Apostle mean when he asks, 'Who has ever understood the Lord's thoughts, or been his counselor?' It hardly seems possible to be one spirit with a person without knowing his thoughts.

Gregory: Holy men do know the Lord's thoughts, Peter, in so far as they are one with Him. This is clear from the Apostle's words, 'Who else can know a man's thoughts, except the man's own spirit that is within him? So no one else can know God's thoughts but the Spirit of God.' To show that he actually knew God's thoughts, St. Paul added: 'And what we have received is no spirit of worldly wisdom; it is the Spirit that comes from God.' And again: 'No eye has seen, no ear has heard, no human heart conceived, the welcome God has prepared for those who love him. To us, then, God has made a revelation of it through his Spirit.'

Peter: If it is true that God's thoughts are revealed to the Apostle by the Holy Spirit, how could he introduce his statement with the words, 'How deep is the mine of God's wisdom, of his knowledge; how inscrutable are his judgments, how undiscoverable his ways!' Another difficulty just occurred to me now as I was speaking. In addressing the Lord, David the Prophet declares, 'With my lips I have pronounced all the judgments of thy mouth.' Surely it is a greater achievement to express one's knowledge than merely to possess it. How is it, then, that St. Paul calls the judgments of God inscrutable, whereas David says he knows them all and has even pronounced them with his lips?

Gregory: I already gave a brief reply to both of these objections when I told you that holy men know God's thoughts in so far as they are one with Him. For all who follow the Lord wholeheartedly are living in spiritual union with Him. As long as they are still weighed down with a perishable body, however, they are not actually united to Him. It is only to the extent that they are one with God that they know His hidden judgments. In so far as they are not yet one with Him, they do not know them. Since even holy men cannot fully grasp the secret designs of God during this present life, they call His judgments inscrutable. At the same time, they understand His judgments and can even pronounce them with their lips; for they keep their hearts united to God by dwelling continually on the words of holy Scripture and on such private revelations as they may receive, until they grasp His meaning. In other words, they do not know the judgments which God conceals but only those which He reveals. That is why, after declaring, 'With my lips I have pronounced all the judgments,' the Prophet immediately adds the phrase, 'of thy mouth,' as if to say, 'I can know and pronounce only the judgments You have spoken to me. Those You leave unspoken must remain hidden from our minds.' So the Prophet and the Apostle are in full agreement. God's decisions are truly unfathomable. But, once His mouth has made them known, they can also be proclaimed by human lips. What God has spoken man can know. Of the thoughts He has kept secret man can know nothing.

Peter: That is certainly a reasonable solution to the difficulties that I raised. If you know any other miraculous events in this man's life, would you continue with them now?

Gregory: (17) Under the direction of Abbot Benedict a nobleman named Theoprobus had embraced monastic life. Because of his exemplary life he enjoyed the saint's personal friendship and confidence. One day, on entering Benedict's room, he found him weeping bitterly. After he had waited for some time and there was still no end to the abbot's tears, he asked what was causing him such sorrow, for he was not weeping as he usually did at prayer, but with deep sighs and lamentation.

'Almighty God has decreed that this entire monastery and everything I have provided for the community shall fall into the hands of the barbarians,' the saint replied. 'It was only with the greatest difficulty that I could prevail upon Him to spare the lives of its members.'

This was the prophecy he made to Theoprobus, and we have seen its fulfillment in the recent destruction of his abbey by the Lombards.[12] They came at night while the community was asleep and plundered the entire monastery, without capturing a single monk. In this way God fulfilled His promise to Benedict, His faithful servant. He allowed the barbarians to destroy the monastery, but safeguarded the lives of the religious. Here you can see how the man of God resembled St. Paul, who had the consolation of seeing everyone with him escape alive from the storm, while the ship and all its cargo were lost.

(18) Exhilaratus, a fellow Roman who, as you know, later became a monk was once sent by his master to Abbot Benedict with two wooden flasks of wine. He delivered only one of them, however; the other he hid along the way. Benedict, who could observe even what was done in his absence, thanked him for the flask, but warned him as he turned to go: 'Son, be sure not to drink from the flask you have hidden away. Tilt it carefully and you will see what is inside.'

Exhilaratus left in shame and confusion and went back to the spot, still wishing to verify the saint's words. As he tilted the flask a serpent crawled out, and at the sight of it he was filled with horror for his misdeed.

(19) Not far from the monastery was a village largely inhabited by people the saintly Benedict had converted from the worship of idols and instructed in the true faith. There were seven nuns living there too, and he used them to send one of his monks down to give them spiritual conferences.

After one of these instructions they presented the monk with a few handkerchiefs, which he accepted and hid away in his habit. As soon as he got back to the abbey he received a stern reproof. 'How is it,' the abbot asked him, 'that evil has found its way into your heart?' Taken completely by surprise, the monk did not understand why he was being rebuked, for he had completely forgotten about the handkerchiefs. 'Was I not present,' the saint continued, 'when you accepted those handkerchiefs from the handmaids of God and hid them away in your habit?' The offender instantly fell at Benedict's feet, confessed his fault, and gave up the present he had received.

(20) Once when the saintly abbot was taking his evening meal, a young monk whose father was a high-ranking official happened to be holding the lamp for him. As he stood at the abbot's table the spirit of pride began to stir in his heart. 'Who is this,' he thought to himself, 'that I should have to stand here holding the lamp for him while he is eating? Who am I to be serving him?'

Turning to him at once, Benedict gave the monk a sharp reprimand. 'Brother,' he said, 'sign your heart with the sign of the cross. What are you saying? Sign your heart!' Then, calling the others together, he had one of them take the lamp instead, and told the murmurer to sit down by himself and be quiet. Later, when asked what he had done wrong, the monk explained how he had given in to the spirit of pride and silently murmured against the man of God. At this the brethren all realized that nothing could be kept secret from their holy abbot, since he could hear even the unspoken sentiments of the heart.

(21) During a time of famine the severe shortage of food was causing a great deal of suffering in Campania. At Benedict's monastery the entire grain supply had been used up and nearly all the bread was gone as well. In fact, when mealtime came, only five loaves could be found to set before the community. Noticing how downcast they were, the saint gently reproved them for their lack of trust in God and at the same time tried to raise their dejected spirits with a comforting assurance. 'Why are you so depressed at the lack of bread!' he asked. 'What if today there is only a little? Tomorrow you will have more than you need.'

The next day 200 measures of flour were found in sacks at the gate of the monastery, but no one ever discovered whose services almighty God had employed in bringing them there. When they saw what had happened, the monks were filled with gratitude and learned from this miracle that even in their hour of need they must not lose faith in the bountiful goodness of God.

Peter: Are we to believe that the spirit of prophecy remained with the servant of God at all times, or did he receive it only on special occasion?

Gregory: The spirit of prophecy does not enlighten the minds of the prophets constantly, Peter. We read in sacred Scripture that the Holy Spirit breathes where He pleases, and we should also realize that He breathes when He pleases. For example, when King David asked whether he could build a temple, the Prophet Nathan gave his consent, but later had to withdraw it. And Eliseus once found a woman in tears without knowing the reason for her grief. This is why he told his servant who was trying to interfere, 'Let her alone, for her soul is in anguish and the Lord has hidden it from me and has not told me.'

All this reflects God's boundless wisdom and love. By granting these men the spirit of prophecy He raises their minds above the world, and by withdrawing it again He safeguards their humility. When the spirit of prophecy is with them they learn what they are by God's mercy. When the spirit leaves them they discover what they are of themselves.

Peter: This convincing argument leaves no room for doubt about the truth of what you say. Please resume your narrative now, if you recall any other incidents in the life of the blessed Benedict.

Gregory: (22) A Catholic layman once asked him to found a monastery on his estate at Terracina. The servant of God readily consented and, after selecting several of his monks for this undertaking, appointed one of them abbot and another his assistant. Before they left he specified a day on which he would come to show them where to build the chapel, the refectory, a house for guests, and the other buildings they would need. Then he gave them his blessing.

After their arrival at Terracina they looked forward eagerly to the day he had set for his visit and prepared to receive the monks who would accompany him. Before dawn of the appointed day, Benedict appeared in a dream to the new abbot as well as to his prior and showed them exactly where each section of the monastery was to stand. In the morning they told each other what they had seen, but, instead of putting their entire trust in the vision, they kept waiting for the promised visit. When the day passed without any word from Benedict, they returned to him disappointed. 'Father,' they said, 'we were waiting for you to show us where to build, as you assured us you would, but you did not come.'

'What do you mean?' he replied. 'Did I not come as I promised?'

'When?' they asked.

'Did I not appear to both of you in a dream as you slept and indicate where each building was to stand? Go back and build as you were directed in the vision.'

They returned to Terracina, filled with wonder, and constructed the monastery according to the plans he had revealed to them.

Peter: I wish you would explain how Benedict could possibly travel that distance and then in a vision give these monks directions which they could hear and understand while they were asleep.

Gregory: What is there in this incident that should raise a doubt in your mind, Peter? Everyone knows that the soul is far more agile than the body. Yet we have it on the authority of holy Scripture that the Prophet Habacuc was lifted from Judea to Chaldea in an instant, so that he might share his dinner with the Prophet Daniel, and presently found himself back in Judea again. If Habacuc could cover such a distance in a brief moment to take a meal to his fellow Prophet, is it not understandable that Abbot Benedict could go in spirit to his sleeping brethren with the information they required? As the Prophet came in body with food for the body, Benedict came in spirit to promote the life of the soul.

Peter: Your words seem to smooth away all my doubts. Could you tell me now what this saint was like in his everyday speech?

Gregory: (23) There was a trace of the marvelous in nearly every thing he said, Peter, and his words never failed to take effect because his heart was fixed in God. Even when he uttered a simple threat that was indefinite and conditional, it was just as decisive as a final verdict.

Some distance from the abbey two women of noble birth were leading the religious life in their own home. A God-fearing layman was kind enough to bring them what they needed from the outside world. Unfortunately, as is sometimes the case, their character stood in sharp contrast to the nobility of their birth, and they were too conscious of their former importance to practice true humility toward others. Even under the restraining influence of religious life they still had not learned to control their tongues, and the good layman who served them so faithfully was often provoked at their harsh criticisms. After putting up with their insults for a long time, he went to blessed Benedict and told him how inconsiderate they were. The man of God immediately warned them to curb their sharp tongues and added that he would have to excommunicate them if they did not. This sentence of excommunication was not actually pronounced, therefore, but only threatened.

A short time afterward the two nuns died without any sign of amendment and were buried in their parish church. Whenever Mass was celebrated, their old nurse, who regularly made an offering for them, noticed that each time the deacon announced, 'The noncommunicants must now leave,' the nuns rose from their tombs and went outside.[13] This happened repeatedly, until one day she recalled the warning Benedict had given them while they were still alive, when he threatened to deprive them of communion with the Church if they kept on speaking so uncharitably.

The grief-stricken nurse had Abbot Benedict informed of what was happening. He sent her messengers back with an oblation and said, 'Have this offered up for their souls during the Holy Sacrifice, and they will be freed from the sentence of excommunication.' The offering was made and after that the nuns were not seen leaving the church any more at the deacon's dismissal of the non-communicants. Evidently, they had been admitted to communion with our blessed Lord in answer to the prayers of His servant Benedict.

Peter: Is it not extraordinary that souls already judged at God's invisible tribunal could be pardoned by a man who was still living in the mortal flesh, however holy and revered he may have been?

Gregory: What of Peter the Apostle? Was he not still living in the flesh when he heard the words, 'Whatever thou shalt bind on earth shall be bound in heaven, and whatever thou shalt loose on earth shall be loosed in heaven'? All those who govern the Church in matters of faith and morals exercise the same power of binding and loosing that he received. In fact, the Creator's very purpose in coming down from heaven to earth was to impart to earthly man this heavenly power. It was when God was made flesh for man's sake that flesh received its undeserved prerogative of sitting in judgment even over spirits. What raised our weakness to these heights was the descent of an almighty God to the depths of our own helplessness.

Peter: Your lofty words are certainly in harmony with these mighty deeds.

Gregory: (24) One time, a young monk who was too attached to his parents left the monastery without asking for the abbot's blessing and went home. No sooner had he arrived there he died. The day after his burial his body was discovered lying outside the grave. His parents had him buried again, but on the following day found the body unburied as before. In their dismay they hurried to the saintly abbot and pleaded with him to forgive the boy for what he had done. Moved by their tears, Benedict gave them a consecrated Host with his own hands. 'When you get back,' he said, 'place this sacred Host upon his breast and bury him once more.'[14] They did so, and thereafter his body remained in the earth without being disturbed again.

Now, Peter, you can appreciate how pleasing this holy man was in God's sight. Not even the earth would retain the young monk's body until he had been reconciled with blessed Benedict.

Peter: I assure you I do. It is really amazing.

Gregory: (25) One of Benedict's monks had set his fickle heart on leaving the monastery. Time and again the man of God pointed out how wrong this was and tried to reason with him but without any success. The monk persisted obstinately in his request to be released. Finally, Benedict lost patience with him and told him to go.

Hardly had he left the monastery grounds when he noticed to his horror that a dragon with gaping jaws was blocking his way. 'Help! Help!' he cried out, trembling, 'or the dragon will devour me.' His brethren ran to the rescue, but could see nothing of the dragon. Still breathless with fright, the monk was only too glad to accompany them back to the abbey. Once safe within its walls, he promised never to leave again. And this time he kept his word, for Benedict's prayers had enabled him to see with his own eyes the invisible dragon that had been leading him astray.

(26) I must tell you now of an event I heard from the distinguished Anthony. One of his father's servants had been seized with a severe case of leprosy. His hair was already falling out and his skin growing thick and swollen. The fatal progress of the disease was unmistakable. In this condition he was sent to the man of God, who instantly restored him to his previous state of health.

(27) Benedict's disciple Peregrinus tells of a Catholic layman who was heavily bur-

dened with debt and felt that his only hope was to disclose the full extent of his misfortune to the man of God. So he went to him and explained that he was being constantly tormented by a creditor to whom he owed twelve gold pieces.

'I am very sorry,' the saintly abbot replied. 'I do not have that much money in my possession.' Then, to comfort the poor man in his need, he added, 'I cannot give you anything today, but come back again the day after tomorrow.'

In the meantime the saint devoted himself to prayer with his accustomed fervour. When the debtor returned, the monks, to their surprise, found thirteen gold pieces lying on top of a chest that was filled with grain. Benedict had the money brought down at once. 'Here, take these,' he told him. 'Use twelve to pay your creditor and keep the thirteenth for yourself.'

I should like to return now to some other events I learned from the saint's four disciples who were mentioned at the beginning of this book.

There was a man who had become so embittered with envy that he tried to kill his rival by secretly poisoning his drink. Though the poison did not prove fatal, it produced horrible blemishes resembling leprosy, which spread over the entire body of the unfortunate victim. In this condition he was brought to the servant of God, who cured the disease with a touch of his hand and sent him home in perfect health.

(28) While Campania was suffering from famine, the holy abbot distributed the food supplies of his monastery to the needy until there was nothing left in the storeroom but a little oil in a glass vessel. One day, when Agapitus, a sub-deacon, came to beg for some oil, the man of God ordered the little that remained to be given to him, for he wanted to distribute everything he had to the poor and thus store up riches in heaven.

The cellarer listened to the abbot's command, but did not carry it out. After a while, Benedict asked him whether he had given Agapitus the oil. 'No,' he replied, 'I did not. If I had, there would be none left for the community.' This angered the man of God, who wanted nothing to remain in the monastery through disobedience, and he told another monk to take the glass with the oil in it and throw it out the window. This time he was obeyed.

Even though it struck against the jagged rocks of the cliff just below the window, the glass remained intact as if it had not been thrown at all. It was still unbroken and none of the oil had spilled. Abbot Benedict had the glass brought back and given to the sub-deacon. Then he sent for the rest of the community and in their presence rebuked the disobedient monk for his pride and lack of faith.

(29) After that the saint knelt down to pray with his brethren. In the room where they were kneeling there happened to be an empty oil-cask that was covered with a lid. In the course of his prayer the cask gradually filled with oil and the lid started to float on top of it. The next moment the oil was running down the sides of the cask and covering the floor. As soon as he was aware of this, Benedict ended his prayer and the oil stopped flowing. Then, turning to the monk who had shown himself disobedient and wanting in confidence, he urged him again to strive to grow in faith and humility.

This wholesome reprimand filled the cellarer with shame. Besides inviting him to trust in God, the saintly abbot had clearly shown by his miracle what marvelous power such trust possesses. In the future who could doubt any of his promises? Had he not in a moment's time replaced the little oil still left in the glass with a cask that was full to overflowing?

(30) One day, on his way to the Chapel of St. John at the highest point of the mountain, Benedict met the ancient Enemy of mankind, disguised as a veterinarian with medicine horn and triple shackle.

'Where are you going?' the saint asked him.

'To your brethren,' he replied with scorn. 'I am bringing them some medicine.'

Benedict continued on his way and after his prayer hurried back. Meanwhile, the evil spirit entered one of the older monks whom he found drawing water and had thrown him to the ground in a violent convulsion. When the man of God caught sight of this old brother in such torment, he merely struck him on the cheek, and the evil spirit was promptly driven out, never to return.

Peter: I should like to know whether he always obtained these great miracles through fervent prayer. Did he ever perform them at will?

Gregory: It is quite common for those who devoutly cling to God to work miracles in both of these ways, Peter, either through their prayers or by their own power, as circumstances may dictate. Since we read in St. John that 'all those who did welcome him he empowered to become the children of God,' why should we be surprised if those who are the children of God use this power to work signs and wonders? Holy men can undoubtedly perform miracles in either of the ways you mentioned, as is clear from the fact that St. Peter raised Tabitha to life by praying over her, and by a simple rebuke brought death to Ananias and Sapphira for their lies. Scripture does not say that he prayed for their death, but only that he reprimanded them for the crime they had committed. Now, if St. Peter could restore to life by a prayer and deprive of life by a rebuke, is there any reason to doubt that the saints can perform miracles by their own power as well as through their prayers?

I am now going to consider two instances in the life of God's faithful servant Benedict. One of them shows the efficacy of his prayer; the other, the marvelous powers that were his by God's gift.

(31) In the days of King Totila one of the Goths, the Arian heretic Zalla, had been persecuting devout Catholics everywhere with the utmost cruelty. No monk or cleric who fell into his hands ever escaped alive. In his merciless brutality and greed he was one day lashing and torturing a farmer whose money he was after. Unable to bear it any longer, the poor man tried to save his life by telling Zalla that all his money was in Abbot Benedict's keeping. He only hoped his tormentor would believe him and put a stop to his brutality. When Zalla heard this, he did stop beating him, but immediately bound his hands together with a heavy cord. Then, mounting his horse, he forced the farmer to walk ahead of him and lead the way to this Benedict who was keeping his money.

The helpless prisoner had no choice but to conduct him to the abbey. When they arrived, they found the man of God sitting alone in front of the entrance reading. 'This is the Abbot Benedict I meant,' he told the infuriated Goth behind him.

Imagining that this holy man could be frightened as readily as anyone else, Zalla glared at him with eyes full of hate and shouted harshly, 'Get up! Do you hear? Get up and give back the money this man left with you?' At the sound of this angry voice the man of God looked up from his reading and, as he glanced toward Zalla, noticed the farmer with his hands bound together. The moment he caught sight of the cord that held them, it fell miraculously to the ground. Human hands could never have unfastened it so quickly.

Stunned at the hidden power that had set his prisoner free, Zalla fell trembling to his knees and, bending his stubborn, cruel neck at the saint's feet, begged for his prayers. Without rising from his place, Benedict called for his monks and had them take Zalla inside for some food and drink. After that he urged him to give up his heartless cruelty. Zalla went away thoroughly humbled and made no more demands on this farmer who had been freed from his bonds by a mere glance from the man of God.

So you see, Peter, what I said is true. Those who devote themselves wholeheartedly to the service of God can sometimes work miracles by their own power. Blessed Benedict checked the fury of a dreaded Goth without even rising to his feet, and with a mere glance unfastened the heavy cord that bound the hands of an innocent man. The very speed with which he performed this marvel is proof enough that he did it by his own power.

And now, here is a remarkable miracle that was the result of his prayer. (32) One day, when he was out working in the fields with his monks, a farmer came to the monastery carrying in his arms the lifeless body of his son. Broken-hearted at his loss, he begged to see the saintly abbot and, on learning that he was at work in the fields, left the dead body at the entrance of the monastery and hurried off to find him. By then the abbot was already returning from his work. The moment the farmer caught sight of him he cried out,

'Give me back my son! Give me back my son!'

Benedict stopped when he heard this. 'But I have not taken your son from you, have I?' he asked.

The boy's father only replied, 'He is dead. Come! Bring him back to life.'

Deeply grieved by his words, the man of God turned to his disciples. 'Stand back, brethren!' he said. 'Stand back! Such a miracle is beyond our power. The holy Apostles are the only ones who can raise the dead. Why are you so eager to accept what is impossible for us?'

But overwhelming sorrow compelled the man to keep on pleading. He even declared with an oath that he would not leave until Benedict restored his son to life. The saint then asked him where the body was. 'At the entrance to the monastery,' he answered.

When Benedict arrived there with his monks, he knelt down beside the child's body and bent over it. Then, rising, he lifted his hands to heaven in prayer. 'O Lord,' he said, 'do not consider my sins but the faith of this man who is asking to see his son alive again, and restore to this body the soul You have taken from it.'

His prayer was hardly over when the child's whole body began once more to throb with life. No one present there could doubt that this sudden stirring was due to a heavenly intervention. Benedict then took the little boy by the hand and gave him back to his father alive and well.

Obviously, Peter, he did not have the power to work this miracle himself. Otherwise he would not have begged for it prostrate in prayer.

Peter: The way facts bear out your words convinces me that everything you have said is true. Will you please tell me now whether holy men can always carry out their wishes, or at least obtain through prayer whatever they desire?

Gregory: (33) Peter, will there ever be a holier man in this world than St. Paul? Yet he prayed three times to the Lord about the sting in his flesh and could not obtain his wish. In this connection I must tell you how the saintly Benedict once had a wish he was unable to fulfill.

His sister Scholastica, who had been consecrated to God in early childhood, used to visit with him once a year. On these occasions he would go down to meet her in a house belonging to the monastery, a short distance from the entrance.

For this particular visit he joined her there with a few of his disciples and they spent the whole day singing God's praises and conversing about the spiritual life. When darkness was setting in, they took their meal together and continued their conversation at table until it was quite late. Then the holy nun said to him, 'Please do not leave me tonight, brother. Let us keep on talking about the joys of heaven till morning.'

'What are you saying, sister?' he replied. 'You know I cannot stay away from the monastery.'

The sky was so clear at the time that there was not a cloud in sight. At her brother's refusal Scholastica folded her hands on the table and rested her head upon them in earnest prayer. When she looked up again, there was a sudden burst of lightning and thunder, accompanied by such a downpour that Benedict and his companions were unable to set a foot outside the door.

By shedding a flood of tears while she prayed, this holy nun had darkened the cloudless sky with a heavy rain. The storm began as soon as her prayer was over. In fact, the two coincided so closely that the thunder was already resounding as she raised her head from the table. The very instant she ended her prayer the rain poured down.

Realizing that he could not return to the monastery in this terrible storm, Benedict complained bitterly, 'God forgive you, sister!' he said. 'What have you done?'

Scholastica simply answered, 'When I appealed to you, you would not listen to me. So I turned to my God and He heard my prayer. Leave now if you can. Leave me here and go back to your monastery.'

This, of course, he could not do. He had no choice now but to stay, in spite of his unwillingness. They spent the entire night together and both of them derived great profit from the holy thoughts they exchanged about the interior life.

Here you have my reason for saying that this holy man was once unable to obtain what he desired. If we consider his point of view, we can readily see that he wanted the sky to remain as clear as it was when he came down from the monastery. But this wish of his was thwarted by a miracle almighty God performed in answer to a woman's prayer. We need not be surprised that in this instance she proved mightier than her brother; she had been looking forward so long to this visit. Do we not read in St. John that God is love? Surely it is no more than right that her influence was greater than his, since hers was the greater love.

Peter: I find this discussion very enjoyable.

Gregory: (34) The next morning Scholastica returned to her convent and Benedict to his monastery. Three days later as he stood in his room looking up toward the sky, he beheld his sister's soul leaving her body and entering the court of heaven in the form of a dove.

Overjoyed at her eternal glory, he gave thanks to God in hymns of praise. Then, after informing his brethren of her death, he sent some of them to bring her body to the monastery and bury it in the tomb he had prepared for himself. The bodies of these two were now to share a common resting place, just as in life their souls had always been one in God.

(35) At another time, the deacon Servandus came to see the servant of God on one of his regular visits. He was abbot of the monastery in Campania that had been built by the late Senator Liberius, and always welcomed an opportunity to discuss with Benedict the truths of eternity, for he, too, was a man of deep spiritual understanding. In speaking of their hopes and longings they were able to taste in advance the heavenly food that was not yet fully theirs to enjoy. When it was time to retire for the night, Benedict went to his room on the second floor of the tower, leaving Servandus in the one below, which was connected with his own by a stairway. Their disciples slept in the large building facing the tower.

Long before the night office began, the man of God was standing at his window, where he watched and prayed while the rest were asleep. In the dead of night he suddenly beheld a flood of light shining down from above more brilliant than the sun, and with it every trace of darkness cleared away. Another remarkable sight followed. According to his own description, the whole world was gathered up before his eyes in what appeared to be a single ray of light. As he gazed at all this dazzling display, he saw the soul of Germanus, the Bishop of Capua, being carried by angels up to heaven in a ball of fire.

Wishing to have someone else witness this great marvel, he called out for Servandus, repeating his name two or three times in a loud voice. As soon as he heard the saint's call, Servandus rushed to the upper room and was just in time to catch a final glimpse of the miraculous light. He remained speechless with wonder as Benedict described everything that had taken place. Then without any delay the man of God instructed the devout Theoprobus to go to Cassino and have a messenger sent to Capua that same night to find out what had happened to Germanus. In carrying out these instructions the messenger discovered that the revered bishop was already dead. When he asked for further details, he learned that his death had occurred at the very time blessed Benedict saw him carried into heaven.

Peter: What an astounding miracle! I hardly know what to think when I hear you say that he saw the whole world gathered up before his eyes in what appeared to be a single ray of light. I have never had such an experience. How is it possible for anyone to see the whole universe at a glance?

Gregory: Keep this well in mind, Peter. All creation is bound to appear small to a soul that sees the Creator. Once it beholds a little of His light, it finds all creatures small indeed. The light of holy contemplation enlarges and expands the mind in God until it stands above the world. In fact, the soul that sees Him rises even above itself, and as it is drawn upward in His light all its inner powers unfold. Then, when it looks down from above, it sees how small everything is that was beyond its grasp before.

Now, Peter, how else was it possible for this man to behold the ball of fire and watch the angels on their return to heaven except with light from God? Why should it surprise us, then, that he could see the whole world gathered up before him after this inner light had lifted him so far above the world? Of course, in saying that the world was gathered up before his eyes I do not mean that heaven and earth grew small, but that his spirit was enlarged. Absorbed as he was in God, it was now easy for him to see all that lay beneath God. In the light outside that was shining before his eyes, there was a brightness which reached into his mind and lifted his spirit heavenward, showing him the insignificance of all that lies below.

Peter: My difficulty in understanding you has proved of real benefit, the explanation it led to was so thorough. Now that you have cleared up this problem for me, would you return once more to your account of blessed Benedict's life?

Gregory: (36) I should like to tell you much more about this saintly abbot, but I am purposely passing over some of his miraculous deeds in my eagerness to take up those of others. There is one more point, however, I want to call to your attention. With all the renown he gained by his numerous miracles, the holy man was no less outstanding for the wisdom of his teaching. He wrote a Rule for Monks that is remarkable for its discretion and its clarity of language. Anyone who wishes to know more about his life and character can discover in his Rule exactly what he was like as an abbot, for his life could not have differed from his teaching.

(37) In the year that was to be his last, the man of God foretold the day of his holy death to a number of his disciples. In mentioning it to some who were with him in the monastery, he bound them to strict secrecy. Some others, however, who were stationed elsewhere he only informed of the special sign they would receive at the time of his death.

Six days before he died he gave orders for his tomb to be opened. Almost immediately he was seized with a violent fever that rapidly wasted his remaining strength. Each day his condition grew worse until finally, on the sixth day, he had his disciples carry him into the chapel, where he received the Body and Blood of our Lord to gain strength for his approaching end. Then, supporting his weakened body on the arms of his brethren, he stood with his hands raised to heaven and as he prayed he breathed his last.

That day two monks, one of them at the monastery, the other some distance away, received the very same revelation. They both saw a magnificent road covered with rich carpeting and glittering with thousands of lights. From his monastery it stretched eastward in a straight line until it reached up into heaven. And there in the brightness stood a man of majestic appearance, who asked them, 'Do you know who passed this way?'

'No,' they replied.

'This,' he told them, 'is the road taken by blessed Benedict, the Lord's beloved, when he went to heaven.'

Thus, while the brethren who were with Benedict witnessed his death, those who were absent knew about it through the sign he had promised them. His body was laid to rest in the Chapel of St. John the Baptist, which he had built to replace the altar of Apollo.

(38) Even in the cave at Subiaco, where he had lived before, this holy man still works numerous miracles for people who turn to him with faith and confidence. The incident I am going to relate happened only recently.

A woman who had completely lost her mind was roaming day and night over hills and valleys, through forests and fields, resting only when she was utterly exhausted. One day, in the course of her aimless wanderings, she strayed into the saint's cave and rested there without the least idea of where she was. The next morning she woke up entirely cured and left the cave without even a trace of her former affliction. After that she remained free from it for the rest of her life.

Peter: How is it that, as a rule, even the martyrs in their care for us do not grant the same great favors through their bodily remains as they do through their other relics? We find them so often performing more outstanding miracles away from their burial places.

Gregory: There is no doubt, Peter, that the holy martyrs can perform countless miracles where their bodies rest. And they do so in behalf of all who pray there with a pure intention. In places where their bodies do not actually lie buried, however, there is danger that those whose faith is weak may doubt their presence and their power to answer prayers. Consequently, it is in these places that they must perform still greater miracles. But one whose faith in God is strong earns all the more merit by his faith, for he realizes that the martyrs are present to hear his prayers even though their bodies happen to be buried elsewhere.

It was precisely to increase the faith of His disciples that the eternal Truth told them, 'If I do not go, the Advocate will not come to you.' Now certainly the Holy Spirit, the Advocate, is ever proceeding from the Father and the Son. Why, then, should the Son say He will go in order that the Spirit may come, when, actually, the Spirit never leaves Him? The point is that as long as the disciples could see our Lord in His human flesh they would want to keep on seeing Him with their bodily eyes. With good reason, therefore, did He tell them, 'If I do not go, the Advocate will not come.' What He really meant was, 'I cannot teach you spiritual love unless I remove my body from your sight; as long as you continue to see me with your bodily eyes you will never learn to love me spiritually.'

Peter: That is a very satisfying explanation.

Gregory: Let us interrupt our discussion for a while. If we are going to take up the miracles of other holy men, we shall need a short period of silence to rest our voices.

Notes

1   A little town about seventy miles northeast of Rome. The saint was born around 480.
2   The Lombards, a Germanic people, left their homes along the upper Danube and invaded Italy in 568, establishing a kingdom there which lasted until 774.
3   Subiaco lies along the Anio River about five miles north of Affile. The lake St. Gregory speaks of gave the site its Latin name of *Sublacum*. It was formed by a dam which Emperor Claudius had built across the river, and lasted until 1305 when the dam was destroyed by floods.
4   Usually identified as Vicovaro, about twenty miles farther down the Anio.
5   St. Gregory is referring to the winding path that led up the mountain. The altitude of Monte Cassino is 1,500 feet.
6   Monte Cassino is about seventy-five miles southeast of Rome. St. Benedict arrived there in 529. In addition to the pagan shrines mentioned by St. Gregory, there was also a very ancient fortress on the summit for the defense of the townspeople below and the surrounding plains. The Abbey of Monte Cassino was built entirely within the walls of the fortress and was for that reason known at first as the Citadel of Campania, as we learn from the full title of this book.
7   St. Martin of Tours.
8   The Ostrogoths were a Germanic people from Eastern Europe who had established their kingdom in Italy under Theodoric in 493. King Totila (541-52) was fighting to re-establish Gothic power there after it had virtually been broken by Emperor Justinian's armies during the previous decade. The following events probably took place when Totila was marching on Naples, which he captured in 543.
9   In southeastern Italy, about 120 miles from Monte Cassino.
10   About five miles from Monte Cassino.
11   Only the priesthood and the diaconate were regarded as sacred or holy orders before the

twelfth century, when the subdiaconate also came to be included among them.

12 Monte Cassino was destroyed by Duke Zotto in 589 and was not rebuilt until 720, under Abbot Petronax.

13 The deacon's words applied to the unbaptized and the excommunicated, who were not allowed to remain for the Mass of the Faithful. Their dismissal took place after the Gospel and sermon.

14 During the first centuries laypeople were permitted to handle the Blessed Sacrament and even keep it in their homes. The practice of placing a consecrated Host on the bodies of those who died in union with the Church was quite common in St. Benedict's time. Cf. A. Rush, *Death and Burial in Christian Antiquity* (Washington 1941) 99-101.

Laws of Ethelbert

Ethelbert of Kent (560-616) was the Anglo-Saxon ruler whose hegemony extended over all Britain south of the Humber. He received Augustine of Canterbury and allowed him to begin his mission of the conversion of the Anglo-Saxons. His law code was probably compiled around 602 and is the earliest Anglo-Saxon legal compilation.

Source: Dorothy Whitelock, *English Historical Documents* vol. 1.

1. The property of God and the Church [is to be paid for] with a twelve-fold compensation; a bishop's property with an eleven-fold compensation; a priest's property with a nine-fold compensation; a deacon's property with a six-fold compensation; a cleric's property with a three-fold compensation; the peace of the Church with a two-fold compensation; the peace of a meeting with a two-fold compensation.

2. If the king calls his people to him, and anyone does them injury there, [he is to pay] a two-fold compensation and 50 shillings to the king.

3. If the king is drinking at a man's home, and anyone commits any evil deed there, he is to pay two-fold compensation.

4. If a freeman steal from the king, he is to repay nine-fold.

5. If anyone kills a man in the king's estate, he is to pay 50 shillings compensation.

6. If anyone kills a freeman, [he is to pay] 50 shillings to the king as "lord-ring".[1]

7. If [anyone] kills the king's own smith or his messenger, he is to pay the ordinary wergild.

8. The [breach of the] king's protection,[2] 50 shillings.

9. If a freeman steals from a freeman, he is to pay three-fold, and the king is to have the fine or all the goods.

10. If anyone lies with a maiden belonging to the king, he is to pay 50 shillings compensation.

11. If it is a grinding slave, he is to pay 25 shillings compensation; [if a slave of] the third [class], 12 shillings.

12. The king's *fedesl* is to be paid for with 20 shillings.

13. If anyone kills a man in a nobleman's estate, he is to pay 12 shillings compensation.

14. If anyone lies with a nobleman's serving-woman, he is to pay 20 shillings compensation.

15. The [breach of a] *ceorl's*[3] protection: six shillings.

16. If anyone lie with a *ceorl's* serving-woman, he is to pay six shillings compensation; [if] with a slave-woman of the second [class], 50 *sceattas*; [if with one of] the third [class], 30 *sceattas*.

17. If a man is the first to force his way into a man's homestead, he is to pay six shillings compensation; he who enters next, three shillings; afterwards each [is to pay] a shilling.

18. If anyone provides a man with weapons, when a quarrel has arisen, and [yet] no injury results, he is to pay six shillings compensation.

19. If highway-robbery is committed, he[4] is to pay six shillings compensation.

20. If, however, a man is killed, he is to pay 20 shillings compensation.

21. If anyone kills a man, he is to pay as an ordinary wergild 100 shillings.

22. If anyone kills a man, he is to pay 20 shillings at the open grave, and within 40 days the whole wergild.

23. If the slayer departs from the land, his kinsmen are to pay half the wergild.

24. If anyone binds a free man, he is to pay 20 shillings compensation.

25. If anyone kills a *ceorl*'s dependant, he is to pay six shillings compensation.

26. If [anyone] kills a *læt*,[5] he is to pay for one of the highest class 80 shillings; if he kills one of the second class, he is to pay 60 shillings; if one of the third class, he is to pay 40 shillings.

27. If a freeman breaks an enclosure, he is to pay six shillings compensation.

28. If anyone seizes property inside, the man is to pay three-fold compensation.

29. If a freeman enters the enclosure, he is to pay four shillings compensation.

30. If anyone kill a man, he is to pay with his own money and unblemished goods, whatever their kind.

31. If a freeman lies with the wife of another freeman, he is to atone with his wergild, and to obtain another wife with his own money, and bring her to the other's home.

32. If anyone thrusts through a true *hamseyld*, he is to pay for it with its value.

33. If hair-pulling occur, 50 *sceattas* [are to be paid] as compensation....

73. If a freewoman, with long hair,[6] commits any misconduct, she is to pay 30 shillings compensation.

74. The compensation for [injury to] a maiden is to be as for a freeman.

75. [Breach of] guardianship over a noble-born widow of the highest class is to be compensated for with 50 shillings.

75.I. that over one of the second class, with 20 shillings; over one of the third class, with 12 shillings; over one of the fourth, with six shillings.

76. If a man takes a widow who does not belong to him, the [penalty for breach of the] guardianship is to be doubled.

77. If anyone buys a maiden, she is to be bought with a [bride] payment, if there is no fraud.

77.I. If, however, there is any fraud, she is to be taken back home, and he is to be given back his money.

78. If she bears a living child, she is to have half the goods, if the husband dies first.

79. If she wishes to go away with the children, she is to have half the goods.

80. If the husband wishes to keep [the children], [she is to have the same share] as a child.

81. If she does not bear a child, [her] paternal kinsmen are to have [her] goods and the "morning-gift".[7]

82. If anyone carries off a maiden by force, [he is to pay] to the owner 50 shillings, and afterwards buy from the owner his consent [to the marriage].

83. If she is betrothed to another man at a [bride] price, he[8] is to pay 20 shillings compensation.

84. If a return [of the woman] takes place, [he is to pay] 35 shillings and 15 shillings to the king.

85. If anyone lies with the woman of a servant while her husband is alive, he is to pay a two-fold compensation.

86. If one servant kills another without cause, he is to pay the full value.

87. If a servant's eye or foot is destroyed, the full value is to be paid for him.

88. If anyone binds a man's servant, he is to pay six shillings compensation.

89. Highway robbery of [or by?] a slave is to be three shillings.

90. If a slave steals, he is to pay two-fold compensation.

Notes

1   Presumably what is called elsewhere a *manbot*. The term used here is obviously ancient, belonging to a time when payments were more often in rings than in currency. Several of the words in this code are either unique, or used only in poetry, which was conservative in its vocabulary.

2   Offences against anyone or any place under the king's protection, but also including various acts showing lack of respect. Other persons than the king had their *mund(byrd)* "(right of giving) protection".

3   Though modern English "churl" is the direct descendant of this word, the sense has changed so much that to use it would be misleading. Its normal Old English meaning is a peasant proprietor.

4   The man who provided the weapon.

5   Only in Kent is there reference to this class, lower than the *ceorl*, but above the slave.

6   This is generally taken to be a distinguishing feature of a free, as opposed to a bond, woman.

7   The gift made by the husband to the bride the morning after the consummation of the marriage.

8   The man who ran off with her.

Bede

History of the English Church and People

Bede (ca. 672-735) spent almost all of his life in the Northumbrian monastery of St. Paul at Jarrow. His writing included exegetical works, chronology, rhetoric, metrics, natural history, and hagiography as well as history. His History of the English Church and People *is the most important narrative source for English history up to 731. Bede was extremely careful in his selection and use of sources, although he carefully molded his work in order to present his own vision of the growth of English Christianity. The following selections present Augustine's mission to England, the life of Bishop Aidan, and the Synod of Whitby.*

Source: Leo Sherley-Price, ed., Bede:*A History of the English Church and People* (Harmondsworth: Penguin Books, 1955).

Book One

CHAPTER 23: *The holy Pope Gregory sends Augustine and other monks to preach to the English nation, and encourages them in a letter to persevere in their mission* [A.D.*596*]

In the year of our Lord 582, Maurice, fifty-fourth in succession from Augustus, became Emperor, and ruled for twenty-one years. In the tenth year of his reign, Gregory, an eminent scholar and administrator, was elected Pontiff of the apostolic Roman see, and ruled it for thirteen years, six months, and ten days. In the fourteenth year of the Emperor, and about the one hundred and fiftieth year after the coming of the English to Britain, Gregory was inspired by God to send his servant Augustine with several other God-fearing monks to preach the word of God to the English nation. Having undertaken this task in obedience to the Pope's command and progressed a short distance on their journey, they became afraid, and began to consider returning home. For they were appalled at the idea of going to a barbarous, fierce, and pagan nation, of whose very language they were ignorant. They unanimously agreed that this was the safest course, and sent back Augustine—who was to be consecrated bishop in the event of their being received by the English—so that he might humbly request the holy Gregory to recall them from so dangerous, arduous, and uncertain a journey. In reply, the Pope wrote them a letter of encouragement, urging them to proceed on their mission to preach God's word, and to trust themselves to his aid. This letter ran as follows:
    'GREGORY, Servant of the servants of God, to the servants of our Lord. My very dear sons, it is better never to undertake any high enterprise than to abandon it when once begun. So with the help of God you must carry out this holy task which you have begun. Do not be deterred by the troubles of the journey or by what men say. Be constant and zealous in carrying out this enterprise which, under God's guidance, you have undertaken: and be assured that the greater the labour, the greater will be the glory of your eternal reward. When Augustine your leader returns, whom We have appointed your abbot, obey him humbly in all things, remembering that whatever he directs you to do will always be to the good of your souls. May Almighty God protect you with His grace, and grant me to see the result of your labors in our heavenly home. And although my office

prevents me from working at your side, yet because I long to do so, I hope to share in your joyful reward. God keep you safe, my dearest sons.

'Dated the twenty-third of July, in the fourteenth year of the reign of the most pious Emperor Maurice Tiberius Augustus, and the thirteenth year after his Consulship: the fourteenth interdiction.'

CHAPTER 24: *Pope Gregory writes commending them to the Bishop of Arles*

The venerable Pontiff also wrote to Etherius, Archbishop of Arles, asking him to offer a kindly welcome to Augustine on his journey to Britain. This letter reads:

'To his most reverend and holy brother and fellow-bishop Etherius: Gregory, servant of the servants of God.

'Religious men should require no commendation to priests who exhibit the love that is pleasing to God; but since a suitable opportunity to write has arisen, We have written this letter to you, our brother, to certify that its bearer, God's servant Augustine, with his companions, of whose zeal we are assured, has been directed by us to proceed to save souls with the help of God. We therefore request Your Holiness to assist them with pastoral care, and to make speedy provision for their needs. And in order that you may assist them the more readily, we have particularly directed Augustine to give you full information about his mission, being sure that when you are acquainted with this, you will supply all their needs for the love of God. We also commend to your love the priest Candidus, our common son in Christ, whom we have transferred to a small patrimony in our church. God keep you safely, most reverend brother.

'Dated the twenty-third day of July, in the fourteenth year of the reign of the most pious Emperor Maurice Tiberius Augustus, and the thirteenth year after his Consulship: the fourteenth indiction.'

CHAPTER 25: *Augustine reaches Britain, and first preaches in the Isle of Thanet before King Ethelbert, who grants permission to preach in Kent* **[A.D.597]**

Reassured by the encouragement of the blessed father Gregory, Augustine and his fellow-servants of Christ resumed their work in the word of God, and arrived in Britain. At this time the most powerful king there was Ethelbert, who reigned in Kent and whose domains extended northwards to the river Humber, which forms the boundary between the north and south Angles. To the east of Kent lies the large island of Thanet, which by English reckoning is six hundred hides in extent; it is separated from the mainland by a waterway about three furlongs broad called the Wantsum, which joins the sea at either end and is fordable only in two places. It was here that God's servant Augustine landed with companions, who are said to have been forty in number. At the direction of blessed Pope Gregory, they had brought interpreters from among the Franks, and they sent these to Ethelbert, saying that they came from Rome bearing very glad news, which infallibly assured all who would receive it of eternal joy in heaven and an everlasting kingdom with the living and true God. On receiving this message, the king ordered them to remain in the island where they had landed, and gave directions that they were to be provided with all necessaries until he should decide what action to take. For he had already heard of the Christian religion, having a Christian wife of the Frankish royal house named Bertha, whom he had received from her parents on condition that she should have freedom to hold and practice her faith unhindered with Bishop Liudhard, whom they had sent as her helper in the faith.

After some days, the king came to the island, and, sitting down in the open air, summoned Augustine and his companions to an audience. But he took precautions that they should not approach him in a house; for he held an ancient superstition that, if they were practisers of magical arts, they might have opportunity to deceive and master him. But the monks were endowed with power from God, not from the Devil, and approached the king carrying a silver cross as their standard and the likeness of our Lord and Saviour painted on a board. First of all they offered prayer to God, singing a litany for the eternal salvation both of themselves and of those to whom and for whose sake they had come. And when, at the king's command, they had sat down and preached the word of life to the king and his court, the king said: 'Your words and promises are fair indeed; but they are new and uncertain, and I cannot accept them and abandon the age-old beliefs that I have held together with the whole English nation. But since you have travelled far, and I can see that you are sincere in your desire to impart to us what you believe to be true and excellent, we will not harm you. We will receive you hospitably and take care to supply you with all that you need; nor will we forbid you to preach and win any people you can to your religion.' The king then granted them a dwelling in the city of Canterbury, which was the chief city of all his realm, and in accordance with his promise he allowed them provisions and did not withdraw their freedom to preach. Tradition says that as they approached the city, bearing the holy cross and the likeness of our great King and Lord Jesus Christ as was their custom, they sang in unison this litany: 'We pray Thee, O Lord, in all Thy mercy, that Thy wrath and anger may be turned away from this city and from Thy holy house, for we are sinners. Alleluia.'

CHAPTER 26: *The life and doctrine of the primitive Church are followed in Kent: Augustine establishes his episcopal see in the king's city*

As soon as they had occupied the house given to them they began to emulate the life of the apostles and the primitive Church. They were constantly at prayer; they fasted and kept vigils; they preached the word of life to whomsoever they could. They regarded worldly things as of little importance, and accepted only the necessities of life from those they taught. They practiced what they preached, and were willing to endure any hardship, and even to die for the truth which they proclaimed. Before long a number of heathen, admiring the simplicity of their holy lives and the comfort of their heavenly message, believed and were baptized. On the east side of the city stood an old church, built in honor of Saint Martin during the Roman occupation of Britain, where the Christian queen of whom I have spoken went to pray. Here they first assembled to sing the psalms, to pray, to say Mass, to preach, and to baptize, until the king's own conversion to the Faith gave them greater freedom to preach and to build and restore churches everywhere.

At length the king himself, among others, edified by the pure lives of these holy men and their gladdening promises, the truth of which they confirmed by many miracles, believed and was baptized. Thenceforward great numbers gathered each day to hear the word of God, forsaking their heathen rites and entering the unity of Christ's holy Church as believers. While the king was pleased at their faith and conversion, it is said that he would not compel anyone to accept Christianity; for he had learned from his instructors and guides to salvation that the service of Christ must be accepted freely and not under compulsion. Nevertheless, he showed greater favour to believers, because they were fellow-citizens of the kingdom of heaven. And it was not long before he granted his teachers in his capital of Canterbury a place of residence appropriate to their station, and gave them possessions of various kinds to supply their wants....

CHAPTER 29: *Gregory sends Augustine the pallium, a letter, and several clergy* **[A.D.** *601***]**

Hearing from Bishop Augustine that he had a rich harvest but few to help him gather it, Pope Gregory sent with his envoys several colleagues and clergy, of whom the principal and most outstanding were Mellitus, Justus, Paulinus, and Rufinianus. They brought with them everything <u>necessary</u> for the worship and service of the Church, including sacred vessels, altar coverings, <u>church ornaments</u>, vestments for priests and clergy, relics of the holy Apostles and martyrs, and many books. Gregory also sent a letter to Augustine, telling him that he had dispatched the *pallium* to him, and giving him directions on the appointment of bishops in Britain. This letter runs as follows:

'To our most reverend and holy brother and fellow-bishop Augustine: Gregory, servant of the servants of God.

'While Almighty God alone can grant His servants the ineffable joys of the kingdom of heaven, it is proper that we should reward them with earthly honours, and encourage them by such recognition to devote themselves to their spiritual labours with redoubled zeal. And since the new Church of the English has now, through the goodness of God and your own efforts, been brought to the grace of God, we grant you the privilege of wearing the *pallium* in that Church whenever you perform the solemnities of the Mass. You are to consecrate twelve bishops in different places, who will be subject to your jurisdiction: the bishop of the city of London will thenceforward be consecrated by his own synod, and will receive the honor of the *pallium* from this apostolic See which, by divine decree, we at present occupy. We wish you also to send a bishop of your own choice to the city of York, and if that city with the adjoining territory accepts the word of God, this bishop is to consecrate twelve other bishops, and hold the dignity of Metropolitan. If we live to see this, we intend to grant him the *pallium* also, but he is to remain subject to your authority. After your death, however, he is to preside over the bishops whom he has consecrated and to be wholly independent of the Bishop of London. Thenceforward, seniority of consecration is to determine whether the Bishop of London or York takes precedence; but they are to consult one another and take united action in all matters concerning Augustus, and the nineteenth after his Consulship: the fourth indiction.'

CHAPTER 32: *Pope Gregory sends letters and gifts to King Ethelbert*

Pope Gregory also sent a letter to King Ethelbert with many gifts of different kinds, wishing to bestow earthly honors on this king who by his exertions and zeal, and to his great joy, had been brought to knowledge of heavenly glory. A copy of this letter follows.

'To our excellent son, the most glorious King Ethelbert, King of the English: the Bishop Gregory.

'The reason why Almighty God raises good men to govern nations is that through them He may bestow the gifts of His mercy on all whom they rule. We know that this is so in the case of the English nation, over whom you reign so gloriously, so that by means of the good gifts that God grants to you He may bless your people as well. Therefore, my illustrious son, zealously foster the grace that God has given you, and press on with the task of extending the Christian Faith among the people committed to your charge. Make their conversion your first concern; suppress the worship of idols, and destroy their shrines; raise the moral standards of your subjects by your own innocence of life, encouraging, warning, persuading, correcting, and showing them an example by your good deeds. God will most surely grant you His rewards in heaven if you faithfully proclaim His Name and truth upon earth; and He whose honor you seek and uphold among your peoples will make your own name glorious to posterity.

'So it was that the devout Emperor Constantine in his day turned the Roman State from its ignorant worship of idols by his own submission to our mighty Lord and God Jesus Christ, and with his subjects accepted Him with all his heart. The result is that his glorious reputation has excelled that of all his predecessors, and he has outshone them in reputation as greatly as he surpassed them in good works. Now, therefore, let Your Majesty make all speed to bring to your subject princes and peoples the knowledge of the One God, Father, Son and Holy Spirit, so that your own merit and repute may excel that of all the former kings of your nation. And when you have thus cleansed your subjects from their sins, you will bear the load of your own sins with greater confidence before the judgment seat of God.

'Our most reverend brother Bishop Augustine has been trained under monastic Rule, has a complete knowledge of holy scripture, and, by the grace of God, is a man of holy life. Therefore I beg you to listen to his advice ungrudgingly, follow it exactly and store it carefully in your memory; for if you listen to him when he speaks in God's name, God himself will listen more readily to the prayers he utters on your behalf. But if you ignore his advice—which God forbid—and disregard him when he speaks for God, how should God pay attention when he speaks for you? Work sincerely and wholeheartedly with him in fervent faith, and support his efforts with all the strength God has given you, so that you may receive a place in the kingdom of Christ, Whose Faith you profess and uphold in your own realm.

'We would also have Your Majesty know what we have learned from the words of Almighty God in holy Scripture, that the end of this present world is at hand and the everlasting kingdom of the Saints is approaching. When the end of the world is near, unprecedented things occur—portents in the sky, terrors from heaven, unseasonable tempests, wars, famines, pestilences, and widespread earthquakes. Not all these things will happen during our own lifetimes, but will all ensue in due course. Therefore, if any such things occur in your own country, do not be anxious, for these portents of the end are sent to warn us to consider the welfare of our souls and remember our last end, so that, when our Judge comes, He may find us prepared by good lives. I have mentioned these matters in this short letter, my illustrious son, in the hope that as the Christian Faith grows more strong in your kingdom, our correspondence with you may become more frequent. So my pleasure in addressing you will keep pace with the joy in my heart at the glad news of the complete conversion of your people.

'I have sent some small presents, which will not appear small to you, since you receive them with the blessing of the blessed Apostle Peter. May Almighty God continue to perfect you in His grace, prolong your life for many years, and after this life receive you among the citizens of our heavenly home. May the grace of heaven preserve Your Majesty in safety.

'Dated the twenty-second day of June, in the nineteenth year of our most pious lord and Emperor Maurice Tiberius Augustus, and the eighteenth after his Consulship: the fourth indiction.'

Book Two

CHAPTER 2: *Augustine urges the British bishops to cement Catholic unity, and performs a miracle in their presence. Retribution follows their refusal* [A.D.603]

Meanwhile, with the aid of King Ethelbert, Augustine summoned the bishops and teachers of the nearest British province to a conference at a place still known to the English as Augustine's Oak, which lies on the border between the Hwiccas and the West Saxons. He began by urging them to establish brotherly relations with him in Catholic unity, and to join with him in God's work of preaching the Gospel to the heathen.

Now the Britons did not keep Easter at the correct time, but between the fourteenth and the twentieth days of the moon—a calculation depending on a cycle of eighty-four years. Furthermore, certain other of their customs were at variance with the universal practice of the Church. But despite protracted discussions, neither the prayers nor the advice nor the censures of Augustine and his companions could obtain the compliance of the Britons, who stubbornly preferred their own customs to those in universal use among Christian Churches. Augustine then brought this lengthy and fruitless conference to a close, saying, 'Let us ask our Lord, *who makes men to be of one mind* in his Father's house, to grant us a sign from heaven and show us which tradition is to be followed, and by what roads we are to hasten our steps towards His kingdom. Bring in some sick person, and let the beliefs and practice of those who can heal him be accepted as pleasing to God and to be followed by all.' On the reluctant agreement of his opponents, a blind Englishman was led in and presented to the British priests, from whose ministry he obtained no healing or benefit. Then Augustine, as the occasion demanded, knelt in prayer to the Father of our Lord Jesus Christ, imploring that the man's lost sight might be restored and prove the means of bringing the light of spiritual grace to the minds of countless believers. Immediately the blind man's sight was restored, and all acknowledged Augustine as the true herald of the light of Christ. The Britons declared that, while they had learnt that what Augustine taught was the true way of righteousness, they could not abandon their ancient customs without the consent and approval of their own people, and therefore asked that a second and fuller conference might be held.

This was arranged, and seven British bishops and many very learned men are said to have attended, who came mainly from their most famous monastery which the English call Bancornaburg [Bangor-is-Coed, co. Flint], then ruled by Abbot Dinoot. Those summoned to this council first visited a wise and prudent hermit, and enquired of him whether they should abandon their own traditions at Augustine's demand. He answered: 'If he is a man of God, follow him.' 'But how can we be sure of this?' they asked. 'Our Lord says, *Take my yoke upon you and learn of Me, for I am meek and lowly in heart*,' he replied. 'Therefore if Augustine is meek and lowly in heart, it shows that he bears the yoke of Christ himself, and offers it to you. But if he is haughty and unbending, then he is not of God, and we should not listen to him.' Then they asked, 'But how can we know even this?' Whereupon Augustine, that man of God, is said to have answered them with a threat that was also a prophecy: if they refused to accept peace with their fellow-Christians, they would be forced to accept war at the hands of enemies; and if they refused to preach to the English the way of life, they would eventually suffer at their hands the penalty of death. And, by divine judgement, all these things happened as Augustine foretold.

Some while after this, the powerful king Ethelfrid, whom I have already mentioned, raised a great army at the City of Legions—which the English call Legacestir [Chester], but which the Britons more correctly call Carlegion—and made a great slaughter of the faithless Britons. Before battle was joined, he noticed that their priests were assembled apart in a safer place to pray for their soldiers, and he enquired who they were and what they had come there to do. Most of these priests came from the monastery of Bangor, where there are said to have been so many monks that although it was divided into seven sections, each under its own head, none of these sections contained less than three hundred monks, all of whom supported themselves by manual work. Most of these monks, who had kept a three-day fast, had gathered to pray at the battle, guarded by a certain Brocmail, who was there to protect them from the swords of the barbarians while they were intent on prayer. As soon as King Ethelfrid was informed of their purpose, he said: 'If they are crying to their God against us, they are fighting against us even if they do not bear arms.' He therefore directed his first attack against them, and then destroyed the rest of the accursed army, not without heavy loss to his own forces. It is said that of the monks who came to pray about twelve hundred perished in this battle, and only fifty escaped by flight. Brocmail and his men took to their heels at the first assault, leaving those whom they should have protected unarmed and exposed to the swordstrokes of the enemy. Thus, long after his death, was fulfilled Bishop Augustine's prophecy that the faithless Britons, who had rejected the offer of eternal salvation, would incur the punishment of temporal destruction.

CHAPTER 3: *Augustine consecrates Mellitus and Justus as bishops: his own death* [**A.D.***604*]

In the year of our Lord 604, Augustine, Archbishop of Britain, consecrated two bishops, Mellitus and Justus. Mellitus was appointed to preach in the province of the East Saxons, which is separated from Kent by the river Thames, and bounded on the east by the sea. Its capital is the city of London, which stands on the banks of the Thames, and is a trading centre for many nations who visit it by land and sea. At this time Sabert, Ethelbert's nephew through his sister Ricula, ruled the province under the suzerainty of Ethelbert, who, as already stated, governed all the English peoples as far north as the Humber. When this province too had received the faith through the preaching of Mellitus, King Ethelbert built a church dedicated to the Holy Apostle Paul in the city of London, which he appointed as the episcopal see of Mellitus and his successors. Augustine also consecrated Justus as bishop of a Kentish city which the English call Hrofescaestir [Rochester] after an early chieftain named Hrof. This lies nearly twenty-four miles west of Canterbury, and a church in honor of Saint Andrew the Apostle was built here by King Ethelbert, who made many gifts to the bishops of both these churches as well as to Canterbury; he later added lands and property for the maintenance of the bishop's household.

When our father Augustine, the beloved of God, died, his body was laid to rest just outside the church of the holy Apostles Peter and Paul, since the church was not yet completed or consecrated. But as soon as it was dedicated, his body was brought inside and buried in the north porch with great honor. This is also the last resting-place of all succeeding archbishops except Theodore and Bertwald, whose bodies lie inside the church, no space remaining in the porch. Almost in the centre of the church stands an altar dedicated in honor of blessed Pope Gregory, at which a priest of the place says solemn mass in their memory each Saturday. On the tomb of Augustine is inscribed this epitaph:

'Here rests the Lord Augustine, first Archbishop of Canterbury, who, having been sent here by blessed Gregory, Pontiff of the City of Rome, and supported by God with miracles, guided King Ethelbert and his people from the worship of idols to the Faith of Christ. He ended the days of his duty in peace, and died on the twenty-sixth day of May in the above King's reign.'

Book Three

Chapter 7: *The West Saxons accept the Faith through the teaching of Birinus and his successors Agilbert and Leutherius* [**A.D.** *635*]

During the reign of Cynegils, the West Saxons, anciently known as the Gewissae, accepted the Faith of Christ through the preaching of Bishop Birinus. He had come to Britain at the direction of Pope Honorius [I], having promised the Pope that he would sow the seeds of our holy Faith in the distant lands beyond the English dominions where no other teacher had been before him. He was consecrated bishop by Asterius, Bishop of Genoa, at the Pope's command; but when he had reached Britain and entered the territory of the Gewissae, he found them completely heathen, and decided that it would be better to begin to preach the word of God among them rather than seek more distant converts. He therefore evangelized that province, and when he had instructed its king, he baptized him and his people. It happened at the time that the most holy and victorious Oswald was present, who greeted King Cynegils as he came from the font, and offered him an alliance most acceptable to God, taking him as his godson, and his daughter as wife. The two kings gave Bishop Birinus the city of Dorcic [Dorchester, Oxon.] for his episcopal see, and there he built and dedicated several churches, and brought many people to God by his holy labours. He also died and was buried there; and many years later, when Haeddi was bishop, his body was translated to Venta [Winchester]and laid in the church of the blessed Apostles Peter and Paul.

On the death of Cynegils, his son Cenwalh succeeded to the throne, but refused to accept the Faith and sacraments of Christ. Not long afterwards he lost his kingdom, for he put away his wife, who was sister of Penda, King of Mercia, and took another woman. This led to war, and Cenwalh was driven out of his kingdom and took refuge with Anna King of the East Angles. There he lived in exile for three years, during which he learned the Christian Faith and received Baptism. For Anna his host was a good man, and blessed with good and holy children, as I shall mention later.

When Cenwalh had been restored to his kingdom, there arrived in the province a bishop from Gaul named Agilbert, who had been studying the scriptures in Ireland for many years. This bishop came to the king, and voluntarily undertook to evangelize the country. Appreciating his learning and enthusiasm, the king asked him to accept an episcopal see and remain in the province as his chief bishop. Agilbert acceded to the king's request, and presided as bishop for many years. Later, however, the king, who understood only Saxon, grew tired of the bishop's foreign speech, and invited to the province a bishop of his own race called Wini, who had been consecrated in Gaul; and dividing his kingdom into two dioceses, he gave Wini the city of Venta - known by the Saxons as Wintancestir - as his see. This action gravely offended Agilbert, whom the king had not consulted in the matter, and he returned to Gaul, where he became Bishop of Paris and ended his days there at an advanced age. Not many years after Agilbert's departure from Britain, Wini was also driven from his bishopric by the king, and took refuge with Wulfhere, King of Mercia, to whom he offered money for the Bishopric of London, and held it till his death. So for a considerable time the province of the West Saxons remained without any bishop.

During this interval King Cenwalh, who had often lost large areas of his kingdom to his enemies, eventually remembered that as he had formerly been driven from his throne because of his infidelity and had been restored to it after his acceptance of the Christian Faith, so he was now justly deprived of God's protection because his kingdom has no bishop. He therefore sent messengers to Agilbert in Gaul, offering him satisfaction and requesting him to return to his bishopric. But Agilbert sent his regrets, and said that it was impossible for him to return, since he was now responsible for his own bishopric and city of Paris. But not wishing to appear unwilling to help, he sent in his place his nephew, the priest Leutherius [a latinized form of the name 'Hlothere], who could be made bishop if the king were agreeable, recommending him as worthy of a bishopric. Both king and people welcomed Leutherius with honour, and asked Theodore, then Archbishop of Canterbury, to consecrate him in their bishop. He was accordingly consecrated at Canterbury, and for many years wisely ruled the West Saxon see with the full support of the synod.

CHAPTER 25: *Controversy arises with the Scots over the date of Easter* [A.D.664]

When Bishop Aidan departed this life, he was succeeded in the Bishopric by Finan, who had been consecrated and sent by the Scots. He built a church in the Isle of Lindisfarne suitable for an episcopal see, constructing it,. however, not of stone, but of hewn oak thatched with reeds after the Scots manner. It was later dedicated by the most reverend Archbishop Theodore in honor of the blessed Apostle Peter. But Eadbert, a later Bishop of Lindisfarne, removed the thatch, and covered both roof and walls with sheets of lead.

About this time there arose a great and recurrent controversy on the observance of Easter, those trained in Kent and Gaul maintaining that the Scottish observance was contrary to that of the universal Church. The most zealous champion of the true Easter was a Scot named Ronan, who had been instructed in Gaul and Italy in the authentic practice of the Church. He disputed against Finan and convinced many, or at least persuaded them to make a more careful enquiry into the truth. But he entirely failed to move Finan, a hot-tempered man whom reproof made more obstinate and openly hostile to the truth. James, formerly the deacon of the venerable Archbishop Paulinus, of whom I have spoken, kept the true and Catholic Easter with all whom he could persuade to adopt the right observance. Also Queen Eanfled and her court, having a Kentish priest named Romanus who followed the Catholic practice, observed the customs she had seen in Kent. It is said that the confusion in those days was such that Easter was sometimes kept twice in one year, so that when the King had ended Lent and was keeping Easter, the Queen and her attendants were still fasting and keeping Palm Sunday. During Aidan's lifetime these differences of Easter observance were patiently tolerated by everyone; for it was realized that, although he was in loyalty bound to retain the customs of those who sent him, he nevertheless labored diligently to cultivate the faith, piety, and love that marks out God's saints. He was therefore rightly loved by all, even by those who differed from his opinion on Easter, and was held in high respect not only by ordinary folk, but by Honorius of Canterbury and Felix of the East Angles.

When Finan, who followed Aidan as bishop, died, he was succeeded by another Irishman, Colman, under whom an even more serious controversy arose about Easter and also about other rules of Church discipline. This dispute rightly began to trouble the minds and consciences of many people, who feared that they might have received the name of Christian in vain. Eventually the matter came to the notice of King Oswy and his son Alchfrid. Oswy thought nothing could be better than the Scots teaching, having been instructed and baptized by the Scots and having a complete grasp of their language. But Alchfrid, who had been instructed in the Faith by Wilfrid—a very learned man who had gone to Rome to study the doctrine of the Church, and spent a long time at Lyons under Dalfin, Archbishop of Gaul, from whom he had received the tonsure—knew that Wilfrid's doctrine was in fact preferable to all the traditions of the Scots. He had therefore given him a monastery with forty hides of land at In-Hrypum [Ripon]. Actually, he had given this not long previously to the adherents of the Scottish customs; but since, when offered the alternative, these preferred to give up the place rather than alter their customs, he then offered it to Wilfrid, whose life and teaching made him a worthy recipient. About this time, Agilbert, Bishop of the West Saxons, whom I have mentioned, had come to visit the province of the Northumbrians. He was a friend both of King Alchfrid and of Abbot Wilfrid and stayed with them for some time, and at the king's request he made Wilfrid a priest in his monastery. He also had with him a priest named Agatho. So when discussion arose there on the questions of Easter, the tonsure, and various other church matters, it was decided to hold a synod to put an end to this dispute at the monastery of Streanaeshalch, which means The Bay of the Beacon, then ruled by the Abbess Hilda, a woman devoted to God. Both kings, father and son, came to this synod, and so did Bishop Colman with his Scots clergy, and Bishop Agilbert with the priests Agatho and Wilfrid. James and Romanus supported the latter, while Abbess Hilda and her community, together with the venerable bishop Cedd, supported the Scots. Cedd, who as already mentioned had long ago been ordained by the Scots, acted as a most careful interpreter for both parties at the council.

King Oswy opened by observing that all who served the One God should observe one rule of life, and since they all hoped for one kingdom of heaven, they should not differ in celebrating the sacraments of heaven. The synod now had the task of determining which was the truer tradition, and this should be loyally accepted by all. He then directed his own bishop Colman to speak first, and to explain his own rite and its origin. Then Colman said: 'The Easter customs which I observe were taught me by my superiors, who sent me here as a bishop; and all our forefathers, men beloved of God, are known to have observed these customs. And lest anyone condemn or reject them as wrong, it is recorded that they owe their origin to the blessed evangelist Saint John, the disciple especially loved by our Lord, and all the churches over which he presided.' When he had concluded these and similar arguments, the king directed Agilbert to explain the origin and authority of his own customs. Agilbert replied: 'May I request that my disciple the priest Wilfrid be allowed to speak in my place? For we are both in full agreement with all those here present who support the traditions of our Church, and he can explain our view in the English language more competently and clearly than I can do through an interpreter.' When Wilfrid had received the king's command to speak, he said: 'Our Easter customs are those that we have seen universally observed in Rome, where the blessed Apostles Peter and Paul lived, taught, suffered, and are buried. We have also seen the same customs generally observed throughout Italy and Gaul when we travelled through these countries for study and prayer. Furthermore, we have learnt that Easter is observed by men of different nations and languages at one and the same time, in Africa, Asia, Egypt, Greece, and throughout the world wherever the Church of Christ has spread. The only people who stupidly contend against the whole world are these Scots and their partners in obstinacy the Picts and Britons, who inhabit only a portion of these two uttermost islands of the ocean.' In reply to this statement, Colman answered: 'It is strange that you call us stupid when we uphold customs that rest on the authority of so great an Apostle, who was considered worthy to lean on our Lord's breast, and whose great wisdom is acknowledged

sidered worthy to lean on our Lord's breast, and whose great wisdom is acknowledged throughout the world.' Wilfrid replied: 'Far be it from us to charge John with stupidity, because he literally observed the Law of Moses at a time when the Church followed many Jewish practices, and the Apostles were not able immediately to abrogate the observances of the Law once given by God, lest they gave offence to believers who were Jews (whereas idols, on the other hand, being inventions of the Devil, must be renounced by all converts). For this reason Paul circumcised Timothy, offered sacrifice in the Temple, and shaved his head at Corinth with Aquila and Priscilla, for no other reason than that of avoiding offence to the Jews. For James said to Paul: "*Thou seest, brother, how many thousands of Jews there are which believe; and they are all zealous of the law.*" But today, as the Gospel spreads throughout the world, it is unnecessary and indeed unlawful for the faithful to be circumcised or to offer animals to God in sacrifice. John, following the custom of the Law, used to begin the Feast of Easter on the evening of the fourteenth day of the first month, not caring whether it fell on the Sabbath or on any other day. But Peter, when he preached in Rome, remembering that it was on the day after the Sabbath that our Lord rose from the dead and gave the world the hope of resurrection, realized that Easter should be kept as follows: like John, in accordance with the law, he waited for moonrise on the evening of the fourteenth day of the first month. And if the Lord's Day, then called the morrow of the Sabbath, fell on the following day, he began to observe Easter the same evening, as we all do today. But, if the Lord's Day did not fall on the day following the fourteenth day of the moon, but on the sixteenth, seventeenth, or any day up to the twenty-first, he waited until that day, and on the Sabbath evening preceding it he began the observance of the Easter Festival. This evangelical and apostolical tradition does not abrogate but fulfil the Law, which ordained that the Passover be kept between the eve of the fourteenth and twenty-first days of the moon of that month. And this is the custom of all the successors of blessed John in Asia since his death, and is also that of the worldwide Church. This is the true and only Easter to be observed by the faithful. It was not newly decreed by the Council of Nicaea, but reaffirmed by it, as Church history records. It is quite apparent, Colman, that you follow neither the example of John, as you imagine, nor that of Peter, whose tradition you deliberately contradict. Your keeping of Easter agrees neither with the Law nor with the Gospel. For John, who kept Easter in accordance with the decrees of Moses, did not keep to the first day after the Sabbath; but this is not your practice, for you keep Easter only on the first day after the Sabbath. Peter kept Easter between the fifteenth and twenty-first days of the moon; you do not, for you keep it between the fourteenth and twentieth days of the month. As a result, you often begin Easter on the evening of the thirteenth day, which is not mentioned in the Law. Nor did our Lord, the Author and Giver of the Gospel, eat the old Passover or institute the Sacrament of the New Testament to be celebrated by the Church in memory of His Passion on that day, but on the fourteenth. Furthermore, when you keep Easter, you totally exclude the twenty-first day, which the Law of Moses particularly ordered to be observed. Therefore, I repeat, you follow neither John nor Peter, the Law nor the Gospel, in your keeping of our greatest Festival.'

Colman in reply said: 'Do you maintain that Anatolius, a holy man highly spoken of in Church history, taught contrary to the Law and the Gospel, when he wrote that Easter should be kept between the fourteenth and twentieth days of the moon? Are we to believe that our most revered Father Columba and his successors, men so dear to God, thought or acted contrary to Holy Scripture when they followed this custom? The holiness of many of them is confirmed by heavenly signs, and their virtues by miracles; and having no doubt that they are Saints, I shall never cease to emulate their lives, customs, and discipline.'

'It is well established that Anatolius was a most holy, learned, and praiseworthy man,' answered Wilfrid; 'but how can you claim his authority when you do not follow his directions? For he followed the correct rule about Easter, and observed a cycle of nineteen years; but either you do not know of this general custom of the Christian Church, or else you ignore it. He calculated the fourteenth day of the moon at Easter according to the

the twentieth to Easter Sunday, regarding it after sunset as the twenty-first day. But it appears that you do not realize this distinction, since you sometimes keep Easter before full moon, that is, on the thirteenth day. And with regard to your Father Columba and his followers, whose holiness you claim to imitate and whose rules and customs you claim to have been supported by heavenly signs, I can only say that when many shall say to our Lord at the day of judgement: *"Have we not prophesied in Thy name, and cast out devils, and done many wonderful works?"* the Lord will reply, *"I never knew you."* Far be it from me to apply these words to your fathers; for it is more than just to believe good rather than evil of those whom one does not know. So I do not deny that they were true servants of God and dear to Him, and that they loved Him in primitive simplicity but in devout sincerity. Nor do I think that their ways of keeping Easter were seriously harmful, so long as no one came to show them a more perfect way to follow. Indeed, I feel that, if any Catholic reckoner had come to them, they would readily have accepted his guidance, as we know that they readily observed such of God's ordinances as they already knew. But you and your colleagues are most certainly guilty of sin if you reject the decrees of the Apostolic See, indeed of the universal Church, which are confirmed by Holy Writ. For, although your Fathers were holy men, do you imagine that they, a few men in a corner of a remote island, are to be preferred before the universal Church of Christ throughout the world? And even if your Columba—or, may I say, ours also if he was the servant of Christ—was a Saint potent in miracles, can he take precedence before the most blessed Prince of the Apostles, to whom our Lord said: *"Thou art Peter, and upon this rock I will build my Church, and the gates of hell shall not prevail against it, and I will give unto thee the keys of the kingdom of heaven"?'*

When Wilfrid had ended, the king asked: 'Is it true, Colman, that these words were spoken to that Peter by our Lord?' He answered: 'It is true, Your Majesty.' Then the king said: 'Can you show that a similar authority was given to your Columba?' 'No,' replied Colman. 'Do you both agree,' the king continued, 'that these words were indisputably addressed to Peter in the first place, and that our Lord gave him the keys of the kingdom of heaven?' Both answered: 'We do.' At this, the king concluded: 'Then, I tell you, Peter is guardian of the gates of heaven, and I shall not contradict him. I shall obey his commands in everything to the best of my knowledge and ability; otherwise, when I come to the gates of heaven, there may be no one to open them, because he who holds the keys has turned away.'

When the king said this, all present, both high and low, signified their agreement and, abandoning their imperfect customs, hastened to adopt those which they had learned to be better.

King Alfred

The following texts relate to King Alfred of Wessex, (849-899). Alfred led the Anglo-Saxon resistance to Danish invasions, united all of England not under Danish rule, and fostered a reform of English political and cultural life.

Alfred's laws were prepared between 871 and 899. Asser had lived and worked with Alfred and had assisted him with his translation of Gregory the Great's Pastoral Care. *Asser used the Anglo-Saxon Chronicle as a source and Einhard's* Life of Charlemagne *as a model. The letter to Edward the Elder shows the importance of Alfred's legal program.*

Source: Dorothy Whitelock, *English Historical Documents* vol. 1.

Dooms

Introduction

I, then, King Alfred, have collected these (dooms) and ordered them to be written down, many of those which our predecessors observed and which were also pleasing to me. And those which were not pleasing to me, by the advice in my *Witan*, I have rejected, ordering them to be observed only as amended. I have not ventured to put in writing much of my own, being uncertain what might please those who shall come after us. So I have here collected the dooms that seemed to me the most just, whether they were from the time of Ine, my kinsman, from that of Offa, king of the Mercians, or from that of Aethelbert, the first of the English to receive baptism; the rest I have discarded. I then, Alfred, king of the West Saxons, have shown these to all my *Witan* who have declared it is the will of all that they be observed...

1. First we direct, what is most necessary, that each man keep carefully his oath and pledge.
1.1. If anyone is wrongfully compelled to either of these, [to promise] treachery against his lord or any illegal aid, then it is better to leave it unfulfilled than to perform it.
1.2. [If, however, he pledges what it is right for him to perform,] and leaves it unfulfilled, let him with humility give his weapons and his possessions into his friends' keeping and be 40 days in prison at a king's estate; let him endure there what penance the bishop prescribes for him, and his kinsmen are to feed him if he has no food himself.
1.3. If he has no kinsmen and has not the food, the king's reeve is to feed him.
1.4. If he has to be forced thither, and will not go otherwise, and he is bound, he is to forfeit his weapons and his possessions.
1.5. If he is killed, he is to lie unpaid for.
1.6. If he escapes before the end of the period, and he is caught, he is to be 40 days in prison, as he should have been before.
1.7. If he gets clear, he is to be outlawed, and to be excommunicated from all the churches of Christ.
1.8. If, however, there is secular surety for him, he is to pay for the breach of surety as the law directs him, and for the breach of pledge as his confessor prescribes for him.

2. If anyone for any guilt flees to any one of the monastic houses to which the king's food-rent belongs, or to some other privileged community which is worthy of honor, he

is to have a respite of three days to protect himself, unless he wishes to be reconciled.

2.1. If during that respite he is molested with slaying or binding or wounding, each of those [who did it] is to make amends according to the legal custom, both with wergild and with fine, and to pay to the community 120 shillings as compensation for the breach of sanctuary, and is to have forfeited his own [claim against the culprit].

3. If anyone violates the king's surety, he is to pay compensation for the charge as the law directs him, and for the breach of the surety with five pounds of pure pennies. The breach of the archbishop's surety or of his protection is to be compensated with three pounds; the breach of the surety or protection of another bishop or an ealdorman is to be compensated with two pounds.

4. If anyone plots against the king's life, directly or by harboring his exiles or his men, he is liable to forfeit his life and all that he owes.

4.1. If he wishes to clear himself, he is to do it by [an oath equivalent to] the king's wergild.

4.2. Thus also we determine concerning all ranks, both *ceorl* and noble: he who plots against his lord's life is to be liable to forfeit his life and all that he owns, or to clear himself by his lord's wergild.

5. Also we determine this sanctuary for every church which a bishop has consecrated: if a man exposed to a vendetta reaches it running or riding, no one is to drag him out for seven days, if he can live in spite of hunger, unless he himself fights [his way] out. If however anyone does so, he is liable to [pay for breach of] the king's protection and of the church's sanctuary—more, if he seizes more from there.

5.1. If the community have more need of their church, he is to be kept in another building, and it is to have no more doors than the church.

5.2. The head of that church is to take care that no one give him food during that period.

5.3. If he himself will hand out his weapons to his foes, they are to keep him for 30 days, and send notice about him to his kinsmen.

5.4. Further sanctuary of the church: if any man has recourse to the church on account of any crime which has not been discovered, and there confesses himself in God's name, it is to be half remitted.

5.5. Whoever steals on Sunday or at Christmas or Easter or on the Holy Thursday in Rogation days; each of those we wish to be compensated doubly, as in the Lenten fast.

6. If anyone steals anything in church, he is to pay the simple compensation and the fine normally belonging to that simple compensation, and the hand with which he did it is to be struck off.

6.1. And if he wishes to redeem the hand, and that is allowed to him, he is to pay in proportion to his wergild.

7. If anyone fights or draws his weapon in the king's hall, and he is captured, it is to be at the king's judgment, whether he will grant him death or life.

7.1. If he escapes, and is afterwards captured, he shall always pay for himself with his wergild, and compensate for the crime, with wergild as with fine, according to what he has done.

8. If anyone brings a nun out of a nunnery without the permission of the king or the bishop, he is to pay 120 shillings, half to the king and half to the bishop and the lord of the church which has the nun.

8.1. If she outlives him who brought her out, she is to have nothing of his inheritance.

8.2. If she bears a child, it is not to have any of that inheritance, any more than the mother.

8.3. If her child is killed, the share of the maternal kindred is to be paid to the king; the paternal kindred are to be given their share.

9. If a woman with child is slain when she is bearing the child, the woman is to be paid for with full payment, and the child at half payment according to the wergild of the father's kin.

9.1. The fine is always to be 60 shillings until the simple compensation rises to 30 shillings; when the simple compensation has risen to that, the fine is afterwards to be 120 shillings.

9.2. Formerly, [the fine] for the stealer of gold, the stealer of stud-horses, the stealer of bees, and many fines, were greater than others; now all are alike, except for the stealer of a man: 120 shillings.

10. If anyone lies with the wife of a man of a twelve-hundred wergild, he is to pay to the husband 120 shillings; to a man of a six-hundred wergild 100 shillings is to be paid; to a man of the *ceorl* class 40 shillings is to be paid.

12. If a man burns or fells the wood of another, without permission, he is to pay for each large tree with five shillings, and afterwards for each, no matter how many there are, with fivepence; and 30 shillings as a fine.

13. If at a common task a man unintentionally kills another [by letting a tree fall on him] the tree is to be given to the kinsmen, and they are to have it from that estate within 30 days, or else he who owns the wood is to have the right to it.

14. If anyone is born dumb, or deaf, so that he cannot deny sins or confess them, the father is to pay compensation for his misdeeds.

15. If anyone fights or draws a weapon in the presence of the archbishop, he is to pay 150 shillings as compensation; if this happens in the presence of another bishop or of an ealdorman, he is to pay 100 shillings compensation.

16. If anyone steals a cow or a brood-mare and drives off a foal or a calf, he is to pay a shilling compensation [for the latter], and for the mothers according to their value.

17. If anyone entrusts to another one of his helpless dependants, and he dies during that time of fostering, he who reared him is to clear himself of guilt, if anyone accuses him of any.

18. If anyone in lewd fashion seizes a nun either by her clothes or her breast without her leave, the compensation is to be double that we have established for a lay person.

18.1. If a betrothed maiden commits fornication, if she is of *ceorl* birth, 60 shillings compensation is to be paid to the surety; and it is to be paid in livestock, cattle [only], and one is not to include in it any slave.

18.2. If she is a woman of a six-hundred wergild, 100 shillings are to be given to the surety.

18.3. If she is a woman of a twelve-hundred wergild, 120 shillings are to be paid to the surety.

19. If anyone lends his weapon to another that he may kill a man with it, they may, if they wish, join him to pay the wergild.

19.1. If they do not join, he who lent the weapon is to pay a third part of the wergild and a third part of the fine.

19.2. If he wishes to clear himself, that in making the loan he was aware of no evil intent, he may do so.

19.3. If a sword-polisher receives another man's weapon to polish it, or a smith a man's tool, they both are to give it back unstained,[1] just as either of them had received it; unless either of them had stipulated that he need not be liable to compensation for it.

20. If anyone entrusts property to another man's monk, without the permission of the monk's lord, and it is lost to him, he who owned it before is to bear the loss.

21. If a priest slays another man, he is to be handed over, and all of the [minster] property which he bought for himself, and the bishop is to unfrock him, when he is to be delivered up out of the minster, unless the lord is willing to settle the wergild on his behalf.

22. If anyone brings up a charge in a public meeting before the king's reeve, and afterwards wishes to withdraw it, he is to make the accusation against a more likely person, if he can; if he cannot, he is to forfeit his compensation.

23. If a dog rends or bites a man to death, [the owner] is to pay six shillings at the first offence; if he gives it food, he is to pay on a second occasion 12 shillings, on a third 30 shillings.
23.1. If in any of these misdeeds the dog is destroyed, nevertheless this compensation is still to be paid.
23.2 If the dog commits more offences, and the owner retains it, he is to pay compensation for such wounds as the dog inflicts, according to the full wergild.

24. If a neat wounds a man, [the owner] is to hand over the neat, or make terms.

25. If anyone rapes a *ceorl*'s slave-woman, he is to pay five shillings compensation to the *ceorl*, and 60 shillings fine.
25.1. If a slave rape a slave-woman, he is to pay by suffering castration.

26 (29). If anyone with a band of men kills an innocent man of a two-hundred wergild, he who admits the slaying is to pay the wergild and the fine, and each man who was in that expedition is to pay 30 shillings as compensation for being in that band.

27 (30). If it is a man of a six-hundred wergild, each man [is to pay] 60 shillings as compensation for being in that band, and the slayer the wergild and full fine.

28 (31). If he is a man of a twelve-hundred wergild, each of them [is to pay] 120 shillings, and the slayer the wergild and the fine.
28.1 (31.1). If a band of men does this and afterwards wishes to deny it[2] on oath, they are all to be accused; and then they are all collectively to pay the wergild, and all one fine, as is accordant to the wergild.

29 (26). If anyone rapes a girl not of age, that is to be the same compensation as for an adult.

30 (27). If a man without paternal kinsmen fights and kills a man, and if then he has maternal kinsmen, those are to pay a third share of the wergild, [and the associates a third; for the third part] he is to flee.[3]
30.1 (27.1). If he has no maternal kinsmen, the associates are to pay half, and for half he is to flee.

31 (28). If anyone kills a man so placed, if he has no kinsmen, he is to pay half to the king, half to the associates.

32. If anyone is guilty of public slander, and it is proved against him, it is to be compensated for with no lighter penalty than the cutting off of his tongue, with the proviso that it be redeemed at no cheaper rate than it is valued in proportion to the wergild.

33. If anyone charges another about a pledge sworn by God, and wishes to accuse him

that he did not carry out any of those [promises] which he gave him, he [the plaintiff] is to pronounce the preliminary oath in four churches, and the other, if he wishes to clear himself, is to do it in twelve churches.

34. Moreover, it is prescribed for traders; they are to bring before the king's reeve in a public meeting the men whom they take up into the country with them, and it is to be established how many of them there are to be; and they are to take with them men whom they can afterwards bring to justice at a public meeting; and whenever it may be necessary for them to have more men out with them on their journey, it is always to be announced, as often as it is necessary for them, to the king's reeve in the witness of the meeting.

35. If anyone binds an innocent *ceorl*, he is to pay him ten shillings compensation.
35.1. If anyone scourges him, he is to pay him 20 shillings compensation.
35.2. If he places him in the stocks, he is to pay him 30 shillings compensation.
35.3. If in insult he disfigures him by cutting his hair, he is to pay him 10 shillings compensation.
35.4. If, without binding him, he cuts his hair like a priest's, he is to pay him 30 shillings compensation.

36. Moreover, it is established; if anyone has a spear over his shoulder, and a man is transfixed on it, the wergild is to be paid without the fine.
36.1. If he transfixed before his eyes, he is to pay the wergild; if anyone accuses him of intention in this act, he is clear himself in proportion to the fine, and by that [oath] do away with the fine,
36.2. if the point is higher than the butt end of the shaft. If they are both level, the point and the butt end, that is to be [considered] without risk.

37. If anyone from one district wishes to seek a lord in another district, he is to do so with the witness of the ealdorman, in whose shire he previously served.
37.1. If he do it without his witness, he who accepts him as his man is to pay 120 shillings compensation; he is, however, to divide it, half to the king in the shire in which the man served previously, half in that into which he has come.
37.2. If he has committed any wrong where he was before, he who now receives him as his man is to pay compensation for it, and 120 shillings to the king as fine.

38. If anyone fights in a meeting in the presence of the king's ealdorman, he is to pay wergild and fine, as it is the law, and before that, 120 shillings to the ealdorman as a fine.
38.1. If he disturbs a public meeting by drawing a weapon, [he is to pay] 120 shillings to the ealdorman as a fine.
38.2. If any of this takes place in the presence of the deputy of the king's ealdorman, or of the king's priest, 30 shillings [is to be paid] as a fine.

39. If anyone fights in the house of a *ceorl*, he is to pay six shillings compensation to the *ceorl*.
39.1. If he draws a weapon and does not fight, it is to be half as much.
39.2. If either of these things happens to a man of a six-hundred wergild, it is to amount to three-fold the compensation to a *ceorl*; [if] to a man of a twelve-hundred wergild, to double that of the man of the six-hundred wergild.
40. Forcible entry into the king's residence shall be 120 shillings; into the archbishop's, 90 shillings; into another bishop's or an ealdorman's, 60 shillings; into that of a man of a twelve-hundred wergild, 30 shillings; into that of a man of a six-hundred wergild, 15 shillings; forcible entry into a *ceorl*'s enclosure, five shillings.
40.1. If any of this happens when the army has been called out, or in the Lenten fast, the compensations are to be doubled.

40.2. If anyone openly neglects the rules of the Church in Lent without permission, he is to pay 120 shillings compensation.

41. The man who holds bookland, which his kinsmen left to him—then we establish that he may not alienate it from his kindred if there is a document or witness [to show] that he was prohibited from doing so by those men who acquired it in the beginning and by those who gave it to him; and that is then to be declared[4] in the witness of the king and of the bishop, in the presence of his kinsmen.

42. Moreover we command: that the man who knows his opponent[5] to be dwelling at home is not to fight before he asks justice for himself.
42.1. If he has sufficient power to surround his opponent and besiege him there in his house, he is to keep him seven days inside and not fight against him, if he will remain inside; and then after seven days, if he will surrender and give up his weapons, he is to keep him unharmed for 30 days, and send notice about him to his kinsmen and his friends.
42.2. If he, however, reaches a church, it is then to be [dealt with] according to the privilege of the church, as we have said before.
42.3. If he [the attacker] has not sufficient power to besiege him in his house, he is to ride to the ealdorman and ask him for support; if he will not give him support, he is to ride to the king, before having recourse to fighting.
42.4. Likewise, if a man run across his opponent, and did not previously know him to be at home, if he will give up his weapons, he is to be kept for 30 days and his friends informed; if he will not give up his weapons, then he may fight against him. If he is willing to surrender, and to give up his weapons, and after that anyone fights against him, he [who does] is to pay wergild or compensation for wounds according to what he has done, and a fine, and is to have forfeited [the right to avenge] his kinsman.
42.5. Moreover we declare that a man may fight on behalf of his lord, if the lord is being attacked, without incurring a vendetta. Similarly the lord may fight on behalf of his man.
42.6. In the same way, a man may fight on behalf of his born kinsman, if he is being wrongfully attacked, except against his lord; that we do not allow.
42.7. And a man may fight without incurring a vendetta if he finds another man with his wedded wife, within closed doors or under the same blanket, or with his legitimate daughter or his legitimate sister, or with his mother who was given as a lawful wife to his father.

43. These days are to be given to all free men, but not to slaves or unfree laborers: 12 days at Christmas, and the day on which Christ overcame the devil, and the anniversary of St Gregory, and seven days at Easter and seven days after, and one day at the feast of St Peter and St Paul, and in harvest-time the whole week before the feast of St Mary, and one day at the feast of All Saints. And the four Wednesdays in the four Ember weeks are to be given to all slaves, to sell them to whomsoever they choose anything of what anyone has given them in God's name, or of what they can earn in any of their leisure moments.[6]

The treaty between Alfred and Guthrum (886-890)

PROLOGUE. This is the peace which King Alfred and King Guthrum and the councillors of all the English race and all the people which is in East Anglia have all agreed on and confirmed with oaths, for themselves and for their subjects, both for the living and those yet unborn, who care to have God's grace or ours.

1. First concerning our boundaries: up the Thames, and then up the Lea, and along the Lea to its source, then in a straight line to Bedford, then up the Ouse to the Watling

Street.

2. This is next, if a man is slain, all of us estimate Englishmen and Dane at the same amount, at eight half-marks[7] of refined gold, except the *ceorl* who occupies rented land, and their [the Danes'] freedmen; these also are estimated at the same amount, both at 200 shillings.

3. And if anyone accuses a king's thegn of manslaughter, if he dares to clear himself by oath, he is to do it with 12 king's thegns; if anyone accuses a man who is less powerful than a king's thegn, he is to clear himself with 12 of his equals and with one king's thegn—and so in every suit which involves more than four mancuses—and if he dare not [clear himself], he is to pay three-fold compensation, according as it is valued.

4. And that each man is to know his warrantor at [the purchase of] men or horses or oxen.

5. And we all agreed on the day when the oaths were sworn, that no slaves nor freemen might go without permission into the army of the Danes, any more than any of theirs to us. But if it happens that from necessity any one of them wishes to have traffic with us, or we with them, for cattle or goods, it is to be permitted on condition that hostages shall be given as a pledge of peace and as evidence so that one may know no fraud is intended.

Old English letter to King Edward the Elder explaining the history of an estate at Fonthill, Wiltshire (899-924, probably early in the reign)

Sire, I will inform you what happened about the land at Fonthill, the five hides which Æthelhelm Higa is claiming. When Helmstan committed the crime of stealing Ethelred's belt, Higa at once began to bring a charge against him, along with other claimants, and wished to win the land from him by litigation. Then he came to me and begged me to intercede for him, because I had stood sponsor to him at his confirmation before he committed that crime. Then—may God repay his soul—he allowed him to be entitled to prove his right against Æthelhelm as regards the land, because of my advocacy and true account. Then he ordered that they should be brought to agreement, and I was one of the men appointed to do it, and Wihtbord and Ælfric, who was then keeper of the wardrobe, and Brihthelm and Wulfhun the Black of Somerton, and Strica and Ubba and more men than I can now name. Then each of them gave his account, and it then seemed to us all that Helmstan should be allowed to come forward with the title-deeds and prove his right to the land, that he had it as Æthelthryth had sold it into Oswulf's possession at a suitable price; and she had told Oswulf that she was entitled to sell it to him because it was her "morning-gift" when she married Æthelwulf. And Helmstan included all this in the oath. And King Alfred had given his signature to Oswulf, when he bought the land from Æthelthryth, that it might thus remain valid, and Edward gave his and Æthelnoth his and Deormod his, and so did each of the men whom one then wished to have. And when we were reconciling them at Wardour, the deed was produced and read, and the signatures were all written on it. Then it seemed to all of us who were at that arbitration that Helmstan was the nearer to the oath on that account.

Then Æthelhelm would not fully assent until we went in to the king and told exactly how we had decided it and why we had decided it; and Æthelhelm stood himself in there with us. And the king stood in the chamber at Wardour—he was washing his hands. When he had finished, he asked Æthelhelm why what we had decided for him did not seem just to him; he said that he could think of nothing more just then than that Helmstan should be allowed to give the oath if he could. I then said that he wished to attempt it, and asked the king to appoint a day for it, and he then did so. And on that appointed day he performed the oath fully. He asked me to help him, and said that he would rather give [the land to me] than that the oath should fail or it ever... Then I said that I would help him to obtain justice, but never to any wrong, on condition that he granted it to me; and he gave me a pledge to that.

And then we rode on that appointed day, I—and Wihtbord rode with me, and Brihthelm rode there with Æthelhelm; and we all heard that he gave the oath in full. Then we all said that it was a closed suit when the sentence had been fulfilled. And, Sire, when will any suit be ended if one can end it neither with money nor with an oath? And if one wishes to change every judgment which King Alfred gave, when shall we have finished disputing? And he then gave me the title-deed just as he had pledged to do, as soon as the oath was given; and I promised him that he might use the land as long as he lived, if he would keep himself out of disgrace.

Then on top of that—I do not know whether it was a year and a half or two years later— he stole the untended oxen at Fonthill, by which he was completely ruined, and drove them to Chicklade, and there he was discovered, and the man who tracked him rescued the traced cattle [?]. Then he fled, and a bramble scratched him in the face; and when he wished to deny it, that was brought in evidence against him. Then Eanwulf Peneard's son, who was the reeve, intervened, and took from him all the property that he owned at Tisbury. I then asked him why he did so, and he said that he was a thief, and the property was adjudged to the king, because he was the king's man. And Ordlaf succeeded to his land; because what he was occupying was held on lease from him, he could not forfeit it. And you then pronounced him an outlaw. Then he sought your father's body, and brought a seal[8] to me, and I was with you at Chippenham. Then I gave the seal to you, and you removed his outlawry and gave him the estate to which he still has withdrawn [?]. And I succeeded to my land, and then in your witness and that of your councillors I gave it to the bishop, five hides in exchange for the land of five hides at Lyddiard. And the bishop and all the community granted me the four hides, and the fifth was subject to tithe. Now, Sire, it is very necessary for me that it may remain as it is now arranged and was before. If it shall be otherwise, then I must and will be satisfied with what seems right to you as a charitable gift.

Endorsement
And Æthelhelm Higa retired from the dispute when the king was at Warminster, in the witness of Ordlaf and Osferth and Odda and Wihtbord and Ælfstan the Bald and Æthelnoth.

Life of King Alfred

To my venerable and most pious lord, ruler of all the Christians of the island of Britain, Alfred, king of the Anglo-Saxons, Asser, lowest of all the servants of God, wishes thousandfold prosperity in both the present and future life, according to his prayers and desires.

Chap. 1. In the year of our Lord's incarnation 849, Alfred, king of the Anglo-Saxons, was born in the royal residence called Wantage, in the shire which is named Berkshire; which shire is thus called from the wood *Berroc*, where box grows very abundantly...[9]

Chap. 2. His mother was called Osburh, a very religious woman, noble in character, noble also by birth; for she was the daughter of Oslac, the renowned cupbearer of King Æthelwulf. This Oslac was by race a Goth, for he was sprung from the Goths and Jutes, namely from the stock of Stuf and Wihtgar, two brothers, and also ealdormen, who received the rule over the Isle of Wight from their uncle King Cerdic and his son Cynric, their cousin. They killed the few British inhabitants of the island whom they could find on it at the place called *Wihtgarabyrig*, for the rest of the inhabitants of the island had either already been killed or had fled as exiles…

Chap. 12. But meanwhile,[10] King Æthelwulf was lingering beyond the sea for some little time, a certain disgraceful thing, contrary to the practice of all Christians, arose to the west of Selwood. For King Æthelbald, son of King Æthelwulf, and Ealhstan, bishop of the church of Somerset, are said to have plotted that King Æthelwulf should not be received again into the kingship when he returned from Rome. This unhappy business, unheard of in all previous ages, very many persons ascribe to the bishop and the ealdorman alone, by whose counsel it is said this deed was done. But there are also many who impute it solely to the royal pride, because that king was stubborn in this affair and in many other wrong acts, as we have heard from certain men's accounts; and this was proved by the outcome of the affair. For as King Æthelwulf was returning from Rome, his son aforesaid, with all his counsellors, or rather conspirators, tried to commit so great a crime as to keep the king out of his own kingdom; but God did not allow it to happen, neither did the nobles of all the Saxon land consent. For, in order that the irremediable danger to the Saxon land from civil war, with father and son at war, or rather with the whole people fighting against one or the other of them, might not grow more fierce and cruel from day to day, the kingdom previously united was by the indescribable forbearance of the father and the assent of all the nobles divided between father and son; and the eastern districts were assigned to the father, the western, on the other hand, to the son. Thus, where the father ought to have reigned by rights, the wicked and stubborn son reigned; for the western part of the Saxon land has always been more important than the eastern.

Chap. 13. When therefore King Æthelwulf arrived from Rome, all the people, as was fitting, rejoiced so greatly at the coming of their lord, that, if he had allowed it, they wished to deprive his stubborn son Æthelbald, with all his counsellors, of any share in the kingdom. But he, as we have said, exercising great forbearance and prudent counsel, lest danger should befall the kingdom, would not have it done thus. And without any opposition or ill-feeling on his nobles' part, he ordered that Judith, daughter of King Charles, whom he had received from her father, was to sit beside him on the royal throne as long as he lived, contrary to the wrongful custom of that nation. For the people of the West Saxons did not allow the queen to sit next the king, or even to be called queen, but "wife of the king".[11]

Chap. 16. Thus King Æthelwulf lived two years after he came back from Rome. During these years, among many other good endeavors in this present life, meditating on his departure on the way of all flesh, he ordered to be written a testamentary, or rather an advisory, letter, so that his sons should not dispute unduly among themselves after their father's death; in this he took care to command in writing in due form, a division of the kingdom between his sons, that is to say the two eldest, of his own inheritance between his sons and daughter and his relations also, and of the money, which he should leave, between the needs of the soul and his sons and also his nobles. Concerning this prudent policy we have decided to record a few examples out of many, for posterity to imitate, namely such as are understood to belong particularly to the necessities of the soul. It is unnecessary to insert the rest, which belong to human dispensation, in this little book, lest by its length it should arouse disgust in the readers and also in those desiring to hear it. For the benefit of his soul then, which he had been zealous to promote in all things from the first flower of his youth, he enjoined that his successors after him until the Day of Judgment were always to supply with food, drink and clothing, one poor man, whether a native or foreigner, from every ten hides throughout all his hereditary land, provided that that land was occupied by men and herds, and had not become waste land. He gave orders also that a great sum of money was every year to be taken to Rome for his soul, namely

300 mancuses, which were to be divided there thus: 100 mancuses in honor of St. Peter, especially for the purchase of oil to fill all the lamps of that apostolic church on Easter eve and likewise at cockcrow, and 100 mancuses in honor of St. Paul on the same terms, for the purchase of oil to fill the lamps on Easter eve and at cockcrow, and 100 mancuses also for the universal apostolic pope.

Chap. 17. But when King Æthelwulf was dead, his son Æthelbald, contrary to God's prohibition and Christian dignity, and also against the usage of all pagans, ascending the bed of his father, married Judith, daughter of Charles, king of the Franks, earning much infamy from all who heard of it; and ruled the government of the kingdom of the West Saxons for two and a half years after his father's death.

Chap. 21. …I think that we should return to what specially incited me to this work; that is to say, that I consider that I should insert briefly in this place the little that has come to my knowledge concerning the character of my revered lord, Alfred, king of the Anglo-Saxons, during his childhood and boyhood.

Chap. 22. Now, he was loved by his father and mother, and indeed by everybody, with a united and immense love, more than all his brothers, and was always brought up in the royal court, and as he passed through his childhood and boyhood he appeared fairer in form than all his brothers, and more pleasing in his looks, his words and his ways. And from his cradle a longing for wisdom before all things and among all the pursuits of this present life, combined with his noble birth, filled the noble temper of his mind; but alas, by the unworthy carelessness of his parents and tutors, he remained ignorant of letters until his twelfth year, or even longer. But he listened attentively to Saxon poems day and night, and hearing them often recited by others committed them to his retentive memory. A keen huntsman, he toiled unceasingly in every branch of hunting, and not in vain; for he was without equal in his skill and good fortune in that art, as also in all other gifts of God, as we have ourselves often seen.

Chap. 23. When, therefore, his mother one day was showing him and his brothers a certain book of Saxon poetry which she held in her hand, she said: "I will give this book to whichever of you can learn it most quickly." And moved by these words, or rather by divine inspiration, and attracted by the beauty of the initial letter of the book, Alfred said in reply to his mother, forestalling his brothers, his elders in years though not in grace: "Will you really give this book to one of us, to the one who can soonest understand and repeat it to you?" And, smiling and rejoicing, she confirmed it, saying: "To him will I give it." Then taking the book from her hand he immediately went to his master, who read it. And when it was read, he went back to his mother and repeated it.

Chap. 24. After this he learnt the daily course, that is, the services of the hours, and then certain psalms and many prayers. He collected these into one book and carried it about with him everywhere in his bosom (as I have myself seen) day and night, for the sake of prayer, through all the changes of this present life, and was never parted from it. But alas, what he principally desired, the liberal arts, he did not obtain according to his wish, because, as he was wont to say, there were at that time no good scholars in all the kingdom of the West Saxons.

Chap. 25. He often affirmed with frequent laments and sighs from the bottom of his heart, that among all his difficulties and hindrances in this present life this was the greatest; that, during the time when he had youth and leisure and aptitude for learning, he had no teachers; but when he was more advanced in years, he did have teachers and writers to some extent, when he was not able to study, because he was harassed, nay, rather disturbed, day and night both with illnesses unknown to all the physicians of this island, and with the cares of the royal office at home and abroad, and also with the invasions of pagans by land and sea. Yet, among all the difficulties of this present life, from infancy unto the present day, he has never abandoned that same insatiable longing, and even now still yearns for it....

Chap. 75. Sons and daughters were born to him by the aforesaid wife, namely Æthelflæd, the first-born, and after her Edward, then Æthelgifu, next Ælfthryth, then Æthelweard, besides those who were snatched away in infancy by an early death....Æthelflæd, when she reached marriageable age, was joined in matrimony to Ethelred, ealdorman of the Mercians. Æthelgifu, devoted to God as a virgin, subjected and consecrated to the rules of the monastic life, entered the service of God. Æthelweard, the youngest, was given over by the divine counsel and the admirable prudence of the king to the pleasures of literary studies, along with almost all the children of noble birth of the whole country, and also many of humble birth, under the diligent care of masters. In that school, books of both languages, Latin, that is, and English, were assiduously read, and they had leisure for writing; so that before they had the strength for manly pursuits, namely hunting and other pursuits which are fitting for noblemen, they were zealous and skilled in the liberal arts. Edward and Ælfthryth were always brought up in the royal court, with great care from their tutors and nurses, and indeed, with great affection from all; and until this day they continue there, showing humility, affability and gentleness to all, whether their countrymen or foreigners, and great obedience to their father. Nor, indeed, are they allowed to live idly and carelessly without a liberal education among the other occupations of this present life which are fitting for nobles; for they have learnt carefully psalms and Saxon books, and especially Saxon poems, and they frequently make use of books.

Chap. 76. Meanwhile the king, in the midst of wars and frequent hindrances of this present life, and also of the raids of the pagans and his daily infirmities of body did not cease, single-handed, assiduously and eagerly with all his might, to govern the kingdom, to practise every branch of hunting, to instruct his goldsmiths and aid his craftsmen, and his falconers, hawkers and dog-keepers, to erect buildings to his own new design more stately and magnificent than had been the custom of his ancestors, to recite Saxon books, and especially to learn by heart Saxon poems, and command others to do so. He also was in the habit of hearing daily the divine office, the Mass, and certain prayers and psalms, and of observing both the day and the night hours, and of visiting churches at night-time, as we have said, in order to pray without his followers knowing. Moreover, he showed zeal for almsgiving, and generosity both to his countrymen and to strangers from all nations, and very great and matchless kindness and pleasantness towards all men, and skill in searching into things unknown. And many Franks, Frisians, men of Gaul, pagans, Welsh, Scots and Bretons willingly submitted to his lordship, both noblemen and men of humble rank; and he ruled them all in accordance with his own honorable nature just like his own people, and loved and honored them, and enriched them with money and rights. Also he was accustomed to listen to the Holy Scripture recited by native clergy, but also, if by chance someone had come from elsewhere, to listen with equal earnestness and attention to prayers along with foreigners. He also loved his bishops and all the ecclesiastical order, his ealdormen and his nobles, his officials and all members of his household, with a wonderful affection. And he himself never ceased among other occupations, day and night, to train their sons, who were being brought up in the royal household, in all good behaviour, and to educate them in letters, loving them no less than his own sons. Yet, as if he had no comfort in all these things and as if he suffered no disquiet from within or without, he complained in anxious sadness by day and night to God and to all who were bound to him in close affection, and lamented with repeated sighs, that Almighty God had not made him skilled in divine wisdom and the liberal arts; emulating in this the pious and most illustrious and rich Solomon, king of the Hebrews, who, despising all present glory and riches, sought first wisdom from God, and also found both, wisdom and present glory, as it is written: "Seek therefore first the kingdom of God and his justice, and all these things shall be granted unto you." But God, who always sees into the inmost thoughts, and prompts our designs and all good desires, and also most amply ordains that good desires may be obtained, and who never prompts anyone to desire well without also ordaining what each man well and justly desires to have, stirred up the king's mind from within, not without; as it is written: "I will hear what the Lord God will speak in me." Whenever he could, he would acquire assistants in his good design, who could help him to the desired wisdom, that he might obtain what he longed for. Forthwith, like the prudent bee, which arises in the summer-time at dawn from its beloved cells and, directing its course in swift flight through the unknown ways of the air, alights upon many and various blossoms of herbs, plants and fruits, and finds and carries home what pleases it most, he turned afar the gaze of his mind, seeking abroad what he had not at home, that is, in his own kingdom.

Chap. 77. And then God, suffering no longer his so good and just complaint, sent for the king's goodwill some consolations, certain lights, as it were, namely Wærferth, bishop of the church of Worcester, a man well versed in the divine Scriptures, who at the king's command first translated clearly and beautifully from Latin into the Saxon language the books of the "Dialogues" of Pope Gregory and his disciple Peter, sometimes giving a paraphrase; and then Plegmund, a Mercian by race, archbishop of the church of Canterbury, a venerable man, endowed with wisdom; also Athelstan and Wærwulf, priests and chaplains, learned men, of Mercian race. King Alfred summoned these four to him from Mercia, and advanced them with great honors and authority in the kingdom of the West Saxons, in addition to those which Archbishop Plegmund and Bishop Wærferth possessed in Mercia. By the teaching and wisdom of all these men, the king's desire was ceaselessly increased and fulfilled. For by day and night, whenever he had any free time, he ordered books to be read before him by such men, nor indeed did he allow himself to be without any of them. Therefore he obtained a knowledge of almost all books, although he could not as yet by himself understand anything from books, for he had not yet begun to read anything.

Chap. 78. But, since in this matter the royal avarice, praiseworthy as it was, was still unsatisfied, he sent messengers across the sea to Gaul to acquire teachers. From there he summoned Grimbald, priest and monk, a venerable man, an excellent singer, most learned in every way in ecclesiastical studies and the divine Scriptures and adorned with all good qualities; and also John, likewise a priest and monk, a man of very keen intelligence and most learned in all branches of the art of literature enriched, and skilled in many other arts. By their teaching the king's mind was much enriched; he endowed and honored them with great authority.

Chap. 79. At that time I also was summoned by the king, and came to the Saxon land from the western and farthest parts of Wales, and when I had decided to come to him through great tracts of country. I reached the province of the South Saxons, which is called Sussex in the Saxon language, led by guides of that race. There I first saw the king in the royal residence which is called Dean. And when I had been kindly received by him, among other topics of conversation, he asked me pressingly to devote myself to his service and to be a member of his court, and to give up for his sake all that I possessed to the north and west of the Severn; and he promised also to give me a greater recompense. And this he did. I replied that I could not make such a promise carelessly and rashly. For it seemed wrong to me to desert for the sake of any worldly honor and power those so holy places in which I had been reared and educated, tonsured, and finally ordained, unless by force and compulsion. To which he said: "If you cannot accede to this, at least grant to me half of your service, so that you may be six months with me and as many in Wales." To which I replied thus: "I cannot promise this easily and rashly without the counsel of my friends." But indeed, since I realized that he desired my services, though I knew not why, I promised that I would return to him six months later, if my life were spared, with such a reply as might be advantageous for me and mine, and acceptable to him. And when this reply seemed good to him, and I had given a pledge to return at the appointed time, on the fourth day we rode away from him and returned to our own land. But when we had left him, a violent fever laid hold of me in the city of Caer and I was grievously afflicted with it day and night for 12 months and a week without any hope of life. And when I did not come to him at the appointed time, as I had promised, he sent letters to me, which explained to him the reason for my delay and declared that I would perform what I had promised if I could recover from that sickness. Therefore, when the sickness left me, I devoted myself, as I had promised the king, to his service, by the advice and permission of all our people, for the benefit of that holy place and all dwelling in it, on this condition, that I should spend six months of every year with him, either, if I could, six months at a time, or otherwise by turns spend three months in Wales and three in the Saxon land, and that land should be benefited by the teaching of St. David, yet in every case in proportion to our strength. For our brethren hoped that they would suffer fewer tribulations and injuries from King Hyfaidd—who often plundered that monastery and the diocese of St. David's, sometimes by driving out the bishops who were in charge of it, as he at one time among these drove out Archbishop Nobis, my kinsman, and me myself—if I were to come to the notice and friendship of that king by any kind of agreement.

Chap. 80. For at that time, and for a long time before, all the districts of the southern part of Wales belonged to King Alfred, and still belong to him; for Hyfaidd with all the inhabitants of the region of Dyfed, compelled by the power of the six sons of Rhodri, had submitted to the royal overlordship; also Hywel, son of Rhys, king of Glywyssing, and Brochwel and Ffernfael, the sons of Merwig, kings of Gwent, compelled by the might and tyranny of Ealdorman Ethelred and the Mercians, of their own accord besought the same king that he would be their lord and protector against their enemies. Also Elise, son of Tewdwr, king of Brecknock, forced by the power of the same sons of Rhodri, with his brothers, finally deserted the friendship of the Northumbrians, from which they had no good, but only injury, and came to the king's presence earnestly beseeching his friendship. And when he had been honorably received by the king, and been accepted by him as his son from the hands of the bishop at confirmation, and been enriched by great gifts, he submitted with all his followers to the king's overlordship, on such terms that he would be obedient to the king in all things, just like Ethelred with the Mercians.

Chap. 81. Nor did they all obtain the king's friendship in vain. For those who desired to increase their earthly power, obtained this; those who desired money, obtained money; those who desired friendship, gained friendship; those who desired both, received both. And all had love and guardianship and protection from every side, in as far as the king with his people could defend himself. When, therefore, I came to him at the royal residence which is called *Leonaford*, I was honorably received by him, and remained with him in his court on that occasion for eight months, during which I read to him whatever books he wished and which we had at hand. For it is his most usual habit either himself to read books aloud or to listen to others who read them, day and night, in the midst of all other occupations of mind and body. And when I had frequently asked his permission to return, and could by no means obtain it, at length when I had made up my mind absolutely to demand his permission, I was summoned to him in the early morning of the eve of our Lord's Nativity, and he delivered to me two letters, in which there was a detailed list of all the things belonging to two monasteries, which in Saxon are called Congresbury and Banwell, and on that same day he delivered to me those two monasteries with everything that was in them, and a very costly silk robe, and a strong man's load of incense, adding these words, that he did not give me these small things because he was unwilling to give greater later on. Indeed at a later time he unexpectedly gave me Exeter, with all the diocese belonging to it, in Saxon territory and in Cornwall, besides innumerable daily gifts of all kinds of earthly riches, which it would be tedious to enumerate here lest it should cause weariness to the readers. But do not let anyone think that I have mentioned such gifts in this place out of any vain glory or in flattery, or for the sake of gaining greater honor; for I call God to witness that I have not done so, but only to make clear to those who do not know, how profuse is his generosity. Then at once he gave me leave to ride to those two monasteries, which were filled with all good things, and thence to return to my own country.

Chap. 87. Also in that same year (887) the oft-mentioned Alfred, king of the Anglo-Saxons, first began by the divine inspiration both to read (Latin) and translate on one and the same day. But, that this may be made clear to those ignorant of it, I will take care to explain the reason for this late start.

Chap. 88. For when we were both sitting one day in the royal chamber talking as was our wont, on all sorts of subjects, it happened that I read to him a passage from a certain book. And when he had listened to it intently with both his ears, and pondered it carefully in the depths of this mind, he suddenly showed me a little book, which he constantly carried in the depths of his bosom, in which were contained the daily course and certain psalms and prayers which he had read in his youth, and he ordered me to write that passage in the same little book. And I, hearing this and perceiving in part his eagerness of mind and also his devout wish to study the divine wisdom, gave great thanks to Almighty God, although silently, with hands outstretched to heaven, who had planted so great devotion for the study of wisdom in the king's heart. But when I found no vacant space in that little book, in which I could write the passage - for it was completely filled with various matters - I hesitated for a little while, principally that I might provoke the king's fine understanding to a greater knowledge of the divine testimonies. And when he urged me to write it as quickly as possible I said to him: "Are you willing that I should write this passage on a separate leaf? For we do not know whether we may not at some time find one or more such passages which may please you; and if this happens unexpectedly, we shall be glad to have kept it apart." And hearing this, he said that it was a good plan. When I heard this I was glad, and hastened to prepare a quire, at the beginning of which I wrote the passage he had commended; and on the same day I wrote by his command no fewer than three other passages which pleased him, in the same quire, as I had foretold. And henceforth as we daily talked together, and searching to this end found other equally pleasing passages, that quire became full; and rightly, as it is written: "The just man builds upon a small foundation and by degrees passes to greater things." Like a most productive bee, travelling far and wide over the marshes in its quest, he eagerly and unceasingly collected many various flowers of Holy Scripture, with which he densely stored the cells of his mind.

Chap. 89. Now, once that passage had been written, he straightway was eager to read and to translate into the Saxon language, and hence to instruct many others. And just as we should learn from that happy thief, who knew the Lord Jesus Christ, his Lord, and indeed the Lord of all, hanging beside him on the venerable gallows of the Holy Cross; for with humble prayers, bending on him his bodily eyes, because he could do nothing else, being all fixed with nails, he called with a lowly voice: "Christ, remember me when thou shalt come into my kingdom", and on the gallows first began to learn the rudiments of the Christian faith; the king likewise, though in a different way, for he was set with royal power, presumed by the instigation of God to begin his first lessons in holy writings on the festival of St. Martin and he (began) to learn those flowers, which had been gathered from various masters, and to bring them all into the compass of one book although in no order, as they came to hand, until it grew almost to the size of a psalter. This book he used to call his 'enchiridion', that is, 'hand-book', because he was most careful to have it at hand by day and night. And he found, as he then said, no little comfort in it....

Chap. 91. The king was pierced by many nails of tribulation, although placed in royal power. For, from his twentieth till his forty-fifth year, in which he now is, he has been constantly afflicted with a most severe attack of an unknown malady, so that he has not a single hour's peace, in which he is not either suffering that infirmity or driven almost to despair by apprehension of it. Moreover he was troubled, and with good reason, by the constant inroads of foreign peoples, which he constantly sustained by land and sea without any peaceful interval. What shall I say of his frequent expeditions and battles against the pagans and the incessant cares of government? What of his daily (solicitude) for the nations, which dwell from the Tyrrhenian Sea to the farthest end of Ireland? Indeed, we have even seen and read letters sent to him along with gifts by the patriarch Elias. What of the cities and towns he restored, and the others, which he built where none had been before? Of the buildings made by his instructions with gold and silver, beyond compare? Of the royal halls and chambers constructed admirably in stone and timber at his command? Of the royal residences in stone, moved at the royal command from their ancient sites and beautifully erected in more suitable places? And what of the great trouble and vexation (besides his illness) he had with his own people, who would voluntarily submit to little or no labor for the common needs of the kingdom? Yet, just as a skillful pilot strives to bring his ship, laden with great riches, to the longed-for safe harbor of his native land, though nearly all his sailors are worn out; he, upheld by divine aid, would not allow the helm of the kingdom he had once received to totter or waver, though set alone in the midst of the raging and manifold whirlpools of this present life. For he most wisely brought over and bound to his own will and to the common profit of the whole kingdom his bishops and ealdormen and nobles, and the thegns who were dearest to him, and also his reeves, to whom, after God and the king, the control of the kingdom seems rightly to belong, by gently instructing, flattering, urging, commanding them, and, after long patience, by punishing sharply the disobedient, and by showing in every way hatred of vulgar folly and obstinacy. But if among these exhortations of the king, his orders were not carried out because of the slackness of the people, or things begun late in time of need were unfinished and of no profit to those who undertook them - for I may tell of fortresses ordered by him and still not begun, or begun too late to be brought to completion - and enemy forces broke in by land or sea, or, as often happened, on every side, the opponents of the royal ordinances then were ashamed with a vain repentance when on the brink of ruin. For by the witness of Scripture I call that repentance vain, by which numberless men sorrow when afflicted with grievous loss for the many ill-deeds they have committed. But though - alas, the pity of it - they are sadly afflicted through this, and moved to tears by the loss of their fathers, wives, children, servants, slaves, handmaids, their labors and all their goods, what help is hateful repentance, when it cannot succor their slain kinsmen, nor redeem captives from odious captivity, nor even can it help themselves, who have escaped, seeing that they have nought with which to sustain their own lives? Grievously afflicted, they then repent with too late repentance, and regret that they have carelessly neglected the king's orders, and with one voice praise the king's wisdom, and promise to fulfill with all their strength what they have before refused, that is, with regard to the building of fortresses and the other things for the common profit of the whole kingdom.

Chap. 92. I do not consider it profitable to pass over in this place his vow and most well-thought-out scheme, which he was never able to put aside by any means either in prosperity or adversity. For when in his usual manner he was meditating on the needs of his soul, among other good acts in which he was actively engaged by day and night, he ordered the foundation of two monasteries; one for monks in the place which is called Athelney, which is surrounded on all sides by very great swampy and impassable marshes, so that no one can approach it by any means except in punts or by a bridge which has been made with laborious skill between two fortresses. At the western end of this bridge a very strong fort has been placed of most beautiful workmanship by the king's command. In this monastery he collected monks of various races from every quarter, and set them therein.

Chap. 93. For at first he had no noble or freeman of his nation who would of his own accord enter the monastic life - apart from children, who by reason of their tender age could not yet choose good or refuse evil - for indeed for many years past the desire for the monastic life had been utterly lacking in all that people, and also in many other nations, although there still remains many monasteries founded in that land, but none properly observing the rule of this way of life, I know not why; whether on account of the onslaughts of foreigners, who very often have invaded by land or sea, or on account of the nation's too great abundance of riches of every kind, which I am much more inclined to think the reason for that contempt of the monastic life. For this reason he sought to gather together monks of different race in that monastery.

Chap. 94. First, he appointed John, priest and monk, by race an Old Saxon, as abbot, and then some priests and deacons from across the sea. But when he still had not with these the number he wanted, he also procured many of that same Gallic race, some of whom, being children, he ordered to be educated in that same monastery, and to be raised to the monastic order at a later time. In that monastery I also saw one of pagan race, brought up there and wearing the monastic habit, quite a young man, and not the lowest among them. FN28

Chap. 98. The aforesaid king also ordered to be built another monastery by the east gate of Shaftesbury, as a habitation for nuns, over which he appointed as abbess his own daughter, Æthelgifu, a virgin dedicated to God. And along with her dwell many other noble nuns serving God in the monastic life in the same monastery. He richly endowed these two monasteries with estates and wealth of all kinds.

Chap. 99. When all this was thus settled, he meditated according to his usual practice what he could still add that would further his pious intentions. Things wisely begun and profitably conceived were profitably continued. For long ago he had heard that it was written in the law that the Lord had promised to repay his tithe many times over, and had faithfully kept his promise. Inspired by this example and wishing to excel the practice of his predecessors, the pious thinker promised that he would faithfully and devoutly with all his heart give to God a half part of his service, both by day and night, and also the half part of all the riches which reached him every year by moderate and just acquisition; and this resolve he strove to carry out skillfully and wisely in as far as human discernment can observe and keep it. But, as was his habit, in order that he might carefully avoid what we are warned against in another place in Holy Scripture: "If thou offer aright, but dost not divide aright, thou sinnest", he considered how he might rightly divide what he willingly devoted to God, and, as Solomon says: "The heart of the king" - that is his counsel - "is in the hand of the Lord." Taking counsel from on high, he ordered his officers first to divide into two equal parts all his annual revenue.

Chap. 100. When this was done, he adjudged that the first part should be devoted to secular uses, and ordered that this should be further divided into three parts. The first of these shares he bestowed annually on his fighting men, and also on his noble thegns who dwelt by turns in his court, serving him in many offices. Now the royal household was always managed in three relays; for the followers of the aforesaid king were prudently divided into three companies, so that the first company resided one month in the royal court on duty day and night, and when the month was over and another company arrived, the first went home and remained there for two months, each seeing to his own affairs. So also the second company, when its month was over and the third company arrived, returned home and stayed there for two months. And also the third, having finished one month of service, went home when the first company arrived, to remain there for two months. And by this arrangement the administration of the royal court is taken in turn at all times of this present life.

Chap. 101. Thus, then, did he grant the first of the three aforesaid shares to such men, to each, however, according to his rank and also to his office; and the second to the craftsmen, whom he had with him in almost countless number, collected and procured from many races, who were men skilled in every kind of earthly craft; and the third share to strangers from every race, who flocked to him from places far and near asking him for money, and even to those who did not ask, to each according to his rank. He gave in a praiseworthy manner with a wonderful liberality, and cheerfully, since it is written: "The Lord loveth a cheerful giver."

Chap. 102. But the second part of all his wealth, which came to him every year from revenue of every kind, and was paid into his treasury, he devoted, as we said a little while back, with all his will, to God, and ordered his officials to divide it most carefully into four equal parts, in such a way, that the first part of this division was to be prudently dispended on the poor of every race who came to him. He used to say in this connexion, that as far as human discretion could ensure it, the saying of the holy Pope Gregory ought to be observed, in which he made a wise observation about the division of alms, saying thus: "Do not give little to whom you should give much, nor much to whom you should give little, nor nothing to whom you should give something, nor anything to whom you should give nothing." And the second part he gave to the two monasteries which he himself had built, and to those serving in them, about which we spoke more fully a little way back; and the third to a school which he had collected very zealously from many nobles of his own race and also boys not of noble birth; and the fourth part to the neighboring monasteries throughout the Saxon kingdom and Mercia. And in some years he also either made gifts, according to his means, to the churches in Wales and Cornwall, Old Brittany, Northumbria, and sometimes even in Ireland, in turn, and to the servants of God dwelling in them, or else he proposed to give them later on, provided his life and prosperity continued.

Chap. 105. When these things had been completely set in order, since he desired as he had vowed to God, to preserve half his service, and to increase it further, in as far as his capacity and his means, and indeed his infirmity, permitted, he showed himself a minute inquirer into the truth of judgments, and this especially because of his care for the poor, on whose behalf he exerted himself wonderfully by day and by night in the midst of his other duties in this present life. For except for him alone, the poor had no helpers throughout that kingdom, or indeed very few; since almost all the magnates and nobles of that land had turned their minds more to the things of this world than to the things of God; indeed, in the things of this world each regarded more his own private advantage than the common good.

Chap. 106. Also he gave attention to judgments for the benefit of his nobles and common people, for in the assemblies of the ealdormen and the reeves they disagreed among themselves, so that hardly one of them would allow to be valid whatever had been judged by the ealdormen or reeves. And compelled by this perverse and obstinate dissension, all desired to submit to the king's judgment, and both parties quickly hastened to do so. But yet anyone who knew that on his side some injustice had been committed in that suit, was unwilling to approach the judgment of such a judge of his own accord, but only against his will, though compelled to come by force of law and covenant. For he knew that there he could not quickly conceal any part of his ill-doing, and no wonder, since the king was in truth a most skilled investigator into the exercise of justice, as in all other matters. For he shrewdly looked into almost all the judgments of his whole country which were made in his absence, to see whether they were just or unjust, and if truly he could discover any wrong in those judgments, he would on his own authority mildly inquire of those judges, either in person or by some of his faithful followers, why they had given so wrong a judgment, whether from ignorance or out of any kind of ill-will, that is, for love or fear of one party, or hatred of the other, or even for greed of anyone's money. And then, if those judges admitted that they had given such judgments because they knew no better in those cases, he wisely and moderately reproved their inexperience and folly, saying thus: "I am amazed at your presumption, that you have by God's favour and mine assumed the office and status of wise men, but have neglected the study and practice of wisdom. I command you therefore either to resign on the spot the exercise of the worldly authority you hold, or to apply yourselves much more zealously to the study of wisdom." When they had heard these words, the ealdormen and reeves hastened to turn themselves with all their might to the task of learning justice, for they were terrified and as if they had been severely punished; so that in a marvellous fashion almost all the ealdormen, reeves and thegns, who had been untaught from their childhood, gave themselves to the study of letters, preferring thus toilsomely to pursue this unaccustomed study rather than resign the exercise of their authority. But if anyone were unable to make progress in learning to read, either by reason of his age or the too great slowness of an unpractised mind, he ordered his son, if he had one, or some other kinsman, or even, if he had no one else, his own man, free man or slave, whom he had long before made to learn to read, to read Saxon books to him day and night whenever he had any leisure. And, greatly sighing from the bottom of their hearts that they had not applied themselves to such studies in their youth, they considered the youth of this age happy, who could have the good fortune to be trained in the liberal arts, accounting themselves unhappy indeed, since they had neither learnt in their youth, nor were able to learn in their old age, though they ardently desired it. But we have dealt on this quickness of old and young to learn to read to add to knowledge of the aforesaid king.

Anglo-Saxon Chronicle

865   In this year the heathen army encamped on Thanet and made peace with the people of Kent. And the people of Kent promised them money for that peace. And under cover of that peace and promise of money the army stole away inland by night and ravaged all east Kent.

866   In this year Ethelbert's brother Ethelred succeeded to the kingdom of the West Saxons. And the same year a great heathen army came into England and took up winter quarters in East Anglia; and there they were supplied with horses, and the East Angles made peace with them.

867   In this year the army went from East Anglia to Northumbria, across the Humber estuary to the city of York. And there was great civil strife going on in that people, and they had deposed their king Osbert and taken a king with no hereditary right, Ælla. And not until late in the year did they unite sufficiently to proceed to fight the raiding army; and nevertheless they collected a large army and attacked the enemy in York, and broke into the city; and some of them got inside, and an immense slaughter was made of the Northumbrians, some inside and some outside, and both kings were killed, and the survivors made peace with the enemy. And the same year Bishop Ealhstan died, and he had held the bishopric of Sherborne for 50 years, and his body is buried in the cemetery there.

868   In this year the same army went into Mercia to Nottingham and took up winter quarters there. And Burgred, king of the Mercians, and his councillors asked Ethelred, king of the West Saxons, and his brother Alfred to help him to fight against the army. They then went with the army of the West Saxons into Mercia to Nottingham, and came upon the enemy in that fortress and besieged them there. There occurred no serious battle there, and the Mercians made peace with the enemy.

869   In this year the raiding army returned to the city of York, and stayed there one year.

870   In this year the raiding army rode across Mercia into East Anglia, and took up winter quarters at Thetford. And that winter King Edmund fought against them, and the Danes had the victory, and killed the king, and conquered all the land. And the same year Archbishop Ceolnoth died.

871   In this year the army came into Wessex to Reading, and three days later two Danish earls rode farther inland. Then Ealdorman Æthelwulf encountered them at Englefield, and fought against them there and had the victory, and one of them, whose name was Sidroc, was killed there. Then four days later King Ethelred and his brother Alfred led a great army to Reading and fought against the army; and a great slaughter was made on both sides and Ealdorman Æthelwulf was killed, and the Danes had possession of the battle-field.

And four days later King Ethelred and his brother Alfred fought against the whole army at Ashdown; and the Danes were in two divisions: in the one were the heathen kings Bagsecg and Healfdene, and in the other were the earls. And then King Ethelred fought against the kings' troop, and King Bagsecg was slain there; and Ethelred's brother Alfred fought against the earls' troop, and there were slain Earl Sidroc the Old, and Earl Sidroc the Younger and Earl Osbearn, Earl Fræna and Earl Harold; and both enemy armies were put to flight and many thousands were killed, and they continued fighting until night.

And a fortnight later King Ethelred and his brother Alfred fought against the army at Basing, and there the Danes had the victory. And two months later, King Ethelred and his brother Alfred fought against the army at *Meretun*, and they were in two divisions; and they put both to flight and were victorious far on into the day; and there was a great slaughter on both sides; and the Danes had possession of the battle-field. And Bishop Heahmind was killed there and many important men. And after this battle a great summer army came to Reading. And afterwards, after Easter, King Ethelred died, and he had reigned five years, and his body is buried at Wimborne minster.

Then his brother Alfred, the son of Æthelwulf, succeeded to the kingdom of the West Saxons. And a month later King Alfred fought with a small force against the whole army at Wilton and put it to flight far on into the day; and the Danes had possession of the battle-field. And during that year nine general engagements were fought against the Danish army in the kingdom south of the Thames, besides the expeditions which the king's brother Alfred and [single] ealdormen and king's thegns often rode on, which were not counted. And that year nine (Danish) earls were killed and one king. And the West Saxons made peace with the enemy that year.

872   In this year the army went from Reading to London, and took up winter quarters there; and then the Mercians made peace with the army.

873   In this year the army went into Northumbria, and it took up winter quarters at Torksey in Lindsey; and then the Mercians made peace with the army.

In this year the army took up winter quarters at Torksey.

874   In this year the army went from Lindsey to Repton and took up winter quarters there, and drove King Burgred across the sea, after he had held the kingdom 22 years. And they conquered all that land. And he went to Rome and settled there; and his body is buried in the church of St. Mary in the English quarter. And the same year they gave the kingdom of the Mercians to be held by Ceolwulf, a foolish king's thegn; and he swore oaths to them and gave hostages, that it should be ready for them on whatever day they wished to have it, and he would be ready, himself and all who would follow him, at the enemy's service.

875   In this year the army left Repton: Healfdene went with part of the army into Northumbria and took up winter quarters by the River Tyne. And the army conquered the land and often ravaged among the Picts and the Strathclyde Britons; and the three kings, Guthrum, Oscetel and Anwend, went from Repton to Cambridge with a great force, and stayed there a year. And that summer King Alfred went out to sea with a naval force, and fought against the crews of seven ships, and captured one ship and put the rest to flight.

876   In this year the enemy army slipped past the army of the West Saxons into Wareham; and then the king made peace with the enemy and they gave him hostages, who were the most important men next to their king in the army, and swore oaths to him on the holy ring[12]—a thing which they would not do before for any nation—that they would speedily leave his kingdom. And then under cover of that, they—the mounted army—stole by night away from the English army to Exeter. And that year Healfdene shared out the land of the Northumbrians, and they proceeded to plough and to support themselves.

877   In this year the enemy army from Wareham came to Exeter; [and the naval force sailed west along the coast] and encountered a great storm at sea, and 120 ships were lost at Swanage. And King Alfred rode after the mounted army with the English army as far as Exeter, but could not overtake them [before they were in the fortress where they could not be reached]. And they gave him hostages there, as many as he wished to have, and swore great oaths and then kept a firm peace. Then in the harvest season the army went away into Mercia and shared out some of it, and gave some to Ceolwulf.

878   In this year in midwinter after twelfth night the enemy army came stealthily to Chippenham, and occupied the land of the West Saxons and settled there, and drove a great part of the people across the sea, and conquered most of the others; and the people submitted to them, except King Alfred. He journeyed in difficulties through the woods and fen-fastnesses with a small force.

And the same winter the brother of Ivar and Healfdene was in the kingdom of the West Saxons [in Devon], with 23 ships. And he was killed there and 840 men of his army with him. And there was captured the banner which they called 'Raven'.

And afterwards at Easter, King Alfred with a small force made a stronghold at Athelney, and he and the section of the people of Somerset which was nearest to it proceeded to fight from that stronghold against the enemy. Then in the seventh week after Easter he rode to 'Egbert's stone' east of Selwood, and there came to meet him all the people of Somerset and of Wiltshire and of that part of Hampshire which was on this side of the sea, and they rejoiced to see him. And then after one night he went from that encampment to Iley, and after another night to Edington, and there fought against the whole army and put it to flight, and pursued it as far as the fortress, and stayed there a fortnight. And then the enemy gave him preliminary hostages and great oaths that they would leave his kingdom, and promised also that their king should receive baptism, and they kept their promise. Three weeks later King Guthrum with 30 of the men who were the most important in the army came [to him] at Aller, which is near Athelney, and the king stood sponsor to him at his baptism there; and the unbinding of the chrism[13] took place at Wedmore. And he was twelve days with the king, and he honored him and his companions greatly with gifts.

879   In this year the army went from Chippenham to Cirencester, and stayed there for one year. And the same year a band of vikings assembled and encamped at Fulham by the Thames. And the same year there was an eclipse of the sun for one hour of the day.

880   In this year the army went from Cirencester into East Anglia, and settled there and shared out the land. And the same year the army which had encamped at Fulham went overseas into the Frankish empire to Ghent and stayed there for a year.

881   In this year the army went farther inland into the Frankish empire, and the Franks fought against them; and the Danish army provided itself with horses after that

battle.

882   In this year the army went farther into the Frankish empire along the Meuse, and stayed there a year. And the same year King Alfred went out with ships to sea and fought against four crews of Danish men, and captured two of the ships—and the men were killed who were on them—and two crews surrendered to him. And they had great losses in killed or wounded before they surrendered.

883   In this year the army went up the Scheldt to Condé, and stayed there for a year. And Pope Marinus sent some wood of the Cross to King Alfred. And that same year Sigelm and Athelstan took to Rome the alms [which King Alfred had promised thither], and also to India to St. Thomas and St. Bartholomew, when the English were encamped against the enemy army at London; and there, by the grace of God, their prayers were well answered after that promise.

884   In this year the army went up the Somme to Amiens, and stayed there a year.

885   In this year the aforesaid army divided into two [one part going east], the other part to Rochester, where they besieged the city and made other fortifications round themselves. And nevertheless the English defended the city until King Alfred came up with his army. Then the enemy went to their ships and abandoned their fortification, and they were deprived of their horses there, and immediately that same summer they went back across the sea. That same year King Alfred sent a naval force from Kent into East Anglia. Immediately they came into the mouth of the Stour and they encountered 16 ships of vikings and fought against them, and seized all the ships and killed the men. When they turned homeward with the booty, they met a large naval force of vikings and fought against them on the same day, and the Danes had the victory.

That same year before Christmas, Charles, king of the Franks, died. He was killed by a boar, and a year previously his brother, who had also held the western kingdom, had died. They were both sons of Louis, who died in the year of the eclipse of the sun. He was the son of that Charles[14] whose daughter Æthelwulf, king of the west Saxons, had married. That same year a large naval force assembled among the Old Saxons and twice in the year there occurred a great battle, and the Saxons had the victory, and with them there were the Frisians.

That same year Charles[15] succeeded to the western kingdom and to all the kingdom on this side of the Mediterranean and beyond this sea, as his great-grandfather[16] had held it, except for Brittany. This Charles was the son of Louis,[17] the brother of the Charles who was the father of Judith whom King Æthelwulf married; and they were sons of Louis.[18] This Louis was the son of the old Charles.[19] This Charles was Pippin's son.

That same year there died the good pope, Marinus, who had freed from taxation the English quarter at the request of Alfred, king [of the West Saxons]. And he had sent him great gifts, including part of the Cross on which Christ suffered.

And that same year the Danish army in East Anglia violated their peace with King Alfred.

886   In this year the Danish army which had gone east went west again, and then up the Seine, and made their winter quarters there at the town of Paris.

That same year King Alfred occupied London; and all the English people that were not under subjection to the Danes submitted to him. And he then entrusted the borough to the control of Ealdorman Ethelred.[20]

887   In this year the Danish army went up past the bridge at Paris, then up along the Seine to the Marne, and then up the Marne as far as Chézy, and stayed there and in the Yonne area, spending two winters in those two places.

And the same year Charles,[21] king of the Franks, died; and six weeks before he died his brother's son Arnulf had deprived him of the kingdom. The kingdom was then divided into five, and five kings were consecrated to it. It was done, however, with Arnulf's consent and they said that they would hold it under him, for not one of them was born to it in the male line but him alone. Arnulf then lived in the land east of the Rhine, and Rudolf[22] succeeded to the middle kingdom and Odo[23] to the western portion; and Berengar[24] and Guido[25] to Lombardy and the lands on that side of the Alps; and they held it with much discord and fought two general engagements, and ravaged the land again and again, and each repeatedly drove out the other.

And the same year in which the army went up beyond the bridge at Paris, Ealdorman Æthelhelm took to Rome the alms of King Alfred and the West Saxons.

888   In this year Ealdorman Beocca took to Rome the alms of the West Saxons and of King Alfred. And Queen Æthelswith, who was King Alfred's sister, died, and her body is buried in Pavia. And the same year Archbishop Ethelred and Ealdorman Æthelwold died in the same month.

889   There was no expedition to Rome in this year, but King Alfred sent two couriers with letters.

890   In this year Abbot Beornhelm took to Rome the alms of the West Saxons and of King Alfred. And the northern king, Guthrum, whose baptismal name was Athelstan, died. He was King Alfred's godson, and he lived in East Anglia and was the first[26] to settle that land.

And the same year the Danish army went from the Seine to St. Lô, which lies between Brittany and France; and the Bretons fought against them and had the victory, and drove them into a river and drowned many of them.

891   In this year the Danish army went east, and King Arnulf with the East Franks, the Saxons and Bavarians fought against the mounted force before the ships arrived, and put it to flight.

And three Scots came to King Alfred in a boat without any oars from Ireland, which they had left secretly, because they wished for the love of God to be in foreign lands, they cared not where. The boat in which they travelled was made of two and a half hides, and they took with them enough food for seven days. And after seven days they came to land in Cornwall, and went immediately to King Alfred. Their names were as follows: Dubslane, Machbethu and Maelinnum. And Swifneh, the best scholar among the Scots, died.

And the same year after Easter, at the Rogation days or before, there appeared the star which is called in Latin *cometa*. Some men say that it is in English the long-haired star, for there shines a long ray from it, sometimes on one side, sometimes on every side.

892   In this year the great Danish army, which we have spoken about before, went back from the eastern kingdom westward to Boulogne, and they were provided with ships there, so that they crossed in one journey, horses and all, and then came up into the estuary of the Lympne with 200 [and 50] ships. That estuary is in East Kent, at the east end of that great wood which we called *Andred*. The wood is from east to west 120 miles long, or longer, and 30 miles broad. The river, of which we spoke before, comes out of the Weald. They rowed their ships up the river as far as the Weald, four miles from the mouth of the estuary, and there they stormed a fortress. Inside that fortification there were a few peasants, and it was only half made.

Then immediately afterwards Hæsten[27] came with 80 ships up the Thames estuary and made himself a fortress at Milton, and the other army made one at Appledore.

893   In this year, that was twelve months after the Danes had built the fortress in the eastern kingdom, the Northumbrians and East Angles had given King Alfred oaths, and the East Angles had given six preliminary hostages; and yet, contrary to those pledges, as often as the other Danish armies went out in full force, they went either with them or on their behalf. And then King Alfred collected his army, and advanced to take up a position between the two enemy forces, where he had the nearest convenient site with regard both to the fort in the wood and the fort by the water, so that he could reach either army, if they chose to come into the open country. Then they went afterwards along the Weald in small bands and mounted companies, by whatever side it was then undefended by the English army. And also they were sought by other bands, almost every day, either by day or by night, both from the English army and from the boroughs. The king had divided his army into two, so that always half its men were at home, half on service, apart from the men who guarded the boroughs. The enemy did not all come out of those encampments more than twice: once when they first landed, before the English force was assembled, and once when they wished to leave those encampments. Then they captured much booty, and wished to carry it north across the Thames into Essex, to meet the ships. Then the English army intercepted them and fought against them at Farnham, and put the enemy to flight and recovered the booty. And the Danes fled across the Thames where there was no ford, and up along the Colne on to an islet. Then the English forced besieged them there for as long as their provisions lasted; but they had completed their term of service and used up their provisions, and the king was then on the way there with the division which was serving with him. When he was on his way there and the other English army was on its way home, and the Danes were remaining behind there because their king had been wounded in the battle, so that they could not move him, those Danes who lived in Northumbria and East Anglia collected some hundred ships, and went south around the coast [And some 40 ships went north around the coast] and besieged a fortress on the north coast of Devon, and those who had gone south besieged Exeter.

When the king heard that, he turned west towards Exeter with the whole army, except for a very inconsiderable portion of the people (who continued) eastwards. They went on until they came to London, and then with the citizens and with the reinforcements which came to them from the west, they went east to Benfleet. Hæsten had then come there with his army which had been at Milton, and the large army which had been at Appledore on the estuary of the Lympne had then also come there. Hæsten had previously built that fortress at Benfleet; and he was then out on a raid, and the large army was at home. Then the English went there and put the enemy to flight, and stormed the fortress and captured all that was within, both goods, and women and also children, and brought all to London; and they either broke up or burnt all the ships, or brought them to London or to Rochester. And Hæsten's wife and two sons were brought to the king; and he gave them back to him, because one of them was his godson, and the other the godson of Ealdorman Ethelred. They had stood sponsor to them before Hæsten came to Benfleet, and he had given the king oaths and hostages, and the king had also made him generous gifts of money, and so he did also when he gave back the boy and the woman. But immediately they came to Benfleet and had made that fortress, Hæsten ravaged his kingdom, that very province which Ethelred, his son's godfather, was in charge of; and again, a second time, he had gone on a raid in that same kingdom when his fortress was stormed.

When the king had turned west with the army towards Exeter, as I have said before, and the Danish army had laid siege to the borough, they went to their ships when he arrived there. When he was occupied against the army there in the west, and the (other) two Danish armies were assembled at Shoebury in Essex, and had made a fortress there, they went both together up along the Thames, and a great reinforcement came to them both from the East Angles, and the Northumbrians. [They then went up along the Thames until they reached the Severn, then up along the Severn.] Then Ealdorman Ethelred and Ealdorman Æthelhelm and Ealdorman Æthelnoth and the king's thegns who then were at home at the fortresses assembled from every borough east of the Parret, and both west and east of Selwood, and also north of the Thames and west of the Severn, and also some portion of the Welsh people. When they were all assembled, they overtook the Danish army at Buttington on the bank of the Severn, and besieged it on every side in a fortress. Then when they had encamped for many weeks on the two sides of the river, and the king was occupied in the west in Devon against the naval force, the besieged were oppressed by famine, and had eaten the greater part of their horses and the rest had died of starvation. They then came out against the men who were encamped on the east side of the river, and fought against them, and the Christians had the victory. And the king's thegn Ordheah and also many other king's thegns were killed, and a very great [slaughter] of the Danes was made, and the part that escaped were saved by flight.

When they came to Essex to their fortress and their ships, the survivors collected again before winter a large army from the East Angles and Northumbrians, placed their women and ships and property in safety in East Anglia, and went continuously by day and night till they reached a deserted city in Wirral, which is called Chester. Then the English army could not overtake them before they were inside that fortress. However, they besieged the fortress for some two days, and seized all the cattle that was outside, and killed the men whom they could cut off outside the fortress, and burnt all the corn, or consumed it by means of their horses, in all the surrounding districts. And that was twelve months after they had come hither across the sea.

894 And then in this year, immediately after that, the Danish went into Wales from Wirral, because they could not stay there. That was because they were deprived both of cattle and the corn which had been ravaged. When they turned back from Wales with the booty they had captured there, they went, so that the English army could not reach them, across Northumbria and into East Anglia, until they came into east Essex on to an island called Mersea, which is out in the sea.

And when the Danish army which had besieged Exeter turned homewards, they ravaged up in Sussex near Chichester, and the citizens put them to flight and killed many hundreds of them, and captured some of their ships.

Then that same year in early winter the Danes who were encamped on Mersea rowed their ships up the Thames and up the Lea. That was two years after they came hither across the sea.

895 And in the same year the aforesaid army made a fortress by the Lea, 20 miles above London. Then afterwards in the summer a great part of the citizens and also of other people marched till they arrived at the fortress of the Danes, and there they were put to flight and four king's thegns were slain. Then later, in the autumn, the king encamped in the vicinity of the borough while they were reaping their corn, so that the Danes could not deny them that harvest. Then one day the king rode up along the river, and examined where the river could be obstructed, so that they could not bring the ships out. And when this was carried out: two fortresses were made on the two sides of the river. When they had just begun that work [and had encamped for that purpose], the enemy perceived that they could not bring the ships out. Then they abandoned the ships and went overland till they reached Bridgnorth on the Severn and built that fortress. Then the English army rode after the enemy, and the men from London fetched the ships, and broke up all which they could not bring away, and brought to London those which were serviceable. And the Danes had placed their women in safety in East Anglia before they left that fortress. Then they stayed the winter at Bridgnorth. That was three years after they had come hither across the sea into the estuary of the Lympne.

896 And afterwards in the summer of this year the Danish army divided, one force going into East Anglia and one into Northumbria; and those that were moneyless got themselves ships and went south across the sea to the Seine.

By the grace of God, the army had not on the whole afflicted the English people very greatly; but they were much more seriously afflicted in those three years by the mortality of cattle and men, and most of all in that many of the best king's thegns who were in the land died in those three years. Of those, one was Swithwulf, bishop of Rochester, and

Ceolmund, ealdorman of Kent, and Brihtwulf, ealdorman of Essex [and Wulfred, ealdorman of Hampshire], and Ealhheard, bishop of Dorchester, and Eadwulf, a king's thegn in Sussex, and Beornwulf, the town-reeve of Winchester, and Ecgwulf, the king's marshal, and many besides them, though I have named the most distinguished.

In the same year the armies in East Anglia and Northumbria greatly harassed Wessex along the south coast with marauding bands, most of all with the warships which they had built many years before. Then King Alfred had 'long ships' built to oppose the Danish warships. They were almost twice as long as the others. Some had 60 oars, some more. They were both swifter and steadier and also higher than the others. They were built neither on the Frisian nor the swifter and steadier Danish pattern, but as it seemed to him himself that they could be most useful. Then on a certain occasion of the same year, six ships came to the Isle of Wight and did great harm there, both in Devon and everywhere along the coast. Then the king ordered (a force) to go thither with nine of the new ships, and they blocked the estuary from the seaward end. Then the Danes went out against them with three ships, and three were on dry land farther up the estuary; the men from them had gone up on land. Then the English captured two of those three ships at the entrance to the estuary, and killed the men, and the one ship escaped. On it also the men were killed except five. These got away because the ships of their opponents ran aground. Moreover, they had run aground very awkwardly; three were aground on that side of the channel on which the Danish ships were aground, and all [the others] on the other side, so that none of them could get to the others. But when the water had ebbed many furlongs from the ships, the Danes from the remaining three ships went to the other three which were stranded on their side, and they then fought there. And there were killed the king's reeve Lucuman, Wulfheard the Frisian, Æbba the Frisian, Æthelhere the Frisian, Æthelfrith the king's *geneat*, and in all 62 Frisians and English and 120 of the Danes. Then, however, the tide reached the Danish ships before the Christians could launch theirs, and therefore they rowed away out. They were then so wounded that they could not row past Sussex, but the sea cast two of them on to the land, and the men were brought to Winchester to the king, and he ordered them to be hanged. And the men who were on the one ship reached East Anglia greatly wounded. That same summer no fewer than 20 ships, men and all, perished along the south coast. That same year died Wulfric, the king's marshal, who was [also] the Welsh-reeve.

897   In this year, nine days before midsummer, Æthelhelm, ealdorman of wiltshire, died; and in this year died Heahstan, who was bishop of London.

900   In this year Alfred the son of Æthelwulf died, six days before All Saints' Day. He was king over the whole English people except for that part which was under Danish rule, and he had held the kingdom for one and a half years less than thirty; and then his son Edward succeeded to the kingdom.

In this year King Alfred died on 26 October; and he had held the kingdom 28 years and half a year; then his son Edward succeeded to the kingdom.

Then the atheling Æthelwold, his father's brother's son,[28] rode and seized the residence at Wimborne and at *Twinham*, against the will of the king and his councillors. Then the king rode with the army till he encamped at Badbury[29] near Wimborne, and Æthelwold stayed inside the residence with the men who had given allegiance to him; and he had barricaded all the gates against him, and said that he would either live there or die there. Then meanwhile the atheling rode away by night, and went to the Danish army in Northumbria, and they accepted him as king and gave allegiance to him. Then the woman was seized whom he had taken without the king's permission and contrary to the bishops' orders—for she had been consecrated a nun.

And in this same year Ethelred, who was ealdorman of Devon, died four weeks before King Alfred....

Notes

1 Without it having been used to commit a crime.

2 i.e. each wishes to deny being the actual slayer.

3 This shows that the payment of their proper share frees the kinsmen from the dangers of a vendetta, even if the whole wergild is not paid. The slayer himself remains exposed if his own third is unpaid.

4 by whoever is contesting the alienation of the land.

5 A man against whom he has a legitimate blood-feud.

6 The rest of the code consists of a tariff of the compensations to be paid for wounds of various kinds and for other injuries.

7 A mark was a Scandinavian weight, by the end of the next century, and perhaps already, about 3440-3520 grains. The amount here stated may represent a recognised Scandinavian wergild, but, if the ratio of gold to silver was approximately 10:1 at this time, it would not be very far from the wergild of the highest English class. *see* Chadwick, *Studies on Anglo-Saxon Institutions*, pp. 50f.

8 Probably a document authenticated by a seal, to show that he had taken an oath at the king's tomb.

9 Here follows his genealogy.

10 *i.e.* while Æthelwulf was away on his visit to Rome in 855.

11 Here follows a story that this custom arose from the evil behaviour of Offa's daughter, Eadburh, wife of Brihtric of Wessex, part of which Asser tells on Alfred's authority.

12 A sacred ring, normally kept in the inner sanctuary of the heathen temples, and worn by the chief at assemblies, is mentioned in the saga literature of Iceland.

13 For eight days after baptism, white robes were worn and a white cloth, bound round the head after the anointment with the chrism. The ceremony of its removal is what is meant here.

14 Charles the Bald.

15 The Fat, deposed in 887.

16 Charles the Great.

17 The German, died 876.

18 The Pious.

19 The Great.

20 The lord of the Mercians, who married Alfred's daughter, Æthelflæd. Under their rule, Mercia preserved its autonomy.

21 Charles the Fat, who died in January 888.

22 Count of Upper Burgundy.

23 Count of Paris.

24 Margrave of Friuli.

25 Duke of Spoleto.

26 *i.e.* of the Danes.

27 Old Norse Hásteinn (*Hastingus*), a viking leader first heard of on the Loire in 866, who afterwards had an active career on the Continent.

28 He was son of King Ethelred, Alfred's elder brother and predecessor.

29 Badbury Rings, a prehistoric earthwork.

Theodore

Penitential

Handbooks of Penance were important texts in insular spirituality. In the course of the seventh and eighth centuries, they spread to the continent and had deep and lasting influence on the development of medieval ethics and spirituality. The penitential of Theodore (ca. 668-690) was one of the most widely disseminated of these handbooks both in England and on the Continent.

Source: John McNeill and Helena M. Gamer, *Medieval Handbooks of Penance: A Translation of the Principal Libri Poenitentiales and selections from related documents* (New York: Columbia University Press, 1938).

Preface

In the name of Christ. Here begins the preface of the booklet which Father Theodore, having been inquired of by different persons, prepared for the remedy of penance. A pupil of the [North]umbrians, to all Catholics of the English, especially to the physicians of souls, as a suppliant [send] blessing and greeting in the Lord Christ.

First, then, beloved, from love of your blessedness, I thought it fitting, to set forth whence I have collected the penitential remedies which follow, in order that the law may not, on account of the age or negligence of copyists, be perpetuated in a confused and corrupted state, as is usual—that law which of old time God gave figuratively by its first promulgator and then later committed to the Fathers, that they should make it known to their sons that another generation should be acquainted with it; to wit, the [law of] penance, which the Lord Jesus, when he was baptized before us all, proclaimed as the instrument of his teaching for those who had no means of healing; saying: "Do penance," etc. For the increase of your felicity, He deigned to send from the blessed see of him to whom it is said, "Whatsoever thou shalt loose on earth shall be loosed also in heaven," one by whom this most wholesome treatment of wounds is to be controlled; "for I," says the Apostle, "have received of the Lord," and I, beloved, have received of you, by God's favour, that which, in turn, I have handed over to you. For the greater part of these [decisions] the presbyter Eoda, of blessed memory, whose surname was "Christian," is said, by true report, to have received in answer to his questions from the venerable prelate Theodore. Supplementing these also is that element which the divine grace has in like manner provided to our unworthy hands, the things which that man is likewise reported to have searched out, from a booklet of the Irish. Concerning this book, the aged [Theodore] is said to have expressed the opinion that the author was an ecclesiastic.

Further, not only many men but also women, enkindled by him through these [decisions] with inextinguishable fervour, burning with desire to quench the thirst, made haste in crowds to visit a man undoubtedly of extraordinary knowledge for our age. Hence there has been found in divers quarters that conflicting and confused digest of those rules of the second book compiled with the cases adjudged. For which reason I implore, brethren, the most kind indulgence of your favour, through Him who was crucified and [who] by the shedding of His blood in life mightily confirmed what He had preached, that, if for the interests of the practical service I have committed any sin of rashness or

275

ignorance, you will defend me before Him with the support of your intercession. For I call to witness the Maker of all things, that so far as I know my own heart, I have done these things for the sake of that kingdom of which He has preached; and if, as I fear, I undertake something beyond my talents, then, you thus assisting me, let your good will toward a work so necessary implore the pardon of my sin before Him. For in all these things equally and without invidious discrimination, according as I am able, I carefully select out of the whole the more useful things I have been able to find, and I have collected them, prefixing headings to them one by one. For I believe that men of good spirit give attention to these things, of whom it is said: "On earth peace to men of good will."

Book One

I. Of Excess and Drunkenness

1. If any bishop or deacon or any ordained person has had by custom the vice of drunkenness, he shall either desist or be deposed.

2. If a monk vomits on account of drunkenness, he shall do penance for thirty days.

3. If a presbyter or a deacon [does this] on account of drunkenness, he shall do penance for forty days.

4. If [the offence is] due to weakness or because he has been a long time abstinent and is not accustomed to drink or eat much; or if it is for gladness at Christmas or Easter or for any festival of a saint, and he then has imbibed no more than is commanded by his seniors, no offence is committed. If a bishop commands it no offence is committed, unless he himself does likewise.

5. If a lay Christian vomits because of drunkenness, he shall do penance for fifteen days.

6. Whoever is drunk against the Lord's command, if he has taken a vow of sanctity, shall do penance for seven days on bread and water, or twenty days without fat; or laymen, without beer.

7. Whoever in wickedness makes another drunk, shall do penance for forty days.

8. Whoever vomits from excess shall do penance for three days.

9. If with the sacrifice of communion, he shall do penance for seven days; if on account of weakness, he is without guilt.

II. Of Fornication

1. If anyone commits fornication with a virgin he shall do penance for one year. If with a married woman, for four years, two of these entire, and in the other two during the three forty-day periods[1] and three days a week.

2. He judged that he who often commits fornication with a man or with a beast should do penance for ten years.

3. Another judgment is that he who is joined to beasts shall do penance for fifteen years.

4. He who after his twentieth year defiles himself with a male shall do penance for fifteen years.

5. A male who commits fornication with a male shall do penance for ten years.

6. Sodomites shall do penance for seven years, and the effeminate man as an adultress.

7. Likewise he who commits this sexual offence once shall do penance for four years. If he has been in the habit of it, as Basil says, fifteen years; but if not, one year less[?] as a woman. If he is a boy, two years for the first offence; if he repeats it, four years.

8. If he does this "in femoribus," one year, or the three forty-day periods.

9. If he defiles himself, forty days.

10. He who desires to commit fornication, but is not able, shall do penance for forty or twenty days.

11. As for boys who mutually engage in vice, he judged that they should be whipped.

12. If a woman practices vice with a woman, she shall do penance for three years.

13. If she practices solitary vice, she shall do penance for the same period.

14. The penance of a widow and of a girl is the same. She who has a husband deserves a greater penalty if she commits fornication.

15. He who ejaculates into the month of another shall do penance for seven years; this is the worst of evils. Elsewhere it was his judgment that both [participants in the offence] shall do penance to the end of life; or twelve years, or as above seven.

16. If one commits fornication with his mother, he shall do penance for fifteen years and never change except on Sundays. But this so impious incest is likewise spoken of by him in another way—that he shall do penance for seven years, with perpetual pilgrimage.

17. He who commits fornication with his sister shall do penance for fifteen years in the way which it is stated above of his mother. But this [penalty] he also elsewhere established in a canon as twelve years. Whence it is not unreasonable that the fifteen years that are written apply to the mother.

18. The first canon determined that he who often commits fornication should do penance for ten years; a second canon, seven; but on account of the weakness of man, on deliberation they said he should do penance for three years.

19. If a brother commits fornication with a natural brother, he shall abstain from all kinds of flesh for fifteen years.

20. If a mother imitates acts of fornication with her little son, she shall abstain from flesh for three years and fast one day in the week, that is until vespers.

21. He who amuses himself with libidinous imagination shall do penance until the imagination is overcome.

22. He who loves a woman in his mind shall seek pardon from God; but if he has spoken [to her], that is, of love and friendship, but is not received by her, he shall do penance for

seven days.

III. Of Thieving Avarice

1. If any layman carries off a monk from the monastery by stealth, he shall either enter a monastery to serve God or subject himself to human servitude.

2. Money stolen or robbed from churches is to be restored fourfold; from secular persons, twofold.

3. Whoever has often committed theft, seven years is his penance, or such a sentence as his priest shall determine, that is, according to what can be arranged with those whom he has wronged. And he who used to steal, when he becomes penitent, ought always to be reconciled to him against whom he has offended and to make restitution according to the wrong he has done to him; and [in such case] he shall greatly shorten his penance. But if he refuses, or is unable, let him do penance scrupulously for the prescribed time.

4. And he who gives notice of stolen goods shall give a third part to the poor; and whoever treasures up goods in excess through ignorance, shall give a third part to the poor.

5. Whoever has stolen consecrated things shall do penance for three years without fat and then [be allowed to] communicate.

IV. Of manslaughter

1. If one slays a man in revenge for a relative, he shall do penance as a murderer for seven or ten years. However, if he will render to the relatives the legal price, the penance shall be lighter, that is, [it shall be shortened] by half the time.

2. If one slays a man in revenge for a brother, he shall do penance for three years. In another place it is said that he should do penance for ten years.

3. But a murderer, ten or seven years.

4. If a layman slays another with malice aforethought, if he will not lay aside his arms, he shall do penance for seven years; without flesh and wine, three years.

5. If one slays a monk or a cleric, he shall lay aside his arms and serve God, or he shall do penance for seven years. He is in the judgment of his bishop. But as for one who slays a bishop or presbyter, it is for the king to give judgment in this case.

6. One who slays a man by command of his lord shall keep away from the church for forty days; and one who slays a man in public war shall do penance for forty days.

7. If through anger, he shall do penance for three years; if by accident, for one year; if by a potion or any trick, seven years or more; if as a result of a quarrel, ten years.

V. Of Those Who Are Deceived by Heresy

1. If one has been ordained by heretics, if he was without blame [in the matter] he ought to be reordained; but if not, he ought to be deposed.

2. If one goes over from the Catholic Church to heresy and afterward returns, he cannot be ordained except after a long probation and in great necessity. Pope Innocent claimed that such a person is not permitted by the authority of the canons to become a cleric

[even] after penance. Therefore if Theodore says this: "only in great necessity," as has been said, he permitted the procedure, who often used to say that he wished that the decrees of the Romans should never be changed by him.

3. If one flouts the Council of Nicea and keeps Easter with the Jews on the fourteenth of the moon, he shall be driven out of every church unless he does penance before his death.

4. If one prays with such a person as if he were a Catholic cleric, he shall do penance for a week; if indeed he neglects this, he shall the first time do penance for forty days.

5. If one seeks to encourage the heresy of these people and does not do penance, he shall be likewise driven out; as the Lord saith: "He that is not with me is against me."

6. If one is baptized by a heretic who does not rightly believe in the Trinity, he shall be rebaptized. This we do not believe Theodore to have said [since it is] in opposition to the Nicene council and the decrees of the synod; as is confirmed in connection with the Arian converts who did not rightly believe in the Trinity.[2]

7. If one gives the communion to a heretic or receives it from his hand, and does not know that the Catholic Church disapproves it, when he afterward becomes aware [of this] he shall do penance for an entire year. But if he knows and [yet] neglects [the rule] and afterwards does penance, he shall do penance for ten years. Others judge that he should do penance for seven years and, more leniently, for five.

8. If one, without knowing it, permits a heretic to celebrate the Mass in a Catholic church, he shall do penance for forty days. If [he does this] out of veneration for him [i.e., for the heretic], he shall do penance for an entire year.

9. If [he does this] in condemnation of the Catholic church and the customs of the Romans, he shall be cast out of the Church as a heretic, unless he is penitent; if he is, he shall do penance for ten years.

10. If he departs from the Catholic church to the congregation of the heretics and persuades others and afterward performs penance, he shall do penance for twelve years; four years outside the church, and six among the "hearers," and two more out of communion. Of these it is said in a synod: They shall receive the communion or oblation in the tenth year.

11. If a bishop or an abbot commands a monk to sing a mass for dead heretics, it is not proper or expedient to obey him.

12. If a presbyter is present where he has sung a mass, and another recites the names of dead persons and names heretics together with Catholics, and after the mass he is aware of it, he shall do penance for a week. If he has done it frequently, he shall do penance for an entire year.

13. But if anyone orders a mass for a dead heretic and preserves his relics on account of his piety, because he fasted much, and he does not know the difference between the Catholic faith and that of the Quatrodecimans, and [if he] afterward understands and performs penance, he ought to burn the relics with fire, and he shall do penance for a year. If one knows, however, and is indifferent, when he is moved to penance he shall do penance for ten years.

14. If anyone departs from God's faith without any necessity and afterwards receives

penance with his whole heart, he shall do penance among the "hearers"; according to the Nicene council, three years without the church among the penitents, and two years in addition out of communion.

VI. Of Perjury

1. He who commits perjury in a church shall do penance for eleven years.

2. He who [commits perjury] however [because] forced by necessity, for the three forty-day periods.

3. But he who swears on the hand of a man[3]—this is nothing among the Greeks.

4. If, however, he swears on the hand of a bishop or of a presbyter or of a deacon or on an altar or on a consecrated cross and lies, he shall do penance for three years. But if on a cross that is not consecrated, he shall do penance for one year.

5. The penance for perjury is three years.

VII. Of Many and Diverse Evils, and What Necessary Things Are Harmless

1. He who has committed many evil deeds, that is, murder, adultery with a woman and with a beast, and theft, shall go into a monastery and do penance until his death.

2. Of money which has been seized in a foreign province from a conquered enemy, that is, from an alien king who has been conquered, the third part shall be given to the church or to the poor, and penance shall be done for forty days because it was the king's command.[4]

3. He who drinks blood or semen shall do penance for three years.

4. There is pardon for evil imaginations if they are not carried out in action, nor yet by intention.

5. Further, Theodore approved reckoning the twelve three-day periods as the equivalent of a year. Also in the case of sick persons, the value of a man or of a female slave for a year, or to give the half of all his possessions, and if he have defrauded anyone, to restore fourfold, as Christ judged. These are the proofs of what we said in the preface about the booklet of the Irish; in which, as in other matters, sometimes he [the author of the Irish booklet] determined these things therein more leniently, as seemed best to him; it set the measure [of penance] for the week.

6. He who eats unclean flesh or a carcass that has been torn by beasts shall do penance for forty days. But if the necessity of hunger requires it, there is no offense, since a permissible act is one thing and what necessity requires is another.

7. If anyone accidentally touches food with unwashed hands, or [if] a dog, a cat, a mouse, or an unclean animal that has eaten blood [touches it] there is no offense; and if one from necessity eats an animal that seems unclean, whether a bird or a beast, there is no offense.

8. If a mouse falls into a liquid it shall be removed and sprinkled with holy water, and if it is alive it may be taken [for food]; but if it is dead, all the liquid shall be poured out and not given to man, and the vessel shall be cleansed.

9. Again, if that liquid in which a mouse or a weasel is submerged and dies and contains much food, it shall be purged and sprinkled with holy water and taken if there is need.

10. If birds drop dung into any liquid, the dung shall be removed from it, and it shall be sanctified with [holy] water, and it shall be clean food.

11. Unwittingly to absorb blood with the saliva in not a sin.

12. If without knowing it, one eats what is polluted by blood or any unclean thing, it is nothing; but if he knows, he shall do penance according to the degree of the pollution.

VIII. Of Various Failings of the Servants of God

1. If a priest is polluted in touching or in kissing a woman he shall do penance for forty days.

2. If a presbyter kisses a woman from desire, he shall do penance for forty days.

3. Likewise if a presbyter is polluted through imagination, he shall fast for a week.

4. For masturbation, he shall fast for three weeks.

5. If any presbyter denies penance to the dying, he is answerable for their souls, since the Lord saith, "On whatever day the sinner is converted, he shall live and die." For true conversion is possible in the last hour, since the Lord sees not only the time but the heart; for the thief in his last hour, by a confession of one moment, merited to be in paradise.

6. A monk or a holy virgin who commits fornication shall do penance for seven years.

7. He who often pollutes himself through the violence of his imagination shall do penance for twenty days.

8. He who when asleep in a church pollutes himself shall do penance for three days.

9. For masturbation, the first time he shall do penance for twenty days, on repetition, forty days; for further offenses fasts shall be added.

10. If "in femoribus," one year or the three forty-day periods.

11. He who defiles himself shall do penance for forty days; if he is a boy, for twenty days or be flogged. If he is in orders, for the three forty-day periods or a year if he has done it frequently.

12. If anyone renounces the world and afterward resumes a secular habit, if he was a monk and after these things performs penance, he shall do penance for ten years and after the first three years, if he has been approved in all his penance in tears and prayers, the bishop can deal more leniently with him.

13. If he was not a monk when he departed from the Church, he shall do penance for seven years.

14. Basil gave judgment that a boy should be permitted to marry before the age of sixteen if he could not abstain; but that if he is already a monk, [and marries], he is both [classed] among bigamists and shall do penance for one year.

IX. Of Those Who Are Degraded or Cannot Be Ordained

1.   A bishop, presbyter, or deacon guilty of fornication ought to be degraded and to do penance at the decision of a bishop; yet they shall take communion. With loss of rank, penance dies, the soul lives.

2.   If anyone after he has vowed himself to God takes a secular habit, he assuredly ought not to proceed a second time to any rank.

3.   Nor ought a woman [in such case] to take the veil; it is far better that she should not come to prominence in the Church.

4.   If any presbyter or deacon marries a strange woman, he shall be deposed before the people.

5.   If he commits adultery with her and it comes to the knowledge of the people, he shall be cast out of the Church and shall do penance among the laymen as long as he lives.

6.   If anyone has a concubine, he ought not to be ordained.

7.   If any presbyter in his own province or in another or wherever he may be found refuses to baptize a sick person who has been committed to him or on account of the exertion of the journey [declines the duty] so that he dies without baptism, he shall be deposed.

8.   Likewise he who slays a man or commits fornication, shall be deposed.

9.   It is not permitted to ordain a boy brought up in a monastery before the age of twenty-five.

10. If anyone, before or after baptism, marries a twice married woman, as in the case of twice married men, he cannot be ordained.

11. If anyone who is not ordained performs baptism through temerity, he is cut off from the Church and shall never be ordained.

12. If through ignorance anyone has been ordained before he is baptized, those who have been baptized by that pagan ought to be [re]baptized, and he himself shall not be ordained [again].

   This, again, is said to have been differently determined by the Roman Pontiff of the Apostolic See, to the effect that not he who baptizes, even if he is a pagan, but the Spirit of God, ministers the grace of baptism; but also this matter was differently decided in the case of a "pagan" presbyter—he who thinks himself baptized, holding the Catholic faith in his works—these cases are differently decided—that is, that he should have been baptized and ordained.

X. Of Those Who Have Been Baptized Twice; How They Shall Do Penance

1.   Those who in ignorance have been twice baptized are not required to do penance for this, except that according to the canons they cannot be ordained unless some great necessity compels it.

2.   However, those who have been baptized a second time, not ignorantly, [which is] as if they crucified Christ a second time, shall do penance for seven years on Wednesdays and Fridays and during the forty-day periods, if it was on account of some fault. But if they

determined [to be baptized] for the sake of cleanness, they shall do penance in this way for three years.

XI. Of Those Who Despise the Lord's Day, and Neglect the Appointed Fasts of the Church of God

1. Those who labour on the Lord's day, the Greeks reprove the first time; the second, they take something from them; the third time, [they take] the third part of their possessions, or flog them; or they shall do penance for seven days.

2. But if on account of negligence anyone fasts on the Lord's day, he ought to abstain for a whole week. If [he does this] a second time, he shall fast for twenty days; if afterwards forty days.

3. If he fasts out of contempt for the day, he shall be abhorred as a Jew by all the Catholic churches.

4. But if he despises a fast appointed in the church and acts contrary to the decrees of the elders, not in Lent, he shall do penance for forty days. But if it is in Lent, he shall do penance for a year.

5. If he does it frequently and it has become habitual to him, he shall be cast out of the Church, as saith the Lord: "He that shall scandalize one of these little ones," etc.

XII. Of the Communion of the Eucharist, or the Sacrifice

1. The Greeks, clergy, and laymen, communicate every Lord's day, and those who do not communicate for three Lord's days are to be excommunicated, as the canons state.

2. Likewise the Romans who so wish, communicate; however those who do not so wish are not excommunicated.

3. The Greeks and Romans abstain from women for three days before the [feast of] loaves of proposition, as it is written in the law.

4. Penitents according to the canons ought not to communicate before the conclusion of the penance; we, however, out of pity give permission after a year or six months.

5. He who receives the sacrament after food shall do penance for seven days. (It is in the judgment of his bishop. This point, that it is in the judgment of the bishop, is not added in some texts.)

6. If the host has become corrupted with dirt accumulated by time it is always to be burned with fire.

7. Moreover, it shall be permitted if necessary that confession be made to God alone. And this [word] "necessary" is not in some codices.

8. He who mislays the host, [leaving it] for beasts and birds to devour, if by accident, he shall fast for three weeks; if through neglect, for the three forty-day periods.

XIII. Of Reconciliation

1. The Romans reconcile a man within the apse; but the Greeks will not do this.

2. The reconciliation of the penitents in the Lord's Supper is by the bishops only—and the penance is ended.

3. If it is difficult for the bishop, he can, for the sake of necessity, confer authority on a presbyter, to perform this.

4. Reconciliation is not publicly established in this province, for the reason that there is no public penance either.

XIV. Of the Penance for Special Irregularities in Marriage

1. In a first marriage the presbyter ought to perform Mass and bless them both, and afterwards they shall absent themselves from church for thirty days. Having done this, they shall do penance for forty days, and absent themselves from the prayer; and afterwards they shall communicate with the oblation.

2. One who is twice married shall do penance for a year; on Wednesdays and Fridays and during the three forty-day periods he shall abstain from flesh; however, he shall not put away his wife.

3. He that is married three times, or more, that is a fourth or fifth marriage, or beyond that number, for seven years on Wednesdays and Fridays and during the three forty-day periods they shall abstain from flesh; yet they shall not be separated. Basil so determined, but in the canon four years [are indicated].

4. If anyone finds his wife to be an adultress and does not wish to put her away but has had her in the matrimonial relation to that time, he shall do penance for two years on two days in the week and [shall perform] the fasts of religion; or as long as she herself does penance he shall avoid the matrimonial relation with her, because she has committed adultery.

5. If any man or woman who has taken the vow of virginity is joined in marriage, he shall not set aside the marriage but shall do penance for three years.

6. Foolish vows and those incapable of being performed are to be set aside.

7. A woman may not take a vow without the consent of her husband; but if she does take a vow she can be released, and she shall do penance according to the decision of a priest.

8. He who puts away his wife and marries another shall do penance with tribulation for seven years or a lighter penance for fifteen years.

9. He who defiles his neighbor's wife, deprived of his own wife, shall fast for three years two days a week and in the three forty-day periods.

10. If [the woman] is a virgin, he shall do penance for one year without meat and wine and mead.

11. If he defiles a vowed virgin, he shall do penance for three years, as we said above, whether a child is born of her or not.

12. If she is his slave, he shall set her free and fast for six months.

13. If the wife of anyone deserts him and returns to him undishonored, she shall do penance for one year; otherwise for three years. If he takes another wife he shall do penance

for one year.

14. An adulterous woman shall do penance for seven years. And this matter is stated in the same way in the canon.

15. A woman who commits adultery shall do penance for three years as a fornicator. So also shall she do penance who makes an unclean mixture of food for the increase of love.

16. A wife who tastes her husband's blood as a remedy shall fast for forty days, more or less.

17. Moreover, women shall not in the time of impurity enter into a church, or communicate—neither nuns nor laywomen; if they presume [to do this] they shall fast for three weeks.

18. In the same way shall they do penance who enter a church before purification after childbirth, that is, forty days.

19. But he who has intercourse at these seasons shall do penance for twenty days.

20. He who has intercourse on the Lord's day shall seek pardon from God and do penance for one or two or three days.

21. In case of unnatural intercourse with his wife, he shall do penance for forty days the first time.

22. For a graver offense of this kind he ought to do penance as one who offends with animals.

23. For intercourse at the improper season he shall fast for forty days.

24. Women who commit abortion before [the foetus] has life, shall do penance for one year or for the three forty-day periods or for forty days, according to the nature of the offense; and if later, that it, more than forty days after conception, they shall do penance for three years as murderesses, that is for three years on Wednesdays and Fridays and in the three forty-day periods. This according to the canons is judged [punishable by] ten years.

25. If a mother slays her child, if she commits homicide, she shall do penance for fifteen years, and never change except on Sunday.

26. If a poor woman slays her child, she shall do penance for seven years. In the canon it is said that if it is a case of homicide, she shall do penance for ten years.

27. A woman who conceives and slays her child in the womb within forty days shall do penance for one year; but if later than forty days, she shall do penance as a murderess.

28. If an infant that is weak and is a pagan has been recommended to a presbyter [for baptism] and dies [unbaptized], the presbyter shall be deposed. ? MAKES NO SENSE

29. If the neglect is on the part of the parents, they shall do penance for one year; and if a child of three years dies without baptism, the father and the mother shall do penance for three years. He gave this decision at a certain time because it happened to be referred to him.

30. In the canon, he who slays his child without baptism [is required to do penance for] ten years, but under advisement he shall do penance for seven years.

XV. Of the Worship of Idols

1. He who sacrifices to demons in trivial matters shall do penance for one year; but he who [does so] in serious matters shall do penance for ten years.

2. If any woman puts her daughter upon a roof or into an oven for the cure of a fever, she shall do penance for seven years.

3. He who causes grains to be burned where a man has died, for the health of the living and of the house, shall do penance for five years.

4. If a woman performs diabolical incantations or divinations, she shall do penance for one year or the three forty-day periods, or forty days, according to the nature of the offense. Of this matter it is said in the canon: He who celebrates auguries, omens from birds, or dreams, or any divinations according to the custom of the heathen, or introduces such people into his houses, in seeking out any trick of the magicians—when these become penitents, if they belong to the clergy they shall be cast out; but if they are secular persons they shall do penance for five years.

5. In the case of one who eats food that has been sacrificed and later confesses, the priest ought to consider the person, of what age he was and in what way he had been brought up or how it came about. So also the sacerdotal authority shall be modified in the case of a sick person. And this matter is to be observed with all diligence in all penance always and rigorously in confession, in so far as God condescends to aid.

Book Two

I. Of the Ministry of a Church, or of Its Rebuilding

1. A church may be placed in another place if it is necessary, and it ought not to be sanctified, except that the priest ought to sprinkle it with [holy] water, and in the place of the altar[5] a cross ought to be set.

2. It is acknowledged that two masses may be celebrated in one day on every altar; and he who does not communicate shall not approach the bread nor the kiss [of peace] in the Mass; and he who eats beforehand is not admitted to this kiss.

3. The lumber of a church ought not to be applied to any other work except for another church or for burning with fire or for the benefit of the brethren in a monastery or to bake bread for them; and such things ought not to pass into lay operations.

4. In a church in which the bodies of dead believers are buried, an altar may not be sanctified; but if it seems unsuitable for consecration, when the bodies have been removed and the woodwork of it has been scraped or washed, it[6] shall be re-erected.

5. But if it was previously consecrated, masses may be celebrated in it if religious men are buried there; but if there is a pagan [buried there], it is better to cleanse it and cast [the corpse] out.

6. We ought not to make steps in front of the altar.

7.   The relics of saints are to be venerated.

8.   If it can be done, a candle should burn near them every night; but if the poverty of the place prevents this, it does them no harm.

9.   The incense of the Lord is to be burned on the natal days of saints out of reverence for the day, since they, as lilies, shed an odour of sweetness and asperge the Church of God as a church is asperged with incense, beginning at the altar.

10.   A layman ought not to read a lection in a church nor sing the Alleluia, but only the psalms and responses without the Alleluia.

11.   As often as they wish, those who dwell in houses may sprinkle them with holy water; and when thou dost consecrate water thou shalt first offer a prayer.

II. Of the Three Principal Orders of the Church

1.   A bishop may confirm in a field if it is necessary.

2.   Likewise a presbyter may celebrate masses in a field if a deacon or the presbyter himself holds in his hands the chalice and the oblation.

3.   A bishop ought not to compel an abbot to go to a synod unless there is also some sound reason.

4.   A bishop determine cases of poor men up to fifty solidi; but the king, if [the amount in litigation] is above that sum.

5.   A bishop or an abbot may keep a criminal as a slave if he [the criminal] has not the means of redeeming himself.

6.   A bishop may absolve from a vow if he will.

7.   Only a presbyter may celebrate masses and bless the people on Good Friday and sanctify a cross.

8.   A presbyter is not obliged to give tithes.

9.   A presbyter must not reveal the sin of a bishop, since he is set over him.

10.   The host is not to be received from the hand of a priest who cannot recite the prayers or the lections according to the ritual.

11.   If a presbyter sings the responses in the Mass, or anything [else], he shall not remove his cope; moreover, he lays it on his shoulders even when he is reading the Gospel.

12.   In the case of a presbyter who is a fornicator, if before he was found out he baptized, those whom he baptized shall be baptized a second time.

13.   If any ordained presbyter perceives that he was not baptized, he shall be baptized and ordained again, and all whom he baptized previously shall be baptized.

14.   Among the Greeks, deacons do not break the holy bread; neither do they say the collect or the "Dominus vobiscum" or the compline.

15. A deacon may not give penance to a layman, but a bishop or a presbyter ought to give it.

16. Deacons can baptize, and they can bless food and drink; they cannot give the bread.

III. Of the Ordination of Various Persons

1. In the ordination of a bishop the mass ought to be sung by the ordaining bishop himself.

2. In the ordination of a presbyter or of a deacon, the bishop ought to celebrate masses as the Greeks are accustomed to do at the election of an abbot or an abbess.

3. In the ordination of a monk, indeed, the abbot ought to perform the mass and complete three prayers over his head; and for seven days he shall veil his head with his cowl, and on the seventh day the abbot shall remove the veil as in baptism the presbyter is accustomed to take away the veil of the infants; so also ought the abbot to do to the monk, since according to the judgment of the fathers it is a second baptism in which, as in baptism, all sins are taken away.

4. A presbyter may consecrate an abbess with the celebration of the mass.

5. In the ordination of an abbot, indeed, the bishop ought to perform the mass and bless him as he bows his head, with two or three witnesses from among his brethren, and give him the staff and shoes.

6. Nuns, moreover, and churches ought always to be consecrated with a mass.

7. The Greeks bless a widow and a virgin together and choose either as an abbess. The Romans, however, do not veil a widow with a virgin.

8. According to the Greeks a presbyter may consecrate a virgin with the sacred veil, reconcile a penitent, and make the oil for exorcism and the chrism of the sick if it is necessary. But according to the Romans these functions appertain to bishops alone.

IV. Of Baptism and Confirmation

1. In baptism sins are remitted; [but] not loose behaviour with women, since the children who were born before the baptism of the parents are in such cases in the same status as those born after their baptism.

2. If indeed she who was married before [her] baptism is not regarded as a wife, it follows that the children who were previously begotten can neither be held to be [true] children nor be called brothers among themselves or sharers of the inheritance.

3. If any pagan gives alms and keeps abstinence and [does] other good works which we cannot enumerate, does he not lose these in baptism? No, for he shall not lose any good, but he shall wash away the evil. This Pope Innocent asserted, taking for example what was done concerning the catechumen Cornelius.

4. Gregory Nazianzen declares that the second baptism is that of tears.

5. We believe no one is complete in baptism without the confirmation of a bishop; yet we do not despair.

6. Chrism was established in the Nicene synod.

7. It is not a breach of order if the chrismal napkin is laid again upon another who is baptized.

8. One person may, if it is necessary, be [god]father to a catechumen both in baptism and in confirmation; however, it is not customary, but [usually] separate persons act as godparents in each [office].

9. No one may act as a godparent who is not baptized or confirmed.

10. However, a man may act as a godparent for a woman in baptism, likewise also a woman may act as a godparent for a man.

11. Baptized persons may not eat with catechumens, nor give them the kiss;[7] how much more [must this regulation be observed] in the case of pagans.

V. The Mass of the Dead

1. According to the Roman Church the custom is to carry dead monks or religious men to the church, to anoint their breasts with the chrism, there to celebrate masses for them and then with chanting to carry them to their graves. When they have been placed in the tomb a prayer is offered for them; then they are covered with earth or stone.

2. On the first, the third, the ninth, and also on the thirtieth day a mass is celebrated for them, and, if they wished it, [a mass] is observed a year later.

3. A mass is celebrated for a dead monk on the day of his burial and on the third day; afterward as often as the abbot decides.

4. It is the custom also for masses to be celebrated for monks each week, and for their names to be recited.

5. Three masses in a year [are sung] for dead seculars, on the third, the ninth, and the thirtieth day, since the Lord rose from the dead on the third day and in the ninth hour "he yielded up the ghost, and the children of Israel bewailed Moses for thirty days.

6. For a good layman there is to be a mass on the third day; for a penitent on the thirtieth day, or on the seventh, after the fast; since his neighbors ought to fast seven days and to make an offering at the altar, as in Jesus Ben Sirach we read: "And the children of Israel fasted for Saul"; afterward, as often as the priest decides.

7. Many say that it is not permissible to celebrate masses for infants of less than seven years; but it is permitted, nevertheless.

8. Dionysius the Areopagite says that he who offers masses for a bad man commits blasphemy against God.

9. Augustine says that masses are to be performed for all Christians, since it either profits them or consoles those who offer or those who seek [to have it done].

10. A presbyter or a deacon who is not permitted to, or who will not, take communion, may not celebrate masses.

VI. Of Abbots and Monks, or of the Monastery

1. Out of humility and with the permission of the bishop an abbot may relinquish his office. But the brethren shall elect an abbot for themselves from among their own number, if they have [a suitable man]; if not, from among outsiders.

2. And the bishop shall not keep an abbot in his office by violence.

3. The congregation ought to elect an abbot after the abbot's death, or while he is alive if he has gone away or sinned.

4. He himself cannot appoint anyone from among his own monks, nor from those without, nor can he give [the office] to another abbot without the decision of the brethren.

5. If, indeed, the abbot has sinned, the bishop cannot take away the property of the monastery, albeit the abbot has sinned; but he shall send him to another monastery, into the power of another abbot.

6. Neither an abbot nor a bishop may transfer the land of a church to another [church] although both are under his authority. If he wishes to change the land of a church, he shall do it with the consent of both [parties].

7. If anyone wishes to set his monastery in another place, he shall do it on the advice of the bishop and of his brethren, and he shall release a presbyter for the ministry of the church in the former place.

8. It is not permissible for men to have monastic women, nor women, men; nevertheless, we shall not overthrow that which is the custom in this region.

9. A monk may not take a vow without the consent of his abbot; if he lacks this, the vow is to be annulled.

10. If an abbot has a monk worthy of the episcopate, he ought to grant this, if it is necessary.

11. A boy may not marry when he has already set before him the vow of a monk.

12. Any monk whom a congregation has chosen to be ordained to the rank of presbyter for them, ought not to give up his former habit of life.

13. But if he is afterwards found to be either proud or disobedient or vicious, and [if] in a better rank [he] seeks a worse life, he shall be deposed and put in the lowest place, or [he shall] make amends with satisfaction.

14. The reception of infirm persons into a monastery is within the authority and liberty of the monastery.

15. Washing the feet of laymen[8] is also within the liberty of a monastery. Except on the Lord's day, it is not obligatory.

16. It is also a liberty of the monastery to adjudge penance to laymen for this is properly a function of the clergy.

VII. The Rite of the Women, or Their Ministry in the Church

1.   It is permissible for the women, that is, the handmaidens of Christ, to read the lections and to perform the ministries which appertain to the confession of the sacred altar, except those which are the special functions of priests and deacons.
[In a minority of manuscripts this canon reads]:
Women shall not cover the altar with the corporal nor place on the altar the offerings, nor the cup, nor stand among ordained men in the church, nor sit at a feast among priests.

2.   According to the canons it is the function of the bishops and priests to prescribe penance.
[For this canon a number of manuscripts have the following:]
No woman may adjudge penance for anyone, since in the canon no one may [do this] except the priests alone.

3.   Women may receive the host under a black veil, as Basil decided.

4.   According to the Greeks a woman can make offerings, but not according to the Romans.

VIII. Of the Customs of the Greeks and of the Romans

1.   On the Lord's Day the Greeks and the Romans sail and ride; they do make bread, nor proceed in a carriage, except only to church, nor bathe themselves.

2.   The Greeks do not write publicly on the Lord's Day; in the case of special necessity, however, they write at home.

3.   The Greeks and the Romans give clothing to their slaves, and they work, except on the Lord's Day.

4.   Greek monks do not have slaves; Roman monks have them.

5.   On the day before the Lord's nativity, at the ninth hour, when mass is ended, that is, the vigil of the Lord, the Romans eat; but the Greeks take supper [only] when vespers and mass have been said.

6.   In the case of plague, both the Greeks and the Romans say that the sick ought to be visited, as [are] other persons, as the Lord commands.

7.   The Greeks do not give carrion flesh to swine but allow the skins and leather [of carrion] to be taken for shoes, and the wool and horns may be taken [but] not for any sacred [use].

8.   The washing of the head is permitted on the Lord's Day, and it is permitted to wash the feet in a solution of lye; but this washing of the feet is not a custom of the Romans.

IX. Of the Communion of the Irish and Britons Who Are Not Catholic in Respect to Easter and the Tonsure.

1.   Those who have been ordained by Irish or British bishops who are not Catholic with respect to Easter and the tonsure are not united to the Church, but [they] shall be confirmed again by a Catholic bishop with imposition of hands.

2.   Likewise also the churches that have been consecrated by these bishops are to be sprinkled with holy water and confirmed by some collect.

3.   Further, we have not the liberty to give them, when they request it, the chrism or the eucharist, unless they have previously confessed their willingness to be with us in the unity of the Church. And likewise a person from among these nations, or anyone who doubts his own baptism, shall be baptized.

X. Of Those Who Are Vexed by the Devil

1.   If a man is vexed by the devil and can do nothing but run about everywhere, and [if he] slays himself, there may be some reason to pray for him if he was formerly religious.

2.   If it was on account of despair, or of some fear, or for some unknown reasons, we ought to leave to God the decision of this matter, and we dare not pray for him.

3.   In the case of one who of his own will slays himself, masses may not be said for him; but we may only pray and dispense alms.

4.   If any Christian goes insane through a sudden seizure, or as a result of insanity slays himself—there are some who celebrate masses for such an one.

5.   One who is possessed of a demon may have stones and herbs, without [the use of] incantation.

XI. Of the Use or Rejection of Animals

1.   Animals which are torn by wolves or dogs are not to be eaten, nor a stag nor a goat if found dead, unless perchance they were previously killed by a man, but they are to be given to swine and dogs.

2.   Birds and other animals that are strangled in nets are not to be eaten by men; nor if they are found dead after being attacked by a hawk, since it is commanded in the fourth [sic] chapter of the Acts of the Apostles to abstain from fornication, from blood, from that which is strangled, and from idolatry.

3.   Fish, however, may be eaten, since they are of another nature.

4.   They do not forbid horse [flesh], nevertheless it is not the custom to eat it.

5.   The hare may be eaten, and it is good for dysentery; and its gall is to be mixed with pepper for [the relief of] pain.

6.   If bees kill a man, they ought also to be killed quickly, but the honey may be eaten.

7.   If by chance swine eat carrion flesh or the blood of a man, we hold that they are not to be thrown away; nor are hens; hence swine that [only] taste the blood of a man are to be eaten.

8.   But as for those which tear and eat the corpses of the dead, their flesh may not be eaten until they become feeble and until a year has elapsed.

9.   Animals that are polluted by intercourse with men shall be killed, and their flesh thrown to dogs, but their offspring shall be for use, and their hides shall be taken. However, when there is uncertainty, they shall not be killed.

1.   Those who are married shall abstain from intercourse for three nights before they communicate.

2.   A man shall abstain from his wife for forty days before Easter, until the week of Easter. On this account the Apostle says: "That ye may give yourselves to prayer."

3.   When she has conceived a woman ought to abstain from her husband for three months before the birth, and afterward in the time of purgation, that is, for forty days and nights, whether she has borne a male or a female child.

4.   It is also fully permitted to a woman to communicate before she is to bear a child.

5.   If the wife of anyone commits fornication, he may put her away and take another; that is, if a man puts away his wife on account of fornication, if she was his first, he is permitted to take another; but if she wishes to do penance for her sins, she may take another husband after five years.

6.   A woman may not put away her husband, even if he is a fornicator, unless, perchance, for [the purpose of his entering] a monastery. Basil so decided.

7.   A legal marriage may not be broken without the consent of both parties.   *TOUGH RULE*

8.   But either, according to the Greeks, may give the other permission to join a monastery for the service of God, and [as it were] marry it, if he [or she] was in a first marriage; yet this is not canonical. But if such is not the case, [but they are] in a second marriage, this is not permitted while the husband or wife is alive.

9.   If a husband makes himself a slave through theft or fornication or any sin, the wife, if she has not been married before, has the right to take another husband after a year. This is not permitted to one who has been twice married.

10.   When his wife is dead, a man may take another wife after a month. If her husband is dead, the woman may take another husband after a year.

11.   If a woman is an adultress and her husband does not wish to live with her, if she decides to enter a monastery she shall retain the fourth part of her inheritance. If she decides otherwise, she shall have nothing.

12.   Any woman who commits adultery is in the power of her husband if he wishes to be reconciled to an adulterous woman. If he makes a reconciliation, her punishment does not concern the clergy, it belongs to her own husband.

13.   In the case of a man and a woman who are married, if he wishes to serve God[9] and she does not, or if he wishes to do so and he does not, or if either of them is broken in health, they may still be completely separated with the consent of both.

14.   A woman who vows not to take another husband after her husband's death and when he is dead, false to her word, takes another and is married a second time, when she is moved by penitence and wishes to fulfill her vow, it is in the power of her husband [to determine] whether she shall fulfill it or not.

15.   Therefore, to one woman who after eleven years confessed [such] a vow, Theodore gave permission to cohabit with the man.

16. And if anyone in a secular habit takes a vow without the consent of the bishop, the bishop himself has power to change the decision if he wishes.

17. A legal marriage may take place equally in the day and in the night, as it is written, "Thine is the day and thine is the night."

18. If a pagan puts away his pagan wife, after baptism it shall be in his power to have her or not to have her.

19. In the same way, if one of them is baptized, the other a pagan, as saith the Apostle, "If the unbeliever depart, let him depart"; therefore, if the wife of any man is an unbeliever and a pagan and cannot be converted, she shall be put away.

20. If a woman leaves her husband, despising him, and is unwilling to return and be reconciled to her husband, after five years, with the bishop's consent, he shall be permitted to take another wife.

21. If she has been taken into captivity by force and cannot be redeemed, [he may] take another after a year.

22. Again, if she has been taken into captivity her husband shall wait five years; so also shall the woman do if such things have happened to the man.

23. If, therefore, a man has taken another wife, he shall receive the former wife when she returns from captivity, and put away the later one; so also shall she do, as we have said above, if such things have happened to her husband.

24. If an enemy carries away any man's wife, and he cannot get her again, he may take another. To do this is better than acts of fornication.

25. If after this the former wife comes again to him, she ought not to be received by him, if he has another, but she may take to herself another husband, if she has had [only] one before. The same ruling stands in the case of slaves from over sea.

26. According to the Greeks it is permitted to marry in the third degree of consanguinity, as it is written in the Law; according to the Romans, in the fifth degree; however, in the fourth degree they do not dissolve [a marriage] after it has taken place. Hence they are to be united in the fifth degree; in the fourth, if they are found [already married] they are not to be separated; in the third, they are to be separated.

27. Nevertheless, it is not permitted to take the wife of another after his death [if he was related] in the third degree.

28. On the same conditions a man is joined in matrimony to those who are related to him, and to his wife's relatives after her death.

29. Two brothers may also have two sisters in marriage, and a father and a son [respectively] a mother and her daughter.

30. A husband who sleeps with his wife shall wash himself before he goes into a church.

31. A husband ought not to see his wife nude.

32. If anyone has illicit connection or illicit marriage, it is nevertheless permissible to eat the food which they have, for the prophet has said: "The earth is the Lord's and the full-

ness thereof."

33. If a man and a woman have united in marriage, and afterward the woman says of the man that he is impotent, if anyone can prove that this is true, she may take another [husband].

34. Parents may not give a betrothed girl to another man unless she flatly refuses [to marry the original suitor]; but she may go to a monastery if she wishes.

35. But if she who is betrothed refuses to live with the man to whom she is betrothed, the money which he gave for her shall be paid back to him, and a third part shall be added; if, however, it is he that refuses, he shall lose the money which he gave for her.

36. But a girl of seventeen years has power over her own body.

37. Until he is fifteen years old a boy shall be in the power of his father, then he can make himself a monk; but a girl of sixteen or seventeen years who was before in the power of her parents [can become a nun]. After that age a father may not bestow his daughter in marriage against her will.

XIII. Of Male and Female Slaves

1. If he is compelled by necessity, a father has the power to sell his son of seven years of age into slavery; after that, he has not the right to sell him without his consent.

2. A person of fourteen [years] can make himself a slave.

3. A man may not take away from his slave money which he has acquired by his labour.

4. If the master of a male and female slave joins them in marriage and the male slave or the female slave is afterward set free, and if the one who is in slavery cannot be redeemed, the one who has been set free may marry a free born person.

5. If any freeman takes a female slave in marriage, he has not the right to put her away if they were formerly united with the consent of both.

6. If anyone acquires [as a slave] a free woman who is pregnant, the child that is born of her is free.

7. If anyone sets free a pregnant slave woman, the child which she brings forth shall be [in a state] of slavery.

XIV. Of Various Matters

1. There are three legitimate fasts in a year for the people; the forty [days] before Easter, when we pay the tithes of the year, and the forty [days] before the Lord's nativity and the forty days and nights after Pentecost.[10]

2. He who fasts for a dead person aids himself. But to God alone belongs knowledge of the dead person.

3. Laymen ought not to be dilatory with respect to their promises, since death does not delay.

4. On no account may the servant of God fight. Let [the matter] be for consultation by

many servants of God.

5. One infant may be given to God at a monastery instead of another, even if [the father] has vowed the other; nevertheless it is better to fulfill the vow.

6. Similarly, cattle of equal value may be substituted if it is necessary.

7. If a king holds the territory of another king, he may give it for [the good of] his soul.

8. If anyone converted from the world to the service of God has any royal specie received from a king, that [specie] is in the power of that king; but if it is from a former king, [now] dead, that which he received shall be as his other goods; it is permissible to give it to God with himself.

9. That which is found on a road may be taken away. If the owner is found, it shall be restored to him.

10. Let the tribute of the church be according to the custom of the province; that is, so that the poor may not so greatly(?) suffer violence on this account in tithes or in any matters.

11. It is not lawful to give tithes except to the poor and to pilgrims, or for laymen [to give] to their own churches.

12. Out of reverence for the new birth, prayer is to be made in the fifty days.[11]

13. Prayer may be [made] under a veil if necessity requires it.

14. The sick may take food and drink at all hours when they desire it or when they are able [to take it] if they cannot [do so] at the proper times.

Epilogue[12]

Our [authors], as we said, have written these [canons] in consultation with the venerable Theodore, archbishop of the English. If some suppose they have in their possession in more satisfactory or better form these two rules,[13] we hope they will well use their own [versions] and not neglect ours, in which the parts which seem corrupted are attributed by all to the fault of both scribes and interpreters—pretty barbarous men—so that by some, even [by] those instructed by him, the defective and incorrect passages are rightly said not to be his decisions. Of these, although they are retained by many here and there and in a confused state, in succeeding books we have been able with the aid of Christ the Lord to set in order impartially according to our ability not a few of the chief things out of them. But being still in doubt about this work, we connect with it passages in certain minor works that are necessary to it, especially in the booklet on penance, which I think can be easily perceived by a discerning person.

It therefore remains further in vindication of our father Theodore to make satisfaction as best we can to you, beloved,[14] who, not finding a full exposition in the utterances of other Catholics, have therefore had recourse to him. In all these matters, I, not undeservedly, entreat you, beloved, who have been judging the difficulties of these [inquiries] that on this account you defend me by your merits on the right hand and on the left, while I strive on your behalf in the welter of these [difficulties], Christ being the judge of the contest, against the threatening blows of calumniators. It is easier for these [calumniators] to defame the laborers than to sweat in the zeal of labour; for some of our people have given themselves to abuse the wisest men of the Church of God by the volubility of their tongues. I refer to St. Jerome whom they call an evil speaker to men, to Augustine whom they call loquacious, and to Isidore whom they call an arranger of glosses. I say nothing of the others, when they say that Gregory, our Apostle, easily uttered what others had earlier expounded, a follower in the beaten paths of other men. From this source I have recently heard (what I shudder to tell) that a certain gross follower of heathen fables is abusing the promulgator of the Law of God and chronicler of the whole history of creation, saying, "What could Moses himself, the magician, either know or say to him?"

What, then, can my defense be, since I, in comparison to those whom I have mentioned, am nothing. Yet, "by the grace of God, I am what I am;" may it not have been void in me through him who is able to create all things of nothing and to bring to pass great things from little. On this account, if any Catholic author finds anything anywhere in these canons that he is able to amend, he shall have permission from us to do this reasonably, in view of the fact that unless the parts that are not to be followed are suppressed, when they are held of equal validity they occasion contention to those to whom it is said: "not in contention and envy; But put ye on the Lord Jesus Christ."

Notes

1 Probably by the "three forty-day periods" frequently assigned in this penitential, those mentioned in Book II, xiv, 1, below, are to be understood. Some modern writers habitually call these "the three lents."

2 The writer has mistaken the canons of Constantinople (381) for those of Nicaea. The council of Constantinople admitted Arians without rebaptism (can. vii, Manis, III, 563). See also the 8th canon of the synod of Arles (314), Mansi, II, 472.

3 Meaning a layman, as indicated by the next canon.

4 The last clause gives the reason for the lightness of the penalty.

5 Meaning, "in the place where the altar formerly stood."

6 Apparently, the altar.

7 That is, "the kiss of peace."

8 The "pedilavium," or ceremonial foot washing, usually accompanied baptism in the Celtic Church.

9 That is, to enter a monastery.

10 These are the "three forty-day periods" ("quadragesimae") frequently referred to in this and some other penitentials.

11 The period between Easter and Pentecost.

12 The epilogue has come down in only two manuscripts, and neither one includes both the beginning and the end. The text is unusually obscure.

13 Probably the two books of the penitential.

14 Literally, "to your love."

Domesday Book

In 1065 William the Conqueror ordered a survey of his kingdom in order to provide him with an exact record of the local contributions to royal taxation. In addition, the inquest was designed to inform him of the manner that England had been divided among his vassals and to settle issues of land disputes which had been continuing since the conquest ten years before. The result was an extraordinarily rich and detailed survey which is an invaluable source for understanding English social, economic, and political structures in the eleventh century.

The survey of Huntingdonshire is fairly typical of the entries. In general, each entry describes the assessment of the manor in hides to the geld. These "hides" are not actual units of land but units of tax assessment. It then states the number of "ploughs", that is, the amount of arable land that can be ploughed each year by a team of 8 oxen. Finally, it states the number of ploughs on the demesne of the manor and the number in the peasant tenures. Finally, it may add miscellaneous information about other resources and its value at the death of Edward the Confessor in 1066 (T.R.E. tempore Regis Edwardi) and in 1086.

Source: David Douglas and G. W. Greenaway (ed.) *English Historical Documents* vol. II (Oxford: Oxford University Press 1953).

Huntingdonshire

In the borough of Huntingdon there are 4 quarters.

In 2 quarters there were *T.R.E.*, and are now, 116 burgesses rendering all customs and the king's geld, and under them there are 100 bordars who help them to pay the geld. Of these burgesses St. Benedict of Ramsey had 10 with sake and soke and every custom except that they paid geld *T.R.E.* Eustace took them away wrongfully from the abbey and they are, with the others, in the king's hand. Ulf Fenisc had 18 burgesses, now Gilbert of Ghent has them with sake and soke except for the king's geld.

The abbot of Ely has 1 toft with sake and soke except for the king's geld.

The bishop of Lincoln had in the site of the castle a messuage with sake and soke which has now disappeared.

Earl Siward had a messuage with a house with sake and soke, quit from all custom, which the Countess Judith has now.

In the site of the castle there were 20 messuages assessed to all customs, and rendering yearly 16 shillings and 8 pence to the king's 'farm'. These do not exist now.

In addition to these, there were and are 60 waste messuages within these quarters. These gave and give their customs. And in addition to these there are 8 waste messuages which *T.R.E.* were fully occupied. These gave all customs.

In the other 2 quarters there were and are 140 burgesses, less half a house, assessed to all customs and the king's geld, and these had 80 haws for which they gave and give all customs. Of these St. Benedict of Ransey had 22 burgesses *T.R.E.* Two of these were quit of all customs, and 30 rendered 10 pence yearly each. All other customs belonged to the abbot, apart from the king's geld.

In these quarters Aluric the sheriff *T.R.E.* had 1 messuage which King William afterwards granted to his wife and sons. Eustace has it now, and the poor man, with his mother, is claiming it. In these 2 quarters there were and are 44 waste messuages which gave and give their customs. And in these 2 quarters Borred and Turchil *T.R.E.* had 1 church with

2 hides of land and 22 burgesses with houses belonging to the same church with sake and soke; Eustace has all this now. Wherefore these men claim the king's mercy; nevertheless these 22 burgesses give every custom to the king.

Geoffrey the bishop has 1 church and 1 house from the aforesaid which Eustace took away from St. Benedict, and the same saint is still claiming them.

In this borough Gos and Hunef had 16 houses *T.R.E.* with sake and soke and toll and team. The Countess Judith has them now.

The borough of Huntingdonshire used to defend itself towards the king's geld for 50 hides as the fourth part of Hurstingstone hundred, but now it does not so pay geld in that hundred, after the king set a geld of money on the borough. From this whole borough 10 pounds came out *T.R.E.* by way of 'Landgable' of which the earl had the third part, and the king two-thirds. Of this rent 16 shillings and 8 pence, divided between the earl and the king, now remain upon 20 messuages where the castle is. In addition to these payments the king had 20 pounds and the earl 10 pounds from the 'farm' of the borough more or less according as each could make disposition of his part. One mill rendered 40 shillings to the king and 20 shillings to the earl. To this borough there belong 2 ploughlands and 40 acres of land and 10 acres of meadow, of which the king with two parts, and the earl with the third part, divide the rent. The burgesses cultivate this land and take it on lease through the servants of the king and the earl. Within the aforesaid rent there are 3 fishermen rendering 3 shillings. In this borough there were 3 moneyers paying 40 shillings between the king and the earl, but now they are not there. *T.R.E.* it rendered 30 pounds; now the same.

In Hurstingstone hundred demesne ploughlands are quit of the king's geld. Villeins and sokemen pay geld according to the hides written in the return, apart from Broughton where the abbot of Ramsey pays geld for 1 hide with the others.

Here are noted those holding lands in Huntingdonshire
1. King William.
2. The bishop of Lincoln.
3. The bishop of Coutances.
4. The abbey of Ely.
5. The abbey of Crowland.
6. The abbey of Ramsey.
7. The abbey of Thorney.
8. The abbey of Peterborough.
9. Count Eustace.
10. The count of Eu.
11. Earl Hugh.
12. Walter Giffard.
13. William of Warenne.
14. Hugh of Bolbec.
15. Eudo, son of Hubert.
16. Sweyn of Essex.
17. Roger of Ivry.
18. Arnulf of Hesdins.
19. Eustace the sheriff.
20. The Countess Judith.
21. Gilbert of Ghent.
22. Aubrey 'de Vere'.
23. William, son of Ansculf.
24. Rannulf, the brother of Ilger.
25. Robert Fafiton.
26. William 'Ingania'.
27. Ralph, son of Osmund.

28. Rohais, the wife of Richard.
29. The king's thegns.

1. The land of the king

Hurstingstone hundred

A manor. In Hartford King Edward had 15 hides assessed to the geld. There is land for 17 ploughs. Rannulf the brother of Ilger keeps it now. There are 4 ploughs now on the demesne; and 30 villeins and 3 bordars have 8 ploughs. There is a priest; 2 churches; 2 mills rendering 4 pounds; and 40 acres of meadow. Woodland for pannage, 1 league in length and half a league in breadth. *T.R.E.* it was worth 24 pounds; now 15 pounds.

Normancross hundred

A manor. In Bottlebridge King Edward had 5 hides assessed to the geld. There is land for 8 ploughs. The king has 1 plough now on the demesne; and 15 villeins have 5 ploughs. There is a priest and a church; 60 acres of meadow and 12 acres of woodland for pannage in Northamptonshire. *T.R.E.* it was worth 100 shillings; now 8 pounds. Rannulf keeps it.

In this manor belonging to the king, and in other manors, the enclosure of the abbot of Thorney is doing harm to 300 acres of meadow.

In Stilton the king's sokemen of Normancross have 3 virgates of land assessed to the geld. There is land for 2 ploughs, and there are 5 ploughing oxen.

In Orton the king has soke over 3-1/2 hides of land in the land of the abbot of Peterborough which was Godwine's.

Toseland hundred

A manor. In Gransden Earl Alfgar had 8 hides of land assessed to the geld. There is land for 15 ploughs. There are 7 ploughs now on the demesne; and 24 villeins and 8 bordars have 8 ploughs. There is a priest and a church; 50 acres of meadow; 12 acres of underwood. From the pasture come 5 shillings and 4 pence. *T.R.E.* it was worth 40 pounds; now 30 pounds. Rannulf keeps it.

Leightonstone hundred

A manor. In Alconbury, and in Gidding, which is an outlying estate, there were 10 hides assessed to the geld. There is land for 20 ploughs. There are now 5 ploughs belonging to the hall on 2 hides of this land; and 35 villeins have 13 ploughs there; 80 acres of meadow. *T.R.E.* it was worth 12 pounds; now the same. Rannulf, the brother of Ilger, keeps it.

A manor. In Keyston King Edward had 4 hides of land assessed to the geld. There is land for 12 ploughs. There are 2 ploughs now on the demesne; and 24 villeins and 8 bordars have 10 ploughs; 86 acres of meadow. Scattered woodland for pannage 5 furlongs in length and 1-1/2 furlongs in breadth. *T.R.E.* it was worth 10 pounds; now the same. Rannulf, the brother of Ilger, keeps it.

A manor. In Brampton King Edward had 15 hides assessed to the geld. There is land for 15 ploughs. There are 3 ploughs now on the demesne; and 36 villeins and 2 bordars have 14 ploughs. There is a church and a priest; 100 acres of meadow. Woodland for pannage half a league in length and 2 furlongs in breadth. Two mills rendering 100 shillings. *T.R.E.* it was worth 20 pounds; now the same. Rannulf, the brother of Ilger, keeps it.

Soke.[1] In Graffham there are 5 hides assessed to the geld. There is land for 8 ploughs. The soke is in Leightonstone hundred. There 7 sokemen and 17 villeins have 6 ploughs now and 6 acres of meadow. Woodland for pannage 1 league in length and 1 league in breadth. *T.R.E.* it was worth 5 pounds; now 10 shillings less.

A manor. In Godmanchester King Edward had 14 hides assessed to the geld. There is land for 57 ploughs. There are 2 ploughs now on the king's demesne on 2 hides of this land; and 80 villeins and 16 bordars have 24 ploughs. There is a priest and a church; 3 mills rendering 100 shillings; 160 acres of meadow; and 50 acres of woodland for pannage. From the pasture come 20 shillings. From the meadows come 70 shillings. *T.R.E.* it was worth 40 pounds; now it is worth the same 'by tale'.

2. The land of the bishop of Lincoln

Toseland hundred

A manor. In 'Cotes' the bishop of Lincoln had 2 hides assessed to the geld. There is land for 3 ploughs. There are 2 ploughs now on the demesne; and 3 villeins have 2 oxen; 20 acres of meadow. *T.R.E.* it was worth 40 shillings; now the same. Thurstan holds it of the bishop.

A manor. In Staughton the bishop of Lincoln had 6 hides assessed to the geld. There is land for 15 ploughs. There are 2-1/2 ploughs on the demesne; and 16 villeins and 4 bordars have 8 ploughs. There is a priest and a church; 24 acres of meadow; 100 acres of underworld. *T.R.E.* it was worth 10 pounds; now the same. Eustace holds it of the bishop. The abbot of Ramsey claims this manor against the bishop.

A manor. In Diddington the bishop of Lincoln had 2-1/2 hides assessed to the geld. There is land for 2 ploughs. There are now 2 ploughs on the demesne and 5 villeins have 2 ploughs. A church, and 18 acres of meadow. Woodland for pannage half a league in length and half in breadth. *T.R.E.* it was worth 60 shillings; now 70 shillings. William holds it of the bishop.

A manor. In Buckden the bishop of Lincoln had 20 hides assessed to the geld. There is land for 20 ploughs. There are now 5 ploughs on the demesne; and 37 villeins and 20 bordars have 14 ploughs. There is a church and a priest; 1 mill worth 30 shillings; 84 acres of meadow. Woodland for pannage 1 league in length and 1 league in breadth. *T.R.E.* it was worth 20 pounds; now 16 pounds and 10 shillings.

Normancross hundred

A manor. In Denton Godric had 5 hides assessed to the geld. There is land for 2 ploughs. There is 1 plough on the demesne; and 10 villeins and 2 bordars have 5 ploughs. There is a church and a priest; 24 acres of meadow and 24 acres of underwood. *T.R.E.* it was worth 100 shillings; now 4 pounds. Thurstan holds it of the bishop.

A manor. In Orton Leuric had 3 hides and 1 virgate of land assessed to the geld. There is land for 2 ploughs and 1 ox. There is now 1 plough on the demesne; and 2 villeins and 9 acres of meadow. *T.R.E.* it was worth 20 shillings; now 10 shillings. John holds it of the bishop. The king claims the soke of this land.

A manor. In Stilton Tovi had 2 hides assessed to the geld. There is land for 2 ploughs and 7 oxen. There is now 1 plough on the demesne; and 6 villeins have 3 ploughs; 16 acres of meadow and 5 acres of underwood. *T.R.E.* it was worth 40 shillings; now the same. John holds it of the bishop. This land was given to Bishop Wulfwig *T.R.E.*

Leightonstone hundred

A manor. In Leighton Bromswold Turchil the Dane had 15 hides assessed to the geld. There is land for 17 ploughs. There are now 6 ploughs on the demesne; and 33 villeins and 3 bordars have 10 ploughs. One mill rendering 3 shillings; 3 knights hold 3 hides less 1 virgate of this land: they have 3 ploughs and 3 villeins with half a plough. There are 30 acres of meadow and 10 acres of underwood. *T.R.E.* the bishop's demesne was worth 20 pounds and it is worth the same now. The land of the knights is worth 60 shillings. Earl Waltheof gave this manor in alms to St. Mary of Lincoln.

In Pertenhall Alwin had 1 virgate of land assessed to the geld. There is land for half a plough. This land is situated in Bedfordshire but renders geld and service in Huntingdonshire. The king's servants claim this land for his use. *T.R.E.* it was worth 5 shillings; now the same. William holds it of Bishop Remigius and ploughs it with his own demesne.

3. The land of the bishop of Coutances

In Hargrave Semar had 1 virgate of land assessed to the geld. There is land for 2 oxen. The soke belongs to Leightonstone hundred. The same man himself holds it of the bishop of Coutances and ploughs there with 2 oxen and has 2 acres of meadow. *T.R.E.* it was worth 5 shillings; now the same.

4. The land of the abbey of Ely

Hurstingstone hundred

A manor. In Colne the abbey of Ely had 6 hides assessed to the geld. There is land for 6 ploughs and in demesne the abbey has land for 2 ploughs apart from the 6 hides. There are now 2 ploughs on the demesne, and 13 villeins and 5 bordars have 5 ploughs; 10 acres of meadow. Woodland for pannage 1 league in length and half a league in breadth; marsh of the same extent. *T.R.E.* it was worth 6 pounds; now 100 shillings.

A manor. In Bluntisham the abbey of Ely had 6-1/2 hides assessed to the geld. There is land for 8 ploughs, and, apart from these hides, the abbey has land for 2 ploughs in demesne. There are now 2 ploughs on the demesne; and 10 villeins and 3 bordars have 3 ploughs. There is a priest and a church; 20 acres of meadow. Woodland for pannage 1 league in length and 4 furlongs in breadth. *T.R.E.* it was worth 100 shillings; now the same.

A manor. In Somersham the abbey of Ely had 8 hides assessed to the geld. There is land for 12 ploughs, and, apart from these hides, the abbey had land for 2 ploughs in demesne. There are now 2 ploughs on the demesne; and 32 villeins and 9 bordars have 9 ploughs. There are 3 fisheries rendering 8 shillings, and 20 acres of meadow. Woodland for pannage 1 league in length and 7 furlongs in breadth. *T.R.E.* it was worth 7 pounds; now 8 pounds.

A manor. In Spaldwick the abbey of Ely had 15 hides assessed to the geld. There is land for 15 ploughs. There are now 4 ploughs on the demesne on 5 hides of this land; and 50 villeins and 10 bordars have 25 ploughs. There is 1 mill rendering 2 shillings; and 160 acres of meadow; and 60 acres of woodland for pannage. *T.R.E.* it was worth 16 pounds; now 22 pounds.

A manor. In Little Catworth, outlying estate of Spaldwick, there are 4 hides assessed to the geld. Land for 4 ploughs; 7 villeins have 2 ploughs there now.

5. The land of the abbey of Crowland

A manor. In Morborne the abbey of Crowland has 5 hides assessed to the geld. There is land for 9 ploughs. There are now 2 ploughs on the demesne on 1 hide of this land; and 16 villeins and 3 bordars have 7 ploughs. There is a church and a priest; 40 acres of meadow; 1 acre of underwood. *T.R.E.* it was worth 100 shillings; now the same.

In Thurning there are 1-1/2 hides assessed to the geld. There is land for 1-1/2 ploughs. The soke belongs to the king's manor of Alconbury. Eustace holds it now from the abbot of Crowland, and had 1 plough there and 1 villein with half a plough and 6 acres of meadow. *T.R.E.* it was worth 20 shillings; now the same.

6. The land of St. Benedict of Ramsey

[This is similarly described as lying in Stukeley; Abbot's Ripton; Broughton; Wistow; Upwood; Holywell; St. Ives; Houghton; Wyton; Warboys; Sawtry; Elton; Lutton; Yelling;

Hemingford Abbots; Offord; Dillington; Gidding; Bythorn; Bringtin; Old Weston; Ellington.]

7. The land of St. Mary of Thorney

[This is similarly described as lying in Yaxley; Stanground; Woodstone; Haddon; Water Newton; Sibson; Stibbington.]

8. The land of St. Peter of Peterborough

[This is similarly described as lying at Fletton; Alwalton; Orton Waterville.]

9. The land of Count Eustace

[This is similarly described as lying at Glatton; Chesterton; Sibson.]

10. The land of the Count of Eu

[This is similarly described as lying at Buckworth.]

11. The land of Earl Hugh

[This is similarly described as lying in Upton; Coppingford.]

12. The land of Walter Giffard

[This is similarly described as lying at Folksworth.]

13. The land of William of Warenne

[This is similarly described as lying at Kimbolton; Keysoe; Catworth.]

14. The land of Hugh of Bolbec

[This is similarly described as lying at Wood Walton.]

15. The land of Eudo, son of Hubert

[This is similarly described as lying at Hamerton.]

16. The land of Sweyn of Essex

[This is similarly described as lying at Waresley.]

17. The land of Roger of Ivry

[This is similarly described as lying at Covington.]

18. The land of Arnulf of Hesdins

[This is similarly described as lying in Offord Cluny.]

19. The land of Eustace the sheriff

[This is similarly described as lying in Sawtry; Caldecot; Washingley; Orton Longueville;

Stilton; Chesterton; Bottlebridge; Swineshead; Catworth; Hargrave; Gidding; Winwick; Thurning; Luddington; Weston; Wooley; Hemingford; Offord; Waresley; Hail Weston; Southoe; Perry; Catworth.]

20. The land of the Countess Judith

[This is similarly described as lying in Conington; Sawtry; Stukeley; Molesworth; 'Cotes'; Eynesbury; Offord; Diddington; Paxton.]

21. The land of Gilbert of Ghent

[This is similarly described as lying in Fen Stanton.]

22. The land of Aubrey 'de Vere'

[This is similarly described as lying in Yelling; Hemingford.]

23. The land of William, son of Ansculf

[This is similarly described as lying in Waresley.]

24. The land of Rannulf, brother of Ilger

[This is similarly described as lying in Everton.]

25. The land of Robert Fafiton

[This is similarly described as lying in Hail Weston; Southhoe.]

26. The land of William 'Ingania'

[This is similarly described as lying in Gidding.]

27. The land of Ralph, son of Osmund

[This is similarly described as lying in Hemingford.]

28. The land of Rohais, wife of Richard fitz Gilbert

Toseland hundred

A manor. In Eynesbury Robert, son of Wimarc, had 15 hides assessed to the geld. There is land for 27 ploughs. Rohais, the wife of Richard, has 7 ploughs on the demesne there now. In the same place St. Neot has from her 3 ploughs on the demesne, and in the same village 19 villeins and 5 bordars have 7 ploughs. There is 1 mill worth 23 shillings, and 1 fishery which is valued with the manor; 65-^{1}/$_2$ acres of meadow. *T.R.E.* it was worth 24 pounds; now it is worth 21 pounds apart from that which is assigned to the food of the monks, which is valued at 4 pounds. William 'Brito' holds 2 hides and 1 virgate of this land from Rohais and has half a plough on the demesne; and 3 villeins and 4 bordars have 1 plough. It is worth 30 shillings.

29. The land of the king's thegns

A manor. In Washingley, Chetelebert had 2-^{1}/$_2$ hides assessed to the geld. There is land for 4 ploughs. He himself holds from the king and has 1 plough there; and 10 villeins have

4 ploughs. There is a church and a priest; 12 acres of meadow. Woodland for pannage 7 furlongs in length and 10-$\frac{1}{2}$ furlongs in breadth. *T.R.E.* it was worth 10 shillings; now the same.

Leightonstone hundred

In Keysoe Alwine had 1 virgate of land assessed to the geld with sake and soke. There is land for 2 oxen. It belongs to Bedfordshire, but gives geld in Huntingdonshire. He himself holds now of the king and has 1 villein there with 2 oxen in a plough. *T.R.E.* it was worth 16 pence; now the same.

A manor. In Catworth Avic had 3 hides assessed to the geld. There is land for 4 ploughs. Eric holds it now of the king. And the same man has under the king 1 hide assessed to the geld. There is land for 1 plough. He has 2 villeins there, and 6 acres of meadow. *T.R.E.* it was worth 40 shillings; now 20 shillings.

In Brampton Elric has 1 hide and 1 virgate of land assessed to the geld. There is land for 10 oxen. There are 3 bordars and 1 plough. It is worth 30 shillings.

A manor. In Wooley Golde and Uluric, his son, had 3 hides assessed to the geld. There is land for 6 ploughs. They themselves now have it from the king. There is 1 plough on the demesne; and 14 villeins have 5 ploughs; 20 acres of meadow. *T.R.E.* it was worth 60 shillings; now the same.

In Sawtry Alwine had half a carucate assessed to the geld. There is land for 6 oxen. His wife holds it now of the king, and has 1 plough there and 2 acres. *T.R.E.* it was worth 10 shillings; now the same.

[Claims]

The jurors of Huntingdon say that the church of St. Mary of the borough and the land which is annexed to it belonged to the church of Thorney, but the abbot gave it in pledge to the burgesses. Moreover, King Edward gave it to Vitalis and Bernard, his priests, and they sold it to Hugh, chamberlain to King Edward. Moreover, Hugh sold it to two priests of Huntingdon, and in respect of this they have the seal of King Edward. Eustace has it now without livery, without writ, and without seisin.

Eustace took away wrongfully the house of Leveve and gave it to Oger of London.

They bear witness that the land of Hunef and Gos was under the hand of King Edward on the day when he was alive and dead and that they held of him and not of the earl. But the jurors say that they heard that King William was said to have given it to Waltheof.

Touching the 5 hides of Broughton the jurors say that it was the land of sokemen *T.R.E.*, but that the same king gave the land and the soke over the men to St. Benedict of Ramsey in return for a service which Abbot Alwin did for him in Saxony, and ever afterwards the saint had it.

The shire bears witness that the land of Bricmer 'Belehorne' was 'reeveland' *T.R.E.* and belonged to the king's 'farm'.

They bear witness that the land of Alwin the priest was to the abbot. ...

They bear witness that Aluric's land of Yelling and Hemingford belonged to St. Benedict and that it was granted to Aluric for the term of his life on the condition that after his death it ought to return to the church, and 'Bocstede' with it. But this same Aluric was killed in the battle of Hastings, and the abbot took back his lands and held them until Aubrey 'de Vere' deprived him of possession.

Touching 2 hides which Ralph, son of Osmund, holds in Hemingford, they say that one of them belonged to the demesne of the church of Ramsey in King Edward's day, and that Ralph holds it against the abbot's will. Touching the other hide, they say that Godric held it from the abbot, but when the abbot was in Denmark, Osmund, Ralph's father, seized it from Sawin the fowler, to whom the abbot had given it for love of the king.

Touching Summerlede they say that he held his land from Turulf who gave it to him, and afterwards from the sons of Turulf, and they had sake and soke over him.

The jurors say that the land of Wulwine Chit of Weston was a manor by itself, and did not belong to Kimbolton, but that nevertheless he was a man of Earl Harold.

Touching a hide and a half of land which was Ælget's, the jurors say that this Ælget held them from Earl Tosti with sake and soke and afterwards of Waltheof.

Godric the priest likewise held 1 hide of land from Earl Waltheof *T.R.E.*, and Eustace holds it now.

They say that the land of Godwine of Weston in no way belonged to Saxi, Fafiton's predecessor.

The men of the shire bear witness that King Edward gave Swineshead to Earl Siward with sake and soke, and so Earl Harold had it, except that the men paid geld in the hundred, and performed military service with them.

Touching the land of Fursa, the soke was the king's. King Edward had soke over 1 virgate of land of Alwin Deule in Pertenhall.

The jurors say that the hide of land which Wulwine Chit had in Catworth was in the king's soke and that Earl Harold did not have it.

In Little Catworth the same Wulwine had 1 hide over which King Edward always had sake and soke. But Wulwine could give and sell the land to whom he wished. But the men of the countess say that the king gave the land to Earl Waltheof.

The shire bears witness that the third part of half a hide which lies in Easton and pays geld in Bedfordshire belongs to the abbot of Ely's manor of Spaldwick. The abbot of Ely thus held it *T.R.E.*, and for five years after the coming of King William. Eustace seized this land wrongfully from the church, and kept it.

The jurors say that Keystone was and is of the 'farm' of King Edward, and although Aluric the sheriff resided in that village, he nevertheless always paid the king's 'farm' therefrom, and his sons after him, until Eustace took the sheriffdom. They have never seen or heard of a seal of King Edward that he put it outside his 'farm'.

Alwold and his brother claim that Eustace took away their land from them, and the men of the shire deny that they have ever seen a seal, or seen anyone who gave Eustace seisin of it.

On the day when King Edward was alive and dead, Gidding was an outlying estate of Alconbury in the king's 'farm'.

The men of the shire bear witness that Buckworth was an outlying estate of Paxton *T.R.E.*

They say that 36 hides of land in Brampton which Richard 'Ingania' claims to belong to the forest were of the king's demesne 'farm', and did not belong to the forest.

They say that Graffham was and is the king's sokeland, and that they have not seen the writ, or anyone who gave legal possession of this to Eustace.

Touching 6 hides in Conington they said they had heard that these formerly belonged to the church of Thorney, and that they were granted to Turchill on condition that after [his] death they ought to return to the church with the other 3 hides in the same village. The jurors said that they had heard this, but they had not seen evidence of it, nor were they present when the arrangement was made.

Touching the land of Tosti of Sawtry, they say that Eric, his brother, bequeathed it to the church of Ramsey after his death and after the death of his brother and sister.

Touching Fletton the jurors say that *T.R.E.* the whole belonged to the church of Peterborough, and so it should.

Touching Leuric's land the jurors say that it was in the king's soke, but Bishop Remigius shows the writ of King Edward by which he gave Leuric with all his land to the bishopric of Lincoln with sake and soke.

Notes

1   This term prefixed to estates in this survey indicates "a group of tenements – united to some manor by the ties of rent, the homage of the peasant landholders, and in most cases their suit of court to the manorial centre".

Einhard

Life of Charles the Great

Einhard (ca. 770-840), originally from the region of Mainz, was raised in the monastery of Fulda and later educated at the court of Charlemagne. He later served Charlemagne and his son Louis the Pious (824-840) in various capacities at court and on diplomatic missions. Displeased with the direction of Louis' reign, he retired from court in the early 820s and wrote his Life of Charlemagne ca. 825/26. The text, which is a classic of medieval biography, demonstrates the author's thorough familiarity with his model Suetonius, but is also an extremely subtle critique of Charlemagne's successor. Like royal biographers after him such as Joinville, biographer of St. Louis IX (see below) Einhard attacks the faults of the reigning monarch by the simple expediency of praising the virtues of his predecessor.

Source: Translated by Samuel Epes Turner

Einhard's Preface

Since I have taken upon myself to narrate the public and private life, and no small part of the deeds, of my lord and foster-father, the most excellent and most justly renowned King Charles, I have condensed the matter into as brief a form as possible. I have been careful not to omit any fact that could come to my knowledge, but at the same time not to offend by a prolix style those minds that despise everything modern, if one can possibly avoid offending by a new work men who seem to despise also the masterpieces of antiquity, the works of most learned and luminous writers. Very many of them, I have no doubt, are men devoted to a life of literary leisure, who feel that the affairs of the present generation ought not to be passed by, and who do not consider everything done today as unworthy of mention and deserving to be given over to silence and oblivion, but are nevertheless seduced by lust of immortality to celebrate the glorious deeds of other times by some sort of composition rather than to deprive posterity of the mention of their own names by not writing at all.

Be this as it may, I see no reason why I should refrain from entering upon a task of this kind, since no man can write with more accuracy than I of events that took place about me, and of facts concerning which I had personal knowledge, ocular demonstration, as the saying goes, and I have no means of ascertaining whether or not any one else has the subject in hand.

In any event, I would rather commit my story to writing, and hand it down to posterity in partnership with others, so to speak, than to suffer the most glorious life of this most excellent king, the greatest of all the princes of his day, and his illustrious deeds, hard for men of later times to imitate, to be wrapped in the darkness of oblivion.

But there are still other reasons, neither unwarrantable nor insufficient, in my opinion, that urge me to write on this subject, namely, the care that King Charles bestowed upon me in my childhood, and my constant friendship with himself and his children after I took up my abode at court. In this way he strongly endeared me to himself, and made me greatly his debtor as well in death as in life, so that were I, unmindful of the benefits conferred upon me, to keep silence concerning the most glorious and illustrious deeds of a man who claims so much at my hands, and suffer his life to lack due eulogy and written memorial, as if he had never lived, I should deservedly appear ungrateful, and be so considered, albeit my powers are feeble, scanty, next to nothing indeed, and not at all adapted to write and set forth a life that would tax the eloquence of a Tully.

I submit the book. It contains the history of a very great and distinguished man; but there is nothing in it to wonder at besides his deeds, except the fact that I, who am a barbarian, and very little versed in the Roman language, seem to suppose myself capable of writing gracefully and respectably in Latin, and to carry my presumption so far as to disdain the sentiment that Cicero is said in the first book of the "Tusculan Disputations" to have expressed when speaking of the Latin authors. His words are: "It is an outrageous abuse both of time and literature for a man to commit his thoughts to writing without having the ability either to arrange them or elucidate them, or attract readers by some charm of style." This dictum of the famous orator might have deterred me from writing if I had not made up my mind that it was better to risk the opinions of the world, and put my little talents for composition to the test, than to slight the memory of so great a man for the sake of sparing myself.

The Life of the Emperor Charles

1. The Merovingian family, from which the Franks used to choose their kings, is commonly said to have lasted until the time of Childeric, who was deposed, shaved and thrust into the cloister by command of the Roman Pontiff Stephen. But although, to all outward appearances, it ended with him, it had long since been devoid of vital strength, and conspicuous only from bearing the empty epithet Royal; the real power and authority in the kingdom lay in the hands of the chief officer of the court, the so–called Mayor of the Palace, and he was at the head of affairs. There was nothing left the King to do but to be content with his name of King, his flowing hair, and long beard, to sit on his throne and play the ruler, to give ear to the ambassadors that came from all quarters, and to dismiss them, as if on his own responsibility, in words that were, in fact, suggested to him, or even imposed upon him. He had nothing that he could call his own beyond this vain title of King and the precarious support allowed by the Mayor of the Palace in his discretion, except a single country seat, that brought him but a very small income. There was a dwelling house upon this, and a small number of servants attached to it, sufficient to perform the necessary offices. When he had to go abroad, he used to ride in a cart, drawn by a yoke of oxen, driven, peasant–fashion, by a ploughman; he rode in this way to the palace and to the general assembly of the people, that met once a year for the welfare of the kingdom, and he returned him in like manner. The Mayor of the Palace took charge of the government and everything that had to be planned or executed at home and abroad.

LINK TO YEARS OF POWER

2. At the time of Childeric's disposition, Pepin, the father of King Charles, held this office of Mayor of the Palace, one might almost say, by hereditary right; for Pepin's father, Charles, had received it at the hands of his father, Pepin, and filled it with distinction. It was this Charles that crushed the tyrants who claimed to rule the whole Frank land as their own, and that utterly routed the Saracens, when they attempted the conquest of Gaul, in two great battles—one in Aquitania, near the town of Poitiers, and the other on the River Berre, near Narbone—and compelled them to return to Spain. This honor was usually conferred by the people only upon men eminent from their illustrious birth and ample wealth. For some years, ostensibly under King Childeric, Pepin, the father of King Charles, shared the duties inherited from his father and grandfather most amicably with his brother, Carloman. The latter, then, for reasons unknown, renounced the heavy cares of an earthly crown and retired to Rome. Here he exchanged his worldly garb for a cowl, and built a monastery on Mt. Oreste, near the Church of St. Sylvester, where he enjoyed for several years the seclusion that he desired, in company with certain others who had the same object in view. But so many distinguished Franks made the pilgrimage to Rome to fulfill their vows, and insisted upon paying their respects to him, as their former lord, on the way, that the repose which he so much loved was broken by these frequent visits, and he was driven to change his abode. Accordingly, when he found that his plans were frustrated by his many visitors, he abandoned the mountain, and withdrew to the Mon-

astery of St. Benedict, on Monte Cassino, in the province of Samnium, and passed the rest of his days there in the exercises of religion.

3.   Pepin, however, was raised, by decree of the Roman Pontiff, from the rank of Mayor of the Palace to that of King, and ruled alone over the Franks for fifteen years or more. He died of dropsy, in Paris, at the close of the Aquitanian war, which he waged with William, Duke of Aquitania, for nine successive years, and left two sons, Charles and Carloman, upon whim, by the grace of God, the succession devolved.

The Franks, in a general assembly of the people, made them both kings, on condition that they should divide the whole kingdom equally between them, Charles to take and rule the part that had belonged to their father, Pepin, and Carloman the part which their uncle, Carloman, had governed. The conditions were accepted, and each entered into possession of the share of the kingdom that fell to him by this arrangement; but peace was *OF COURSE NOT CHARLES* only maintained between them with the greatest difficulty, because many of Carloman's party kept trying to disturb their good understanding, and there were some even who plotted to involve them in a war with each other. The event, however, showed the danger to have been rather imaginary than real, for at Carloman's death his widow fled to Italy with her sons and her principal adherents, and without reason, despite her husband's brother, put herself and her children under the protection of Desiderius, King of the Lombards. Carloman had succumbed to disease after ruling two years in common with his brother, and at his death Charles was unanimously elected King of the Franks.

4.   It would be folly, I think, to write a word concerning Charles' birth and infancy, or even his boyhood, for nothing has ever been written on the subject, and there is no one alive now who can give information of it. Accordingly, I have determined to pass that by as unknown, and to proceed at once to treat of his character, his deeds, and such other facts of his life as are worth telling and setting forth, and shall first give an account of his deeds at home and abroad, then of his character and pursuits, and lastly of his administration and death, omitting nothing worth knowing or necessary to know.

5.   His first undertaking in a military way was the Aquitanian war, begun by his father, but not brought to a close; and because he thought that it could be readily carried through, he took it up while his brother was yet alive, calling upon him to render aid. The campaign once opened, he conducted it with the greatest vigor, notwithstanding his brother withheld the assistance that he had promised, and did not desist or shrink from his self-imposed task until, by his patience and firmness, he had completely gained his ends. He compelled Hunold, who had attempted to seize Aquitania after Waifar's death, and renew the war then almost concluded, to abandon Aquitania and flee to Gascony. Even here he gave him no rest, but crossed the River Garonne, built the castle of Fronsac, and sent ambassadors to Lupus, Duke of Gascony, to demand the surrender of the fugitive, threatening to take him by force unless he were promptly given up to him. Thereupon Lupus chose the wiser course, and not only gave Hunold up, but submitted himself, with the province which he ruled, to the King.

6.   After bringing this war to an end and settling matters in Aquitania (his associate in authority had meantime departed this life), he was induced, by the prayers and entreaties of Hadrian, Bishop of the city of Rome, to wage war on the Lombards. His father before him had undertaken this task at the request of Pope Stephen, but under great difficulties, for certain leading Franks, of whom he usually took counsel, has so vehemently opposed his design as to declare openly that they would leave the king and go home. Nevertheless, the war against the Lombard King Astolf had been taken up and very quickly concluded. Now, although Charles seems to have had similar, or rather just the same grounds for declaring war that his father had, the war itself differed from the preceding one alike in its difficulties and its issue. Pepin, to be sure, after besieging King Astolf a few days in Pavia, had compelled him to give hostages, to restore to the Romans the cities and castles that

he had taken, and to make oath that he would not attempt to seize them again: but Charles did not cease, after declaring war, until he had exhausted King Desiderius by a long siege, and forced him to surrender at discretion; driven his son Adalgis, the last hope of the Lombards, not only from his kingdom, but from all Italy; restored to the Romans all that they had lost; subdued Hruodgaus, Duke of Friuli, who was plotting revolution; reduced all Italy to his power, and set his son Pepin as king over it.

At this point I should describe Charles's difficult passage over the Alps into Italy, and the hardships that the Franks endured in climbing the trackless mountain ridges, the heaven-aspiring cliffs and ragged peaks, if it were not my purpose in this work to record the manner of his life rather than the incidents of the wars that he waged. Suffice it to say that this war ended with the subjection of Italy, the banishment of King Desiderius for life, the expulsion of his son Adalgis from Italy, and the restoration of the conquests of the Lombard kings to Hadrian, the head of the Roman Church.

7.   At the conclusion of this struggle, the Saxon war, that seems to have been only laid aside for the time, was taken up again. No war ever undertaken by the Frank nation was carried on with such persistence and bitterness, or cost so much labor, because the Saxons, like almost all the tribes of Germany, were a fierce people, given to the worship of devils, and hostile to our religion, and did not consider it dishonorable to transgress and violate all law, human and divine. Then there were peculiar circumstances that tended to cause a breach of peace every day. Except in a few places, where large forests or mountain ridges intervened and made the bounds certain, the line between ourselves and the Saxons passed almost in its whole extent through an open country, so that there was no end to the murders, thefts and arsons on both sides. In this way the Franks became so embittered that they at last resolved to make reprisals no longer, but to come to open war with the Saxons. Accordingly war was begun against them, and was waged for thirty-three successive years with great fury; more, however, to the disadvantage of the Saxons than of the Franks. It could doubtless have been brought to an end sooner, had it not been for the faithlessness of the Saxons. It is hard to say how often they were conquered, and, humbly submitting to the King, promised to do what was enjoined upon them, gave without hesitation the required hostages, and received the officers sent them from the King. They were sometimes so much weakened and reduced that they promised to renounce the worship of devils, and to adopt Christianity, but they were no less ready to violate these terms than prompt to accept them, so that it is impossible to tell which came easier to them to do; scarcely a year passed from the beginning of the war without such changes on their part. But the King did not suffer his high purpose and steadfastness—firm alike in good and evil fortune—to be turned from the task that he had undertaken; on the contrary, he never allowed their faithless behaviour to go unpunished, but either took the field against them in person, or sent his counts with an army to wreak vengeance and exact righteous satisfaction. At last, after conquering and subduing all who had offered resistance, he took ten thousand of those that lived on the banks of the Elbe, and settled them, with their wives and children, in many different bodies here and there in Gaul and Germany. The war that had lasted so many years was at length ended by their acceding to the terms offered by the King; which were renunciation of their national religious customs and the worship of devils, acceptance of the sacraments of the Christian faith and religion, and union with the Franks to form one people.

8.   Charles himself fought but two pitched battles in this war, although it was long protracted—one on Mount Osning, at the place called Detmold, and again on the bank of the river Hase, both in the space of little more than a month. The enemy were so routed and overthrown in these two battles that they never afterwards ventured to take the offensive or to resist the attacks of the King, unless they were protected by a strong position. A great many of the Frank as well as of the Saxon nobility, men occupying the highest posts of honor, perished in this war, which only came to an end after the lapse of thirty-two years. So many and grievous were the wars that were declared against the Franks in the mean-

time, and skillfully conducted by the King, that one may reasonably question whether his fortitude or his good fortune is to be more admired. The Saxon war began two years before the Italian war; but although it went on without interruption, business elsewhere was not neglected, nor was there any shrinking from other equally arduous contests. The King, who excelled all the princes of his time in wisdom and greatness of soul, did not suffer difficulty to deter him or danger to daunt him from anything that had to be taken up or carried through, for he had trained himself to bear and endure whatever came, without yielding in adversity, or trusting to the deceitful favors of fortune in prosperity.

9.　In the midst of this vigorous and almost uninterrupted struggle with the Saxons, he covered the frontier by garrisons at the proper points, and marched over the Pyrenees into Spain at the head of all the forces that he could muster. All the towns and castles that he attacked surrendered, and up to the time of his homeward march he sustained no loss whatsoever; but on his return through the Pyrenees he had cause to rue the treachery of the Gascons. That region is well adapted for ambuscades by reason of the thick forests that cover it; and as the army was advancing in the long line of march necessitated by the narrowness of the road, the Gascons, who lay in ambush on the top of a very high mountain, attacked the rear of the baggage train and the rear guard in charge of it, and hurled them down to the very bottom of the valley. In the struggle that ensued, they cut them off to a man; they then plundered the baggage, and dispersed with all speed in every direction under cover of approaching night. The lightness of their armor and the nature of the battle ground stood the Gascons in good stead on this occasion, whereas the Franks fought at a disadvantage in every respect, because of the weight of their armor and the unevenness of the ground. Eggihard, the King's steward; Anselm, Count Palatine; and Roland, Governor of the March of Brittany, with very many others, fell in this engagement. This ill turn could not be avenged for the nonce, because the enemy scattered so widely after carrying out their plan that not the least clue could be had to their whereabouts.

[margin handwriting: SONG OF ROLAND; A LOSS FOR CHARLES]

10.　Charles also subdued the Bretons, who live on the sea coast, in the extreme western part of Gaul. When they refused to obey him, he sent an army against them, and compelled them to give hostages, and to promise to do his bidding. He afterwards entered Italy in person with his army, and passed through Rome to Capua, a city in Campania, where he pitched his camp and threatened the Beneventans with hostilities unless they should submit themselves to him. Their duke, Aragis, escaped the danger by sending his two sons, Rumold and Grimold, with a great sum of money to greet the King, begging him to accept them as hostages, and promising for himself and his people compliance with all the King's commands, on the single condition that his personal attendance should not be required. The King took the welfare of the people into account rather than the stubborn disposition of the Duke, accepted the proffered hostages, and released him from the obligation to appear before him in consideration of his handsome gift. He retained the younger son only as hostage, and sent the elder back to his father, and returned to Rome, leaving commissioners with Aragis to exact the oath of allegiance, and administer it to the Beneventans. He stayed in Rome several days in order to pay his devotions at the holy places, and then came back to Gaul.

11.　At this time, on a sudden, the Bavarian war broke out, but came to a speedy end. It was due to the arrogance and folly of Duke Tassilo. His wife, a daughter of King Desiderius, was desirous of avenging her father's banishment through the agency of her husband, and accordingly induced him to make a treaty with the Huns, the neighbors of the Bavarians on the east, and not only to leave the King's commands unfulfilled, but to challenge him to war. Charles' high spirit could not brook Tassilo's insubordination, for it seemed to him to pass all bounds; accordingly he straightway summoned his troops from all sides for a campaign against Bavaria, and appeared in person with a great army on the river Lech, which forms the boundary between the Bavarians and the Alemanni.

After pitching his camp upon its banks, he determined to put the Duke's disposition to the test by an embassy before entering the province. Tassilo did not think that it was for his own or his people's good to persist, so he surrendered himself to the King, gave the hostages demanded, among them his own son Theodo, and promised by oath not to give ear to anyone who should attempt to turn him from his allegiance; so this war, which bade fair to be very grievous, came very quickly to an end. Tassilo, however, was afterward summoned to the King's presence, and not suffered to depart, and the government of the province that he had had in charge was no longer intrusted to a duke, but to counts.

12. After these uprisings had been thus quelled, war was declared against the Slavs who are commonly known among us as Wilzi, but properly, that is to say in their own tongue, are called Welatabians. The Saxons served in this campaign as auxiliaries among the tribes that followed the King's standard at his summons, but their obedience lacked sincerity and devotion. War was declared because the Slavs kept harassing the Abodriti, old allies of the Franks, by continual raids, in spite of all commands to the contrary. A gulf of unknown length, but nowhere more than a hundred miles wide, and in many parts narrower, stretches off towards the east from the Western Ocean. Many tribes have settlements on its shores; the Danes and Swedes, whom we call Northmen, on the northern shore and all the adjacent islands; but the southern shore is inhabited by the Slavs and Aïsti, and various other tribes. The Welatabians, against whom the King now made war, were the chief of these; but in a single campaign, which he conducted in person, he so crushed and subdued them that they did not think it advisable thereafter to refuse obedience to his commands.

13. The war against the Avars, or Huns, followed, and, except for the Saxon war, was the greatest that was waged; he took it up with more spirit than any of his other wars, and made far greater preparations for it. He conducted one campaign in person in Pannonia, of which the Huns then had possession. He intrusted all subsequent operations to his son, Pepin, and the governors of the provinces, to counts even, and lieutenants. Although they most vigorously prosecuted the war, it only came to a conclusion after a seven years' struggle. The utter depopulation of Pannonia, and the site of the Khan's palace, now a desert, where not a trace of human habitation is visible, bear witness how many battles were fought in those years, and how much blood was shed. The entire body of the Hun nobility perished in this contest, and all its glory with it. All the money and treasure that had been years amassing was seized, and no war in which the Franks have ever engaged within the memory of man brought them such riches and such booty. Up to that time the Huns had passed for a poor people, but so much gold and silver was found in the Khan's palace, and so much valuable spoil taken in battle, that one may well think that the Franks took justly from the Huns what the Huns had formerly taken unjustly from other nations. Only two of the chief men of the Franks fell in this war—Eric, Duke of Friuli, who was killed in Tarsatch, a town on the coast of Liburnia, by the treachery of the inhabitants; and Gerold, Governor of Bavaria, who met his death at Pannonia, slain, with two men that were accompanying him, by an unknown hand while he was marshalling his forces for battle against the Huns, and riding up and down the line encouraging his men. This war was otherwise almost a bloodless one so far as the Franks were concerned, and ended most satisfactorily, although by reason of its magnitude it was long protracted.

14. The Saxon war next came to an end as successful as the struggle had been long. The Bohemian and Linonian wars that next broke out could not last long; both were quickly carried through under the leadership of the younger Charles. The last of these wars was the one declared against the Northmen called Danes. They began their careers as pirates, but afterward took to laying waste the coasts of Gaul and Germany with their large fleet. Their King Godfred was so puffed with vain aspirations that he counted on gaining empire over all Germany, and looked upon Saxony and Frisia as his provinces. He had already subdued his neighbors the Abodriti, and made them tributary, and boasted that he

would shortly appear with a great army before Aix–la–Chapelle, where the King held his court. Some faith was put in his words, empty as they sound, and it is supposed that he would have attempted something of the sort if he had not been prevented by a premature death. He was murdered by one of his own bodyguard, and so ended at once his life and the war that he had begun.

15. Such are the wars, most skillfully planned and successfully fought, which this most powerful king waged during the forty–seven years of his reign. He so largely increased the Frank kingdom, which was already great and strong when he received it at his father's hands, that more than double its former territory was added to it. The authority of the Franks was formerly confined to that part of Gaul included between the Rhine and the Loire, the Ocean and the Balearic Sea; to that part of Germany which is inhabited by the so–called Eastern Franks, and is bounded by Saxony and the Danube, the Rhine and the Saale—this stream separates the Thuringians from the Sorabians; and to the country of the Alemanni and Bavarians. By the wars above mentioned he first made tributary Aquitania, Gascony, and the whole of the region of the Pyrenees as far as the River Ebro, which rises in the land of the Navarrese, flows through the most fertile districts of Spain, and empties into the Balearic Sea, beneath the walls of the city of Tortosa. He next reduced and made tributary all Italy from Aosta to Lower Calabria, where the boundary line runs between the Beneventans and the Greeks, a territory more than a thousand miles long; then Saxony, which constitutes no small part of Germany, and is reckoned to be twice as wide as the country inhabited by the Franks, while about equal to it in length; in addition, both Pannonias, Dacia beyond the Danube, and Istria, Liburnia, and Dalmatia, except the cities on the coast, which he left to the Greek Emperor for friendship's sake, and because of the treaty that he had made with him. In fine, he vanquished and made tributary all the wild and barbarous tribes dwelling in Germany between the Danube, all of which speak very much the same language, but differ widely from one another chiefly in customs and dress. The chief among them are the Welatabians, the Sorabians, the Abodriti, and the Bohemians, and he had to make war upon these; but the rest, by far the larger number, submitted to him of their own accord.

16. He added to the glory of his reign by gaining the goodwill of several kings and nations; so close, indeed, was the alliance that he contracted with Alfonso, King of Galicia and Asturias, that the latter, when sending letters or ambassadors to Charles, invariably styled himself his man. His munificence won the kings of the Scots also to pay such deference to his wishes that they never gave him any other title than lord, or themselves than subjects or slaves: there are letters from them extant in which these feelings in his regard are expressed. His relations with Aaron, King of the Persians, who ruled over almost the whole of the East, India excepted, were so friendly that this prince preferred his favor to that of all the kings and potentates of the earth, and considered that to him alone marks of honor and munificence were due. Accordingly, when the ambassadors sent by Charles to visit the most holy sepulchre and place of resurrection of our Lord and Savior presented themselves before him with gifts, and made known their master's wishes, he not only granted what was asked, but gave possession of that holy and blessed spot. When they returned, he dispatched his ambassadors with them, and sent magnificent gifts, besides stuffs, perfumes, and other rich products of the Eastern lands. A few years before this, Charles had asked him for an elephant, and he sent the only one that he had. The Emperors of Constantinople, Nicephorus, Michael, and Leo, made advances to Charles, and sought friendship and alliance with him by several embassies; and even when the Greeks suspected him of designing to wrest the empire from them, because of his assumption of the title Emperor, they made a close alliance with him, that he might have no cause of offense. In fact, the power of the Franks was always viewed by the Greeks and Romans with a jealous eye, whence the Greek proverb "Have the Frank for your friend, but not for your neighbor."

17. This King, who showed himself so great in extending his empire and subduing foreign nations, and was constantly occupied with plans to that end, undertook also very many works calculated to adorn and benefit his kingdom, and brought several of them to completion. Among these, the most deserving of mention are the basilica of the Holy Mother of God at Aix-la-Chapelle, built in the most admirable manner, and a bridge over the Rhine at Mayence, half a mile long, the breadth of the river at this point. This bridge was destroyed by fire the year before Charles died, but, owing to his death so soon after, could not be repaired, although he had intended to rebuild it in stone. He began two palaces of beautiful workmanship—one near his manor called Ingelheim, not far from Mayence; the other at Nimeguen, on the Waal, the stream that washes the south side of the island of the Batavians. But, above all, sacred edifices were the object of his care throughout his whole kingdom; and whenever he found them falling to ruin from age, he commanded the priests and fathers who had charge of them to repair them, and made sure by commissioners that his instructions were obeyed. He also fitted out a fleet for the war with the Northmen; the vessels required for this purpose were built on the rivers that flow from Gaul and Germany into the Northern Ocean. Moreover, since the Northmen continually overran and laid waste the Gallic and German coasts, he caused watch and ward to be kept in all the harbors, and at the mouths of rivers in all the harbors, and at the mouths of rivers large enough to admit the entrance of vessels, to prevent the enemy from disembarking; and in the South, in Narbonensis and Septimania, and along the whole coast of Italy as far as Rome, he took the same precautions against the Moors, who had recently begun their piratical practices. Hence, Italy suffered no great harm in his time at the hands of the Moors, nor Gaul and Germany from the Northmen, save that the Moors got possession of the Etruscan town of Civita Vecchia by treachery, and sacked it, and the Northmen harried some of the islands in Frisia off the German coast.

18. Thus did Charles defend and increase as well as beautify his kingdom, as is well known; and here let me express my admiration of his great qualities and his extraordinary constancy alike in good and evil fortune. I will now forthwith proceed to give the details of his private and family life.

  After his father's death, while sharing the kingdom with his brother, he bore his unfriendliness and jealousy most patiently, and, to the wonder of all, could not be provoked to be angry with him. Later he married a daughter of Desiderius, King of the Lombards, at the instance of his mother; but he repudiated her at the end of a year for some reason unknown, and married Hildegard, a woman of high birth, of Suabian origin. He had three sons by her—Charles, Pepin, and Louis—and as many daughters—Hruodrud, Bertha, and Gisela. He had three other daughters besides these—Theoderada, Hiltrud, and Ruodhaid—two by his third wife, Fastrada, a woman of East Frankish (that is to say, German) origin, and the third by a concubine, whose name for the moment escapes me. At the death of Fastrada, he married Liutgard, an Alemannic woman, who bore him no children. After her death he had three concubines—Gersuinda, a Saxon, by whom he had Adaltrud, Regina, who was the mother of Drogo and Hugh; and Ethelind, by whom he had Theodoric. Charles' mother, Berthrada, passed her old age with him in great honor; he entertained the greatest veneration for her; and there was never any disagreement between them except when he divorced the daughter of King Desiderius, whom he had married to please her. She died soon after Hildegard, after living to see three grandsons and as many granddaughters in her son's house, and he buried her with great pomp in the Basilica of St. Denis, where his father lay. He had an only sister, Gisela, who had consecrated herself to a religious life from girlhood, and he cherished as much affection for her as for his mother. She also died a few years before him in the nunnery where she had passed her life.

19. The plan that he adopted for his children's education was, first of all, to have both boys and girls instructed in the liberal arts, to which he also turned his own attention. As soon as their years admitted, in accordance with the customs of the Franks, the boys had

to learn horsemanship, and to practice war and the chase, and the girls to familiarize themselves with cloth–making, and to handle distaff and spindle, that they might not grow indolent through idleness, and he fostered in them every virtuous sentiment. He only lost three of all his children before his death, two sons and one daughter, Charles who was the eldest, Pepin, whom he had made King of Italy, and Hruodrud, his oldest daughter, whom he had betrothed to Constantine, Emperor of the Greeks. Pepin left one son, named Bernard, and five daughters, Adelaide, Atula, Guntrada, Berthaid, and Theoderada. The King gave a striking proof of his fatherly affection at the time of Pepin's death: he appointed the grandson to succeed Pepin, and had the granddaughters brought up with his own daughters. When his sons and his daughter died, he was not so calm as might have been expected from his remarkably strong mind, for his affections were no less strong, and move him to tears. Again, when he was told of the death of Hadrian, the Roman Pontiff, whom he had loved most of all his friends, he wept as much as if he had lost a brother, or a very dear son. He was by nature most ready to contract friendships, and not only made friends easily, but clung to them persistently, and cherished most fondly those with whom he had formed such ties. He was so careful of the training of his sons and daughters that he never took his meals without them when he was at home, and never made a journey without them; his sons would ride at his side, and his daughters follow him, while a number of his bodyguard, detailed for their protection, brought up the rear. Strange to say, although they were very handsome women, and he loved them very dearly, he was never willing to marry any of them to a man of their own nation or to a foreigner, but kept them all at home until his death, saying that he could not dispense with their society. Hence, though otherwise happy, he experienced the malignity of fortune as far as they were concerned; yet he concealed his knowledge of the rumors current in regard to them, and of the suspicions entertained of their honor.

20. By one of his concubines he had a son, handsome in face, but hunchbacked, named Pepin, whom I omitted to mention in the list of his children. When Charles was at war with the Huns, and was wintering in Bavaria, this Pepin shammed sickness, and plotted against his father in company with some of the leading Franks, who seduced him with vain promises of the royal authority. When his deceit was discovered, and the conspirators punished, his head was shaved, and he was suffered, in accordance with his wishes, to devote himself to a religious life in the monastery of Prüm. A formidable conspiracy against Charles had previously been set on foot in Germany, but all the traitors were banished, some of them without mutilations, others after their eyes had been put out. Three of them only lost their lives; they drew their swords and resisted arrest, and, after killing several men, were cut down, because they could not otherwise be overpowered. It is supposed that the cruelty of Queen Fastrada was the primary cause of these plots, and they were both due to Charles' apparent acquiescence in his wife's cruel conduct, and deviation from the usual kindness and gentleness of his disposition. All the rest of his life he was regarded by everyone with the utmost love and affection, so much so that not the least accusation of unjust rigor was ever made against him.

21. He liked foreigners, and was at great pains to take them under his protection. There were often so many of them, both in the palace and the kingdom, that they might reasonably have been considered a nuisance; but he, with his broad humanity, was very little disturbed by such annoyances, because he felt himself compensated for these great inconveniences by the praises of his generosity and the reward of high renown.

22. Charles was large and strong, and of lofty statute, though not disproportionately tall (his height is well known to have been seven times the length of his foot); the upper part of his head was round, his eyes very large and animated, nose a little long, hair fair, and face laughing and merry. Thus his appearance was always stately and dignified, whether he was standing or sitting; although his neck was thick and somewhat short, and his belly rather prominent; but the symmetry of the rest of his body concealed these defects. His

gait was firm, his whole carriage manly, and his voice clear, but not so strong as his size led one to expect. His health was excellent, except during the four years preceding his death, when he was subject to frequent fevers; at the last he even limped a little with one foot. Even in those years he consulted rather his own inclinations than the advice of physicians, who were almost hateful to him, because they wanted him to give up roasts, to which he was accustomed, and to eat boiled meat instead. In accordance with the national custom, he took frequent exercise on horseback and in the chase, accomplishments in which scarcely any people in the worlds can equal the Franks. He enjoyed the exhalations from natural warm springs, and often practiced swimming, in which he was such an adept that none could surpass him; and hence it was that he built his palace at Aix–la–Chapelle, and lived there constantly during his latter years until his death. He used not only to invite his sons to his bath, but his nobles and friends, and now and then a troop of his retinue or bodyguard, so that a hundred or more persons sometimes bathed with him.

23. He used to wear the national, that is to say, the Frank, dress—next his skin a linen shirt and linen breeches, and above these a tunic fringed with silk; while hose fastened by bands covered his lower limbs, and shoes his feet, and he protected his shoulders and chest in winter by a close–fitting coat of otter or marten skins. Over all he flung a blue cloak, and he always had a sword girt about him, usually one with a gold or silver hilt and belt; he sometimes carried a jeweled sword, but only on great feastdays or at the reception of ambassadors from foreign nations. He despised foreign costumes, however handsome, and never allowed himself to be robed in them, except twice in Rome, when he donned the Roman tunic, chlamys, and shoes; the first time at the request of Pope Hadrian, the second to gratify Leo, Hadrian's successor. On great feastdays he made use of embroidered clothes and shoes bedecked by a golden buckle, and he appeared crowned with a diadem of gold and gems, but on other days his dress varied from the common dress of the people.

24. Charles was temperate in eating, and particularly so in drinking, for he abominated drunkenness in anybody, much more in himself and those of his household; but he could not easily abstain from food, and often complained that fasts injured his health. He very rarely gave entertainments, only on great feastdays, and then to large numbers of people. His meals ordinarily consisted of four courses, not counting the roast, which his huntsmen used to bring in on the spit; he was more fond of this than any other dish. While at table, he listened to reading or music. The subjects of the readings were the stories and deeds of olden time: he was fond, too, of St. Augustine's books, and especially of the one entitled "The City of God." He was so moderate in the use of wine and all sorts of drink that he rarely allowed himself more than three cups in the course of a meal. In summer, after the midday meal, he would eat some fruit, drain a single cup, put off his clothes and shoes, just as he did for the night, and rest for two or three hours. He was in the habit of awaking and rising from bed four or five times during the night. While he was dressing and putting on his shoes, he not only gave audience to his friends, but if the Count of the Palace told him of any suit in which his judgement was necessary, he had the parties brought before him forthwith, took cognizance of the case, and gave his decision, just as if he were sitting on the judgement seat. This was not the only business that he transacted at this time, but he performed any duty of the day whatever, whether he had to attend to the matter himself, or to give commands concerning it to his officers.

25. Charles had the gift of ready and fluent speech, and could express whatever he had to say with the utmost clearness. He was not satisfied with command of his native language merely, but gave attention to the study of foreign ones, and in particular was such a master of Latin that he could speak it as well as his native tongue; but he could understand Greek better than he could speak it. He was so eloquent, indeed, that he might have passed for a teacher of eloquence. He most zealously cultivated the liberal arts, held those

those who taught them in great esteem, and conferred great honors upon them. He took lessons in grammar of the deacon Peter of Pisa, at that time an aged man. Another deacon, Albin of Britain, surnamed Alcuin, a man of Saxon extraction, who was the greatest scholar of the day, was his teacher in other branches of learning. The King spent much time and labor with him studying rhetoric, dialectics, and especially astronomy; he learned to reckon, and used to investigate the motions of the heavenly bodies most curiously, with an intelligent scrutiny. He also tried to write, and used to keep tablets and blanks in bed under his pillow, that at leisure hours he might accustom his hand to form the letters; however, as he did not begin his efforts in due season, but late in life, they met with ill success.

26. He cherished with the greatest fervor and devotion the principles of the Christian religion, which had been instilled into him from infancy. Hence it was that he built the beautiful basilica at Aix-la-Chapelle, which he adorned with gold and silver and lamps, and with rails and doors of solid brass. He had the columns and marbles for this structure brought from Rome and Ravenna, for he could not find such as were suitable elsewhere. He was a constant worshipper at this church as long as his health permitted, going morning and evening, even after nightfall, besides attending mass; and he took care that all the services there conducted should be administered with the utmost possible propriety, very often warning the sextons not to let any improper or unclean thing be brought into the building or remain in it. He provided it with a great number of sacred vessels of gold and silver and with such a quantity of clerical robes that not even the doorkeepers who fill the humblest office in the church were obliged to wear their everyday clothes when in the exercise of their duties. He was at great pains to improve the church reading and psalmody, for he was well skilled in both, although he neither read in public nor sang, except in a low tone and with others.

27. He was very forward in succoring the poor, and in that gratuitous generosity which the Greeks call alms, so much so that he not only made a point of giving in his own country and his own kingdom, but when he discovered that there were Christians living in poverty in Syria, Egypt, and Africa, at Jerusalem, Alexandria, and Carthage, he had compassion on their wants, and used to send money over the seas to them. The reason that he zealously strove to make friends with the kings beyond the seas was that he might get help and relief to the Christians living under their rule. He cherished the Church of St. Peter the Apostle at Rome above all other holy and sacred places, and heaped its treasury with a vast wealth of gold, silver, and precious stones. He sent great and countless gifts to the popes, and throughout his whole reign the wish that he had nearest at heart was to re-establish the ancient authority of the city of Rome under his care and by his influence, and to defend and protect the Church of St. Peter, and to beautify and enrich it out of his own store above all other churches. Although he held it in such veneration, he only repaired to Rome to pay his vows and make his supplications four times during the whole forty-seven years that he reigned.

28. When he made his last journey thither, he had also other ends in view. The Romans had inflicted many injuries upon the Pontiff Leo, tearing out his eyes and cutting out his tongue, so that he had been compelled to call upon the King for help. Charles accordingly went to Rome, to set in order the affairs of the Church, which were in great confusion, and passed the whole winter there. It was then that he received the titles of Emperor and Augustus, to which he at first had such an aversion that he declared that he would not have set foot in the Church the day that they conferred, although it was a great feast-day, if he could have foreseen the design of the Pope. He bore very patiently with the jealousy which the Roman emperors showed upon his assuming these titles, for they took this step very ill; and by dint of frequent embassies and letters, in which he addressed them as brothers, he made their haughtiness yield to his magnanimity, a quality in which he was unquestionably much their superior.

29. It was after he received the imperial name that, finding the laws of his people very defective (the Franks have two sets of laws, very different in many particulars), he determined to add what was wanting, to reconcile the discrepancies, and to correct what was vicious and wrongly cited in them. However, he went no further in this matter than to supplement the laws with a few capitularies, and those imperfect ones; but he caused the unwritten laws of all the tribes that came under his rule to be compiled and reduced to writing. He also had the old rude songs that celebrate the deeds and wars of the ancient kings written out for transmission to posterity. He began a grammar of his native language. He gave the months names in his own tongue, in place of the Latin and barbarous names by which they were formerly known among the Franks. He likewise designated the winds by twelve appropriate names; there were hardly more than four distinctive ones in use before. He called January, Wintarmanoth; February, Hornung; March, Lentzinmanoth; April, Ostarmanoth; May, Winnemanoth; June, Brachmanoth; July, Heuvimanoth; August, Aranmanoth; September, Witumanoth; October, Windumemanoth; November, Herbistmanoth; December, Heilagmanoth. He styled the winds as follows; Subsolanus, Ostroniwint; Eurus, Ostsundroni; Euroauster, Sundostroni; Auster, Sundroni; Austro–Africus, Sundwestroni; Africus, West–sundroni; Zephyrus, Westroni; Caurus, Westnordroni; Circius, Nordwestroni; Septentrio, Nordroni; Aquilo, Nordostroni; Vulturnus, Ostnordroni.

30. Toward the close of his life, when he was broken by ill–health and old age, he summoned Louis, King of Aquitania, his only surviving son by Hildegard, and gathered together all the chief men of the whole kingdom of the Franks in a solemn assembly. He appointed Louis, with their unanimous consent, to rule with himself over the whole kingdom, and constituted him heir to the imperial name, placing the diadem upon his son's head, he bade him be proclaimed Emperor and Augustus. This step was hailed by all present with great favor, for it really seemed as if God had prompted him to it for the kingdom's good; it increased the King's dignity, and struck no little terror into foreign nations. After sending his son back to Aquitania, although weak from age he set out to hunt, as usual, near his palace at Aix–la–Chapelle, and passed the rest of the autumn in the chase, returning thither about the first of November. While wintering there, he was seized, in the month of January, with a high fever, and took to his bed. As soon as he was taken sick, he prescribed for himself abstinence from food, as he always used to do in case of fever, thinking that the disease could be driven off, or at least mitigated, by fasting. Besides the fever, he suffered from a pain in the side, which the Greeks called pleurisy; but he still persisted in fasting, and in keeping up his strength only by draughts taken at very long intervals. He died January twenty–eighth, the seventh day from the time he took to his bed, at nine o'clock in the morning, after partaking of the holy communion, the seventh–second year of his age and the forty–seventh of his reign.

31. His body was washed and cared for in the usual manner, and was then carried to the church, and interred amid the greatest lamentations of all the people. There was some question at first where to lay him, because in his lifetime he had given no directions as to his burial; but at length all agreed that he could nowhere be more honorably entombed than in the very basilica that he had built in the town at his own expense, for the love of God and our Lord Jesus Christ, and in honor of the Holy and Eternal Virgin, His Mother. He was buried there the same day that he died, and a gilded arch was erected above his tomb with his image and an inscription. The words of the inscription were as follows: "In this tomb lies the body of Charles, the Great and Orthodox Emperor, who gloriously extended the kingdom of the Franks, and reigned prosperously for forty–seven years. He died at the age of seventy, in the year of our Lord 814, the 7th Indiction, on the 28th day of January."

32. Very many omens had portended his approaching end, a fact that he had recognized as well as others. Eclipses both of the sun and moon were very frequent during the last

three years of his life, and a black spot was visible on the sun for the space of seven days. The gallery between the basilica and the palace, which he had built at great pains and labor, fell in sudden ruin to the ground on the day of the Ascension of our Lord. The wooden bridge over the Rhine at Mayence, which he had caused to be constructed with admirable skill, at the cost of ten years' hard work, so that it seemed as if it might last forever, was so completely consumed in three hours by an accidental fire that not a single splinter of it was left, except what was under water. Moreover, one day in his last campaign into Saxony against Godfred, King of the Danes, Charles himself saw a ball of fire fall suddenly from the heavens with a great light, just as he was leaving camp before sunrise to set out on the march. It rushed across the clear sky from right to left, and everybody was wondering what was the meaning of the sign, when the horse which he was riding gave a sudden plunge, head foremost, and fell, and threw him to the ground so heavily that his cloak buckle was broken and his sword belt shattered; and after his servants had hastened to him and relived him of his arms, he could not rise without their assistance. He happened to have a javelin in his hand when he was thrown, and this was struck from his grasp with such force that it was found lying at a distance of twenty feet or more from the spot. Again, the palace at Aix-la-Chapelle frequently trembled, the roofs of whatever buildings he tarried in kept up a continual crackling noise, the basilica in which he was afterwards buried was struck by lightening, and the gilded ball that adorned the pinnacle of the roof was shattered by the thunderbolt and hurled upon the bishop's house adjoining. In this same basilica, on the margin of the cornice that ran around the interior, between the upper and lower tiers or arches, a legend was inscribed in red letters, stating who was the builder of the temple, the last words of which were **Karolus Princeps.** The year that he died it was remarked by some, a few months before his decease, that the letters of the word **Princeps** were so effaced as to be no longer decipherable. But Charles despised, or affected to despise, all these omens, as having no reference whatever to him.

33. It had been his intention to make a will, that he might give some share in the inheritance to his daughters and the children of his concubines; but it was begun too late and could not be finished. Three years before his death, however, he made a division of his treasures, money, clothes, and other movable goods in the presence of his friends and servants, and called them to witness it, that their voices might insure the ratification of the disposition thus made. He had a summary drawn up of his wishes regarding this distribution of his property, the terms and text of which are as follows:

"In the name of the Lord God, the Almighty Father, Son, and Holy Ghost. This is the inventory and division dictated by the most glorious and most pious Lord Charles, Emperor Augustus, in the 811th year of the Incarnation of our Lord Jesus Christ, in the 43rd year of his reign in France and 37th in Italy, the 11th of his empire, and the 4th Indiction, which considerations of piety and prudence have determined him, and the favor of God enabled him, to make of his treasures and money ascertained this day to be in his treasure chamber. In this division he is especially desirous to provide not only that the largess of alms which Christians usually make of their possessions shall be made for himself in due course and order out of his wealth, but also that his heirs shall be free from all doubt, and know clearly what belongs to them, and be able to share their property by suitable partition without litigation or strife. With this intention and to this end he first divided all his substance and movable goods ascertained to be in his treasure chamber on the day aforesaid in gold, silver, precious stones, and royal ornaments into three lots, and has subdivided and set off two of the said lots into twenty-one parts, keeping the third entire. The first two lots have been thus subdivided into twenty-one parts because there are in his kingdom twenty-one recognized metropolitan cities, and in order that each archbishopric may receive by way of alms, at the hands of his heirs and friends, one of the said parts, and that the archbishop who shall then administer its affairs shall take the part given to it, and share the same with his suffragans in such manner that one third shall go to the

Church, and the remaining two–thirds be divided among the suffragans. The twenty–one parts into which the first two lots are to be distributed, according to the number of recognized metropolitan cities, have been set apart from one another, and each has been put aside by itself in a box labeled with the name of the city for which it was destined. The names of the cities to which this alms or largess is to be sent are as follows: Rome, Ravenna, Milan, Friuli, Grado, Cologne, Mayence, Salzburg, Treves, Sens, Besançon, Lyons, Rouen, Rheims, Arles, Vienne, Moutiers-en-Tarantaise, Embrun, Bordeaux, Tours, and Bourges. The third lot, which he wishes to be kept entire, is to be bestowed as follows: While the first two lots are to be divided into the parts aforesaid, and set aside under seal, the third lot shall be employed for the owner's daily needs, as property which he shall be under no obligation to part with in order to the fulfillment of any vow, and this as long as he shall be in the flesh, or consider it necessary for his use. But upon his death, or voluntary renunciation of the affairs of this world, this said lot shall be added to the aforesaid twenty-one parts; the second shall be assigned to his sons and daughters, and to the sons and daughters of his sons, to be distributed among them in just and equal partition; the third, in accordance with the custom common among Christians, shall be devoted to the poor; and the fourth shall go to the support of the men servants and maid servants on duty in the palace. It is his wish that to this said third lot of the whole amount, which consists, as well as the rest, of gold and silver, shall be added all the vessels and utensils of brass, iron, and other metals, together with the arms, clothing, and other movable goods, costly and cheap, adapted to divers uses, as hangings, coverlets, carpets, woolen stuffs, leathern articles, pack–saddles, and whatsoever shall be found in his treasure chamber and wardrobe at that time, in order that thus the parts of the said lots may be augmented, and the alms distributed reach more persons. He ordains that his chapel—that is to say, its church property, as well as that which he has provided and collected as that which came to him by inheritance from his father—shall remain entire, and not be disserviced by any partition whatever. If, however, any vessel, books, or other articles be found therein which are certainly known not to have been given by him to the said chapel, whoever wants them shall have them on paying their value at a fair estimation. He likewise commands that the books which he has collected in his library in great numbers shall be sold for fair prices to such as want them, and the money received therefrom given to the poor. It is well known that among his other property and treasures there are three silver tables, and one very large and massive golden one. He directs and commands that the square silver table, upon which there is a representation of the city of Constantinople, shall be sent to the Basilica of St. Peter the Apostle at Rome, with the other gifts destined therefor; that the round one, adorned with a delineation of the city of Rome, shall be given to the Episcopal Church at Ravenna; that the third, which far surpasses the other two in weight and in beauty of workmanship, and is made in three circles, showing the plan of the whole universe, drawn with skill and delicacy, shall go, together with the golden table, fourthly above mentioned, to increase that lot which is to be devoted to his heirs and to alms.

This deed, and the dispositions thereof, he has made and appointed in the presence of the bishops, abbots, and counts able to be present, whose names are hereto subscribed: Bishops—Hildebald, Ricolf, Arno, Wolfar, Bernoin, Laidrad, John, Theodulf, Jesse, Heito, Waltgaud. Abbots—Fredugis, Adalung, Angilbert, Irmino. Counts—Walacho, Meginher, Otulf, Stephen, Unruoch, Burchard, Meginhard, Hatto, Rihwin, Edo, Ercangar, Gerold, Bero, Hildiger, Rocculf."

Charles's son Louis, who by the grace of God succeeded him, after examining this summary, took pains to fulfill all its conditions most religiously as soon as possible after his father's death.

Selected Capitularies

The most important source for understanding Carolingian cultural, administrative, and social reform programs are the capitularies, directives used by the central administration to communicate with local authorities. The following examples show the range of these instruments and the various problems of Frankish society they attempt to address. They include the capitularies of Herstal, 779; Paderborn, 785; Saxons, 797; Frankfurt, 794; De literis colendis; De villis; Capitulaire missorum generale 802; Capitularia missorum Specialia, 802.

Source: H. R. Lyon and John Percival, *The Reign of Charlemagne: Documents on Carolingian Government and Administration* (New York: St. Martin's Press, 1975).

Herstal, 779

In the eleventh auspicious year of the reign of our lord and most glorious king, Charles, in the month of March, there was made a capitulary whereby, there being gathered together in one synod and council the bishops and abbots and illustrious counts, together with our most pious lord, decisions were agreed to concerning certain appropriate matters in accordance with God's will.

1   Concerning the metropolitans, that suffragan bishops should be placed under them in accordance with the canons, and that such things as they see needing correction in their ministry they should correct and improve with willing hearts.

2   Concerning bishops: where at present they are not consecrated they are to be consecrated without delay.

3   Concerning the monasteries that have been based on a rule, that they should live in accordance with that rule; and that convents should preserve their holy order, and each abbess reside in her convent without intermission.

4   That bishops should have authority over the priests and clerks within their dioceses, in accordance with the canons.

5   That bishops should have authority to impose correction on incestuous people, and should have the power of reproving widows within their dioceses.

6   That no one should be allowed to receive another's clerk, or to ordain him to any rank.

7   Concerning tithes, that each man should give his tithe, and that these should be disposed of according to the bishop's orders.

8   Concerning murderers and other guilty men who ought in law to die, if they take refuge in a church they are not to be let off, and no food is to be given to them there.

9   That robbers who are caught within an immunity area should be presented by the justices of that area at the count's court; and anyone who fails to comply with this is to lose his benefice and his office. Likewise a vassal of ours, if he does not carry this out, shall lose his benefice and his office; anyone who has no benefice must pay the fine.

10   Concerning a man who commits perjury, that he cannot redeem if except by losing his hand. But if an accuser wishes to press the charge of perjury they are both to go to the ordeal of the cross; and if the swearer wins, the accuser is to pay the equivalent of his wergeld. This procedure is to be observed in minor cases; in major cases, or in cases involving free status, they are to act in accordance with the law.

11   Concerning the judgement of, and punishment inflicted upon robbers, the synod have ruled that the testimony given by the bishops is probably equivalent to that of the count, provided there is no malice or ill will, and there is no intervention in the case except in the interests of seeing justice done. And if he [the judge] should maim a man through hatred or ill intent and not for the sake of justice, he is to lose his office and is to be subject to the laws under which he acted unjustly and to the penalty which he sought to inflict.

12   The heads of procedure which our father of happy memory decided upon for his hearings and for his synods; these we wish to preserve.

13   Concerning the properties of the churches from which the *census* now comes, the tithes and ninths should be paid along with that *census*; likewise tithes and ninths are to be given for those properties from which they have not so far come—from fifty *casati* one shilling, from thirty *casati* half a shilling, and from twenty a *tremissis* [*i.e.* fourpence]. And concerning precarial holdings, where they are now they are to be renewed, and where they are not they are to be recorded. And a distinction should be made between the precarial holdings established by our authority and those which they establish of their own volition from the property of the church itself.

14   Concerning the raising of an armed following, let no one dare to do it.

15   Concerning those who give tribute in candles, and those who are free by deed or charter, the long standing arrangements are to be observed.

16   Concerning oaths entered into by swearing together in a fraternity, that no one should dare to perform them. Moreover, concerning alms-giving, and fire and shipwreck, even though men enter into fraternities they are not to dare to swear to them.

17   Concerning travellers who are going to the palace or anywhere else, that no one should dare to assault them with an armed band. And let no one presume to take away another's crop when the fields are enclosed, unless he is going to the host or is acting as one of our *missi*; anyone who dares to do otherwise shall make amends for it.

18   Concerning the tolls that have before now been forbidden, let no one exact them except where they have existed from of old.

19   Concerning the sale of slaves, that it should take place in the presence of a bishop or count, or in the presence of an archdeacon or *centenarius*, or in that of a *vicedominus* or a count's justice, or before well-known witnesses; and let no one sell a slave beyond the march. Anyone who does so must pay the fine as many times over as the slaves he sold; and if he does not have the means to pay he must hand himself over in service to the count as a pledge, until such time as he can pay off the fine.

20   Concerning coats of mail, that no one should dare to sell them outside our kingdom.

21   If a count does not administer justice in his district he is to arrange for our *missus* to be provided for from his household until justice has been administered there; and if a vassal of ours does not administer justice, then the count and our *missus* are to stay at his

house and live at his expense until he does so.

22   If anyone is unwilling to accept a payment instead of vengeance he is to be sent to us, and we will send him where is likely to do least harm. Likewise, if anyone is unwilling to pay a sum instead of vengeance or to give legal satisfaction for it, it is our wish that he be sent to a place where he can do no further harm.

23   Concerning robbers, our instructions are that the following rules should be observed; for the first offence they are not to die but to lose an eye; for the second offence the robber's nose is to be cut off; for the third offence, if he does not mend his ways, he must die.

Mantua, 781

Concerning the various provisions which we have made known to all men at the general assembly held at Mantua.

1   Concerning the administration of justice in God's Church, in the matter of widows and orphans, and others who need protection, it is our wish and our special instruction that all bishops, abbots and counts shall both give and accept full justice according to the law.

2   This we have decided, that everyone who has a claim shall make it three times to his count, and shall find suitable men to give truthful witness that he made the claim and was unable to secure justice as a result of it; and if anyone does otherwise, and brings his claim prematurely to the palace, he shall pay the legal penalty.

3   Further, the count shall declare before witnesses on their behalf that he was willing to give them justice, and he shall have his notary write everything down, namely, what claim they made and what justice they received; so that when the people have made their claim the counts can have no excuse unless it is abundantly clear that they were willing to give them justice; also, that the count himself or his advocate can testify by an oath that there was no negligence in giving them justice, and we can know through their report whether they made the claim to them or not.

4   Let this be known to all men, that if anyone makes a claim after the case has been legally closed, he must either receive 15 strokes of the rod or be made to pay 15 shillings.

5   Let no one receive another's priest and allow him to celebrate mass before he has been interviewed and examined by the local bishop.

6   When a bishop goes the round of his parishes, let the count or his agent [*sculdhais*] give him assistance, so that he can perform his ministry in full, according to the canons.

7   Let no one sell Christian or pagan slaves or arms of any kind or stallions outside our kingdom; anyone who does so must be made to pay our fine, and if he is unable to bring the slaves back he must pay their worth.

8   With regard to tolls; let no one presume to levy a toll except in accordance with ancient custom, and let it be levied only in places recognized by law from of old; anyone who levies it unlawfully must make payment according to the law, and in addition must pay our fine to our *missi*.

9   Concerning the coinage: after the first day of August let no one dare to give or receive the pennies now current; anyone who does so is to pay our fine.

10   Concerning brigands who rarely come before our *missi*: let the counts seek them out, and keep them on bail or in custody until the *missi* return to them....

Paderborn, 785 (Capitulary concerning the parts of Saxony)

1   Decisions were taken first on the more important items. All were agreed that the churches of Christ which are now being built in Saxony and are consecrated to God should have no less honor than the temples of idols had, but rather a greater and more surpassing honor.

2   If anyone takes refuge in a church, let no one presume to drive him out of that church by force; rather let him be in peace until he is brought to plead his case, and in honor of God and in reverence for the saints of the church let his life and all his members be respected. But let him pay for his offense according to his means and according to what is decided; and after this let him be brought to the presence of our lord the king, who shall send him wherever in his mercy he shall decide.

3   If anyone makes forcible entry to a church, and steals anything from it by violence or stealth, or if he sets fire to the church, let him die.

4   If anyone in contempt of the Christian faith should spurn the holy Lenten fast and eat meat, let him die; but let the priest enquire into the matter, lest it should happen that someone is compelled by necessity to eat meat.

5   If anyone kills a bishop or a priest or a deacon, he shall likewise pay with his life.

6   If anyone is deceived by the devil, and believes after the manner of pagans that some man or some woman is a witch and eats people, and if because of this he burns her or gives her flesh to someone to eat or eats it himself, let him pay the penalty of death.

7   If anyone follows pagan rites and causes the body of a dead man to be consumed by fire, and reduces his bones to ashes, let him pay with his life.

8   If there is anyone of the Saxon people lurking among them unbaptized, and if he scorns to come to baptism and wishes to absent himself and stay a pagan, let him die.

9   If anyone sacrifices a man to the devil, and after the manner of pagans offers him as a victim to demons, let him die.

10   If anyone takes counsel with pagans against Christians, or wishes to persist with them in hostility to Christians, let him die; and anyone who treacherously approves of this against the king or against Christian people, let him die.

11   If anyone is shown to be unfaithful to our lord the king, let him suffer the penalty of death.

12   If anyone rapes the daughter of his lord, he shall die.

13   If anyone kills his lord or his lady, he shall be punished in the same way.

14   However, if anyone has committed these capital crimes and has gone undetected, and goes of his own accord to a priest and is willing to make his confession and undergo a penance, he shall be excused the death penalty on the priest's testimony.

15   On the lesser items all were agreed. For each and every church the people in the area

who attend it are to provide a farmstead and two manses of land; and for every 120 men among them, be they noble or free or *lidi*, they are to give a male and a female slave to the church.

16   This too was decided, with Christ's blessing, that of any revenue which comes to the royal fisc, whether it be from infringement of the peace or a ban of any kind [*sive in frido sive in qualecumque banno*], or from any other payment due to the king, a tithe is to be given to the churches and the clergy.

17   Likewise, in accordance with God's command, we instruct all men to give a tithe of their substance and labor to their churches and clergy; and let nobles, free men and *lidi* alike make partial return to God for what he has given to each and every Christian.

18   On Sundays there are to be no assemblies or public gatherings, except in cases of great need or when an enemy is pressing; rather let all attend church to hear the word of God, and give their time to prayers and lawful occupations. Likewise on the greater feast days they should gather to serve God and his Church, and put off secular business.

19   Likewise it was decided to include in these enactments that all infants should be baptized within the year; we have decided further, that if anyone scorns to offer an infant for baptism before a year has gone by, and does not consult a priest or obtain his permission, he shall, if he is of noble birth, pay 120 shillings to the fisc, if he is a free man, 60 shillings, and if he is a *lidus* 30.

20   If anyone contracts a forbidden or unlawful marriage, he shall pay 60 shillings if he is a noble, 30 if he is a free man, and 15 if he is a *lidus*.

21   If anyone offers prayers to springs or trees or groves, or makes an offering after the manner of the gentiles and consumes it in honor of demons, he shall pay 60 shillings if he is a noble, 30 if he is a free man, and 15 is he is a *lidus*. But if they do not have the means to pay at once, they are to be placed in the service of the church until such time as the shillings are paid.

22   It is our order that the bodies of Christian Saxons shall be taken to the church's cemeteries and not to the pagan burial grounds.

23   We have decided to hand over the diviners and sooth-sayers to the churches and the clergy.

24   With regard to robbers and other criminals who flee from one country to another, if anyone receives them into his power, and keeps them with him for seven nights for any purpose other than to bring them to justice, let him pay our fine. Likewise, if the count lets such a man abscond, and refuses to bring him to justice, and can give no reason for so doing, let him lose his office.

25   With regard to sureties, let no one, under any circumstances, dare to use another man as a surety; anyone who does this shall pay our fine.

26   Let no one take it upon himself to bar the way to any man coming to us to appeal for justice; if anyone tries to do this he shall pay our fine.

27   If any man is unable to find a surety, his property is to be placed in distraint until he finds one. But if he dares to enter his house in defiance of the ban, let him forfeit ten shillings or one ox in payment for the ban, and in addition pay in full his original debt. And if the surety does not keep him to the appointed day, let him lose whatever he stood to lose

in his capacity as surety; but let him who was debtor to the surety pay back double the loss that he caused his surety to suffer.

28 With regard to payments and rewards: let no one take reward against an innocent person [*cf*. Psalm 15.4]; if anyone dares to do this, he must pay our fine. And if, which God forbid, it should happen that a count does it, let him lose his office.

29 Let all the counts endeavor to be at peace and concord with one another: and if it should happen that some disagreement or quarrel should arise among them, they must not scorn our help in settling it.

30 If anyone kills a count or conspires to kill him, his inheritance shall be made over to the king and he shall be subject to his jurisdiction.

31 We have given authority to the counts, within the areas assigned to them, to impose a fine of up to 60 shillings for feuds or other major crimes; but for minor offences we have fixed the limits of the count's fine at 15 shillings.

32 If anyone has to give an oath to a man, let him swear that oath in church on the appointed day; and if he scorns to swear, let him give a pledge; and anyone who shows himself negligent must pay 15 shillings and afterwards give full satisfaction in the case.

33 With regard to perjury, the law of the Saxons is to apply.

34 We forbid the Saxons to come together as a body in public gatherings, except on those occasions when our *missus* assembles them on our instructions; rather, let each and every count hold court and administer justice in his own area. And the clergy are to see to it that this order is obeyed.

Concerning the Saxons, 797

1 In the seven hundred and ninety-seventh year of the incarnation of Our Lord Jesus Christ, and in the thirtieth and twenty-fifth years respectively of the reign of our lord and most mighty king, Charles, there being assembled together at the palace at Aix at his bidding on the twenty-eighth day of October the reverend bishops and abbots and the illustrious counts, and there being also gathered together the Saxons from the several regions—from Westphalia, from Angaria and from Eastphalia—they did all with one mind agree and ordain that for those matters for which the Franks pay 60 shillings if they have offended against the king's ban, the Saxon shall likewise pay, if they have done something contrary to the ban. The matters in question are these: first that the Church, and then that widows, orphans and humble folk generally, should be left in rightful peace and quiet; that no one should dare to commit rape or violence or arson within the neighborhood; and that no one should presume to hold back from military service in defiance of the king's ban.

2 Those who offend in any of the eight matters mentioned are to pay, Saxons and Franks alike, 60 shillings.

3 It was agreed by all the Saxons that, in all cases where Franks are bound by law to pay 15 shillings, the noble Saxons shall pay 12 shillings, free men 5, and *lidi* 3.

4 This also they decided, that when any case is settled within a district by the local authorities, the people of the district are to receive 12 shillings as a fine [*pro districtione*] in the usual way, and they are to have this concession also in payment of the wergeld which it was their custom to have. But if cases are settled in the presence of the royal *missi*,

the people are to have these 12 shillings as wergeld and the royal *missus* is to receive another 12 on the king's behalf, on the grounds that he has been troubled with the matter. If, however, the case is carried through to the palace for a settlement in the king's presence, then both of the 12 shilling payments, that for wergeld and that owed to the local people, making 24 shillings in all, are to be paid to the king's account, on the grounds that the settlement was not arrived at in the district concerned. And if there is anyone who is unwilling to abide by what his neighbors have decided in his district, and who comes to the palace for this reason, and if it is there decided that the original decision was just, he must on the first occasion, as explained above, pay 24 shillings to the king's account; and if he then goes away and refuses to abide by it or to make a just settlement, and is again brought to the palace for this reason and judged, let him pay the 24 shillings twice over; and if, in spite of this, he is detained and brought to the palace for the same reason a third time, let him pay for it three times over to the king.

5   If any noble is summoned to court and refuses to come, let him pay four shillings; free men are to pay two shillings and *lidi* one.

6   In the matter of priests, it was decided that if anyone should presume to do harm to them or to their men, or should take anything from them unlawfully, he should pay back everything to them and make amends twice over.

7   Concerning the king's *missi*, it was decided that if a *missus* should happen to be killed by them [the Saxons], he who dared to do it should pay for him three times over. Likewise, for anything done to their men, they should see that threefold restoration is made and payment given according to their law.

8   Concerning fire-raising, it was decided that no one should dare to do so in his district out of anger or enmity or for any other spiteful motive: there should, however, be an exception if a man is so rebellious that he refuses to accept a court's decision and cannot be otherwise restrained; and if he refuses to come to us and be judged in our presence; in such a case a common hearing should be declared and all the people in the district must come, and if they are unanimous in this court the fine can be raised in order to restrain him. When at this hearing a common course of action is agreed upon, let it be carried out in accordance with their own law, and not through any anger or spiteful intent, but only in order to restrain a man for us. If anyone dares to raise a fire in any other circumstances, let him, as is said above, pay 60 shillings.

9   Likewise, seeing that our lord the king, for the sake of peace and for [preventing] feuds and for other important reasons, wishes to impose a stronger fine [*bannum*], it was decided, with the consent of the Franks and of his faithful Saxons, according to his decision, as the case demands and as opportunity allows, to double the 60 shilling payment; and if anyone goes against this order, let him pay 100 shillings, or even up to a thousand.

10   Concerning the criminals who should (according to the Saxon law code) incur the death penalty, it was decided by all that whoever of them seeks refuge in the royal prerogative it shall be part of that prerogative either to hand the criminal back for punishment, or with their consent to remove him and his wife and family and all his goods from the district, and settle them inside his kingdom or in the march or wherever he wishes, and to have possession of him as though dead.

11   Note should be taken of the proper equivalents of the Saxon shillings; a yearling calf of either sex, in autumn when it is put to byre, is to count for one shilling; likewise in spring, when it comes out of the byre; but afterwards, as it grows older, it should increase in value proportionately. Of oats, the Bortrini must give 40 bushels for a shilling, and of rye 20 bushes; those to the south, however, must give 30 bushels of oats for a shilling and

15 bushels of rye. Of honey, the Bortrini must give one and a half *siccli* for a shilling, while those of the south are to give two *siccli*. Likewise of winnowed barley they are to give the same amount as of rye for one shilling. In silver, 12 pennies make a shilling. And in other media of exchange the values shall be the equivalents in each case.

The Synod of Frankfurt, 794

1   A gathering, under God's blessing, in accordance with the apostolic authority and the order of our most pious lord king, Charles, in the twenty-sixth year of his reign, of all the bishops and priests of the kingdom of the Franks, of Italy, of Aquitaine and Provence in synod and council, among whom, in the holy assembly, was the most gentle king himself. Whereat, under the first and foremost head, there arose the matter of the impious and wicked heresy of Elipandus, bishop of the see of Toledo, and Felix, bishop of Urgel, and their followers, who in their erroneous belief concerning the Son of God assert adoption: this heresy did all the most holy fathers above mentioned repudiate and with one voice denounce, and it was their decision that it should be utterly eradicated from the Holy Church.

2   There was presented for discussion the matter of the new synod of the Greeks, organized at Constantinople on the subject of the adoration of images, in which it was stated that they regarded as anathema those images of the saints which did not have a bearing on the service or adoration of the Holy Trinity; our most holy fathers aforementioned repudiated it and despised all such adoration and service, and argued in condemning it.

3   After this had been dealt with a decision was reached concerning Tassilo, the cousin of our lord king, Charles, who had formerly been duke of Bavaria. He took his stand in the midst of the most holy council, asking pardon for the sins that he had committed, both for those which he had perpetrated in the time of our lord king, Pippin, against him and against the kingdom of the Franks, and for those later ones committed under our lord and most pious king, Charles, in which he had shown himself to be a breaker of his word. He begged to be thought worthy of indulgence from the king, and appeared to do so in all humility, since he wholeheartedly repudiated all anger and scandalous behavior on his part and all things committed against the king to which he had been party. Moreover, all his rights and properties, everything that should lawfully belong to himself or his sons or daughters in the duchy of Bavaria, he disowned and renounced, and forswearing all claims to it for the future irrevocably surrendered it, and along with his sons and daughters commended it to the mercy of the king. Wherefore our lord [the king], moved with pity, both forgave the said Tassilo graciously for the sins he had committed, restored full favor to him, and with compassion received him in love and affection, so that from henceforth he might be secure in the mercy of God. And so he ordered three copies of this decision to be written to the one effect; one he ordered to be kept in the palace, another to be given to the said Tassilo for him to keep by him in the monastery, and the third to be deposited in the chapel of the sacred palace.

4   Our most pious lord the king, with the consent of the holy synod, gave instructions that no man, whether he be cleric or layman, should ever sell corn in time of abundance or in time of scarcity at a greater price than the public level recently decided upon, that is a *modius* of oats one penny, a *modius* of barley two pennies, a *modius* of rye three pennies, a *modius* of wheat four pennies. If he should wish to sell it in the form of bread, he should give 12 loaves of wheat bread, each weighing two pounds, for one penny, and for the same price 15 of equal weight of rye bread, 20 of barley bread of the same weight, and 25 of oat bread of the same weight. For the public corn of our lord the king, if it should be sold, the price is to be two *modii* of oats for a penny, one *modius* of barley for a penny, two pence for a *modius* of rye, and three for a *modius* of wheat. Anyone who holds a benefice of us should take the greatest possible care that, if God but provide, none of the slaves

of the benefice should die of hunger; and anything that remains above what is necessary for the household he may freely sell in the manner laid down.

5   Concerning the pennies, you should be fully aware of our edict, that in every place, in every city and in every market these new pennies must be current and must be accepted by everyone. Provided they bear the imprint of our name and are of pure silver and of full weight, if anyone should refuse to allow them in any place, in any transaction of buying and selling, he shall, if he is a free man, pay 15 shillings to the king, and, if he is of servile status and the transaction is his own, shall lose the transaction or be flogged naked at the stake in the presence of the people; but if he has done it on his lord's orders, the lord, if it is proved against him, shall pay the 15 shillings.

6   It was ordained by our lord the king and by the holy synod that bishops should administer justice in their parishes. And if any person from among the abbots, priests, deacons, sub-deacons, monks, and other clerics, or anyone else in the parish should refuse to obey his bishop, let them come to their metropolitan, and let him decide the case along with his suffragans. Our counts also are to come to the bishops' courts. And if there is anything which the metropolitan bishop cannot put right or settle, then let the accusers finally come to us, with the accused and with letters from the metropolitan, that we may know the truth of the matter.

7   It was ruled by our lord the king and by the holy synod that a bishop should not move from one city to another, but should stay and take care of his church; likewise a priest or a deacon should stay in his church according to the canons.

8   With regard to the dispute between Ursio, bishop of Vienne and the advocate of Elifantus, bishop of Arles, there were read letters of St Gregory, Zosimus, Leo and Symmachus, which made it clear that the church of Vienne should have four suffragan sees, with itself as the fifth over them, and that the church at Arles should have nine suffragan sees under its authority. As to the question of Tarantaise and Embrun and Aix, an embassy was arranged to the apostolic see; and whatever may be decided by the pontiff of the Church of Rome shall be adhered to.

9   It was ruled also by the same our lord the king and by the holy synod that Peter the bishop [of Verdun] should assert before God and his angels and, in the presence of two or three others, as though he were receiving consecration, or indeed in the presence of his archbishop, should swear that he had not conspired for the death of the king or against his kingdom nor been unfaithful to him. The said bishop, since he could find no one with whom he could swear, decided for himself that he would, as God's man, go before the judgement of God, and testify without relics and without the holy gospels and solely in the presence of God that he was innocent of these matters, and that in accordance with his innocence God should help this his man, who was bound to submit to his judgement and did so. Yet it was not by order of the king or by the decision of the holy synod but by his own free will that he submitted to God's judgement, and was acquitted by Our Lord and found innocent. Nevertheless, our king in his mercy bestowed his favor on the said bishop and endowed him with his former honors, and would not allow a man whom he perceived to merit nothing harmful to be without honor as a result of the charge alleged against him.

10   It was ruled by our lord the king and decided by the holy synod that Gaerbodus, who said he was a bishop but had no witnesses of his consecration, and yet had sought episcopal insignia from Magnardus the metropolitan bishop (who declared moreover that he was not ordained deacon or priest according to canonical prescription), should be deposed by the said metropolitan or by the other bishops of the province from that rank of bishop which he claimed to have.

11 That monks should not go out for secular business nor to engage in lawsuits, unless they do so in accordance with the precepts of the rule itself.

12 That men should not become recluses unless the bishop of the province and the abbot have previously approved of them, and they are to enter upon their place of retreat according to their arrangements.

13 That an abbot should sleep alongside his monks according to the rule of St Benedict.

14 That greedy men should not be chosen as cellarers in the monasteries, but that such men should be chosen as the rule of St Benedict instructs.

15 Concerning a monastery where there are bodies of saints; that it should have an oratory within its cloister where the peculiar and daily office may be done.

16 We have heard that certain abbots, led on by greed, require a payment on behalf of those entering their monastery. Therefore we and the holy synod have decided that under no circumstances shall money be required for receiving brothers into a holy order, but that they should be received in accordance with the rule of St Benedict.

7 That an abbot should not be chosen, when the king so orders, in the congregation, except by the consent of the local bishop.

18 That whatever sin is committed by the monks, we do not allow the abbots under any circumstances to blind them or inflict the mutilation of members upon them, unless the discipline of the rule provides for it.

19 That priests, deacons, monks and clerks should not go into taverns to drink.

20 That a bishop should not be permitted to be ignorant of the canons and the rule.

21 That the Lord's day should be observed from evening to evening.

22 That it should not be proper to consecrate bishops in small towns and villages.

23 Concerning other men's slaves, that they should not be taken in by anyone, and should not be ordained by bishops without their lords' permission.

24 Concerning clerks and monks, that they should remain steadfast in their chosen way of life.

25 That in general, tithes and ninths (or the *census*) should be paid by all who owe them, in respect of benefices and Church property, according to the earlier enactments of our lord the king; and every man should give the lawful tithe in respect of his property to the Church. For we have been informed that in that year when the severe famine broke out there was an abundance of empty corn eaten by demons, and voices of reproach were heard.

26 That the church buildings and their roofs should be repaired and restored by those who hold benefices dependent on them. And where, on the testimony of trustworthy men, it is found that they have in their own houses any wood or stone or tiles that were previously on the church buildings, they must restore to the church everything that has been taken from it.

27 Concerning clerks, that they should under no circumstances move from one church

to another, nor be taken in without the knowledge of the bishop and letters of commendation from the diocese to which they belonged, lest it should happen that discord arise in the Church as a result. And wherever such men are found, they must all return to their own church; and let no one dare to keep such a man by him once his bishop or abbot has indicated his wish to have him back. And if it should happen that the lord does not know where he should look for his clerk, let the man with whom he is staying keep him in custody and not allow him to wander elsewhere, until such time as he is restored to his lord.

28 That men should not be ordained without restriction [*absolute*].

29 That each and every bishop should give good teaching and instruction to those placed in his charge, so that there will always in God's house be found men who are worthy to be chosen according to the canons.

30 Concerning clerks who quarrel among themselves or who act in opposition to their bishop, they are to take all the measures that the canons prescribe. And if it should happen that a quarrel arises between a clerk and a layman, the bishop and the count should meet together and should with one mind decide case between them according to what is right.

31 Concerning plots and conspiracies, that they should not occur; and where they are discovered they are to be crushed.

32 That monasteries should be guarded according to the provisions of the canons.

33 That the catholic faith of the Holy Trinity, the Lord's Prayer and the Creed should be preached and handed on to all men.

34 Concerning the stamping out of greed and covetousness.

35 Concerning the practice of hospitality.

36 Concerning criminals, that they should not be allowed to accuse their superiors or their bishops.

37 Concerning absolution in time of emergency.

38 Concerning priests who have been disobedient towards their bishops; they must under no circumstances communicate with the clerks who live in the king's chapel, unless they have made their peace with their bishop, lest it should happen that excommunication according to the canons should come upon them as a result.

39 If a priest is caught in a criminal act, he should be brought before his bishop and be dealt with according to the ruling of the canons. And if it should happen that he wishes to deny the offence, and his accuser is unable to offer proof of it, and the matter cannot be settled before his bishop, then the decision should be referred to their whole council.

40 Concerning girls who have been deprived of their parents; they should, under the supervision of bishops and priests, be entrusted to suitably sober women, in accordance with the teachings of canonical authority.

41 That no bishop should abandon his proper see by spending his time elsewhere, nor dare to stay on his own property for more than three weeks. And the relatives or heirs of a bishop should in no circumstance inherit after his death any property which was acquired by him after he was consecrated bishop, either by purchase or by gift; rather, it

should go in full to the church. Such property as he had before then shall, unless he make a gift from it to the Church, pass to his heirs and relatives.

42 That no new saints should be revered or invoked in prayers, nor memorials of them erected by the wayside; only those are to be venerated in church which have been deservedly chosen on the basis of their passions or their lives.

43 Concerning the destruction of trees and groves, let the authority of the canons be observed.

44 That the chosen judges should not be rejected by either side in a dispute.

45 Concerning their witnesses, let the canons be observed. And small children should not be compelled to swear an oath, as the Guntbadingi do.

46 Concerning young girls, at what time they are to take the veil and what are to be their occupations before the age of 25, the writings of the canons should, if necessary, be consulted.

47 Concerning abbesses who do not live according to the canons or the monastic rule: the bishops are to make inquiries and give notice to the king, so that they may be deprived of their office.

48 Concerning offerings which are made to the Church or for the use of the poor, the provisions of the canons are to be observed; such funds are not to be dispensed except by those appointed by the bishop.

49 Concerning priests, and not ordaining them before their thirtieth year.

50 That when the sacred mysteries are accomplished all men should be peaceable towards one another during the rites of mass.

51 Concerning not reciting names until an oblation is offered.

52 That no one should believe that God cannot be prayed to except in three languages only; since God can be prayed to, and man listened to if his prayers are just, in any language.

53 That no bishop or priest should be allowed to be ignorant of the sacred canons.

54 Concerning churches which are built by free men; it is allowed to bestow them as gifts, or to sell them, provided that no church is destroyed and the daily offices are observed.

55 Our lord the king informed the holy synod that he had permission of the holy see, that is of Pope Hadrian, to keep Angilramnus the archbishop permanently in his place to deal with ecclesiastical matters. He asked the synod that he might be allowed to have bishop Hildebald there on the same terms as he had Angilramnus, he had the apostolic permission. The whole synod agreed, and decided that he should be in the palace to deal with ecclesiastical matters.

56 He suggested that the holy synod should think it right to accept Alcuin into its fellowship and prayers, since he was a man of learning in the doctrines of the Church. All the synod agreed to the suggestion of our lord the king, and accepted him into their fellow-

ship and their prayers.

Charles the Great on the study of literature, end of the eighth century

We, Charles, by the grace of God king of the Franks and Lombards and patrician of the Romans, to Abbot Baugulf and all your congregation and our faithful teachers [*oratoribus*] entrusted to your charge, send affecting greeting in the name of Almighty God.

Be it known to your devotion, most pleasing in the sight of God, that we, along with our faithful advisers, have deemed it useful that the bishoprics and monasteries which through the favor of Christ have been entrusted to us to govern should, in addition to the way of life prescribed vy their rule and practice of holy religion, devote their efforts to the study of literature and to the teaching of it, each according to his ability, to those on whom God has bestowed the capacity to learn; that, just as the observance of a rule gives soundness to their conduct, so also an attention to teaching and learning may give order and adornment to their words, and those who seek to please God by living aright may not fail to please him also by rightness in their speaking. For it is written, 'Either by your words shall you be justified, or by your words shall you be condemned [Matthew 12.27].' For although it is better to do what is right than to know it, yet knowledge comes before action. Thus each man must first learn what he wishes to carry out, so that he will know in his heart all the more fully what he needs to do, in order that his tongue may run on without stumbling into falsehood in the praise of Almighty God. For since falsehood is to be shunned by all men, how much more should it be avoided, as far as they are able, by those who have been chosen for this one purpose, that they should give special service to truth. Letters have often been sent to us in these last years from certain monasteries, in which was set out what the brothers there living were striving to do for us in their holy and pious prayers; and we found that in most of these writings their sentiments were sound but their speech uncouth. Inwardly their pious devotions gave them a message of truth, but because of their neglect of learning their unskilled tongues could not express it without fault. And so it came about that we began to fear that their lack of knowledge of writing might be matched by a more serious lack of wisdom in the understanding of holy scripture. We all know well that, dangerous as are the errors of words, yet much more dangerous are the errors of doctrine. Wherefore we urge you, not merely to avoid the neglect of the study of literature, but with a devotion that is humble and pleasing to God to strive to learn it, so that you may be able more easily and more rightly to penetrate the mysteries of the holy scriptures. For since there are figures of speech, metaphors and the like to be found on the sacred pages, there can be no doubt that each man who reads them will understand their spiritual meaning more quickly if he is first of all given full instruction in the study of literature. Let men be chosen for this work who have the will and ability to learn and also the desire to instruct others; and let it be pursued with an eagerness equal to my devotion in prescribing it. For we want you, as befits the soldiers of the Church, to be inwardly devout and outwardly learned, pure in good living and scholarly in speech; so that whoever comes to see you in the name of God and for the inspiration of your holy converse, just as he is strengthened by the sight of you, so he may be instructed also by your wisdom, both in reading and chanting, and return rejoicing, giving thanks to Almighty God. Therefore, if you wish to keep our favor, do not neglect to send copies of this letter to all your suffragans and fellow bishops, and to all the monasteries.

'De Villis,' end of the eighth century

1   It is our wish that those of our estates which we have established to minister to our needs shall serve our purposes and not those of other men.

2   That all our people shall be well looked after, and shall not be reduced to penury by anyone.

3   That the stewards shall not presume to put our people to their own service, and shall not compel them to give their labor or to cut wood or to do any other work for them; and they shall accept no gifts from them, neither a horse nor an ox, nor a cow, nor a pig, nor a sheep, nor a piglet, nor a lamb, nor anything other than bottles of wine, vegetables, fruit, chickens and eggs.

4   If anyone of our people does harm to our interests through theft or any other neglect of duty, let him make good the damage in full, and in addition let him be punished by whipping according to the law, except in the case of murder or arson, for which a fine may be exacted. As far as concerns other men, let the stewards be careful to give them the justice to which they have a right, as the law directs. Our people, as we have said, are to be whipped in preference to being fined. Free men, however, who live on our crown lands [*fiscis*] and estates shall be careful to pay for any wrong they may have done, according to their law; and whatever they may give as their fine, whether it be cattle or any other form of payment, shall be assigned to our use.

5   Wherever it falls to our stewards to see that our work is done, whether it be sowing or ploughing, harvesting, haymaking or gathering of grapes, let each one of them, at the appropriate time and place, supervise the work and give instructions as to how it should be done, so that everything may be successfully carried out. If a steward is not in his district, or cannot get to a particular place, let him send a good messenger from among our people, or some other man who can be trusted, to look after our affairs and settle them satisfactorily; and the steward shall be especially careful to send a reliable man to deal with this matter.

It is our wish that our stewards shall pay a full tithe of all produce to the churches that are on our estates, and that no tithe of ours shall be paid to the church of another lord except in places where this is an ancient custom. And no clerics shall hold these churches except our own or those from our people or from our chapel.

7   That each steward shall perform his service in full, according to his instructions. And if the necessity should arise for his service to be increased, let him decide whether he should add to the manpower or to the days spent in performing it [*si servitium debeat multiplicare vel noctes*].

8   That our stewards shall take charge of our vineyards in their districts, and see that they are properly worked; and let them put the wine into good vessels, and take particular care that no loss is incurred in shipping it. They are to have purchased other, more special, wine to supply the royal estates. And if they should buy more of this wine than is necessary for supplying our estates they should inform us of this, so that we can tell them what we wish to be done with it. They shall also have slips from our vineyards sent for our use. Such rents from our estates as are paid in wine they shall send to our cellars.

9   It is our wish that each steward shall keep in his district measures for *modii* and *sextaria*, and vessels containing eight *sextaria*, and also baskets of the same capacity as we have in our palace.

10   That our mayors and foresters, our stablemen, cellarers, deans, toll-collectors and other officials shall perform regular services, and shall give pigs in return for their holdings: in place of manual labor, let them perform their official duties well. And any mayor who has a benefice, let him arrange to send a substitute, whose task it will be to carry out the manual labor and other services on his behalf.

11   That no steward, under any circumstances, shall take lodgings for his own use or for his dogs, either among our men or among those living outside our estates.

12   That no steward shall commend a hostage of ours on our estates.

13   That they shall take good care of the stallions, and under no circumstances allow them to stay for long in the same pasture, lest it should be spoiled. And if any of them is unhealthy, or too old, or is likely to die, the stewards are to see that we are informed at the proper time, before the season comes for sending them in among the mares.

14   That they shall look after our mares well, and segregate the colts at the proper time. And if the fillies increase in number, let them be separated so that they can form a new herd by themselves.

15   That they shall take care to have our foals sent to the winter palace at the feast of St Martin.

16   It is our wish that whatever we or the queen may order any steward, or whatever our officials, the seneschal or the butler, may order them in our name or in the name of the queen, they shall carry out in full as they are instructed. And whoever falls short in this through negligence, let him abstain from drinking from the moment he is told to do so until he comes into our presence or the presence of the queen and seeks forgiveness from us. And if a steward is in the army, or on guard duty, or on a mission, or is away elsewhere, and gives an order to his subordinates and they do not carry it out, let them come on foot to the palace, and let them abstain from food and drink until they have given reasons for failing in their duty in this way; and then let them receive their punishment, either in the form of a beating or in any other way that we or the queen shall decide.

17   A steward shall appoint as many men as he has estates in his district, whose task it will be to keep bees for our use.

18   At our mills they are to keep chickens and geese, according to the mill's importance—or as many as possible.

19   In the barns on our chief estates they are to keep not less than 100 chickens and not less than 30 geese. At the smaller farms they are to keep not less than 50 chickens and not less than 12 geese.

20   Every steward is to see that the produce is brought to the court in plentiful supply throughout the year; also, let them make their visitations for this purpose at least three or four times.

21   Every steward is to keep fishponds on our estates where they have existed in the past, and if possible he is to enlarge them. They are also to be established in places where they have not so far existed but where they are now practicable.

22   Those who have vines shall keep not less than three or four crowns of grapes.

23   On each of our estates the stewards are to have as many byres, pigsties, sheepfolds and goat-pens as possible, and under no circumstances are they to be without them. They are also to have cows provided by our serfs for the performance of their service, so that the byres and plough-teams are in no way weakened by service on our demesne. And when they have to provide meat, let them have lame but healthy oxen, cows or horses which are not mangy, and other healthy animals; and, as we have said, our byres and plough-teams must not suffer as a result of this.

24   Every steward is to take pains over anything he is to provide for our table, so that everything he gives is good and of the best quality, and as carefully and cleanly prepared

335

as possible. And each of them, when he comes to serve at our table, is to have corn for two meals a day for his service; and any other provisions, whether in flour or in meat, are similarly to be of good quality.

25 They are to report on the first of September whether or not there will be food for the pigs.

26 The mayors are not to have more land in their districts than they can ride through and inspect in a single day.

27 Our houses are to have continuous watch-fires and guards to keep them safe. And when our *missi* and their retinues are on their way to or from the palace, they shall under no circumstances take lodging in the royal manor houses, except on our express orders or those of the queen. And the count in his district, or the men whose traditional custom it has been to look after our *missi* and their retinues, shall continue, as they have done in the past, to provide them with pack-horses and other necessities, so that they may travel to and from the palace with ease and dignity.

28 It is our wish that each year in Lent on Palm Sunday, which is also called Hosanna Sunday, the stewards shall take care to pay in the money part of our revenue according to our instructions, after we have determined the amount of our revenue for the year in question.

29 With regard to these of our men who have cases to plead, every steward is to see to it that they are not compelled to come into our presence to make their plea; and he shall not allow a man to lose, through negligence, the days on which he owes service. And if a serf of ours is involved in a lawsuit outside our estates, his master is to do all he can to see that he obtains justice. And if in a given place the serf has difficulty obtaining it, his master shall not allow him to suffer as a result, but shall make it his business to inform us of the matter, either in person or through his messenger.

30 It is our wish that from all the revenue they shall set aside what is needed for our purposes; and in the same way they are to set aside the produce with which they load the carts that are needed for the army, both those of the householders and those of the shepherds, and they shall keep a record of how much they are sending for this purpose.

31 That in the same way each year they shall set aside what is necessary for the household workers and for the women's workshops; and at the appropriate time they are to supply it in full measure, and must be in a position to tell us how they have disposed of it, and where it came from.

32 That every steward shall make it his business always to have good seed of the best quality, whether bought or otherwise acquired.

33 After all these parts of our revenue have been set aside or sown or otherwise dealt with, anything that is left over is to be kept to await our instructions, so that it can be sold or held in reserve as we shall decide.

34 They are to take particular care that anything which they do or make with their hands—that is, lard, smoked meat, sausage, newly-salted meat, wine, vinegar, mulberry wine, boiled wine, garum, mustard, cheese, butter, malt, beer, mead, honey, wax and flour—that all these are made or prepared with the greatest attention to cleanliness.

35 It is our wish that tallow shall be made from fat sheep and also from pigs; in addition, they are to keep on each estate not less than two fatted oxen, which can be used for mak-

ing tallow there or can be sent to us.

36 That our woods and forests shall be well protected; if there is an area to be cleared, the stewards are to have it cleared, and shall not allow fields to become overgrown with woodland. Where woods are supposed to exist they shall not allow them to be excessively cut or damaged. Inside the forests they are to take good care of our game; likewise, they shall keep our hawks and falcons in readiness for our use, and shall diligently collect our dues there. And the stewards, or our mayors or their men, if they send their pigs into our woods to be fattened, shall be the first to pay the tithe for this, so as to set a good example and encourage other men to pay their tithe in full in the future.

37 That they shall keep their fields and arable land in good order, and shall guard our meadows at the appropriate time.

38 That they shall always keep fattened geese and chickens sufficient for our use if needed, or for sending to us.

39 It is our wish that the stewards shall be responsible for collecting the chickens and eggs which the serfs and manse-holders contribute each year; and when they are not able to use them they are to sell them.

40 That every steward, on each of our estates, shall always have swans, peacocks, pheasants, ducks, pigeons, partridges and turtle doves, for the sake of ornament.

41 That the buildings inside our demesnes, together with the fences around them, shall be well looked-after, and that the stables and kitchens, bakeries and wine-presses, shall be carefully constructed, so that our servants who work in them can carry out their tasks properly and cleanly.

42 That each estate shall have in its store-room beds, mattresses, pillows, bed-linen, table-cloths, seat-covers, vessels of bronze, lead, iron and wood, fire-dogs, chains, pot-hangers, adzes, axes, augers, knives and all sorts of tools, so that there is no need to seek them elsewhere or to borrow them. As to the iron tools which they provide for the army, the stewards are to make it their business to see that these are good, and that when they are returned they are put back into the storeroom.

43 They are to supply the women's workshops with materials at the appropriate times, according to their instructions—that is, linen, wood, woad, vermilion, madder, wool-combs, teazles, soap, oil, vessels and the other small things that are needed there.

44 Two thirds of the Lenten food shall be sent each year for our use—that is, of the vegetables, fish, cheese, butter, honey, mustard, vinegar, millet, panic, dry or green herbs, radishes, turnips, and wax or soap and other small items; and as we have said earlier, they are to inform us by letter of what is left over, and shall under no circumstances omit to do this, as they have done in the past, because it is through those two thirds that we wish to know about the one third that remains.

45 That every steward shall have in his district good workmen—that is, blacksksmiths, gold- and silver-smiths, shoemakers, turners, carpenters, shield-makers, fishermen, falconers, soap-makers, brewers (that is, people who know how to make beer, cider, perry or any other suitable beverage), bakers to make bread for our use, net-makers who can make good nets for hunting or fishing or fowling, and all the other workmen too numerous to mention.

46 That the stewards shall take good care of our walled parks, which the people call

brogili, and always repair them in good time, and not delay so long that it becomes necessary to rebuild them completely. This should apply to all buildings.

47   That our hunters and falconers, and the other servants who are in permanent attendance on us at the palace, shall throughout our estates be given such assistance as we or the queen may command in our letters, on occasions when we send them out on an errand or when the seneschal or butler gives them some task to do in our name.

48   That the wine-presses on our estates shall be kept in good order. And the stewards are to see to it that no one dares to crush the grapes with his feet, but that everything is clean and decent.

49   That our women's quarters shall be properly arranged—that is, with houses, heated rooms and living rooms; and let them have good fences all round, and strong doors, so that they can do our work well.

50   That each steward shall determine how many horses there should be in a single stable, and how many grooms with them. Those grooms who are free men, and have benefices in the district, shall live off those benefices. Similarly the men of the fisc, who hold manses, shall live off them. And those who have no holding shall receive their food from the demesne.

51   Every steward is to take care that dishonest men do not conceal our seed from us, either under the ground or elsewhere, thus making the harvest less plentiful. Similarly, with the other kinds of mischief, let them see to it that they never happen.

52   It is our wish that the men of the fisc, our serfs, and the free men who live on our crown lands and estates shall be required to give all men the full and complete justice to which they are entitled.

53   That every steward shall take pains to prevent our people in his district from becoming robbers and criminals.

54   That every steward shall see to it that our people work well at their tasks, and do not go wasting time at markets.

55   It is our wish that the stewards should record, in one document, any goods or services they have provided, or anything they have appropriated for our use, and, in another document, what payments they have made; and they shall notify us by letter of anything that is left over.

56   That every steward in his district shall hold frequent hearings and dispense justice, and see to it that our people live a law-abiding life.

57   If any of our serfs should wish to say something to us about his master in connection with our affairs, he is not to be prevented from coming to us. And if a steward should learn that his subordinates wish to come to the palace to lodge a complaint against him, then that steward shall present his arguments against them at the palace, and give reason why we should not be displeased at hearing their complaint. In this way we wish to find out whether they come from necessity or merely on some pretext.

58   When our puppies are entrusted to the stewards they are to feed them at their own expense, or else entrust them to their subordinates, that is, the mayors and deans, or cellarers, so that they in their turn can feed them from their own resources—unless there should be an order from ourselves or the queen that they are to be fed at their own ex-

pense. In this case the steward is to send a man to them, to see to their feeding, and is to set aside food for them; and there will be no need for the man to go to the kennels every day.

59 Every steward shall, when he is on service, give three pounds of wax and eight *sextaria* of soap each day; in addition, he shall be sure to give six pounds of wax on St Andrew's Day, wherever we may be with our people, and a similar amount in mid-Lent.

60 Mayors are never to be chosen from among powerful men, but from men of more modest station who are likely to be loyal.

61 That each steward, when he is on service, shall have his malt brought to the palace; and with him shall come master-brewers who can make good beer there.

62 That each steward shall make an annual statement of all our income, from the oxen which our ploughmen keep, from the holdings which owe ploughing services, from the pigs, from rents, judgement-fees and fines, from the fines for taking game in our forests without our permission and from the various other payments; from the mills, forests, fields, bridges and ships; from the free men and the hundreds which are attached to our fisc; from the markets; from the vineyards, and those who pay their dues in wine; from hay, firewood and torches, from planks and other timber; from waste land; from vegetables, millet and panic; from wool, linen and hemp; from the fruits of trees; from larger and smaller nuts; from the graftings of various trees; from gardens, turnips, fishponds; from hides, skins and horns; from honey and wax; from oil, tallow and soap; from mulberry wine, boiled wine, mead and vinegar; from beer and from new and old wine; from new and old grain; from chickens and eggs and geese; from the fishermen, smiths, shield-makers and cobblers; from kneading troughs, bins or boxes; from the turners and saddlers; from forges and from mines, that is, from iron- or lead-workings and from workings of any other kind; from people paying tribute; and from colts and fillies. All these things they shall set out in order under separate headings, and shall send the information to us at Christmas time, so that we may know the character and amount of our income from the various sources.

63 With regard to all the things mentioned so far, our stewards should not think it hard of us to make these demands, since it is our wish that they likewise should be able to make demands of their subordinates without giving offence. And all the things that a man ought to have in his house or on his estates, our stewards shall have on our estates.

64 That our carts which go to the army as war-carts shall be well constructed; their coverings shall be well-made of skins, and sewn together in such a way that, should the necessity arise to cross water, they can get across rivers with the provisions inside and without any water being able to get in—and, as we have said, our belongings can get across safely. It is also our wish that flour—12 *modii* of it—should be placed in each cart for our use; and in those carts which carry wine they are to place 12 *modii* according to our measurement, and they are also to provide for each cart a shield, a lance, a quiver and a bow.

65 That the fish from our fishponds shall be sold, and others put in their place, so that there is always a supply of fish; however, when we do not visit the estates they are to be sold, and our stewards are to get a profit from them for our benefit.

66 They are to give an account to us of the male and female goats, and of their horns and skins; and each year they are to bring to us the newly-salted meat of the fattened goats.

67 With regard to vacant manses and newly acquired slaves, if they have any surplus which they cannot dispose of, they are to let us know.

68 It is our wish that the various stewards should always have by them good barrels bound with iron, which they can send to the army and to the palace, and that they should not make bottles of leather.

69 They shall at all times keep us informed about wolves, how many each of them has caught, and shall have the skins delivered to us. And in the month of May they are to seek out the wolf cubs and catch them, with poison and hooks as well as with pits and dogs.

70 It is our wish that they shall have in their gardens all kinds of plants: lily, roses, fenugreek, costmary, sage, rue, southernwood, cucumbers, pumpkins, gourds, kidney-beans, cumin, rosemary, caraway, chick-pea, squill, gladiolus, tarragon, anise, colocynth, chicory, ammi, sesili, lettuces, spider's foot, rocket salad, garden cress, burdock, penny-royal, hemlock, parsley, celery, lovage, juniper, dill, sweet fennel, endive, dittany, white mustard, summer savory, water mint, garden mint, wild mint, tansy, catnip, centaury, garden poppy, beets, hazelwort, marshmallows, mallows, carrots, parsnip, orach, spinach, kohlrabi, cabbages, onions, chives, leeks, radishes, shallots, cibols, garlic, madder, teazles, broad beans, peas, coriander, chervil, capers, clary. And the gardener shall have house-leeks growing on his house. As for trees, it is our wish that they shall have various kinds of apple, pear, plum, sorb, medlar, chestnut and peach; quince, hazel, almond, mulberry, laurel, pine, fig, nut and cherry trees of various kinds. The names of apples are: *gozmaringa, geroldinga, crevedella, spirauca*; there are sweet ones, bitter ones, those that keep well, those that are to be eaten straightaway, and early ones. Of pears they are to have three or four kinds, those that keep well, sweet ones, cooking pears and the late-ripening ones.

General Capitulary for the *missi*, spring 802

1 Concerning the commission despatched by our lord the emperor. Our most serene and most Christian lord and emperor, Charles, has selected the most prudent and wise from among his leading men, archbishops and bishops, together with venerable abbots and devout laymen, and has sent them out into all his kingdom, and bestowed through them on all his subjects the right to live in accordance with a right rule of law. Wherever there is any provision in the law that is other than right or just he has ordered them to inquire most diligently into it and bring it to his notice, it being his desire, with God's help, to rectify it. And let no one dare or be allowed to use his wit and cunning, as many do, to subvert the law as it is laid down or the emperor's justice, whether it concerns God's churches, or poor people and widows and orphans, or any Christian person. Rather should all men live a good and just life in accordance with God's commands, and should with one mind remain and abide each in his appointed place or profession: the clergy should live a life in full accord with the canons without regard for base gain, the monastic orders should keep their life under diligent control, the laity and secular people should make proper use of their laws, refraining from ill-will and deceit, and all should live together in perfect love and peace. And the *missi* themselves, as they wish to have the favor of Almighty God and to preserve it through the loyalty they have promised, are to make diligent inquiry wherever a man claims that someone has done him an injustice; so everywhere, and amongst all men, in God's holy churches, among poor people, orphans and widows, and throughout the whole people they may administer law and justice in full accordance with the will and the fear of God. And if there be anything which they themselves, together with the counts of the provinces, cannot correct or bring to a just settlement, they should refer it without any hesitation to the emperor's judgement along with their reports. And in no way, whether by some man's flattery or bribery, or by the excuse of blood relationship with someone, or through fear of someone more powerful, should anyone hinder the right and proper course of justice.

2   Concerning the promise of fealty to our lord the emperor. He has given instructions that in all his kingdom all men, both clergy and laity, and each according to his vows and way of life, who before have promised fealty to him as king, should now make the same promise to him as Caesar; and those who until now have not made the promise are all to do so from 12 years old and upwards. And that all should be publicly informed, so that each man may understand how many important matters are contained in that oath—not only, as many have thought until now, the profession of loyalty to our lord the emperor throughout his life, and the undertaking not to bring any enemy into his kingdom for hostile reasons, nor to consent to or be silent about anyone's infidelity towards him, but also that all men may know that the oath has in addition the following meaning within it.

3   [First,] that everyone on his own behalf should strive to maintain himself in God's holy service, in accordance with God's command and his own pledge, to the best of his ability and intelligence, since our lord the emperor himself is unable to provide the necessary care and discipline to all men individually.

4   Second, that no man, through perjury or any other craft or deceit, or through anyone's flattery or bribery, should in any way withhold or take away or conceal our lord the emperor's serf, or his landmark, or his land, or anything that is his by right of possession; and that no one should conceal the men of his fisc who run away and unlawfully and deceitfully claim to be free men, nor take them away by perjury or any other craft.

5   That no one should presume to commit fraud or theft or any other criminal act against God's holy churches or against widows or orphans or pilgrims; for the lord emperor himself, after God and his saints, has been appointed their protector and defender.

6   That no one should dare neglect a benefice held of our lord the emperor, and build up his own property from it.

7   That no one should presume to ignore a summons to the host from our lord the emperor, and that no count should be so presumptuous as to dare to excuse any of those who ought to go with the host, either on the pretext of kinship or through the enticement of any gift.

8   That no one should presume to subvert in any way any edict or any order of our lord the emperor, nor trifle with his affairs nor hinder nor weaken them, nor act in any other way contrary to his will and his instructions. And that no one should dare to be obstructive about any debt or payment that he owes.

9   That no one in court should make a practice of defending another man in an unlawful manner, by arguing the case weakly through a desire for gain, by hampering a lawful judgement by showing off his skill in pleading, or by presenting a weak case in an attempt to do his client harm. Rather should each man plead for himself, be it a question of tax or debt or some other case, unless he is infirm or unacquainted with pleading; for such men the *missi* or the chief men who are in the court or a judge who knows the case can plead it before the court, or if necessary a man can be provided to plead, who is approved by all parties and has a good knowledge of the case at issue; this, however, should only be done at the convenience of the chief men or *missi* who are present. At all events, it must be done in accordance with justice and the law; and no one should be allowed to impede the course of justice by offering a reward or a fee, by skilful and ill-intentioned flattery, or by the excuse of kinship. And let no one make an unlawful agreement with anyone, but let all men be seriously and willingly prepared to see that justice is done.

10-24   [These sections are all on ecclesiastical matters, dealing with the duties and conduct of clergy, monks, etc.]

25 That the counts and *centenarii* should strive to see that justice is done, and should have as assistants in their duties men in whom they can have full confidence, who will faithfully observe justice and the law, will in no wise oppress the poor, and will not dare, for flattery or a bribe, to conceal in any manner of concealment any thieves, robbers or murderers, adulterers, evil-doers and performers of incantations and auguries, and all other sacrilegious people, but rather will bring them to light, that they may receive correction and punishment according to the law, and that with God's indulgence all these evils may be removed from among our Christian people.

26 That the justices should give right judgement according to the written law, and not according to their private opinions.

27 We ordain that no one in all our kingdom, whether rich or poor, should dare to deny hospitality to pilgrims; that is, no one should refuse a roof, a hearth and water to any pilgrims who are travelling the country in the service of God, or to anyone who is journeying for love of God or for the salvation of his soul. And if a man should be willing to offer any further benefit to such people, let him know that God will send him the best reward, as he himself said: 'Whoso shall receive one such little child in my name receiveth me'; and in another place, 'I was a stranger, and ye took me in [Matthew 18.5; 25.35].'

28 Concerning the commissions coming from our lord the emperor. The counts and the *centenarii* should, as they are desirous of the favor of our lord the emperor, provide for the *missi* who are sent upon them with all possible attention, that they may go about their duties without any delay; and he has given instructions to all men that it is their duty to make such provision, that they suffer no delay to occur anywhere, and that they help them to go upon their way with all haste, and make such provision for this as our *missi* may require.

29 Concerning those poor men who owe payment of the royal fine and to whom the lord emperor in his mercy has given remission; the counts or *missi* are not to have the right for their part to bring constraint upon people so excused.

30 Concerning those whom the lord emperor wishes, with Christ's blessing, to have peace and protection in his kingdom, that is, those who have thrown themselves upon his mercy, those who, whether Christians or pagans, have desired to offer any information, or who from poverty or hunger have sought his intervention; let no one dare to bind them in servitude or take possession of them or dispose of them or sell them, but rather let them stay where they themselves choose, and live there under the lord emperor's protection and in his mercy. If anyone should presume to transgress this instruction, let him know that a man so presumptuous as to despise the lord emperor's orders must pay for it with the loss of his life.

31 For those who administer the justice of our lord the emperor let no one dare to devise harm or injury, nor bring any hostility to bear upon them. Anyone who presumes to do so must pay the royal fine; and if he is guilty of a greater offence, the orders are that he be brought to the king's presence.

32 Murder, by which a great multitude of our Christian people perish, we ordain should be shunned and avoided by every possible means; Our Lord himself forbade hatred and enmity among his faithful, and murder even more. How can a man feel confident that he will be at peace with God, when he has killed the son most close to himself? Or who can believe that Christ Our Lord is on his side, when he has murdered his brother? It is, moreover a great and unacceptable risk with God the Father and Christ the ruler of heaven and earth to arouse the hostility of men. With men, we can escape for a time by hiding, but even so by some chance of fortune we fall into our enemy's hands; but where can a man

escape from God, from whom no secrets are hid? What rashness to think to escape his anger! For this reason we have sought, by every kind of precept, to prevent the people entrusted to us for ruling from perishing as a result of this evil; for he who feels no dread at the anger of God should not receive mild and benevolent treatment from us; rather would we wish a man who had dared to commit the evil act of murder to receive the severest of punishments. Nevertheless, in order that the crime should not increase further, and in order that serious enmity should not arise among Christians when they resort to murders at the persuasion of the devil, the guilty person should immediately set about making amends, and should with all possible speed pay the appropriate recompense to the relatives of the dead man for the evil he has done to them. And this we firmly forbid, that the parents of the dead man should dare in any way to increase the enmity arising from the crime committed, or refuse to allow peace when the request is made; rather, they should accept the word given to them and the compensation offered, and allow perpetual peace, so long as the guilty man does not delay payment of the compensation. And when a man sinks to such a depth of crime as to kill his brother or a relative, he must betake himself immediately to the penance devised for him, and to do as his bishop instructs him and without any compromising. He should strive with God's help to make full amends, and should pay compensation for the dead man according to the law and make his peace in full with his kinsmen; and once the parties have given their word let no one dare to arouse further enmity on the matter. And anyone who scorns to pay the appropriate compensation is to be deprived of his inheritance pending our judgement.

33 We forbid absolutely the crime of incest. If anyone is stained by wicked fornication he must in no circumstances be let off without severe penalty, but rather should be punished for it in such a way that others will be deterred from committing the same offence, that filthiness may be utterly removed from our Christian people, and that the guilty person himself may be fully freed from it through the penance that is prescribed for him by his bishop. The woman concerned should be kept under her parents' supervision subject to our judgement. And if such people are unwilling to agree to the bishop's judgement concerning their improvement they are to be brought to our presence, mindful of that exemplary punishment for incest imposed by Fricco upon a certain nun.

34 That all should be fully and well prepared for whenever our order or announcement may come. And if anyone then maintains that he is not ready and disregards our instructions he is to be brought to the palace—and not he alone, but all those who presume to go against our edict or our orders.

35 That all bishops and their priests should be accorded all honor and respect in their service of God's will. They should not dare to stain themselves or others with incestuous unions. They should not presume to solemnize marriages until the bishops and priests, together with the elders of the people, have carefully inquired to see if there be any blood relationship between the parties, and should only then give their blessing to the marriage. They should avoid drunkenness, shun greediness, and not commit theft; disputes and quarrels and blasphemies, whether in normal company or in a legal sense, should be entirely avoided; rather, they should live in love and unity.

36 That all men should contribute to the full administration of justice by giving their agreement to our *missi*. They should not in any way give their approval to the practice of perjury, which is a most evil crime and must be removed from among our Christian people. And if anyone after this is convicted of perjury he should know that he will lose his right hand; but he is also to be deprived of his inheritance subject to our judgement.

37 That those who commit patricide or fratricide, or who kill an uncle or a father-in-law or any of their kinsmen, and who refuse to obey and consent to the judgement of our bishops, priests, and other justices, are for the salvation of their souls and for the carrying out

of the lawful judgement to be confined by our *missi* and counts in such custody that they will be safe, and will not pollute the rest of the people, until such time as they are brought to our presence. And in the meantime they are not to have any of their property.

38 The same is to be done with those who are arraigned and punished for unlawful and incestuous unions, and who refuse to mend their ways or submit to their bishops and priests, and who presume to disregard our edict.

39 That no one should dare to steal our beasts in our forests; this we have forbidden already on many occasions, and we now firmly ban it again, that no one should do it any more and should take care to keep the faith which everyone has promised to us and desires to keep. And if any count or *centenarius* or vassal of ours or any of our officials should steal our game he must at all costs be brought to our presence to account for it. As for the rest of the people, anyone who steals the game in this way should in every case pay the appropriate penalty, and under no circumstances should anyone be let off in this matter. And if anyone knows that it has been done by someone else, in accordance with the faith he has promised to us to keep and has now to promise again he should not dare to conceal this.

40 Finally, therefore, from all our decrees we desire it to be known in all our kingdom through our *missi* now sent out: among the clergy, the bishops, abbots, priests, deacons, clerks, and all monks and nuns, that each one in his ministry or profession should keep our edict or decree, and when it is right should of his good will offer thanks to the people, give them help, or if need be correct them in some way. Similarly for the laity, in all places everywhere, if a plea is entered concerning the protection of the holy churches, or of widows or orphans or less powerful people, or concerning the host, and is argued on these cases, we wish them to know that they should be obedient to our order and our will, that they maintain observance of our edict, and that in all these matters each man strive to keep himself in God's holy service. This in order that everything should be good and well-ordered for the praise of Almighty God, and that we should give thanks where it is due; that where we believe anything to have gone unpunished we should so strive with all earnestness and willingness to correct it that with God's help we may bring it to correction, to the eternal reward both of ourselves and of all our faithful people. Similarly concerning the counts and *centenarii*, our officers (*ministerialibus*), we wish all the things above mentioned in our deliberations to be known. So be it.

Special Capitularies for the *missi*, 802.

Capitulary for the missi *for Paris and Rouen*
In Paris, Meaux, Melun, Provins, Estampes, Chartres and Poissy: Fardulfus and Stephanus. In Le Mans, Exmes, Lisieux, Bayeux, Coutances, Avranches, Evreux and Merey, and for that part of the Seine and Rouen: Bishop Magenardus and Madelgaudus.
Capitulary for the missi *for Orleans*
First, for the city of Orleans on the Seine, by the direct route, then to Troyes, with the whole of its region, then to Langres, from Langres to the town of Besançon in Burgundy, from there to Autun, and afterwards to the Loire as far as Orleans: those sent are Archbishop Magnus and Count Godefredus.

1 Concerning the oath of fealty, that all should reaffirm it.

2 Concerning bishops and the clergy, whether they are living according to the canons, and whether they are well acquainted with them and are carrying them out.

3 Concerning abbots, whether they are living according to a rule or according to the canons, and whether they are well acquainted with that rule or those canons.

4   Concerning the monasteries where there are monks, whether they live according to the rule in cases where it is part of their vows.

5   Concerning convents, whether the nuns live according to a rule or to the canons, and concerning their cloisters.

6   Concerning secular laws.

7   Concerning perjury.

8   Concerning murder.

9   Concerning adultery and other unlawful acts, whether committed in bishoprics and monasteries and convents or among laymen.

10   Concerning those men who have plundered our benefices and made up their private holdings. Likewise concerning the property of the churches.

11   Concerning those Saxons who have our benefices in Frankia, in what way they cultivate them, and with what degree of care.

12   Concerning the oppressions of poor free men, who owe military service and are oppressed by the justices.

13   That all men be well prepared for whatever order may come from us.

13a Concerning the preparation of ships around the coast.

13b Concerning the free men who live around the coastal regions; if a message should come to them instructing them to come and give assistance, and they refuse to obey it, each of them must pay twenty shillings, a half to his lord and a half to the people. If one of them is a *lidus* he must pay fifteen shillings to the people and give his back to be flogged. If he is a serf he must pay ten shillings to the people and receive the flogging.

14   Concerning the commissions coming to us and the *missi* sent out by us.

15   Concerning those whom we wish to have peace and protection throughout the kingdoms which by the favor of Christ belong to us.

16   Concerning those men who have been killed in administering our justice.

17   Concerning tithes and ninths and the dues to God's churches, that they should be at pains to pay them and to make good what is wanting.

18   Concerning the ban of our lord the emperor and king, and those things for which it has been our wont to exact a fine, that is, violence offered to churches, to widows or orphans or those unable to defend themselves, and rape, and failure to observe a decree concerning the host, that those who offend against the king in these respects should make full reparation.

18a That they make careful enquiries among the bishops, abbots, counts, abbesses and all our vassals, to see what degree of mutual harmony and friendship they have in their various districts, or whether there appears to be any discord among them; and that they be careful to report to us the whole truth of these matters, confirmed by their oath. That all of them should have good administrators [*vicedomos*] and advocates.

19 In addition, they are to enquire into and settle any matter that may be necessary, whether in our jurisdiction or in that of the churches, concerning widows, orphans, minors, and all other persons. And whatever they find that needs correcting, let them take pains to correct it to the best of their ability; what they cannot correct they must have referred to our presence.

The oath whereby I reaffirm that from this day forth, being of sound mind and with no evil intent from my part to his, I am a faithful subject of our lord and most pious emperor, Charles, son of King Pippin and Queen Berthana, for the honor of his kingdom, as a man ought lawfully to be towards his lord; so help me God, and these relics of the saints here situated, for all the days of my life with all my will and with what intelligence God has given me, I will so attend and consent.

Again: the oath whereby I affirm. I am a faithful servant of our lord and most pious emperor, Charles, son of King Pippin and Queen Berthana, as a man lawfully ought to be towards his lord, for his kingdom and for his right. And this oath which I have sworn I shall willingly keep to the best of my knowledge and ability, from this day forth, so help me God, who created heaven and earth, and these relics of saints.

DID THEY REALLY CARE SO MUCH FOR THE ORPHANS & WIDOWS OR WAS THAT JUST ALOT OF FORMAL TALK?

Charters of Cluny

The monastery of Cluny received gifts of land, churches, and monasteries throughout the tenth, eleventh, and twelfth centuries. These and other property transactions were preserved in written form, i.e. in charters. The charters from the tenth century that were preserved at Cluny are among the richest primary sources for that period. Although unprecedented in number, the charters of Cluny are not unlike those made for other monasteries. Except for the foundation of Chartres, the following were all drawn up for members of one family, later known as the Grossi. This family is discussed by Georges Duby, La société, pp. 336-46 and in his article, "Lineage, Nobility, and Knighthood," in The Chivalrous Society, *pp. 59-80 as an example of a newly established castellan lineage. The Grossi are also studied most recently in Constance Bouchard,* Sword, Mitre and Cloister, *pp 160–167 and 300–307. The family relationships were as follows:*

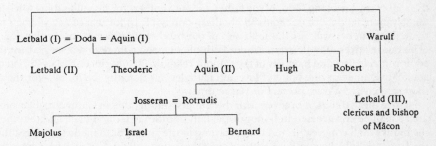

(The Majolus of this family was *not* the same person as the Majolus who was abbot of Cluny 954-994.)

The documents presented here illustrate the ways in which a pious family and a monastery related to one another through the medium of land. These charters raise numerous issues connected with the history of religion; the meaning of property; the uses of written instruments; the uses of land and dependents; the memories that people had of families, land, crimes, and acts of piety; ideas about the church; and the gift exchange system of the early middle ages.

Sources: Select Historical Documents; A. Bruel: Recueil des Chartres de l'Abbaye de Cluny. (Paris: imprimerie Nationale, 1876-84) translated by Barbara Rosenwein.

The Foundation Charter of Cluny[1]

To all right thinkers it is clear that the providence of God has so provided for certain rich men that, by means of their transitory possessions, if they use them well, they may be able to merit everlasting rewards. As to which thing, indeed, the divine word, showing it to be possible and altogether advising it, says: "The riches of a man are the redemption of his soul." (Prov. xiii.) I, William, count and duke by the grace of God, diligently pondering this, and desiring to provide for my own safety while I am still able, have considered it advisable—nay, most necessary, that from the temporal goods which have been conferred upon me I should give some little portion for the gain of my soul. I do this, indeed, in order that I who have thus increased in wealth may not, perchance, at the last be accused of having spent all in caring for my body, but rather may rejoice, when fate at last shall snatch all things away, in having reserved something for myself. Which end, indeed, seems attainable by no more suitable means than that, following the precept of Christ: "I will make his poor my friends" (Luke xvi. 9), and making the act not a temporary but a lasting one, I should support at my own expense a congregation of monks. And this is my trust, this my hope, indeed, that although I myself am unable to despise all things, nevertheless, by receiving despisers of the world, whom I believe to be righteous, I may receive the reward of the righteous. Therefore be it known to all who live in the unity of the faith and who await the mercy of Christ, and to those who shall succeed them and who shall continue to exist until the end of the world, that, for the love of God and of our Savior Jesus Christ, I hand over from my own rule to the holy apostles, Peter, namely, and Paul, the possessions over which I hold sway, the town of Cluny, namely, with the court and demesne manor, and the church in honor of St. Mary the mother of God and of St. Peter the prince of the apostles, together with all the things pertaining to it, the vills, indeed, the chapels, the serfs of both sexes, the vines, the fields, the meadows, the woods, the waters and their outlets, the mills, the incomes and revenues, what is cultivated and what is not, all in their entirety. Which things are situated in or about the country of Macon, each one surrounded by its own bounds. I give, moreover, all these things to the aforesaid apostles—I, William, and my wife Ingelberga—first for the love of God; then for the soul of my lord king Odo, of my father and my mother; for myself and my wife—for the salvation, namely, of our souls and bodies;—and not least for that of Ava who left me these things in her will; for the souls also of our brothers and sisters and nephews, and of all our relatives of both sexes; for our faithful ones who adhere to our service; for the advancement, also, and integrity of the catholic religion. Finally, since all of us Christians are held together by one bond of love and faith, let this donation be for all,—for the orthodox, namely, of past, present or future times.

I give these things, moreover, with this understanding, that in Cluny a regular monastery shall be constructed in honor of the holy apostles Peter and Paul, and that there the monks shall congregate and live according to the rule of St. Benedict, and that they shall possess, hold, have and order these same things unto all time. In such wise, however, that the venerable house of prayer which is there shall be faithfully frequented with vows and supplications, and that celestial converse shall be sought and striven after with all desire and with the deepest ardour; and also that there shall be sedulously directed to God prayers, beseechings and exhortations as well for me as for all, according to the order in which mention has been made of them above. And let the monks themselves, together with all the aforesaid possessions, be under the power and dominion of the abbot Berno, who, as long as he shall live, shall preside over them regularly according to his knowledge and ability. But after his death, those same monks shall have power and permission to elect any one of their order whom they please as abbot and rector, following the will of God and the rule promulgated by St. Benedict,—in such wise that neither by the intervention of our own or of any other power may they be impeded from making a purely canonical election. Every five years, moreover, the aforesaid monks shall pay to the church of the apostles at Rome ten shillings to supply them with lights; and they shall have the protection of those same apostles and the defence of the Roman pontiff; and those monks may, with their whole heart and soul, according to their ability and knowledge, build up the aforesaid place. We will, further, that in our times and in those of our successors, according as the opportunities and possibilities of that place shall allow, there shall daily, with the greatest zeal to be performed there works of mercy towards the poor, the needy, strangers, and pilgrims. It has pleased us also to insert in this document that, from this day, those same monks there congregated shall be subject neither to our yoke, nor to that of our relatives, nor to the sway of any earthly power. And, through God and all his saints, and by the awful day of judgment, I warn and abjure that no one of the secular princes, no count, no bishop whatever, not the pontiff of the aforesaid Roman see, shall invade the property of these servants of God, or alienate it, or diminish it, or exchange it, or give it as a benefice to any one, or constitute any prelate over them against their will. And that such unhallowed act may be more strictly prohibited to all rash and wicked men, I subjoin the following, giving force to the warning. I adjure ye, oh holy apostles and glorious princes of the world, Peter and Paul, and thee, oh supreme pontiff of the apostolic see, that, through the canonical and apostolic authority which ye have received from God, ye do remove from participation in the holy church and in eternal life, the robbers and invaders and alienators of these possessions which I do give to ye with joyful heart and ready will; and be ye protectors and defenders of the aforementioned place of Cluny and of the servants of God abiding there, and of all these possessions—on account of the clemency and mercy of the most holy Redeemer. If any one—which Heaven forbid, and which, through the mercy of the God and the protection of the apostles I do not think will happen—whether he be a neighbor or a stranger, no matter what his condition or power, should, through any kind of wild attempt to do any act of violence contrary to this deed of gift which we have ordered to be drawn up for the love of almighty God and for reverence of the chief apostles Peter and Paul; first, indeed, let him incur the wrath of almighty God, and let God remove him from the land of the living and wipe out his name from the book of life, and let his portion be with those who said to the Lord God: Depart from us; and, with Dathan and Abiron whom the earth, opening its jaws, swallowed up, and hell absorbed while still alive, let him incur everlasting damnation. And being made a companion of Judas let him be kept thrust down there with eternal tortures, and, lest it seem to human eyes that he pass through the present world with impunity, let him experience in his own body, indeed, the torments of future damnation, sharing the double disaster with Heliodorus and Antiochus, of whom one being coerced with sharp blows and scarcely escaped alive; and the other, struck down by the divine will, his members putrefying and swarming with vermin, perished most miserably. And let him be a partaker with other sacrilegious persons who presume to plunder the treasure of the house of God; and let him, unless he come to his senses, have as enemy and as the one who will refuse him entrance into the blessed paradise, the key-bearer of the whole hierarchy of the church, and, joined with the latter, St. Paul; both of whom, if he had wished, he might have had as most holy mediators for him. But as far as the worldly law is concerned, he shall be required, the judicial power compelling him, to pay a hundred pounds of gold to those whom he has harmed; and his attempted attack, being frustrated, shall have no effect at all. But the validity of this deed of gift, endowed with all authority, shall always remain inviolate and unshaken, together with the stipulation subjoined. Done publicly in the city of Bourges. I, William, commanded this act to be made and drawn up, and confirmed it with my own hand.

(Signed by Ingelberga and a number of bishops and nobles.)

Charters of the Grossi Family

Charter # 802[1] (March, 951)

To all who consider the matter reasonably, it is clear that the dispensation of God is so designed that if riches are used well, these transitory things can be transformed into eternal rewards. The Divine word showed that this was possible, saying "Wealth for a man is the redemption of his soul," and again, "Give alms and all things are yours."

We, that is, I, Doda, a woman, and my son Letbald [II], carefully considering this fact, think it necessary that we share some of the things that were conferred on us, Christ granting, for the benefit of our souls. We do this to make Christ's poor our friends, in accordance with Christ's precept and so that He may receive us, in the end, in the eternal tabernacle.

Therefore, let it be known to all the faithful that we—Doda and my son Letbald—give some of our possessions, with the consent of lord Aquin [I], my husband, for love of God and his holy Apostles, Peter and Paul,[2] to the monastery of Cluny, to support the brothers [i.e. monks] there who ceaselessly serve God and His apostles. [We give] an allod[3] that is located in the *pagus*[4] of Mâcon, called Nouville.[5] The serfs [servi] that live there are: Sicbradus and his wife, Robert, Eldefred and his wife and children, Roman and his wife and children, Raynard and his wife and children, Teutbert and his wife and children, Dominic and his wife and children, Nadalis with her children, John with his wife and children, Benedict with his wife and children, Maynard with his wife and children, another Benedict with his wife and children, and a woman too...[6] with her children.

And we give [land in] another *villa*[7] called Colonge and the serfs living there: Teotgrim and his wife and children, Benedict and his wife and children, Martin and his children, Adalgerius and his wife and children, [and] Sicbradus.

And [we give] a *mansus*[8] in Culey and the serfs there: Andrald and his wife and children, Eurald and his wife and children. And [we give] whatever we have at Chazeux along with the serf Landrad who lives there. We also give a little harbor on the Aar river[9] and the serfs living there: Agrimbald and Gerald with their wives and children.

In addition, we give an allod in the *pagus* of Autun, in the *villa* called Beaumont and the serfs living there. John, Symphorian, Adalard and their wives and children, in order that [the monks] may, for the love of Christ, receive our nephew, Adalgysus, into their society.[10]

[We give] all the things named above with everything that borders on them: vineyards, fields, buildings, serfs of every sex and age, ingress and egress, with all mobile and immobile property already acquired or to be acquired, wholly and completely. We give all this to God omnipotent and His apostles for the salvation of our souls and for the soul of Letbald [I], the father of my son, and for the salvation of Aquin [I], my husband, and of all our relatives and finally for all the faithful in Christ, living and dead.

Moreover, I, the aforesaid Letbald, uncinch the belt of war, cut off the hair of my head and beard for divine love, and with the help of God prepare to receive the monastic habit in the monastery [of Cluny]. Therefore, the property that ought to come to me by paternal inheritance I now give [to Cluny] because of the generosity of my mother and brothers. [I do so] in such a way that while [my mother and brothers] live, they hold and possess it. I give a *mansus* in Fragnes, along with the serf Ermenfred and his wife and children, to [my brother] Theoderic, *clericus*,[11] and after his death let it revert to [Cluny]. And I give another *mansus* at Verzé with the serf Girbald and his wife and children to my brother Hugo. In the *pagus* of Autun I give to [my brother] Aquin [II] the allod that is called Dompierre-les-Ormes, and the serf Benedict and his wife and their son and daughter. [I give Aquin also] another allod in Vaux, and the serfs Teutbald and his wife and children and Adalgarius. [I give all this] on condition that, if these brothers of mine [Hugh and Aquin], who are laymen, die without legitimate offspring, all these properties will go to the monastery as general alms.

If anyone (which we do not believe will happen) either we ourselves (let it not happen!) or any other person, should be tempted to bring a claim in bad faith against this charter of donation, let him first incur the wrath of God, and let him suffer the fate of Datan and Abiran and of Judas, the traitor of the Lord. And unless he repents, let him have the apostles [Peter and Paul] bar him from the celestial kingdom. Moreover, in accordance with earthly law, let him be forced to pay ten pounds. But let this donation be made firm by us, with the stipulation added. S[ignum][12] of Doda and her son Letbald, who asked that it be done and confirmed. S. of Aquin, who consents. S. of Hugo. S. of Evrard. S. of Walo. S. of Warembert. S. of Maingaud. S. of Giboin. S. of Leotald. S. of Widald. S. of Hemard. S. of Raimbald. Dated in the month of March in the 15th year of the reign of King Louis.[13] I, brother Andreas, *levite*,[14] undersign at the place for the secretary.

I, Majolus, humble abbot [of Cluny] by the will of God, and the whole congregation of brothers of the monastery of Cluny. We have decided to grant something from the property of our church to a certain cleric, named Letbald [III] for use during his lifetime, and we have done so, fulfilling his request.

The properties that we grant him are located in the *pagus* of Mâcon, in the *ager*[16] of Grevilly, in a *villa* called Collonge: *mansi*, vineyards, land, meadows, woods, water, and serfs of both sexes and whatever else we have in that place, which came to us from Raculf.[17] And we grant two *mansi* at Boye and whatever we have there. And in Massy, one *mansus*. And in "Ayrodia" [not identified], in a place called Rocca, we give *mansi* with vineyards, land, woods, water, and serfs of every sex and age; and we grant all the property of Chassigny [a place near Lugny that has disappeared]: vineyards, land, meadows, woods, water, mills and serfs and slaves. And at "Bussiacus" [near St-Huruge], similarly [we grant] *mansi*, vineyards, lands, meadows, and woods. And at "Ponciacus" [not id.] [we give] *mansi*, vineyards, land. Just as Raculf gave these things to us in his testament, so we grant them to [Letbald] on the condition that he hold them while he lives and after his death these things pass to Cluny. And let him pay 12 denars every year to mark his taking possession (*in vestitura*).

We also grant to him other property that came from lord Letbald [I], his uncle: a *mansus* at La Verzée and another at Bassy and another at Les Légères, and again another in Fragnes and another in Chazeux. And again a *mansus* in the *pagus* of Autun, at Dompierre-les-Ormes and another in Vaux and the serfs and slaves of both sexes that belong to those *mansi*. Let him hold and possess these properties as listed in this *precaria*[18] for as long as he lives. And when his mortality prevails—something no man can avoid—let this property fall to [Cluny] completely and without delay. [Meanwhile] let him pay 12 denars every year, on the feast day of Apostles Peter and Paul.

I have confirmed this decree with my own hand and have ordered the brethren to corroborate it, so that it will have force throughout his lifetime. S. of lord Majolus, abbot. S. of Balduin, monk. S. of Vivian. S. of John. S. of Arnulf. S. of Costantinus. S. of Tedbald. S. of Joslen. S. of Grimald. S. of Hugo. S. of Rothard. S. of Ingelbald. S. of Achedeus. S. of Vuitbert. S. of Ingelman. Dated by the hand of Rothard, in the 25th year of the reign of King Lothar.

Charter # 1577 (Nov. 12, 981–Nov. 11, 982)

To this holy place, accessible to our prayers [et cetera].[19] I, Rotrudis, and [my husband] Josseran, and my sons, all of us give to God and his holy Apostle, Peter and Paul, and at the place Cluny, half of a church[20] that is located in the *pagus* of Mâcon, named in honor of St. Peter, with everything that belongs to it, wholly and completely, and [property in] the *villa* that is called Curtil-sous-Buffières. There [we give] a field and a meadow that go together and have the name *ad Salas*. This land borders at the east on a *via publica*[21] and a man-made wall; at the south on a meadow; at the west on a *via publica*, and similarly at the north. [I make this gift] for the salvation of the soul of my husband Josseran, and [for the soul of my son] Bernard. Done at Cluny. Witnesses: Rotrudis, Josseran, Bernard, Israel, Erleus, Hugo, Odo, Raimbert, Umbert. Ingelbald wrote this in the 28th year of the reign of King Lothar.

Charter # 1845 (990-991)

By the clemency of the Savior a remedy was conceded to the faithful: that they could realize eternal returns on His gifts if they distributed them justly. Wherefore, I, Majolus,[22] in the name of God, give to God and his holy apostles Peter and Paul and at the place Cluny some of my property which is located in the county of Lyon, in the *villa* "Mons" [not id.]. It consists of a *mansus indominicatus*[23] with a serf named Durannus and his wife, named Aldegard, and their children, and whatever belongs or appears to belong to this *mansus*, namely fields, vineyards, meadows, woods, pasturelands, water and water courses, that is already acquired or will be acquired, whole and complete. I make this donation first for my soul and for my burial [in Cluny's cemetery] and for the soul of my father Josseran and of my mother Rotrudis and of my brothers, and for the souls of my *parentes*[24] and for the salvation of all the departed faithful, so that all may profit in common. [I give it] on the condition that I may hold and possess it while I live, and that every year I will pay a tax of 12 denars on the feast day of the Prince of the Apostles [i.e. St. Peter]. After my death, let [the property] go to Cluny without delay.

But if anyone wants to bring any bad-faith claim against this donation, let him first incur the wrath of the Omnipotent and all His saints; and unless he returns to his senses, let him be thrust into Hell with the devil. As in the past, let this donation remain firm and stable, with the stipulation added. Done publicly at Cluny. S. of Majolus, who asks that it be done and confirmed. S. of Bernard, S. of Israel, S. of Arleius, S. of Bernard, S. of Hubert. Aldebard, *levita*, wrote this in the 4th year of the reign of Hugh [Capet].

Charter # 2508 (994–1030?)[25]

Notice of a quitclaim that took place at Cluny in the presence of lord Rainald, venerable prior at that place; and of other monks who were there, namely Walter, Aymo, Amizon, Warner, Lanfred, Locerius, Giso; and of noblemen: Witbert, Robert, Ildinus, Gislebert, Bernard, and Hugo. In the first place, let all, present and future, know that a long and very protracted quarrel between the monks of Cluny and Majolus[26] finally, by God's mercy, came to this end result: first that he [Majolus] quit his claim to the land which Oddo and Teza [Oddo's] daughter[27] destined for us and handed over by charter: the woods in *Grandi Monte* with its borders [as follows]: on the east [it borders on] its own inheritance ([namely] passing between mountains and through wasteland and across the castle of Teodoric; on the south [it borders on] *terra francorum*[28]; on the west and north [it borders on] land of St. Peter. [Majolus] draws up this notice at this time so that he may reunite himself with the favor of St. Peter and the brothers, and so that he may persevere in future as a faithful servant in the service of St. Peter. S. Hugo, S. Witbert, S. Robert, S. Ildinus, S. Gislebert, S. Bernard.

Charter # 2946 (?1018–1030)[29]

In the name of the incarnate Word. I, Raimodis, formerly the wife of the lord Wichard, now dead, and now joined in matrimony to lord Ansedeus, my husband; with the consent and good will [of Ansedeus], I give or rather give again some land which is called Chazeux to St. Peter and Cluny. [I give it] for the soul of my husband Wichard. This land once belonged to St. Peter and Cluny. But the abbot and monks gave it as a precarial gift to lord Letbald [III], a certain cleric who afterwards became bishop of Mâcon. Letbald, acting wrongly, alienated [the land] from St. Peter and gave it to Gauzeran to make amends for killing Gauzeran's relative, Berengar.

Therefore I give it again to St. Peter for the soul of my husband Wichard, and for Gauzeran, Wichard's father. I also give a slave named Adalgarda and her children, and [I give] the whole inheritance for the soul of my husband Wichard, and of my daughter Wiceline, and for my own soul.

If anyone wants to bring false claim against this donation, let him not prevail, but let him pay a pound of gold into the public treasury. S. of Raimodis, who asked that this charter be done and confirmed. S. of Ansedeus. S. of another Ansedeus. S. of Achard. S. of Walter. S. of Costabulus. S. of Ugo.

Notes

1   Sept. 11, 910 AD.

2   Cluny was dedicated to the Apostles Peter and Paul.

3   An allod was land that was owned outright, in contrast to land held in fief, for example.

4   A Roman administrative subdivision.

5   Almost all the places mentioned in these charters are within about ten miles from the monastery of Cluny.

6   Effaced in the manuscript.

7   In this region a *villa* was normally not a great estate nor a village, but rather a small district in which many landowners held land.

8   A *mansus* (plural: *mansi*) was, strictly speaking, a farming unit. In the context of Doda's charter, she is probably thinking of a "demesne mansus", an outsize farming unit that included the *mansi* of dependents.

9   A tributary of the Rhin (*not* the Rhine) river.

10   Possibly Adalgynsus is to become a monk; but it is more likely that he is to become a special "friend" of the monastery for whom prayers will be said.

11   i.e. a priest

12   Usually laymen did not sign charters; rather they made marks or signs (their *signum*) which was copied by the scribe in front of their name. The S refers to this sign.

13   A Carolingian king of the area that would later become France between 936-954.

14   i.e. a deacon.

15   This charter is dated in this way because the scribe dated it in the 25th year of the reign of King Lothar, the son of King Louis, whose rule began on November 12, 954.

16   The *pagus* of Mâcon was divided into subdivisions called *agri* (singular: *ager*). There were perhaps ten or more *villae* in each *ager*.

17   Raculf was probably a member of this family whose precise relationship has not been established.

18   This document is in fact an excellent example of a precarial donation. It was a conditional grant of land *by* the monastery to someone outside of the monastery for his (or her) lifetime.

19   A formula considered so commonplace that it did not need to be fully written out. Consider the formula today, "Sincerely yours," which is so familiar that the full sentence, "Be assured that I remain sincerely yours," (or something on that order) is usually left out.

20   Churches could be given in whole or in part, and with or without their tithes (which often belonged not to the holder of the church but to the local bishop). See Giles Constable, *Monastic Tithes*.

21   A dirt road. There was a very extensive network of roads in the area around Cluny, left from the Roman period.

22   *Not* the abbot.

23   This is the "demesne mansus" referred to above.

24   Meaning much more than a nuclear family, but perhaps not quite as much as a clan.

25   The scribe did not give a date. But we know that Rainald was prior at Cluny beginning in 994, and that Majolus died c. 1030; these give us, respectively, the *terminus post quem* and the *terminus ante quem* of the document.

26   The same man as the donor above.

27   These were probably relatives of Majolus.

28   Probably land of free peasants.

29   This date was suggested by Maurice Chaume, on the basis of other charters elsewhere that tell us at what date Raimodis, the donor in this charter, became a widow.

Miracles of Saint Foy

Saint Foy (Faith) was traditionally reputed to have been a girl of twelve martyred at Agen in 303. In the ninth century monks from the monastery of Conques stole her relics and brought them to their monastery where, they became the object of a major pilgrimage from the tenth century. The body of the saint was kept in a case reliquary while the head was venerated in a golden statue which represented the young woman seated in glory.

Bernard of Angers, a student of Fulbert of Chartres (ca. 960–1028) and later director of the episcopal school in Angers, made three pilgrimages to Conques and, although at first skeptical of the cult, was entirely won over to the saint. His book of her miracles helped to spread the cult of Saint Foy across Europe and also served as a model for hagiographical dossiers for other cults.

Source: A. Bouillet, ed. *Liber miraculorum Sancte Fidis* (Paris: Alphonse Picard, 1897).

Concerning Vuitbert whose eyes, having been gouged out, were restored by Saint Foy

In the region of Rodez where reposes the blessed virgin Foy, in the vicus of Conques, there lived a priest named Gerald, who is still alive. He had a godson who was attached to him both by kinship and by episcopal confirmation named Vuitbert, who was his domestic servant and a competent administrator of his property. Once this Vuitbert went to Conques to celebrate the feast. When the solemn vigil was completed the next morning, that is the very day of the feast, as he was returning home, by bad fortune he encountered his lord who had been moved against him by an inexplicable evil zeal. This priest, when he saw him in the garb of a pilgrim, began with words of peace, but then was roused to aggressive abuse: "Well, Vuitbert, I see you have become a Roman." (this was the way the people of the area called pilgrims). He answered, "Yes, master, I am returning from the feast of Saint Foy." Then after speaking amicably of various things, the priest gave him permission to depart. But after he had gone on a little way, looking over his back this priest of the Jewish treason, if one can call one contaminated by such a sacrilege a priest, ordered his servant to wait a bit for him. Vuitbert complied and suddenly the priest ordered him to be encircled and held by his men.

When he saw this, shaking with fear, he asked of what crime he was accused, but the evil man gave only this response: "You did me wrong and are planning even worse things. This is why I want for reparations nothing less than your own eyes," and would not describe any more openly the nature of the offense as if from modesty. It is unjust for a priest to make judgment based on his own jealousy since the cause of this evil had arisen from the suspicion of debauchery with women. Vuitbert, since he was ignorant of the affair, confidently offered to vindicate himself of all culpability. "My lord," he said, "if you would openly indicate all the crimes of which you suspect me, I am prepared to refute them legally. I am unable to determine by what law I ought to incur your wrath and that of your followers. The priest replied, "Enough, enough, of your superficial excuses; the sentence has been pronounced: your eyes will be torn out."

But Vuitbert, seeing the priest stand firm in his gladiatorial resolve and seeing the hour of his irreparable destruction imminent, and discerning no other opportunity of defending himself but prayer, although despairing of his safety, made this plea: "Lord, pardon me! If not for my innocence, at least for the love of God and of Saint Foy for the love of whom I am now wearing the holy habit of a pilgrim."

At these words the wild monster, not taking seriously either God or his saint, contorted by rage, vomited forth the poison of blasphemy which he had in his heart: "Neither God not Saint Foy will save you today! You will not be able to escape my hands by invoking them. And don't expect that out of reverence for the habit of a pilgrim I would consider you worthy and inviolable since you have so evilly harmed me." This said, he ordered the man be thrown down and that his eyes be torn out. But when he could force none of his three men whose names we omit because of the horror of this barbarity, to carry out such a deed, ordering them at least to hold him down and descending from his horse, he tore out the eyes of his godson with the same fingers which were consecrated to holding the body of Christ and tossed them away.

These things did not happen without the presence of the heavenly power, which does not abandon men who call upon divine assistance and is always near those calling on it in truth and which passes judgment for those enduring injury. Those who were present immediately saw a snow white dove, or as the doer of this evil deed claimed, a magpie. This magpie or dove took up the bloody eyes of the poor unfortunate and rising high above the earth carried them toward Conques.

Nor should one wonder if God entrusted magpies with the task of protecting the eyes in this desert of a place since he had preserved the life of Elias in the desert by means of ravens. Or by chance, as the divinity wished, unknown birds may have come, which could be thought of neither as magpies nor as doves. In truth there is no ambiguity between the two types of birds since the servants saw a white dove, but the priest was unable to see anything but a pie which is distinctive by its black and white. But because God shows himself terrible to the evildoer and mild to the just, it may be that for the innocent and for those grieving with a clear conscience at the sight of such evil a white species of bird was seen while it appeared mixed to the evil doer. Nevertheless when the wicked priest saw this, he was overcome with remorse and began to cry profusely, at which one of his companions told him that it was too late and in vain to act in such a way. After he departed, he never again celebrated the mass either because he did not dare to do so having perpetrated such a crime or, as is more likely, because he altogether neglected it because of worldly concerns.

The mother of this Gerald, profoundly upset by the great wrong done to an innocent person, received Vuitbert into her home and provided for everything he needed with great charity until he was well. For during this same time he had gone before her, not on the order of his lord but rather to show her the more severe than usual atrocity which on her word her son had caused, by which false zeal she felt wounded in her heart. Once he was well in the same year he sought his food in the art of a public entertainer and so well accepted his injury that as he was accustomed to say he did not worry about not having eyes, so much did the desire for gain and the pleasure of amusing delight him.

A year passed. The day before the vigil of Saint Foy, he had fallen to sleep when he saw before him a young girl of indescribable beauty. Her appearance was like that of an angel. Her face shone and appeared with droplets of rose and scarlet. Her expression surpassed all human beauty. Her size was as had been read that it was in the time of her passion, that of an adolescent, not yet of mature age. She wore majestic clothing entirely brocaded of gold and surrounded by a variety of subtle colors. Her wide sleeves, carefully pleated, fell to her feet. She wore on her head a diadem decorated with four gems from which radiated extraordinary light. The smallness of her body seems to me to have signified nothing more than that at the time of her passion, as we have said, one reads that she had been a youth.

The beauty of her mouth, in so far as it was given to the one to which this vision appeared to see, and her marvelous clothing, were not, I believe, without cause, for these were in themselves glorious symbols. We can see that the so to speak too large clothes represented the armour or protection of overflowing faith. The golden radiance properly represents the illumination of spiritual grace. What could the delicacy of the colors and the pleated sleeves mean unless they offered the trace of divine wisdom? On the most important part of the body, that is the head, were seen four gems, which remind us of the four principal virtues, prudence, fortitude, justice and temperance. Since Saint Foy had the knowledge and perfection of these virtues and, deeply filled with the Holy Spirit she cultivated in the depths of her loving heart those other virtues derived from these, she was altogether pleasing to the Most-High. Moreover, not ignorant of the greatest good she offered herself to holy martyrdom as a willing and pure sacrifice to Christ. There remains the beauty of her face. We mentioned it first according to the order of our account, reserving its mystery for the end because it presents us with the culmination and the end of all life, that is, charity. It is right that charity be represented by white which surpasses all the colors by its brilliance. It is right to understand charity, the most perfect of virtues, which we place before the ruddiness which suggests martyrdom. This is not absurd because no one obtains the grace of martyrdom without the eminence of charity. Saint Foy heroically protected this virtue when for His love she faced with bravery a horrible death.

Thus the saint, leaning on the bedpost, softly touched the right cheek of the sleeper and whispered to him, "Vuitbert, are you asleep?" He answered, "Who is there?" "I am Saint Foy," she replied. "My lady, why have you come to me?" "Simply to see you." Vuitbert thanked her, and Saint Foy replied, "Do you know me?" He recognized her as if he had already seen her and answered, "Yes, I see you well, my lady, and I recognize you perfectly." "Tell me how you are and how your affairs are doing." "Very well, my Lady, and all is going very well. Everything succeeds for me by the grace of God." "What," she said, "how can all be going well when you cannot see the light of the heavens?" But he, as happens in dreams, thought that he could see although he could not. This last question reminded him of his torn out eyes. "How could I see," he asked, "when, last year, while returning from your feast, alas, I lost my eyes by the brutality of an unjust master?" The saint said, "He offended God too much and raised the anger of the Creator, he who harmed you so seriously in your body without your having merited it. But if tomorrow, on the vigil of my martyrdom, you go to Conques, and you buy two candles and place one before the altar of the Holy Savior, the other before the altar where my bodily clay is placed, you will merit to enjoy the complete restoration of your eyes. For with a great supplication concerning the injury done you I moved the piety of the divine Judge to mercy. I bothered God by my incessant prayers until I obtained for you this cure." After these words she still insisted and urged him to go to Conques and encouraged him because he hesitated before the expense. "A thousand people, whom you have never before seen," she said, "will give to you. Besides, so that you can easily complete the present business, go quickly at dawn to the church of this parish, (this was the parish of he who had deprived him of his eyes which since ancient times was called Espeyrac) and hear Mass there, and you will receive six pence." He thanked her as a benefactor deserved and the celestial power left him.

He awoke immediately and went to the church where he told his vision. People thought that he was delirious. But not at all discouraged, he went through the crowd asking each in order to obtain twelve pence. Finally a certain Hugo, moving apart from the others, opened his purse and offered him six pence and one obole, that is, a little more than the vision had announced. This first success increased his confidence. What more can I say? He arrived at Conques, told his vision to the monks, bought the candles, presented them to the altar, and started the vigil before the golden statue of the holy martyr.

Around midnight it seemed to him that he could see as though two small glowing berries, no larger than the fruit of a laurel, came from above and buried themselves deeply into his gouged eye sockets. At the shock, his thoughts became muddled and he fell asleep. But at the hour of lauds the chanting of the psalms awoke him and he seemed to see spots of light and the silhouettes of people moving about, but he had an unbelievable headache and only half conscious he thought that he was dreaming. Gradually coming out of his stupor, he began to distinguish more clearly forms and finally himself again he recalled the vision he had seen. He raised his hands to his eyes and touched those windows of his flesh returned to the light and entirely reconstituted. He went to tell his neighbors and broke forth in praises for the immeasurable magnificence of Christ. This causes an indescribable rejoicing. Each person asked himself if he was dreaming or if he had actually seen an extraordinary miracle. The most amazed were those who had known him the longest.

Among these things something ridiculous and worthy of applause happened. Since he was a man of the purest simplicity, the fear entered his heart that perhaps that Gerald who had torn out his eyes might come to the public feast and again if he should by chance encounter him he might once more by the force of his hand remove the glory of his eyes in his wrath. Therefore amongst the confusion of the common crown he attempted to slip away unseen. Since he was not yet certain of the gift of recovering his sight a great bewilderment took over him when by chance hurrying with the tightly packed crowd to the church he came opposite an ass which he saw as clear as day. When he had admired it, rebuking its owner with severity, he said, "You, whoever you are, you fool, move your ass so that you do not block travellers." When the former was absolutely certain of what had happened, he withdrew quickly and hurried to find a certain knight known to him whose city (castle) was situated on a high cliff whence it was protected by nature such that it appeared inaccessible to all sorts of siege machines, not further from Conques than sixteen miles. After he had fled to this castle because of the protection of its impregnable valleys, with difficulty he at last returned (to Conques) because of the many entreaties and promises of security made by the monks. When many people coming from far and near hurried there desiring to see him because of this unheard-of miracle, as they left rejoicing they gave him many gifts. And this is what Saint Foy had said to him in the vision as we said, "A thousand men whom you have never seen will give to you," naming a finite number, as is customary in the Scriptures, for an infinite one.

Next, so that he might be better known and established in the place, abbot Arlaldus of happy memory who has recently died, with the common agreement of the brothers, gave him the task of selling wax which was extremely abundant here by the hand of God. From whence, when he had gathered together with many complaints he began, as is the nature of men, to become swollen with pride, and when there appeared in his soul the desire of a woman, he immediately forgot the dignity of the miracle worked in him. But in order that this might not be borne unavenged, suddenly the revenge of the holy virgin caused the misfortune that one of the man's eyes was blinded, not totally, and when he was led to the remedy of penance, she entirely restored his vision. Later on he again and again fell into the habit of wallowing in lust, and pursued by divine vengeance, he lost the vision of one eye, and recovered it when he repented. We could write as many chapters of miracles as often as this happened, were our purpose not to avoid excess. At last, when this had happened to him without cease, he lost the use of both his eyes. For this reason, in order to do more perfect penance, after cutting his beard and receiving the tonsure, he bound himself over to the clerical order. Although this ignorant and illiterate layman did this, nevertheless it was founded in love of God and thus he merited to recover his eyesight. Thus finally after so many lashings of correction, the impatience of his lust which could be said to have heaped up filth in him, was not punished corporally any further. Now this old man, reduced by evil actions to the lowest value and poverty, now is nourished by the public alms of the brothers, and he is content with his diminished condition and for the most part the support offered him in his twilight years. He rejoices in the fame of such a restoration, altogether secure from the fickleness of frivolity.

Thus I, a witness of the truth of divine providence, have painted without any falsification, as is contained in this writing, what I received from the mouth of this Vuitbert. Nor did I add anything for a more decorative effect nor do I think that I can escape unpunished if I think to celebrate in a lying style this eternal friend and beloved of God Saint Foy, who it is known suffered the deadly sentence of martyrdom for truth which is Christ. Finally, since many whose authority is sufficiently accepted have accepted prodigious things even though they happened much before their own time only based on the testimony of those who were not present at the events and who were intent to describe them in the most elegant manner, why should I allow things which took place in my own time and which I saw with my own eyes, and concerning which the people of the Auvergne, Rouergue, the Toulousin, and other regions present indisputable testimony, which pertain to our duty of teaching, disappear from memory? Especially since this thing which we have just finished describing with such little adornment almost violently forces such an insignificant person as myself to presume to present a subject so dangerous and arduous.

In this region there are few people trained in writing, I do not know whether by sloth or ignorance (since there are many who glory in the profession of learning who never show themselves learned by their works), but these writers, ungrateful for their gifts, have either wilfully neglected these great events or been entirely ignorant of them. Therefore I declare that it is better to be accused of audacity than to incur the guilt of negligence provided that I attempt to write down in letters what by no means he can do if writing for posterity is to be served without having the reproach of doubt or the condemnation of truth. So that there should be no doubt that this above mentioned Vuitbert was not immediately cured by divine mercy there, but in truth as was said above lost his eyes,, he was without health for a whole year. Moreover he showed the taking of his eyes by evil means to many of his neighbors and when this had been recognized by all He cured him at last. Thus this miracle was no less than that of the man born blind in the Gospel possibly even more astonishing. But we recall what the Truth had promised: "He who believes in me, the works which I do he too will do, and he will even do greater things because I go to the Father."

XI Concerning those who, robbing St. Foy, suddenly perished in the collapse of a roof.

There was another miracle of divine vengeance, but in a time before my arrival, which encourages the ecclesiastics and those devotedly serving the divine cult in the house of God and which terrified those who violently rob the goods of the holy church of God or who claim the inheritance of the saints as their own right. For in this time there are many whom we can justly term antichrists, who are so blinded by ambition that they dare to invade church rights, that they not only do not revere the offices of sacred ministry but they even attack them not only with invective and with beatings, but even afflict them with death. We have seen canons, monks and abbots despoiled of their honor and deprived of their goods and destroyed by death. We have seen bishops, some condemned by proscription, others expelled from their bishopric without cause, others cut down with the sword, and even burned by Christians in terrible flames for the defense of ecclesiastical rights, if in truth one can call those people Christians, who attack the order of Christian religion, they who stand opposed to Christ and to truth in all things. Because these undergo no punishment in the present life, they are not terrified by celestial vengeance. Rather they hope that there will never be any vengeance and there are even those who do not believe in a future judgment because in doing evil they have always enjoyed success and in following their own wills they have always escaped punishment. They have never experienced any hint of vengeance and therefore what they hear about vengeance of Christ they consider to be fables. Therefore it is necessary that the divine avenger punish some of them even in this world, lest they becomes so elated by their impunity that it appear a trivial thing to irritate God. It is also needed so that prowling folly, which rejects the sweet yoke of Christ and disdains the warnings of holy correction might be so bridled by the suffering of present punishments so that it will impose a limit on its own malice lest it be more severely punished or that it might repent altogether and return to health. Then those who prepared their soul similarly for a like deed might be terrified by such an example and might repent of their intended evil, and might hurry in penance to the society of the sons of light. But having spoken about these things first, let us come now to that end toward which we hurry.

There was in the region of Cahors a noble woman, Doda, lord of Castelnau on the

Dordogne. She had unjustly occupied an estate of Saint Foy which is called Alans. At the moment of her death, concerned about the salvation of her soul, she returned this property to the monastery of Conques. Hildegar, the son of her daughter, succeeded her, rich in the abundance of wealth as well as in the honor of office. He ruled from this famous castle in the territory of Albi called Penne, and he again dared to invade once more the same property and to take it from the monastery of Conques. For this reason the monks, in order to recover their property through the justice of the divine judge from the hand of this most violent robber, as was their custom, decided to go to in procession with the populace carrying as was the custom, the venerable effigy of the holy virgin. I shall explain later my feelings about this image, which might appear to be an object of superstition. There it happened that a knight of Hildegar (the grandson of Doda), whose name we forget and right now we are not able to return to Conques in order to ask for it, was reveling on Christmas, was dining in the midst of splendid knights and a succession of servants. Having consumed more wine than he was accustomed, among other things bodily abused the servants of Saint Foy, called them vile manure, protesting that he was amused to see the monks carrying their statue, a mask or sham worthy of ridicule and spittle, onto the contested estate. He would not be scared away by this nor would he defend his lord's rights any less violently and strenuously. Rather it seemed simple if he were to show how altogether vile this statue was by trampling it under foot. It would be tedious to tell how many times, three and four or more, he repeated such insults and laughter, when suddenly, the terrible sound of a divine storm was heard. It suddenly destroyed the balcony, the structure of the upper story collapsed, and all of the roof fell in. However, of the whole multitude who were present, only the blasphemer, his wife, and his five servants were killed. And so that no one might think that the house collapsed and that these men were killed by chance; the seven bodies were found thrown far out of the windows. Their remains lie in the cemetery of Saint-Antoin in the region of Albi.

Listen, robbers and devastators of Christian estates: the punishments of God are ineluctable and just are his judgments. His vengeance cedes place to no power; if it hold back for a time, it will strike with more force in the future. If you escape it in the present, a harsher punishment awaits you: that of eternal fire.

XII The processions of Saint Foy

There are many and undeniable indications that divine justice exercises a terrible judgment upon those who speak against Saint Foy. We will tell about one most extraordinary event when we speak about the image of the holy martyr. It is an ancient custom in all of Auvergne, Rodez, Toulouse and the neighboring regions that the local saint has a statue of gold silver, or some other metal according to their means. This statue serves as a reliquary for the head of the saint or for a part of his body. The learned might see in this a superstition and a vestige of the cult of demons, and I myself who am but an ignoramus had the same impression the first time that I saw the statue of Saint Gerard enthroned on the altar resplendent with gold and stones, with an expression so human that the simple people sense that they are being watched by the gaze of an inquisitor and they pretend that it winks at pilgrims whose prayers it answers. I admit to my shame that turning to my friend Bernerius and laughing I whispered to him in Latin, "What do you think of the idol? Wouldn't Jupiter or Mars be happy with it?" And Bernerius was inspired to add rather ingenuous pleasantries and to revile the statue. We were not wrong: when one adores the true God, it is inappropriate and absurd to make images of plaster, wood or bronze except for the image of the Lord crucified that Christian piety makes with love to celebrate the memory of the passion of the Lord and which all of the holy Church has adopted. As for saints, it is sufficient that the truthful books or frescoes on walls recall their memory. For we do not tolerate statues of saints for any reason, unless as an ancient abuse and an eradicable and inborn custom of the ignorant. In certain regions these images take on such an importance that if, for example, I had the misfortune to express my reflections on the image of St. Gerard out loud, I would have had to pay dearly for my crime.

Three days later we arrived at Saint Foy. At the moment that we entered the monastery it happened by chance that the back of the sanctuary where the holy image is kept was open. We approached but the crowd was such that we could not prostrate ourselves like so many others already lying on the floor. Unhappy, I remained standing, fixing my view on the image and murmuring this prayer, "Saint Foy, you whose relics rest in this sham, come to my assistance on the day of judgment." And this time again I looked at my companion the scholastic Bernerius from out of the corner because I found it outrageous that all of these rational beings should be praying to a mute and inanimate object. My idle talk or little understanding nevertheless did not come from a clean conscience, because I should not have disrespectfully called a sacred image, which is not consulted for divination by means of sacrifices like an idol but is rather for revering the memory of a martyr in honor of the highest God, a sham like those of Venus of Diana. Later I greatly regretted to have acted so stupidly toward the saint of God. This was because among other miracles Don Adalgerius, at that time dean and later as I have heard, abbot (of Conques and Figeac), told me a remarkable account of a cleric named Oldaric. One day when the venerable image had to be taken to another place, because he thought himself smarter than the others, his heart was so twisted that he restrained the crowd from bringing offerings and he insulted and belittled the image of the saint with various insults. The next night, a lady of imposing severity appeared to him: "You," she said, "how dare you insult my image?" Having said this, she flogged her enemy with a staff which she was seen to carry in her right hand. He survived only long enough to tell the vision in the morning.

Thus there is no place left for arguing whether the effigy of Saint Foy ought to be venerated since it is clear that he who reproached the holy martyr nevertheless retracted his reproach, nor is it a spurious idol where nefarious rites of sacrifice or of divination are conducted, but rather a plus memorial of the holy virgin before which great numbers of faithful decently and eloquently implore her efficacious intercession for their sins. And what is more wisely to be recognized, the container of the relics of the saints was made as a votive offering of the craftsman in the form of that person and is by far a more precious treasure than the ark of the covenant was of old. In the statue of Saint Foy her whole head is preserved, which is surely one of the most noble pearls of the celestial Jerusalem. Out of consideration of her merits, the divine goodness effects such prodigies that I have never heard the like concerning any other saint in our time. Therefore the image of Saint Foy is not something which ought to be destroyed or vituperated, especially since it has never led anyone to fall back into the error of paganism nor has it lessened the virtues of the saints nor caused the slightest harm to religion.

XXVIII That Saint Foy performs great miracles at synods and concerning the boy in whom a fourfold miracle was worked.

Nor do I think it should be omitted that among the many bodies of saints which are carried to councils as is the custom of the region, Saint Foy, holding as it were the first place, shows forth the glory of miracles. Among the many of these there are two which we do not think tedious to recount in this book. The most reverend Arnaldus, bishop of Rodez (1025-1031) convoked a synod in his dioceses to which the various bodies of the saints were carried from the various communities of monks and canons. The battle lines of the saints were arranged in tents and pavilions in the field of St. Felix which is about one mile from the town. The golden majesty of Saint Amantius, likewise confessor and bishop, the golden reliquary of Saint Saturninus, martyr, and the golden image of Mary, the mother of God, and the golden majesty of Saint Foy especially adorned the field. There was present in addition many relics of the saints whose number will not be estimated in the present writing. Here one famous and miraculous event was chosen by the All-powerful to glorify his faithful follower. A boy born blind and lame, deaf and mute, was carried by his kinsmen and placed below the image which occupied the sublime position of honor. After remaining here for about one hour, he merited divine medicine. And made entirely well by the gift of grace, he rose up speaking, hearing, seeing and happily walking about on his feet without difficulty. When the cries of the vulgar masses wnet up at such a wonder, the lords in attendance at the council, who were deliberating a bit removed, began to ask each other saying, "What does this cry from the people mean? The countless Bertilda (of Rouergue d. ca. 1015) answered them, " What else could this be, unless it is Saint Foy "joking around as usual." Then, when the event has been investigated, filled with wonder and joy, everyone urged the whole assembly to the praise of God, contemplating frequently with great joy that the venerable lady had said that Saint Foy was playing.

Fulbert of Chartres

Letter to William of Aquitaine

In 1020 Bishop Fulbert of Chartres (ca. 960–1028) wrote Duke William V of Aquitaine (ca. 960–1030) on the duties of lords and vassals. This ideal image of feudal relations can be contrasted with the brutal realities in the two documents which follow.

Source: Recueil des historiens des Gaules et de la France, X, 463.

Fulbert, bishop, to the glorious duke of the Aquitanians William.

Invited to write something concerning the form of fealty, I have briefly noted for you the following things from the authority of books. He who swears fealty to his lord must always remember these six things: harmless, safe, honorable, useful, easy, possible. Harmless, that is, he must not harm his lord in his body. Safe, he must not harm him in his secrets or in the fortifications by which he is able to be safe. Honorable, so that he must not harm him in his justice or in other affairs which are seen to pertain to his honor. Useful, that he might not be harmful to him in his possessions. Easy or possible, so that he not make difficult any good which his lord could easily do nor make anything impossible that is difficult. It is just that the vassal avoid these evils, but he does not merit his holding for so doing, for it is not enough that he abstain from evil unless he does what is good.

Therefore it remains that he should give his lord counsel and aid in these same six above mentioned things if he wishes to be seen worthy of his benefice and to be safe in the fealty he has sworn. The lord should act toward his vassal reciprocally in all these things. If he does not do so, he deserves to be considered of bad faith, just as the vassal, if he were caught in collusion or in doing or in consenting to them, would be perfidious or perjured.

I would have written to you at greater length if I had not been occupied with many other things, both the restoration of our city and of our church which have recently been totally consumed by a horrendous fire. Although for a time we could not be turned away from this loss, through the hope in the consolation of God and of you we once more breathe.

Hugh of Lusignan

Agreement Between Lord And Vassal

Around 1020/25 Hugh of Lusignan, a powerful and ambitious chatelain in Poitou, wrote or dictated his account of his relations with William V of Aquitaine over the previous decades. Hugh contended that he had been unjustly deprived of lands and castles that had belonged to his ancestors. His description of his treatment at the hands of his lord provides unique glimpses into the realities of feudal relationships in the eleventh century.

Source: Ed. Jane Martindale, *English Historical Review* 84 (1969) pp. 528–548. Tr. George Beech.

William Count of the Aquitanians had an agreement with Hugh the Chiliarch to the effect that when Viscount Roso dies he [William] would give him his honor in commendation. Roho the bishop saw and heard this and he kissed the arm of the Count. Then Viscount Savary seized from Hugh land which he [Hugh] held from Count William and when the Viscount died the Count promised Hugh that he would make no agreement or accord with Ralph the dead man's brother until the land had been restored. This he said in the presence of all, but afterwards he secretly gave him [Ralph] the land. Hugh had an agreement with Viscount Ralph that he would marry his daughter [Ralph's] in return for that estate or for a larger one, or for other things. When the Count heard of this he was greatly angered and went humbly to Hugh and said to him, "Don't marry Ralph's daughter, I will give you whatever you want from me and you will be my friend before everyone else except my son." And Hugh did what the Count ordered him to do and out of love and fidelity he secretly rejected the woman. At the same time it happened that Joscelin of Parthenay castle died, and the Count said that he would turn over his honor and wife [Joscelin's] to Hugh, but that if he [Hugh] refused to accept them, he would no longer have confidence in him. In this affair Hugh did not encourage the Count at all in his own behalf or in anyone else's, nor did he discourage him. Thinking it over, he said to the Count, "I will do everything you order me to do." Making an agreement with Count Fulk, the Count promised to give him [i.e. Fulk] something from his own benefices in place of that one. Fulk then promised that he would give to Hugh those things which belonged to him. As a part of this agreement the Count called for Viscount Ralph and said to him, "Hugh will not keep the agreement which he has with you because I forbid him to. But Fulk and I have an agreement that we will give him [i.e. Hugh] the honor and wife of Joscelin and we do this to punish you because you don't keep faith with me." And when Ralph heard this he was deeply sorry and said to the Count, "For the sake of God do not do that," and the Count said, "Make a pledge to me that you will not give him your daughter nor keep your agreement with him and I likewise will see that he does not possess the honor or the wife of Joscelin." And they did thus so that Hugh got neither the one nor the other. Ralph left to go to Count William who was in Montreuil castle, sending a message to Hugh that they should talk with one another. This was done and Ralph said to Hugh, "I tell you these things in advance in the faith that you will not reveal me; give me a pledge that you will aid me against Count William and I will keep your agreement and I will aid you against all men." But out of love for Count William Hugh refused to do this and Hugh and Ralph parted angrily. Then Ralph started war with Count William and out of love for the Count, Hugh went to war with Ralph and suffered greatly.

When Ralph died Hugh asked the Count to restore to him the land which Ralph had seized from him. The Count said to Hugh, "I will not make an agreement with Viscount Josfred, the nephew of Ralph, nor with the men of Thouars castle, until I return your land." But the Count by no means did this but left and made an agreement with Viscount Josfred and with the men of Thouars castle and did not make an agreement with Hugh; and Hugh did not get his land but on account of the evil deed which Hugh did for the Count, Josfred started a war with Hugh and burned Mouzeuil castle and seized Hugh's knights and cut off their hands and did enough else. The Count in no way aided Hugh nor did he make an honest agreement between them, but Hugh in addition to this lost his land and on account of his assistance to the Count he lost still another which he was holding peacefully. And when Hugh saw that he was not going to get his land he seized 43 of the best knights of Thouars and he could have had justice and peace and his land back. And if he had been willing to accept a ransom he could have had 40,000 *soildi*. When the Count heard of this he ought to have been happy but he was angry and sent for Hugh saying to him, "Give me the men." And Hugh answered him, "Why do you ask these things of me my lord? It is only your fidelity [i.e. your lack of it] which causes me to lose things." The Count then said, "I don't ask you for them in order to do you wrong but because you are mine [i.e. my vassal] to do my will [i.e. to act according to my wishes] and so that everyone may know as a result of our agreement according to which I will get the men, that I will make an agreement with you that you will get your lands back and be re-paid for the evil done you or else I will return the men to you. Believe and trust me and if anything should turn out badly for you, you will know because it was I who betrayed you." Then Hugh trusted in him and in God and handed over the men to the Count under such an agreement. Later on Hugh lost his land and got neither justice nor the men back.

The Count of the Poitevins and Bishop Gilbert had an agreement among themselves with Hugh's Uncle Joscelin. It concerned Vivonne castle to the effect that after the death of Bishop Gilbert the castle should go to Joscelin. While still alive the Bishop had the men of that castle commend themselves [i.e. become vassals of] to Joscelin and turned over the tower to him; after the death of both men the Count made an agreement between Bishop Isembert and Hugh to the effect that half of the castle should be Hugh's, half from the demesne and two parts from the fiefs of the vassals. Therefore the Count had Hugh commend himself to Bishop Isembert. Then he took the best estate from them.

A Tribune named Aimery seized the castle called Civray from his lord Bernard and this castle was rightfully Hugh's as it had been his father's. Because of his anger at Aimery Count William urged Hugh to become the vassal of Bernard for that part of the castle which had belonged to his father so that both [i.e. Bernard and Hugh] could do war with Aimery. But Hugh did not want to be the vassal of Bernard. The Count let this request wait for a year and then growing angrier he urged Hugh all the more to become the vassal of Bernard. When a year had passed the Count came with great wrath to Hugh and said to him, "Why don't you make an agreement with Bernard? You owe so much to me that if I should tell you to make a peasant into a lord you should do it. Do what I tell you and if it should turn out badly for you, come and see me about it." Hugh believed him and became the man [i.e. vassal] of Bernard for the fourth part of the said castle. As his pledge to Hugh Bernard gave the Count and four hostages. The Count said to Hugh, "Commend those hostages to me under such conditions that if Bernard should not keep those agreements made to you on faith, I will turn them over to you to custody and by my faith will be your helper." The Count promised this very strongly to Hugh [how strongly he himself well knows]. And Hugh trusted in his lord and took up a just war on account of the above castle and suffered great losses in men and other things. And the Count started to build a castle for him called Couhe but did not finish it but he spoke with Aimery and gave up the castle to him [i.e. Aimery] and in no way aided Hugh.

Later the Count became upset with Aimery on account of the castle called Chize which Aimery had seized and Hugh and the Count went to war together against him. He [i.e. the Count] beseiged the castle of Malavallis in return for the evil deed which Aimery had done to him and captured it, and Hugh aided him as best he could. Before Hugh left the Count the latter promised him, just as a lord ought to promise satisfaction to his vassal, that he would make no agreement with Aimery nor have anything to do with him without Hugh, and that Malavallis would not be built without his [i.e. Hugh's] advice. But the Count did make an agreement with Aimery and permitted him to build Malavallis without the advice of Hugh. As long as Aimery lived Hugh got nothing back with respect to the aforesaid matters.

After the death of Aimery a great war began between the son of Aimery [also named Aimery] and Hugh. At the same time Hugh came to the Count and said to him, "Things are going badly for me now, my Lord, in that I have no part of the fief which you caused me to acquire." The Count answered him, "I am going to make a pact with them [i.e. Aimery's son and his men] which, if they keep it well, should be fine: if not, I will build the castle which I started." And the castle was constructed on the advice of Bernard who hitherto had assisted Hugh in the war. Then the men of Civray, when they saw how Hugh was oppressing them, were no longer able to hold out and made an agreement with Bernard giving him the castle and admitting him into it without consulting Hugh. Now both Bernard and Aimery were at war against Hugh and he was alone against them. Coming to the Count Hugh said to him, "My Lord, I am doing very badly because the lord of whom I became a vassal at your advice has just taken away my fief. I beg and urge you through the faith which a lord ought to render to his vassal that you see to it that I get either a favorable pact or my fief as you pledged to me, or that you turn over to me the hostages which I commended to you, and that in addition you aid me as you pledged to me." The Count, however, neither aided him nor made an agreement with him nor gave over his hostages, but gave them back to Bernard with no strings attached.

After this a war started between Bernard, Aimery, and Hugh. And when Hugh saw that the Count aided him in no way he went to seek the advice of Gerald the Bishop of Limoges and they both left to move against Bernard in La Marche where they built a castle. But the Count who ought to have aided Hugh seized the castle from him and burned it. And he [i.e. the Count] and his son ordered all their men that no one should help Hugh unless he wished to die. Then Bernard in consultation with his men decided that they should do evil to Hugh on the advice of the Count and they [i.e. Bernard and his men] appointed a deadline fifteen days away. During those fifteen days the Count arranged a truce between Bernard and Hugh. Three days before the end of the truce the Count took Hugh along with his host to Apremont castle and a meeting was held in his castle. From there the Count went to Blaye where he was to have a meeting with Count Sancho and he told Hugh that he should come along. And Hugh responded, "My Lord, why do you ask me to go with you? You yourself know how short is the truce which I have with Bernard and he is threatening to do me ill." The Count said to him "Don't fear that they will do anything to you as long as you are with me," and he [i.e. the Count] took him along with him for force and against his wishes. And while they were staying at the meeting place Hugh's men heard that Bernard was attacking him. They sent a message to Hugh that he should come. Then Hugh said to the Count, "Bernard is attacking me." And the Count said, "Do not fear that they should have dared to attack you. Besides you would have needed that they attack in order that I might put them [i.e. Bernard and his men] to confusion and give you assistance." And in the very same hour the Count sent directions to Hugh through his own men that he should go on ahead and then he [the Count] followed him. When Hugh reached Lusignan Bernard was at Confolens castle and had captured the *burg* and the *barrium* [i.e. the cleared area and houses around the *burg*] and had burned everything except the spoils and the men taken prisoners, and had done enough other evil deeds. A messenger ran up to Hugh and said to him, "Bernard has your wife besieged in the old castle which is left over from the fire." Coming to the Count Hugh said to him, "My Lord, now help me because my wife is besieged." But the Count gave him no aid nor advice at all, and Bernard and his men turned back and did much harm to Hugh and his men, more than he could bear, fifty thousand *solidi* worth. And Hugh suffered this damage during the truce which the Count offered him at Blaye.

Not long after this Hugh went to Gencay castle and burned it and seized the men and women and took everything with him; and proceeding to the Count he said to him, "My Lord, give me permission to build the castle which I burned." And the Count said to him, "How can you build a castle when you are Fulk's vassal? He will demand it from you and you won't be able to keep it unless you turn it over to him." Hugh said, "My Lord, when I became the vassal of Fulk I told him that his men were seizing things which belonged to me and that if I was able to regain possession of them I would do it, but that I want to do this in such a way as to remain his vassal. And Fulk said to me, 'If you get angry at them, don't get angry at me.'" And when the Count heard that Fulk and Hugh had such an agreement he was pleased and said to Hugh, "Build the castle under such an agreement that if I am able to buy your share and mine from Count Fulk, one part [i.e. of the castle] will be mine and the other yours." And Hugh built the castle. Then Fulk asked the Count for it and the Count responded, "Ask Hugh for it." Then Fulk did this and Hugh responded, "When I became your vassal, I told you that if I was able to seize the castles from my enemies I would do it and that I would hold it [sic] from you, and I want to do this because this castle which you are demanding belonged to my relatives and I have a better right to it than those who were holding it." And Fulk said to him, "How can you, who are my vassal, hold something which I did not give you, against my will?" Then Hugh sought again the advice of the Count. The Count told him, "If he is willing to give you pledges that your enemies will not have the castle then you can't keep it; if not, keep it, because he will not be able to accuse you [i.e. of breaking feudal custom]." Hugh then asked Fulk to give him hostages, but he gave none saying, "I am going to see the Count and I will give him the hostages, and he can give you some of his own," and then the conference turned into an angry one. Fulk demanded Hugh's castle of the Count. "I will never give it up without pledges," said Hugh. Then the Count said to him, "I will give you a pledge; tell me which ones you want." Hugh said, "Get the ones you want from Count Fulk and give me what I'm asking for. Give me the man who has custody of the tower of Melle so that if Aimery should get the castle without my advice and evil should happen to me, that man will turn the tower over to me." The Count said to him, "I will not do this because it is not in power to do it." Then Hugh said, "If you want to do this with Melle, make the same agreement with regard to Chize." But the Count was willing to do neither the one nor the other; and Hugh and his men saw that the Count was dealing badly with them, and they parted in anger. Then Hugh sent all kinds of necessities into the castle and intended to hold it against all comers if they would not give him pledges. Then the Count came outside his *civitatem* [presumably Poitiers] and asked Hugh to come to him and through Count William of Angouleme ordered him to submit himself to the mercy of the Count because he [i.e. the Count] could not change the situation which called for him to aid Fulk and he was fearful of losing [the friendship of] either Fulk or Hugh. Then Hugh committed himself to the friendship and trust of the Count his Lord and did this out of love for him [the Count] because he [i.e. the Count] was certain that Fulk had not been badly led. And the Count said, "Let Hugh do this for me and I will give him my faith just as a Lord ought to do to his vassal, and if evil should happen to him he will know that it was I who betrayed him and he will never trust in me again." And Hugh responded, "My Lord has spoken to me in such a way about many things and as a result has led me away [i.e. from my original opposition to him]." And not a single one of Hugh's men would advise him to trust the Count. But the Count reminded Hugh of all the good things which he had done for him and pressed him with his love and requests and appeals; then Hugh said to the Count, "I will trust every thing to you, but watch out lest you do me evil, for if you do, I will not be faithful to you nor will I serve you, nor will I render fidelity to you; but on account of the fact that I will be separated from you and you are not able to give me pledges, I want you to give me my fief as a hostage that [in case of your violation] I will never serve you and [I want you to] release me from that oath which I made to you." And the Court answered, "Gladly." And Hugh against the wishes of his men had turned the castle over to the Count under such an agreement that Aimery would not get possession of it without his [i.e. Hugh's] advice and that evil should not happen to him. When these reservations had been heard, Hugh accepted [and the Count gave] his fief as a pledge under such an agreement that if the Count should mislead him with regard to the agreement about Gencay, he would never again render service to him [as a vassal]. And the Count released him from the oaths so that he would never observe them and without any malevolence [on the part of the Count]. And the Count handed over Gencay without consulting Hugh and was given money and some domaine land. And it went very badly for Hugh with men killed, houses burned, booty taken, lands seized, and many other things which in truth cannot be enumerated. When this had ended the Count gave Hugh a respite and promised that he would give him a benefice either of something which was his by right or of something which would be pleasing to him. But when this period passed the Count did nothing for Hugh but sent an order to him, "Don't wait because I am not going to do anything for you. If all the world were mine I would not give you as much as a finger could hold with regard to this matter." When Hugh heard this he went to the court of the Count and informed him of his rights but it profited him not a bit. This saddened Hugh and in the presence of all who were there he renounced his allegiance to the Count except what he owed for the city [i.e. Poitiers] and his own person.

Before either Hugh or his men did any evil the men of the Count seized a benefice from Hugh's men in the name of war. When Hugh saw this he went to Chize castle which had been his uncle's but which Peter was holding unjustly, and whence much harm was being done to Hugh. He seized the tower and threw out Peter's men. And Hugh did this because he thought he had a right to it since it had belonged to his father or others of his relatives and he was losing that right. And when the Count heard of this he was greatly saddened and sent an order to Hugh that the letter should turn over to him the tower which he had taken away from Peter. Hugh sent back to the Count that he [the Count] should turn over to him [Hugh] his father's honor and the other things which he had seized in it, and in addition the entire honor which had belonged to Joscelin and which the Count had given him. The Count thought this over and then they arranged for a conference. The Count said to Hugh, "I will not give you those honors which you ask of me, but I will give you that honor which your uncle's—the castle, the tower, and the entire honor—under such an agreement that you no longer demand of me that honor which was your father's, or others of your relatives, nor anything which you claim as your right." When he heard this Hugh greatly mistrusted the Count in that the latter with evil intent had taken much away from him in the past, and he said to the Count, "I don't dare to do this because I'm afraid that you'll threaten me with evil as you have done with regard to many other things." The Count said to Hugh, "I will make such pledges to you that you will no longer distrust me." Hugh asked him, "What kind of pledges?" The Count said, "I will produce a serf who will undergo an ordeal for you so that you will not doubt that the agreement which we make among ourselves will be kept nor that harm will ever again be done to you with regard to those affairs of the past, but the agreement will be kept firmly without any evil intent." When Hugh heard the Count speak in this manner he said, "You are my Lord, I will not accept a pledge from you, but I will simply rely on the mercy of God and of yourself." The Count said to Hugh, "Give up all those claims over which you have quarreled with me in the past and swear fidelity to me and my son and I will give you your uncle's honor or something else of equal value in exchange for it." Then Hugh said, "My Lord, I beg you through God and this blessed crucifix which is made in the figure of Christ that you do not make me do this if you and your son were intending to threaten me with trickery." And the Count said, "On my honor my son and I will do this without trickery." Hugh then said, "And when I shall have sworn fidelity to you, you will demand Chize castle of me, and if I should not turn it over to you, you will say that it is not right that I deny you the castle which I hold from you, and if I should turn it over to you, you and your son will seize it [i.e. and keep it] because you will have given nothing in pledge except the mercy of God and yourself." The Count said, "We will not do that, but if we should demand it of you, don't turn it over to us." Under the terms of such an agreement, or *finis* as it was also called, that the Count and his son should render fidelity to Hugh with no evil intentions, they received Hugh as their vassal in faith and trust. And they had Hugh abandon everything which he claimed from the past. And he swore fidelity to them and they gave him the honor of his uncle Joscelin just as the latter held it one year before he died.

Here end the agreements between the Count and Hugh.

Liudbrand of Cremona

A Chronicle of Otto's Reign

Liudbrand of Cremona (ca. 920-927) was raised in the court of King Hugo of Italy before becoming chancellor of King Berengar II. After breaking with Berengar, he went to the court of Otto I who named him bishop of Cremona and sent him on various diplomatic missions. He was the author of a history of Italy, Germany, and Byzantium between 888 and 949 directed against Berengar which he called Antapodosis *(Retaliation), an account of his unsuccessful attempt to arrange a marriage for Otto II with a Byzantine princess, and the following text, a justification of Otto I's Italian policy.*

· Source: F.A. Wright, *The Works of Liudprand of Cremona* (London: George Routledge and Sons, Ltd., 1930).

Ch. I.   Berengar and Adalbert were reigning, or rather raging, in Italy, where, to speak the truth, they exercised the worst of tyrannies, when John, the supreme pontiff and universal pope, whose church had suffered from the savage cruelty of the aforesaid Berengar and Adalbert, sent envoys from the holy church of Rome, in the persons of the cardinal deacon John and the secretary Azo, to Otto, at that time the most serene and pious king and now our august emperor, humbly begging him, both by letters and a recital of facts, for the love of God and the holy apostles Peter and Paul, whom he hoped would remit his sins, to rescue him and the holy Roman church entrusted to him from their jaws, and restore it to its former prosperity and freedom. While the Roman envoys were laying these complaints, Waldpert, the venerable archbishop of the holy church of Milan, having escaped half-dead from the mad rage of the aforesaid Berengar and Adalbert, sought the powerful protection of the above mentioned Otto, at that time king and now our august emperor, declaring that he could no longer bear or submit to the cruelty of Berengar and Adalbert and Willa, who contrary to all human and divine law had appointed Manasses Bishop of Arles to the see of Milan. He said that it was a calamity for his church thus to intercept a right that belonged to him and to his people. After Waldpert came Waldo Bishop of Como, crying out that he also had suffered a like insult at the hands of Berengar, Adalbert and Willa. With the apostolic envoys there also arrived some members of the laity, among them the illustrious marquess Otbert, asking help and advice from his most sacred majesty Otto, then king now emperor.

Ch. II.   The most pious king was moved by their tearful complaints, and considered not himself but the cause of Jesus Christ. Therefore, although it was contrary to custom, he appointed his young son Otto as king, and leaving him in Saxony collected his forces and marched in haste to Italy. There he drove Berengar and Adalbert from the realm at once, the more quickly inasmuch as it is certain that the holy apostles Peter and Paul were fighting under his flag. The good king brought together what had been scattered and mended what had been broken, restoring to each man his due possessions. Then he advanced on Rome to do the same again.

Ch. III.   There he was welcomed with marvellous ceremony and unexampled pomp, and was anointed as emperor by John the supreme bishop and universal pope. To the church he not only gave back her possessions but bestowed lavish gifts of jewels, gold and silver. Furthermore Pope John and all the princes of the city swore solemnly on the most precious body of Saint Peter that they would never give help to Berengar and Adalbert. Thereupon Otto returned to Pavia with all speed.

Ch. IV.   Meanwhile Pope John, forgetful of his oath and the promise he had made to the sacred emperor, sent to Adalbert asking him to return and swearing that he would assist him against the power of the most sacred emperor. For the sacred emperor had so terrified this Adalbert, persecutor of God's churches and of Pope John, that he had left Italy altogether and had gone to Fraxinetum and put himself under the protection of the Saracens. The righteous emperor for his part could not understand at all why Pope John was now showing such affection to the very man whom previously he had attacked in bitter hatred. Accordingly he called together some of his intimates and sent off to Rome to inquire if this report was true. On his messengers' arrival they got this answer, not from a few chance informants, but from all the citizens of Rome:—"Pope John hates the most sacred emperor, who freed him from Adalbert's clutches, for exactly the same reason that the devil hates his creator. The emperor, as we have learned by experience, knows, works and loves the things of God: he guards the affairs of church and state with his sword, adorns them by his virtues, and purifies them by his laws. Pope John is the enemy of all these things. What we say is a tale well known to all. As witness to its truth take the widow of Rainer his own vassal, a woman with whom John has been so blindly in love that he has made her governor of many cities and given to her the golden crosses and cups that are the sacred possessions of St Peter himself. Witness also the case of Stephana, his father's mistress, who recently conceived a child by him and died of an effusion of blood. If all else were silent, the palace of the Lateran, that once sheltered saints and is now a harlot's brothel, will never forget his union with his father's wench, the sister of the other concubine Stephania. Witness again the absence of all women here save Romans: they fear to come and pray at the thresholds of the holy apostles, for they have heard how John a little time ago took women pilgrims by force to his bed, wives, widows and virgins alike. Witness the churches of the holy apostles, whose roof lets the rain in upon the sacrosanct altar, and that not in drops but in sheets. The woodwork fills us with alarm, when we go there to ask God's help. Death reigns within the building, and, though we have much to pray for, we are prevented from going there and soon shall be forced to abandon God's house altogether. Witness the women he keeps, some of them fine ladies who, as the poet says, are as thin as reeds by dieting, others everyday buxom wenches. It is all the same to him whether they walk the pavement or ride in a carriage and pair. That is the reason why there is the same disagreement between him and the holy emperor as there is of necessity between wolves and lambs. That he may go his way unchecked, he is trying to get Adalbert, as patron, guardian and protector".

Ch. V.   When the envoys on their return gave this report to the emperor, he said:— "He is only a boy, and will soon alter if good men set him an example. I hope that honorable reproof and generous persuasion will quickly cure him of these vices; and then we shall say with the prophet:—'This is a change which the hand of the Highest has brought'". He added:—"The first thing required by circumstances is that we dislodge Berengar from his position on Montefeltro. Then let us address some words of fatherly admonition to the lord pope. His sense of shame, if not his own wishes, will soon effect a change in him for the better. Perchance if he is forced into good ways, he will be ashamed to get out of them again".

Ch. VI.   This done, the emperor went on board ship and sailed down the Po to Ravenna. Thence he advanced to Montefeltro, sometimes called St Leo's Mountain, and besieged the fort in which Berengar and Willa had taken refuge. Thereupon the aforesaid Pope John sent Leo, then the venerable chief notary of the holy Roman church and now in that same see successor to Saint Peter chief of the apostles, together with Demetrius, one of the most illustrious of the Roman princes, as envoy to the holy emperor. By their mouths he declared that it was not surprising if in the heat of youth he had hitherto indulged in childish follies; but now the time had come when he would fain live in a different fashion. He also cunningly alleged that the holy emperor had sheltered two of his disloyal subordinates, Bishop Leo and the cardinal deacon John, and that he was now breaking his sworn promise by letting them take an oath of allegiance not to the Pope but to the Emperor. To the envoys the emperor gave this answer: "I thank the pope for the change and improvement in his ways that he promises. As for the violation of pledges that he charges me with, judge yourselves if the accusation be true. We promised to restore all the territory of Saint Peter that might fall into our hands: and for that reason we are now striving to drive Berengar with all his household from yonder fort. How can we restore this territory to the pope, if we do not first wrest it from the hands of violent men and bring it under our control? As for Bishop Leo and the cardinal deacon John, his disloyal subordinates, whom he accuses us of having welcomed, we have neither seen them in these days nor welcomed them. The lord pope sent them to Constantinople to do us damage, and on their way, we are told, they were taken prisoners at Capua. We are also informed that with them was arrested a certain Saleccus, a Bulgarian by birth and an Hungarian by training, who is an intimate friend of the lord pope, and also a reprobate named Zacheus, a man quite ignorant of all literature sacred or profane, whom the lord pope has recently consecrated as bishop, with the intention that he should preach to the Hungarians a campaign against us. We would not have believed that the lord pope would have acted thus, whoever told us; but his letter, sealed with leaden seals and bearing his signature, compels us to think that it is true".

Ch. VII.   This done, the emperor sent Landohard the Saxon bishop of Minden and Luidprand the Italian bishop of Cremona to Rome in company with the pope's envoys, to satisfy the lord pope that no blame attached to him. Furthermore the righteous emperor bade the soldiers of their guard to prove the truth of his words in single combat if the pope refused to believe him. The aforesaid bishops Landohard and Luitbrand came before the lord pope at Rome, and although they were received with all due honour they saw clearly with what scorn and indifference he was prepared to treat the holy emperor. They explained everything in order, as they had been told to do, but the pope refused to be satisfied wither with an oath or with a single combat and persisted in being obdurate. Still, a week later he craftily sent John, Bishop of Narni, and Benedict, cardinal deacon, back to the lord emperor with his envoys, thinking that by their tricks he could delude a man whom it is exceptionally difficult to deceive. Before they got back, however, Adalbert at the pope's invitation had left Fraxinetum and reached Civita Vecchia; whence he set out for Rome and there, so far from being repudiated by the pope, as he should have been, received from him an honorable welcome.

Ch. VIII.   While these things were going on, the fierce heat of the dog days kept the emperor away from the hills of Rome. But when the sun had entered the sign of the Virgin and brought a temperate change, he collected his forces, and at the secret invitation of the Romans drew near to the city. Yet why do I say "secret", when the greater part of the Roman princes forced their way into the castle of St Paul and giving hostages invited the holy emperor to enter. Why make a long tale? When the emperor pitched his camp in the vicinity, the pope and Adalbert made their escape together from Rome. The citizens welcomed the holy emperor and all his men into their town, promising again to be loyal and adding under a strong oath that they would never elect or ordain a pope except with the consent and approval of the august Cæsar Otto the lord emperor and his son King Otto.

Ch. IX.   Three days later at the request of the bishops and people of Rome a synod was held in the church of St Peter, attended by the emperor and the Italian archbishops.

The deacon Rodalf acted in place of Ingelfred patriarch of Aquileia, who had been seized by a sudden sickness in that city; Waldpert came from Milan, Peter from Ravenna; Archbishop Adeltac and Landohard, bishop of Minden, represented Saxony; Otker, bishop of Spires, France. The Italian bishops were Hubert of Parma, Liudprand of Cremona, Hermenard of Reggio; the Tuscans, Conrad of Lucca, Everard of Arezzo, the bishops of Pisa, Sienna, Florence, Pistoia, Peter of Camerino, the bishop of Spoleto; the Romans, Gregory of Albano, Sico of Ostia, Benedict of Porto, Lucidus of Gavio, Theophylact of Palestrina, Wido of Selva Candida, Leo of Velletri, Sico of Bieda, Stephen of Cervetri, John of Nepi, John of Tivoli, John of San Liberato, Romanus of Ferentino, John of Norma, John of Veroli, Marinus of Sutri, John of Narni, John of Sabina, John of Gallese, the bishops of Civita, Castellana, Alatri, Orte, John of Anagni, the bishop of Trevi, Sabbatinus of Terracina. There were also present: Stephen cardinal archpriest of the parish Balbina, Dominic of the parish Anastasia, Peter of the parish Damascus, Theophylact of the parish Chrysogonus, John of the parish Equitius, Peter of the parish Pamachius, Adrian of the parish Caecilia, Adrian of the parish Lucina, Benedict of the parish Sixtus, Theophylact of the parish Four Crowned Saints, Stephen of the parish Sabina, Benedict cardinal archdeacon, John deacon, Bonofilius chief cardinal deacon, George second cardinal deacon, Stephen assistant, Andrew treasurer, Sergius chief warden, John sacristan, Stephen, Theophylact, Adrian, Stephen, Benedict, Azo, Adrian, Romanus, Leo, Benedict, Leo, Leo, Leo notaries, Leo chief of the school of singers, Benedict subdeacon in charge of the offertories, Azo, Benedict, Demetrius, John, Amicus, Sergius, Benedict, Urgo, John, Benedict subdeacon and steward, Stephen arch-acolyte with all the acolytes and district deacons. Representing the princes of Rome were Stephen son of John, Demetrius Meliosi, Crescenti de Caballo Marmoreo, John Mizina, Stephen de Imiza, Theodore de Rufina, John de Primicerio, Leo de Cazunuli, Rihkard, Pietro de Canapanaria, and Benedict with his son Bulgamin. The commoner Peter, also called Imperiola, together with the whole body of Roman soldiery was in attendance.

Ch. X.   When all had taken their seats and complete silence was established, the holy emperor began thus: "How fitting it would have been for the lord pope John to be present at this glorious holy synod. I ask you, holy fathers, to give your opinion why he has refused to attend this great gathering, for you live as he does and share in all his interests", Thereupon the Roman bishops and the cardinal priests and deacons together with the whole population said:—"We are surprised that your most holy wisdom deigns to ask us this question: even the inhabitants of Iberia and Babylonia and India know the answer to it. John is not now even one of those who come in sheep's clothing and within are ravening wolves: his savageness is manifest, he is openly engaged in the devil's business, and he makes no attempt at disguise". The emperor replied:—"It seems to us right that the charges against the pope should be brought forward seriatim, and that the whole synod should then consider what course we should adopt". Thereupon the cardinal priest Peter got up and testified that he had seen the pope celebrate mass without himself communicating. John bishop of Narni and John cardinal deacon then declared that they had seen the pope ordain a deacon in a stable and at an improper season. Benedict cardinal deacon with his fellow deacons and priests said that they knew the pope had been paid for ordaining bishops and that in the city of Todi he had appointed a bishop for ten years. On the question of his sacrilege, they said, no inquiries were necessary; knowledge of it was a matter of eyesight not of hearsay. As regards his adultery, though they had no visual information, they knew for certain that he had carnal acquaintance with Rainer's widow, Stephana his father's concubine, the widow Anna, and his own niece, and that he had turned the holy palace into a brothel and resort for harlots. He had gone hunting publicly: he had blinded his spiritual father Benedict who died of his injuries: he had caused the death of cardinal subdeacon John by castrating him: he had set houses on fire and appeared in public equipped with sword, helmet and cuirass. To all this they testified; while everyone, clergy and laity alike, loudly accused him of drinking wine for love of the devil. At dice, they said, he asked the aid of Jupiter, Venus, and the other demons; he did not celebrate matins nor observe the canonical hours nor fortify himself with the sign of the cross.

Ch. XI.   When he had heard this, as the Romans could not understand his native Saxon tongue, the emperor bade Luitbrand bishop of Cremona to deliver the following speech in the Latin language to all the Romans. Accordingly he got up and began thus: "It often happens, and we know it by experience that men set in high positions are besmirched by the foul tongue of envy: the good displease the bad, even as the bad displease the good. For this reason we still regard as doubtful the charge against the pope which the cardinal Benedict read out and communicated to you, and we are uncertain whether it originated from zeal for righteousness or from impious envy. Therefore, unworthy as I am, by the authority of the position that has been granted me I call upon you all by the Lord God, whom no one, even if he wishes, can deceive, and by his holy mother the pure virgin Mary, and by the most precious body of the chief of apostles, in whose church this is now being read, cast no foul words against the lord pope nor accuse him of anything that he has not really done and that has not been witnessed by men on whom we can rely". Thereupon the bishops, the priests, the deacons, the rest of the clergy, and the whole Roman people cried out as one man:—"If Pope John has not committed all the shameful crimes that the deacon Benedict read out to us and done things even worse and more disgusting than those, may the most blessed Peter, whose verdict closes the gates of heaven against the unworthy and opens them for the righteous, never free us from the chains of our sins: may we be held fast in the bonds of anathema and at the last day be set on the left hand with those who said to the Lord God: 'Depart from us, we would have no knowledge of thy ways'. If you do not give us credence, at least you ought to believe the army of our lord the emperor, against whom the pope advanced five days ago, equipped with sword, shield, helmet and cuirass. It was only the intervening waters of the Tiber that saved him from being taken prisoner in that garb". Then the holy emperor said:—"There are as many witnesses to that as there are fighting men in our army". So the holy synod pronounced: "If it please the holy emperor, let a letter be sent to the lord pope, that he come here and purge himself from all these charges". Thereupon a letter was sent to him as follows:—

Ch. XII.   "To the supreme pontiff and universal pope lord John, Otto, august emperor by the grace of God, together with the archbishops and bishops of Liguria, Tuscany, Saxony and France, sends greeting in the name of the Lord. When we came to Rome in God's service and inquired of your sons, the Roman bishops, cardinal priests and deacons, and the whole body of the people besides, concerning your absence, and asked them what was the reason that you were unwilling to see us, the defenders of your church and your person, they brought out such foul and filthy tales about you that we should be ashamed of them, even if they were told about actors. That your highness may not remain in complete ignorance we set down some of them briefly here; for though we would fain give them all seriatim, one day is not enough. Know then that you are charged, not by a few men but by all the clergy and laity alike, of homicide, perjury, sacrilege and of the sin of unchastity with your own kinswoman and with two sisters. They tell me too something that makes me shudder, that you have drunk wine for love of the devil, and that in dice you have asked the help of Jupiter, Venus and the other demons. Therefore we earnestly beg your paternal highness not to refuse under any pretence to come to Rome and clear yourself of all these charges. If perchance you fear the violence of a rash multitude, we declare under oath that no action is contemplated contrary to the sanction of the holy canons."

Ch. XIII.   After reading this letter, the pope sent the following reply: "Bishop John, servant of God's servants, to all the bishops. We hear say that you wish to make another pope. If you do, I excommunicate you by Almighty God, and you have no power, to ordain no one or celebrate mass".

Ch. XIV.   When this answer was read in the holy synod, the following clergy, who had been absent at the previous meeting, were present: from Lorraine, Henry Archbishop of Trèves; from Aemilia and Liguria, Wido of Modena, Gezo of Tortona, Sigulf of Piacenza. The synod returned the following reply to the lord pope:—"To the supreme pontiff and universal lord pope John, Otto, august emperor by the grace of God, and the holy synod assembled at Rome in God's service, send greeting in the Lord's name. At our last meeting of the sixth of November we sent you a letter containing the charges made against you by your accusers and their reasons for bringing them. In the same letter we asked your highness to come to Rome, as is only just, and to clear yourself from these allegations. We have now received your answer, which is not at all of a kind suited to the character of this occasion but is more in accordance with the folly of rank indifference. There could be no reasonable excuse for not coming to the synod. But messengers from your highness ought certainly to have put in an appearance here, and assured us that you could not attend the holy synod owing to illness or some such insuperable difficulty. There is furthermore a sentence in your letter more fitting for a stupid boy than a bishop. You excommunicated us all if we appointed another bishop to the see of Rome, and yet gave us power to celebrate the mass and ordain clerical functionaries. You said:—'You have no power to ordain no one'. We always thought, or rather believed, that two negatives make an affirmative, if your authority did not weaken the verdict of the authors of old. However, let us reply, not to your words, but to your meaning. If you do not refuse to come to the synod and to clear yourself of these charges, we certainly are prepared to bow to your authority. But if — which Heaven forbid! — under any pretence you refrain from coming and defending yourself against a capital charge, especially when there is nothing to stop you, neither a sea voyage, nor bodily sickness, nor a long journey, then we shall disregard your excommunication, and rather turn it upon yourself, as we have justly the power to do. Judas, who betrayed, or rather who sold, Our Lord Jesus Christ, with the other disciples received the power of binding and loosing from their Master in these words:—'Verily I say unto you, Whatsoever ye shall bind on earth shall be bound in heaven: and whatsoever ye shall loose on earth shall be loosed in heaven'. As long as Judas was a good man with his fellow disciples, he had the power to bind and loose. But when he became a murderer for greed and wished to destroy all men's lives, whom then could he loose that was bound or bind that was loosed save himself, whom he hanged in the accursed noose?" This letter was written on the twenty-second day of November and sent by the hand of the cardinal priest Adrian and the cardinal deacon Benedict.

Ch. XV.   When these latter arrived at Tivoli, they could not find the pope: he had gone off into the country with bow and arrows, and no one could tell them where he was. Not being able to find him they returned with the letter to Rome and the holy synod met for the third time. On this occasion the emperor said: "We have waited for the pope's appearance, that we might complain of his conduct towards us in his presence: but since we are now assured that he will not attend, we beg you earnestly to listen to an account of his treacherous behaviour. We hereby inform you, archbishops, bishops, priests, deacons, clerics, counts, judges and people, that Pope John being hard pressed by Berengar and Adalbert, our revolted subjects, sent messengers to us in Saxony, asking us for the love of God to come to Italy and free him and the church of St Peter from their jaws. We need not tell you how much we did for him with God's assistance: you see it to-day for yourselves. But when by my help he was rescued from their hands and restored to his proper place, forgetful of the oath of loyalty which he swore to me on the body of St Peter, he got Adalbert to come to Rome, defended him against me, stirred up tumults, and before my soldiers' eyes appeared as leader in the campaign equipped with helmet and cuirass. Let the holy synod now declare its decision". Thereupon the Roman pontiffs and the other clergy and all the people replied: "A mischief for which there is no precedent must be cauterized by methods equally novel. If the pope's moral corruption only hurt himself and not others, we should have to bear with him as best we could. But how many chaste youths by his example have become unchaste? How many worthy men by association with him have become reprobates? We therefore ask your imperial majesty that this monster, whom no virtue redeems from vice, shall be driven from the holy Roman church, and another be appointed in his place, who by the example of his goodly conversation may prove himself both ruler and benefactor, living rightly himself and setting us an example of like conduct". Then the emperor said: "I agree with what you say; nothing will please me more than for you to find such a man and to give him control of this holy universal see".

Ch. XVI. At that all cried with one voice:—"We elect as our shepherd Leo, the venerable chief notary of the holy Roman church, a man of proved worth deserving of the highest sacerdotal rank. He shall be the supreme and universal pope of the holy Roman church, and we hereby reprobate the apostate John because of his vicious life". The whole assembly repeated these words three times, and then with the emperor's consent escorted the aforesaid Leo to the Lateran Palace amid acclamations, and later at the due season in the church of St Peter elevated him to the supreme priesthood by holy consecration and took the oath of loyalty towards him.

Ch. XVII. When this had been arranged the most holy emperor, hoping that he could stay at Rome with a few men and not wishing the Roman people to be burdened with a great army, gave many of his soldiers leave to return home. John, the so-called pope, hearing of this and knowing how easily the Romans could be bribed, sent messengers to the city, promising the people all the wealth of St Peter and the churches, if they would fall upon the pious emperor and the lord pope Leo and impiously murder them. Why make a long tale? The Romans encouraged, or rather ensnared by the fewness of the emperor's troops and animated by the promised reward, at once sounded their trumpets and rushed in hot haste upon the emperor to kill him. He met them on the bridge over the Tiber, which the Romans had barricaded with wagons. His gallant warriors, well trained in battle with fearless hearts and fearless swords, leaped forward among the foe, like hawks falling on a flock of birds, and drove them off in panic without resistance. No hiding place, neither basket nor hollow tree trunk nor filthy sewer, could protect them in their flight. Down they fell, and as usually happens with such gallant heroes, most of their wounds were in the back. Who of the Romans then would have escaped from the massacre, had not the holy emperor yielded to the pity, which they did not deserve, and called off his men still thirsting for the enemies' blood.

Ch. XVIII. After they were all vanquished and the survivors had given hostages, the venerable pope Leo fell at the emperor's feet and begged him to give the hostages back and rely on the people's loyalty. At the request of the venerable pope Leo the holy emperor gave back the hostages, although he knew that the Romans would soon start the trouble I am about to relate. He also commended the pope to the Romans' loyalty, a lamb entrusted to wolves; and leaving Rome hastened towards Camerino and Spoleto where he had heard that Adalbert was to be found.

Ch. XIX. Meanwhile the women, with whom the so-called pope John was accustomed to carry on his voluptuous sports, being many in numbers and noble in rank, stirred up the Romans to overthrow Leo, whom God and they themselves had chosen as supreme and universal pope, and bring John back again into Rome. This they did; but by the mercy of God the venerable pope Leo escaped from their clutches and with a few attendants made his way to the protection of the most pious emperor Otto.

Ch. XX. The holy emperor was bitterly grieved at this insult, and to avenge the expulsion of the lord pope Leo and the foul injuries done by the deposed John to the cardinal deacon John and the notary Azo, one of whom had his right hand cut off, and the other his tongue, two fingers and his nose, he got his army together again and prepared to return to Rome. But before the holy emperor's forces were all assembled, the Lord decreed that every age should know how justly Pope John had been repudiated by his bishops and all the people, and how unjustly afterwards he had been welcomed back. One night when John was disporting himself with some man's wife outside Rome, the devil dealt him such a violent blow on the temples that he died of the injury within a week. Moreover at the prompting of the devil, who had struck the blow, he refused the last sacraments, as I have frequently heard testified by his friends and kinsmen who were at his death bed.

Ch. XXI. At his death the Romans, forgetful of the oath they had taken to the holy emperor, elected Benedict cardinal deacon as pope, swearing moreover that they would never abandon him but would defend him against the emperor's might. Thereupon the emperor invested the city closely and allowed no one to get out with a whole skin. Siege engines and famine completed the work, and finally in spite of the Romans he got possession of the city again, restored the venerable Leo to his proper place, and bade Benedict the usurper to appear before him.

Ch. XXII. Accordingly the supreme and universal pope the lord Leo took his seat in the church of the Lateran and with him the most holy emperor Otto, together with the Roman and Italian bishops, the archbishops of Lorraine and Saxony, the bishops, priests, deacons and the whole Roman people whose names will be given later. Before them appeared Benedict, the usurper of the apostolic chair, brought in by the men who had elected him and still wearing the pontifical vestments. To him the cardinal archdeacon Benedict addressed the following charge: "By what authority or by what law, O usurper, are you now wearing this pontifical raiment, seeing that our lord the venerable pope Leo is alive and here present, whom you and we elected to the supreme apostolic office when John had been accused and disowned? Can you deny that you swore to our lord the emperor here present that you and the other Romans would never elect nor ordain a pope without the consent of the emperor and his son King Otto?" Benedict replied:— "Have mercy upon my sin". Then the emperor, revealing by his tears how inclined he was to mercy, asked the synod not to pass hasty judgment upon Benedict. If he wished and could, let him answer the questions and defend his case: if he had neither the wish nor the power but confessed his guilt, then let him for the fear of God have some mercy shown to him. Thereupon Benedict flung himself in haste at the feet of the lord pope Leo and the emperor, and cried out: "I have sinned in usurping the holy Roman see." He then handed over the papal cloak and gave the papal staff which he was holding to pope Leo, who broke it in pieces and showed it to the people. Next the pope bade Benedict to sit down on the ground and took from him his chasuble and stole. Finally he said to all the bishops: "We hereby deprive Benedict, usurper of the holy Roman apostolic chair, of all pontifical and priestly office: but by reason of the clemency of the lord emperor Otto, by whose help we have been restored to our proper place, we allow him to keep the rank of deacon, not at Rome but in exile, which we now adjudge against him".

Pope Gregory VII and King Henry IV

The Investiture Controversy

Although the investiture controversy was a pan-European phenomenon, the critical eleventh-century phase most affected the development of the Empire. The contest between Gregory VII (1073-1085) and emperor Henry IV (1056-1106) was largely a propaganda war fought for the allegiance of the German episcopate and nobility. The series of letters of Gregory and Henry present the positions of each side and their attempts to best their opponents in public opinion.

Source: Theodor E. Mommsen and Karl F. Morrison, *Imperial Lives and Letters of the Eleventh Century* (New York: Columbia U. Press, 1962); Ephraim Emerton, *The Correspondence of Pope Gregory VII* (New York: Columbia University Press, 1932).

The Correspondence of Pope Gregory VII

Book III, 3 (July 20, 1075.)

Gregory ... to King Henry, greeting ...

Among other praiseworthy actions, my beloved son, to which you are reported to have risen in your efforts at self-improvement, there are two that have specially commended you to your holy mother, the Roman church: first, that you have valiantly withstood those guilty of Simony; and second, that you freely approve, and strenuously desire to enforce, the chastity of the clergy as servants of God. For these reasons you have given us cause to expect of you still higher and better things with God's help. Wherefore we earnestly pray that you may hold fast by these, and we beseech our Lord God that he may deign to increase your zeal more and more.

But now, as regards the church of Bamberg, which according to the ordinance of its founder [King Henry II] belongs to the Holy and Apostolic See as the shoulder to the head, that is, as a most intimate member, by a certain special bond of duty, we are greatly disturbed and we are forced by the obligation of our office to come to the rescue of its distress with all our powers. That simoniac so-called bishop Hermann, summoned to a Roman synod this present year, failed to appear. He came within a short distance of Rome, but there halted and sent forward messengers with ample gifts, trying, with his well-known trickery, to impose upon our innocence and, if possible, to corrupt the integrity of our colleagues by a pecuniary bargain. But when this turned out contrary to his hopes, convinced of his own damnation he hastily retreated and, soothing the minds of the clergy who were with him by smooth and deceitful promises, declared that if he were able to regain his own country he would resign his bishopric and enter the monastic life.

How he kept these promises Your Highness, beloved son, well knows. With increasing audacity he plundered the clergy who were upholding the welfare and the honor of their church, and had not your royal power restrained him, as we are informed, he would have completely ruined them. After careful consideration of these outrages we removed him from his episcopal and priestly office. Further, as he dared to oppress the church of Bamberg, under the apostolic patronage of St. Peter, more cruelly and more harshly than

377

before, we placed him in the bonds of anathema until he should lay down his usurped dignity and, nevertheless, present himself for trial before the Apostolic See.

Now, therefore, most excellent son, we ask Your Highness and urge you by our dutiful obligation to take counsel with men of piety and so to regulate the affairs of that church according to God's order, that you may be worthy of divine protection through the intercession of St. Peter, in whose name and under whose patronage the church was founded.

What I have written regarding this case to our colleague Siegfried, bishop of Mainz, and the clergy and people of Bamberg, you may learn with certainty from the letters dispatched to them.[1]

To King Henry IV, Admonishing Him to Show More Deference to the Holy See and Its Decrees
Book III, 10, p. 263. Dec. 8, 1075 [or Jan. 8, 1076].

Gregory, bishop, servant of God's servants, to King Henry, greeting and the apostolic benediction — but with the understanding that he obeys the Apostolic See as becomes a Christian king.

Considering and weighing carefully to how strict a judge we must render an account of the stewardship committed to us by St. Peter, prince of the Apostles, we have hesitated to send you the apostolic benediction, since you are reported to be in voluntary communication with men who are under the censure of the Apostolic See and of a synod. If this is true, you yourself know that you cannot receive the favour of God nor the apostolic blessing unless you shall first put away those excommunicated persons and force them to do penance and shall yourself obtain absolution and forgiveness for your sin by due repentance and satisfaction. Wherefore we counsel Your Excellency , if you feel yourself guilty in this matter, to make your confession at once to some pious bishop who, with our sanction, may impose upon you a penance suited to the offense, may absolve you and with your consent in writing may be free to send us a true report of the manner of your penance.

We marvel exceedingly that you have sent us so many devoted letters and displayed such humility by the spoken words of your legates, calling yourself a son of our Holy Mother Church and subject to us in the faith, singular in affection, a leader in devotion, commending yourself with every expression of gentleness and reverence, and yet in action showing yourself most bitterly hostile to the canons and apostolic decrees in those duties especially required by loyalty to the Church. Not to mention other cases, the way you have observed your promises in the Milan affair, made through your mother and through bishops, our colleagues, whom we sent to you, and what your intentions were in making them is evident to all. And now, heaping wounds upon wounds, you have handed over the sees of Fermo and Spoleto — if indeed a church may be given over by any human power to persons entirely unknown to us, whereas it is not lawful to consecrate anyone except after probation and with due knowledge.

It would have been becoming to you, since you confess yourself to be a son of the Church, to give more respectful attention to the master of the Church, that is, to Peter, prince of the Apostles. To him, if you are of the Lord's flock, you have been committed for your pasture, since Christ said to him: "Peter, feed my sheep," and again: "To thee are given the keys of Heaven, and whatsoever thou shalt bind on earth shall be bound in Heaven and whatsoever thou shalt loose on earth shall be loosed in Heaven." Now, while we, unworthy sinner that we are, stand in his place of power, still whatever you send to us, whether in writing or by word of mouth, he himself receives, and while we read what is written or hear the voice of those who speak, he discerns with subtle insight from what spirit the message comes. Wherefore Your Highness should beware lest any defect of will toward the Apostolic See be found in your words or in your messages and should pay due reverence, not to us but to Almighty God, in all matters touching the welfare of the Christian faith and the status of the Church. And this we say although our Lord deigned to declare: "He who heareth you heareth me; and he who despiseth you despiseth me."

We know that one who does not refuse to obey God in those matters in which we have spoken according to the statutes of the holy fathers does not scorn to observe our admonitions even as if he had received them from the lips of the Apostle himself. For if our Lord, out of reverence for the chair of Moses, commanded the Apostles to observe the teaching of the scribes and pharisees who sat thereon, there can be no doubt that the apostolic and gospel teaching, whose seat and foundation is Christ, should be accepted and maintained by those who are chosen to the service of teaching.

At a synod held at Rome during the current year, and over which Divine Providence willed us to preside, several of your subjects being present, we saw that the order of the Christian religion had long been greatly disturbed and its chief and proper function, the redemption of souls, had fallen low and through the wiles of the Devil had been trodden under foot. Startled by this danger and by the manifest ruin of the Lord's flock we returned to the teaching of the holy fathers, declaring no novelties nor any inventions of our own, but holding that the primary and only rule of discipline and the well-trodden way of the saints should again be sought and followed, all wandering paths to be abandoned, For we know that there is no other way of salvation and eternal life for the flock of Christ and their shepherds except that shown by him who said: "I am the door and he who enters by me shall be saved and shall find pasture." This was taught by the Apostles and observed by the holy fathers and we have learned it from the Gospels and from every page of Holy Writ.

This edict [against lay investiture], which some who place the honor of men above that of God call an intolerable burden, we, using the right word, call rather a truth and a light necessary for salvation, and we have given judgment that it is to be heartily accepted and obeyed, not only by you and your subjects but by all princes and peoples who confess and worship Christ — though it is our especial wish and would be especially fitting for you, that you should excel others in devotion to Christ as you are their superior in fame, in station and in valour.

Nevertheless, in order that these demands may not seem to you too burdensome or unfair we have sent you word by your own liegemen not to be troubled by this reform of an evil practice but to send us prudent and pious legates from your own people. If these can show in any reasonable way how we can moderate the decision of the holy fathers [at the Council] saving the honor of the eternal king and without peril to our own soul, we will condescend to hear their counsel. It would in fact have been the fair thing for you, even if you had not been so graciously admonished, to make reasonable inquiry of us in what respect we had offended you or assailed your honor, before you proceeded to violate the apostolic decrees. But how little you cared for our warnings or for doing right was shown by your later actions.

However, since the long-enduring patience of God summons you to improvement, we hope that with increase of understanding your heart and mind may be turned to obey the commands of God. We warn you with a father's love that you accept the rule of Christ, that you consider the peril of preferring your own honor to his, that you do not hamper by your actions the freedom of that Church which he deigned to bind to himself as a bride by a divine union, but, that she may increase as greatly as possible, you will begin to lend to Almighty God and to St. Peter, by whom also your own glory may merit increase, the aid of your valour by faithful devotion.

Now you ought to recognize your special obligation to them for the triumph over your enemies which they have granted you, and while they are making you happy and singularly prosperous, they ought to find your devotion increased by their favor to you. That the fear of God, in whose hand is all the might of kings and emperors, may impress this upon you more than any admonitions of mine, bear in mind what happened to Saul after he had won a victory by command of the prophet, how he boasted of his triumph, scorning the prophet's admonitions, and how he was rebuked by the Lord, and also what favor followed David the King as a reward for his humility in the midst of the tokens of his bravery.

Finally, as to what we have read in your letters and do not mention here we will give you no decided answer until your legates, Radbod, Adalbert and Odescalcus, to whom we entrust this, have returned to us and have more fully reported your decision upon the matters which we commissioned them to discuss with you.

The Roman Lenten Synod of 1076
Book III, 10(a), (Feb. 14-20, 1076).

In the year of the Incarnation 1075, our lord Pope Gregory held a synod at Rome in the church of Our Savior which is called the Constantiniana. A great number of bishops and abbots and clergy and laymen of various orders were present.

At this synod, among the decrees promulgated was the excommunication of Siegfried, archbishop of Mainz, in the following form:

In accordance with the judgment of the Holy Spirit and by authority of the blessed Apostles Peter and Paul, we suspend from every episcopal function, and exclude from the communion of the body and blood of the Lord, Siegfried, archbishop of Mainz, who has attempted to cut off the bishops and abbots of Germany from the Holy Roman Church, their spiritual mother — unless perchance in the hour of death, and then only if he shall come to himself and truly repent. Those who voluntarily joined his schism and still persist in their evil deeds, we also suspend from all episcopal functions. Those, however, who consented against their will we allow time until the feast of St. Peter; but if within that term they shall not have given due satisfaction in person or by messengers in our presence, they shall thenceforth be deprived of their episcopal office.

Excommunication of the bishops of Lombardy
The bishops of Lombardy who, in contempt of canonical and apostolic authority, have joined in a sworn conspiracy against St. Peter, prince of the Apostles, we suspend from their episcopal functions and exclude them from the communion of Holy Church.

[Here follows a list of excommunications of prelates and laymen beyond the Alps, ending with the proclamation against King Henry IV.]

Excommunication of Henry IV
O blessed Peter, prince of the Apostles, mercifully incline thine ear, we [sic] pray, and hear me, thy servant, whom thou hast cherished from infancy and hast delivered until now from the hand of the wicked who have hated and still hate me for my loyalty to thee. Thou art my witness, as are also my Lady, the Mother of God, and the blessed Paul, thy brother among all the saints, that thy Holy Roman Church forced me against my will to be its ruler. I had no thought of ascending thy throne as a robber, nay, rather would I have chosen to end my life as a pilgrim than to seize upon thy place for earthly glory and by devices of this world. Therefore, by thy favor, not by any works of mine, I believe that it is and has been thy will, that the Christian people especially committed to thee should render obedience to me, thy especially constituted representative. To me is given by thy grace the power of binding and loosing in Heaven and upon earth.

Wherefore, relying upon this commission, and for the honor and defense of thy Church, in the name of Almighty God, Father, Son and Holy Spirit, through thy power and authority, I deprive King Henry, son of the emperor Henry, who has rebelled against thy Church with unheard-of-audacity, of the government over the whole kingdom of Germany and Italy, and I release all Christian men from the allegiance which they have sworn or may swear to him, and I forbid anyone to serve him as king. For it is fitting that he who seeks to diminish the glory of thy Church should lose the glory which he seems to have.

And, since he has refused to obey as a Christian should or to return to the God whom he has abandoned by taking part with excommunicated persons, has spurned my warnings which I gave him for his soul's welfare, as thou knowest, and has separated himself from thy Church and tried to rend it asunder, I bind him in the bonds of anathema in thy stead and I bind him thus as commissioned by thee, that the nations may know and be convinced that thou art Peter and that upon thy rock the son of the living God has built his Church and the gates of hell shall not prevail against it.

A General Apology to All the Faithful in Germany
Epistolae collectae, Book IV, 14   1076.

Gregory ... to all bishops, dukes, counts and other loyal defenders of the faith in Germany, greeting ...

We hear that certain among you are in doubt regarding our excommunication of the king and are asking whether he was lawfully condemned; also whether our sentence was pronounced with due deliberation and under authority of a legal right of inquiry. We have therefore taken pains to make clear the understanding of all by what motives, as our conscience bears witness, we were led to this act of excommunication. And we do this, not so much in order to make public by our own complaint the several cases which, alas! are only too well known, as to silence the accusations of those who feel that we took up the sword of the spirit rashly and were moved rather by our own impulses than by a holy fear and a zeal for justice.

While we were still in the office of deacon, sinister and dishonorable rumors came to us regarding the conduct of the king, and we sent him frequent admonitions both by letter and by legates, for the sake of the imperial station and personal character of his father and mother as well as from our hope and wishes for his improvement, warning him to desist from his evil ways and, mindful of his noble birth and station, so to order his life as would be fitting for a king and, God willing, for an emperor. And later, when we had reached the dignity of Supreme Pontiff — unworthy as we were — and he had grown in years and in vice, we, knowing that God would require his soul at our hands the more strictly now that authority and freedom were given to us above all others, besought him the more earnestly in every way, by argument, by persuasion and by threats, to amend his life. He replied with frequent letters of devotion, pleading his frail and fickle youth and the evil counsels of those in power at his court and promising from day to day that he would comply with our instructions — he promised in words, but in fact he trampled them under foot with ever-increasing misbehaviour.

In the meantime we summoned to repentance certain of his intimates by whose intrigues and advice he had profaned bishoprics and many monasteries, for money installing wolves instead of shepherds. We ordered them, while there was still time, to give back the church property, which they had received with sacrilegious hand through this accursed commerce, to its rightful owners and to give satisfaction to God for their sins by penitential service. But when we learned that they refused to do this after due time and continued in their accustomed evil ways, we cut them off from the communion and body of the whole Church as guilty of sacrilege and as servants and members of the Devil, and we warned the king to banish them from his household and from his counsels and to desist from all association with them as persons under excommunication.

But again, when the Saxon uprising against the king was gaining strength and he saw that the resources and defenses of the kingdom were failing him to a great extent, he wrote us a letter of supplication full of humility. In this letter he confessed his fault before Almighty God and St. Peter and ourself and besought us by our apostolic authority to correct his offenses in church affairs against the canon law and the decrees of holy fathers. He also promised to obey us in all respects and to give us his faithful aid and counsel. And afterward, being admitted to penance by our colleagues and legates, Humbert, bishop of Palestrina, and Gerald, bishop of Ostia, whom we had sent to him, he reaffirmed all these promises in their hands, taking his oath by the sacred scarfs which they wore around their necks.

Then some time later, after a battle with the Saxons, he performed his sacrifices of gratitude to God for his victory by promptly breaking his vows of amendment, fulfilling none of his promises, receiving the excommunicated persons into his intimate counsels and bringing ruin upon the churches as he had done before.

With the greatest grief, then, although we had lost almost all hope of his improvement after he had treated with scorn the gifts of the heavenly king, we decided to make a further attempt, desiring rather that he should listen to apostolic gentleness than that he should suffer from our severity. We therefore wrote warning him to remember his promises and consider to whom they had been made; not to imagine that he could deceive God, whose anger when he begins to give judgment is the more severe the longer his patience has endured; and not to dishonour God, who has honored him, or use his power in contempt of God and in despite of apostolic authority, knowing as he does that God resists the proud but shows favor to the humble.

Besides this, we sent to him three clergymen, his own subjects, through whom we gave him private warnings to do penance for his crimes, horrible to describe, but known to many and published through many lands and for which the authority of law, human and divine, commands that he should not only be excommunicated until he should give due satisfaction, but should be deposed from his royal office without hope of restitution.

Finally we warned him that, unless he should exclude the excommunicated persons from his intimacy, we could pass no other sentence upon him but that, being cut off from the Church, he should join the fellowship of the condemned, with whom, rather than with Christ, he has chosen to take his part. And yet, if he were willing to listen to our warnings and reform his conduct, we called upon God — and we call upon him still — to bear witness how greatly we should rejoice in his honor and his welfare, and with what affection we should welcome him into the bosom of Holy Church as one who, being the chief of a nation and ruling over a widespread kingdom, is bound to be the defender of the Catholic peace and righteousness.

On the other hand, his actions prove how little he cares either for our written words or for the messages sent by our legates. He was angered that anyone should reprove or correct him, and could not be led back to any improvement, but, carried away by a still greater fury of self-confidence, he did not stop until he had caused almost all the bishops in Italy and as many as he could in Germany to suffer shipwreck of their faith and had compelled them to refuse the obedience and honor which they owed to St. Peter and the Apostolic See and which had been granted to these by Our Lord Jesus Christ.

When, therefore, we saw that we had reached the limit: namely, first, that he refused to give up his relations with those who had been excommunicated for sacrilege and the heresy of Simony; second, because he was not willing, I will not say to perform, but even to promise repentance for his crimes, for the penance which he had sworn to in the hands of our legates was a fraudulent one; finally, because he had dared to divide the body of Christ, that is, the unity of the Church — for all these crimes, I say, we excommunicated him through the decision of a council. Since we could not bring him back to the way of salvation by gentle means, we tried, with God's help, to do so by severity, and if — which God forbid! — he should not be afraid even of the severest penalty, our soul should at least be free from the charge of negligence or timidity.

If, then, anyone thinks that this sentence was imposed illegally or without reason, if he is willing to apply common sense to the sacred law he will take our part, will listen patiently to what is taught, not by ourself but by divine authority, and is sanctioned by the unanimous opinion of the holy fathers, and he will agree with us. We do not believe that any true believer who knows the canon law can be caught by this error and can say in his heart, even though he dare not openly proclaim it, that this action was not well taken. Nevertheless, even if — which God forbid! — we had bound him with this chain without due cause or in irregular form, the judgment is not to be rejected on this ground, as the holy fathers declare, but absolution is to be sought in all humility.

Now do you, my beloved, who have not desired to forsake the righteousness of God on account of the wrath of the king or of any danger, take no thought of the folly of those who "shall be consumed for their cursing and lying," but stand fast like men and comfort yourselves in the Lord. Know that you are on the side of him who, as unconquered king and glorious victor, will judge the living and the dead, rendering to each one according to his works. Of his manifold rewards you may be assured if you remain faithful to the end and stand firm in his truth. For this we pray God without ceasing, that he may give you strength to be established by the Holy Spirit in his name. May he turn the heart of the king to repentance and cause him to understand that we and you love him far more truly than those who now favor and support his evil doing.

And if, under God's blessing, he shall return to his senses, no matter what he may be plotting against us, he shall find us always ready to receive him back into holy communion in accordance with your affectionate counsel.

To All in Authority in Germany, Urging Their Support in His Struggle with Henry IV
Book IV, 1, (July 25, 1076).

Gregory ... to all his brethren in Christ, bishops, abbots and priests, dukes, princes and knights, all dwellers in the Roman Empire who truly love the Christian faith and the honor of St. Peter, greeting ...

We render thanks to Almighty God, who for the exceeding love he bore to us did not spare his own son, but gave him for us all, to protect and govern his Church, beyond all our deserts, beyond the expectation even of good men. You know, beloved brethren, that in this time of peril when Antichrist is busy everywhere by means of his members, scarce one is to be found who truly loves God and his honor, or who prefers his commands rather than earthly profit and the favor of the princes of this world. But he who rejects not his own and daily changes sinners from his left side to his right has looked upon you with calm and favoring countenance and has set you up against his enemies to the healing of many nations, that it might please you rather to be steadfast in the perils of this present life than to set the favor of men above the glory and honor of the eternal king. So doing you will not pass over with deaf ears that saying of the prince of the Apostles, "Ye are a chosen generation, a royal priesthood," and also, "We ought to obey God rather than men."

You well know, my brethren, for how long a time our Holy Church has had to bear the unheard-of wickedness and manifold wrongdoing of the king—would that I could call him Christian or [truly] your king—and what misfortunes it has suffered at his hands under the lead of our ancient enemy. Already during our diaconate we sent him words of warning out of our affection for him and our devotion to his parents, and after we came to the priestly office — unworthy as we are — frequently and earnestly have we striven, with the help of pious men, to bring him to his senses. But how he has acted against all this, how he has rendered evil for good, and how he has raised his heel against St. Peter and striven to rend in twain the Church which God entrusted to him you know, and it has been spread abroad throughout the world. But, since it belongs to our office to regard men and not their vices, to resist the wicked that they may repent, and to abhor evil but not men, we admonish you by authority of St. Peter, prince of the Apostles, and call upon you as our beloved brethren to endeavor in every way to snatch him from the hand of the Devil and rouse him to a true repentance, that we may be able with God's help to bring him back in brotherly love into the bosom of that Church which he has sought to divide. This, however, in such ways that he may not be able by some fraud to disturb the Christian faith and trample our Holy Church under his feet.

But if he will not listen to you and shall choose to follow the Devil rather than Christ and shall prefer the counsel of those who have long been under excommunication for simoniacal heresy to yours, then we shall find ways under divine inspiration to rescue the already declining Church Universal by serving God rather than man.

Now do you, my brethren and fellow priests, by authority of St. Peter, receive and bring back into the bosom of our Holy Mother Church as many as shall repent of those who have not been ashamed to set the king above Almighty God and to deny the law of Christ, if not in words, at least by their deeds — as the Apostle says, "They profess that they know God; but in works they deny him" — these receive, that you may be worthy to rejoice in Heaven with the angels of God. In all things keep before your eyes the honor of your holy father, the prince of the Apostles. But all those, bishops or laymen, who, led astray by fear or the favor of men, have not withdrawn from association with the king, but by favoring him have not feared to hand over the king's soul and their own to the Devil — have no dealings or friendship with these unless they shall repent and perform the proper acts of penance. For these are they who hate and slay their own souls and the king's as well, and are not ashamed to throw the kingdom, their fatherland and the Christian faith into confusion. For, as we are subject to the word of the prophet: "If thou speakest not to warn the wicked from his wicked way ... his soul will I require at thine hand," and again, "Cursed be he that shall hold back his sword from blood," that is, shall hold back the word of reproof from smiting those of evil life, so they, unless they obey, are subject to the wrath of the divine judgment and to the penalties of idolatry, as Samuel bears witness. And God is our witness that we are moved against evil princes and faithless priests by no question of worldly advantage, but by our sense of duty and by the power of the Apostolic See which continually weighs upon us. It were better for us, if need were, to pay the debt of mortality at the hands of tyrants rather than to consent in silence to the ruin of the Christian law through fear or for any advantage. We know what our fathers said: "He who does not oppose evil men out of regard for his station gives his consent; and he who removes not that which ought to be cut out is guilty of the offense."

May Almighty God, from whom all good things proceed, guard and strengthen your hearts through the merits of Our Lady, the Queen of Heaven, and the intercession of the blessed Apostles Peter and Paul, and may he always pour upon you the grace of his Holy Spirit that you may do what is pleasing to him. May you be worthy to rescue his Bride, our Mother, from the jaws of the wolf, and may you attain to his supreme glory, cleansed of all your sins.

To Bishop Hermann of Metz, in Defense of the Excommunication of Henry IV
Book IV, 2, (Aug. 25, 1076).

Gregory ... to Hermann, bishop of Metz, greeting ...

You have asked a great many questions of me, a very busy man, and have sent me an extremely urgent messenger. Wherefore I beg you to bear with me patiently if my reply is not sufficiently ample.

The bearer will report to you as to my health and as to the conduct of the Romans and the Normans in regard to me. As to the other matters about which you inquire — would that the blessed Peter himself, who is many times honored or wronged in me his servant, such as I am, might give the answers!

There is no need to ask me who are the excommunicated bishops, priests or laymen; since beyond a doubt they are those who are known to be in communication with the excommunicated king Henry — if, indeed, he may properly be called king. They do not hesitate to place the fear and favor of men before the commands of the eternal King nor to expose their king to the wrath of Almighty God by giving him their support.

He too feared not to incur the penalty of excommunication by dealing with followers who had been excommunicated for the heresy of Simony nor to draw others into excommunication through their dealings with him. How can we think of such things but in the words of the Psalmist: "The fool hath said in his heart there is no God," or again: "They are all gone astray in their wills."

Now to those who say: "A king may not be excommunicated," although we are not bound to reply to such a fatuous notion, yet, lest we seem to pass over their foolishness impatiently we will recall them to sound doctrine by directing their attention to the words and acts of the holy fathers. Let them read what instructions St. Peter gave to the Christian community in his ordination of St. Clement in regard to one who had not the approval of the pontiff. Let them learn why the Apostle said, "Being prompt to punish every disobedience"; and of whom he said, "Do not even take food with such people." Let them consider why Pope Zachary deposed a king of the Franks and released all his subjects from their oaths of allegiance. Let them read in the records [*registra*] of St. Gregory how in his grants to certain churches he not merely excommunicated kings and dukes who opposed him but declared them deprived of their royal dignity. And let them not forget that St. Ambrose not only excommunicated the emperor Theodosius but forbade him to stand in the room of the priests within the church.

But perhaps those people would imagine that when God commended his Church to Peter three times saying, "Feed my sheep," he made an exception of kings! Why do they not see, or rather confess with shame that, when God gave to Peter as leader the power of binding and loosing in heaven and on earth he excepted no one, withheld no one from his power? For if a man says that he cannot be bound by the ban of the Church, it is evident that he could not be loosed by its authority, and he who shamelessly denies this cuts himself off absolutely from Christ. If the Holy Apostolic See, through the princely power divinely bestowed upon it, has jurisdiction over spiritual things, why not also over temporal things? When kings and princes of this world set their own dignity and profit higher than God's righteousness and seek their own honor, neglecting the glory of God, you know whose members they are, to whom they give their allegiance. Just as those who place God above their own wills and obey his commands rather than those of men are members of Christ, so those of whom we spoke are members of Antichrist. If then spiritual men are to be judged, as is fitting, why should not men of the world be held to account still more strictly for their evil deeds?

Perchance they imagine that royal dignity is higher than that of bishops; but how great the difference between them is, they may learn from the difference in their origins. The former came from human lust of power; the latter was instituted by divine grace. The former constantly strives after empty glory; the latter aspires ever toward the heavenly life. Let them learn what Anastasius the pope said to Anastasius the emperor regarding these two dignities, and how St. Ambrose in his pastoral letter distinguished between them. He said: "If you compare the episcopal dignity with the splendor of kings and the crowns of princes, these are far more inferior to it than lead is to glistening gold." And knowing this, the emperor Constantine chose, not the highest, but the lowest seat among the bishops; for he knew that God resists the haughty, but confers his grace upon the humble.

Meantime, be it known to you, my brother, that, upon receipt of letters from certain of our clerical brethren and political leaders we have given apostolic authority to those bishops to absolve such persons excommunicated by us as have dared to cut themselves loose from the king. But as to the king himself, we have absolutely forbidden anyone to dare to absolve him until we shall have been made certain by competent witnesses of his sincere repentance and reparation; so that at the same time we may determine, if divine grace shall have visited him, in what form we may grant him absolution, to God's glory and his own salvation. For it has not escaped our knowledge that there are some of you who, pretending to be authorized by us, but really led astray by fear or the favor of men, would presume to absolve him if I [*sic*] did not forbid them, thus widening the wound instead of healing it. And if others, bishops in very truth, should oppose them, they would say that these were actuated, not by a sense of justice, but by personal hostility.

Moreover ordination and consecration by those bishops who dare to communicate with an excommunicated king become in the sight of God an execration, according to St. Gregory. For since they in their pride refuse to obey the Apostolic See, they incur the charge of idolatry, according to Samuel. If he is said to be of God who is stirred by divine love to punish crime, certainly he is not of God who refuses to rebuke the lives of carnal men so far as in him lies. And if he is accursed who withholds his sword from blood—that is to say, the word of preaching from destroying the life of the flesh — how much more is he accursed who through fear or favor drives his brother's soul into everlasting perdition! Furthermore you cannot find in the teaching of any of the holy fathers that men accursed and excommunicated can convey to others that blessing and that divine grace which they do not fear to deny by their actions.

Meanwhile, we order you to ask our brother, the venerable archbishop of Trier, to forbid the bishop of Toul to interfere in the affairs of the abbess of Remiremont and, with your assistance, to annul whatever action he has taken against her.

But, concerning Matilda, daughter to us both and faithful servant of St. Peter, I will do as you wish. I am not yet quite clear as to her future status — *deo gubernante*. I wish you, however, clearly to understand that although I remember her late husband Godfrey as a frequent offender against God, I am not affected by his enmity toward me nor by any other personal feeling, but moved by my fraternal affection for you and by Matilda's prayers I pray God for his salvation.

May Almighty God, through the mediation of Mary, Queen of Heaven, ever virgin, and the authority of the blessed Apostles Peter and Paul granted by him to them, absolve you and all our brethren who uphold the Christian faith and the dignity of the Apostolic See from all your sins, increase your faith, hope and charity and strengthen you in your defense of his law that you may be worthy to attain to everlasting life.

To All the Faithful in Germany, Counseling Them to Choose a New King in the Event that Henry IV Can Not Be Brought to Repentance
Book IV, 3, (Sept. 3, 1076).

Gregory ... to all the beloved brethren in Christ, fellow bishops, dukes, counts and all defenders of the Christian faith dwelling in the kingdom of Germany, greeting and absolution from all their sins through the apostolic benediction.

If you weigh carefully the decree in which Henry, king so-called, was excommunicated in a holy synod by judgment of the Holy Spirit, you will see beyond a doubt what action ought to be taken in his case. It will there be seen why he was bound in the bondage of anathema and deposed from his royal dignity, and that every people formerly subject to him is released from its oath of allegiance.

But because, as God knows, we are not moved against him by any pride or empty desire for the things of this world, but only by zeal for the Holy See and our common mother, the Church, we admonish you in the Lord Jesus and beg you as beloved brethren to receive him kindly if with his whole heart he shall turn to God, and to show toward him not merely justice which would prohibit him from ruling, but mercy which wipes out many crimes. Be mindful, I beg you, of the frailty of our common human nature and do not forget the pious and noble memory of his father and his mother, rulers the like of whom cannot be found in this our day.

Apply, however, the oil of kindness to his wounds in such a way that the scars may not grow foul by neglect of the wine of discipline and thus the honor of Holy Church and of the Roman Empire fall in widespread ruin through our indifference. Let those evil counselors be far removed from him, who, excommunicated for the heresy of Simony, have not scrupled to infect their master with their own disease and by diverse crimes have seduced him into splitting our Holy Church in twain and have brought upon him the wrath of God and of Saint Peter. Let other advisors be given him who care more for his advantage than their own and who place God above all earthly profit. Let him no longer imagine that Holy Church is his subject or his handmaid but rather let him recognize her as his superior and his mistress. Let him not be puffed up with the spirit of pride and defend practices invented to check the liberty of Holy Church, but let him observe the teaching of the holy fathers which divine power taught them for our salvation.

But if he shall have given you reliable information as to these and other demands which may properly be made upon him, we desire that you give us immediate notice by competent messengers so that, taking counsel together, we may with God's help decide upon the right course of action. Above all, we forbid, in the name of St. Peter, that any one of you should venture to absolve him from excommunication until the above-mentioned information shall have been given to us and you shall have received the consent of the Apostolic See and our renewed answer. We are distrustful of the conflicting counsels of different persons and have our suspicions of the fear and favor of men.

But now, if through the crimes of many [others] — which God forbid! — he shall not with whole heart turn to God, let another ruler of the kingdom be found by divine favor, such an one as shall bind himself by unquestionable obligations to carry out the measures we have indicated and any others that may be necessary for the safety of the Christian religion and of the whole empire. Further, in order that we may confirm your choice — if it shall be necessary to make a choice — and support the new order in our time, as we know was done by the holy fathers before us, inform us at the earliest possible moment as to the person, the character and the occupation of the candidate. Proceeding thus with pious and practical method you will deserve well of us in the present case and will merit the favour of the Apostolic See by divine grace and the blessing of St. Peter, prince of the Apostles.

As to the oath which you have taken to our best beloved daughter, the empress Agnes, in case her son should die before her, you need have no scruples, because, if she should be led by over-fondness for her son to resist the course of justice or, on the other hand, should defend justice and consent to his deposition, you will know how to do the rest. This, however, would seem to be advisable: that when you have come to a firm decision among yourselves that he shall be removed, you should take counsel with her and with us as to the person to be entrusted with the government of the kingdom. Then either she will give her assent to the common judgment of us all, or the authority of the Apostolic See will release all bonds which stand in the way of justice.

With regard to the excommunicated persons, I remind you that I have already given to those of you who defend the Christian faith as bishops should authority to absolve them, and I hereby confirm this — provided only that they truly repent and with humble hearts apply for penance.

To the German Princes, Giving an Account of Canossa
Book IV, 12, (End of Jan., 1077).

Whereas, for love of justice you have made common cause with us and taken the same risks in the warfare of Christian service, we have taken special care to send you this accurate account of the king's penitential humiliation, his absolution and the course of the whole affair from his entrance into Italy to the present time.

According to the arrangement made with the legates sent to us by you we came to Lombardy about twenty days before the date at which some of your leaders were to meet us at the pass and waited for their arrival to enable us to cross over into that region. But when the time had elapsed and we were told that on account of the troublous times — as indeed we well believe — no escort could be sent to us, having no other way of coming to you we were in no little anxiety as to what was our best course to take.

Meanwhile we received certain information that the king was on the way to us. Before he entered Italy he sent us word that he would make satisfaction to God and St. Peter and offered to amend his way of life and to continue obedient to us, provided only that he should obtain from us absolution and the apostolic blessing. For a long time we delayed our reply and held long consultations, reproaching him bitterly through messengers back and forth for his outrageous conduct, until finally, of his own accord and without any show of hostility or defiance, he came with a few followers to the fortress of Canossa where we were staying. There, on three successive days, standing before the castle gate, laying aside all royal insignia, barefooted and in coarse attire, he ceased not with many tears to beseech the apostolic help and comfort until all who were present or who had heard the story were so moved by pity and compassion that they pleaded his cause with prayers and tears. All marveled at our unwonted severity, and some even cried out that we were showing, not the seriousness of apostolic authority, but rather the cruelty of a savage tyrant.

At last, overcome by his persistent show of penitence and the urgency of all present, we released him from the bonds of anathema and received him into the grace of Holy Mother Church, accepting from him the guarantees described below, confirmed by the signatures of the abbot of Cluny, of our daughters, the Countess Matilda and the Countess Adelaide, and other princes, bishops and laymen who seemed to be of service to us.

And now that these matters have been arranged, we desire to come over into your country at the first opportunity, that with God's help we may more fully establish all matters pertaining to the peace of the Church and the good order of the land. For we wish you clearly to understand that, as you may see in the written guarantees, the whole negotiation is held in suspense, so that our coming and your unanimous consent are in the highest degree necessary. Strive, therefore, all of you, as you love justice, to hold in good faith the obligations into which you have entered. Remember that we have not bound ourselves to the king in any way except by frank statement — as our custom is — that he may expect our aid for his safety and his honor, whether through justice or through mercy, and without peril to his soul or to our own.

To Hermann of Metz, in Defense of the Papal Policy toward Henry IV
Book VIII, 21, (March 15, 1081).

Gregory ... to his beloved brother in Christ, Hermann, bishop of Metz, greeting ...

We know you to be ever ready to bear labor and peril in defense of the truth, and doubt not that this is a gift from God. It is a part of his unspeakable grace and his marvelous mercy that he never permits his chosen ones to wander far or to be completely cast down; but rather, after a time of persecution and wholesome probation, makes them stronger than they were before. On the other hand, just as among cowards one who is worse than the rest is broken down by fear, so among the brave one who acts more bravely than the rest is stirred thereby to new activity. We remind you of this by way of exhortation that you may stand more joyfully in the front ranks of the Christian host, the more confident you are that they are the nearest to God the conqueror.

You ask us to fortify you against the madness of those who babble with accursed tongues about the authority of the Holy Apostolic See not being able to excommunicate King Henry as one who despises the law of Christ, a destroyer of churches and of the empire, a promoter and partner of heresies, nor to release anyone from his oath of fidelity to him; but it has not seemed necessary to reply to this request, seeing that so many and such convincing proofs are to be found in Holy Scripture. Nor do we believe that those who abuse and contradict the truth to their utter damnation do this as much from ignorance as from wretched and desperate folly. And no wonder! It is ever the way of the wicked to protect their own iniquities by calling upon others like themselves; for they think it of no account to incur the penalty of falsehood.

To cite but a few out of the multitude of proofs: Who does not remember the words of our Lord and Savior Jesus Christ: "Thou art Peter and on this rock I will build my Church, and the gates of hell shall not prevail against it. And I will give thee the keys of the kingdom of heaven and whatsoever thou shalt bind on earth shall be bound in heaven and whatsoever thou shalt loose on earth shall be loosed in heaven." Are kings excepted here? Or are they not of the sheep which the Son of God committed to St. Peter? Who, I ask, thinks himself excluded from this universal grant of the power of binding and loosing to St. Peter unless, perchance, that unhappy man who, being unwilling to bear the yoke of the Lord, subjects himself to the burden of the Devil and refuses to be numbered in the flock of Christ? His wretched liberty shall profit him nothing; for if he shakes off from his proud neck the power divinely granted to Peter, so much the heavier shall it be for him in the day of judgment.

This institution of the divine will, this foundation of the rule of the Church, this privilege granted and sealed especially by a heavenly decree to St. Peter, chief of the Apostles, has been accepted and maintained with great reverence by the holy fathers, and they have given to the Holy Roman Church, as well in general councils as in their other acts and writings, the name of "universal mother." They have not only accepted her expositions of doctrine and her instructions in [our] holy religion, but they have also recognized her judicial decisions. They have agreed as with one spirit and one voice that all major cases, all especially important affairs and the judgments of all churches ought to be referred to her as to their head and mother, that from her there shall be no appeal, that her judgments may not and cannot be reviewed or reversed by anyone.

Thus Pope Gelasius, writing to the emperor Anastasius, gave him these instructions as to the right theory of the principate of the Holy and Apostolic See, based upon divine authority:

Although it is fitting that all the faithful should submit themselves to all priests who perform their sacred functions properly, how much the more should they accept the judgment of that prelate who has been appointed by the supreme divine ruler to be superior to all priests and whom the loyalty of the whole later Church has recognized as such. Your Wisdom sees plainly that no human capacity [concilium] whatsoever can equal that of him whom the word of Christ raised above all others and whom the reverend Church has always confessed and still devotedly holds as its Head.

So also Pope Julius, writing to the eastern bishops in regard to the powers of the same Holy and Apostolic See, says:

You ought, my brethren, to have spoken carefully and not ironically of the Holy Roman and Apostolic Church, seeing that our Lord Jesus Christ addressed her respectfully [decenter], saying, "Thou art Peter and upon this rock I will build my church, and the gates of hell shall not prevail against it; and I will give thee the keys of the kingdom of heaven." For it has the power, granted by a unique privilege, of opening and shutting the gates of the celestial kingdom to whom it will.

To whom, then, the power of opening and closing in Heaven is given, shall he not be able to judge the earth? God forbid! Do you remember what the most blessed Apostle Paul says: "Know ye not that we shall judge angels? How much more things that pertain to this life?"

So Pope Gregory declared that kings who dared to disobey the orders of the Apostolic See should forfeit their office. He wrote to a certain senator and abbot in these words:

If any king, priest, judge or secular person shall disregard this decree of ours and act contrary to it, he shall be deprived of his power and his office and shall learn that he stands condemned at the bar of God for the wrong that he has done. And unless he shall restore what he has wrongfully taken and shall have done fitting penance for his unlawful acts he shall be excluded from the sacred body and blood of our Lord and Savior Jesus Christ and at the last judgment shall receive condign punishment.

Now then, if the blessed Gregory, most gentle of doctors, decreed that kings who should disobey his orders about a hospital for strangers should be not only deposed but excommunicated and condemned in the last judgment, how can anyone blame us for deposing and excommunicating Henry, who not only disregards apostolic judgments, but so far as in him lies tramples upon his mother the Church, basely plunders the whole kingdom and destroys its churches — unless indeed it were one who is a man of his own kind?

As we know also through the teaching of St. Peter in his letter touching the ordination of Clement, where he says: "If any one were friend to those with whom he [Clement] is not on speaking terms, that man is among those who would like to destroy the Church of God and, while he seems to be with us in the body, he is against us in mind and heart, and he is a far worse enemy than those who are without and are openly hostile. For he, under the forms of friendship, acts as an enemy and scatters and lays waste the Church." Consider then, my best beloved, if he passes so severe a judgment upon him who associates himself with those whom the pope opposes on account of their actions, with what severity he condemns the man himself to whom the pope is thus opposed.

But now, to return to our point: Is not a sovereignty invented by men of this world who were ignorant of God subject to that which the providence of Almighty God established for his own glory and graciously bestowed upon the world? The Son of God we believe to be God and man, sitting at the right hand of the Father as High Priest, head of all priests and ever making intercession for us. He despised the kingdom of this world wherein the sons of this world puff themselves up and offered himself as a sacrifice upon the cross.

Who does not know that kings and princes derive their origin from men ignorant of God who raised themselves above their fellows by pride, plunder, treachery, murder — in short, by every kind of crime — at the instigation of the Devil, the prince of this world, men blind with greed and intolerable in their audacity? If, then, they strive to bend the priests of God to their will, to whom may they more properly be compared than to him who is chief over all the sons of pride? For he, tempting our High Priest, head of all priests, son of the Most High, offering him all the kingdoms of this world, said: "All these will I give thee if thou wilt fall down and worship me."

Does anyone doubt that the priests of Christ are to be considered as fathers and masters of kings and princes and of all believers? Would it not be regarded as pitiable madness if a son should try to rule his father or a pupil his master and to bind with unjust obligations the one through whom he expects to be bound or loosed, not only on earth but also in heaven? Evidently recognizing this the emperor Constantine the Great, lord over all kings and princes throughout almost the entire earth, as St. Gregory relates in his letter to the emperor Mauritius, at the holy synod of Nicaea took his place below all the bishops and did not venture to pass any judgment upon them but, even addressing them as gods, felt that they ought not to be subject to his judgment but that he ought to be bound by their decisions.

Pope Gelasius, urging upon the emperor Anastasius not to feel himself wronged by the truth that was called to his attention said: "There are two powers, O august Emperor, by which the world is governed, the sacred authority of the priesthood and the power of kings. Of these the priestly is by so much the greater as they will have to answer for kings themselves in the day of divine judgment;" and a little further: "Know that you are subject to their judgment, not that they are to be subjected to your will."

In reliance upon such declarations and such authorities, many prelates have excommunicated kings or emperors. If you ask for illustrations: Pope Innocent excommunicated the emperor Arcadius because he consented to the expulsion of St. John Chrysostom from his office. Another Roman pontiff deposed a king of the Franks, not so much on account of his evil deeds as because he was not equal to so great an office, and set in his place Pippin, father of the emperor Charles the Great, releasing all the Franks from the oath of fealty which they had sworn to him. And this is often done by Holy Church when it absolves fighting men from their oaths to bishops who have been deposed by apostolic authority. So St. Ambrose, a holy man but not bishop of the whole Church, excommunicated the emperor Theodosius the Great for a fault which did not seem to other prelates so very grave and excluded him from the Church. He also shows in his writings that the priestly office is as much superior to royal power as gold is more precious than lead. He says: "The honor and dignity of bishops admit of no comparison. If you liken them to the splendor of kings and the diadem of princes, these are as lead compared to the glitter of gold. You see the necks of kings and princes bowed to the knees of priests, and by the kissing of hands they believe that they share the benefit of their prayers." And again: "Know that we have said all this in order to show that there is nothing in this world more excellent than a priest or more lofty than a bishop."

Your Fraternity should remember also that greater power is granted to an exorcist when he is made a spiritual emperor for the casting out of devils, than can be conferred upon any layman for the purpose of earthly dominion. All kings and princes of this earth who live not piously and in their deeds show not a becoming fear of God are ruled by demons and are sunk in miserable slavery. Such men desire to rule, not guided by the love of God, as priests are, for the glory of God and the profit of human souls, but to display their intolerable pride and to satisfy the lusts of their mind. Of these St. Augustine says in the first book of his Christian doctrine: "He who tries to rule over men — who are by nature equal to him — acts with intolerable pride." Now if exorcists have power over demons, as we have said, how much more over those who are subject to demons and are limbs of demons! And if exorcists are superior to these, how much more are priests superior to them!

Furthermore, every Christian king when he approaches his end asks the aid of a priest as a miserable suppliant that he may escape the prison of hell, may pass from darkness into light and may appear at the judgment seat of God freed from the bonds of sin. But who, layman or priest, in his last moments has ever asked the help of any earthly king for the safety of his soul? And what king or emperor has power through his office to snatch any Christian from the might of the Devil by the sacred rite of baptism, to confirm him among the sons of God and to fortify him by the holy chrism? Or — and this is the greatest thing in the Christian religion — who among them is able by his own word to create the body and blood of the Lord? or to whom among them is given the power to bind and loose in Heaven and upon earth? From this it is apparent how greatly superior in power is the priestly dignity.

Or who of them is able to ordain any clergyman in the Holy Church — much less to depose him for any fault? For bishops, while they may ordain other bishops, may in no wise depose them except by authority of the Apostolic See. How, then, can even the most slightly informed person doubt that priests are higher than kings? But if kings are to be judged by priests for their sins, by whom can they more properly be judged than by the Roman pontiff?

In short, all good Christians, whomsoever they may be, are more properly to be called kings than are evil princes; for the former, seeking the glory of God, rule themselves rigorously; but the latter, seeking their own rather than the things that are of God, being enemies to themselves, oppress others tyrannically. The former are the body of the true Christ; the latter, the body of the Devil. The former rule themselves that they may reign forever with the supreme ruler. The power of the latter brings it to pass that they perish in eternal damnation with the prince of darkness who is king over all the sons of pride.

It is no great wonder that evil priests take the part of a king whom they love and fear on account of honors received from him. By ordaining any person whomsoever, they are selling their God at a bargain price. For as the elect are inseparably united to their Head, so the wicked are firmly bound to him who is head of all evil — especially against the good. But against these it is of no use to argue, but rather to pray God with tears and groans that he may deliver them from the snares of Satan, in which they are caught and after trial may lead them at last into knowledge of the truth.

So much for kings and emperors who, swollen with the pride of this world, rule not for God but for themselves. But since it is our duty to exhort everyone according to his station, it is our care with God's help to furnish emperors, kings and other princes with the weapons of humility that thus they may be strong to keep down the floods and waves of pride. We know that earthly glory and the cares of this world are wont especially to cause rulers to be exalted, to forget humility and, seeking their own glory, strive to excel their fellows. It seems therefore especially useful for emperors and kings, while their hearts are lifted up in the strife for glory, to learn how to humble themselves and to know fear rather than joy. Let them therefore consider carefully how dangerous, even awesome is the office of emperor or king, how very few find salvation therein, and how those who are saved through God's mercy have become far less famous in the Church by divine judgment than many humble persons. From the beginning of the world to the present day we do not find in all authentic records [seven] emperors or kings whose lives were as distinguished for virtue and piety as were those of a countless multitude of men who despised the world — although we believe that many of them were saved by the mercy of God. Not to speak of Apostles and Martyrs, who among emperors and kings was famed for his miracles as were St. Martin, St. Antony and St. Benedict? What emperor or king ever raised the dead, cleansed lepers or opened the eyes of the blind? True, Holy Church praises and honors the emperor Constantine, of pious memory, Theodosius and Honorius, Charles and Louis, as lovers of justice, champions of the Christian faith and protectors of churches, but she does not claim that they were illustrious for the splendor of their wonderful works. Or to how many names of kings or emperors has Holy Church ordered churches or altars to be dedicated or masses to be celebrated?

Let kings and princes fear lest the higher they are raised above their fellows in this life, the deeper they may be plunged in everlasting fire. Wherefore it is written: "The mighty shall suffer mighty torments." They shall render unto God an account for all men subject to their rule. But if it is no small labor for the pious individual to guard his own soul, what a task is laid upon princes in the care of so many thousands of souls! And if Holy Church imposes a heavy penalty upon him who takes a single human life, what shall be done to those who send many thousands to death for the glory of this world? These, although they say with their lips, *mea culpa*, for the slaughter of many, yet in their hearts they rejoice at the increase of their glory and neither repent of what they have done nor regret that they have sent their brothers into the world below. So that, since they do not repent with all their hearts and will not restore what they have gained by human bloodshed, their penitence before God remains without the fruits of a true repentance.

Wherefore they ought greatly to fear, and they should frequently be reminded that, as we have said, since the beginning of the world and throughout the kingdoms of the earth very few kings of saintly life can be found out of an innumerable multitude, whereas in one single chair of successive bishops — the Roman — from the time of the blessed Apostle Peter nearly a hundred are counted among the holiest of men. How can this be, except because the kings and princes of the earth, seduced by empty glory, prefer their own interests to the things of the Spirit, whereas pious pontiffs, despising vainglory, set the things of God above the things of the flesh. The former readily punish offenses against themselves but are not troubled by offenses against God; the latter quickly forgive those who sin against them but do not easily pardon offenders against God. The former, far too much given to worldly affairs, think little of spiritual things; the latter, dwelling eagerly upon heavenly subjects, despise the things of this world.

All Christians, therefore, who desire to reign with Christ are to be warned not to reign through ambition for worldly power. They are to keep in mind the admonition of that most holy pope Gregory in his book on the pastoral office: "Of all these things what is to be followed, what held fast, except that the man strong in virtue shall come to his office under compulsion? Let him who is without virtue not come to it even though he be urged thereto." If, then, men who fear God come under compulsion with fear and trembling to the Apostolic See where those who are properly ordained become stronger through the merits of the blessed Apostle Peter, with what awe and hesitation should men ascend the throne of a king where even good and humble men like Saul and David become worse! What we have said above is thus stated in the decrees of the blessed pope Symmachus — though we have learned it by experience: "He, that is St. Peter, transmitted to his successors an unfailing endowment of merit together with an inheritance of innocence;" and again: "For who can doubt that he is holy who is raised to the height of such an office, in which if he is lacking in virtue acquired by his own merits, that which is handed down from his predecessor is sufficient. For either he [Peter] raises men of distinction to bear this burden or he glorifies them after they are raised up."

Wherefore let those whom Holy Church, of its own will and with deliberate judgment, not for fleeting glory but for the welfare of multitudes, has called to royal or imperial rule — let them be obedient and ever mindful of the blessed Gregory's declaration in that same pastoral treatise: "When a man disdains to be the equal of his fellow men, he becomes like an apostate angel. Thus Saul, after his period of humility, swollen with pride, ran into excess of power. He was raised in humility, but rejected in his pride, as God bore witness, saying: 'Though thou wast little in thine own sight, wast thou not made the head of the tribes of Israel?'" and again: "I marvel how, when he was little to himself he was great before God, but when he seemed great to himself he was little before God." Let them watch and remember what God says in the Gospel: "I seek not my own glory," and, "He who would be first among you, let him be the servant of all." Let them ever place the honor of God above their own; let them embrace justice and maintain it by preserving to everyone his right; let them not enter into the counsels of the ungodly, but cling to those of religion with all their hearts. Let them not seek to make Holy Church their maid-servant or their subject, but recognizing priests, the eyes of God, as their masters and fathers, strive to do them becoming honor.

If we are commanded to honor our fathers and mothers in the flesh, how much more our spiritual parents! If he that curseth his father or his mother shall be put to death, what does he deserve who curses his spiritual father or mother? Let not princes, led astray by carnal affection, set their own sons over that flock for whom Christ shed his blood if a better and more suitable man can be found. By thus loving their own son more than God they bring the greatest evils upon the Church. For it is evident that he who fails to provide to the best of his ability so great and necessary an advantage for our holy mother, the Church, does not love God and his neighbor as befits a Christian man. If this one virtue of charity be wanting, then whatever of good the man may do will lack all saving grace.

But if they do these things in humility, keeping their love for God and their neighbor as they ought, they may count upon the mercy of him who said: "Learn of me, for I am meek and lowly of heart." If they humbly imitate him, they shall pass from their servile and transient reign into the kingdom of eternal liberty.

The Letters of Henry IV

Henry declares to the Roman clergy and people that Hildebrand is his enemy. He sends them a copy of his decree of deposition (Letter 11) and exhorts them to take a new pope after forcing Hildebrand to step down (1076).

Henry, King by the grace of God, sends grace, greeting, and every good thing to the clergy and people of the entire holy Roman Church:

That fidelity is believed firm and unshaken which is always kept unchanged for one whether he is present or absent — fidelity altered neither by the extended absence of him to whom it is owed nor through the wearisome passage of a long time. We know that this is the sort of fidelity which you keep for us; we are thankful, and we ask that it continue unchanged. Specifically, we ask that just as you act now, so in the future you will steadfastly be friends of our friends and enemies of our enemies.

Noting particularly among the latter the monk Hildebrand, we urge you to enmity against him, since we have found him to be an assailant and an oppressor of the Church, as well as a waylayer of the Roman commonwealth, and of our kingdom, as may be known clearly from the following letter sent to him by us:

[In the original of Letter 10, the full text of Letter 11 is given here. Letter 10 continues:]

This is the text of our letter to the monk Hildebrand, which we have also written to you so that our will may be both yours and ours — nay rather, so that your love may bring satisfaction to God and to us. Rise up against him, therefore, O most faithful, and let the man who is first in the faith be first in his condemnation. We do not say, however, that you should shed his blood, since after his deposition life would indeed be a greater penalty for him than death. We say rather that if he prove unwilling to descend, you should force him to do so and receive into the Apostolic See another, elected by us with the common counsel of all the bishops and of yourselves, one who will be willing and able to cure the wounds which that man has inflicted upon the Church.

Henry charges Hildebrand with having stolen his hereditary privileges in Rome, striven to alienate Italy, abused the bishops, and threatened his office and his life. He reports the sentence of deposition issued by the Diet of Worms, and as patrician of the Romans, he commands him to descend from the throne of St. Peter (1076).

Henry, King by the grace of God, to Hildebrand:

Although hitherto I hoped for those things from you which are expected of a father and obeyed you in all respects to the great indignation of our vassals,[2] I have obtained from you a requital suitable from one who was the most pernicious enemy of our life and kingly office. After you had first snatched away with arrogant boldness all the hereditary dignity owed me by that See, going still further you tried with the most evil arts to alienate the kingdom of Italy.[3] Not content with this, you have not feared to set your hand against the most reverend bishops, who are united to us like most cherished members and have harassed them with most arrogant affronts and the bitterest abuses against divine and human laws. While I let all these things go unnoticed through patience, you thought it not patience but cowardice and dared to rise up against the head itself, announcing, as you know, that (to use your own words) you would either die or deprive me of my life and kingly office.

Judging that this unheard of defiance had to be confuted not with words, but with action, I held a general assembly of all the foremost men of the kingdom, at their supplication. When they had made public through their true declaration (which you will hear from their own letter) those things which they had previously kept silent through fear and reverence, they took public action to the end that you could no longer continue in the Apostolic See. Since their sentence seemed just and righteous before God and men, I also give my assent, revoking from you every prerogative of the papacy which you have seemed to hold, and ordering you to descend from the throne of the city whose patriciate is due me through the bestowal of God and the sworn assent of the Romans.

Renunciation of Gregory VII by the German Bishops (Synod of Worms, 1076)

Siegfried, archbishop of Mainz, Udo of Trier, William of Utrecht, Herman of Metz, Henry of Liége, Ricbert of Verden, Bido of Toul, Hozeman of Speier, Burchard of Halberstadt, Werner of Strassburg, Burchard of Basel, Otto of Constance, Adalbero of Würzburg, Rupert of Bamberg, Otto of Regensburg, Egilbert of Freising, Ulric of Eichstäatt, Frederick of Münster, Eilbert of Minden, Hezilo of Hildesheim, Benno of Osnabrück, Eppo of Naumburg, Imadus of Paderborn, Tiedo of Brandenburg, Burchard of Lausanne, and Bruno of Verona, to Brother Hildebrand:

When you had first usurped the government of the Church, we knew well how, with your accustomed arrogance, you had presumed to enter so illicit and nefarious an undertaking against human and divine law. We thought, nevertheless, that the pernicious beginnings of your administration ought to be left unnoticed in prudent silence. We did this specifically in the hope that such criminal beginnings would be emended and wiped away somewhat by the probity and industry of your later rule. But now, just as the deplorable state of the universal Church cries out and laments, through the increasing wickedness of your actions and decrees, you are woefully and stubbornly in step with your evil beginnings.

Our Lord and Redeemer impressed the goodness of peace and love upon his Faithful as their distinctive character, a fact to which there are more testimonies than can be included in the brevity of a letter. But by way of contrast, you have inflicted wounds with proud cruelty and cruel pride, you are eager for profane innovations, you delight in a great name rather than in a good one, and with unheard-of self-exaltation, like a standard bearer of schism, you distend all the limbs of the Church which before your times led a quiet and tranquil life, according to the admonition of the Apostle. Finally, the flame of discord, which you stirred up through terrible factions in the Roman church, you spread with raging madness through all the churches of Italy, Germany, Gaul, and Spain. For you have taken from the bishops, so far as you could, all that power which is known to have been divinely conferred upon them through the grace of the Holy Spirit, which works mightily in ordinations. Through you all administration of ecclesiastical affairs has been assigned to popular madness. Since some now consider no one a bishop or priest save the man who begs that office of Your Arrogance with a most unworthy servility, you have shaken into pitiable disorder the whole strength of the apostolic institution and that most comely distribution of the limbs of Christ, which the Doctor of the Gentiles so often commends and teaches. And so through these boastful decrees of yours — and this cannot be said without tears — the name of Christ has all but perished. Who, however, is not struck dumb by the baseness of your arrogant usurpation of new power, power not due you, to the end that you may destroy the rights due the whole brotherhood? For you assert that if any sin of one of our parishioners comes to your notice, even if only by rumour, none of us has any further power to bind or to loose the party involved, for you alone may do it, or one whom you delegate especially for this purpose. Can anyone schooled in sacred learning fail to see how this assertion exceeds all madness?

We have judged that it would be worse than any other evil for us to allow the Church of God to be so gravely jeopardized — nay rather, almost destroyed — any longer through these and other presumptuous airs of yours. Therefore, it has pleased us to make known to you by the common counsel of all of us something which we have left unsaid until now: that is, the reason why you cannot now be, nor could you ever have been, the head of the Apostolic See.

In the time of the Emperor Henry [III] of good memory, you bound yourself with a solemn oath that for the lifetime of that Emperor and for that of his son, our lord the glorious King who now presides at the summit of affairs, you would neither obtain the papacy yourself nor suffer another to obtain it, insofar as you were able, without the consent and approbation either of the father in his lifetime or of the son in his. And there are many bishops today who were witnesses of this solemn oath, who saw it then with their own eyes and heard it with their own ears. Remember also that in order to remove jealous rivalry when ambition for the papacy tickled some of the cardinals, you obligated yourself with a solemn oath never to assume the papacy both on the plea and on the condition that they did the same thing themselves. We have seen in what a holy way you observed each of these solemn vows. Again, when a synod was celebrated in the time of Pope Nicholas [II], in which one hundred twenty-five bishops sat together, it was decided and decreed under anathema that no one would ever become pope except by the election of the cardinals and the approbation of the people, and by the consent and authority of the king. And of this council and decree, you yourself were author, advocate, and subscriber.

In addition to this, you have filled the entire Church, as it were, with the stench of the gravest of scandals, rising from your intimacy and cohabitation with another's wife who is more closely integrated into your household than is necessary. In this affair, our sense of decency is affected more than our legal case, although the general complaint is sounded everywhere that all judgments and all decrees are enacted by women in the Apostolic See, and ultimately that the whole orb of the Church is administered by this new senate of women. For no one can complain adequately of the wrongs and the abuse suffered by the bishops, whom you call most undeservedly sons of whores and other names of this sort.

Since your accession was tainted by such great perjuries, since the Church of God is imperiled by so great a tempest arising from abuse born of your innovations, and since you have degraded your life and conduct by such multifarious infamy, we declare that in the future we shall observe no longer the obedience which we have not promised to you. And since none of us, as you have publicly declared, has hitherto been a bishop to you, you also will now be pope to none of us.

Henry charges Hildebrand with having thrown the whole Church into confusion and with having threatened his life and office. He declares that Hildebrand was not ordained of God, but is damned by the precept of St. Paul and by the judgment of all Henry's bishops; and he commands him to descend from the Apostolic See (1076).

Henry, King not by usurpation, but by the pious ordination of God, to Hildebrand, now not Pope, but false monk:

You have deserved such a salution as this because of the confusion you have wrought; for you left untouched no order of the Church which you could make a sharer of confusion instead of honor, of malediction instead of benediction.

For to discuss a few outstanding points among many: Not only have you dared to touch the rectors of the holy Church — the archbishops, the bishops and the priests, anointed of the Lord as they are — but you have trodden them under foot like slaves who know not what their lord may do. In crushing them you have gained for yourself acclaim from the mouth of the rabble. You have judged that all these know nothing, while you alone know everything. In any case, you have sedulously used this knowledge not for edification, but for destruction, so greatly that we may believe Saint Gregory, whose name you have arrogated to yourself, rightly made this prophesy of you when he said: "From the abundance of his subjects, the mind of the prelate is often exalted, and the thinks that he has more knowledge than anyone else, since he sees that he has more power than anyone else."

And we, indeed, bore with all these abuses, since we were eager to preserve the honor of the Apostolic See. But you construed our humility as fear, and so you were emboldened to rise up even against the royal power itself, granted to us by God. You dared to threaten to take the kingship away from us — as though we had received the kingship from you, as though kingship and empire were in your hand and not in the hand of God.

Our Lord, Jesus Christ, has called us to kingship, but has not called you to the priesthood. For you have risen by these steps: namely, by cunning, which the monastic profession abhors, to money; by money to favor; by favor to the sword. By the sword you have come to the throne of peace, and from the throne of peace you have destroyed the peace. You have armed subjects against their prelates; you who have not been called by God have taught that our bishops who have been called by God are to be spurned; you have usurped for laymen the bishops' ministry over priests, with the result that these laymen depose and condemn the very men whom the laymen themselves received as teachers from the hand of God, through the imposition of the hands of bishops.

You have also touched me, one who, though unworthy, has been anointed to kingship among the anointed. This wrong you have done to me, although as the tradition of the holy Fathers has taught, I am to be judged by God alone and am not to be deposed for any crime unless — may it never happen — I should deviate from the Faith. For the prudence of the holy bishops entrusted the judgment and the deposition even of Julian the Apostate not to themselves, but to God alone. The true pope Saint Peter also exclaims, "Fear God, honor the king." You, however, since you do not fear God, dishonour me, ordained of Him.

Wherefore, when Saint Paul gave no quarter to an angel from heaven if the angel should preach heterodoxy, he did not except you who are now teaching heterodoxy throughout the earth. For he says, "If anyone, either I or an angel from heaven, preach any other gospel unto you than that which we have preached unto you, let him be accursed." Descend, therefore, condemned by this anathema and by the common judgment of all our bishops and of ourself. Relinquish the Apostolic See which you have arrogated. Let another mount the throne of Saint Peter, another who will not cloak violence with religion but who will teach the pure doctrine of Saint Peter.

I, Henry, King by the grace of God, together with all our bishops, say to you: Descend! Descend!

In this encyclical letter to his bishops, Henry admonishes them to help the beleaguered Church against Hildebrand, who has destroyed the peace between the kingship and the priesthood and has recently abused royal envoys. He invites them to participate in an assembly at Worms on Whitsun (1076).

Henry, King by the grace of God, sends to A., the grace, greeting, and love which he sends not to all men, but only to a few:

In the greatest affairs there is need for the greatest counsels of the greatest men, who externally should have power and within should not be lacking in good will, so that they may be both willing and able to deliberate well about that matter for which they wish well. For in the advancement of any enterprise, neither power without good will nor good will without power is useful. O most faithful subject, you possess, we think, each of these in equal proportion. To tell the truth, although as one of the great, you possess great power, your good will for our advantage and for that of our kingdom grows even greater than this great power — if we know you well and have properly noted your fidelity. From past actions faithfully done, the hope grows that future actions will be done yet more faithfully. We trust to your love, however, that your fidelity may not fall short of our hope, since from the fidelity of none of the kingdom's princes do we hope for greater things than from yours. Thus until this very time, we have rejoiced not only in what past affairs reveal but also in your promise of things still to be hoped for.

Let your good will stand by us, therefore, together with your power at this opportune time, the good will for which not only our need is earnestly longing, but also that of all your fellow bishops and brethren, nay rather, that of the whole oppressed Church. Certainly, you are not ignorant of this oppression. Only see to it that you do not withdraw assistance from the oppressed Church, but rather that you give your sympathy to the kingship and to the priesthood. Just as hitherto the Church was exalted by each of these offices, so now, alas, it is laid low, bereft of each; since one man has arrogated both for himself, he has injured both, and he who has neither wanted nor was able to be of benefit in either has been useless in each.

To keep you in suspense no longer as to the name of the man under discussion, learn of whom we speak: it is the monk Hildebrand (a monk indeed in habit), so-called pope who, as you yourself know clearly, presides in the Apostolic See not with the care of a pastor but with the violence of a usurper and from the throne of peace dissolves the bond of the one catholic peace. To cite to a few things among many: without God's knowledge he has usurped for himself the kingship and the priesthood. In this deed he held in contempt the pious ordinance of God, which especially commanded these two — namely, the kingship and the priesthood — should remain, not as one entity, but as two. In his Passion, the Savior Himself meant the figurative sufficiency of the two swords to be understood in this way: When it was said to him, "Lord, behold there are two swords here," He answered, "It is enough," signifying by this sufficient duality, that the spiritual and the carnal swords are to be used in the Church and that by them every hurtful thing is to be cut off. That is to say, He was teaching that every man is constrained by the priestly sword to obey the king as the representative of God but by the kingly sword both to repel enemies of Christ outside and to obey the priesthood within. So in charity the province of one extends into the other, as long as neither the kingship is deprived of honor by the priesthood nor the priesthood is deprived of honor by the kingship. You yourself have found out, if you have wanted to discover it, how the Hildebrandine madness has confounded this ordinance of God; for in his judgment, no one may be a priest unless he begs that [honor] from his arrogance. He has also striven to deprive me of the kingship — me whom God has called to the kingship (God, however, has not called him to the priesthood) — since he saw that I wished to hold my royal power from God and not from him and since he himself had not constituted me as king. And further, he threatened to deprive me of kingship and life, neither of which he had bestowed.

Although he often contrived these outrages against us, and others like them, as you yourself know, nonetheless he was not satisfied unless from day to day he cast new and coarse sorts of affliction upon us, as he recently showed in dealing with our envoys. This paper is not sufficiently long to set forth how he handled those messengers of ours; how demeaningly he afflicted them; how cruelly he imprisoned them; and when they had been imprisoned, how he harmed them with nakedness, cold, hunger and thirst, and blows. Finally, he ordered them to be led about through the middle of the city to offer a spectacle to all, after the example of the martyrs. So you may believe and say that in common with the tyrant Decius he rages and torments the saints.

Wherefore, be not ashamed, most cherished friend, be not ashamed to satisfy the petition we make in common with your fellow bishops: that you come to Worms at Pentecost and hear many things there with the other princes, a few of which this letter mentions, and advise us what is to be done. For you are besought by the love of your fellow bishops, admonished through the advantage of the Church, and bound by the honor of our life and of the whole kingdom.

The Promise of Henry IV to Gregory VII (Promissio Oppenheimensis, 1076)

Admonished by the counsel of our vassals, I promise to maintain a due obedience in all things to the Apostolic See and to you, Pope Gregory.[4] I shall take care to emend with dutiful reparation whatever diminution of the honor of that See or of your own honor is seen to have arisen through us.

Since certain rather serious schemes which I am supposed to have against that same See and Your Reverence are now at issue, at a fitting time, either I shall clear them away through the prayer of innocence or through the help of God or at that very time I shall gladly undertake suitable penance for them.

It is also altogether fitting, however, for Your Sanctity not to ignore those things which have been spread abroad about you and which bear scandal to the Church. But after this scruple has also been removed from the public conscience, it is fitting that the universal tranquility of the Church as well as that of the kingdom be made firm through your wisdom.

Henry declares to his princes that he wishes to obey and to render satisfaction to Pope Gregory; he exhorts them to follow his example and to obtain release from excommunication (1076).

Henry, King by the grace of God, sends the glorious esteem of his good will to archbishops, bishops, dukes, margraves, counts, and to every order of dignity:

We have learned by the assertion of our vassals that on behalf of Our Mercy some men have detracted from the Apostolic See and its venerable pontiff, the Lord Pope Gregory. For this reason, it has pleased us, on beneficial counsel, to change our former position and after the fashion of our predecessors and ancestors to reserve in all respects due obedience to that same sacrosanct See and to the Lord Pope Gregory, who is known to serve as its head. It has also pleased us to make amends with fitting reparation if anything serious has been done against him.

We wish that you also admonished by the example of Our Serenity, like us, will not refuse to show solemn [obedience] to Saint Peter and to his vicar. And may whosoever know that they are bound by his ban strive to be absolved formally by this same Lord Pope Gregory.

Henry informs his mother, the Empress-dowager Agnes, that at a recent Diet he was persuaded to allow the case of the bishops who had deserted him to be discussed at another assembly in the near future. He grants her petition (1074-1076).

To the mother of blessing and well-being, Henry, King by the grace of God, sends love from his whole heart and whatever is better and beyond:

Since it is right for you to know well how we progress, we want to send you word, inasmuch as you are our dearest mother, of what this Curia and assembly has ordered and ratified. After much consideration of our case, we were finally overcome by the apostolic legation and by the counsel and persuasion of all our vassals, many of whom were present, and we granted and permitted the restitution of the deserter-bishops. Nonetheless, we did this in such a fashion that in whatever manner we wish, we may continue warily to watch these men in the interests of our side until the day we have set to consider their case. Know that those same legates of the pope are awaiting that day and time here.

But for the sake of that good faith which we have in you, ask earnestly of God that our cause may receive its long-expected outcome. As for that, however, which you have asked of us, most certainly you will receive it on that condition which you wish and of which you have notified us. In addition [you will receive] whatever we can grant to your love.

The Vow of Henry IV to Gregory VII at Canossa (1077).

Oath of Henry, King of the Germans.

Before the date the Lord Pope Gregory is to set, I, King Henry, shall bring about justice according to his judgment or harmony according to his counsel with regard to the complaint and objection now being made against me by archbishops, bishops, dukes, counts, the other princes in the realm of the Germans, and those who follow them by reason of the same objection. If a concrete obstacle hinder me or him, I shall be ready to do the same when that hindrance has been overcome. Also, if the same Lord Pope Gregory should wish to go beyond the mountains to other lands, he, those who are among his retainers or guards, and those who are sent by him or come to him from any region, will be safe in coming, staying, and going thence, from any harm to life and limb and from capture by me and by those whom I can control. Moreover, no other difficulty prejudicial to his honor will occur with my assent; and should any person create one for him, I shall help him [Gregory] in good faith, according to my ability.

Done at Canossa, 28 January, the fifteenth Indiction.

Decree of the Synod of Brixen (1080)

In the year of the incarnation of the Lord 1080, with the most serene King Henry IV as moderator, in the twenty-sixth year of his reign, on the seventh day before the Kalends of July, on the fifth day of the week, in the third indiction, when an assembly of thirty bishops and of the leaders of the army, not only of Italy but also of Germany, was gathered at Brixen in Bavaria by royal order, of one accord a voice came forth as though from the mouth of all complaining terribly against the cruel madness of one false monk, Hildebrand, also called Pope Gregory VII. It complained that the ever-unconquered King suffered this madness to rage untouched for so long, when Paul, the vessel of election, witnesses that the prince does not carry a sword without cause and Peter, the first of the Apostles, cries out that the king not only is supreme but that governors are to be sent by him specifically for the punishment of evildoers and for the praise of the good. In fulfillment of these sayings it seemed just to this most glorious King and to his princes that the judgment of the bishops with the sentence of divine censure ought to issue against this Hildebrand before the material sword went forth against him, with the consequence that the royal power might resolve to prosecute him with greater freedom after the prelates of the Church had first deposed him from his proud prelacy.

Which of the Faithful knowing him would fear to let fly the shaft of damnation against him? From the time he entered the world, this man strove to procure position for himself[5] over men through vain glory, without the support of any merits; to set dreams and divinations, his own and those of others, ahead of divine dispensation; to appear a monk in habit and not to be one by profession; to judge himself exempt from ecclesiastical discipline, subject to no master; to devote himself more than laymen to obscene theatrical shows; publicly for the sake of filthy lucre, to attend to the tables of the money changers on the porch of them who do business? And so from these pursuits, he garnered his money and, supplanting the abbot, usurped the abbacy of Saint Paul.

Thereafter, seizing the archdiaconate, he led a certain man named Mancius astray by guile so that man sold him his own office. And against the will of Pope Nicholas, a popular tumult attending his action, he forced his advancement to the stewardship of Saint Peter's. Finally, he is convicted of having murdered four Roman pontiffs with violent deaths. His instrument was poison administered at the hands of one of his intimates, namely, John Braciutus. Although he repented too late, while others still kept silent this ministrant of death himself bore witness to these deeds with dire cries, pressed by the nearness of his own death. And then, on the same night in which the funeral rites of Pope Alexander were lovingly performed in the basilica of the Savior, this oft-mentioned plague-bearer fortified the gates of the Roman city and the and the bridges, the towers and the triumphal arches, with detachments of armed men. When a military force has been brought together, like an enemy he occupied the Lateran Palace. And lest the clergy should dare oppose him, since no one wished to elect him, he terrified them by threatening them with death upon the unsheathed swords of his followers. He sprang upon the long-occupied throne before the body of the dead man reached its tomb. But when certain of the clergy wanted to remind him of the decree of Pope Nicholas (which was promulgated with the threat of anathema by one hundred twenty-five bishops and with the approval of this same Hildebrand and which stated that if anyone presumed to be pope without the assent of the Roman prince, he should be considered by all not pope, but an apostate), he denied that he knew there was a king anywhere, and he asserted that he could adjudge the decrees of his predecessors void.

What more? Not only Rome, indeed, but the Roman world itself, bears witness that he has not been elected by God but that he has most impudently thrust himself upward through force, fraud, and money. His fruits reveal his root; his words show his intent. He it was who subverted ecclesiastical order, who threw the rule of the Christian empire into turmoil, who plotted death of body and soul for the catholic and pacific King, who defended a king who was a breaker of vows and a traitor, who sowed discord among those in concord, strife among the peaceful, scandals among brothers, divorce among the married, and who shook whatever was seen to stand in quiet amidst those who lived piously.

Wherefore, as was said before, we who have been gathered together through the agency of God, supported by the legates and letters of the nineteen bishops who assembled at Mainz on the holy day of last Pentecost, pass judgment against that same most insolent Hildebrand: for he preaches acts of sacrilege and arson; he defends perjuries and murders; long a disciple of the heretic Beringer, he places in question the catholic and apostolic Faith in regard to the Body and Blood of the Lord; he is an open devotee of divinations and dreams, and a necromancer working with an oracular spirit;[6] and therefore he wanders beyond the limits of the true Faith. We judge that canonically he must be deposed and expelled and that, unless he descends from this See after hearing these words, he is forever damned.

I, Hugh Candidus,[7] cardinal priest of the holy Roman Church, from the Title of Saint Clement in the third district of the city, have assented to this decree promulgated by us, and I have subscribed it in the name of all the Roman cardinals.

I, Diepold, archbishop of Milan, have subscribed.

I, Kuono, bishop of Brescia, have subscribed.

I, Otto, bishop-elect of Tortona, have subscribed.

I, William, bishop of Pavia, have subscribed.

I, Reginald, bishop of Belluno, have subscribed.

I, Sigebod, bishop of Verona, have subscribed.

I, Dionysius, bishop of Piacenza, have subscribed.

Udo, bishop of Asti. I have subscribed.

I, Hugh, bishop-elect of Firmo, have subscribed.

Milo of Padua has subscribed.

I, Conrad, bishop of Utrecht, have subscribed.

Henry, the patriarch [of Aquileia], has subscribed.

Didald, bishop of Vicenza, has subscribed.

Regenger, bishop of Vercelli, has subscribed.

Rupert, bishop of Bamberg, has subscribed.

Norbert, bishop of Chur, has subscribed.

Eberhard, bishop of Parma, has subscribed.

Roland, by the grace of God, bishop of Treviso, most willingly has subscribed.

Arnold, bishop of Cremona, has subscribed.

Arnold, bishop of Bergamo, has subscribed.

I, Diedo, bishop of Brandenburg, have subscribed.

Leomar, archbishop of the holy church of Hamburg.

I, Werner, by the grace of God, bishop of Bobbio, have subscribed.

I, Altwin, bishop of Brixen, have subscribed.

I, Meginward, bishop of Freising, have subscribed.

I, Burchard, bishop of Lausanne, have subscribed.

I, Conrad, bishop of Genoa, have subscribed.

Henry, King by the grace of God. I have subscribed.

Henry praises the constancy of the clergy and people of Rome and announces his imminent arrival at Rome to assume his hereditary dignity (the Imperial office), to remove the conflicts of kingship and priesthood and to restore all things to peace and unity (1081).[8]

Henry, King by the grace of God, sends to the clergy and the Roman people, to the greater and lesser [feudatories], his affection in the most sincere expression of his favor and best wishes:

From many accounts of the elder nobles of our empire we have learned with what great fidelity and benevolence you honored our father of sacrosanct memory and with what great acts of honor he advanced publicly and privately both the dignity of your church and the universal grandeur of the Roman name. Nor, indeed, after his death did you cherish us in our infancy with less love and reverence. On all counts you stood beside us with faithful constancy as far as was possible in the face of the wickedness of certain pestilential and proud men. The helplessness of our youth was at first our plea for not responding to your enduring love with due requital by granting you our favor. And after we put on the man, so great a madness of tyrannical perfidy swelled up against us that supreme necessity forced us to direct the entire concern of our effort toward crushing it.

But now since we have cut off with the sword both the life and the pride of those most bitter enemies, not by our power but by that of God, and in large part have set in order the members of the disrupted and sundered Empire, we intend to come to you. Our specific aim is to receive from you, by the common assent and favor of you all, our due and hereditary dignity and to bestow with every kind of honor the thanks which you deserve. We are surprised, however, that when our approach became better known, no legation from you came to us in the customary manner. For that reason we have refrained from sending our envoys to you. You yourselves know with what infamous abuse our envoys, honored and venerable men, were afflicted in the last year by him from whom such conduct was least fitting, in a manner exceeding the inhumanity of all barbarians.

This is the very thing with which those disturbers of peace and concord charge us. They scatter word among you that we come meaning to diminish the honor of Saint Peter, the prince of the apostles, and through our own power to overturn the commonwealth of you all. Indeed, these tactics accord with their usual conduct. But we tell the truth to you in good faith, for it is altogether our will and resolve to visit you peacefully, as far as is within us, and then, having considered the advice of all of you especially, and of our other vassals, to remove from our midst the long-lasting discord of the kingship and the priesthood, and to recall all things to peace and unity in the name of Christ.

Notes

1   In December, 1075, almost six months to the day after Henry's great victory on the Unstrut over the Saxons, Gregory, prosecuting the policy he had begun at his Lenten Synod earlier in 1075, threatened to excommunicate Henry should he not shun the company of the bishops excommunicated at the Synod, obey the synodal edict against lay investiture, and conform to Pa-

pal orders in regard to Imperial churches in Italy. Henry received Gregory's letters early in 1076 and vigorously accepted their implicit challenge, dispatching at once the first four letters reprinted here and summoning the Synod of Brixen, where the majority of German bishops joined him in pronouncing Gregory's deposition.

2 The Latin original is *fidelis*, a word which appears frequently throughout Henry IV's letters. At the risk of imprecision, the requirements of translation have forced a rendering as either "vassal" or "subject." The reader should not be misled, however, by the modern meaning of "vassal": *Fidelis* denoted no servile status, but, to the contrary, indicated a man who had taken an oath of "fealty" (*fidelitas*) to an overlord — and invariably, therefore, a *fidelis* was a person of high station within feudal political society.

3 A reference to Gregory's denial of Henry's right to name Tedald archbishop of Milan and to fill the sees of Fermo and Spoleto.

4 In joining battle with Gregory, Henry severely miscalculated his strength. While most of the German bishops supported him against Gregory, a great number of temporal princes led by his old enemies Welf of Bavaria, Rudolf of Swabia, and Berthold of Carinthia took the opportunity to rebel against their excommunicate King. The threat of revolt in Saxony also revived immediately. In October, 1076, Henry's army gathered at Oppenheim, facing the rebel army at Tribur just opposite them across the Rhine. Fearing the results of open battle, Henry offered this promise to the Papal legates who were with his enemies; it was accepted and, with the understanding that points at issue between Henry and Gregory's partisans would be settled at a future meeting, both armies disbanded. In the 1076 letter to the princes reprinted here, Henry declared his altered policy to his supporters and urged them to conform themselves to it. For their part, the rebellious princes sent a legation to Gregory, asking him to go to Germany the next February to arbitrate the conflict between them and their King. Gregory accepted these proposals and was making his way toward Germany when Henry intercepted him at Canossa and, after making his submission, was released from excommunication.

5 "Se commendare," in the feudal sense of commending oneself to a lord in order to gain lands and position.

6 Probably a reference to the prophecy Gregory made at the Lenten Synod of 1080, after he had excommunicated Henry for the second time: "Be it known to all of you, that if he does not repent before the feast of St. Peter, he will be killed or deposed. If it does not happen thus, no one need believe me ever again." Bonizo, *Liber ad Amicum*, chap. 9, *MGH LdL.*, I, 616. Sigebert of Gembloux (*Chronicon, MGH SS.*, VI, 369) reports, "Pope Hildebrand predicted, as though it had been divinely revealed to him, that the false king was to die in this year. Indeed, he predicted the truth; but the conjecture about the false king deceived him, since, according to his construction, the prediction referred to King Henry." Sigebert refers to the death of Rudolf of Rheinfelden.

7 At first a supporter of Gregory, he turned to the royalists within a year of Gregory's election, charging that it was uncanonical, and became a leader of the Synod of Worms (1076).

8 Between Canossa and Gregory's Lenten Synod of 1080, the Papacy took no major part in German affairs. Toward the end of this period, however, Gregory gave his support openly to the antiking Rudolf of Rheinfelden, whom Henry defeated and killed in battle in January, 1080. This defeat and Henry's steadfast refusal to obey Gregory's edicts against lay investiture led to Gregory's second excommunication of the King at his Lenten Synod two months after Rudolf's death. Henry's position in Germany was then quite strong, and, in addition, the greater part of the German and Lombard bishops declared for him in this new crisis, rejecting Gregory as pope at the Synods of Bamberg and Mainz and electing Archbishop Wibert of Ravenna as his successor at the Synod of Brixen. With ample forces, Henry entered Italy early in 1080 to execute the judgments of his bishops; he then sent this letter to the people of Rome. Armed resistance to his march through the lands of his cousin, Mathilda of Tuscany, a stanch supporter of the reformed Papacy, kept him from Rome almost a year. Late in 1082 he withdrew from Tuscany, and in 1083 he began his brief and victorious siege of Rome.

The Concordat of Worms

The first phase of the investiture controversy ended in September 1122 with a compromise between Calixtus II and Henry V– the Concordat of Worms of September, 1122..

Source: Henry Bettenson, ed. *Documents of the Christian Church* (London: Oxford University Press, 1963).

Agreement of Pope Calixtus II.

I, Calixtus, Bishop, servant of the servants of God, do grant to thee, beloved son, Henry – by the grace of God Emperor of the Romans, Augustus – that the elections of bishops and abbots of the German kingdom, who belong to that kingdom, shall take place in thy presence, without simony or any violence; so that if any dispute shall arise between the parties concerned, thou, with the counsel or judgement of the metropolitan and the co-provincial bishops, shalt give consent and aid to the party which has the more right. The one elected shall receive the regalia from thee by the sceptre and shall perform his lawful duties to thee on that account. But he who is consecrated in the other parts of thy empire [i.e. Burgundy and Italy] shall, within six months, and without any exaction, receive the regalia from thee by the sceptre, and shall perform his lawful duties to thee on that account (saving all rights which are known to belong to the Roman church). Concerning matters in which thou shalt make complaint to me, and ask aid – I, according to the duty of my office, will furnish aid to thee. I give unto thee true peace, and to all who are or have been of thy party in this conflict.

Edict of the Emperor Henry V

In the name of the holy and indivisible Trinity I, Henry, by the grace of God Emperor of the Romans, Augustus, for the love of God and of the holy Roman church and of our lord Pope Calixtus, and for the salvation of my soul, do surrender to God, and to the holy apostles of God, Peter and Paul, and to the Holy Catholic Church, all investiture through ring and staff; and do grant that in all the churches that are in my kingdom or empire there may be canonical election and free consecration. All the possessions and regalia of St. Peter which, from the beginning of this discord unto this day, whether in the time of my father or in mine have been seized, and which I hold, I restore to that same Holy Roman Church. And I will faithfully aid in the restoration of those things which I do not hold. The possessions also of all other churches and princes, and of all other persons lay and clerical which have been lost in that war: according to the counsel of the princes, or according to justice, I will restore, as far as I hold them; and I will faithfully aid in the restoration of those things which I do not hold. And I grant true peace to our lord Pope Calixtus, and to the Holy Roman Church, and to all those who are or have been on its side. And in matters where the Holy Roman Church shall ask aid I will grant it; and in matters concerning which it shall make complaint to me I will duly grant to it justice. All these things have been done by the consent and counsel of the princes. Whose names are here adjoined: Adalbert archbishop of Mainz; F. archbishop of Cologne; H. bishop of Ratisbon; O. bishop of Bamberg; B. bishop of Spires; H. of Augsburg; G. of Utrecht; Ou. of Constance; E. abbot of Fulda; Henry, duke; Frederick, duke; S. duke; Pertolf, duke; Margrave Teipold; Margrave Engelbert; Godfrey, count Palatine; Otto, count Palatine; Berengar, count.

I, Frederick, archbishop of Cologne and arch-chancellor, have ratified this.